LIES AND THE BRONTËS

MONICA KENDALL

LIES
and the
BRONTËS

The Quest for the Jenkins Family

Best wishes

Monica Kendall

SilverWood

Published in 2021 by SilverWood Books

SilverWood Books Ltd
14 Small Street, Bristol, BS1 1DE, United Kingdom
www.silverwoodbooks.co.uk

Copyright © Monica Eve Kendall 2021
Map 1 © SilverWood Books from the author's original document
Family Trees © SilverWood Books from the author's original document

ISBN 978-1-80042-005-2 (hardback)

British Library Cataloguing in Publication Data
A CIP catalogue record for this book is
available from the British Library

Page design and typesetting by SilverWood Books

To my darling mother
Dorice Margaret Kendall née Jenkins
1919–2015

'Do you like the truth? It is well for you. Adhere to that preference – never swerve thence.'

— Charlotte Brontë, *Shirley*, p. 165

Once known in any detail and any scope, every life is something extraordinary, full of particular drama and tension and surprise, often containing unimagined degrees of suffering or heroism, and invariably touching extreme moments of triumph and despair, though frequently unexpressed. The difference lies in the extent to which one is eventually recorded, and the other is eventually forgotten.

— Richard Holmes, *Footsteps*, p. 208

the biographer works in words

— Leon Edel, *Writing Lives*, p. 16

And immediately
Rather than words comes the thought of high windows:
The sun-comprehending glass,
And beyond it, the deep blue air, that shows
Nothing, and is nowhere, and is endless.

— Philip Larkin, 'High Windows'

Contents

List of Illustrations   VIII
Acknowledgements   XI
Note on the Transcriptions of Letters   XV
List of Abbreviations   XVI

1 The Search Begins   1
2 Evan: 'In the sweet shire of Cardigan'   14
3 Ystrad Meurig: 'Far from the Concourse of Men'   45
4 David: Chelsea and Yorkshire, 1807–1813   63
5 Eliza: The Ancestors   91
6 Eliza: Moving On   126
7 Cambridge: 'I was the Dreamer, they the Dream'   158
8 Belgium, 1814–1823: *'C'est le feu!'*   199
9 Yorkshire and Brussels, 1824–1825: School, Death and Marriage   222
10 Evan Embattled, 1826–1829:
     The Button-maker's Grandson and the Scottish Bishop   246
11 Revolution and a Love Triangle, 1830–1831   270
12 Chaplain to the King   314
13 The Brontës Come to Brussels, 1842: The Trial of Common Sense   356
14 Charlotte Returns to Brussels, 1843:
     A Faithless-looking Youth, a Welsh Pony and Possible Forgery   394
15 'Why should we weep or mourn': Schoolboys and Death   421
16 'between Life & death'   448
17 Coda   473

Notes   477
Select Bibliography   553
Index   565

Illustrations

Jacket: Ferdinand de Braekeleer, *The Ceremony of the Inauguration of King Leopold I, 21 July 1831* (1856). © Royal Museums of Fine Arts of Belgium, Brussels. Photo: J. Geleyns – Art Photography

Plates

1   The graves of Evan and Eliza Jenkins and their son Edward, Brussels City Cemetery in Evere, February 2014. Author's photo.

2   Llanbadarn Odwyn church and churchyard, Ceredigion. Author's photo.

3   John Thomas, *Revd John Williams, Ystradmeurig (1745–1818)* (1885), print, courtesy of Llyfrgell Genedlaethol Cymru/The National Library of Wales.

4   Canolfan Edward Richard Centre, Ystrad Meurig. Author's photo.

5   Cartoon of a visit to Ystrad Meurig (Noel Ford, 2012), Canolfan Edward Richard Centre, courtesy of Margaret Ford.

6   *Chelsea Old Church* (1788), courtesy of Kensington and Chelsea Archives.

7   F.P. Thompson's map of Chelsea (1836) showing David's school, courtesy of Kensington and Chelsea Archives.

8   Portrait of Rev. David Jenkins, incumbent of Pudsey St Lawrence (c.1850) (West Yorkshire Archive Service, Leeds: BDP88/8).

9   Portrait of Provost Alexander Livingston of Countesswells (c.1750). © Aberdeen City Council (Art Gallery & Museums Collections).

10 Eliza Jenkins and daughter Helen (c.1860). Author's photo.

11   Engraving of St Ninian's Church and Manse, North Leith (nineteenth century?), from John Russell, *The Story of Leith* (London: Thomas Nelson and Sons, [1922]), p. 165.

12   Margaret Wyndham née Jay (1860s), courtesy of Dalwood Restoration Association.

13   François Gailliard, *Scène de carnaval sur le boulevard Anspach* (1886) (Musée de la Ville de Bruxelles – Maison du Roi).

14   The Chapel Royal, Brussels (postcard, 1905–8). © Archives de la Ville de Bruxelles.

15   Interior view of the Chapel Royal, Brussels. Author's photo.

16   *The Prince of Orange Pressed by the Crowd* (anonymous lithograph, c.1830) (Bibliothèque Royale de Belgique; Wikimedia Commons).

17   Lieven de Winne, *Portrait of King Leopold I* (1860–1). © Royal Museums of Fine Arts of Belgium, Brussels. Photo: Guy Cussac, Brussel.

18   Comte de Buisseret, *La place Royale* (1832) (Musée de la Ville de Bruxelles – Maison du Roi).

19   The Isabelle Quarter in 1843, showing the pensionnat © Selina Busch, from Eric Ruijssenaars, *The Pensionnat Revisited: More Light Shed on the Brussels of the Brontës* (Printed by Nuance Zaandam, 2003), p. 37.

20   George Richmond, *Portrait of Charlotte Brontë* (1850). © National Portrait Gallery, London.

21   Samuel Laurence, *Portrait of Elizabeth Gaskell* (1854) (The University of Manchester Library), courtesy of The Elizabeth Gaskell Family Collection.

22   Edward Jenkins (1865). Author's photo.

23   Edward Jenkins, family and friends (before 1873). Author's photo.

24   Edward and John Jenkins in the *Almanack of the Church of the Resurrection*. Author's photo.

25   Engraving of the laying of the stone for the unbuilt Church of the Resurrection (1864) after a photograph by Ghémar, *Illustrated London News*, 23 April 1864, p. 384, courtesy of The British Library.

26   Sketch of Lixmount House, near Edinburgh, courtesy of Erica Fairfax-Lucy of Charlecote Park, Warwickshire. Photo: Frank Storr.

Maps

1   Belgium and the Netherlands   XVIII

2   Brussels, the lower town: from *Plan de Bruxelles et des faubourgs* (1839)   XIX

3   Brussels, the upper town: from *Plan de Bruxelles et des faubourgs* (1839)   XX

4   Brussels, the Isabelle Quarter in 1843 © Selina Busch, from Eric
     Ruijssenaars, *The Pensionnat Revisited: More Light Shed on the Brussels
     of the Brontës* (Printed by Nuance Zaandam, 2003), p. 8   XXI

Family Trees

1   The family of Evan and David Jenkins   XXII

2   Eliza's descent from a Huguenot martyr   XXIII

3   Eliza's Scottish descent   XXIV

Acknowledgements

I couldn't have written this book without the generous research and friendship of Marcia Watson: we are fifth cousins once removed, and removed additionally by 9,000 miles. We had been briefly in contact years before when she asked to republish my article about the Jenkins school in New York. When I first got annoyed with the fabrications about my ancestors we were serendipitously reconnected thanks to Helen MacEwan of the Brussels Brontë Group. This has been an incredible journey of discovering my great-great-grandparents and their role in the Brontë story, and one of the most rewarding results has been my internet encounter with Marcia of Perth, Australia. I bet our ancestors – the sisters Eliza and Margaret Jay – would be pleased, maybe stunned. It would be daft to thank her in my notes for every bit of research she passed on, but it included many wills and much on our Jay family, and also, for example, on Catherine Phelps and Miss Morse, and she found a devastating advertisement from November 1849 at the last stages of my writing. She was like an archaeologist in the next trench to me: while she painstakingly uncovered not just the bones, but the beads and postholes, in my trench I would carry off the bones I found but maybe miss some beads, and definitely postholes. Then she would offer her finds up to me, and from my European perspective I put them in a historical and literary context. Marcia was also a great sounding board, though of course my interpretations are my own; she was patient at calming my more wild conjectures, while I was not bad at reinterpreting hers. She also helped in transcribing some letters – my first encounter with a crossed family letter was one of fright – and she provided invaluable family trees that have been refined over the years, which I have simplified for this book.

I must thank also Robyn Crosslé and the team at the University of New England, New South Wales, Australia, for their incredible transcription work on the numerous letters in the Wyndham archive. Especially when I was reading a scan of a crossed letter it was so helpful to be able to check my efforts against their transcription. I then had the luxury of discovering or emending a few words. Thanks so much to Don Seton Wilkinson and Marcia for sending me the transcribed letters, and to Bill Oates at the University of New England who was the ideal archivist: he sent me the catalogue and was prompt and happy to send me the scans I requested. Again thanks to Don for giving me permission to use the photograph of Margaret Wyndham née Jay on behalf of the Dalwood Restoration Association. I also particularly want to thank Jane Horton for agreeing to do the index on such a long book: our professional relationship goes back several years; we finally met in person at the Hay on Wye book festival in 2019 when I was still finishing my book.

A special thank you to Margaret and John Powell and the mug of tea in their special house.

There are many other people I want to thank who made my research so much easier and enjoyable. I attempted this list in chronological order, which is going back over more than six years of research, and have slightly failed, but it takes me back geographically over my scholar adventure, since I first discovered that my Jenkins ancestors knew the Brontës:

Helen MacEwan of the Brussels Brontë Group; Roger Cox; Doug Whiteley, churchwarden, Pudsey parish church; Jacqueline Charade, Chapel Royal, Brussels; Jonathan Rush and Adam Green, Trinity College Library, Cambridge; Mike Morrogh, Shrewsbury School; Paul Westney and Celia Bailey Jones, Canolfan Edward Richard Centre, Ystrad Meurig, Ceredigion; Nathan Williams and Nicholas Melia, Borthwick Institute for Archives; Helen Palmer, County Archivist, Ceredigion; Sarah Roberts, University of Wales Trinity Saint David, Lampeter; Sara Slinn; Beryl Evans, Cardiganshire Family History Society/ Cymdeithas Hanes Teuluoedd Ceredigion; Chris Theaker, Nanteos Mansion, Ceredigion; Julian Reid, Merton College, Oxford; Michael Freeman, Ventnor; John Lovell, Woodford Historical Society; Diane Wilson, Parish Administrator, St Mary's Church, Andover; Rev. Richard Burge, Hartshead; Aaldert Prins and Patricia Quaghebeur, KADOC, Leuven, Belgium; Sarah Prince for giving me permission to use the portrait of her great-great-great-grandmother Elizabeth

Gaskell; Margaret Ford for giving me permission to use the cartoon by her husband Noel Ford (1942–2019); Peter Stubbs for sending me the image of St Ninian's Church in Leith; Selina Busch for giving me permission to use her plan and drawing of the Isabelle Quarter in 1843; Sarah Laycock at the Brontë Parsonage Museum; Erica Fairfax-Lucy of Charlecote Park for her helpful emails and for giving me permission to use the sketch of Lixmount, and Frank Storr who originally photographed it and found it on his memory stick. There is a story there which fittingly may stand for the generosity I have received over the long years of research. Frank told me that the late Sir Edmund Fairfax-Lucy brought it into the National Trust office to be photographed a few years ago. The sketch used to hang in the Morning Room, but Sir Ed, a celebrated painter, liked to rearrange things, so his widow Erica and Frank will hunt for it. Another quest.

I also thank the staff at the following: Aberdeen Art Gallery & Museums; Archives de la Ville de Bruxelles; Balliol College Archives & Manuscripts, Oxford; The British Library; Brontë Society & Brontë Parsonage Museum; Cumbria Archive & Local Studies Centre, Whitehaven; Holy Trinity Church, Brussels; John Hay Library, Brown University, Rhode Island; The John Rylands Library, University of Manchester; Lambeth Palace Library, London; London Metropolitan Archives; National Library of Wales/Llyfrgell Genedlaethol Cymru; Northamptonshire Record Office; Oriel College Archives, Oxford; Pepys Library, Magdalene College, Cambridge; Royal Collection Trust; Scottish Genealogist; the West Yorkshire Archive Service, Leeds; and the Wordsworth Trust, Dove Cottage, Grasmere.

And I am so grateful to Helen Hart, Alice van Raalte and the team at SilverWood.

I thank the following institutions for giving me permission to quote from manuscripts in their care, many of whose staff were working remotely during the Coronavirus pandemic:

Balliol College Archives, University of Oxford: Morier Family Papers, Class C, Box 1, 1788–92, Quoted by kind permission of the Master and Fellows of Balliol College; Bedfordshire Archives Service: OR2298/5b, letter from Theresa Rouse-Boughton to her father, 13 June 1853; Borthwick Institute for Archives, University of York: Ordination papers of David Jenkins, Ord.D.1810 and Ord.P.1811, York Diocesan Archive; The British Library: Add. MS 61805, Stonestreet journal; The Brontë Parsonage Museum: letters by Abraham Dixon; courtesy of the Curwen Estate and Cumbria Archive and Local Studies Centre, Whitehaven: DCU/3, Curwen Family papers; the General Secretary of the Diocese of London,

Richard Gough: the ordination bundles of Rev. Evan Jenkins held at the LMA; Hampshire Record Office: Malmesbury papers: 9M73/G410, note from Andrew Dalziel [Dalzel] (1746–1806), 27 June 1777; John Hay Library, Brown University: Ms.52.298, T. Westwood, 'Letter, 1869, November 21, Brussels, Belgium'; Lambeth Palace Library: letters in FP Howley 4, 5, 7, 24 and FP Blomfield 48, 59, 65; Mitchell Library, State Library of New South Wales: MLMSS 139, letters to William Branwhite Clarke; The National Library of Wales/Llyfrgell Genedlaethol Cymru: various; Norfolk Record Office: BUL 1/15/1-54 561 x 9, copy letter from Sir George Hamilton Seymour; Northamptonshire Archives Service: C(A) Box 15/95, Papers of the Cartwright family of Aynho, letter from Bishop Howley to Rev. Holworthy, 24 April 1826; Shropshire Archives: SA 807/568, letter from M. Bright to Augusta Bright, 24 February 1846?; University of New England (UNE), NSW, Australia: Regional Collection: Dinton–Dalwood Letters 1827–88, acc. no. A109; and the Wordsworth Trust: letters from Dora and Edward Quillinan.

I thank Faber and Faber Ltd for permission to use an extract from Philip Larkin's 'High Windows' as an epigraph. The epigraph from Richard Holmes's *Footsteps: Adventures of a Romantic Biographer* is reprinted by permission of HarperCollins Publishers Ltd © Richard Holmes 1985.

Note on the
Transcriptions of Letters

Unless otherwise noted, in my transcription of unpublished letters I have used the following conventions: used spaced en dashes; single quote marks; lowered superscripts; retained abbreviated words; retained capital initials when they seem intentional. My cuts are shown as [...]. Original authorial additions are shown within angled brackets: \ /. Uncertain readings with ? before the conjectured word, or noted in square brackets. For published letters I have followed the conventions of their editor other than replacing em dashes with spaced en dashes.

Abbreviations

ACAD	A Cambridge Alumni Database, University of Cambridge, online (based on *Alumni Cantabrigienses*)
Balliol	Balliol College Oxford Archives, Morier family papers, Class C, Box 1, 1788–92
BL	The British Library
BNA	The British Newspaper Archive
CB	Charlotte Brontë
CCEd	Clergy of the Church of England database, 1540–1835, online
Clarke Papers	Clarke family papers, ML MSS 139/5, Mitchell Library, State Library of New South Wales, Sydney, Australia
FP	Fulham Papers: papers of the Bishops of London, Lambeth Palace Library
Haworth BPM	Brontë Parsonage Museum, Haworth, West Yorkshire
Kadoc	Documentatie- en Onderzoekscentrum voor Religie, Cultuur en Samenleving, Leuven, Belgium
Lambeth	Lambeth Palace Library, London
Letters I, II, III	Charlotte Brontë, *The Letters of Charlotte Brontë*, Volume One: *1829–1847*, ed. Margaret Smith (Oxford: Clarendon Press, 1995); Volume Two: *1848–1851* (2000); Volume Three: *1852–1855* (2004)
LMA	London Metropolitan Archives
NLW	The National Library of Wales, Aberystwyth
ODNB	*Oxford Dictionary of National Biography*, online. I have given the date of the latest year on their website.

OS	Ordnance Survey
TNA	The National Archives, Kew, London
VCH	Victoria County History, British History Online
Whitehaven	Cumbria Archive Centre, Whitehaven: Curwen Family of Workington Hall, 1358–1929: DCU/3
Wyndham	University of New England (UNE) Regional Collection, NSW, Australia: Dinton–Dalwood Letters 1827–88, acc. no. A109

1. Belgium and the Netherlands

North Sea

NETHERLANDS

GERMANY

•Amsterdam

The Hague•   •Leiden
                    Utrecht
              •Rotterdam

          •Dordrecht

Ostend•   •Antwerp
      •Bruges   Mechelen
          •Ghent   •(Malines)
                      Leuven
•Calais   BELGIUM Brussels• •(Louvain)   •Aachen
                          •Tervuren   (Aix-la-
•Boulogne   •Liège   Chapelle)
          •Lille   •Waterloo
              •Ghlin   Chaudfontaine• •Spa
              •Mons   •Namur

FRANCE   LUXEMBOURG

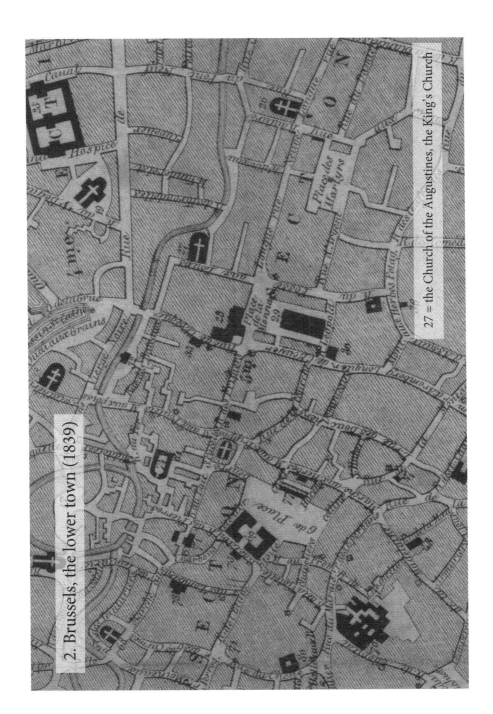

2. Brussels, the lower town (1839)

27 = the Church of the Augustines, the King's Church

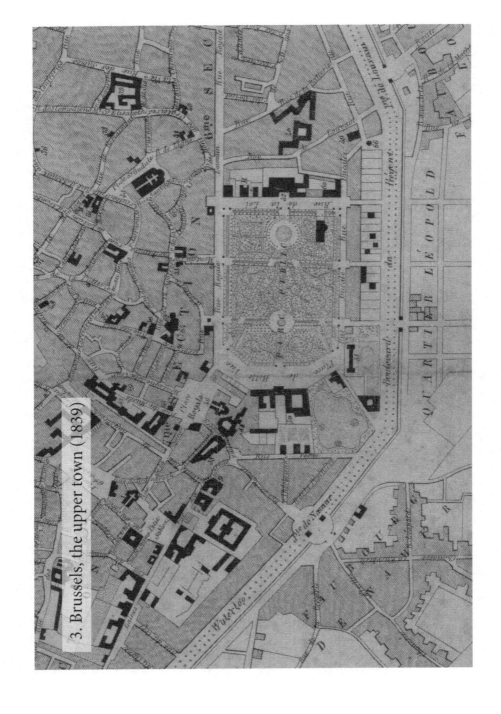

3. Brussels, the upper town (1839)

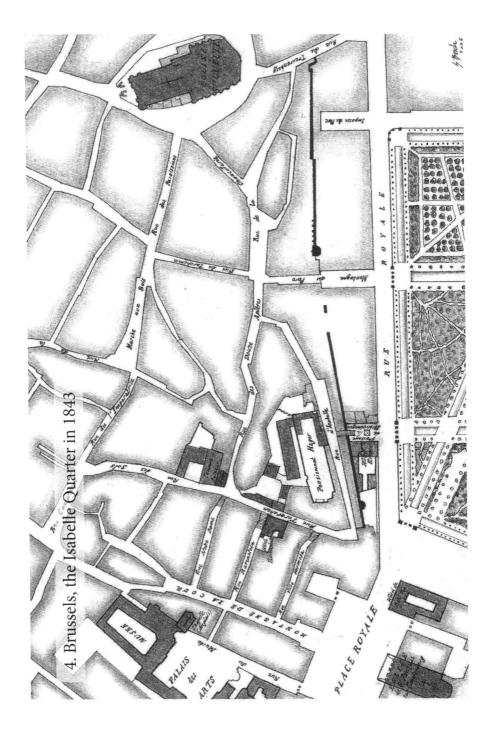

4. Brussels, the Isabelle Quarter in 1843

1. The family of Evan and David Jenkins

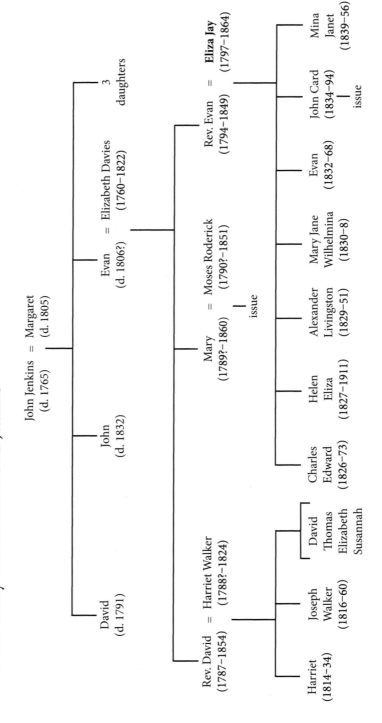

John Jenkins = Margaret
(d. 1765)   (d. 1805)

David
(d. 1791)

John
(d. 1832)

Evan = Elizabeth Davies
(d. 1806?)   (1760–1822)

3
daughters

Rev. David = Harriet Walker
(1787–1854)   (1788?–1824)

Mary = Moses Roderick
(1789?–1860)   (1790?–1851)

Rev. Evan = **Eliza Jay**
(1794–1849)   (1797–1864)

Harriet
(1814–34)

Joseph
Walker
(1816–60)

David
Thomas
Elizabeth
Susannah

Charles
Edward
(1826–73)

Helen
Eliza
(1827–1911)

Alexander
Livingston
(1829–51)

Mary Jane
Wilhelmina
(1830–8)

Evan
(1832–68)

John Card
(1834–94)

Mina
Janet
(1839–56)

issue

issue

2. Eliza's descent from a Huguenot martyr

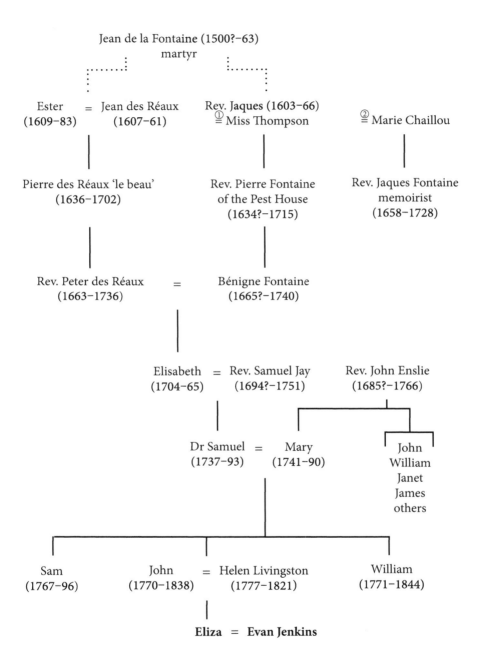

Jean de la Fontaine (1500?–63)
martyr

Ester (1609–83) = Jean des Réaux (1607–61)

Rev. Jaques (1603–66)
① = Miss Thompson

② = Marie Chaillou

Pierre des Réaux 'le beau' (1636–1702)

Rev. Pierre Fontaine
of the Pest House
(1634?–1715)

Rev. Jaques Fontaine
memoirist
(1658–1728)

Rev. Peter des Réaux (1663–1736) = Bénigne Fontaine (1665?–1740)

Elisabeth (1704–65) = Rev. Samuel Jay (1694?–1751)

Rev. John Enslie (1685?–1766)

Dr Samuel (1737–93) = Mary (1741–90)

John
William
Janet
James
others

Sam (1767–96)

John (1770–1838) = Helen Livingston (1777–1821)

William (1771–1844)

Eliza = Evan Jenkins

3. Eliza's Scottish descent

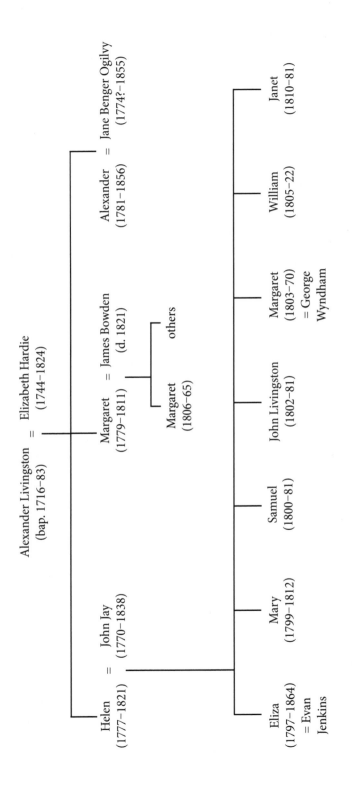

One

The Search Begins

Once below a time in Cardiganshire, there was a poor tenant farmer's son, the third child of a third son, whose father died when he was twelve. Between the mountains and the sea, this boy might have spent his days supporting his mother and sister by working on the farm, his head bent to the earth, his heart to the black cattle. But a pony ride away, in the middle of this Welsh nowhere, something else offered: the other world of a unique school – learning English, Latin, Greek, Hebrew. A decade after Byron, the young man arrived at Trinity College, Cambridge; he died chaplain to a king. This is his story and that of the woman he married – my ancestors – and of their close encounter with the Brontë sisters.[1]

* * *

February rain in the Evere cemetery in Brussels. I stood at the grave of my great-great-grandparents and wondered if they would like me.

That was in 2014, four months after my research had begun. Sometime later I read Richard Holmes's *Footsteps* – notes on his search for Robert Louis Stevenson, Mary Wollstonecraft, Shelley … He writes: 'When I travelled alone I craved after intimacy with my subject […] I came often to feel excluded, left behind, shut out from the magic circle of his family. I wanted to get in among them, to partake in their daily life, to understand what Shelley called the "deep truth" of their situation.'[2] Holmes wonders if that was because of some imbalance in his own character. Perhaps because I was searching for my own family my lack of confidence at the graveside spoke of an even graver lack of identity, or an impossible yearning to belong to a family that might be happier than my own. But reading Holmes, I knew that I was not alone. I was also on an addictive search: in my case for my Jenkins ancestors, friends of the Brontës, whose lives had been largely ignored, their dates muddled, first names unresearched, stories made up. What were they like? No one knew; no one had attempted to know.

The epigraph to Julian Barnes's novel *Flaubert's Parrot* is an extract from a letter by Gustave Flaubert of 1872: 'When you write the biography of a friend, you must do it as if you were taking *revenge* for him.'[3] It is partly true that other than curiosity there is an element of revenge in my research and writing. Reducing my ancestors to ciphers because they seemed far too dull to investigate, each biographer of the Brontës copying the last one, some fabricating, few querying dubious sources. I wanted to tell the story of the Jenkins family who knew Charlotte Brontë in Brussels for two years and Emily for nine months, or who knew Patrick Brontë in West Yorkshire for forty years – this is a triple biography. But I also wanted to share my search: after the slog up and down cul-de-sacs, after the blackened fingers wading through folder after folder in an archive, those Eureka moments of utter delight, the moments when one new piece of jigsaw joined up with two others. I was also set on a strange but fabulous task of looking in famous novels for glimpses of my family.

My footsteps led me not only to rain-soaked cemeteries, but to hot canals in Holland, the soft green hills of mid-Wales (also rain-soaked), a massive church in West Yorkshire, the cobbled waterside at Leith and misty seashore of Aberdeen. I have ensconced myself with digital camera and pencil in archives in Oxford, Cambridge, Aberystwyth, Whitehaven, York, London and Leuven. I have devoured biographies, novels and essays, and squinted at cross-writing in Victorian letters that miraculously survived white ants, sea voyages and human destruction. I hope my family, long in their graves in West Yorkshire, Brussels, London or old Cardiganshire, will look kindly on my attempt. Unlike Bernard's humdrum biographer in Virginia Woolf's *The Waves*, I uncover the 'torn bits of stuff, stuff with raw edges',[4] not tack them together, to show, as Richard Holmes so movingly and eloquently says in an epigraph I have chosen for my book, 'every life is something extraordinary'.

* * *

I hardly know what swelled to my throat as I read her letter – such a vehement impatience of restraint & steady work, such a strong wish for wings – wings such as wealth can furnish – such an urgent thirst to see – to know – to learn – something internal seemed to expand boldly for a minute[5]

With these words of excitement, of frustration, Charlotte Brontë wrote to Ellen Nussey in August 1841 after reading their friend Mary Taylor's letter about her trip on the Continent, about what she had seen, 'pictures the most exquisite – & cathedrals the most venerable'. Charlotte felt trapped as a governess, 'the living in other people's houses – the estrangement from one's real character'. Her wish for wings was still alive two months later, as she again wrote to Ellen, 'I burn to go somewhere else – I think Nell I see a chance of getting to Brussels'.[6] And in between those two letters, she had written the most important letter of her life: to her Aunt Branwell.

Elizabeth Branwell had joined the Brontë household after her sister Maria, Charlotte's mother, had died when Charlotte was five. She had a small income and savings and in 1841 she had offered to lend some money to help the three sisters set up a school. Emily was living at home after abandoning a teaching job; the youngest, Anne, was also unhappy as a governess. But the letter from Mary Taylor fired Charlotte with a new vision and she had to convince her aunt that some of the money would be even better used to finance six months at a school abroad for herself and Emily (Anne could go later). Charlotte used all her powers of persuasion: the education is superior in Brussels, it is cheap, her French would be vastly improved and (in Mrs Gaskell's version of the letter) her old school friend Mary Taylor (aged twenty-four) was at a 'first-rate establishment' there, though that would be too expensive (perhaps half hoping that Aunt Branwell might say, but that doesn't sound too expensive). And most importantly, she stressed respectability and propriety: Mary 'with the assistance of Mrs. Jenkins, the wife of the British Chaplain, would be able to secure me a cheap and decent residence and respectable protection'.[7] Rev. and Mrs Jenkins were my great-great-grandparents.

Charlotte's letter to her Aunt Branwell was successful. In February 1842, 25-year-old Charlotte, her younger sister Emily and her father Rev. Patrick journeyed from Haworth to Brussels. They were accompanied by Charlotte's friend Mary Taylor and Mary's brother Joe, a frequent traveller, later portrayed as Martin Yorke in *Shirley*.

Charlotte's first biographer, her friend Elizabeth Gaskell, quotes from Charlotte's letter to her aunt and then tells us: 'Reference has been made in her letters to Mrs. Jenkins, the wife of the chaplain of the British Embassy. At the request of his brother – a clergyman, living not many miles from Haworth, and an acquaintance of Mr. Brontë's – she made much inquiry, and at length, after some discouragement in her search, heard of a school which seemed in every respect desirable.' This was the pensionnat of Madame Heger. 'Mr. Brontë took his daughters to the Rue d'Isabelle, Brussels; remained one night at Mr. Jenkins'; and straight returned to his wild Yorkshire village.'

Mrs Gaskell remarks how miserably shy the girls were, and adds: 'Mrs. Jenkins told me that she used to ask them to spend Sundays and holidays with her, until she found that they felt more pain than pleasure from such visits. Emily hardly ever uttered more than a monosyllable. Charlotte was sometimes excited sufficiently to speak eloquently and well – on certain subjects; but before her tongue was thus loosened, she had a habit of gradually wheeling round on her chair, so as almost to conceal her face from the person to whom she was speaking.'

The final mention of Mrs Jenkins in the biography is a few pages later: Mrs Gaskell says there was another English family where Charlotte was a welcome guest 'where, I suspect, she felt herself more at her ease than either at Mrs. Jenkins', or the friends whom I have mentioned'.[8] I will discuss Mrs Gaskell's references to the Jenkinses in a later chapter.

* * *

So my Jenkins family knew two of the most famous authors in English literature, and my great-great-grandmother was mentioned and quoted in one of the most famous biographies ever written (in 1857), yet absolutely nothing passed down in my family. Nor had I ever heard that I had a great-great-great-uncle who was a clergyman in Yorkshire and knew Patrick Brontë. Clergymen seemed to abound in my mother's family, but none, I thought, in Yorkshire.

However, what I certainly did know was that my mother's Jenkins family had lived in Brussels for much of the nineteenth century. I had been told about Rev. Evan Jenkins, who had been born 'somewhere' in Wales (no one knew where) and had gone to Cambridge University. According to my mother, someone once said to him, maybe in the 1820s, 'Why not go to Brussels.' And off he went. Somehow/somewhere he had been ordained, but most important of all – and this we definitely knew – he had been made honorary chaplain to Leopold I, King of the Belgians – Victoria and Albert's dearest uncle.

My mother had inherited a huge Victorian family Bible. The name in ink at the top of the page inserted inside the front cover is that of my great-grandfather. It reads: 'John Card Jenkins M.A. 4th son of Revd Evan Jenkins M.A. […] born at Bruxelles October 16th 1834 / died at Bruxelles September 26th 1894.' Below is John's mother's name, then come John's wife's name, that of her parents, her birth and death dates, and a list of John and Mary's eight children, born between 1866 and 1877, all in 'Bruxelles', nearly all baptized in the Chapel Royal there. All the children have notes on their dates of birth and death, and their sponsors at baptism. There are no dates or any other details for Evan and his wife. There is no mention of John's siblings. What it does, however, state is what no book about the Brontës has ever provided: the first name and maiden name of the Brontës' 'Mrs Jenkins': my great-great-grandmother was born Eliza Jay.

We had also inherited large albums or scrapbooks created by three of John and Mary's daughters, my great-aunts. They are crammed with pasted-in photos, often uncaptioned, newspaper clippings, wedding invitations, concert and amateur dramatic programmes … mainly from the 1880s onwards, though some photos are obviously older and not all taken in Brussels (there is a photo of great-grandmother Mary with her four sisters that is all crinolines in *Little Women* style, taken sometime in the 1860s, probably in Shropshire). Sometimes I went through these with my mother, to try and name the faces or hear any other stories about my English and Welsh ancestors. Her father, John Card Jenkins (the younger; 'Jack'), had founded a prep school for boys in New York in 1904, which is still going. Every year we were sent the school magazine and on a university acting trip to New York in the 1970s I had visited the school. In 2000, due to the magic of email, I got in closer contact and, probably because I had said something about the Brussels roots of the school, and why it was called St Bernard's, I was asked to write about the school's founder, my grandfather, and his growing up in the British community there. My great-aunts' albums and their newspaper clippings were my main, invaluable source, but I also used the internet to describe nineteenth-century Brussels to New Yorkers. I wrote:

My grandmother, Connie, told her daughter – my mother – that Brussels was a glamorous place to grow up in. It was a city of cafés and new wide boulevards. There were balls attended by royalty and the diplomatic community, soirées dansantes at the palace, bazaars, the lawn tennis club over which it was reported the British flag 'gracefully floats', cricket, rugby, garden parties, fancy fairs, and amateur theatricals. Brussels in the last decades of the nineteenth century was the 'gayest little capital in Europe', to quote one newspaper report of the time (echoing Thackeray in *Vanity Fair* of 1847).

In this city in June 1815 the Duchess of Richmond held her famous ball before the battle of Waterloo, which took place about fifteen miles south of the city; the great French painter David died in exile in the year Jack's grandfather arrived (David drew that haunting picture of Marie Antoinette on her way to the guillotine); Emily and Charlotte Brontë came to study languages in the early 1840s, and Charlotte returned to teach and found unrequited love; in the very same decade Karl Marx was working on the Communist Manifesto.[9]

There is one error, as my recent research has proved: Jack's grandfather Evan didn't arrive in 1825 – the year of Jacques-Louis David's death in a road accident in Brussels – but I was only a few years out. There is a large lacuna, however: the school magazine article was also posted on the internet, but no one got in touch to say: but haven't you read Elizabeth Gaskell's *Life of Charlotte Brontë*? – your Jenkins family knew the Brontës well.

But one contact was made that was to prove outstandingly important. An Australian, Marcia Watson, wrote to the school asking for permission to reprint it in a magazine, *Dalwood House Newsletter*. We corresponded briefly. She was a distant cousin: our common ancestor being John Jay, the father of 'Mrs Jenkins'. I was descended from John Jay's eldest daughter, Eliza; Marcia, and seemingly thousands of Australians, were descended from a younger daughter, Margaret, who had emigrated to New South Wales with her husband George Wyndham in the 1820s. The purpose of the newsletter was to rally support and funds to restore Dalwood House, George and Margaret's home in the Hunter Valley. He had established the oldest surviving vineyard in Australia. He was also the son of gentry in Wiltshire, related to the Wyndhams of Petworth House, Sussex. Despite Eliza's family being rather lowly in comparison, Marcia had researched the Jenkins descendants and sent what she had unearthed so far. I already knew that my great-grandfather Rev. John had an older brother, Rev. Edward, but I now had names and dates for their siblings. I was intrigued, and thought: one day I will have time to research further myself …

I carefully put the Jenkins family tree in my filing cabinet and forgot about it for thirteen years.

* * *

In autumn 2013 I copy-edited a monograph for an academic publisher that included a chapter on Charlotte Brontë's extraordinary novel *Villette* (a fictional name for Brussels).[10] Memories surfaced that my family were there at the same time, so I decided to buy it. Then, coincidentally, a cousin asked for the number of the Jenkins home in rue St-Bernard in Brussels, where we know they had a school in the second half of the nineteenth century, as her daughter was about to visit. She emailed back telling me to google this combination: Brussels, Brontë, Jenkins. She had just idly tried doing that combination as she explored her Jenkins roots and had found something amazing. And thus I came across a blog on the Brussels Brontë Group website about finding the whereabouts of the Jenkins home in Chaussée d'Ixelles: the house that Charlotte and Emily had 'visited' on several occasions in 1842–3. It had been posted in November 2010 and was titled 'The Jenkinses' House in Ixelles'. It was headed: *'Brian Bracken reports on an important discovery concerning the location of the house of the Rev. Evan Jenkins, the British chaplain in Brussels whose home was so often visited by the Brontë sisters'* and it began: 'The Jenkins family played an important role in the Brontë Brussels story.'[11] I was astounded. The Brontë sisters *knew* my ancestors?

My research took off. I began to email total strangers, including Helen MacEwan of the Brussels Brontë Group. I knew I had to go to Brussels. Helen suggested a good time would be in February 2014 for Eric Ruijssenaars's talk for the Group on the Isabelle Quarter where the Brontë sisters had stayed and learned. I booked my Eurostar ticket for the new year.

But first, I had much reading to do. I obviously turned first to Elizabeth Gaskell's famous biography of 1857. Then, thinking that a lot of research must have been done on the Jenkins family in the past 150 years, I bought Winifred Gérin's biography of Charlotte, published by the Clarendon Press in 1967. Winifred Bourne came from a well-off Surrey family with its fair share of tragedies and went to Newnham College, Cambridge just after World War I to read History and English without being specially academic.[12] She was encouraged to switch from History to French as she had little aptitude for it, a rather telling clue for what I was to find in her biography of Charlotte Brontë. Leon Edel, the biographer of Henry James, was adamant: 'The writing of lives is a department of history and is closely related to the discoveries of history. It can claim the same skills.'[13] In her late twenties Winifred married a Belgian musician, Eugène Gérin, and settled in Paris. There were no children. After their escape from Nazi-occupied France to England they were involved in intelligence work (Winifred as a personal assistant). Eugène died suddenly in 1945, and his widow eventually began writing plays, including one on Charlotte Brontë and her Belgian teacher, M. Heger. Winifred remarried, to a much younger man whom she met at Haworth, and she began writing biographies of the Brontë siblings, while he wrote one on Patrick Brontë. Winifred's biography of Charlotte Brontë in 1967 won much praise and several awards.

I turned first to the index and to Gérin's bits about the Jenkinses. She gives Rev. Evan Jenkins his full name for the first time, and names his brother as Rev. David Jenkins – who was Patrick Brontë's acquaintance (or friend) in West

Yorkshire. Though, alas, Mrs Jenkins still remained without a first name. But there were a few more additions to Mrs Gaskell's account that made me at first intrigued, and actually excited.

The first addition was that the Brontës were fetched from their hotel on arrival in February 1842 by the Jenkinses, and that Mrs Jenkins introduced the Brontës to Madame Heger. Gérin's source for this is 'Chadwick: evidence derived from Mrs Jenkins herself, ch. 15'. This Chadwick knew my great-great-grandmother? Was there somewhere another first-hand account of my ancestor? Then there are further additions by Gérin that are not in Mrs Gaskell's biography, the most lengthy being as follows, which needs to be given in full:

> The visits to Mrs. Jenkins, by which many such a Sunday walk ended, were fraught with as much discomfort to the hosts as to the guests, so unable in their shyness were the Brontës to sustain the slightest small-talk with strangers. In the recollection of the Jenkins's sons, John and Edward (later, in succession to their father, chaplain and assistant chaplain to the Chapel Royal), who were sent to escort the Brontë girls from the pensionnat – or from church – to the other end of the Chaussée d'Ixelles (No. 304) where they lived, there was opposed to them a wall of silence which no tentative conversation on their part could breach. After several such frustrating attempts to make themselves agreeable, the brothers told their mother they had had enough, and she, seeing how patently unhappy Emily Brontë was in particular, herself put an end to the situation. *What was the use, she later asked Mrs. Chadwick, if no one derived any pleasure, and if what was intended as a kindness was regarded in the light of an imposition?*[14]

I gave a half cheer for new material and then stopped. Some things didn't sound right – actually far from it – especially regarding 'John and Edward'. What was Gérin's source? I should have guessed: it was: 'Chadwick, E: *In the Footsteps of the Brontës*, 1914, ch. 15–20'. How could Gérin give a source *six chapters long* for just one anecdote? No wonder her Cambridge college decided that she had no aptitude for history. I obviously had to turn to Chadwick's biography of the Brontës. I ordered the book and waited impatiently for it to arrive.

In chapter 18 of Mrs Chadwick's book, she writes:

> Mrs. Jenkins said that she gave up asking them to her home on Sundays and holidays as she saw that it gave them more pain than pleasure

That copies Mrs Gaskell. Then there is new material:

> and the two sons of Mrs. Jenkins – John and Edward – who were sent to the pensionnat to escort the Brontes when they were invited to their home, declare that they were most shy and awkward, and scarcely exchanged a word with them during the journey.[15]

Then Mrs Chadwick copies another bit from Mrs Gaskell. That is all. So, it was clear: Winifred Gérin in her 1967 book took some of her new material about 'John and Edward' from Mrs Chadwick – *and made the rest up*. And claimed, on no evidence at all, that Mrs Chadwick had talked to Mrs Jenkins. Gérin's whole account about the Jenkinses' sons and Mrs Jenkins's supposed comment was complete and utter fiction. Why was I so sure that the mention of John and Edward couldn't possibly be true? Because I knew that in 1842, when the Brontës arrived in Brussels, John was seven. He was my great-grandfather. Also, I knew that he was the fourth son in the family, eight years younger than Edward. John did not do any escorting.

So what about Mrs Chadwick talking to Mrs Jenkins? Could there be any truth in that at all? I researched Mrs Ellis Chadwick: censuses and her marriage certificate are now online, but could have been discovered at any time before. On 23 July 1885, Esther Alice Miller, 23-year-old daughter of a mill manager in Stockport, married Ellis Henry Chadwick, a schoolmaster in Haworth.[16] Three years later they were living in Bradford, where their first son was born (the firstborn, a daughter, had died in Haworth, as she states in her book). In the 1890s the family moved south towards London; in the 1901 and 1911 censuses they were in Enfield, Middlesex, from where she wrote the Preface to her Brontë book in 1914.[17] She died in Dorset in 1929 in her late sixties. If Mrs Chadwick interviewed Mrs Jenkins then she was a veritable Infant Prodigy, since she had to have interviewed Mrs Jenkins before she was three years old: Eliza Jenkins died in May 1864, Esther Chadwick was born in July 1861.[18]

Why is the escorting story as fictionalized by Winifred Gérin damaging? Because she had made up a story about people whom she didn't know, whom she didn't bother to research, and she had also sloppily flung a 'source' at it. The Jenkins family in her story come off badly: these invented boys whining to their mother; Mrs Jenkins gossiping about how socially inept the Brontë women were … We can all agree that they were shy because of other evidence, but a biographer should be on oath to avoid fiction.[19] There is also another damaging fabrication by Gérin that no one seems to have questioned. It concerns the very last day that Charlotte spent in Belgium – but I shall come to that in a later chapter.

Every biographer to the present day copies this invented 'John and Edward' escorting story.[20] They do not question the fabricated dialogue in Gérin's 1967 book, or her wholly inadequate sources, nor question how and when she thought that Mrs Chadwick had spoken to Mrs Jenkins about the Brontë sisters, when it is impossible from the dates that she did. Nor is it likely that Mrs Chadwick met Edward or John, because Rev. Edward died when Mrs Chadwick was eleven; Rev. John died in 1894, both in Brussels. It seems clear from her book *In the Footsteps* that Esther Chadwick didn't go to Brussels until at least 1910 – she describes the Pensionnat Heger as already demolished.[21] Chadwick may have been researching her biography for years before it was published in 1914, but I am confident that she never met any of the Jenkins family to check her garbled story, nor did she claim that she did. It is a great pity, since Edward and John's sister Helen, who certainly knew the Brontës as a teenager, moved to Paddington, West London from Brussels in the 1890s. In the 1901 census, aged seventy-three, she was living at 23 Formosa Street, next door to her sister-in-law Meliora ('Lora'), Rev. Edward's widow. It is a street of elegant houses in the area near the Regent's Canal known as Little Venice, only twelve miles south of Mrs Chadwick's home in Enfield.

But the escorting story, however fabricated, mainly by Gérin, nagged at me. In the wildest rumour there is often a tiny nugget of truth. Esther Chadwick perhaps heard a garbled memory from someone who knew the names Rev. Edward and Rev. John, though not personally to put them in the right order or realize that John couldn't possibly have done any 'escorting'. If you lived in the English 'village' community in Brussels in the mid-nineteenth century, you certainly would have known them, or of them, but by the time Chadwick was writing in the second decade of the twentieth century the story would be at second or third hand. It seems she met one of the Wheelwright sisters who had been taught for a few months in Brussels by the Brontë sisters, but Frances was a child at the time and apparently didn't attend Rev. Jenkins's church services so was unlikely to know Mrs Jenkins.[22] Chadwick also says she talked to a Belgian, Mademoiselle de Bassompierre, who was also at the Heger pensionnat with the Brontës, but there is no evidence that she knew the Jenkinses either.[23] It is possible that Mrs Chadwick was lying about having met her: her account is merely a slight embroidering of de Bassompierre's letter (in French) in the *Brontë Society Transactions* of 1913. Chadwick's knowledge of French seems poor as she turns 'Miss Emily était beaucoup moins brillante que sa soeur' (Miss Emily was much less brilliant than her sister) into the opposite: 'Mdlle de Bassompierre became very fond of Emily, and considered her superior to Charlotte in every way'.[24] Fabrications abound in biographies, but writing the complete opposite of what is in front of you is perhaps rarer.

Simply pondering on the escorting story led me nowhere. Then one day I spotted an end note I had missed in a recent biography. I did a double take; I read it again with huge excitement. The author was obviously not aware of what she had found. It led me on a small trail of footnotes in other works at the British Library and even on my own bookshelf … But that revelation must wait for when we get to 1842 in this book.

* * *

Rather incensed and perplexed by what I had found, I was eager to get to Brussels at last. I had a lot of places to visit and people to meet. February 2014 arrived and off I went to St Pancras from my home near Little Venice for my first research trip. It was the same month that Charlotte, Emily and their father had journeyed, on their first trip to the Continent, 172 years before.

The train pulled in on a Friday morning at the fairly insalubrious Gare du Midi. I had arranged to meet Helen MacEwan of the Brussels Brontë Group at the cemetery in Evere a few hours later, where she and others had discovered many of my Jenkins family in four graves. It was a generous offer. Without her book, *Down the Belliard Steps*, it would have taken me much longer to discover that the old Protestant cemetery had been closed in the late nineteenth century and bodies moved to Evere. One grave, she said, included Rev. Evan and Eliza Jenkins and some of their children; next to him was their eldest son, my great-great-uncle Rev. Edward (he of the 'escorting story'). Then a short distance away was his younger brother, my great-grandfather Rev. John and family; and opposite him was my great-uncle Edward (another Rev. Charles Edward Jenkins). He had been an Anglican priest in England but had come back to Brussels in 1928 to minister at the Church of the Resurrection, the church built by my family. Sadly, he died of pneumonia only a few years later. He was the last Jenkins clergyman, but 1825 to 1931 (with gaps) is a good stretch for a family of clergymen in a foreign city, who all died far too young.

There was a tram and bus strike, so I got a taxi from near my hotel in the rue du Marché aux Poulets (glorious name for an unprepossessing cobbled street in the old part with a couple of casinos) and was early at the cemetery. I retreated into the office: it was a bitterly cold drizzly day and the office was a warmer place to wait for Helen. 'Two people came before to ask about the Jenkinses,' I was told.

She meant Helen and Renate of the Group. The staff were enormously helpful as I tried to find out if my other great-grandfather was buried there (Ernest Rust Hodson, who had taken over St Bernard's School from the Jenkins family in 1887). They found nothing on him and suggested I go to the City Hall at Ixelles next time I came to Brussels. (I did on another occasion, and I found the site of his grave on a grassy hilltop when the trams weren't on strike.)

But then the woman suddenly brought me a buff folder, labelled: 'Concession de sépulture de la famille Jenkins'. At first I skimmed through its contents, a bit annoyed at my rusty French: but I could tell they were all documents and letters about moving Rev. Evan, wife Eliza and some of their children's bodies from the old Protestant cemetery – the same one Charlotte had been to so often – to the new Evere cemetery. There was a letter in French by my great-grandfather, Rev. John, dated November 1887, from 27 rue St-Bernard, that moved me most: simply seeing his handwriting and understanding his efforts to move his parents, a sister and a brother to the new cemetery. It can't have been easy emotionally.

When Helen arrived she took me to the four Jenkins graves. I don't know precisely what I felt. Excited, yes, but I wasn't sure if Rev. Evan and Eliza, or their son, my great-grandfather Rev. John, might approve of me or my research. But I knew it was good they were together, and that Rev. John had moved his parents and some siblings here, and he was here too with some of his family. Some plastic lay in the broken slab of Rev. John's grave; his elder brother Rev. Edward's grave slab was split; great-uncle Edward's 1930s cross had toppled.

Before I visited the graves, when I went through my great-aunts' albums over the years, I felt I was getting to know them well. Yet the graves were almost those of strangers. But I had gleaned something from looking at the 1887–8 documents in the Jenkins folder. There I felt some kind of kinship. Maybe it was simply that kind, unsolicited move by the woman behind the counter to hand me the Jenkins folder: to one of the family. Members of the Brussels Brontë Group had deciphered the names on the graves. (In the drizzle I could barely see anything.) The new knowledge I had now was confirmation of a rather large brood in the Brussels Jenkins family when Charlotte and Emily arrived in 1842.

Piecing together information from the grave slab, from research in Australia, my great-aunts' albums and other sources, Rev. Evan and Eliza Jenkins had seven children. Only six were living in 1842: their fourth child, Mary Jane Wilhelmina, had died at the age of eight in Ostend in July 1838. It was a boy-noisy, overflowing household for Charlotte and Emily to be confronted with on their visits to the Jenkins family. And, as I found out, theirs were not the only boys in the house.

* * *

I wrote a (rather long) account of my research trip, with a full bibliography, which was posted on 26 March 2014 on the Brussels Brontë Group site. Of course it contains errors, but a lot of it is sound research that holds up. Titled 'Brussels, Brontë, Jenkins: My Great-great-grandparents Rev. Evan and Eliza Jenkins and the Brontës', it relates my first discoveries, including my finding of fabrication in the escorting story that people seemed so fond of.[25] I have had no response to it, and the latest biographer copied again the old, now discredited escorting story made up by Chadwick and Gérin.

* * *

Why is it important to expose the fiction and find out about the Jenkinses? These words of the wonderful, pioneering American academic Richard Altick (d. 2008) are by a master of the craft who says why he believed it was important to know about the lives of authors, including the people they knew:

> behind the book is a man or woman whose character and experience of life cannot be overlooked in any effort to establish what the book really says. The quality of a writer's imagination, the genetic and psychological factors that shaped his personality and determined the atmosphere of his inner being, the occurrences, large and small, that fed the store from which he drew the substance of his art: all these must be sought, examined, and weighed if we are to arrive at a valid understanding of what he intended when he put pen to paper.[26]

In an earlier book, *The Scholar Adventurers* (first published in 1950), Altick seemed to reassure me about the fabrications I had found and guide my steps: 'There is no major literary figure whose biography has been innocent of falsehoods and half-truths, placed there by an early memoirist and then uncritically repeated from writer to writer – and usually embroidered in transmission – until at last they are disproved by the researcher.'[27] I took up the baton and my scholar adventure began.

Two

Evan

'In the sweet shire of Cardigan'

Here is a fairy tale.[1]

A long time ago, when war raged in far-off lands, there was a wild country, part encircled by bleak mountains and ancient bog, part lapped by the sea. Ceredigion, Cardiganshire. A poor, troubled, isolated country; most land was in the hands of the few, the lead and silver mines poisoned both fish and men.

Above the Vale of Aeron, in a one-roomed cottage, a farmer lay dying. It was December; rain was falling again. Outbuildings were poorly repaired, fencing derelict, the land was sodden mud and not even his own; he was the third son, who had sunk below the status of a gentleman claimed by his father. The landlord, owner of vast estates, had died young, unexpectedly, leaving a hapless widow, her son a minor. The agent was soon to go insane. Inside the cottage, around the dying man, were his remaining family. His eldest son had gone off to seek his fortune and was now far away. His wife sat by his bed, exhausted, beyond tears. His teenage daughter knelt by her mother, tucked next to the spinning wheel. The farmer hoped that the little he had saved would help his daughter to find a husband with land, but she looked with longing at the young labourer who strode up the hill from the nearby village and helped with the ploughing and the hay harvest. In the corner of the cottage, away from the smoking peat fire, sat his beloved second son, only just turned twelve. Quiet, dark-haired, small and scared. What would happen to him?

Horse's hooves, a rap on the door. A family friend had arrived hastily from his farm near Lampeter. He had brought paper and ink. More importantly, in

14

a world of Welsh, he had brought English and his writing skills. He sits by the dying man to write down his final wishes, translating: the one pound, a token of love to his elder son who has left home; the huge sum of fifty pounds to his daughter so that she will find favour in the eyes of a gentleman. There is little else to leave other than cattle. His wife and young son are to be his executors. Maybe the friend from Lampeter queries this. But the farmer is adamant. With one last effort he tries to sign his name. He knows how to, he is the son of a gentleman and learned how to read and write. But all he can manage is the first letter of his surname, a rounded 'J'. Not long after, he is buried in the local churchyard. He will never have a headstone.

In a fairy tale the younger son would struggle up from his birth in poverty, he would turn his back on the plough, study strange languages, seek more learning in a city of dreaming spires amidst the fens, then he would journey across the seas to a country far far away and become the confidant of a king. Is this a fairy tale?

* * *

On my return from Brussels in February 2014 my research proper began in confusion. Nowadays it seems easy to look online for a nineteenth-century Cambridge graduate and for an Anglican clergyman before 1835, but the record in *Alumni Cantabrigienses* was unclear. It listed just one Evan Jenkins who had been at Cambridge in the first thirty years of the nineteenth century, but it was undecided about this man's later career: he could have become rector of Dowlais in Glamorgan (the site of the ironworks in Merthyr Tydfil in South Wales) or he became Chaplain in Brussels. Both men had sons who went to Cambridge. This man, whichever he was, was admitted sizar (age '20') at Trinity College, on 22 December 1817, son of Evan, born at Aberystwyth, Cardiganshire. Matriculated Michaelmas 1818, BA in 1823, MA in 1829. Was this my Evan or the Glamorgan Evan? Any Brontë researcher who got that far seems to have given up at this point. Margaret Smith, in her edition of Charlotte Brontë's letters, is cautious, saying that Brussels Evan was '*probably* a graduate of Trinity College Cambridge [...] but the entry in *Venn* is confused'.[2] It was obviously alarming for a descendant: not because I minded about whether Evan was a Cambridge graduate, but because of the lying that would have been involved if he wasn't. John Venn the younger, who continued his father's work and published the relevant volume of Cambridge students in 1947, had tried but failed to link the Jenkins student with the right clergyman, which is not surprising after over a hundred years, especially when a clergyman worked abroad, but it was a disappointment.

I turned to the database of clergymen before 1835.[3] This surely would clear up matters. There were three by the name of Evan Jenkins with a start date of 1800. Only one fitted the bill, and was 'Chaplain: Brussels, Royal chapel 26/03/1835'. That was him, but ... BA at Oxford, Trinity. Well, I didn't mind Oxford, but that was a surprise. Clicking on the BA carried on the confusion, in that the Evan ordained deacon in May 1825 had hailed from Oxford, but the apparently same Evan ordained priest seven months later had been at Cambridge. I dashed off a letter to the Oxford college – who replied that he certainly wasn't there. And at least the Clergy database did link my Evan with Cambridge and Brussels. Panic was over, puzzles remained: why had Oxford crept into the records, and what exactly was Evan's age? If the Cambridge record was correct that he was twenty in December 1817, how did he get to be thirty in the clergy record less than eight years later when he was ordained as a deacon? If Brontë writers give Evan Jenkins a birthdate they follow the Cambridge record, thus that he was born c.1797. But if his deacon ordination record was correct then he was older, born c.1794. Why does that matter? If he was twenty when he started at Cambridge then he was only slightly older than the average intake. But at twenty-three he was a mature student who would have been earning a living, and to be a student at that age was a serious decision.

Thanks to the Clergy database I now had the relevant bishop who conducted the ordinations. Ordination documents can be wondrous documents for family researchers, or be missing, or be too scant to add anything – but to find if they still exist you need to know the diocese, and then the hands-on research can begin. Evan was ordained by the Bishop of London, William Howley (three years later appointed Archbishop of Canterbury), as deacon and then priest in 1825, and I discovered that the ordination 'bundles' were therefore now in the London Metropolitan Archives, a tube ride away along the Circle Line towards the City in Clerkenwell – apt name, Clerks' Well, for a repository of ordination documents.

I had never seen ordination papers before but I hoped that they would definitively establish that the Evan 'born in Aberystwyth' c.1794 (or 1797) at Trinity College, Cambridge was indeed my Evan in Brussels. There was also the oddity of why the only appointment mentioned in the Clergy database referred to a licence in Brussels as late as 1835, when according to family tradition he had been a clergyman there much longer.

At the Clerkenwell archives on a morning in June I ordered the Bishop's Act Books for the period of his ordinations and for the curious licence of 1835. There were also records of the Chapel Royal, Evan's church, dating from around his time. I had also of course ordered the ordination bundles, but I was so nervous that neither 'bundle' would be in the box, or that they would provide little or nothing new, that I looked at the Act Books first. For 1825 it read in a neat hand: 'At an Ordination held in the Chapel Royal Saint James's Palace on Sunday the Twenty ninth day of May instant the Lord Bishop of London admitted the 38 following named Persons into Holy Orders / Deacons […] Evan Jenkins, B.A., Trinity Coll. Oxon [age] 30.' So Oxon (Oxford) was the clerk's error in 1825 and not a modern error. But might the clerk also have got his age wrong? It seems unlikely, age was much more important than the educational establishment: to be ordained a man had to be twenty-three. In Brussels I had been given a copy of Evan's death registration in the Chapel Royal book in which his age was given as fifty-four on the date of his death on 23 September 1849, thus born c.1794, but I wanted further evidence: a date of baptism or even birth, and a place, an address.

In an equally fine hand, Evan's ordination in 1825 as priest was recorded on Sunday, 'the 18th day of December'. He was one of nine so ordained, all from Cambridge colleges, except for one from Oxford. Two were at Trinity College, Cambridge: Evan and William Goode. Then there was a list of seven men, all bracketed together as 'Literate' and 'Colonial'. Literate meaning that they were well schooled in Latin and presumably Greek, but not graduates of Oxbridge. It demonstrates that the Bishop of London was the bishop 'in charge' of clergymen who served abroad, and that almost half the ordained priests on that day were not students at Oxford or Cambridge. No priest's age is noted. According to the Clergy database, William Goode was six years younger than Evan and later spent his priesthood in London. It is unlikely that they had met before or since, but it is interesting that Rev. Goode was also 'fast-tracked' into priesthood. Normally it took a year between being ordained deacon and priest, but Evan was ordained priest after seven months; William Goode after only six months. I later found out the reason for Evan being 'fast-tracked'; maybe Rev. Goode's position was similar.

I was putting off the moment. The box in which I might find Evan's ordination bundles was put on my desk at the window. Serious people either side of me were studying documents with a fierce intensity, tapping at their laptops, wrapped in their own past worlds. Collections of ordination papers really are called 'bundles' correctly: they are small bundles of folded-over paper – letters, testimonials if you are lucky – tied together by a ribbon. I found one with his name on it. It was the priest bundle.

The very first letter within the bundle was definitive. Addressed to the Bishop of London and dated 17 October 1825, it started: 'Whereas our well beloved in Christ Evan Jenkins Bachelor of Arts of Trinity College Cambridge hath declared to us his intention of offering himself as candidate for the sacred office of a Priest'. It was a letter testimonial of his 'learning and good behaviour' by two people who had known him for 'two years and upwards', the two people being W.H. Holworthy 'Chaplain to His B.M.'s Embassy' and Streynsham Master 'A.M. Officiating Minister at the Chapel Royale Brussels'. There was no more mystery. Evan wasn't 'probably' at Trinity College, Cambridge, he was definitely there. The Evan at Trinity was the one who went to Brussels, not the one in Dowlais, Glamorgan.

I had read that priest bundles were usually less informative than deacon bundles, and indeed there were only two other items in the bundle, but one was of immense importance and was a thrilling discovery: it was a note from Evan's older brother David of his baptism and, what I had only dared to hope for, his place of birth:

'1794
Novr. 19. Evan fil. Evan Jenkins Penycastell'
The above is a true copy from the Register Book of Baptisms of Llanbadarn Odyn extracted Sep^t. 21st 1824 by me
D. Jenkins perpetual curate of
Pudsey, Yorkshire

And below the note someone, presumably the Bishop of London's secretary, had worked out Evan's age:

1825
<u>1794</u>
31

So not born in Aberystwyth – which was presumably the nearest large town – but in a village or farmhouse called Penycastell in the parish of Llanbadarn Odyn, neither of which I had heard of, but which names have become so familiar over the years. And Evan was baptized in November 1794, so born maybe a week or so before. I gave out a little yelp of utter delight as I sat at my window desk in Clerkenwell. I had to go to Wales ... Where was this parish?

The final item in the priest bundle was a letter from Evan dated 10 November 1825 to the bishop's secretary. He explains why the certificate of his baptism is late – it simply hadn't arrived in time to be sent on for his deacon ordination in

May. Presumably his deacon testimonials were sufficient to waive the need for proof of his date of birth at that stage. Though there is an oddity here: surely the post wasn't that bad in those days? Why did it take over seven months to go from (presumably) David in West Yorkshire (after a trip to mid-Wales) to Evan in Brussels?

I turned to the deacon bundle. It was fatter. There were more testimonials, including a very florid one from Trinity College dated 18 September 1824. There was also an important note from St John's College, Cambridge: 'Mr. E. Jenkins of Trinity College has attended the lectures of the Norrisian Professor' dated 16 December 1819, and signed by the Professor, T. Calvert.[4] These were essential lectures for those intending to be clergymen (frankly, the only lectures). The dates of both documents were additional confirmation that the Cambridge Evan Jenkins was the Brussels Evan Jenkins. All the finds in the ordination papers belong to my later chapters, as do an unravelling of the odd 1835 licence and the wrong age of '20' in the Trinity College register. I now needed to find Penycastell, somewhere near Aberystwyth, somewhere in the parish of Llanbadarn Odyn, somewhere in the old county of Cardiganshire. Was it a farm or a village? Did it still exist?

* * *

A very important event had occurred a few months before my ordination bundle discoveries: I had re-established contact with my distant cousin in Perth, Western Australia: Marcia Watson. Both of us are descended from John Jay, the father of the Brontës' Mrs (Eliza) Jenkins. Marcia is descended from Eliza's younger sister Margaret, who had married George Wyndham of Dinton, Wiltshire, and emigrated to New South Wales in the 1820s. As I noted above, Marcia had been in touch years before with St Bernard's School in New York to republish my piece about the Jenkinses in Brussels. The revived contact came about through an email I received on my return from Brussels from the splendid founder of the Brussels Brontë Group, Helen MacEwan. Helen wrote that she had received an email two years before from someone enquiring about Evan Jenkins who seemed to be a cousin of mine. Marcia's name rang a bell. I tentatively emailed and so began the start of a truly wonderful collaboration, not only on this book but on my previous one on another member of my family in Brussels.[5]

Marcia is a vastly experienced genealogist, can cope well with Dutch (whereas my forte is French and rusty Latin), and has the patience and skills to navigate foreign sites and digitalized newspapers. Thus in this rich research month in June 2014, Marcia sent me copies of Evan's marriage and death registrations, the latter kept at Ixelles, where he had died, in the house that the Brontë sisters knew well. The methodical Ixelles registration gives the exact age (in French) at which a person dies. In Evan's case, on 23 September 1849 he was fifty-four years, ten months and thirteen days old, born at Aberystwyth. It can't quite be trusted since wife Eliza's age is wrong (she was certainly older than 'forty-three' – or is that what she told the witnesses?!), but it fits well with his baptismal date of 19 November, giving him a birthdate of 10 November 1794. To give some context: that makes him about two years younger than Percy Bysshe Shelley and one year older than John Keats (both of whom will make another appearance in this book – they are not random mentions).

In the marriage registration of Evan Jenkins and Eliza Jay, which took place in Brussels in July 1825, Evan is 'of Aberystwyth in the County of Cardigan in South Wales'. But my hunt was on for Penycastell, his actual place of birth in Cardiganshire.[6] The parish it was in – Llanbadarn Odyn or Odwyn – was not hard to find on the internet. It is a small parish west of the market town of Tregaron in mid-Wales. (Everything below the southernmost reaches of Snowdonia is in South Wales, that is, below the river Dyfi and the town of Machynlleth, but 'South Wales' can conjure up the far south of Wales with its coal-mining and iron and steelworks, so 'mid-Wales' can be more descriptive of this area.)

Llanbadarn Odwyn apparently means the 'very white' church of St Padarn, a sixth-century abbot-bishop to whom the isolated little church is dedicated.[7] To the north, near Aberystwyth, Llanbadarn Fawr refers to the 'great' church of St Padarn (or Paternus), site of his monastery. According to the twelfth-century *Vita sancti Paterni*, Padarn was born in Armorica, north-west Gaul, and arrived in Wales via Ireland. He confronted 'a certain tyrant', Arthur, who tried to steal his tunic, but the ground swallowed Arthur up to his chin until Arthur repented.[8] This is apparently an early reference to King Arthur, though tunic-stealing seems outside his usual line of work. The parish is bordered on the west by the Afon Aeron, and sliced through the middle by the Sarn Helen, the Roman road – a fiercely straight road on the OS map that seems to suddenly stop in another parish further south, at the sites of a Roman fort and bath house, as any sensible road should. Sarn Helen may refer to another Celtic saint, Elen, who is remembered as a prolific road builder in the fourth century. She appears in *The Mabinogion*, in 'The Dream of the Emperor Maxen'.[9] It seems that the knowledge of building roads rather died out in Cardiganshire from then until the turnpike roads (and subsequent Rebecca riots) of the mid-nineteenth century. There is a quote from Catherine Hutton in 1787 displayed in the wonderful Ceredigion Museum in Aberystwyth about journeying from Llanidloes (thirty miles to the east, now in the county of Powys) over the bleak Cambrian Mountains to Aberystwyth:[10]

> In the evening, with the hill above Montgomery full in my remembrance, and the knowledge that four horses were necessary for the hills before us, I went into the kitchen and asked Mr. Parry if anybody ever came back alive from Aberystwith. He said there were some 'fou bonks,' to be sure, but that people did come back alive; and our head coachman comforted us still further by observing that he had several times, generally once or twice a year, taken people thither in safety.[11]

The quote made me appreciate not only the poor roads, but the enormous challenge of getting *out* of Cardiganshire. Another displayed quote in the museum, this time from 1840, showed the progress, but emphasized the earlier isolation: 'Good roads and steam have almost annihilated time and space, and London can be reached from Aberystwyth in 24 hours when formerly it required that time to accomplish the distance from Aberystwyth to Shrewsbury.'[12] It is seventy miles to Shrewsbury, over the border into England, and two days is how long a horse might take. Now we can dash by train in just under two hours – though the 'dash' can turn into a shuffle. I spent a long time recently at Welshpool waiting for the west-bound train – 'an asthmatic caterpillar' our driver called it – to limp past on the single track. There is still a way to go before time and space are annihilated in getting to North and mid-Wales from England.

I stared at every name on the OS map within the parish boundaries – there aren't that many names among these low hills. Penycastell was not there nor any variation. It means 'top or head of the castle'. There were no castles, just one 'non-Roman fort' that might be relevant, but I forgot about it.[13] Penycastell was perhaps a farmhouse that had disappeared. But I should have realized that nothing much changes in this part of Wales: buildings and names just don't disappear. There were a number of Penycastells with hyphens or not in Wales, none in this area, though I was rather attracted by a palatial farmhouse of that name I found on the internet, but Port Talbot was a bit far away, and not even in the same county. Then I just struck lucky as I idly searched: I clicked on an 1890 map of the area and found it – Pen-castell! The line of Sarn Helen was unmistakable, some of the names were also on the OS map; and just to the west of Sarn Helen, the bent line of a minor road matched that on the 1890 map. And on the modern map there were still a few buildings on that spot. I highlighted it with a blob of yellow and wanted to immediately leap on a train. Was it a farm? Still a farm? Marcia had just sent me another useful document – the marriage certificate of Evan's brother Rev. David to his second wife in Pudsey, West Yorkshire in 1848: Evan and David's father had been a farmer.

* * *

The small town of Tregaron is inland, an hour's bus ride south-east of Aberystwyth on the Bay of Cardigan/Irish Sea. I thought, in that excited June, to make it my base for three days. I could take the train from London to Aberystwyth and storm the National Library of Wales to see all the material on anyone called 'Evan Jenkins' or variants who lived near Tregaron at the turn of the nineteenth century (two or three possibles found so far), and make sorties with my backpack into the neighbouring parish of Llanbadarn Odwyn to try and find Penycastell and the little church that was marked by a cross on the modern map.

I also had another reason to visit: to see what was left of Evan's school, as recorded in the Trinity College, Cambridge register. I haven't mentioned Evan's school, Ystradmeurig, until now: this is partly because it is so important and so extraordinary that it will have a chapter of its own. Incidentally, spaces or not, capitals or not, hyphens or not in Penycastell and Ystradmeurig can vary, do vary. Welsh-born T.E. Lawrence ('of Arabia') made the following comments in reply to the proofreader of his *Revolt in the Desert* (an abridgement of *Seven Pillars of Wisdom* made in 1926) about the spelling of various names:

> Proofreader: Jeddah and Jidda used impartially throughout. Intentional?
> Lawrence: Rather! […]
> Proofreader: Jedha, the she-camel, was Jedhah on Slip 40.
> Lawrence: She was a splendid beast. […]
> Proofreader: Author is addressed 'Ya Auruns', but on Slip 56 was 'Aurans'.
> Lawrence: Also Lurens and Runs: not to mention 'Shaw'. More to follow, if time permits.
> Proofreader: Sherif Abd el Mayin of Slip 68 becomes el Main, el Mayein, el Muein, el Mayin, and le Muyein.
> Lawrence: Good egg. I call this really ingenious.[14]

* * *

On my trip to Wales in June 2014, my first spot of research was at the National Library of Wales, on the hill above the sea in Aberystwyth. Outside the station, the last on the line, I pulled my suitcase onto the bus heading uphill to the monumental twentieth-century building that is one of the largest libraries in the UK. Aberystwyth has been a seaside resort since the 1770s. It saw more tourism during the French and Napoleonic Wars as Britons were unable to get to the Continent and flocked instead to Wales and the Lake District in search of the picturesque or a watering place and a spot of bathing. Catherine Hutton, travelling with her parents at the elderly age of thirty-one, survived the dangerous journey to Aberystwyth described above. In his gloriously whimsical book of 1903: *Cardiganshire: A Personal Survey of Some of Its Antiquities, Chapels, Churches, Fonts, Plate, and Registers*, with 'Numerous Illustrations', George Eyre Evans ('Minister of the Gospel and Member of the Cambrian Archaeological Association') begins with Catherine Hutton on her first visit to Wales in July 1787.[15] Evans had delightedly found her account in *Reminiscences of a Gentlewoman of the Last Century*, compiled from her diary and letters by her cousin. She was the daughter of William Hutton, 'the historian of Birmingham', who was a friend of the polymath Dissenter Dr Joseph Priestley.

The interesting Mr Hutton walked back to Shrewsbury (not entirely intentionally), leaving his wife and daughter at the Talbot Inn in Aberystwyth to enjoy boiled chicken and mutton chops, and rediscover the use of their legs in a stroll along the promenade. Mother and daughter were soon persuaded to move out of the inn, as Catherine relates, 'it was found that we did not drink a sufficient quantity of wine with it, and a hint was given us of a private lodging'. This is seven years before Evan was born; to some hoteliers today that might sound familiar. Having moved out of the inn, Catherine comments on the price of fish and meat, and adds: 'The common people complain that the sea bathers have raised the provisions to an enormous price.' Tourists were a nuisance as long ago as 1787. Catherine later wrote to her brother about staying in Aberystwyth that summer: 'it was the only place I ever left wishing that I might not see it again', but she did admire the 'magnificent mountains of Wales'. These short quotes give the impression of a woman one might move to another carriage to avoid, but her letters portray a forthright, witty woman. She was a friend of Byron's half-sister Augusta Leigh, corresponded with Charles Dickens, was a novelist, dress historian and pudding maker. After the hell of the Birmingham anti-Dissenter riots of 1791, when mobs destroyed the houses of the Huttons and Dr Priestley, she explored Wales many more times.

* * *

Back (or forward) to the twenty-first century, I had ordered three items at the monumental National Library in Aberystwyth in June 2014. I felt scruffy and laden after a five hours' train trip from London via Birmingham. I was also damping down any idea that I would have a Eureka moment with what I had ordered. One was a Jenkins will from a bundle called 'Cardiganshire wills, 1805–1847', the second was a marriage bond of 1785 for an Evan Jenkin, yeoman, that sounded equally unpromising (Jenkin not Jenkins, and yeoman?), and the third was 'cartographic material' of Peny Castell in the parish of Llanbadarn Odwyn that sounded rather promising. That was all I could find and I was sceptical about two of them. I had excitedly told cousin Marcia of my discovery in the ordination papers about Penycastell. Two weeks before my trip, she emailed back. So far all I had known was that Evan had an older brother David (friend of Patrick Brontë), but now Marcia wrote from Perth:

> Surfing around the internet to avoid housework and shopping, I looked at the 1841 census. Moses Roderick is living at Pencastell and the family seems to have lived there for years. He came from Llangeitho, not too far away, and he married a Mary Jenkins in 1817. All it says is she was from Llanbadarnodwyn.[16]

There is something wonderful about having a 'research assistant' that is also utterly irritating. It was brilliant news and such a straightforward research thing to do that I hadn't thought of, but there I was on a bubble with a scenario in my head, and it burst. Mary. They had a sister? The census stated that she was fifty in 1841, so she would have been born about 1791 – which was well placed between David in 1787 and Evan in 1794. But I fought to prevent my image of those 'lonely brothers' being disrupted. I replied, totally irrationally, but surely 'every other woman in Wales' is called Mary Jenkins. Or maybe there are other Pencastells in Llanbadarn Odwyn. I asked, 'Do we know if Evan or David made a will' that might name her? I really resisted this 'intrusion' of a sister. Marcia calmly replied that it was the only Pencastell/Penycastell in that parish, and I immediately felt contrite.

* * *

In a vast room at the National Library with only a small scattering of other researchers, I unwrapped the ribbon around the bundle of 'Cardiganshire wills, 1805–1847'. They were in a collection of personal papers and letters acquired by Evan Richards, ale-house keeper, who farmed in the nineteenth century at Nanthenfoel, a farm about twelve miles south-west of Tregaron. The papers had been donated in 1983 by Mrs Estyn Evans of Belfast. There were eleven wills from five different parishes, though five of the wills were of people who lived in the parish of Llanbadarn Odwyn. None were apparently proved. They seemed a random collection dating over forty years. But not entirely random: David Richards of Glanywern, a farm near the river Aeron, about ten miles west of Tregaron, had witnessed several of the wills or was named as a trustee. Perhaps he was the father of Evan Richards and somehow this odd little collection had been kept safe, and maybe even travelled across the water to Ireland and then back again. Amongst them was a will by 'Evan Jenkins of p. Llanbadarn Odwyn, farmer, 8 Dec. 1806'.

I unfolded the small piece of paper sceptically. It was the texture of a dry autumn leaf that could crumble any moment. The hand was scratchy but educated and legible. Right at the top of the page, with hardly any margin, it began: 'In the Name of God Amen. I Evan Jenkins of'. My heart missed a beat. What he was 'of' had been split over two lines but was unmistakable: 'of Peny-castell'. I can't remember now if I cried or laughed, or just stopped breathing for a moment. But would the right people be named in it? After a short preliminary it continued: 'I give & bequeath unto my Beloved Son David Jenkins the sum of One Pound [...] also I give & bequeath unto my Beloved Daughter Mary Jenkins the sum of Fifty Pounds and her Chamber'. So, David and Evan did indeed have a sister. The 'chamber' is interesting: a room of her own, but perhaps meaning also the furniture and furnishings in it. Her father continued: 'Also I constitute name and appoint my Beloved Wife and my Beloved Son Evan Jenkins to be my Sole Executors to them I give all the rest and residue of my goods cattle chattles and effects of what kind and nature they be and after the Disease of my beloved wife my will is that her share is to be divided betwixt my said Daughter Mary and my said Son Evan [...] in the year year [sic] of our Lord 1806.'

Alas, the beloved wife is not named. At the age of nineteen, son David has a token one pound and no share in what remains nor a role as executor. One could read a family quarrel into that, but perhaps the father had set his elder son off on the right path in life: the father's job was done. But there is no mention of his younger son Evan's future: no money or wishes for his education. The will implies that twelve-year-old Evan's future lay on the farm, even after his mother's death. I looked across the south reading room, through the window, to the low yellow and green hills under the June sun above the sea. On the table in front of me lay my great-great-great-grandfather's will, and the landscape outside was now part of my background, but if the younger Evan hadn't left Wales, I wouldn't be here.

At the bottom of the will was the name of a witness that seemed to be 'Grace Davies' 'by mark' – the mark like a shrunken balloon, and then farmer Evan Jenkins's name and the florid 'J' that he had attempted for his mark. Below both names was that of David Richards, the other witness, who I presume had written the will following Evan's dictation. It was just an extraordinary survival, but so frustrating – not least: what was the 'beloved wife's' first name?

I turned next to look at the marriage bond of 1785. The parish was right – 'Llanbadarn Odyn'. The date was certainly possible since David was born in 1787 – but the surname was Jenkin not Jenkins. This Evan Jenkin was a yeoman, which suggested that he owned land. He could also sign his name. The letters were carefully and slowly shaped, with a few decorative squiggles, and bore no resemblance to the florid 'J' mark of the will some twenty years later. I photographed it and handed it in. Until I knew the beloved wife's name – which I might never know – I had to dismiss it.

Finally I turned to the map of 'Peny Castell in the parish of Llanbadarn Odyn'. It was part of the Nanteos estate records – a name that meant nothing to me at the time but turned out to be one of the largest estates in Cardiganshire. It was a rough sketch of the fields belonging to the farm, numbered, annotated (in English though with Welsh field names), with acreages alongside, in fading writing. In total, Penycastell was a farm of just over forty-seven acres.[17] There was a mixture of arable and pasture surrounding a garden, presumably where the farmhouse stood. Neighbours were named – proprietors, not occupiers – one of whom was the famous Thomas Johnes of Hafod, another major landholder in Cardiganshire; but there was also the name David Jenkins, maybe a relation who actually owned land. The catalogue said the map was c.1807. I learnt from an archivist that the date was because of the watermark and its similarity to other estate papers. If so, it was at the time of farmer Evan's death. Thomas Johnes of Hafod lived until 1816, so c.1807 for the map fitted with him. But 'David' Jenkins became a puzzle.

On the back was a note that was not easy to decipher: 'This farm was held under a lease for 21 years which expired abt. 5 years ago. The Buildings are ?resting upon Props, a proof amongst many of the neglect of the agent in not forcing the lessee to have the Buildings in repair.' It was clear, whatever the actual date of the map, that Evan had been a tenant farmer. It made me angry that this agent should have *forced* Evan to repair buildings for which, perhaps, he had no means or his health was too poor. The note ended: 'This farm should fetch 20 [pounds].' I left the library with mixed feelings of excitement at having found so much and depression on behalf of my ancestors: Evan died, perhaps only in early middle age, in a tumbledown farm that the owners might casually and callously sell at any time. There are frequent reports of poor harvests because of bad weather in this period, even famine, and many rents were doubled or trebled during the Napoleonic Wars because of war taxation, both of which could have impoverished tenant farmer Evan and led to his early death.[18]

But now it was time to try and find Penycastell. I retrieved my suitcase and got a bus heading south to Tregaron.

* * *

In summer 1794 (the year of 'Brussels' Evan's birth), Great Britain had been at war with Revolutionary France for just over a year. King Louis and Marie Antoinette had been guillotined, but in July came the death of Robespierre and the end of the Reign of Terror. On the British side of the Channel, two Cambridge University students decided on a walking tour in Wales. One was a serious old Etonian; the other was an excitable, overdramatic, brilliant, overgrown child who had already enjoyed his share of debauchery and radical politics, had written the odd poem and run off to join the army (he was discharged back to Cambridge after a few months).[19] Unfortunately for us, the book of their walk in Wales was written by the former, and not by Samuel Taylor Coleridge.

According to Coleridge's pre-eminent biographer Richard Holmes, the walking tour was newly fashionable for students, who would dress as tramps, stay at local inns, climb, walk, swim, chat with 'the common people' and commune with Nature.[20] Coleridge and his fellow student Joseph Hucks walked over five hundred miles in July and early August in a loop from Gloucester in England, north and west into Anglesey, and then down through the mountains of Snowdonia. 'While tramping,' Holmes writes, 'Coleridge fuelled himself with vast supplies of bread, cheese and brandy. He insisted on climbing Penmaenmawr without a guide: they got lost, ran out of water, and were then benighted and thought they were pursued by monsters.'[21] Wending their way home to England south through the lower hills of Cardiganshire must have been an anticlimax – or a restful relief. They stopped for the night in the small market town of Tregaron, having walked almost thirty miles from Aberystwyth via the cataract at the Devil's Bridge. Did Coleridge chat excitedly to local farmers? Regale the denizens of the inn with radical political ideas? This is what Hucks writes: 'Tregarron is a miserable hole, in the which however we were constrained to sleep, and to break the windows in our bed rooms to let in the fresh air.' That's it. He continues: 'We took a guide from thence to Llanindovrey, over the lonely and trackless mountains of Cardiganshire; it rained hard the whole way.'[22] Perhaps the mutual incomprehension by the Welsh- and English-speakers meant there was nothing else to relate, even when your companion is Coleridge; or maybe the students were just tired and wet.

Unfortunately Tregaron and its inhabitants fare no better from a visitor eleven years after Coleridge and Hucks broke the inn windows. Richard Vaughan Yates, the son of a Unitarian minister in Liverpool, in his 'A tour in Wales' of 1805, was struck by the primitiveness of the inhabitants of Tregaron. Its people were 'in a state bordering on barbarism in their dress, their habitations and their manners, which are extremely rude', though he liked one of the inns (presumably the windows could be opened).[23] By 1821 the manners of the inhabitants, or the perception of their manners, had improved slightly. This is Rev. R.H. Newell in his book of advice to amateur artists on the scenic possibilities in Wales and exactly where to 'station' their easels:

> Tregaron is a miserable village of straggling thatched cottages; and though it has a church, wooden bridge, and mountainous back ground, I could find no station worth your trying. There are two poor public houses without signs. I got a decent bed at one of them, and you will probably procure little else except civility and eggs, but both of them cheap enough, the latter are sometimes even ten a penny! The church is the only tolerable building, and much better than might be looked for in so secluded a place.[24]

From miserable hole to civility and eggs is a kind of progress in almost thirty years. But what none of them was interested in was that Tregaron was a drovers' town. It was the hub for gathering in the Welsh black cattle from south Cardiganshire, Pembrokeshire and Carmarthenshire before they were herded slowly over the Cambrian Mountains to the hamlet of Abergwesyn, and thence onto London.[25] The railways brought a halt to the centuries' long tradition in the mid-nineteenth century, but young Evan and his family knew well the frenzy of this great event. No doubt his father's cattle were led off to England along the old drovers' way. In those days there were at least half a dozen inns in Tregaron. When I got off my bus on that June afternoon after a morning in the library, I booked into the only one left, Y Talbot, in the small, tranquil main square. I didn't encounter hordes of cattle being shod and led off for their hundreds of miles' walk, but I did later meet a jogger – that can sum up one difference in Tregaron between, say, 1814 and 2014. I was sitting staring at my OS map at the table outside the Talbot Hotel one gorgeous sunny morning after breakfast. A jogger stopped: he wanted to be sure which the drovers' road was – that way or that. Having never been to Tregaron before in my life, but quite quick at bluffing that I am brilliant with maps, I pointed: that way, I said. I *think* I was right. I never saw him again.

* * *

I am a walker, a rambler. I wear a map carrier around my neck, also a whistle, a compass, with gaiters on my legs, various layers, poles to hand. I was walking on the moors near Haworth in bleak early April, and having got to Top Withens (a contender for 'Wuthering Heights') I was improvising a circular walk back to the hotel, following my map. I met a couple of male walkers who greeted me:

'A real hiker – first we've met,' one exclaimed.

'Am I real?!'

'You have all the dangly bits.'

I held my head high after that. I am relieved that they hadn't seen me going astray right at the start out of Haworth nor getting bogged down in a field near Stanbury on the way back having 'mislaid' the footpath. I once read a story of a female climber on Mount Everest who got disorientated. Another climber came across her and asked if she was lost. 'Oh no, not lost; I just don't know where I am right now.' That's me as a walker.

My aim that Saturday morning, after my first night at Y Talbot in Tregaron, was to try and find if the Jenkins home at Penycastell farm still existed. I was going to aim for the yellow blob that I had placed on my map, where I'd marked the crooked side road, following what seemed to be footpaths. It looked really straightforward: follow the footpaths west with a few zigzags around fields. I counted up the kilometre squares: four and a bit (roughly three miles), which meant it should take an hour to get to the Roman road – Sarn Helen – and then look for a crooked side road. There were some contours but they were fairly widely spaced, so it was just an undulating walk. Easy!

I still cannot understand how it actually took me well over two hours to find Sarn Helen, considering that I am the proud owner of 'dangly bits'. I remember well the lush fields on the banks of the Teifi: because I went round in a circle at least twice trying to find the bridge over the river, which does a meander here, banked by over-six-foot-tall reeds that I peered through trying to find some way of crossing. When I calmed down and looked at the map properly it was obvious: I was on the wrong side of the field boundary. I tried the neighbouring field and peered down at the river again: a little footbridge! I slithered down the bank, hoping no one had seen me being so inept … or trespassing. Then I was across the water-lilied and glistening Teifi into rich green pasture dotted with sheep, thinking that my ancestors might have walked this way often on their way to market. It was beautiful. I got lost again.

The challenge of footpaths in summer is that vegetation can overwhelm them, especially if there are no other ramblers or even dog-walkers (I saw no one else walking at all). But I finally found the first farm I had been aiming for and a farmer waved at me – astonished to see anyone walking, warning me that I was trespassing again? Luckily he was simply being friendly and obviously curious. Pummelled and battered by vegetation, I eventually found myself in a hollow way, and then a little climb up to – a road! It could only be Sarn Helen, a modern B road, slumbering under a blue June sky with enormous, ominous cumulus clouds piling up overhead. I found a chapel that seemed to be marked on my map (if I was indeed on the right road). It was named 'Llwynpiod' on a plaque on the mosaic-grey-stoned front wall. I should have taken more notice but I snapped it and walked on. The crooked side road was nearby. I felt incredibly nervous. If it was still a working farm there might be no one around, or dogs that barked and nipped me. I might have come all this way only to have to turn back, my tail between my nipped legs.

There was a cottage in a dip ahead – no name sign at all announced what it was. There was a neat small green lawn, honeysuckle and yellow roses rambling along a wooden fence. I looked through an open door. There was a fair-haired, middle-aged woman standing there in sweater and trousers.

'Um, I'm looking for Penycastell. Do you –?'
I pronounced castell in the appalling English way, not knowing that a Welsh 'lisp' was required: casteth. But she replied in an English accent: 'Yes.' She looked startled. We were, after all, in the sort of middle of nowhere. I stammered out my Jenkins story and was invited in. Not long after, I was sitting in the large room of an old cottage. There were thick, whitewashed stone walls, wooden beams, flagstone floor stretching from a wood-burning stove to the furnishings of a modern kitchen/dining room, an elegant red spiral staircase in the corner, and a door leading into a new annexe that contained a sitting-room. In my hands was a mug of tea. I thought: yesterday I was reading about my great-great-great-grandfather dying in this room; just over two hundred years later, here I am with a mug of tea. There was a framed coloured plan hanging on the wall of the 'Lands of Peny Castell [...] The Property of Wm. Edwd. Powell Esqr' – a later map than the c.1807 sketch. I learnt that William Edward Powell, inheritor of the Nanteos estate, was only eighteen – a minor – when his tenant farmer Evan Jenkins wrote that will on his deathbed. Perhaps teenage Mary's 'chamber' was up a wooden

ladder where the red spiral staircase now stood.

Margaret's husband John came back from Tregaron shortly after. He looked equally startled. They were 'incomers' from England but had been living there for years, maybe undisturbed until I arrived. But how hospitable they were. They even took a photo of me in their house with my camera, and John walked up one of the hills in their garden with me to show the view over the Vale of Aeron and escorted me part of the way up the lane and across a few fields to the church of Llanbadarn Odwyn. They owned maybe twelve acres that they let out to farmers. And I think he mentioned the 'fort' on the map (the 'castell') that had once been investigated, and was on their land – but my head was spinning and I didn't take it in. It is a truly lovely spot.

* * *

Penycastell lies in between two rivers, the Aeron and the Teifi; and since the eighteenth century it also lies between two religions. The tiny church of St Padarn – Llanbadarn Odwyn – was a ten-minute walk from the old farmhouse. White stone posts on either side of a wide iron gate gave a glimpse into the churchyard surrounding the grey-stone medieval church. Overhead, after John left me, the white cumulus clouds were rapidly turning into grey cumulonimbus. Beyond the tall green grass swaying between the headstones, beyond a squat yew and elegant Scots pines, were the low hills, a darker green, on the far side of the Aeron river to the west. The ancient church stood perched on its hill, a lovingly restored remnant of an older religion in Wales, on a possibly Celtic site, between the Methodist centre of Llangeitho, the village at the bottom of the hill on the Aeron that I was about to visit, and the Methodist Llwynpiod chapel I had passed that morning on Sarn Helen.

Of course not 'two religions': Methodism was a movement that started in the eighteenth century within the established Anglican Church that only broke away in 1811. But there must have been repercussions within the Jenkins family. Farmer Evan's two sons, David and Evan, became Anglican clergymen after his death – respected members of the established church. Their sister Mary married a Calvinistic Methodist, Moses Roderick from Llangeitho, who was prominent in the Llwynpiod chapel. The current, restored chapel was built in 1803, but the original had been half a century older. And yet the first headstone I noticed as I creaked open the iron gate of the more ancient Anglican church was the large headstone by the path commemorating Mary and Moses Roderick of Pencastell, and next to them the headstone of a son, also Moses Roderick, baptized (I later discovered) as a Welsh Calvinistic Methodist, all mid-nineteenth-century. But

I so wanted to see if there was any trace of Mary's father, farmer Evan, and his wife, she who had (as yet) no name. Could I find her name on a gravestone here? It was becoming an obsession. John, the new owner of Penycastell, had said that they would be cutting the grass in the churchyard in due course and would look for any Jenkinses. I was undertaking a fruitless and frankly insane search. As the heavens opened, I stared forlornly around at mostly illegible gravestones amidst the thigh-high wet grass and retreated into the tiny church.

Eglwys Llanbadarn Odwyn is a simple jewel of a church. Plain white walls, wooden pews the length of the little nave, plain glass windows, a simple beamed roof. On display was a fresh notice with the name of the priest in charge with his *rhif symudol* (mobile number). The caption to a black-and-white photograph taken outside the church of clergymen grouped either side of the 'Lord Bishop of St David's' stated that it had been reopened in 1952. I later learned that it had been in a very poor state in the nineteenth century. It is possible that none of the family of farmer Evan, wife, and children David, Mary and Evan had been able to worship there, but Mary was buried here and so must have been her father, farmer Evan.[26]

It was lunchtime, the sun had come out again, and I was hungry. The map showed a track from the church, and then a footpath going steeply down to the road at the valley floor, which led to Llangeitho, parallel to the river Aeron. There was an enticing blue symbol for a pub, but a walker learns to be sceptical. The little Aeron has its source in the Mynydd Bach between Tregaron and Aberystwyth. Below Llangeitho the river continues south-west for five miles to Tal-sarn, where it turns north-west towards the sea at Aberaeron on Cardigan Bay. Dylan and Caitlin Thomas stayed at Tal-sarn for a while during the Second World War, and their daughter Aeronwy was so-called because she was conceived on the banks of the Aeron.[27]

The track from the church led me to pastureland that sloped steeply down beyond a farm gate to the river. I had somehow missed the footpath. I studied the map: at the bottom of the steep pasture was Pantbeudy Hall, further north along the road I was aiming for. I began retracing my route along the track: finally, cunningly concealed behind gigantic ferns, there seemed to be a way down through jungle. Alas, I had no machete, but I had my walking poles to hack my way downhill to reach the country road and the village. Llangeitho has a prominent white marble statue of the famous Welsh Methodist preacher Daniel Rowland (d. 1790) in its churchyard, and a pub – that didn't open until the evening. But it had a shop and I sat on a bench in the village square in between showers with a sandwich, recovering from yet another pummelling by Welsh vegetation, and wondering about Methodism versus the established church and whether it had created an irreparable rupture in the Jenkins family.

Rev. Daniel Rowland was born only two miles downstream c.1711 and became the leader of Welsh Methodism from about 1750.[28] He was based in Llangeitho, where he was the Anglican curate, first to his father and then to his son. Thousands flocked to this quiet village to hear his sermons. At first he was known as the 'angry cleric' because of the way he chastised sinners. The historian John Davies says: 'The message of the revivalists was terrifyingly simple: eternal torment in hell would be the fate of those who did not have a personal awareness of Christ's suffering and sacrifice. This message, together with descriptions of the torments of the damned, was the theme of Daniel Rowland's eloquent sermons', though he apparently mellowed as he grew older.[29] Methodist meetings were often theatrical events, with vigorous hymn singing and the exultant 'jumping' of those who felt they had been saved. Living so close to this fervour, did the Jenkinses get caught up in the excitement and this heavy emphasis on the seriousness of religion, or hold aloof, preferring low-key traditional services? They remained questions as I sat on my bench, perhaps on the very site of Rowland's chapel, built for him by his parishioners when he was ejected from his curacy at the church.

In West Yorkshire in the 1830s, Charlotte and Branwell Brontë waxed satirical about Methodism in their Angrian stories. Charlotte's Methodist preacher told his congregation: '"Filthy rags are we [...] refuse of the Kennel, Thieves murderers, slanderers, false-swearers." Amen, Amen! groaned every hearer from his inmost soul.'[30] In her 1849 novel *Shirley*, set in 1811–12, the Methodist 'Revd' Moses Barraclough is a drunkard, a wooden-legged, hypocritical leader of the local Yorkshire Luddites, 'roaring at a revival or a love-feast' with 'cat-like, trustless eyes'.[31] However, the trio of Anglican curates are also viewed with a satirical eye. It seems that, despite his children's sardonic views, Patrick Brontë generally got on well with Wesleyan Methodists;[32] in Wales, however, Methodism was, or became, Calvinistical not Wesleyan: they believed in predestination, that only the 'elect' had been chosen by God, a harsher creed.

I had one more adventure during my stay in Tregaron, but that belongs to the next chapter. It was now time to find out if David Jenkins's ordination papers had survived. It had seemed from his father's 1806 will that he was no longer in Wales; we know that four years later he was a curate at Dewsbury with Patrick Brontë.[33] Where had he spent the years until he was able to be ordained at twenty-three? What I discovered was surprising, and there was another find that was even more important.

* * *

A week later I was on the train to York, clutching a mauve and turquoise plan of the modern campus of the University of York. The archives of the diocese of York are held in the new building of the Borthwick Institute for Archives, which was somewhere amongst the maze of 'mauve' buildings, conveniently near a bus stop – if I managed to get off at the right bus stop. It would take at least three hours of travelling, so I'd exchanged emails with the archives assistant Nathan to try to ensure that there would be something for me to see. Having checked the Clergy database online, I gave him the deacon ordination date in July 1810 and that David went to Dewsbury in West Yorkshire as a curate. At first he replied: 'I have checked the indexes for a Rev. David Jenkins for you – there is no entry for a David, but there is one for a Davis whose details appear to match.' I kept calm: I had a good feel for typos. Nathan then reported back that he was indeed David in the papers – and the papers had survived. He booked me in for noon.

The familiar cardboard boxes of ordination bundles were ready for me. In the deacon bundle was a note from someone called Thomas Edwards, dated Chelsea 22 June 1810.[34] It read: 'These are to certify that Mr David Jenkins lived with me as Lat. & Gk. Master abt three years & a half, during that period he conducted himself with the greatest propriety, as a true Christian, and as a person well affected to the present Government in Church and State.' David had taught Latin and Greek in, of all places, Chelsea – London. Today, the name Chelsea, on the River Thames, conjures up elegant houses with wealthy occupants, expensive cafés, the once trendy King's Road. It was more of a riverside suburb then, but going at the age of nineteen from a small tenanted farm in the middle of nowhere to teach classics to well-scrubbed sons of the London gentry seemed so bizarre. Three years and a half – that meant he had arrived in London around the time of his dying father's will. Perhaps he had still been at home in Wales when the will was made. I needed to ponder it and look at the other testimonials, though I was amused by the formulaic 'well affected to the present Government'. In June 1810 George III was popular and months away from his final madness, but the government was weak, led by Prime Minister Spencer Percival, and not expected to last long. And abroad, Napoleon was about to annexe the 'Kingdom of Holland' into the French Empire. An isolated Britain and a tottering government sound familiar two hundred years later.

But then another piece of paper caught my eye and I looked in astonishment

34

at what I had found. I had found her name! It was an affidavit from Elizabeth Jenkins, dated 25 April 1809, County of Cardigan:

> The Voluntary affidavit of Elizabeth Jenkins of Pencastell in the Parish of Lanbadarn Odin in the said County of Cardigan widow of Evan Jenkins deceased late of the same Husbandman.
>
> She Deposeth that she had a son by her said Husband of the name of David but that no Register being kept at the time of this Birth on account of the Parish Church of Lanbadarn odin being at that time in Ruines, that the said David was baptised at Pencastell aforesaid and that it being necessary to ascertain the age of her said son David Jenkins She this said Mother declareth that she was delivered of him on the second day of February in the year of our Lord one thousand seven hundred and eighty seven.

And mother Elizabeth signed the document with her mark (a tall cross shape) before the local Justice of the Peace, a Mr Lloyd. A woman on the other side of the table in the research room looked up enquiringly – maybe I yelped a little – she was perhaps a genealogical researcher too, because when I whispered in excitement that I had just discovered the name of my three times great-grandmother she smiled understandingly.

David Jenkins's deacon and priest ordination papers were brimming with stuff. I photographed, made notes, but just wanted to dash home to London to get at my laptop – what was the name of the woman on the marriage bond who had married Evan Jenkin, yeoman, the one that I had dismissed? Was it also Elizabeth? Had I found the other half of young Evan's family?

When I finally got home, shaky fingers tried to find the right photo file. There it was: Evan Jenkin, of the parish of Llanbadarn Odyn, had agreed in November 1785 to marry Elizabeth Davies, of the parish of Caron (another name for Tregaron). There might be two Evan Jenkinses getting married around that time in the parish, but two Evans marrying two Elizabeths? And it was a perfect date for producing David in February 1787. I had tried to guess her name from those of her son Evan's daughters: Rev. Evan and Eliza had three – Helen Eliza, Mary Jane Wilhelmina and Mina Janet. I had even researched the idea of Wilhelmina as a Welsh or Irish name. The obvious had stared me in the face but it hadn't occurred to me that Eliza Jenkins's mother-in-law would also be an Elizabeth. It was now clear that Rev. Evan and Eliza in Brussels had named their first daughter with the names of their mothers.

* * *

The women universally wear a petticoat and a jacket fitting close to the waist, of striped woollen cloth and a man's hat. A blue coat many of them had, but it is reserved for dress, and in common they wear a long piece of woollen cloth wrapped around the waist. I have a hundred times seen a woman carrying a pitcher of water on her head, a child or loaf in this wrapper and knitting as she walked along.[35]

The later correspondent of Dickens, Catherine Hutton, writing from Aberystwyth in 1787. That Welsh top hat is such a distinctive style for the women of Cardiganshire in the eighteenth and nineteenth centuries that I was given a Welsh doll wearing a top hat when I was small, perhaps when my family went on their one holiday to Wales. Great-great-great-grandmother Elizabeth Jenkins née Davies dressed like that. An anonymous writer in 1828 wrote that 'the black hat is the most expensive article of dress and rather becoming'. He or she added: 'the country people often go barefoot, indeed, shoes are rather an incumbrance in climbing hills and traversing rugged ground, black stockings are worn without feet but with a narrow slip passing over the upper part of the foot and bound by a loop around the second toe; there is a good reason for this, they have so much walking in bog land and their feet often wet with its yellow waters that stockings would be a great inconvenience.'[36] Some fell runners prefer to run without shoes; in the past it was often a practical choice rather than extreme poverty.

Sheep aren't mentioned in farmer Evan Jenkins's will but it is probable that Elizabeth spun wool and knitted. In the 1850s the weirdly admirable Norfolk-born George Borrow walked through Wales, which resulted in his famous travel book *Wild Wales*. He has a very plodding style, writing down every exchange he makes from the greetings to the goodbyes, but he is so endearing and so in love with Welsh poetry that you forgive him and invite him into your home. Somewhere in the Conwy valley, in North Wales, he arrives at a cottage, 'just inside the door of which sat a good-looking middle-aged woman engaged in knitting, the general occupation of Welsh females'.

'Good-day,' said I to her in Welsh. 'Fine weather.'
'In truth, sir, it is fine weather for the harvest.'
'Are you alone in the house?'
'I am, sir, my husband has gone to his labour.'

Borrow interrogates her, in his usual manner, and then asks what I am particularly interested in, thinking of Elizabeth Jenkins not able to sign her name in the affidavit:

> 'Can you read?'
> 'I can, sir.'
> 'Have you any books?'
> 'I have the Bible, sir.'
> 'Will you show it me?'
> 'Willingly, sir.'
> Then getting up she took a book from a shelf and handed it to me at the same time begging me to enter the house and sit down [...] On opening the book the first words which met my eye were 'Gad i mi fyned trwy dy dir!' Let me go through your country. Numbers xx. 22.
> 'I may say these words,' said I, pointing to the passage. 'Let me go through your country.'
> 'No one will hinder you, sir, for you seem a civil gentleman.'
> 'No one has hindered me hitherto. Wherever I have been in Wales I have experienced nothing but kindness and hospitality, and when I return to my own country I will say so.'[37]

Perhaps Elizabeth Jenkins and other women like her could also read the Bible in Welsh, even if they couldn't sign their names.

Another endearing author with a very different, ornate style and a very different personality also tramped around Wales: the 'opium-eater' Thomas De Quincey. Fifty years before the middle-aged George Borrow walked his methodical, indefatigable way through all of Wales, the middle-class schoolboy De Quincey ran away from Manchester Grammar School. Barely five-foot tall, not quite seventeen, the academically gifted De Quincey escaped from school in July 1802, suffering from depression, ill health and desperate for freedom.[38] Nineteen years later his account of his childhood and subsequent opium addiction, the sensational *Confessions of an English Opium-Eater*, was published first as articles in the *London Magazine*. Having walked first to Chester to see his widowed mother, he was intent on reaching the mountains and wild open air of North Wales. Not having enough money to always stay at inns he often slept outdoors, but near the lake of Tal-y-llyn, ten miles north of 'the sweet solitudes of Cardiganshire', a kind 'family of young people' gave him a bed in their cottage.[39]

There is a fairy-tale element in the story of his stay with 'four sisters and three brothers, all grown-up, and remarkable for elegance and delicacy of manners'. He says that they spoke English, 'an accomplishment not often met with in so many members of one Welsh family, especially in villages remote from the high road', but they couldn't write. So De Quincey wrote letters on their behalf: 'a letter about prize-money for one of the brothers' and 'two letters to sweethearts for two of the sisters'. They were so delighted with De Quincey that they begged him to stay. But, alas, after three days their parents arrived home from an annual Methodist meeting at Caernarfon. 'The parents returned with churlish faces, and *"Dym Sassenach"* (*no English*) in answer to all my addresses. I saw how matters stood; and so, taking an affectionate leave of my kind and interesting young hosts, I went my way.' De Quincey adds: 'I easily understood that my talent for writing love-letters would do as little to recommend me with two sexagenarian Welsh Methodists as my Greek Sapphics or Alcaics.'[40] Here are fascinating social details of what may have been happening in the rest of Wales around 1800: the young Welsh able to speak and even read English, but the schooling was so limited that few could write; while the Methodist elders are suspicious, overly serious and backward looking. The historian John Davies quotes Richard Greaves in 1773: 'Methodism has reintroduced the powers of darkness in an age of enlightenment.'[41]

According to Elizabeth Jenkins's affidavit of 1809, the parish church of Llanbadarn Odwyn was in ruins in the 1780s, and probably remained so. It is thus likely that both David and his younger brother Evan went to the Methodist chapel on Sarn Helen on Sundays, which was then still part of the Church of England. Yet they learnt English, Latin and Greek. The Enlightenment was still alive and available to some of the poorest.

Now that I had Elizabeth's name, I could cross-check the relationships and names mentioned in Davies wills. Elizabeth's brother Rees Davies died only a few months before her husband in October 1806. Rees was a widower, with no surviving children, living in the Davies family's parish of Caron (Tregaron). He left no livestock and less than £35, divided mainly among his two brothers and two of his nephews – eldest sons of a brother and sister. The residue was left to his sisters: Elizabeth and Jane. Oddly, even though his brother-in-law farmer Evan Jenkins was one of his executors, nothing was left to Evan's son David, his sister Elizabeth's eldest son, although David's sister Mary was bequeathed his feather bed. Mary's 'chamber' is getting quite snug. It is clear that Rees was Elizabeth Jenkins's brother since it was noted after his death that the executor Evan Jenkins had died before 28 April 1807. Was sixteen-year-old David's future so assured because of his Latin and Greek that his uncle didn't need to include him in his will? Perhaps.

A picture of the Jenkins family of Llanbadarn Odwyn also emerges from a few wills, though unfortunately all the sons are called David, John and Evan; the daughters Anne, Mary and Elizabeth. But after some bafflement as I tangled up two generations with the same names, I could glimpse the story of the unlucky third son, farmer Evan. His father, John Jenkins, was a gentleman, and his will of 1765 leaves land as well as money, including two oxen, eight cows, fourteen cattle and calves, three horses and seventy-nine sheep. There are three sons – David, John and our farmer Evan – and three daughters. Patriarch John leaves to his wife Margaret the tenements of Glan y Gors and Pentre Padarn for ten years so that she can maintain their youngest children, they then will pass to his eldest son, David. This David, who was possibly born in the late 1740s, will also acquire the title of gentleman with ownership of the lands. These farms, Glangors and Pentre-Padarn, are marked on the modern OS map, either side of the Roman road, Sarn Helen. I had walked south down Sarn Helen after my trips to Penycastell and Llangeitho, heading back to Tregaron, and had no idea that all the lush undulating land to the left and right of me had once belonged to the Jenkins family.

The c.1807 map of Penycastell had mentioned a David Jenkins as the owner of some of the neighbouring land, but unless that date was wrong, it was an error, since this David died in 1791, leaving all the land to his brother, the second son, John, who was then aged forty. And his was the gravestone that the Cardiganshire Family History Society recorded in the churchyard of Llanbadarn Odwyn, who died at the incredible age of eighty-one:

Er coffadwriaeth am Mr John Jenkins, Glangorsfawr yn y plwyf hwn, m 20 Hyd. 1832 (81)
[In remembrance of Mr John Jenkins, of Glangorsfawr in this parish, d. 20 October 1832 (81)]

'Mr' John Jenkins – farmer Evan's elder brother was a gentleman, as was his father. However, I mustn't get too proud of their status: 'the majority of the Welsh belonged to the degree of gentleman', writes historian John Davies, and 'in England, the genealogical pride of a poor Welsh *uchelwr* (gentleman) was an object of derision.'[42] Indeed, Charlotte Brontë pours scorn, in *Shirley*, on the Irish curate Peter Malone: 'Mr Malone's father termed himself a gentleman: he was poor and in debt, and besottedly arrogant; and his son was like him.'[43] Her Irish grandfather had been a farm labourer, and father Patrick had only acquired the status of gentleman and entry into the middle class with his degree at Cambridge and his ordination. Evan in Brussels was to mix with royalty and the nobility; despite the derision of the English, it could have boosted his confidence that his grandfather and uncle were gentlemen. Anthony Trollope in his 1858 novel *Doctor Thorne* is well aware of the importance attached to being a 'gentleman' when he introduces his protagonist, who, despite this frailty of pride in his lineage, has a heart of gold:

> No man plumed himself on good blood more than Dr Thorne; no man had greater pride in his genealogical tree [...] no man had a stronger theory as to the advantage held by men who have grandfathers over those who have none, or have none worth talking about [...] He had a pride in being a poor man of a high family.[44]

Tenant farmer Evan's elder brother John outlived his son, and the lands in Llanbadarn Odwyn passed to his grandson David, with additional lands in the neighbouring parish. But this David was the last of the Jenkins male line. He died at twenty-eight and was buried with his grandfather in 1842, leaving his estate to a female cousin, Mary Evans. Along with the Rodericks at Penycastell, this branch of the Jenkinses was Calvinistic Methodist: David left money 'towards repairing the meeting house of Llwynpiod', the chapel on Sarn Helen. In the wills there is no mention of the Jenkinses who had emigrated to Yorkshire and Brussels. Welsh families were traditionally very close, but distance and religion perhaps had utterly separated this family.[45]

But what of the landless third son, farmer Evan? I think, from reading his mother Margaret's will, that she had tried to help. Margaret died in 1805, at a venerable age, having outlived her husband by forty years. In his father's will of 1765 our farmer Evan had been given just five shillings – it is possible that he was about five when his father died. Brother David gave him yearly interest from £20 at his death in 1791, but again no land. However, mother Margaret, living at Glanygors with her long-lived son John when she made her will in 1798, stated:

> First I Give Devise and Bequeath that messuage tenement and lands with appurtenances commonly called and known by the name of Sarnele situate

lying and being in the Parcel of Gwynfil within the Parish of Llandowy [Llanddewi-Brefi] being in the said County now in the tenure occupation and possession of my son Evan Jenkin unto him the said Evan Jenkin my said son his heirs and assigns forever.

I like her determined 'first' – her second son John now owned everything, but she wanted to make sure her youngest son owned something. Sarnele lay just over the border in the next parish and comprised four fields, of just over thirteen acres. It is a corruption of Sarn Helen; the land lies east of the Roman road, adjacent to the land belonging to Glanygors. The year 1798 for Margaret's will is coincidentally (or not) the date of the Land Redemption Tax records, the only ones that survive for Wales: in it, Sarnele is owned by John Jenkins. I can envisage a family quarrel between Margaret and her elder son which led to her defiantly making her will in her younger son's favour. Margaret's will was proved in April 1805, Evan died about eighteen months later, and there is no mention of land in his will. It looks like Evan's surviving brother John successfully objected that his mother couldn't give away this land, even if Evan was farming it. In the 1840s it indeed belonged to brother John's descendants.

In a short story by Elizabeth Gaskell, 'Half a Life Time Ago', published in 1855, the selfish Michael is keen on marrying Susan because she will inherit a farm: 'He, too, should have land like his brother – land to possess, to cultivate, to make profit from, to bequeath.'[46] It ends unhappily for Michael. The fate of the Jenkins third son was to be merely a tenant farmer until his early death in his forties. The population in Cardiganshire was increasing rapidly and land was scarce; if it did become available it was sometimes too expensive for the native farmers to buy. Hence there was emigration to America, south to the mines, or to London. Farmer Evan had possibly started renting Penycastell when he turned twenty-one – that would fit neatly with the comments on the back of the c.1807 map that it had been held on a lease for twenty-one years which had expired five years before. But interestingly the censuses reveal that Penycastell remained in the hands of his descendants, through his daughter Mary, right into the twentieth century. Only then did the Powells of Nanteos sell it. It is time to turn to the Powells, the owners of Penycastell. But before I do, there is one oddity.

In the previous chapter I mentioned that my grandfather apparently had no idea where in Wales the family had come from. In September 1894, my grandfather's father died in Brussels – Rev. John Card Jenkins, the one who didn't escort the Brontë sisters when he was seven. My grandfather's elder brother,

Edward, aged twenty-one, went to register the death. Rev. John Card was born in Brussels, died in Brussels. Yet the record of his son's registration reads:

> John Card Jenkins, pasteur protestant, président du Comité central du Culte anglican en Belgique, décédé le vingt six de ce mois [...] rue de Stassart, 16, résidant même maison, domicilié à Penycastel (Cardigan, Angleterre)

'Domiciled at Penycastel (Cardigan, England).' Did Edward think his father had been born in Wales? Or was he trying to emphasize that his father was 'English' rather than Belgian? Or it could simply indicate how little children know about their parents. But how had he known the name Penycastell? Grandfather Evan had died over forty years before, yet the name of the farmhouse, and the county it was in, had lingered. Perhaps Rev. John Card had been in touch with his Welsh cousins, maybe even visited, but to record it as his 'home' is strange. John Card would have been curious about his second name, which was surely his father's nostalgic reaching out to the county of his birth – Cardiganshire. It may be unique to this family. The choice of name for Evan's last son was a yearning moment of *hiraeth am Gymru* by a Welshman in a foreign country, which resonated even two generations later.

* * *

The estates of the gentry dominated Wales.[47] At the end of the nineteenth century, the Powells at Nanteos, the Pryse family at Gogerddan and the Vaughans (who became Earls of Lisburne from the eighteenth century) at Trawscoed together owned over 100,000 acres of Cardiganshire. Their mansions lay near Aberystwyth. Until the 1530s the Church had owned about a quarter of the land in Wales. At the dissolution of the monasteries not only did the land pass into the ownership of the gentry, but so did most of the church livings. Until 1920, the majority of Anglican clergymen in Wales were appointed to their livings by laymen.[48]

Nanteos, meaning 'nightingale stream', is a beautifully restored Georgian mansion, now a luxury hotel, a few miles south-east of Aberystwyth. In 1690, William Powell, who lived on the next-door estate, married Avarina, the heiress of Nanteos; the Powells clung on to the Nanteos estate despite the usual profligacy, resultant huge debts, absenteeism, and dodgy lawyers and agents until the 1950s. One of the more interesting of the Powells was George Powell (1842–82), who championed Icelandic literature and was a close friend (or lover) of the poet Algernon Swinburne; it seems that they were both fond of flagellation. But, alas, he is after my period. The Palladian mansion that replaced the earlier house was started in 1739 for William and Avarina's son Thomas, who married the wealthy daughter of a London businessman and became a Member of Parliament; he voted in the House but never spoke: he was there for the status, not for the politics.[49]

When farmer Evan leased his farm from the Powells in the 1780s, it is possible that Penycastell had been owned by the Nanteos estate for a long time.[50] Thomas Powell MP had no children, so the estate passed to his brother, the Rev. Dr William Powell, and then at his death in 1780 to Rev. William's son, another Thomas, who inherited the vast estates at the age of thirty-five. He had ambitious plans for the Nanteos demesne – a lake, elegant walks, Gothic ruins – and huge debts. A portrait of him shows a delicate, feminine face, with nicely shaped eyebrows.[51] Whether his debts would have been made manageable under his tenure will never be known since he died suddenly in 1797, leaving a feckless widow, Eleanor, who spent most of her time in London adding to the debts, or hiding in Ireland to escape creditors. There were four surviving children of the marriage; the eldest was only nine when his father died prematurely. The Nanteos estate was thus left for years in the hands of a succession of dubious agents. Just after the heir (William Edward Powell) came of age in 1809 he was informed by his maternal grandfather: 'Your Agent Hugh Hughes is declared insane and incapable of all Business [...] *At all hazards at all events, come down* and *preside* at your Rent Day which is at hand. *Let not an hour be lost as warned and advised.*'[52] Perhaps this Hughes had had a hand in the c.1807 map of Penycastell with its note regretting that a previous agent had not forced Evan Jenkins to repair his buildings after years of neglect of their tenants by the Powells.

William Edward Powell comes straight out of a three-volume novel. After Oxford he purchased an expensive commission in the Royal Horse Guards, entertained lavishly in Bath, married unwisely, cruelly neglected his wife, who may eventually have committed suicide (in 1822), and had a secret mistress and family in London, to whom he was also a blackguard. But in middle age it seems he reformed: he moved to Wales to preside over his estate, a pillar of the Cardiganshire community, dying there in 1854.[53]

My Jenkins family may not have been allowed through the front door, but in May 2015 I bought a ticket for 'cream tea and tour' at Nanteos. Munching my way through a gorgeously laden cream and strawberry scone, gazing at the lawns through the vast windows of the drawing-room, I felt like a scruffy interloper: I was dressed for hiking, not for elegance. But Chris gave me a long, fascinating tour. His enthusiasm was engaging: it is a fine house – the ornate music room, the spacious, slightly sloping first-floor corridor, the original glass ... The house wasn't pompous, but I had misgivings. Finally he showed me an eighteenth-century lead pipe running down the outside of the square Palladian house. Several people had inscribed their names on it over the centuries. At child's height I made out a name: Jenkins. Maybe one day at the start of the nineteenth century a tenant farmer had brought his youngest child to rent day. Bored with the grown-ups, the boy had wandered outside to practise his new skill. Education would give him an utterly different life. And to Evan's school I now turn.

Three

Ystrad Meurig

'Far from the Concourse of Men'

School: Ystradmeiric
County: Cardiganshire
Masters Name: Rev. J. Williams

– admissions book entry for Evan Jenkins,
Trinity College, Cambridge, 1817–18

In his affectionate account of a ramble through Cardiganshire published in 1903, George Eyre Evans, admirer of Catherine Hutton's description of her unsatisfactory holiday in Aberystwyth, and towering figure in the study of Welsh antiquities, describes Ystrad Meurig as 'this virile school, high in eminence for its classical work'.[1] But he laments that the small school building, then almost one hundred years old, was really in need of updating and enlarging. However, the building it had replaced, where young Evan Jenkins had studied in the first decade of the nineteenth century, troubled this Unitarian Minister of the Gospel more.

When I first read 'Ystradmeiric' as Evan's school in the admissions book at Trinity College, it meant precisely nothing.[2] I envisaged something like old Shrewsbury School – Tudor, stone-built and rather grand in appearance though with dodgy toilet facilities. In the Cambridge register Ystradmeiric appeared in no more need of explanation than might 'Eton' or 'Westminster'. Evan's school was indeed stone-built – but it was a church. A small ancient church with seemingly no windows. Further, it wasn't near a town, it was rural, remote and sat between a ruined Norman castle and an even more romantically ruined Cistercian abbey known in its anglicized version as Strata Florida. Ystrad and Strata are the same words, both mean 'vale' or 'valley'. Ystrad Meurig is the vale of the river Meurig, perhaps named after a Welsh prince; Strata Florida in Welsh is Ystrad Fflur – the vale of flowers (the abbey was settled on the banks of the Fflur brook). David Robinson's subtitle for his splendid book on Cistercian abbeys is 'far from the concourse of men', which would beautifully describe the school as well as the abbey.[3] As for 'Meurig', sometimes anglicized as Maurice, there is unfortunately no hard proof that America was named after Richard Ameryk or Amerike (ap Meurig), a Bristol merchant who may have been a patron of the Venetian John Cabot's voyage to the new world in 1497.[4]

In the previous chapter I said that I had a third adventure when I stayed at Tregaron in June 2014. On a beautiful summer's morning I left my Talbot inn to walk six miles north along a disused railway embankment through the ancient bog of Cors Caron. The river Teifi runs through it. The river's source lies just two miles east of Strata Florida in one of the pools on a barren mountain top. The sixteenth-century antiquary John Leland described the source, Llyn Teifi, thus:

> Of al the Pooles none stondith in so rokky and stony Soile as Tyve doth, that hath withyn hym many Stonis. The ground al about Tyve, and a great Mile of toward Stratfler [Strata Florida] is horrible with the sighte of bare Stones, as Cregeryi Mountains be.[5]

The 'horrible' had not yet become romantic. However, the landscape near the source in the Cambrian Mountains had once been thick with woodland, and the white monks' profitable sheep-keeping had started the deforestation that Leland deplored.[6] But there was nothing horrible in sight as I walked through the peat bog along the line of the dismantled Manchester & Milford railway to the village of Ystrad Meurig. It was quiet, lush green and hot, the odd fluffy white cloud dancing under the warm blue sky. In the distance to the west, among light and dark shades of green in a flat landscape, a blue thin Teifi curled its way in the direction of Tregaron. The 'furtive snipe' spotted by Rev. Rees in the 1930s was being particularly furtive.[7] I must have heard and seen skylarks; red kite, curlews and hen harriers were promised by the noticeboard that invited me to the boardwalks nearer the young river. But I welcomed the shade of the trees along the straight path, while bay horses and Jersey cows grazed the meadows, and white beak sedge, sphagnum moss and bog asphodel (*llafn y bladur*) lay undiscovered as I resisted the temptation to try the boardwalks: I had a school appointment.

There is an apocryphal story about the school and its founder, Edward Richard (1714–77).[8] It is great fun, and could well have several elements of truth in it, dating back to around the 1760s:

The patriotic Edward Richards, the founder of the Grammar School at Ystrad Meurig, who was considered equal as a teacher to Arnold of Rugby, or Butler of Shrewsbury, was one day conversing with one of the principals of the University of Oxford about their scholars. There was no end to the praise which the learned Oxonian was bestowing on his students. Mr. Richards at last declared that he believed that the best boys of Ystrad Meurig were quite equal in learning to the students of Oxford.

'O dear,' uttered the other, 'there is no comparison between them.'

'Well,' said Mr. Richards, 'the best plan is to examine them, and I will lay a hundred pounds on my pupils against an equal sum on the side of your scholars.'

When the appointed day for the examination came, Mr. Richards ordered twelve of his scholars to be dressed like common labourers, and to be posted at different stations on the road, about a mile or so from Ystrad Meurig, each student possessing a shovel and mattock with orders how to act when the strangers came in view. At last the Oxonians made their appearance on ponies, and enquired the distance to Ystrad Meurig of the first labourer they met, and the answer was given in pure Latin. They asked the same question to the second, and were answered in classical Greek, and so with the third, when he also answered in excellent Hebrew.

The Oxonians were confounded, and wanted to turn back, saying, 'If the common labourers about here are so proficient in the learned languages what must be the expertness of the best scholars?'

When the Oxonians arrived in the village they were greatly disappointed in witnessing a long straw-thatched college, and a large fire on the ground in one end, made of turf from the bog of Glanteifi. The students were also dressed in cord trousers and grey coats, constructed of home-made cloth, sitting around the fire discoursing freely in the learned languages. Moreover, the Oxonians were so disheartened that they did not attempt the contest, but returned to the University cherishing a higher opinion of 'Little Wales' and the too-often despised Welshmen.

47

What was equally extraordinary was that Edward Richard was not a clergyman, had never been to university and was the second son of a tailor, Thomas, who also ran the village inn with his wife Gwenllian.[9]

The couple seem to have had enough money, and ambition, to send Edward's elder brother Abraham to board at grammar schools in Hereford, just over the border in England, and Carmarthen, forty miles away. Then, at the age of twenty-two, in 1732, he matriculated at Jesus College, Oxford, the 'Welsh college'. What is most mysterious, though, is that he was apparently a gentleman-commoner there.[10] That was only one rank in status below a nobleman. An 'aristocracy of wealth' Thomas de Quincey called such students: fees were double. It seems unbelievable that the son of an inn-keeper/tailor could have been so exalted, especially one who lived in a thatched cottage with one door. He is recorded in *Alumni Oxonienses* merely as a 'pleb'.[11]

The story of the school I was on my way to visit starts with Abraham and a tragedy. Abraham began teaching boys in his village during the vacations from Oxford, including his younger brother. But Edward, at nineteen, preferred climbing Cadair Idris and Pumlumon, his head full of Welsh poetry, to studying the classics. One day Abraham rode to a village across the Afon Ystwyth on some business. He called at an inn for refreshment, then set off to ride home. That was the last time he was seen alive. His mangled corpse was later found in the river, the pony unharmed. Conjecture ranged from murder, to his short sight in not seeing the steep drop of a path in the wood. It was an awful and untimely end for a man of such promise, and it may have been shortly followed by the death of their father Thomas, but it galvanized Edward and changed his life.

Edward went to study briefly at Carmarthen grammar school and then under Rev. John Pugh, who was proficient in many languages, including Greek and Hebrew. The tradition goes that Edward resumed his brother's school in the village church, next door to his thatched home, in 1734, when he was twenty, taking in young boys for an elementary education, including from local gentry families. The school was successful, but after a few years Edward was dissatisfied. He wanted to teach older boys, his ambition lay in higher education, but he wasn't educated enough. He closed his school and for several years studied hard by himself: classics, mathematics and theology, usually starting his studies at four in the morning in the cold church. In about 1746 he reopened the school for older boys, perhaps from the age of thirteen, to train them for the professions, especially as clergymen in the Church of England. It can be seen as the first 'university' in Wales, an Oxbridge college by the ancient bogs of Cors Caron.

Edward Richard not only had a gift for teaching, he had a gift for friendship, what we today call networking skills. He was welcomed into the homes of the local gentry – the educated, elite families of Cardiganshire – the Powells of Nanteos, the Vaughans and Lloyds. My main source, Osborne-Jones in 1934, wonders again about the supposed humble origins of the family in such a class-conscious age, and I, less discreetly, wonder if inn-keeper/tailor Thomas was maybe not the boys' father. Edward's mother Gwenllian kept house for her son until her death in old age in 1763 and any family secrets went to the grave with her; Edward never married. In an important deed of 1757, Edward endowed a perpetual grammar school at Ystrad Meurig from the income of a farm near the village. The local gentry, their heirs and successors were trustees, including Rev. William Powell of Nanteos and headed by the Bishop of St David's. The deed stated that the school was for the teaching of the principles of the Church of England and 'as far beyond the Grammar as the master for the time being should be capable'.[12] The pupils were initially to come from the parish, but if sufficient pupils couldn't be found there, then from the county as a whole, and a number came from outside Cardiganshire. He soon had over fifty pupils.

Equally important, and absolutely vital, was his foundation of a library at the school.[13] Edward Richard bought books when he could, but he was adept at using his gentry network and former pupils for gifts of books, from England as well as Wales. The books were stored in a room created at the west end of the little church. No contemporary catalogue exists so it is not possible to say exactly what books were collected before his death in 1777, and what were collected by his successors, including Rev. John Williams, Edward Richard's pupil and young Evan's headmaster. But some donors are known from inscriptions in the books themselves, and we can be fairly confident that Evan, and presumably elder brother David, thumbed through these.[14] An edition of the *Letters of Pliny* of 1757 was given by Wilmot Vaughan, third Viscount Lisburne and Lord Lieutenant of Cardiganshire, in 1760. Donated by others were editions of the Greek poet Theocritus, of Cicero, Seneca, Thucydides, Lucian, Quintilian. Other than the classics there were also books on history, law, mathematics, navigation, anatomy, astronomy, philosophy, poetry, travels and, above all, religion, including the New Testament in Greek and Arabic, as well as English, Latin, Greek and Hebrew grammars, and Dr Johnson's *Dictionary* of 1755. Most books were in English, Latin or Greek – it seems that the Welsh-language books in his library were removed at some stage. As a Welsh poet himself, Edward Richard encouraged learning in the native tongue, which set the school apart from those in Bangor, Brecon or Carmarthen, which followed the English tradition.

Edward Richard made his will in February 1777. He wrote: 'To my Executors: My Will is to do Good to the present Age and no less to Posterity. Let Charity prevail over self-Interest, and my Effects be disposed of to the best Advantage, and the Money laid out in Books for the Library [...] Let the School and Library be kept in good Repair, and improved to the utmost of your Power.'[15] The school *and* library: in this philistine era of cuts to libraries in the UK, it is sad to acknowledge that over two hundred years later there are those who do not understand the vital necessity of books and self-education. Edward Richard died less than a week later, aged sixty-three. He was a big man, fond of good food and wine, and it is said that eight bearers were required to carry his large coffin, which was laid to rest in the old church.[16]

* * *

On my two-hour Sunday walk along the railway embankment, I eventually crossed a bridge over the Teifi as the shallow river entered the Cors Caron from its mountain source. My path ended at a country lane. The lane curved on either side, with no sign of a village, and I didn't know which way to walk to Ystrad Meurig – left or right? I studied the map, which was of no help. A car stopped. 'Monica?', the elderly driver asked through the open window. Either word had spread that a middle-aged female walker looking puzzled at a map was probably called Monica, or it was Dr Paul Westney whom I had arranged to meet at the Canolfan Edward Richard. It was the latter, and I happily hopped in for a short drive to the centre. After Edward Richard's death in 1777, his former pupil Rev. John Williams was appointed headmaster, and so began the golden years of its fame. But to run ahead a little, in about 1812 the Bishop of St David's, now Thomas Burgess, strongly suggested that a proper school building should be erected to replace the use of the little church, which was somewhat irregular, and it was this building that I was about to see, saved and restored by Dr Westney. It is possible that Evan, when he was a senior pupil, was able to use the new building.

A single-storey white-painted hall building with Gothic windows sat next to a grey, late nineteenth-century church. I was shown the church first by Mike, churchwarden and an old boy – the school next door had lasted for different purposes until the 1970s, and he had attended for two years in his twenties. He was enthusiastic and informative, but the church interior – white walls, neat pews, lots of windows – had no atmosphere for me. Mike described the smaller footprint of the church that Evan had known, and pointed to the old stone tablet in memory of Edward Richard that had been re-erected in the 1898 building; he lay below the flagstones, hopefully undisturbed by the destruction of the little church he had studied and taught in. The two buildings lay within a large oval grassy churchyard, defined by its dry-stone wall. Prominent among the tombs were four within a railed enclosure: one was the tomb of Rev. John Williams, Evan's schoolmaster. Paul Westney took over guiding duties in the school, now the local arts and community centre. Several women were printing in the modern extension that abutted the 1812 hall. Paul led me into the small library, now used as an office, and after the sparkling brightness of the exterior here was a hint of the early nineteenth century. White-painted wooden cupboards lined the walls, but on opening each door I could see unpainted wood covered with schoolboy graffiti, dating back to 1819. I could imagine Evan helping to carry the books from the damp and dark of the old church to the newly built library cupboards.

On the wall was a large portrait of Rev. John Williams – a late nineteenth-century photograph of a drawing that old boys had commissioned of him in his last years. A big man (it must go with the job) with shiny white hair, round glasses perched on his forehead, a bemused faint smile on his lips, his eyes reflecting, not meeting the viewer. A book lies open on the side table next to his wooden chair – apparently the very chair used by Edward Richard – and large tomes line shelves behind him: he is portrayed in the library I was standing in. He looks avuncular, but that is perhaps deceptive: he is a man with keen eyes whom you would not want to cross, a teacher who would notice that you had copied from some other pupil your translation of Epictetus or Cicero, and you would know never to do it again before he even spoke a word. He holds a small round snuff box, useful to soothe away any irritation pupils might offer him. He could be irascible: there is a story told to a later headmaster in 1886 by John Jenkins, a man in his eighties who had worked for the church and school during Rev. Williams's time. Williams, dressed as usual in black, with spurs on his boots, often visited friends at Cwrt Mawr, a mansion near Llangeitho. He would ride home worse for drink, and his servant (John Jenkins's father) had to meet him on the way. Rev. Williams, a strong man, had no fear of riding through rivers, which terrified the servant, and one day Rev. Williams fell off his horse, got up again and rode fast home, leaving his servant trailing. The next day he whipped the servant because he was not at home to greet him.[17] Presumably he also used corporal punishment on his pupils, but not only did old boys resident in London commission the portrait of him, in 1815 they also presented him with a magnificent silver cup.[18]

Schoolmaster John Williams was born in 1745 in the nearby village of Swyddffynnon, the son of a Methodist 'exhorter' and blacksmith.[19] John and his brothers were educated by Edward Richard; one, Evan, became a publisher in the

Strand, London; another, David, became a clergyman and produced a son who was Physician Extraordinary to Queen Victoria in the 1870s.[20] Edward Richard's main aim had been to improve the dreadful state of learning among the Welsh clergy; he detested Methodism and banned his pupils from going to Llangeitho to hear Daniel Rowland preach, but sons of Methodists were welcomed in the school, and several pupils became renowned Methodist preachers. John Williams turned away from his father's Methodism – perhaps due to the influence of Edward Richard – and in turn warned his pupils against the movement. But one day his own sons defied him. Rev. Williams was set to punish them when one son said that he had heard when his father was young that he had leaped and jumped as much as anyone else. (In the popular mind, Welsh Calvinistic Methodists 'jumped' and Quakers 'quaked'.)

At the age of twenty, John Williams was appointed headmaster of Cardigan grammar school, and was ordained deacon in 1768, not yet twenty-three. He did not stay long in Cardigan, next appearing in the 1770s in Herefordshire, as a curate and schoolteacher.[21] He fell ill and obtained leave to visit his native village in Wales in 1777 at the time of Edward Richard's death. He was encouraged to try for the vacant headship, and was appointed by the trustees at Nanteos at the age of thirty-two. Shortly after, he married the daughter of the High Sheriff of Cardiganshire. He delighted in farming, held several curacies and was influential in the Welsh Church, which Edward Richard had never been. He was known as 'Yr Hen Syr' – 'the old sir'; Osborne-Jones says that the title 'had reference to his sense of discipline and his masterful manner'.[22]

With Rev. John Williams you get the sense of a man not only central to the education and culture of Wales, which Edward Richard had been, but of substance in the wider British landscape: two of his sons were friends of Sir Walter Scott. Evan Jenkins would have known both sons well. The elder son, David (1785?–1823), Fellow of Wadham College, Oxford, was to succeed his father as head at Ystrad Meurig in 1818, and was assistant master for some years before that, from when Evan was sixteen. Unfortunately he died at an early age, and was buried alongside his parents in the churchyard. A phrase from the Welsh *englyn* on his tomb translates as 'a man of enlightened understanding and perfect appearance'.[23] His brother John (1792–1858) was almost contemporary with Evan. The younger John Williams's career fascinated me as I tried to find what drove David and Evan Jenkins to leave Wales.[24]

If we assume that Evan's older brother David was also at Ystrad Meurig (there are no surviving records), then the younger John Williams, son of the headmaster, may have been viewed as the star of the school by both the Jenkins brothers. Five years younger than David, John left to teach in Chiswick at about the same time that David also started teaching in London – in 1807, at the age of only fifteen. But rather than teaching until he reached the age for ordination, John went up to Balliol College, Oxford in 1810, graduating at the age of twenty-two with first-class honours, and was ordained deacon the following year. At Balliol he made friends with the handsome John Gibson Lockhart, future son-in-law of Walter Scott, who was also a classical star. John Williams junior spent four unhappy years teaching at Winchester College, and was forced to resign because of a schoolboy rebellion (the pupils occupied the roof and the military were called in). In 1820, Bishop Thomas Burgess appointed John to Lampeter grammar school and gave him a living there. It was probably as a result of John's friendship with Lockhart that Scott sent his second son to Lampeter, and then campaigned to have John appointed rector of a new school, the Edinburgh Academy, where John started in 1824. Scotland, Scott believed, was in desperate need of higher standards of classical education, which it seemed only this Welshman could supply. 'He is a heaven-born teacher,' Scott declared in 1827.[25] John even apparently inspired Scott to write a 'Welsh' romance, *The Betrothed* (1825), set in the Welsh Marches in the twelfth century, focusing on an imperilled, high-born Norman damsel. But the Welsh are uncouth barbarians who talk 'gibberish', and are largely peripheral to the story in which the noble behaviour of the good Normans holds Scott's interest.[26] John Williams conducted Scott's funeral service in the ruined Dryburgh Abbey in 1832. A year later he was made Archdeacon of Cardigan. His own funeral service in 1858, a long way from Wales in Bushey, Hertfordshire, was led by a former pupil of his, the gifted Edinburgh-born Archibald Tait, recently made Bishop of London after an appalling family tragedy, and installed as Archbishop of Canterbury ten years later.[27]

Another pupil also went straight from school to London to teach classics.[28] John Hughes (1787–1860), just four months younger than David Jenkins, was the son of a mayor of Aberystwyth. He was classical master at a large school in Putney for about eighteen months, returning to Wales to be ordained in January 1811, six months later than David. They must have seen each other in London: Putney is only a couple of miles upstream along the Thames from Chelsea. And indeed the young John Williams at Chiswick was only a short boat ride upstream from Putney. Hughes is an interesting comparison with David: both were evangelicals, both were teaching until they could reach the age for ordination, both searching for a curacy so that they could be ordained – a man couldn't be ordained until he was offered a curacy. They may have networked together.

After six years near Conwy on the north coast of Wales, Hughes moved as curate to a parish near Coventry in the Midlands, but was not offered the living because of his evangelicalism; he moved to Deddington, near Oxford, and attracted crowds to hear his preaching, including John Henry Newman – a convert to Calvinist evangelicalism but who later moved in the opposite direction, to become a Roman Catholic cardinal and saint. Hughes subsequently acquired livings in Wales and a prebendal stall in Brecon, then, as with John Williams junior, the archdeaconry of Cardigan. He became important in revitalizing Welsh Anglicanism, especially in tackling the ruinous condition of many of the church buildings; he also published a great deal in Welsh and English. Did his talent for preaching and his energy out-class David Jenkins's? Or was it luck and living a bit longer? I wonder if David looked at his former classmate's career with envy or with pleasure, or a mixture of both.

Many of Edward Richard's pupils in the eighteenth century became poets, Celtic scholars, preachers and clergymen, both Nonconformist and of the established church. Osborne-Jones lists as one of the alumni successes Rev. Thomas Richards, 'a clergyman who did much good work',[29] but, alas, he doesn't make it to *The Dictionary of Welsh Biography*, which demands a bit more than good works among those it includes. Listed in the Welsh *Dictionary*, born between 1736 and 1818, are about twenty considered as eminent Welshmen who were educated at the school, including Rev. John Williams, father and son. Most became clergymen, as well as being musicians, poets or scholars. About a third went on to Oxford, none to Cambridge. Evan Jenkins's decision to go to Cambridge was therefore not inspired by the normal destination of some pupils at Ystrad Meurig. I went up many cul-de-sacs of research before the pivotal name – and the solution to the mystery – was handed to me. But that is for another chapter.

* * *

Back at my tour of the school in June 2014, Paul Westney took me into the hall with Gothic windows where classes had been held from 1812 onwards, when Evan was eighteen. As with many schools of the period, all classes were held in one room, with different masters presiding in different parts of the room. At one stage during Rev. Williams's headship, there were said to have been 176 pupils all crammed into the hall, which seems an impossible squash, though the normal number was between seventy and one hundred pupils. But there was one more room, I was mistaken that there was no upper storey. At the top of a staircase was a room curiously named 'the Vatican' where the headmaster presided, and from the balcony Rev. Williams could view the entire hall, keeping an eye on the assistant master (his son) and on any idle or disruptive pupil. But at least the hall had abundant daylight. On display were two sepia photos of the original church before it was demolished. There were possibly two narrow windows near the west end, though it was hard to tell from the angle from which the photographs were taken, but otherwise the stone walls were blank, and it looks cold, but they must have had a fire: in Tregaron church in the mid-nineteenth century, Rev. Rees recalls his mother saying that a fireplace was built on the lower steps of the spiral stairway of the steeple, with each child bringing some turf fuel.[30] In comparison, the new school hall with its high-beamed roof, large windows and fireplace – now covered over – was a palace, even though it was hard to believe that one hundred pupils could be taught in there at the same time, though the Welsh are small, as George Borrow tells us in the mid-nineteenth century.[31]

I took a slightly different route back to the Talbot Inn via Pontrhydfendigaid, two miles to the east towards Strata Florida, following the course of the Teifi. I may even have stopped for a glass of something in the garden of the Black Lion Hotel before rejoining the railway embankment further south after strolling through hills among grazing and incurious sheep. Even on a pony it was a long way from Evan's home at Penycastell, surely too far for him to ride there and back in a day. So probably, like most of the boys, he lived in lodgings, just as Wordsworth had done when he attended Hawkshead grammar school. Wordsworth lived with Ann and Hugh Tyson for eight years during the school terms, from 1779, when he was just nine, to 1787 when he left for Cambridge. The Tysons were childless and took in between three and eight schoolboy lodgers. Wordsworth's mother had died the year before, and, as Stephen Gill comments, 'it was Wordsworth's good fortune to be placed with someone who gave him not a lodging but a real home'.[32]

I found an amusing advertisement in the Welsh newspaper *The Cambrian*, dated 2 May 1807. Amusing because the ad could be found today, over two hundred years later, addressed at parents looking to acquire a house near a good school. It advertises a substantial farm to be let, on which the proprietor, John Lloyd of Mabws, has 'expended a considerable sum in the repairs and embellishments', and not only is it 'more commodious than can be seen any where in the county of Cardigan, excepting at the mansion-houses of gentlemen', it is 'adjacent to the celebrated School of Ystradmeyric [which] causes it to be particularly eligible for those who require Education for their Children'. But an additional attraction was that the new occupier could entertain 'Boarding Scholars'. The ad continues: 'N.B. Boarding-houses are in much request for Ystradmeyric School.' A nice bit of extra income, but an extra expense to be found by parents – in 1823 a new headmaster at the school advertised fees of forty guineas per annum for boarders; four guineas for day scholars.[33]

* * *

I had questions. Evan's father died around December 1806, when Evan was twelve, leaving no mention of his education in his will. What age did Evan start at Ystrad Meurig, and who paid, who encouraged him? A 'free' grammar school is not that free. And at what age did he leave? All I knew was that he started at Cambridge in October 1818. I had twelve years to fill in. But there are no surviving school records for that period. Also, if he didn't start at Ystrad Meurig until 1807 or 1808, where had he got an elementary education from?

As for the cost of schooling Evan, or whether even to send him to school, I can imagine an extended family conference, as in George Eliot's *The Mill on the Floss*, published in 1860 but set decades earlier. Cardiganshire families were close, so after farmer Evan's death, Jenkins and Davies uncles might have gathered together with his mother Elizabeth, including no doubt a few aunts – though hopefully they were less irritating aunts than in Eliot's novel who came to the mill to discuss Tom Tulliver's 'eddication'. Mr Tulliver has a fair amount of money and doesn't want Tom to be a miller like himself, instead he imagines him as an engineer or surveyor or auctioneer, like Mr Riley, in 'the ample white cravat and shirt-frill', but above all educated enough not to be duped by a lawyer.[34] He wants to take Tom out of his current school to make a 'scholard' of him. Mr Riley approves of the idea: 'Better spend an extra hundred or two on your son's education, than leave it him in your will.' Mr Riley unfortunately recommends the wrong type of education for Tom: an Oxford clergyman who can take one or two boys as pupils in his home. Mr Tulliver is at first dubious: 'Wouldn't a parson be almost too high-learnt to bring up a lad to be a man o' business?' But Mr Riley reassures him: 'O my dear Tulliver [...] you're quite under a mistake about the clergy; all the best schoolmasters are of the clergy. The schoolmasters who are not clergymen, are a very low set of men generally.' But the reader knows that Tom learning Latin is a ludicrous idea, as does Tom himself: at thirteen he is not interested in books, he is a practical boy. The aunts and uncles are astonished. Aunt Glegg says, 'I should like to know what good is to come to the boy, by bringin' him up above his fortin.'[35] The one character who would have benefited from a classical education is the book-devourer Maggie, Tom's younger sister. But as with the 1807 advertisement I mentioned above, where by 'children' you are of course meant to understand 'boys', Maggie is not allowed that kind of education.

So the Davies and Jenkins uncles might have gathered at Penycastell to talk about young Evan: Uncle John Jenkins of nearby Glanygors who had inherited all the family land and maybe felt a little ashamed at not allowing farmer Evan to inherit the four fields of Sarnele that their mother had wished; Uncle William Hughes, who had married Evan's aunt Mary; widow Elizabeth's brothers, Uncles John and William Davies; and Uncle Walter Evans, who had married her sister Jane. Perhaps they gave advice, perhaps they pledged money and help with running the farm. Unlike the fictional Tullivers, they were familiar with a classical education and with clergymen as teachers. Some of them, including deceased farmer Evan, might have attended Ystrad Meurig, even if just for a few years, and perhaps there was family pride that nineteen-year-old David was teaching the classics in London and might become a clergyman. Some of David and Evan's cousins could also have attended the school. David was under age and could have little say in the decision, but his example was a strong argument in favour of sending Evan to the same school. And if he was bright enough, then his future as a clergyman would be assured. No doubt no one thought of sister Mary: she would marry.

But I wonder if Mary had a bit of a Maggie Tulliver in her. Someone had taught her to write – maybe her father or her brothers: in the Llanbadarn Odwyn marriage register in June 1817, when Mary was in her mid-twenties, her new husband Moses Roderick marked his name with a cross; Mary signed it. It is, admittedly, a poor signature – she misses out the first 'n' in Jenkins, and turns the i into a u (perhaps that is Welsh spelling) – but it comes across as a confident attempt. I admire the inventiveness of the 'J': possibly slightly flustered, she turns the tail the wrong way and compensates with an extra squiggle. But there might be another family story there, not just the fluster of a new bride, which I look at in another chapter. Sadly, in the 1832 birth register of one of their children, Mary just marks with a cross. Had she forgotten how to write? Or did she not want to show up her husband again?

* * *

My other question, about what formal schooling Evan might have had before the age of thirteen, is answered simply as: probably none. The Anglican mission, the Society for Promoting Christian Knowledge (SPCK), founded in London in 1698, established charity schools in Wales for those too poor to attend the few grammar schools. Most of their schools were in South Wales and taught through the medium of English, though the society did publish books in Welsh.[36] A few decades later a more widespread initiative was undertaken by a clergyman and his patroness to spread literacy in Welsh throughout the principality. It was such a success that Catherine the Great, Empress of Russia, demanded a report about these 'circulating schools' in 1764.[37] Rev. Griffith Jones was a farmer's son, who was appointed rector of Llanddowror, Carmarthenshire in 1716. Pockmarked and asthmatic, he was a fiery preacher and a huge inspiration to the younger generation of Welsh Methodists such as Daniel Rowland. Jones disapproved of the SPCK's emphasis on teaching in English in their charity schools, and in 1731 he began his itinerant schools to teach the Anglican catechism and Bible reading to adults and children in Welsh. Part-time teachers would settle in a barn, cottage or parish church for a few months to teach reading skills to all ages. Bright pupils, whether farmers or labourers or their children, could become fluent Welsh readers in less than two months. With the help of patrons such as Madam Bridget Bevan of the Vaughan family, by the time of his death in 1761 there were over 3,000 schools throughout Wales. Geraint Jenkins says that 'there is a strong case for claiming that he was the greatest Welshman of the eighteenth century'. The historian John Davies estimates that almost half the population of Wales had learnt to read in these schools. It was a limited education; Griffith Jones said that 'the purpose of this spiritual charity is not to make gentlemen, but Christians and heirs to eternal life'.[38] But 'children' meant girls as well as boys. After Griffith Jones's death, Madam Bevan, from her home in Laugharne (where Dylan Thomas later had his boathouse home), kept the circulating schools going until her own death in 1779.[39] The work of the schools was taken up by the new Sunday schools, an initiative of the Methodists.

It is therefore likely that Evan's mother Elizabeth taught her three children to read Welsh, and that this was reinforced by Sunday school in the nearby Llwynpiod Methodist chapel. Whether she could speak any English is hard to determine, but it is likely that her husband, as the son and brother of 'gentlemen', could. At this time the gentry were largely monoglot English-speakers, so those just one notch below would also need to speak English. And the presence of Ystrad Meurig grammar school would have ensured that a fair number had an education that could be passed on informally, even if these farming alumni had had no inclination to learn more than a little Latin and less Greek. Elder brother David may well have taught Evan more than enough for him to feel at ease when he arrived at the school for his first lessons in English and Latin grammar, mathematics and divinity.

* * *

The next mystery is when did Evan leave school? Soon after his arrival at the see of St David's in 1803, the English-born Bishop Thomas Burgess licensed Ystrad Meurig and three other grammar schools in Wales to prepare candidates for the Church. He was licensing what had already been happening at Ystrad Meurig for over fifty years: both Edward Richard and Rev. John Williams had provided an education for clergymen equivalent to that at Oxford or Cambridge because so few men in Wales could afford to go to the English universities. Bishop Burgess was a good friend of Wales (he remained at the see of St David's for over twenty years, until 1825, when he moved to the see of Salisbury at the age of sixty-eight), but he probably saw that he too was part of the problem of the dire state of the Anglican Church in Wales: he was English. The majority of the lower clergy were poorly educated Welsh-speakers, not considered as gentlemen; whereas all the bishops were English.[40] In 1794, Coleridge's pedestrian university friend Joseph Hucks was taken aback by the short encounter they had with one Welsh clergyman near Bala, North Wales, some sixty miles north of Ystrad Meurig:

Whilst we were at dinner in a little ale-house [...] we had a glance at the clergyman, who happened to enter the house at that very time; his appearance altogether bespoke an inferiority of condition, disgraceful to that respectable body of which he was a member; upon observing us, he abruptly went out, while our landlady informed us, with an air of triumph, as if he was something superior to the rest of mankind, that 'that was the parson.' He was standing near the house when we went out, and wishing to enter into conversation with him, I desired him to inform me which was the direct road to Bala; he appeared somewhat confused, and waving his hand towards the way we had enquired for, answered only by the monosyllable 'that,' and walked hastily away. I felt much hurt, and at the same time a great degree of admiration, both at his truly laconic answer, as well as at his manner of address, in which pride seemed to be struggling with poverty [... this circumstance] bears some credible testimony to the common report of the shameful and scanty provision made for the Welsh clergy; which by no means enables them to assume that character so essentially necessary to the ministers of christianity.[41]

Hucks gives examples of the minute amount of money given to Welsh curates, such as 'the curate of Silian, Cardiganshire, 6 young children, 15l. [pounds] per annum'. Hucks blames the incumbent who does no work, receives the tithes, and pays his curate little.[42] But that may have been the problem in England; in Wales the tithes were paid for the most part to the lay landowners, who rarely paid the clergyman they had appointed adequately, necessitating him to acquire as many livings as possible (pluralism) in order to simply keep his family out of poverty.[43] Hucks was also a snob. He wrote: 'undeniably there are numerous examples of apparent cheerfulness and content to be found amongst the poor inhabitants of a mud-built cottage; but are not the social endearments of domestic life (the only source of enjoyment amongst the lower order of mankind), too often imbittered by repeated difficulties and distresses'.[44] But he is a paternalistic snob since he believes that the lower orders were capable of improvement, and one way would be to pay the clergy better so that they could actually look like gentlemen. His snobbishness about 'the lower orders' was of course typical of his age and throughout the nineteenth century and beyond, which is partly why Wordsworth's 'lyrical ballads' about the lower orders such as the elderly shepherd Michael, the vagrant woman and the idiot boy were so startling in 1798 and 1800. The joke is that the gentlemen from Oxford, Hucks and Coleridge, were walking around Wales dressed as tramps with knapsacks on their backs.

Bishop Burgess also laid down that seven years' education in the classics, Hebrew and theology were essential for a clergyman coming straight from the Welsh grammar schools he licensed. Again, he was probably following the practice at Ystrad Meurig established by Edward Richard.[45] The SPCK were also involved: they funded prizes (known as premiums) and scholarships. There is a notice in *The Cambrian*, dated 9 September 1809 (when Evan was fourteen), by the society, which includes: 'Premiums of 20s. worth of Books for the best Recitation of Sermons, at the licensed Grammar Schools, were adjudged to the following Scholars: [...] John Hughes, of Ystradmeurig School, aged 20' (this is probably the John Hughes who taught in Putney for a while). David Williams at the same school, aged twenty-one, was also awarded a premium for his abridgement of a sermon. The notice then announced the premiums to be competed for in 1810, including for the best essay on Hebrew as 'indispensable to the full understanding of the Scriptures', for the 'best Singer of plain Psalmody' and for the best pupils at the Easter examinations. Finally it announced that 'Daniel Evans, of Ystradmeirig School, aged 19, and John Jones, of Cardigan School, aged 19, were elected Exhibitioners at Ystradmeirig School'. The school is a highly competitive establishment for higher education, now at the height of its success, but the irony is that Bishop Burgess was responsible for the end of its days of glory: he promoted the establishment in Lampeter of a college purely for the training of clergy. St David's College, Lampeter was opened in 1827 and was the first university in Wales.

Until 1827, however, Ystrad Meurig school provided many of the candidates for ordination at twenty-three. But as with David Jenkins, who had left at nineteen, not all stayed until their twenties. This was possibly because the age at starting at the school was fairly fluid, or in the case of the son of the headmaster, John Williams junior, he had learnt all his father and eldest brother could teach him. There may also have been the matter of the money that could be earned from teaching before they were ordained. It seems probable that Evan also left at nineteen or twenty: there are a few other clues that I shall look at later, but one obvious clue is that he wasn't ordained straight from school to a Welsh curacy, as several of his school fellows were. But I think there was also a wanderlust – that was eventually to take him to Brussels – and ambition. I have mentioned the dire straits of the lower clergy in Wales; a better living might be found in England – indeed brother David had been ordained to a curacy in Yorkshire in 1810 because of contacts he had made in London. So maybe the teenage Evan, writing essays on the use of Hebrew, declining irregular Greek verbs, trying to master English and Latin, was dreaming of the land east, beyond the Cambrian Mountains.

In the spring of 1812, another teenager, this time English and from a far more privileged background than Evan, was dreaming of the land west, towards the setting sun.[46] Only twenty miles east of Ystrad Meurig a young man, aged nineteen, came to Nantgwillt in the Elan valley, close to the town of Rhayader, with his pretty new wife, even younger than him. Expelled from Oxford only the year before as a result of his publication of a pamphlet on atheism, he had eloped with Harriet Westbrook, a *mésalliance* that his father had dreaded. The couple were keen to settle on a farm they had found on the east side of the Cambrian Mountains and to gather there a community of radical, like-minded friends. But Percy Bysshe Shelley's father turned his request for money down. And so continued a life on the move, a life of exile, the cruel abandonment of Harriet, another elopement with Mary Godwin. How could this unsettled, angry young man fired with genius fit in the same world as the young Welsh scholar only twenty miles away, who would one day appear to be the quintessential mid-Victorian clergyman? I was intrigued by this strange juxtaposition of lives that didn't seem to belong in the same Britain. And then I realized that in a novel being written at exactly this time those two worlds had collided: Jane Austen's *Mansfield Park*, published in 1814. On the one hand Austen depicts the unsettled threesome of the Bertram sisters and Henry Crawford – the elopements, the challenging of society's mores in behaviour and sexual conduct that leads only to unhappiness or tragedy, which it did in Harriet Shelley's case.

There is also Mary Crawford's contempt for clergymen, displayed when she learns with horror that the man she is attracted to, Edmund Bertram, is considering taking orders: 'what is to be done in the church? Men love to distinguish themselves, and in either of the other lines [lawyer, soldier, sailor], distinction may be gained, but not in the church. A clergyman is nothing.'[47] It is hardly on the scale of Shelley's rage against Christianity ('Oh how I wish I were the Antichrist'),[48] but reflects much of contemporary society's derision towards the Church and its representatives. The young scholars of Ystrad Meurig might have seconded Edmund's defence: 'I cannot call that situation nothing, which has the charge of all that is of the first importance to mankind', and he is strongly supported by his cousin Fanny Price.

But of course the raging Shelley is hardly a simple combination of Henry's lax attitude to love and his sister Mary's dismissive attitude to the Church; he also contains the spirit of Fanny. Surely, unlike Edmund, he would have responded to Fanny's wish to go out onto the lawn to look for Cassiopeia in the night sky, and been moved by Fanny's remarkable speech as she looks through the drawing-room windows at the darkened garden – 'Here's what may tranquillize every care, and lift the heart to rapture! When I look out on such a night as this, I feel as if there could be neither wickedness nor sorrow in the world; and there certainly would be less of both if the sublimity of Nature were more attended to, and people were carried more out of themselves by contemplating such a scene.'[49] Shelley wrote the only poem that makes me cry, 'Ode to the west wind' – west again. And Shelley would have pounced into the discussion when Fanny famously asks Sir Thomas Bertram about the slave trade.[50]

In 1812, for a few months in spring, two young men divided physically only by the Cambrian Mountains, divided far more by class and ideology, symbolized the two sides of the coin of a wartime society battered by revolutionary ideas coming from across the Channel: one young man striving to educate himself and fit in; the other courageously, but naively, fighting to change that society. The 200-acre estate in the Elan valley that Shelley hoped to lease was subsequently drowned by a Victorian reservoir, his first wife Harriet drowned in the Serpentine, Shelley drowned at the age of just twenty-nine in the Gulf of Spezia.

In my next chapter I turn to Evan's elder brother David Jenkins, and his route from classics master in Chelsea to his encounter with Patrick Brontë in West Yorkshire.

Four

David

Chelsea and Yorkshire, 1807–1813

Will you have the goodness, Sir, to inform me, whether I can get
Licensed to this curacy, be inducted into Hartsheath Living, and obtain
License for non-residence, in time, to give a Title to a Gentleman, who
intends to offer himself a candidate for Holy Orders, at his Graces next
ordination?

– Patrick Brontë, letter to Thomas Porteus,
secretary to the Archbishop of York, 6 June 1810[1]

I will explore this revelatory letter – misunderstood or ignored by Brontë
biographers who have not attempted to identify the 'Gentleman' – below. But
to go back three years. I will presume that nineteen-year-old David Jenkins left
Wales for London shortly after his father's death, perhaps in January 1807 for
the start of the school term. It is the year remembered for the abolishment of the
slave trade in the British Empire, for well over twenty years fought for by many
evangelicals, William Wilberforce in particular, Hull-born MP for Yorkshire
and friend of William Pitt the Younger. The previous year had seen the death
of Pitt at only forty-six, Prime Minister almost continuously since the age of
twenty-four, detested by some for his wartime repressive measures and taxes, and
also the death of Charles James Fox, Pitt's larger than life rival on the opposite
benches, detested by King George III. It was the end of an era in Britain, not
only with the deaths of the two big beasts of British politics, but also with the

funeral of Lord Nelson. Yet on the Continent, Napoleon continued his rampage, seemingly unstoppable; he had declared a blockade of Britain and was beginning his invasion of the Russian Empire. It was an unstable and frightening time. Yet in 1807 Wordsworth published his paeon to the morning beauty of London and the River Thames, 'Composed Upon Westminster Bridge': 'Earth has not any thing to shew more fair: / Dull would he be of soul who could pass by / A sight so touching in its majesty [...] Ne'er saw I, never felt, a calm so deep!'[2] That beauty at dawn is still there, still breathtaking, yet commuters stride to their offices across the river looking neither left nor right.

The testimonials for David in his deacon ordination papers, written a few years later, indeed suggest that he arrived in Chelsea early in 1807. Candidates for ordination needed testimonials by clergymen who had known them for three years.[3] Many are vague, giving the formula of 'three years and upwards', and may not have known the candidate well. But Thomas Edwards, his headmaster in Chelsea, is more precise. Writing on 22 June 1810, he states, as I mentioned above, that 'Mr David Jenkins lived with me as Lat & Gk Master abt three years & a half[,] during that period he conducted himself with the greatest propriety'. His son, also Thomas, was a Fellow of Trinity Hall, Cambridge and wrote that he had known David for the usual imprecise 'three years & upwards'. During this time 'he has resided with Mr. Edwards of Chelsea as Classical Assistant in his School, and I declare from my own personal knowledge of the said Mr. David Jenkins that I have every reason to think well of his moral and religious principles'. It is interesting that David includes these two testimonials as neither were the beneficed clergymen required, although lawyer Thomas, as a college Fellow, might have been acceptable to the archbishop. Perhaps David's friends in London urged him to have these extra testimonials as he hadn't been to university, and it was important to make clear that he had the required Latin and Greek.

Where was Mr Edwards's school in Chelsea? On the cover of the deacon ordination bundle it states: 'David Jenkins at Mr. Edwards Academy Chelsea near London'. No street name. I found the son, Thomas Edwards, in *Alumni Cantabrigienses*. He was admitted pensioner (that is, paying full fees), aged seventeen, at Pembroke College, Cambridge in 1793, so he was about thirty, eleven years older than David, when the latter arrived in London. Thus his father, 'Master of Chelsea Academy, Middlesex', was maybe in his sixties. The son gained his LLD (Doctor of Laws) in 1805, when he was Advocate of the Court of Arches – this was an ecclesiastical court of the Church of England, based in the City of London. The short paragraph in *ODNB* about him says that in 1805 he was also advocate at Doctors' Commons, and that he 'took considerable interest in social questions'.[4] So the son was a rising lawyer and either lived with his father in Chelsea, or visited often enough to know David well. It was an impressive testimonial to have, maybe a useful contact, perhaps also someone who discussed with David social issues – poverty, the Luddites, children working in factories – that he was to confront as a clergyman in Yorkshire in the early years of the industrial revolution.

I found the school in *The Survey of London* published in 1913. Under the heading 'Cheyne House, Upper Cheyne Row: Historical Notes' it states:

> Cheyne House, during the end of the 18th century and the first half of the 19th, was a school, and is marked on Thompson's map as 'Cheyne House Academy.' Faulkner says it was carried on in 1829 by Dr. Felix, and formerly by Mr. Edwards. It comprised in 1800 two houses.

The *Survey* adds that it was 'now in a derelict condition'.[5] Upper Cheyne Row is a short street that still exists. I had found Edwards; the significant name of Dr Felix I took no notice of until much later.

The Kensington and Chelsea Archives, in the library near Kensington High Street in London, have F.P. Thompson's map of 1836, and a large table to spread it on. The map is dedicated to the Earl Cadogan, the head of the family who owned, and still own, much of Chelsea, and the map declares that it has been made 'from a new and actual survey'. The 'village' of Chelsea is shaped like a camel's head resting on the River Thames that bends south after the wooden Battersea Bridge.[6] To the west (the camel's mouth) the village ends at Chelsea Creek, beyond which is Fulham and then Putney; to the north the boundary with Kensington is the road to Fulham; the ears reach to Knightsbridge and the tip of Hyde Park; beyond the back of the head is Belgravia and Pimlico, and beyond that Westminster. The eye of the camel is the new church for the parish, St Luke's, consecrated in 1824, desperately needed for the expanding population that couldn't fit into the famous Old Church on the river. Running straight through the 'camel's head' is the private King's road, created for Charles II as part of his route to Hampton Court. The neck of the camel is taken up with the Royal Chelsea Hospital for old soldiers, designed by Sir Christopher Wren, apocryphally from an idea by Nell Gwyn, now famous for the Chelsea Flower Show in May.[7] 'Cheyne House Academy' was indeed marked in Upper Cheyne Row – south of the King's road, midway between the old Battersea Bridge and the Apothecaries' Garden, which lies just west of the Royal Hospital. This ancient botanical garden is now known as Chelsea Physic Garden; it was saved for posterity by Sir Hans Sloane (d. 1753), whose collection of curiosities and manuscripts led to the foundation of the British Museum.

There were numerous schools in Chelsea, for girls as well as boys, from the seventeenth century onwards;[8] it was then a healthy spot amid fields and market gardens but near to London. If you walked along the meandering Thames from the wooden Battersea Bridge to Wordsworth's wooden Westminster Bridge – there were in 1807 no bridges in between these two – it might take about an hour, less in a public boat. The Anglo-Irish satirist, cleric and creator of Gulliver, Jonathan Swift, declared when he stayed for a few months in Church Lane (now Old Church Street) in 1711 that 'it is two good miles [to London] and just five thousand seven hundred and forty-eight steps'. He counted them! (Swift was on a health kick.) When it was wet, Swift took the sixpenny stage from the White Horse Inn on the corner of the lane and the riverbank, though he complained about walking on a lovely day in May when it was 'bloody hot'.[9]

The actress and poet Mary 'Perdita' Robinson, mistress of George IV when he was Prince of Wales, attended a girls' seminary in Chelsea from 1768. The school closed in 1770 due to the intoxication of its head, Meribah Lorrington, who died in a workhouse. The author Rev. Weeden Butler kept a classical school in Cheyne Walk from the 1770s, retiring more than forty years later in 1814.[10] No doubt he was known to David Jenkins. Rev. Butler was morning preacher at the fashionable Charlotte Street chapel in Pimlico, and lecturer at two City churches, as well as chaplain to the Duke of Kent.[11] His eldest son, also Weeden (1772–1831), took over the school; another son, George, was senior wrangler (the best mathematician of his year at the exams) at Cambridge and became headmaster of Harrow School in succession to Dr Joseph Drury in 1805 – despite Byron and other schoolboys' vocal opposition (see chapter 10). Anthony Trollope remembered bitterly the flogging that Dr Butler inflicted when he was a small boy.[12]

The recent Victoria County History comments that the school where David Jenkins taught, kept by Thomas Edwards, was a 'well reputed boys' academy' and that it was one of the largest schools with fifty-three pupils, but that is an error.[13] Its source is the 'Population Book of St Luke's Parish Chelsea, Middlesex' of 1801, which survives in the Kensington and Chelsea Archives. It is a 'census' of the number of people living in each house. On page 43 of the handwritten record, 'Thomas Edwards School' consists of forty-seven males and six females, giving a total of fifty-three 'persons', not schoolboys. This number would include the headmaster and his wife, teachers and servants, so the probable number of boy pupils would be forty. I now needed to find the school where David taught, or its ghost, on the ground.

* * *

One of the main sources for the 1913 *Survey of London* was Thomas Faulkner. In the early nineteenth century, Faulkner hit on a winning idea of writing about the history of Chelsea. He was born in neighbouring Fulham in 1777 and kept a stationer's and bookshop in Paradise Row in Chelsea (a small row of Georgian houses, later flattened to create Royal Hospital Road, which visitors to the annual Chelsea Flower Show will know well). His first book in 1805 was an account of the Royal Hospital. Then five years later he published *An Historical and Topographical Description of Chelsea and its Environs*, with the snappy subtitle: *Interspersed with Biographical Anecdotes of Illustrious and Eminent Persons Who Have Resided in Chelsea During the Three Preceding Centuries*. It is said that he may have been aided by Weeden Butler junior.[14] But Butler contributed a dedicatory poem in which he states that he didn't help him: 'Faulkner! Thine unassisted labour proves / How well thy heart can trace the scene it loves.'[15] The frontispiece engraving shows a quizzical man looking older than his early thirties, well pleased with himself as he displays his book. Faulkner dedicated the book to 'the Honourable and Right Reverend Brownlow, Lord Bishop of Winchester'. Brownlow was the bishop's first name; his surname was North.[16] He was half-brother to Lord North, Prime Minister in the 1770s and early 1780s, so it is hardly surprising that Brownlow North was made Bishop of Winchester in 1781. His London home was Winchester House in Chelsea, to the east of Cheyne Row, where he died in 1820. The bishops' ancient London seat had been in Southwark, where the beautiful medieval rose window still survives, but that had got so dilapidated that an Act of Parliament enabled him to buy a house in Chelsea, which in turn was abandoned after his death.

In his Preface, Faulkner thanks the Honourable and Reverend Gerald Valerian Wellesley, Rector of Chelsea, and Rev. John Rush, Curate of Chelsea – clergymen well known to David, and Faulkner has an impressive list of subscribers, headed by members of the royal family, but also including R. Davy, Florist, King's Road, and a relation: Mr. J. Faulkner, 115 Jermyn Street, Bricklayer to her Royal Highness the Princess Charlotte of Wales, as well as Messrs Fifield and Simonds, Churchwardens of Chelsea, who witnessed David's 'Si Quis' the same year (see below). The Weeden Butlers, father and son, appear, but no Thomas Edwards, father or son, nor David Jenkins, who may have earned far too little to be able to subscribe but perhaps he often browsed in Faulkner's shop and read the book.

In 1829 Faulkner published a second edition in which he revised his potpourri of sites and history to substitute a selection of guided walks through Chelsea.[17] It would have been fun to follow one as I tried to see what David had known between 1807 and 1810, but I floundered almost immediately: Faulkner's first turning right off the King's Road towards the river, known at the time as Cook's Grounds – a lane between fields of cows leading to Upper Cheyne Row – is now Glebe Place, with a terrace of later houses worth at least £5 million each, and the old way into the Row is blocked by the eccentric 50 Glebe Place, with tower, roof sculptures and climbing ivy, built in 1880–5. Next to it, at 49, is a Charles Rennie Mackintosh-designed studio house that was built in the school's garden, completed in 1921. So instead, with Faulkner in hand but supplemented by modern research, I will follow David as he arrives in Chelsea for the first time and finds the school.[18]

* * *

I imagine that David rode the twenty miles to Aberystwyth from Penycastell farmhouse. His mother Elizabeth and sister Mary tearful, wondering if they would ever see him again; little brother Evan envious. On the second day he took the stagecoach to the Welsh border, perhaps having been able to lodge for the night with family friends. He would sit outside on the coach – it was usually four inside and eight outside, though probably more were squeezed on top. There is an advertisement displayed in the Ceredigion Museum in Aberystwyth, dated June 1816: 'The Public are respectfully informed that a Coach will start On Wednesday the Twelfth [sic] day of June instant, from the Kings Head Inn, Kington, At Five o'Clock in the Morning, and arrive at Aberystwith at Seven o'Clock the same Evening. Also, a Coach will leave Aberystwith the same Morning at Six o'Clock, and arrive at Kington at Eight o'Clock the same Evening.' The ancient market town of Kington in Herefordshire is near the border, on Offa's Dyke. Thus, nine years after David travelled this route, it took fourteen hours to cover just over fifty miles.

The advertisement then promises that at Kington this coach will meet with the London coach, which leaves at four o'clock in the morning, two days a week, via Leominster and Oxford, arriving at the Bull and Mouth, London 'on the following Mornings by Eight o'Clock'. This next stage will thus take twenty-eight hours, sitting outside, having little sleep, cold and wet, only stopping to change horses, have a quick bite and a toilet break. In 1807 the fare sitting outside was 16s

just from Aberystwyth to Kington – contrast that with the one pound that David
had received in his father's will: travelling by coach was enormously expensive.
He would have arrived at London's Bull and Mouth Inn groggy, unshaven and
very hungry. He had been on the road for three days and he still had to get to
Chelsea. The Bull and Mouth coaching inn was in St Martin's-Le-Grand, near St
Paul's Cathedral; it was demolished at the end of the nineteenth century.[19] David
possibly had advice to then get the Chelsea coach for the last few miles south-west,
and maybe he was met at the White Horse coaching inn on the Chelsea riverbank
by lawyer Thomas Edwards, the son of his new employer.

The Chelsea coach travelled along what is now the Fulham Road and turned
left into Church Lane – the oldest road in Chelsea. The coach then crossed the
private King's road – narrow, quiet, lined with nursery gardens and a few villas,
abode of the florist Mr Davy with his auriculas, hyacinths and tulips, and greenhouse
plants from Japan, China and North America.[20] Only those who had a copper pass
were allowed to ride through the King's road. Today it is famous for the fun and
abandon of the Swinging Sixties, its miniskirts and kaftans; but fifty years later,
when I strolled down it in 2017, the traffic was noisy, polluting, and the village that
was once here had been destroyed, just as the 1870s creation of the Embankment
parallel to it, and its modern traffic along the Thames, killed off the old Chelsea
along the river. But two hundred years ago, after the stunning cacophony of the
City, David had entered a quieter and leafier haven.

On the left as he travelled down Church Lane he would see the high brick
wall of the rectory. In 1807 the rector was, as mentioned in the subscription to
Faulkner's book, the Anglo-Irish Gerald Valerian Wellesley, younger brother of
Arthur, the future Duke of Wellington. Rev. Gerald was to sign David's 'Si Quis'
in 1810 – rather like marriage banns, this was a public announcement in church
that this person was desirous of being ordained and if anyone knew a reason why
he shouldn't, then they should make their views known. But he didn't contribute
a testimonial for David. He is a shadowy figure, especially compared with his
elder brothers. The eldest, Richard, second Earl of Mornington, had just returned
to England from his authoritarian stint as a workaholic Governor-General of
Bengal; he was under a cloud as Parliament investigated his actions there and
rumours spread of his affairs with actresses. The future Duke of Wellington, then
Major General Sir Arthur Wellesley, was in his late thirties, had recently been
knighted for his victories in India and had just made a strange and ultimately
unhappy marriage with an old flame, Kitty, a woman he had not seen for twenty
years. His younger brother Rev. Gerald had become rector of Chelsea in 1805,

bringing his wife and children to the restored rectory and its huge garden; he was to remain as rector of Chelsea, later at the new church of St Luke's, until 1832. However, all was not as dull as it sounds: his wife Lady Emily, daughter of the first Earl Cadogan, later committed adultery and deserted him, and he was refused a bishopric by the Prime Minister Lord Liverpool, who wrote to his brother the Duke of Wellington in 1826 that 'no clergyman living separate from his wife ought to be raised to the Bench'.[21] But he wasn't too constrained financially. When David knew him he was also chaplain at Hampton Court, rector in Staines, prebendary at Westminster and then St Paul's, and vicar in West Ham, Essex.[22] The high wall enclosing the rectory garden still exists, as does the rectory, although swallowed up by wings and other modern additions. It is apparently the most expensive house in London, with its garden only second in size to that of Buckingham Palace.

When David finally descended at the inn from his perch on the coach, the peace of Church Lane was lost in the human noise along the river bank. Spreading to the east as far as the Apothecaries' Garden, along what is now Cheyne Walk, were wharves, boathouses, taverns and breweries, an ironmonger and a butcher's, interspersed with mostly eighteenth-century houses. A low wall separated the bank from the river, but the river sometimes flooded and flowed into cellars. Opposite the inn stood the Old Church with its tall brick tower, which Faulkner states in 1810 'is now in a very ruinous condition, and ought to be immediately repaired or taken down'.[23] The name 'Old Church' stuck after the Gothic Revival St Luke's was built in the 1820s. The church was well known because of its connection to the great humanist Sir Thomas More, imprisoned by Henry VIII for his refusal to swear to the Act of Succession because it rejected papal jurisdiction, and beheaded in 1535 for denying the king's new title of supreme head of the church in England.[24] Here More had worshipped and endowed a chapel: the only part of the church to survive the bombing in April 1941. The church was rebuilt after the Second World War with such care that it is difficult to notice it is a rebuild when you sit in one of the high-walled wooden pews surrounded by Gothic niches and Renaissance carving, the fan tracery, arches, and wonderful monuments with kneeling and recumbent figures. Since 1969, a golden-faced statue of Sir Thomas – golden presumably because of his elevation to sainthood in 1935 – has sat outside his church, insensible to the traffic noise of the Embankment. Ironically his church is now Church of England, with the Queen as Supreme Governor, while fellow Roman Catholics worship in a late nineteenth-century church around the corner. But his uncompromising stand for integrity resonates, as do his wit and his love of Greek and Latin, and strong belief in education for women, even though his persecution of Protestant heretics makes him a controversial figure. Sir Hans Sloane gave five folio books to the church that are still chained to the bookcase; among them are two volumes of Foxe's *Book of Martyrs*, dating to 1684, which include accounts of some who suffered martyrdom at the hands of More.[25] But for Thomas Faulkner in 1810 he was a great man: 'who, for his judgment, humility, devotion, sweetness of temper, contempt of the world, and true greatness of mind, was the ornament of his own, and may be an example to every age'.[26]

Sir Hans Sloane – Irish-born royal physician and collector – bought More's house, then known as Beaufort House, in 1738.[27] Sloane is regarded by some as a villain since he allowed More's great house to be destroyed a few years later.[28] Thomas Faulkner has lengthy sections on More, describing his monument in the church (with its lengthy biographical inscription, written by More and 'vetted by Erasmus'[29]) and the disputed site of his manor house, built in the 1520s. It is now believed that the wide and noisy Beaufort Street runs straight over the site of the house as it approaches Battersea Bridge, and buried below the Embankment is More's private landing stage. In the 1966 film *A Man for All Seasons*, based on the play by Robert Bolt, Henry VIII (Robert Shaw) arrives by barge to visit More (Paul Scofield) and inexplicably leaps off the barge into the mud instead of using the landing steps. It may be a cue to display Henry's loud, disconcerting laugh, or a good way to fudge a shot of the Thames (actually Beaulieu river in Hampshire) with a completely different location of the swathe of idyllic green lawn in front of More's house (played by Studley Priory, Oxfordshire).

Lawyer Thomas Edwards might well have talked about lawyer Thomas More as he led David past Lawrence Street in 1807 and to the next turning left, Cheyne Row. Lawrence Street was then a cul-de-sac, ending at what was misleadingly called Monmouth House. This was instead a terrace of four houses across the top of the street, named after one of its early residents – Anna, the widow of James, Duke of Monmouth, bastard son of Charles II, executed by his hated uncle James II in 1685 after a failed rebellion. Monmouth had preferred his mistress to his wife; the latter married again and survived him by almost fifty years.[30] Faulkner also mentions that the author Tobias Smollett lived in one of the other terraced houses in the mid-eighteenth century, and wishes that more people read his books, rather than the rubbish puffed up by friends of 'meaner' authors.[31] When I explored Lawrence Street I called in at the Cross Keys pub, dating from 1708 according to the blue plaque, once haunt of J.M.W. Turner, presumably disguised as 'Mr Booth', and Dylan Thomas. They would barely recognize it: trendy bare-brick walls on the inside with distressed wood and Chelsea prices. On a chalk board, the all-day bar menu was headed by truffle brie on toast with spiced honey.

Before turning into Cheyne Row, David would see the Tudor brick remains of Shrewsbury House, one of the ambitious Bess of Hardwick's many houses accumulated during her four marriages in the sixteenth century – another being Chatsworth, now the vast and resplendent home in Derbyshire of the Duke and Duchess of Devonshire. Shrewsbury House in Chelsea had a subterranean passage leading towards Kensington, which Faulkner says had lately been explored.[32] Beyond it along the river bank was Winchester House. David may have visited the bishop there, and this new Latin and Greek master would surely have been shown the bishop's haul from a trip to Italy: murals from Herculaneum and Etruscan vases.[33] At the top of Cheyne Row David would turn right into a short street of eighteenth-century terraced houses. The ninth house along on the north side, at the corner with Cook's Ground, with its market gardens, meadows and Huguenot chapel, was the school. In 1913 it was reported that the floors were falling in and it was later demolished. On its site now squats a twentieth-century house, largely hidden by a high fence, adorned with cctv cameras. There exists, however, a photo of the school taken in 1913. The house was originally built early in the eighteenth century for the Duchess of Hamilton and was altered and added to, so that by 1807 its façade was similar to the terraced houses next door, close to the road behind a railing. It was of two storeys with dormer windows in the roof.[34] David might have had a bedroom behind one of the windows in the attic. Although it would have been quieter than the houses on the riverbank, Thomas Carlyle, who moved into a nearby house in Cheyne Row less than thirty years later and stayed for the rest of his life, complained about the noise of the hawkers, crowing of cocks, barking of dogs, carts rattling over cobbles and once even a noisy Punch and Judy show below his window, and installed a 'silent' room.[35]

* * *

After three years at the school, David was offered a title for orders – a curacy in Yorkshire – and was therefore able to apply for ordination as a deacon. He acquired a testimonial from three clergymen: John Rush, curate at the Old Church and later its incumbent when the new St Luke's was built, and two lecturers at City churches – John Evans, at James Garlickhythe church, and Joseph Patten Rose at St Ann's Aldersgate. 'Lecturer' meant that they specialized in sermons and were paid for out of church funds, and were presumably evangelical. There is too little information about them to establish whether David might have attended their sermons because they were particularly fine or evangelically notable, and the City was a long way to go. Perhaps they were simply friends of Rev. Rush, who visited Chelsea frequently enough to agree to sign David's testimonial, and recognized David as a kindred spirit.

Rev. John Rush, however, crops up quite frequently, much more so than his rector, Rev. Wellesley. He was the same age as the rector: the latter a graduate of Cambridge; Rush a graduate of Oxford, with a Bachelor of Laws degree, and in his late thirties when David arrived. What is interesting is that when Rush was appointed curate to Rev. Wellesley at Chelsea Old Church he had just acquired a living at Hartwell in Buckinghamshire – he was a non-resident rector, employing his own curate. I found evidence for the appointment of one of his curates in the unlikeliest of archives, which I will come to in another chapter. Such was the way with pluralism, and the need to earn enough for one's family – John Rush resided in the place where he was curate, not where he was the rector. And that is exactly what my research found to be Patrick Brontë's aim in Yorkshire, as I discuss below. Chelsea was obviously a better place to live for Rev. John Rush and his family: no doubt education for his children was an important factor. One son had a sad fate: there is a memorial in the chancel to Henry Rush, aged twenty-six, who drowned in the Thames in 1839.[36] Thomas Faulkner mentions Rev. Rush in his book, chairing a meeting in 1809 on how to celebrate George III's fiftieth year on the throne. Though Napoleon was hammering the Austrian army, the tide was turning in Britain's favour in the Peninsular War under Sir Arthur Wellesley, so there was positive news to celebrate as well as the jubilee. The most important resolution at this committee was not for fireworks, ox roasting or street parties – though no doubt they took place – but a subscription to 'relieve and regale the poor on that day'. It is an impressive decision: two shillings each were subsequently given to 5,009 poor persons and children, though the poor in the workhouse had to do their bit by showing how grateful they were. The sun shone on the day itself, Wednesday 25 October; there was divine service in the Old Church and a sermon preached by Rev. Rush (not Rev. Wellesley). The 2nd battalion of the Queen's Royal Volunteers assembled on parade in Sloane Square and marched to Battersea Bridge, where they fired a *feu-de-joie*, which was answered by a discharge of fifty pieces of cannon.[37] Surely the boys had the day off school and, escorted by David and other teachers, waved and cheered, thrilled to have a break from Greek verbs.

* * *

So how did David Jenkins get a curacy in West Yorkshire? It depended on the people you knew, the contacts you made. Which one of the people who wrote or signed testimonials in Chelsea passed his name on to Rev. John Buckworth in Dewsbury, or indeed to Rev. Patrick Brontë? It is not clear which of these two David was recommended to, as shown by the extract from the letter from Patrick Brontë at the start of this chapter, which I will explore below. Or it could have been a connection within the Welsh community – there were more Welsh living in London than in any town in Wales.[38] This was a cut-throat, competitive world, but for some young men getting a curacy was as easy as getting a job in your father's firm. Edmund Bertram in Jane Austen's *Mansfield Park* (1814) has no need to network or grovel to a patron: his father has two livings in his gift; the only slight downside is that Edmund has to wait a short while for the second to fall into his lap. For Jane Austen's brother Henry it was just as easy: when his bank failed in 1816 and he decided to become a clergyman he got the curacy at Chawton, where Jane had written *Mansfield Park* – the living belonged to his uncle.[39]

The stupid, obsequious Mr Collins in *Pride and Prejudice* (written 1790s; published 1813), we are told, made no helpful contacts ('useful acquaintance') at Oxford or Cambridge, but 'a fortunate chance had recommended him to Lady Catherine de Bourgh when the living of Hunsford was vacant'.[40] At twenty-five he had presumably managed to get a curacy after graduation, so after his usual year as deacon he had been ordained priest at Easter before getting the valuable living around October.[41] Jane Austen gives no indication about where he was between graduation and Hunsford in Kent, or how he had been brought to Lady Catherine's notice. She might even be teasing her readers when she has Elizabeth tell Mr Wickham that 'Lady Catherine de Bourgh [...] has very lately given him a living. I hardly know how Mr. Collins was first introduced to her notice, but he certainly has not known her long.'[42] Chance can be a factor, but it was usually connections – that all-important word. The prudent, steady Charlotte Lucas, eyes wide open when she marries the appalling Mr Collins, startles us at her last significant appearance in the novel with her worldly cynicism, but she shouldn't surprise us: she clearly understands how her world works. When Charlotte begins to realize that Mr Darcy is in love with her friend Elizabeth, the chapter ends thus:

> In her kind schemes for Elizabeth, she sometimes planned her marrying Colonel Fitzwilliam. He was beyond comparison the pleasantest man; he certainly admired her, and his situation in life was most eligible; but, to

counterbalance these advantages, Mr. Darcy had considerable patronage in the church, and his cousin could have none at all.[43]

Charlotte has realized what a benefit it would be to her clergyman husband and herself if her friend Elizabeth were to marry Mr Darcy. And here we have a possible future Mrs Proudie – Trollope's memorable bishop's wife – as Charlotte realizes how important her friend's marriage would be for her own situation. Later in the novel, Mr Bennet also sees the huge advantage if Mr Collins can switch his allegiance to a more useful connection than Lady Catherine: 'Elizabeth will soon be the wife of Mr. Darcy,' Mr Bennet writes to Mr Collins. 'Console Lady Catherine as well as you can. But, if I were you, I would stand by the nephew. He has more to give.'[44]

* * *

To try and work out how David Jenkins had got his first curacy in Dewsbury as assistant to Rev. John Buckworth in 1810, I looked at how Patrick Brontë had got there.[45] Patrick had done well at St John's College, Cambridge and had obtained an important prize on graduation in 1806: a curacy in one of the livings owned by Trinity College.[46] His vicar at Wethersfield, Essex, Dr Joseph Jowett, was Regius Professor of Civil Law at Cambridge, and was non-resident in his parish except during the summer vacation. So Patrick was in sole charge for much of the time, for a stipend of £60 a year: a situation that was the norm in this period, and certainly not, as Barker says, 'a rather uncomfortable position for a newly ordained clergyman in his first curacy'.[47] In 1809 Patrick took a new post as a curate in Wellington, Shropshire, probably recommended by a college friend who was a curate in nearby Shrewsbury. The incumbent at Wellington, John Eyton, was a zealous evangelical and the son of the squire who owned the living. He was apparently in poor health and needed two curates, whom of course he had to pay – presumably he had an adequate private income from his father. He was also younger than Patrick. It was there, from his evangelical friends in Shropshire, that Patrick learnt of the need for a curate in Dewsbury, yet again as assistant to a younger man, John Buckworth, with poor health and evangelical zeal. Barker suggests that he accepted the curacy because he longed to go to Yorkshire 'which was regarded by the Evangelicals as a sort of "Promised Land" of opportunity'.[48] Patrick thus moved to Dewsbury in December 1809, aged thirty-two, just under a year after arriving in Wellington.

I rather discount Yorkshire being the overriding attraction for Patrick in favour of the lure of acquiring a living of his own at Hartshead, a few miles west of Dewsbury. It was a living in the gift of the incumbent of Dewsbury, Rev. Buckworth. For Patrick in his early thirties, who was considering starting a family as soon as he could find a wife, to have a living of his own was a priority. We can only assume that that was part of the deal with Buckworth – for otherwise why exchange one sickly evangelical clergyman for another?[49] There was one problem, however: the incumbent of Hartshead-cum-Clifton was still officially in post, and he was younger than Patrick. The Rev. William Lucas of Hartshead had been appointed by Rev. Buckworth's predecessor. Did Rev. Buckworth offer the carrot of the (as yet non-vacant) living to Patrick because Lucas was even more sickly than Rev. Buckworth and expected to die or resign soon?

This was the somewhat confused situation that David Jenkins was to find when he left Chelsea and schoolteaching, and arrived in Dewsbury in July 1810 as a newly ordained curate only seven months after Patrick Brontë had arrived there as curate, and who still didn't have his living at Hartshead.

* * *

I quoted from a letter by Patrick Brontë at the start of this chapter. It is referred to by Barker,[50] but she doesn't understand it and is selective in quoting from it. No one has realized before now that the 'Gentleman' referred to in the letter was David Jenkins, nor is it explored what Patrick was trying to do. So to understand this murky world of clergymen in the early nineteenth century I need to quote more of it. Patrick's letter is addressed to Thomas Porteus, secretary to the Archbishop of York,[51] and it was sent by Patrick from Dewsbury on 6 June 1810, when he had been curate there for six months:

> I thank you for your information – I have got certificates for three years of my ministry, reckoning back from this period. The living of Hartshett [Hartshead] is small: salary only 62£ a year. I am not at present licensed to the curacy of Dewsbury. Will you have the goodness, Sir, to inform me, whether I can get Licensed to this curacy, be inducted into Hartsheath Living, and obtain License for non-residence, in time, to give a Title to a Gentleman, who intends to offer himself a candidate for Holy Orders, at his Graces next ordination? As my Vicar is at Oxford, taking his Master of Arts Degree, and the journey from this to London[52] so far, it will be a most desirable thing for me if I can get all done without leaving this place.

His Grace's 'next ordination' after the date of this letter was 15 July 1810.[53] Just over a month later. And indeed David Jenkins was ordained on that day as deacon by the Archbishop of York. In early June, therefore, Patrick Brontë was trying to get his living at Hartshead so that he could give a title for orders to David as his curate there. But obviously he failed: no doubt the archbishop's secretary replied that there wasn't enough time. So Patrick must have asked Rev. Buckworth to offer David the title for orders instead, maybe in a flurry of correspondence if Buckworth still hadn't returned to Dewsbury, while David waited in Chelsea, hoping that it wouldn't all fall through. We can piece together what probably happened from David's ordination papers, especially the letter that Rev. John Buckworth wrote to the Archbishop of York. In fact there are two letters by Buckworth to the archbishop on one folded sheet of paper, both dated 20 June 1810.

The first letter is the formal offer of a title for orders:

These are to certify Your Grace, that I John Buckworth, Clerk, A.M, Vicar of Dewsbury in the County of York, & Your Grace's Diocese, do hereby nominate & appoint David Jenkins of Chelsea, Middlesex, to perform the office of a Curate in my Church of Dewsbury aforesaid, & do promise to allow him the yearly sum of fifty pounds for his maintenance in the same, humbly beseeching Your Grace to grant him your Licence to serve the said Cure.

Within the folded sheet of paper is another letter from him, dated also 20 June 1810, from Dewsbury Vicarage:

Herewith I have transmitted a Title for Orders in behalf of Mr David Jenkins from whom you will receive the remaining necessary papers in the course of the present week. Having just understood that the Ordination is to take place on July 15 I have requested him to lose no time in sending these to you. Feeling a persuasion that he will give satisfaction [to your] Grace in his examination.

It seems therefore that Rev. Buckworth had arrived back in Dewsbury some days before Wednesday 20 June. If they had not already communicated by letter, Patrick told him then that the next ordination was imminent and that there was no time for he himself to give David a title for orders. Thus they presumably agreed that David should be appointed formally to Dewsbury, but that his main position would be at Hartshead, and some arrangement was made about who was to pay David the minimum stipend of £50. Rev. Buckworth then wrote to David in Chelsea about the situation. David hurriedly got further testimonials from Thomas Edwards and son, and sent his papers to the archbishop on 22 June – Rev. Buckworth had given him very little time.

However, the vital 'Si Quis' in the Old Church in Chelsea had not yet taken place. David apologized to the archbishop's secretary that the 'Si Quis' couldn't be done until Sunday 24 June, 'owing to a mistake'. One can sense the excitement and nerves that David must have felt, afraid that the prize might slip away. I wonder whether other curacy opportunities had been within his grasp before but had failed to materialize. There is an indication that a possible curacy had been in the air in the spring of 1809, since his mother had made her affidavit in April stating the date that David was born. But he was only just twenty-two then, so maybe he was forced to wait another year.

Patrick Brontë also comes across as urgently keen to acquire David as a curate. If we had only Rev. Buckworth's letters to the archbishop, we would assume that Buckworth was behind giving the curacy to David; but with the evidence of Patrick's letter, it is clear that Patrick was the instigator. And the reason? Patrick needed the income from both the Hartshead living and the Dewsbury curacy – where he intended to reside – but he couldn't do both jobs without help. He needed a curate at Hartshead. It seems unlikely that he and David had already met, but not impossible: they may have met in London. But it was more likely a recommendation passed on by colleagues that there was a highly educated, sound young man with evangelical sentiment who was prepared to accept a curacy in Yorkshire with a stipend of £50 a year. Interestingly, Rev. Buckworth had previously had difficulties in getting a curate. In the *Memoir* written in his memory, which I will discuss more below, selections from his letters and diaries are given. In a letter written 9 July 1807, Buckworth remarks: 'I have had several prospects of obtaining assistance, but have been singularly disappointed.' He adds about one man: 'He declined accepting my title, on the ground of distance from his friends.' Patrick Brontë (in December 1809) seems to have been the first curate to accept a position with Buckworth, three years after Buckworth had been nominated to the living of Dewsbury, where he had been curate, at the age of twenty-six.[54]

When David arrived in Yorkshire in July 1810 he would know that he was beholden primarily to Patrick for his first step on the ladder as a clergyman.[55] Brontë biographers either ignore David or give him a passing mention, confused about his role at Patrick's living at Hartshead, and minimize him to the extent of virtually writing him out of history. But linking Patrick's 6 June letter and David's ordination papers it becomes much clearer about what was going on in June and July 1810. However, before investigating Patrick and David's relationship, initially as fellow curates in Yorkshire, and what kind of man Rev. Buckworth was, I needed to take a trip to Dewsbury and Hartshead.

* * *

My trip was blessed by the extraordinary interest taken by the Vicar at Hartshead, Rev. Richard Burge. I had searched for St Peter's Hartshead on the internet in cold early 2018 and left a telephone message just to find out when the church was open. This ended up, many months later, with Rev. Richard arranging to pick me up at Dewsbury Minster to take me to his church in Hartshead for coffee/tea and cakes, but doing in addition something so thoughtful and unsolicited.

Before then, in freezing rainy February, after an initial phone conversation with Rev. Richard, I emailed him about my research into Rev. David Jenkins and his time as curate in Dewsbury and Hartshead, and his links to Patrick Brontë. In turn, Richard said that he had given a talk about Patrick Brontë – his predecessor at St Peter's in Hartshead – to the Brontë Society. We agreed that a good time for me to come was on the first Saturday in June. Out of the blue in April I received an email from Richard: 'I have hopefully organised for something that I trust will be a great surprise and joy for you when you come over that day.'

I had no idea what the surprise would be. What could there be? – my great-great-great-uncle had been a curate at Hartshead and Dewsbury for several years at the same time as Patrick Brontë, and he was mostly ignored, except for a brief mention by Juliet Barker. The booklets on sale that I later found in Dewsbury Minster confirmed his disappearance there. So, intrigued, in June I travelled from my new home in North Wales, staying in a motel in Manchester for the night, about an hour away from Dewsbury. I got a train early the next morning north-east to Dewsbury in West Yorkshire, arriving before nine. I had read Barker's description of early nineteenth-century Dewsbury, and read online about it now being a vibrant Asian community, but at that hour (and yet on a Saturday) it was dull and empty, all shop shutters down, no café that I was hoping for. I traipsed downhill from the railway station through deserted streets, past a Pentecostal church that had once been Methodist, towards the minster (in their day, All Saints parish church) where they had been curates. The Nonconformist churches scattered around me resonated something of their own experience. The retail 'park' around the ancient minster had maybe killed off activity in the lanes down from the station. Opposite the one little supermarket open at that time, near the minster, the sight of an ugly 'shopping mall' depressed me. Inside the supermarket I found friendliness but no orange juice. On the other side of a dual-carriage road was the building I was looking for – All Saints, now the minster.

That is perhaps an unfair description by someone who saw Dewsbury for less than an hour – dual carriageways, ugly road signs, a shop not selling something as basic as fruit juice. But two hundred years before, this Yorkshire woollen town was in a far worse state. In Charlotte Brontë's 'Luddite' novel *Shirley* (published in 1849) she describes this area of the West Riding of Yorkshire in 1811–12, when her father (and David Jenkins) had lived here:

> The period of which I write was an overshadowed one in British history, and especially in the history of the northern provinces. War was then at its height [...] National honour was become a mere empty name, of no value in the eyes of many, because their sight was dim with famine; and for a morsel of meat they would have sold their birthright.
>
> The 'Orders in Council,' provoked by Napoleon's Milan and Berlin decrees, and forbidding neutral powers to trade with France, had, by offending America, cut off the principal market of the Yorkshire woollen trade, and brought it consequently to the verge of ruin [...] At this crisis certain inventions in machinery were introduced into the staple manufactures of the north, which, greatly reducing the number of hands necessary to be employed, threw thousands out of work, and left them without legitimate means of sustaining life. A bad harvest supervened. Distress reached its climax.[56]

All Saints, Dewsbury, a minster in the Anglo-Saxon period and restored to that status in 1993, sits squashed in between the dual carriageway, a sports hall and a soulless retail park.[57] The church looked squat and bypassed, hunkered down within its lawn, its trees and mauve rhododendrons, its old tombstones. One grave cover to the north of the church laments the death of Jeremiah Clay, who died on 7 April 1811, aged twenty-six, 'Whose Soul was Goodness' yet 'Cropt like a Flower he wither'd'. Either David, Patrick or the vicar John Buckworth conducted the funeral – we don't know. The first two would learn, much later, the grief of losing children in their twenties.

The philistines of the 1960s levelled the medieval Moot Hall, once next to the fourteenth-century vicarage, to make way for the dual carriageway.[58] The vicarage had been pulled down in 1884 when the church was enlarged. Yet, inside, the church soars. It is spacious, modern in feel, welcoming. It is really bigger on the inside. It would be unrecognizable to Patrick Brontë and David Jenkins. The church is even reconfigured so that the altar is now at the west end (which caused me endless moments of indecision as the guidebook's description of 'north' and 'south' made no sense to me, used to reckoning an altar as lying at the east end of a church). But what I took, at first, in my architectural ignorance, to be the most modern part of the church – with its spacious crown glass windows – turned out to be its Georgian glory. They would have known those huge windows: just what David would install at his enormous new church in Pudsey, a few miles north, in the 1820s. Whereas the 'Gothic' aisle on the other side, which looked so ancient, was late Victorian fakery.

I had arrived early at the minster – before its advertised opening at 9 a.m. – and hovered in the early June drizzle as blue buses and cars swished past me. But a volunteer helper, sheltering in her car, spotted me, and warmly took me into the church by a side door and through its refectory – soon, I discovered, the refuge of the destitute, the desperate for food, coffee and compassionate human contact. I bought all the booklets they had on offer and began exploring their heritage centre with its fragments of an Anglo-Saxon preaching cross and medieval grave covers, its pristine, informative display boards. One board stated that the name Dewsbury probably derived from *Dewi's burh* – Dewi is 'British', or Welsh, for David. David Jenkins may have known that he had arrived at a town, a *burh* or fortification, called after his namesake before the pagan Anglo-Saxons arrived, perhaps not long after the demise of Roman Britain. This was long before the arrival in Yorkshire of St Paulinus in the seventh century, who represented the second introduction of Christianity into Britain, from Rome, centuries after the arrival of Welsh/British Christianity. Also on display in the heritage centre was a pewter chalice, 'Reputed to have been used by the Rev'd Patrick Brontë – 1809–1811', the label noted. And by Rev. David Jenkins, I thought I might scrawl on it …

In the church was a glowing brass plaque to Patrick Brontë's less than two years as a curate, erected by the Brontë Society. And in the booklets he was described as the sole, hard-working, only curate … Not fair. Not true. This traces back to Juliet Barker's book. 'In Dewsbury,' she writes, 'Patrick had his hands full. John Buckworth performed a marriage on the day his new curate arrived, 5 December 1809, but thereafter the full burden of the church offices was carried almost singlehandedly by Patrick. In the sixteen months of his curacy he personally performed nearly 130 marriages.' The full burden

... almost singlehandedly? She adds: 'Four hundred and twenty-six baptisms were carried out in the parish church [...] Most onerous of all was the number of burials. At first these averaged around twenty a month, but then they rose sharply: from October 1810 to February 1811 there were over fifty a month, peaking at seventy-three in November when, on two occasions, there were eight burials in one day.'[59] This is picked up by one of the booklets I bought: *The Church at Dewsbury*. The author writes, in a section about Patrick Brontë: 'his workload was enormous – 420 baptisms and well over 40 burials per month'. But only the parish register for *marriages* includes the name of the curate or minister. The registers for funerals and baptisms did not include the minister's name until 1813. David Jenkins arrived as co-curate in July 1810: those numerous burials and baptisms were shared. Patrick Brontë was sole curate for only seven months.[60]

Although I got slightly cross at my forebear being written out of a little bit of history, his share of the work unfairly and dishonestly magicked away, I was suddenly cheered by a figure who appeared in the church: Rev. Richard Burge. He hailed me and sped me off to his church of St Peter at Hartshead through the spring rain and the urban sprawl. But before I turn to this, my next adventure, I need to look at Rev. John Buckworth. Who was this evangelical vicar who had employed Patrick Brontë and David Jenkins?

* * *

Rev. John Buckworth is an odd man, hard to read. The anonymously edited *Memoir* written about him after his death in 1835 (when he was fifty-six) has its jolting peculiarities, as if all was not what it seemed. But first an extract from the eulogy printed in the *Memoir* by one of his later curates, Rev. Frederick Reyroux (an Oxford graduate, licensed as curate in 1829):

> I feel it well nigh impossible to overrate the character of this revered and beloved individual. For thirty years he presided over an extensive and populous Parish, nearly half of which time he laboured with astonishing zeal, activity, and success; and the remaining half [...] was spent in almost continual pain and suffering, brought on by his former unremitting attention to his sacred duties. During his active life, 'the mind that was in Christ Jesus' shone brightly forth in his exemplary humility, meekness, and charity [...] I can truly say, I never could, if I may so speak, lay my hand on a single foible in the character and conversation of the Vicar of Dewsbury.[61]

Juliet Barker in her book *The Brontës* falls for this: 'Cheerful, kind and courteous, John Buckworth was outstanding, even among Evangelicals, for his personal faith and humility and for his public exertions on behalf of his parishioners [...] [H]e was a talented preacher; determined to save sinners, he went about it with characteristic energy.'[62] It is surprising, then, that only one former curate contributed to this memoir. Regarding his preaching, though, an unnamed clergyman is less eulogistic: 'His endowments might not perhaps be considered of the very highest order, but still of so respectable a class as to render him highly acceptable, and eminently useful.'[63] 'Useful' is the pre-eminent word of approbation in evangelical circles, but he damns with faint praise, and why is he anonymous?

Why am I sceptical? John Buckworth was born in Lincolnshire in 1779, over eighty miles south of Dewsbury, and was sent to Oxford University as a promising, pious young man, who had been converted, or, as we might say today, 'born again', when he was sixteen – and subsequently refused (apparently 'mildly') to work in his employer's chemist shop on Sundays. The extracts from his diaries in the *Memoir*, written when he was nineteen or twenty, seem to show a genuine 'conversion', but I distrust the trope of the 'suffering saint' that runs through the *Memoir*, though he seems to have fainted rather a lot. He was thirty years a minister – all spent at Dewsbury, and, according to the quotation from his former curate, and the evidence in the *Memoir*, he spent about fifteen years of his ministry dying, yet mostly in lovely places, well away from the industrial North and his parishioners: in 1813 (after Patrick and David had left him) he went to Shrewsbury for six months; he preached there and looked for pious young men, but it looks like an extended holiday. And the *Memoir* states that even before Shrewsbury 'he had suffered much from ill health; and was, at one period, entirely unable to take any public duty for thirteen months' and went off to Wales, particularly to Bala (a lakeside town). Presumably Patrick or David or the next curate was left in charge ... for over a year. From 1817, the author of the *Memoir* states, 'the state of his health prevented him from preaching, except at long intervals, and obliged him to be much from home', implying that for the last eighteen years of his life he did very little work as a minister and was mostly on vacation. In 1818 Buckworth was in Scarborough for ten weeks, a seaside resort on the Yorkshire coast. He has palpitations and 'dare not see any of my relatives'. He spent the whole winter of 1821 in the south of England – at Box Hill in Surrey, a lovely spot then and now. The winter of 1829 he spent in the seaside resort of Torquay in Devon, and went there again in 1831. But he was in Dewsbury when he died in April 1835. One would expect that someone who was so debilitated by illness would be skeletal, but his editor writes that 'towards the middle of his life [he was] rather inclined to stoutness'.[64] I wonder if he had diabetes.

Evangelicalism was a movement that had grown out of the eighteenth-century Enlightenment, and flourished amongst all Protestant Christian denominations. The four key characteristics were: the experience of conversion – turning away from sin and towards Christ; activism – frequent preaching, laborious pastoral work, sending out missionaries; devotion to the Bible – all spiritual truth was to be found in it; and stress on Christ's sacrificial death on the cross.[65] If a non-evangelical can admire their activism in social reform (and the anti-slave trade campaign was their great triumph), the wailing and beating of breasts at conversions can be an immediate turn-off. The *Memoir* reports that at one time 'the power of God was remarkably displayed in the conversion of sinners from darkness to light, by means of the preaching and other labours of Mr. Buckworth. In one year, upwards of sixty persons joined themselves to the Lord [...] In his Diary, he remarks, "What great things hath God wrought by such a poor, feeble, and unworthy instrument."' In Shrewsbury in 1813 he called on a woman who had been convinced by him that she was a poor and ignorant sinner: 'We wept together tears of gratitude, and when I proposed prayer, she went for two of her neighbours to unite with us. It was a tender and sweet season indeed!'[66] Frances Trollope would have snorted in derision.

Frances Trollope's novel *The Vicar of Wrexhill*, set in a village in the New Forest in Hampshire in the 1830s, was published in 1837, only one year later than John Buckworth's eulogistic *Memoir* (had she read it?). The eponymous evangelical vicar is discovered to be a fraud, but not before he almost destroys a family and (almost) rakes in the money by marrying a 'converted' and gullible widow, Mrs Mowbray of Mowbray Park. Frances Trollope is angry about the devastation among families that was caused by 'this fearful superstition':[67]

If all other circumstances left it a matter of doubt whether evangelical influence (as it is impiously called) were productive of good or evil, the terrible power which it is so constantly seen to have of destroying family union must be quite sufficient to settle the question. Any person who will take the trouble to inquire into the fact, will find that family affection has been more blighted and destroyed by the workings of this fearful superstition than by any other cause of which the history of man bears record.

Rev. Cartwright is a melodramatic monster, and not everyone is swayed by his piety or his preaching. A neighbour, Lady Harrington, comments:

> 'Personally I know nothing of this Mr. Cartwright; – we never leave our parish church and our excellent Dr. Broughton, to run after brawling extempore preachers; – but I have been told by one or two of our neighbours who do, that he is what is called a *shining light*: which means, being interpreted, a ranting, canting, fanatic.'[68]

But the widow, and teenage Fanny, the widow's youngest child, succumb. When the widow leaves for London to prove her late husband's will that leaves her everything, disinheriting her eldest son and daughters, Rev. Cartwright turns his attention to Fanny – he invites her to pray for her mother in the library of Mowbray Park:

> But though conscious that the mode of prayer in which she was now so unexpectedly invited to join was very unlike what she was used to, her unbounded love and admiration for Mr. Cartwright rendered it absolutely impossible for her to conceive it wrong, and she prepared herself to pray with all the fervour of her young and ardent spirit [...]
>
> Mr. Cartwright began, almost in a whisper, to utter his extemporary prayer. It first invoked a blessing on *the little knot of united hearts* that now offered their homage to the Lord, and then proceeded to ask, in flowing periods, for exemption from all dangers likely to beset travellers by land for 'our beloved sister in the Lord who is this day gone forth' [...] then, his rich and powerful voice resounding through the room, his eyes raised to the ceiling, and his clasped and extended hands stretched out before him, he burst into an ecstasy of enthusiastic rantings, in which he besought blessings on the head of Fanny.

Frances Trollope comments on the horrors, to her, of what she is describing:

> It is impossible to repeat such language as Mr. Cartwright and those who resemble him think fit to use in their extemporary devotions, without offending against that sensitive horror of profanation which happily still continues to be one of the strongest feelings in the minds of Christians not converted – *i.e.* perverted from the solemn reverence our church enjoins

in the utterance of every word by which we venture to approach the Deity
[...] While imploring Heaven to soften the heart of poor Fanny, who knelt
weeping beside him like a Niobe, he rehearsed her talents and good qualities,
earnestly praying that they might not be turned by the Prince of Darkness
into a snare.[69]

I am reminded of Frances Trollope's description of a ranting evangelical when
I read about Rev. John Buckworth.

* * *

After a five-mile drive west from Dewsbury Minster to Hartshead in June 2018,
Rev. Richard Burge produced his surprise – he had purloined the parish register
of 1810–12 from the archive in Wakefield. He wasn't sure that he had got the
right register, but it was. I was deeply touched. In the little church at Hartshead,
Richard laid it on a table, and opening it I could see immediately my great-
great-great-uncle David Jenkins's signature after performing his first marriage
at Hartshead on 9 August 1810. In fact he performed two marriages on that
day at St Peter's. Seeing the actual record is so different from looking at a scan,
and especially seeing the register in the building where he had signed it and
performed the marriages. Rev. Richard's kind deed had brought David into the
present: the 23-year-old Welshman at the start of his career in the church over
two hundred years ago was almost palpable. He had been forgotten or ignored,
but he was remembered that day in 2018. Richard showed me the Jacobean
table that Patrick Brontë and David Jenkins had used as the communion table.
I was disabused of the notion that the gorgeous little church was the one they
had known – it had been razed to the ground in the Victorian period and
rebuilt, though reusing the Norman arch. But perched on its hill, the view over
fields for miles into the distance would have been their view as well. A local
resident appeared with her laptop, on the hunt for cousins – frequently family
researchers turned up at this monthly church gathering. Since her family had
lived in the area for hundreds of years it was not surprising that David Jenkins's
name, as curate, was written alongside those of her ancestors in the register,
but it was an extraordinary moment when Richard took our photograph in the
church, knowing that two people who had never met before – a Londoner living
in North Wales, and Jacky, a West Yorkshire denizen – had ancestors who had
known each other so well and just here, in this place. Rev. Richard drove me
back to Dewsbury station after an enchanted morning.

* * *

It was now time to study the parish registers for Hartshead[70] and Dewsbury to try to work out David Jenkins's role according to the name of the clergyman who performed the marriages and who signed the register off at the end of the year. Starting in March 1810, Rev. William Hanwell Lucas, the incumbent, makes no appearance. The 'officiating minister' who signed off the year that March was Rev. Joseph Ogden. He was no doubt a local priest who was helping out in the absence of Lucas. Ogden doesn't have an entry in the Clergy database, but a possible son does (John Ogden); the database includes the entry from *Alumni Cantabrigienses* stating that John matriculated at Magdalene College, Cambridge in 1797 and his father was Rev. Joseph of Scholes, Yorks. There are a few places called Scholes in Yorkshire, but the most likely is a mere two miles north of Hartshead. If this is the correct identification, Joseph Ogden was then perhaps in his sixties.

Joseph Ogden also performed all three marriages at St Peter's Hartshead between April and June. After David Jenkins's arrival in July, David performed all the marriages, as 'curate', from 9 August 1810 until 28 March 1811 (nine marriages). Although we don't know who performed the funerals and baptisms, it seems clear that David had been primarily appointed to be the curate at Hartshead so that Patrick could continue as curate at Dewsbury, together with holding the living at Hartshead. And indeed, as the new (non-resident) incumbent, Patrick signed off the register at the end of March 1811. But from August 1811 Patrick starts officiating at the marriages as 'minister', and David only performed one more marriage there – as 'curate of Dewsbury', not just 'curate', on 27 April 1812, as if to underline that his curateship was now located in Dewsbury and not in Hartshead. So Patrick's attempt to remain as curate of Dewsbury while holding the living at Hartshead had ended for some reason. Juliet Barker in *The Brontës* is puzzled by this 'delay in Patrick's removal to Hartshead',[71] but it is not strange when it is realized that Patrick was attempting to be a curate in one place and hold a living in another, just as Rev. John Rush was doing in Chelsea.

In the All Saints, Dewsbury parish register, David's name appears only occasionally: his first marriage there was on 6 August 1810, a few days before his first marriages at Hartshead.[72] But Patrick as 'curate' performed all the other marriages in 1810 after David's arrival (forty-five). It is therefore even clearer that Patrick's main job was to continue as curate in Dewsbury. It is not 'surprising', as Juliet Barker writes, that 'Patrick continued to sign the registers at Dewsbury as "curate" (he would have been entitled to write "Officiating Minister")'[73] – no, Patrick was still the curate at Dewsbury.

The change comes in spring 1811. The last time Patrick signs himself as curate in Dewsbury is 11 March. Thereafter David Jenkins performs most of the marriages, and on 20 May Patrick signs himself as 'Minister'. Therefore he had given up his Dewsbury curacy between March and May 1811. Perhaps David and Patrick also swapped their residence then – Patrick moving to lodgings in Hartshead and David moving to the vicarage or lodgings at Dewsbury. David's priest ordination papers are another useful indicator. The ordination at the archbishop's palace at Bishopthorpe took place on Sunday 21 July 1811.[74] The testimonial as to his good character is signed by John Buckworth, P. Brontë, Minister of Hartshead, and Edward Kilvington, Minister of Ossett. It also confirms that David had arrived in Dewsbury the previous year on the same day as his deacon ordination: we 'do testify, from our personal knowledge of the life & behaviour of the said David Jenkins since the 15th day of July last past [1810] that he hath since that time lived piously, soberly & honestly, applied himself diligently to his studies and (as far as we know or believe) never wrote or maintained any thing contrary to the Doctrine or Discipline of the Church of England'. Also in the bundle is a letter from John Buckworth: 'I [...] do hereby nominate & appoint David Jenkins to perform the office of a Curate in my Church of Dewsbury aforesaid & do promise to allow him the yearly sum of 50 pounds for his maintenance in the same'.[75] Patrick could have nominated David as his curate at Hartshead, as he had intended a year before, but minds had changed: David was now definitely the curate at Dewsbury. And to underline this, on the same day as David's ordination as priest, Patrick acquired an 'assistant curate', John Hall, for a lesser stipend of £40. He was ordained deacon on the same day that David Jenkins was ordained priest.[76]

In David's priest bundle the 'Si Quis', performed in the church at Dewsbury, is signed by Patrick, 'Minister of Hartshead', and not John Buckworth. Finally there is a deposition by David's mother Elizabeth as to his date of birth, dated 12 July. Why another confirmation of David's birthdate was needed in York is puzzling. Had the secretary mislaid her affidavit of the previous year? Or was the secretary being particularly punctilious? David would have had to write speedily to Wales and hope the deposition arrived in time for his ordination.

Clergymen would not be careless when signing a register as 'curate', 'minister' or 'officiating minister'. David last signed himself as 'curate' at Dewsbury the following year, in August 1812, and at his next marriage, on 27 September, he signed himself as 'officiating minister': thus indicating that he had had a preferment. The dates of licences are not a good guide to exactly when a clergyman took up a post. For example, Patrick's licence for Hartshead is dated 27 September 1811, but it is clear that he was regarded as minister in March, when he signed off the register. John Buckworth was without a curate for several months in the autumn of 1812 and had to perform most of the marriages until the arrival of his new curate, Thomas Smith, in November.

David Jenkins was licensed as perpetual curate at the chapel of ease in Pudsey on 21 June 1814, but he had been accepted as minister by September 1812. After two years at Dewsbury, he had got the reward of a living of his own. During those two years he had worked closely with Patrick Brontë, first as his curate in Hartshead (practically if not formally), then taking over from Patrick as the curate at Dewsbury the following year. With Rev. Buckworth so often away, or ill, or involved in training missionaries, the Irishman and the Welshman managed both parishes and the Sunday school together. On 29 July 1813 (seven months after Patrick married Maria Branwell), David married a local girl, Harriet Walker, of the neighbouring parish of Thornhill, a village on the other side of the river Calder to Dewsbury. The man whom they asked to marry them in Harriet's church was Patrick.

For two years Patrick and David were close colleagues, with Patrick, ten years older than David, possibly acting as his mentor. Now they both had livings of their own, and both were married and starting families. Pudsey is only eight miles north of Hartshead, and the same distance from Thornton, where Patrick and his wife Maria moved in 1815. There is no evidence, but it is likely that the families met each other from time to time. Patrick's first child (Maria) was born in 1814, followed a few months later by David's (Harriet), who were later to be together at the same school at Cowan Bridge (Charlotte Brontë's Lowood in *Jane Eyre*) before tragedy struck. David had completed his family with five surviving children by 1823, to Patrick's six by 1820. Even with the Brontë family's move to Haworth in 1820 (only an extra four miles west), there could have been contact. But later evidence makes me wonder if close contact ended in the 1820s – which I will come to in a later chapter. However, it is clear that David was not just 'an acquaintance' of Patrick's, as most books have it.[77]

Certain evidence that David was minister at Pudsey long before the licensing date, is that in the Thornhill marriage register for his wedding in July 1813 he is described as 'Calverley Clerk' – the chapel of All Saints, Pudsey, was in the large ancient parish of Calverley. The discrepancy in the date he actually arrived in Pudsey and the traditional start date of his tenure as minister was that the incumbent, Rev. William Howorth, was ill but didn't die until June 1814.[78] It is possible, though, that he had resigned by August 1813, for David signed himself on that date for the first time as Perpetual Curate in the Pudsey burials register; before that he signed himself as Officiating Minister.[79] Howorth was in his late seventies, so those who had offered the living to David knew he didn't have too long to wait until his official licence was confirmed. Curates desperately seeking a living of their own were what we might call today 'ambulance chasers', perhaps unfairly since there were few other options. During his time at Hartshead and Dewsbury, David had attracted attention: he may have preached well, or had his name passed on to the Calverley vicar, Thomas Faber, keen to appoint a good man to replace the dying Howorth.

David was to stay in Pudsey for the rest of his life, just over forty years, and bring in a revolution there with the building of a huge new church. It is from there that the only image of him originates. It is a strange drawing: the forehead is poorly drawn – it slopes at an odd angle. It is almost a caricature, but his features resemble those of his eldest nephew – Evan and Eliza's first son, Edward. Rev. Richard Burge told me that he thought it was a Welsh face. His piercing eyes are formidable.

It is time to leave David Jenkins and Patrick Brontë as they start on married life, in charge of their own parishes. When I return to them in the 1820s, tragedy will confront both of them.

Five

Eliza

The Ancestors

she was always [...] of very active habits

> – Letter from Jane Livingston to her niece Margaret,
> 1836, commenting about Margaret's older sister Eliza[1]

I do not think that Eliza's continued residence on the Continent, and the society she there meets, have been of any advantage to her, but she is much attached to that horrid place that willingly she will never quit it.

> – Letter from Eliza's brother John Livingston Jay
> to their sister Margaret, 1840[2]

The obtuse, self-satisfied John Livingston Jay was then in his late thirties. For forty-two years he worked at the Royal Hospital, Greenwich, rising steadily, slowly through the ranks of clerks. He even wrote a history of the hospital; it has been lost, but I imagine it as thorough and worthy (and excruciatingly dull). Eliza and younger brother John Livingston came from a family always on the move – Scottish merchants with offices in Aberdeen and Rotterdam, Huguenots escaping from France to Holland, Spitalfields or Norwich, a talented boy from Suffolk who went from university in Glasgow to be a wine merchant and minister in Dordrecht, an uncle trading in Smyrna, another who had fought in the

Peninsular War, a grandfather who studied at Leiden University – with its canals, its ancient botanical garden – because his Nonconformism denied him education at Oxbridge. The family were largely Scottish and French seasoned in a Dutch marinade.

And then there was their father – John Jay: variously merchant, schoolteacher, church elder – who moved his family to three different countries (on one occasion, at least, to escape creditors). Maybe Eliza and her siblings – she was the eldest – just wanted to stay put once they had found a home of their own: Eliza in Brussels, Samuel the lawyer in London, John Livingston in Greenwich, Margaret in New South Wales, where she emigrated with her husband George Wyndham in the 1820s; the youngest, Janet, moved in with her brother John L. and took to staying on the sofa. Eliza commented that she would lose the use of her legs.[3] The letters written to Margaret in Australia over the years by her family are a tremendous survival, though patchy. They are not the only letters by Eliza or about Eliza, but they are family letters, with all the honesty and ghastliness that families engender among themselves. In researching Eliza's childhood, with the minimum of facts to start with, one comment by an aunt stood out as particularly nasty. Here is Aunt Jane, wife of the Peninsular War hero, writing to her favourite niece Margaret in 1836:

> Eliza over exerted herself, she was always [you] know, of very active habits – I cannot say why it is – but I fancy your children are handsomer than Eliza's […] I always loved you better.[4]

Perhaps nastiness ran in the family, since Eliza's Australian nephew Alward, on a trip to Europe in the 1850s, reports back to his mother Margaret: 'Aunt Eliza is very thin & shrivelled – looks aged – but is full of activity & energy.'[5] Eliza was then only fifty-six, but I am thrilled that her activity, her energy, was the feature that dominated from her childhood into middle age. Rather wrinkles than a female ancestor who lay all day on a sofa.

But there was no picture of her, I had no idea what she looked like. The following is a story of gut instinct, perseverance and being right (probably) all along.

* * *

My first research trip to Brussels in February 2014 had been a veritable footslog to almost everywhere I could go that was relevant. On my last day I walked from the Etangs d'Ixelles (the ponds) up the hilly rue des Champs Elysées. After Evan's death in 1849, Eliza and her children had moved here. It was a road parallel to Chaussée d'Ixelles where they had lived when the Brontës visited, with newly built houses and gardens. This is where Mrs Gaskell visited Eliza in 1856. I was looking for no. 61 – I had that number on one family document. I found it at the top of the hill, with views north-west to the centre of Brussels and south to the forest. I photographed it at numerous different angles. I claimed this as the house that the Jenkinses had lived in or used as a school at some period in the second half of the nineteenth century. A researcher in Brussels told me I was probably wrong as house numbers had changed since then. So there the matter rested.

Many months later I was flicking again through a great-aunt's scrapbook (who had been born in Brussels). I froze at a page of tiny brown and cream photographs. Top left was a building and a road I recognized: surely that was no. 61 rue des Champs Elysées. Surely that was the one I had photographed, although there were differences after 150 years. I glanced at a few of the other tiny photos on the page: I recognized John Card (Evan and Eliza's youngest son, my great-grandfather) with a full beard, and great-great-uncle Edward with his side whiskers. They were with family and friends in a garden at the back of a similar white house. Those photos had been taken before 1873, when Edward had died.

Then I glanced down at an equally small (c.3 x 2 in.) brown photo at the bottom of the page; the elderly lady sitting composedly in a chair looked straight back at me. Behind her stood a young woman, eyes down – she had blinked. At first I was unsure, then almost-certainty grew: this attractive older woman in mourning could be Eliza. There were no captions. The portion of the house behind the two figures, with its closed shutters, was different from the house and its lawn where Edward and John Card were posing, so maybe it was taken earlier outside another house (Eliza died in 1864). Also pasted on the page were more small sepia photographs that resembled others taken in the 1860s – the height of the crinoline expansion – which I guessed had been taken in Shropshire. Maybe my great-aunt some thirty years later had known that these photos of relatives were of a similar date and so pasted them on the same page. I needed experts to comment on the dresses 'Eliza' and the young woman – possibly her eldest daughter Helen – wore before I got too convinced, before I discovered that the dates of their clothes couldn't possibly be before 1864. I phoned the Victoria & Albert Museum in South Kensington.

I then lived just across the park from the V&A, so having managed to precariously scan the page (huge heavy album on small scanner) I went to the costume collection as advised. There was just one dress from the 1860s and the bones of a crinoline – they really didn't help. I wandered disconsolately to the circular information desk by the entrance and explained my predicament. The man was sympathetic and then whispered that I should go to the arts library just before 2.30. He wouldn't say more. It was rather mysterious. I wondered if I should check to see if anyone had heard us. Outside the arts library before this witching hour were a few people sitting on benches, all clutching something – a picture, or a bag. We edgily looked at each other as I sat on a sofa nearby. After a while I asked the guard at the entrance to the library what was going to happen: he knew nothing. But when I asked a fellow sofa-sitter holding a print what she knew, she told me it was 'opinions day'.

A V&A staff member with hanging badge arrived and led us all 'backstage'; there were over a dozen of us by then. We climbed a huge flight of dingy steps and sat down again. A photography expert was announced. I had wanted to see a costume expert and was embarrassed that I had a poor scan of a tiny photo, but she said without any prompting from me that it looked later 1850s/early 1860s. I was then led up and downstairs almost back to the library to see the fashion expert, Jenny. She said that the younger, standing Helen was definitely wearing a crinoline, so it was taken after 1856, whereas Eliza was not and was wearing mourning, and her hairstyle was of an earlier period. She reckoned the photo was taken in the early 1860s. The date fitted Eliza, in her sixties, and daughter Helen, in her thirties.

Eliza has a slim, attractive face. Her hair is fair, or maybe grey, and beribboned in a softer (old-fashioned) style than her daughter's severe scrape back. She gazes steadily at the photographer, alert, intelligent, almost smiling – because I think the photographer is her son 'Coco', her youngest, John Card, who is mentioned in a letter as keen on photography.[6] I think I have a definite photo of Helen twenty years later when she was headmistress of the school at no. 61 in 1879. It is a sepia school photo in which she sits surrounded by her girls and other teachers, and is partially captioned by my great-aunt, who was a pupil. Poor Helen is terribly ugly in that photo and it's easy to see how the blinking young woman in the crinoline turned into the proud headmistress of a girls' boarding school, with close-set eyes, huge bald forehead and unflattering scraped-back hair: Helen did not inherit her mother's looks. But the clincher for me that the older woman in the earlier photo was the Brontës' Mrs Jenkins was her close resemblance to an oil painting of her grandfather, Alexander Livingston, merchant and provost of Aberdeen (1750–2), owner of an estate known as Countesswells, father of the Peninsular War hero I mentioned above. The portrait is in Aberdeen, the artist unknown. It is a strange portrait, since, although he was probably in his thirties when the painting was made, the face below the wig looks childlike. But he is fair, with the same steady gaze, the same slim face and long nose as his granddaughter Eliza.

There is just one photograph of Eliza's sister Margaret Wyndham, who moved to Australia. Taken around 1865 when she was in her early sixties, she is in three-quarters profile, looking steadily away from the camera. She wears a crinoline and shown standing, one hand lightly on a chair. Unlike the fair Eliza, she has dark hair. The Prussian explorer Ludwig Leichhardt visited the Wyndhams at their home in the Hunter Valley in December 1842 and described Margaret in her late thirties: 'She is a woman of noble bearing and probably from a very good family. She is tall, but well-proportioned, has black hair and a fine complexion, large expressive eyes, friendly most of the time, but brimming with conversation. She told me that she and her husband taught their children themselves.'[7] There is no obvious likeness between the two women in the photographs, but nothing so dissimilar that they couldn't be sisters. Perhaps if Eliza resembled the Livingstons of her mother's family, Margaret took after her father John Jay's family. Leichhardt's comments about 'noble bearing' and 'very good family' are useful indicators for Eliza, even if they are the gallant remarks of a man appreciating a good-looking woman. Leichhardt disappeared on one of his expeditions into the Australian interior six years later. No trace was ever found of him. His last expedition inspired Patrick White's novel *Voss* (1957).

One triumphant note on no. 61 rue des Champs Elysées that I was told couldn't possibly be no. 61 over 150 years later: I went back to Brussels the next year with a copy of the 1860s/70s photo of the house. Yet back in the rue, comparing buildings and views down the hilly road, I frustratingly couldn't match any building with the photocopy, and drew suspicious glances as I prowled up and down. There was a similar house, but it was on the wrong side of the road and I went home baffled. It took me a long time to realize that the photo must have been printed from the wrong side of the glass negative. No. 61, where Helen Jenkins had presided as headmistress from around the age of forty in 1867 (her pensionnat is listed in the Almanac), where family and friends had posed for the camera one summer's day, was still no. 61. And because of the survival of that house, I had found on that same page in the scrapbook the photograph of Eliza.

* * *

Eliza's maternal grandfather, Alexander Livingston of Countesswells, was a third-generation Aberdonian merchant. Her mother Helen was born when he was in his sixties and on his second marriage (the first had been childless) to Elizabeth

Hardie, almost thirty years younger than him. Elizabeth was a native of Bo'ness in West Lothian and had moved to Rotterdam in 1763 after the death of her parents, when she was nineteen, perhaps to work as a governess.[8] Could Charlotte Brontë have heard about her from Eliza Jenkins? Alexander Livingston died in Rotterdam when his first child, Helen, was five, so there would be few personal memories to pass on to Helen's children, but his obvious eminence and success would have been an important legacy in a world of social hierarchies and 'sets'. His only son – the later Peninsular War hero – was named after him. Eliza and Evan Jenkins's second son also bore the same names. Even if it was because the war hero was a godfather, the choice reflected Eliza's family pride that she wanted to make public. I will come to the naming of their first child later, but find fascinating the contrast between second son – Alexander Livingston Jenkins – and third son – who was just Evan Jenkins, after his father and paternal grandfather. Poor Evan the younger became the black sheep of the family: was it due to his Welsh name, or to the lack of a middle name? When the Brontë sisters arrived in Brussels in 1842 and met the family, Alexander was twelve, his younger brother Evan nine. Was Alexander polite, quietly getting on with his homework, while Evan was dashing around being a nuisance, inheritor of the energy of his mother?

The little I know about their ancestor, the bewigged provost Alexander Livingston, comes from the splendidly named *The Livingstons of Callendar and their Principal Cadets: The History of an Old Stirlingshire Family* – which rather inspires me to order a kilt with the right tartan.[9] Starting as a merchant in Aberdeen in the 1730s, he made a fortune in Rotterdam, returning to Aberdeen to buy the nearby estate of Countesswells in 1750 and be elected provost. As a shipowner he traded with Virginia and invested there, where members of his family lived. Then he lost everything. It seems he set up a linen factory in Aberdeen which failed, and thus lost his holdings in Virginia and his estate in Scotland. But his behaviour to his creditors was as exemplary and honest as Sir Walter Scott's was later to be, and they presented him with a dinner service, pieces which were still preserved among his descendants over a hundred years later – perhaps through the war hero and his wife, Aunt Jane. Indeed, the portrait of the provost seems to have been in their possession, since their grandson, Rev. Samuel Ogilvy Baker, presented it to the City of Aberdeen in 1913. *The Livingstons of Callendar* states that the former provost then made another fortune, but gives no details.

The provost had three children, all born in Rotterdam: Eliza's mother Helen; another daughter Margaret, who married James Bowden, and moved to Edmonton near London; and one son, war hero Alexander. The children inherited their father's substantial estate: Helen's share was about £12,000.[10] When he was eighteen, Alexander the younger bought a commission as cornet with the 12th Light Dragoons with their famous motto of 'Ich Dien', and served in Egypt with his regiment in 1801, when Cairo and Alexandria were taken from the French. He then married the daughter of a baronet, 'Aunt Jane' – Jane Benger Ogilvy, daughter of Sir David Ogilvy, fifth Baronet of Barras, Kincardine in Fife – and added his wife's surname to his own, apparently also inheriting the Ogilvy estate in Forfarshire. In 1809 he took part in the successful invasion of the French island of Martinique, and over the following few years he served with the 60th Royal Rifles in the Peninsular War. He was severely wounded during the successful Anglo-Portuguese night assault of the French-held fortress of Ciudad Rodrigo on 19 January 1812, ordered by Wellington. Over one thousand Allies were killed or wounded, more than twice the number of French casualties. Captain Livingston survived but had an arm amputated. In the census of 1841 he was living with Jane in Somerset with four servants, and despite his war wounds he died at the age of seventy-five, having long outlived both his sisters. With such an uncle and aunt, and such a grandfather, Eliza could hold her head high in most social sets.

There is a family tradition in Australia that Eliza's sister Margaret brought no money at all to her marriage into the gentry family of George Wyndham, to which they didn't object because she was so delightful, but I find that unlikely. Of course some patriarchs did leave everything just to the eldest son, but it was regarded as selfish, and William Wilberforce condemned it.[11] Maybe the 'nothing' that Margaret brought with her included a remnant of her Livingston grandfather's fortune, perhaps 'one thousand pounds in the 4 per cents' that is all Elizabeth Bennet has as a portion, and which Mr Collins loftily regards as so insignificant that he stresses he doesn't mind her having little money when he makes his proposal of marriage ('To fortune I am perfectly indifferent, and shall make no demand of that nature on your father, since I am well aware that it could not be complied with').[12]

I tried to catch a glimpse of the eighteenth-century provost and merchant Alexander Livingston when I walked around Aberdeen one summer's day. A few buildings remain in Old Aberdeen around the university, founded in 1495, but perhaps only part of the 'Mither Kirk' – St Nicholas – would be familiar to him in the utterly transformed new town. New Aberdeen and its harbour would be as alien to him as modern Rotterdam after the bombing of the Second World War. I walked along the beach, from the river Dee to the Don. It was June but fog lay clammily heavy over the sea and the dunes. There were three colours in the landscape: grey, brown and murky green, with a fleck of white from the seagulls. It was wonderfully atmospheric. I don't know if he lost any ships to the deep or to pirates. One had been called *Alexander and Ann*, after his first wife, née Kennedy. When he lost his fortune in the 1750s he presumably sold the ship in order to pay his creditors. I turned away from the sea to follow the Don and walked over its ugly modern bridge through the shrubbery to the quiet otherworldly Brig o' Balgownie, the spacious medieval bridge completed for Robert the Bruce, according to legend, and where the child Byron passed his time in the 1790s. It had once been on an important trade route but was now silent. In the fog over the North Sea and on this beautifully crafted ancient bridge with its Gothic arch I caught a sense of these Aberdonian merchants, of their ceaseless activity and the dangers of losing it all in one sea storm, or on one unexpectedly foggy summer's day. That does not seem to have happened to his son-in-law, his daughter Helen's husband John Jay – Eliza's father – whose downfall seems less straightforward. To the Jays, Eliza's paternal ancestors, I now turn.

* * *

In Alexandre Dumas's (quasi-comic) historical novel *The Three Musketeers*, written over two hundred years after the final devastating siege of the last Huguenot stronghold of La Rochelle (1627–8), there is a great set piece during the siege. Athos (secretly comte de la Fère and the husband of the evil Milady) needs a private conference with his friends Porthos, Aramis and D'Artagnan. To get some privacy he organizes a wager among other soldiers who keep disturbing them that the four can eat a picnic breakfast for an hour in the bastion St Gervais – taken overnight from the Huguenot Rochellais but in danger of being retaken that morning.[13] D'Artagnan is aghast: they will all be killed. At the bastion, the Rochellais and French corpses are arranged upright with guns in their hands by one of the Musketeers' servants to deter the advancing Rochellais troops while they drink wine, continue their breakfast and discuss their plans for dealing with Milady. It is funny, a bit gruesome and rather splendid; but the Rochellais corpses and advancing troops – desperately trying to fight for their Calvinist Protestant religion against powerful Cardinal Richelieu and the French Catholic state – might include Eliza Jenkins's ancestors through her father, John Jay. Not so comic after all. Over half the population of La Rochelle (maybe 20,000) died during the siege in 1627–8, and this probably included several of her des Réaux and Fontaine ancestors (who intermarried from at least 1629), though no burial records survive.[14]

What do survive, however, are the picaresque, pacy, honest memoirs of the Huguenot Rev. Jaques Fontaine (1658–1728), half-brother of Eliza's three times great-grandfather, Rev. Pierre Fontaine (1634?–1715). Both brothers kept their Protestant faith and escaped from the persecution in France – Jaques ending up in Ireland, Pierre in London. Very few memoirs by Huguenots who escaped France survive. Surely Eliza would have known about them: they were written by Jaques (in French) in 1722 for his children, who mostly emigrated to America, but were published by a descendant in New York in 1838 as *A Tale of the Huguenots*; an abridged version, *Memoirs of a Huguenot Family*, was published in 1853.[15] The 1838 edition could have found its way into the Jenkins home and been a topic of conversation. The French writer and historian Prosper Mérimée wrote a caustic review of the 1853 *Memoirs* in a Paris journal. Seemingly in favour of the persecution of the Huguenots ('the austerity of the whole sect seemed a hateful and ridiculous mask to a light-hearted nation'), the atheist Mérimée at least appreciates Jaques Fontaine's personality and his storytelling:

> I have just finished reading this little book with a great deal of interest. The author of these memoirs, Jacques Fontaine […], engages our sympathies at once. He is one of those odd men […] who were perhaps unbearable in their time, but of whom […] we cannot help being fond. Minister by profession, clothmaker or merchant by necessity, soldier on occasion and really by inclination, Jacques Fontaine is a mixture of contrasts who, under the pen of Sir Walter Scott, would have made a fortune in a novel.[16]

That is indeed praise from the writer of the novella *Carmen*, who admired, and translated, Pushkin, Turgenev and Gogol.

There is no place in my book to retell Jaques's bloody fights with French pirates in Co. Cork, Ireland, but invaluable for Eliza's story is his account of their ancestors, and his own eventual escape as the persecution intensified, which might be similar to the flight of her ancestors to the Netherlands and England in 1685. This was the year of the notorious Revocation of the Edict of Nantes, issued by Louis XIV, when the Huguenots (the nickname for the French Calvinists) no longer had the right to practise their religion and were forced to convert (often violently) or flee. The Edict of Nantes had been promulgated by King Henri IV in 1598. It had guaranteed Huguenots certain rights and religious liberty. The Revocation of the Edict signalled the end of any form of toleration, and the start of a flood of French refugees – to the Netherlands, England, America, South

Africa and elsewhere – taking with them, and away from France, their skills of silk-weaving, wine-making, and Protestant industry and morality.

* * *

Jaques Fontaine mentions his half-brother Pierre several times in his memoirs – Eliza's three times great-grandfather – who became chaplain at the Pest House in London (an almshouse used for Huguenot refugees and no longer a hospital for plague victims). There is much on their ancestors, going as far back as the dawn of the Reformation itself, though current research on the records shows discrepancies, and even a possible missing generation. The earliest ancestor Jaques knew about was Jean de la Fontaine, who was from the county of Maine in north-west France and entered the service of King François I in the mid-1520s, where he was commissioned into the elite cavalry of the king's army. Jean's descendant, memoirist Jaques's father, dropped the noble 'de la' as he despised the idleness of the aristocracy, and as a minister he rejected its vanity. I wonder if dinner-table talk at the Jenkinses' home had turned to Eliza's French ancestors when Charlotte was there. In *Villette* she says of Polly's father Mr Home that he was 'of mixed French and Scottish origin, and had connections now living in France, of whom more than one wrote *de* before his name, and called himself noble'.[17]

François I was a great patron of the arts, who invited Leonardo da Vinci to France, where he spent his last years: alas, dying in 1519, about five years before Jean de la Fontaine arrived at court as a young man. But he may have seen the picture Leonardo brought with him from Italy: the *Mona Lisa*. Both Jean and his father embraced Protestantism as soon as it arrived in France in the 1530s. As King's Officer under François's successors, Jean was protected from the persecution of Protestants, but he was no longer safe when he resigned his commission in 1562. Jaques Fontaine describes what happened:

In 1563 they sent executioners from the town of Le Mans who went to his house at night, seized him unaware, and when he least expected it, dragged him out of doors and cut his throat. His wife, seven or eight months with child, followed, hoping to persuade them to change their minds. She received the same treatment from the barbarians. His valet, who thought he could rescue him, shared the glory of his master and mistress. Thus God distributed four crowns of martyrdom to His faithful servants and transported the soul of the babe to heaven, before he came into the world.[18]

Eliza was therefore descended from French Protestant martyrs.

Jaques writes that the murdered couple's surviving children fled to the safety of the Protestant stronghold of La Rochelle, a seaport on the Atlantic Ocean, where one of them, Eliza's ancestor Jaques de la Fontaine (1547?–1633), became Commander of the Chain Tower. This was an important role, since a huge chain was connected from it to the St Nicolas Tower and barred the entrance to the harbour at night.[19] He may have been directly involved in combating the fourteen-month siege of 1627–8, led by Cardinal Richelieu, when Dumas's musketeers enjoyed a picnic among the Rochellais corpses. Famine and disease finally forced the Huguenots to surrender unconditionally. The memoirist adds a curious and comical anecdote about the commander: it seems that his third wife tried to poison him, but he recovered and she was condemned to be hanged:

> Someone requested her pardon of Henry IV who was at La Rochelle. The King demanded to see the man she had poisoned, and when my grandfather appeared before him he cried out 'Hang her! Hang her! Ventre saint gris! He is the handsomest man in my kingdom'! I have seen his portrait [...] He had a full face, white and rosy, and handsome features. He had a majestic air and a blonde beard mingled with the white hairs of age, which reached to his waist. They say also that he had a handsome and well-proportioned physique.[20]

Henri IV became King of France in 1589 and was assassinated in May 1610, so there is a discrepancy with Jaques's account of wives number two and three (whom he says didn't produce children), since the commander's daughter Ester, supposedly from the first marriage, was born in 1609, not giving much time for the commander to marry twice more before the king's death a year later. Ester married Jean des Réaux, 'a good merchant of La Rochelle' in 1629. 'All our des Reaux relatives are descended from them,' our memoirist Jaques Fontaine adds.[21] The families were to be further linked when two of the commander's descendants, a Fontaine and a des Réaux, married in the 1690s. But the discrepancy about the number of wives is not the only problem with this account. No Jaques (de la) Fontaine has been found so far in the La Rochelle registers before 1600. But surely the commander, the handsomest man in the kingdom, with his waist-length blonde beard, existed – memoirist Jaques says he had seen his portrait, and he seems too splendid to make up.

* * *

Before the 'great persecutor' Louis XIV revoked the Edict of Nantes in October 1685, Jaques Fontaine states, intolerance and random persecution had caused many Protestants to flee. Ester's son – our memoirist's cousin Pierre des Réaux (Eliza's three times great-grandfather) – a widower, escaped with his children, aged between twelve and twenty-one, to the Netherlands in January 1685. He was a successful grease and tallow merchant and called 'le beau Réaux' because he was handsome, says our memoirist, who stayed with him in La Rochelle and 'after our flight' in Norwich, England. How perilous that flight was can be gleaned from Jaques Fontaine's account of his own escape with his fiancée in November that year: 'I saw that it was necessary either to die or to leave France.' Jaques secretly found an English captain who was willing to take him and a few others to England, despite the guards at sea and on land aiming to prevent anyone leaving. They waited for the ship on the designated beach, but that was aborted since the authorities learnt about it and they had to scatter among the dunes and hide in the nearby port of La Tremblade, south of La Rochelle. About twenty of them hid in one man's house: 'All day he was terrified, for there was a fine of 1,000 crowns for anyone who concealed a Protestant.' At night he ordered them to leave, which Jaques regarded as 'rather uncivil'.[22] (Maybe it is the English translation, but with Jaques tut-tutting at his frightened host's probably sensible advice to seek shelter elsewhere under the cover of darkness, I agree with Mérimée's comment that although perhaps 'unbearable' at times, Jaques was a man of whom 'we cannot help being fond'.)

The English captain was keen on earning money from the desperate Protestants, or maybe he was a genuine sympathizer. After about five days of their hiding he told them to get hold of a little sailing boat and he would pick them up in the sea north of La Tremblade. They were to raise and lower their sail three times, as would he in reply. But after the refugees had spotted the English ship, a French frigate, used for searching ships to stop Protestants from escaping, also caught sight of the English ship. If the refugees were caught, the men would be sent to the galleys, and the women to convents. 'We were in fear which cannot be expressed in writing nor imagined by those who have not felt it […] What would they think a small boat was doing there at anchor, an unsafe place even for large ships? We were less than a cannon shot away.' The frigate searched the ship fruitlessly and ordered the English captain to sail on, away from Jaques's boat. It was too hazardous for Jaques and his companions to sail back to La Tremblade, but to remain at anchor would arouse suspicion. Jaques prayed and suddenly came up with a scheme, as he often did in his life, though many of his schemes ultimately failed. He told the master of the boat to hide the refugees under an old sail and to pretend to be drunk, and thus 'accidentally' hoist the sail three times to alert the English captain that they were there. The master managed to convince the French frigate that they were waiting for the wind to change, while falling around drunk, hoisting the sail seemingly by mistake three times, and successfully alerting the English captain to wait for them. The little boat then launched out into the open sea to chase after the English ship, but Jaques was afraid that the frigate had seen them change course: 'We were again in extreme fear. Instant death would have been sweet to any of us. A long persecution and the galleys seemed more threatening, because our faith might be destroyed.' But they reached the ship and boarded: 'A happy day for us who had run more risks in fleeing our country, family, friends, and property, than the greediest people take to gain them.' It took Jaques and his fiancée eleven days' sailing to find sanctuary in the Bristol Channel and a welcome in Barnstaple in Devon – at the start of many more adventures.[23]

* * *

Jaques's half-brother Pierre Fontaine, Eliza's ancestor, was over twenty years older, from their father's first marriage to an Englishwoman, a Miss Thompson, who was handsome, from a good family and played the spinet well. Their father, also Rev. Jaques Fontaine (1603–66), had been educated at the famous Huguenot university in western France, the Academy of Saumur, as Pierre was to be. Founded in 1593, it was forced to close about a hundred years later, at the time of the Revocation. Jaques says of his father (Eliza's four times great-grandfather) that he 'was a genius' who dedicated himself to the holy ministry and was loved by his Protestant flock; he was a teetotaller, 'lived on vegetables', was 'fervent and, consequently, exceptionally moving'. His second son, Pierre, the half-brother, was 'a handsome man, fair, finely formed and strong. He was elected minister and colleague of my father in the church of Vaux [on the Atlantic coast, south of La Rochelle], and continued as its minister from my father's death until the church was destroyed.' Jaques describes how his half-brother was imprisoned for several months and then banished from France after the Revocation because he was a minister. He fled to London, but was not allowed to take his eldest daughters with him, though they escaped a few years later. Pierre became minister at the Pest House, 'loved and cherished by all who knew him, for he was a man of the most open manner and the best heart you can imagine'. It is obvious how close the half-brothers were: 'How often has this good and tender brother left his wife's bed both in France and in London, to be with me in another room, so we might resume our conversations? [...] He was always dearer to me than my own brother and we always had something new to discuss.'²⁴ Perhaps the wives were glad of a good night's sleep. Jaques's wife, though, was a feisty, tough woman, well capable of shooting at privateers in Ireland, so I doubt if she felt neglected. The Pest House was a large empty house near Bunhill Fields in East London, north-east of St Paul's Cathedral, when, in 1681, it was given for the use of French Protestant refugees. Suitably, Bunhill Fields was much used by Nonconformists to bury their dead without the use of the Anglican ceremony in the Common Prayer Book. It contains a monument to John Bunyan (d. 1688), whose *Pilgrim's Progress* was an important source for *Jane Eyre*. Rev. Pierre Fontaine was employed to officiate at daily services for sick, poor or mad Huguenot inmates in 1688, and he was still there in 1705; he appears to have conformed to the Church of England and episcopalianism. This was possibly a condition of his employment. It is odd that our memoirist Jaques makes no comment on this, since he himself adamantly refused to conform. The Pest House was later replaced by a new building, La Providence, the French Hospital, founded in 1718.²⁵

* * *

Jaques's cousin, the widowed, 'beau' Pierre des Réaux (Eliza's three times great-grandfather), as I mentioned above, fled France in January with his children before the Revocation. They maybe also travelled secretly, and perilously, by boat, but this time to the Netherlands. They settled near Dordrecht, a major seaport at the meeting of three rivers, whose pre-eminence was to be gradually taken over by Rotterdam. Pierre's sister, who renounced Calvinism, claimed his property in France. Pierre's second son Arnold (born about 1666 in La Rochelle), who became a successful merchant in South Holland, had a godfather named Arnout Walraven, who was probably Dutch, so there may have been business connections a long time before the family fled.²⁶ It may be just a coincidence that the witchlike Madame Walravens in Charlotte Bronte's *Villette* has a similar name, or perhaps it was a surname Charlotte heard mentioned at the Jenkins home in Brussels and relished its Gothic resonance.

Beau Pierre's eldest son Peter, Eliza's great-great-grandfather, had studied as a youth in Saumur and then, after his widowed father and the children fled, Peter studied further in Dordrecht.²⁷ In his twenties, as a new minister in the Dutch Church (when he still had to take his final exams), he was sent to the malarial marshlands of Canvey Island in the Thames estuary in 1688 to look after the Dutch community there.²⁸ This was only three years after this French Huguenot had arrived in Holland – he must have picked up Dutch very rapidly and been an impressive young man for the Dutch Church to select a foreigner for a post in England – or maybe no one else wanted to go to an island where a newcomer could die of malaria, or the 'ague', so quickly. I have walked the Saxon Shore Way trail on the opposite side of the Thames estuary: it is the land of Dickens's *Great Expectations* – wild and bleak, amid eery fog and an otherworldly light where estuary meets the North Sea, and it is easy to imagine escaped prisoners hiding among the gravestones. I find it intriguing that the Dutch found asylum on an island in the Thames.[29] The main settlers arrived in the early 1600s, though there is evidence that there were earlier settlers, fleeing the persecution of the notorious Catholic Duke of Alba, the governor of the Spanish Netherlands, in the previous century. With their experience of land reclamation, the Dutch built sea walls, reclaimed the land and began arable farming for the first time in these marshes. The first Dutch minister was elected in 1631 and permission was given by Charles I to erect their own chapel, which was used by the Dutch until 1704, though not without conflict with the local English, especially during the Dutch Wars of the mid-seventeenth century. But Peter des Réaux arrived in 1688 or 1689, when the new (joint) monarch of England was a Protestant Dutchman, William of Orange. It is possible that Peter was the first minister the island community had had for some years, thanks to the Glorious Revolution headed by William and Mary.

Rev. Peter des Réaux stayed on Canvey Island for about six years and married his Huguenot cousin Bénigne Fontaine, the eldest daughter of Jaques Fontaine's beloved half-brother Pierre, the minister at the Pest House in London. Peter and Bénigne ended up in Norwich, Norfolk around 1694, where he was the minister at the Dutch church. The memoirist Jaques Fontaine describes Bénigne (Eliza's great-great-grandmother) as 'pretty and well-made', but has little regard for Peter: 'He was a little negligent in the education of his children, of whom I believe he had 17 or 18,' but only two or three of the boys survived to adulthood. He adds, damningly, that the sons 'resembled neither father nor mother nor any of the Fontaines, for they were wicked and caused extreme pain and anxiety to their friends and relatives. I do not know where they are nor what has become of them, nor can I say anything of the daughters.'[30] But we know what became of one daughter, Elisabeth des Réaux, who was eighteen at the time Jaques was writing his memoirs, and was to become Eliza's great-grandmother, as Elisabeth Jay.

* * *

Eliza's pedigree as regards Protestant ministers (and indeed martyrs) is daunting. I had known about the nineteenth-century Jenkins clergymen in Brussels, but only from my cousin Marcia in Australia and her sources, especially the amazing memoirs by Rev. Jaques Fontaine, have I learned that behind Evan Jenkins's wife Eliza Jay is not only a whole chain of ministers going back to the 1600s, but a zeal that goes back to the very beginnings of the Reformation – zealous for their reformed faith, martyred, persecuted and forced to be refugees. A strong fibre of Protestantism surely coursed through Eliza's consciousness that might have made her a keen anti-Catholic, wary of the Catholic school she had recommended to the Brontës. Eliza's stock is resolutely Calvinist, Presbyterian, Huguenot: hence that unwavering, frank look at her son's camera in the photograph? This is a woman confident of her roots.

Peter and Bénigne's daughter Elisabeth – Eliza's great-grandmother, and the couple's eleventh child – was born in Norwich, where her father was not only minister to the Dutch church, but also elected pastor of the French church in 1712.[31] Elisabeth was baptized at the medieval church of St Peter Hungate on 28 May 1704, now a centre for medieval art, and was apprenticed to a milliner as a teenager. Sometime in her twenties she and a sister were staying in Rotterdam with their uncle Arnold: both women were named as executors of his will for his estate in Holland. Later, their father left them another substantial sum, most of which had come from his brother, the merchant Arnold. A year after her uncle's death, when she was thirty, Elisabeth married an Englishman in Rotterdam. And I now turn to the English Jays, and Elisabeth's husband, Rev. Samuel Jay.

* * *

There must have been stories in the family in the 1800s about fugitive Huguenot ancestors, but by the time of Eliza's Australian great-niece it had become garbled as she remembered her grandmother Margaret, Eliza's sister living in Australia:

> Her [Margaret's] family had come to England originally as French Huguenot refugees; their name was De Geai. Another branch of the family took refuge in Holland, and grandmama visited distant cousins there as a young girl.[32]

This is probably muddling two ancestors: the English Jays and French des Réaux, with the French descent more interesting because more exotic ('De Geai' may be a misguided attempt to transform Jay into French).[33] But Elisabeth des Réaux's English husband – Eliza's great-grandfather, Rev. Samuel Jay – is also interesting and it is a pity that Charlotte May Wright had no anecdotes about him.

Samuel Jay, a bright Nonconformist child, was born about 1694 in Clare, Suffolk, a once wool-rich town with a large Gothic church on the banks of the river Stour, upriver from what was to become 'Constable country'.[34] If you look down at the little town of Clare and its antique shops from a nearby small hill, it is hard to imagine a boy leaving from there in the early eighteenth century to go as far away as the University of Glasgow, becoming a Protestant minister in the Netherlands and marrying a Huguenot descendant in Rotterdam. But Clare had a strong Presbyterian tradition. East Anglia was a hotbed of Puritanism in the sixteenth century, and Parliamentarian during the Civil Wars. 'Samuel' is an Old Testament name often used by Puritans. We cannot trace his family further back in Clare – Jay is a common Suffolk name – but he is recorded at Glasgow University from March 1711, when he was about seventeen, graduating in 1714. He was noted in the records as 'Anglo-Britannus'. He was one of the first students to get an endowment to study there by a Welsh Presbyterian, Dr Daniel Williams.[35] A nice Welsh connection in Eliza's ancestry.

In the eighteenth century, English Nonconformists who wanted a university education couldn't go to Oxford or Cambridge (since they would have to subscribe to the Thirty-Nine Articles of the Church of England) and went to Leiden or Utrecht in the Netherlands, or to Glasgow or Edinburgh. In the list of men studying Theology during Samuel's time at Glasgow is Joannes (John) Enslie, a Scot.[36] He was also to become Eliza's great-grandfather since John's daughter later married Samuel's son. John Enslie was about ten years older than Samuel. He was recommended to the Scottish church in Rotterdam in 1724 by Alexander Dunlop, the Professor of Greek at Glasgow. Scottish Presbyterians had first settled in Rotterdam in the early seventeenth century to escape Stuart persecution at home. The early nineteenth-century chronicler of the church, Rev. William Steven, the then minister at the Scottish church in Rotterdam, put it more passionately, describing 'the talents and ardent piety of our non-conforming ancestors, who were forced to seek shelter abroad during the domineering ascendancy of prelacy'. After the Glorious Revolution of 1688, Presbyterianism became once again the established religion in Scotland and many Scots went home, but in Rev. Enslie's time there were still Scottish residents and visiting merchants and mariners, and a new church was opened in 1697, later bombed in the Second World War. The consistory of the Scottish congregation in Rotterdam, 'being fully informed of [Enslie's] learning, eloquence, and other needful gifts […] and being persuaded, that, by reason of his piety and other excellent qualifications, he shall be found very fit for edifying, and doing all good service to the church and people of God in this city', urged him to come to Rotterdam instead of taking up a post near Kirkcudbright in south-west Scotland.[37] But it wasn't entirely up to him – there was a fierce struggle between Kirkcudbright presbytery and the Scottish congregation in Rotterdam, which the latter finally won, and Rev. John Enslie arrived in Rotterdam in June 1725.

Rev. Steven later describes 'our eldest minister, Mr Enslie', as head of the Scottish community, going to The Hague on the city's yacht in June 1747 to congratulate the Prince of Orange on his accession to the stadtholdership.[38] This was Prince William IV, first hereditary Stadtholder of the United Provinces of the Netherlands. Enslie 'wished many blessings to his government, person, and family: whereunto his Highness returned a most gracious answer'. It is maybe a day's sail from Rotterdam north to The Hague along the waterways, but to do so on the city's yacht, maybe resplendent with flags and bunting on a sunny June day, sounds like an awesome and deliberately splendid way of travel for a proud little community. The English Presbyterians tagged along since they were temporarily without a minister, and Enslie represented both communities. It was a time of upheaval, and the odd outbreak of violence, so it was probably felt important to make the new Stadtholder aware of his British residents.[39] Eliza would have read this book in the 1830s, maybe even contributed to it, since several members of her family are mentioned in it, Jays as well as Enslies, including her father. Eliza was surely proud that her husband, Rev. Evan Jenkins, as head of his own community in Brussels, no doubt had similar audiences with his Prince of Orange (though without the yacht), William I, King of the Netherlands, who, until the Revolution of 1830, was also king of the country that was to become Belgium. King William I was the grandson of the Prince of Orange whom her great-grandfather had congratulated. I wouldn't be surprised if the Brontë sisters were regaled with this anecdote, and no doubt a copy of Steven's book was (prominently) lying around the Jenkinses' house in Brussels. Interestingly, Evan is mentioned in the book, despite the fact that he was neither Presbyterian (and he accepted prelates – bishops – no doubt to Steven's horror) nor in Rotterdam,[40] but before his mention in the book we have a description of Rev. Enslie's death and details of all his children. My instinct sees Eliza behind some of this (and possibly her Enslie cousins in the Netherlands or Belgium: some were living in Brussels at this time), and indeed Steven's note has as source 'Baptismal Register, and Private Information':

In the month of July 1759, Mr. Enslie, having completed the thirty-fourth year of his ministry, was declared *Emeritus*, with full stipend. He resided at Rotterdam until his death, which took place, after a long illness, April 4th, 1766, at the venerable age of eighty-one. This event called forth an elegiac poem from the pen of Mrs. Elizabeth Wolf Bekker, a Dutch lady, who usefully employed her leisure hours in writing or translating works on religious subjects. An admirable painting and striking likeness of Mr. Enslie, gifted by the family, is in the possession of Consistory. In his person he was of short stature, with small features and an expressive countenance. By his wife, Mrs. Jane Tod, to whom he was married in 1728, and who predeceased him, Mr. Enslie had ten children, of whom the following six survived him.[41]

I will spare the reader for now (some will crop up later as they are important in Eliza's story) the fairly scanty details of the six, who included merchants based in Rotterdam and Smyrna in Turkey, others living in Glasgow, Edinburgh and Essex. The last child Steven mentions is Mary Enslie, who married the son of Rev. Samuel Jay, Rev. Enslie's classmate at Glasgow University. To Rev. Samuel I now return, though, first, a reflection on why I think Eliza passed on information to Rev. Steven about her family. In 1831 she wrote a letter to her husband Evan's friend Rev. William Clarke in which she comments that her spouse 'is very backwards in going forwards'.[42] This is in connection with which church the new (Protestant) King of the Belgians will attend in Brussels, and I think it is so telling about Eliza: eager to promote her husband and her family, but above all confident about her own impressive Protestant roots.

It is not known when Eliza's Suffolk-born great-grandfather, Rev. Samuel Jay, was ordained or when he moved to the Netherlands. But he married the Huguenot descendant Elisabeth des Réaux in Rotterdam in 1734 when he was about forty, ten years older than Elisabeth. A first son died young, and in 1737 their second and only child, also named Samuel, was born in the town. It is possible that Rev. Samuel was a wine merchant with a sideline as a minister. Many documents have gone missing, but it is known that he was appointed minister of the combined congregations of the Merchant Adventurers and Presbyterian churches in Wine Street (Wijnstraat), Dordrecht in 1742. His duties as minister seem light since there were only four marriages and twenty baptisms there until his death in 1751.[43] An ancestor who was a wine merchant and lived in Wine Street – it was a marvellous reason for a trip.

* * *

In July 2016 I planned to visit four towns in the Netherlands connected to Eliza's ancestors: Dordrecht (also known as Dordt or Dort), Rotterdam, Leiden and Utrecht. It was maybe partly logistics – how to get from one town to the other – and partly descriptions in guidebooks that made me decide to base myself for three nights in Dordrecht. Maybe it was the fascinating B&B I found on the internet, or maybe it was a gene memory, for not only was Rev. Samuel based there in the eighteenth century, but his wife Elisabeth's ancestors, the des Réaux family, had lived there in the seventeenth after fleeing the intolerant and barbaric French Catholic state. I struck lucky: the old watery port of Dordrecht, the oldest city in South Holland, is utterly gorgeous. It is the most southerly of my four towns, and to get to it I had first to change at Brussels for a train to Rotterdam, and then backtrack south-east. But other than arriving by boat, it is the best way to arrive because the view of the islands that make up Dordrecht is wonderful from the railway bridge that crosses the Oude Maas (Meuse) river, a distributary of the Rhine. The first bit of my trudge, pulling my suitcase from the station at Dordrecht, was nondescript modern, but then I got to the old houses, the canals and rivers. My B&B, 'The Luthiers', was on the Voorstraat, around the corner from where the three rivers meet, run by violin and guitar makers Lucienne and Wout, who tried to teach me how to pronounce Leiden in the Dutch (not German) way, and nourished me with freshly made strawberry smoothies for breakfast.

Where the three rivers meet – the Beneden Merwede, the Oude Maas and the Noord – is also the start of the narrow, curving, cobbled Wijnstraat (Wine Street) on the next island. It begins at the grandiose fourteenth-century city gate known as the Groothoofdspoort, adorned with a relief of the Dordrecht maiden surrounded by city shields. Ships, waterbuses and barges passed by on the wide, sun-sparkling river, going to Antwerp, Rotterdam and Germany. I watched them as I sipped a glass of wine under a sunshade at one of the cafés. As a major port it would have been even busier with sailing ships and the unloading of cargo in Rev. Jay and Elisabeth's time in the 1740s, and also much smellier in the summer heat as sewage discharged into the canals. I wandered down Wijnstraat to find where their house had been, opposite the church, at no. 160. Neither building remained, but it had the atmosphere of an ancient street as it curved towards the Grote Kerk. The Merchant Adventurers'/Presbyterian church had been pulled down in 1840, but as I stood near the little Wijnbrug (Wine Bridge) that crossed back onto the island I was staying on, I admired the impressive white-and-grey pilastered mid-nineteenth-century house, topped by a fancy, gilt clock, that stood on the site among the brick Dutch gables of older houses at no. 160 Wijnstraat. Their house and the church were no more, but the number and the name of the street, the closeness to the footbridge over the canal, were the same. When Suffolk-born Rev. Samuel died in Dordrecht in 1751 after only nine years of his posting here, perhaps in his late fifties, Elisabeth went to England, maybe only to deal with his will, returning to live in the Netherlands at Schiedam, near

Rotterdam, famous for its gin and tall windmills, where she died fourteen years later aged sixty, leaving an only son, Eliza's grandfather. It is interesting that Dr Samuel Jay, born in Rotterdam, and surely raised mainly there and in Dordrecht, chose to move to England, while his son (Eliza's father, John Jay) eventually did the opposite. There seems to have been a tug in the family between living in the Netherlands (and later Belgium) or in England or Scotland, or maybe, with their languages and rootlessness, they felt at home in both Britain and northern Europe and simply moved where the political, religious or commercial winds blew.

* * *

Dordrecht still embraces a past that would be recognized by those alive three hundred years ago. Rotterdam is another story. The best part of Rotterdam is the one-hour trip by waterbus from Dordrecht, bettered only by the one-hour trip back. Arrival is at first exhilarating as the soothing flat green Dutch landscape and picturesque windmills of Kinderdijk are shoved aside by modern buildings thrusting into the sky, and the waterbus glides under the long, elegant late twentieth-century Erasmus Bridge. But once you step off the boat it is like stepping through a crack in time into a soulless future of raucous ugliness where nothing is remembered. German bombers, and the subsequent firestorm, utterly destroyed the medieval city on 14 May 1940, and thus any building or street connected to Eliza's family: her mother's Scottish merchant family as well as her father's. I looked for Leuvehaven, where her parents had lived after their marriage in 1796 and where she was born. In her day it was the busy old port area, near where my waterbus had halted. Today it is a metro station on a vast expanse of road, with a plethora of street signs and brutal high-rises. After a few hours I fled back to Dordrecht.

Rev. Jay and Elisabeth's only son Samuel attended the university at Leiden to study medicine from 1755 when he was about eighteen, finally graduating as a doctor in 1762, with a dissertation on rickets.[44] Leiden is less than an hour by train, north from Dordrecht. I attempted my new Dutch pronunciation of Leiden as I tried to buy a ticket, only to be met with bafflement, so I resorted to my German pronunciation. It is a beautiful town, where the first Protestant university in the Netherlands was established after the revolt against the Spanish in the sixteenth century, with a myriad of canals and hanging baskets crammed with petunias. In Dr Samuel's day there were more dead dogs and cats in the canals than petunias hanging over them, but old university buildings still line the banks. Shakespeare's Sonnet 30 was displayed in large letters on the white wall of one house; some of the lines were oddly appropriate: 'When to the sessions of sweet silent thought / I summon up remembrance of things past'. It was broiling, so I looked for shade in the oldest garden in the Netherlands, the Hortus Botanicus. The medical student Samuel would have spent many hours here, when the layout was very formal, and where the first tulips in Western Europe were planted in the 1590s. Perhaps he took planting memories from here to England. In his late twenties he married Mary, daughter of his father's Glasgow University classmate, Rev. Enslie, in November 1765, ten months after the death of his mother. At first they lived in Rotterdam but after a few years they moved across the Channel to the port of Southampton in Hampshire, though he continued to have business interests in Rotterdam, purchasing books for academics in Britain, including Dr David Skene (who corresponded with Linnaeus).[45] Again, like so many in Eliza's family, he was based for a while in two countries. Although he had studied medicine rather than theology, he was still involved in his family's religion: he became an elder at the French church in Southampton, where two of his three sons were born, including Eliza's father John (in January 1770). But soon the family moved thirty miles north to Andover – and that is where he and Mary break through the barrier of the monochrome past, because of the survival of letters now kept in Oxford.

* * *

Several months before I went to the Netherlands all I knew about Dr Samuel Jay were his dates, his profession as a physician and his (supposed) place of death in Andover, 'a neat and solid market-town', remarked William Cobbett, farmer and radical writer, in 1822.[46] Idly I did a search on the internet: 'Samuel Jay Andover'. Maybe I might find something about an eighteenth-century physician who lived north of the port of Southampton, seventy miles west of London. I didn't expect anything other than family sites with the wrong Jays. But amazingly I struck gold: Dr Samuel and 'Mrs Jay' were mentioned in a biography by Henry McKenzie Johnston, called *Ottoman and Persian Odysseys: James Morier, Creator of Hajji Baba of Ispahan and his Brothers*, published in 1998. I looked up James Morier in *ODNB*: diplomatist and novelist (1782–1849), born in Smyrna, parents Isaac Morier, consul-general of the Levant Company at Constantinople from 1804, and Clara, daughter of David Van Lennep, the Dutch consul-general and president of the Dutch Levant Company. 'His father was of Huguenot descent' and James was educated at schools in Andover and Wimbledon. His major work was the novel about Hajji Baba, published in 1824, which reached 'critical acclaim for its humorous and perceptive portrayal of Persian life'.[47] Thackeray possibly mentions him in passing in his novel *Pendennis* (1848–50), under the name of Bedwin

Sands, author of *Eastern Ghazuls*.[48] Earlier, in *Vanity Fair* (1847–8), 'Bedwin Sands' has a prominent role in organizing the charades at Gaunt House, when Becky Sharp achieves the height of her success in society:

> Young Bedwin Sands, then an elegant dandy and Eastern traveller, was manager of the revels. An Eastern traveller was somebody in those days, and the adventurous Bedwin, who had published his quarto, and passed some months under the tents in the desert, was a personage of no small importance. In his volume there were several pictures of Sands in various Oriental costumes; and he travelled about with a black attendant of most unprepossessing appearance, just like another Brian de Bois Guilbert [the villain in Scott's *Ivanhoe*]. Bedwin, his costumes, and black man were hailed at Gaunt House as very valuable acquisitions.[49]

Regardless of whether Thackeray lampooned James Morier as an Eastern dandy, or whether the dandy was a composite creation, what was Morier's connection to Eliza's grandfather Dr Samuel Jay in Andover, Hampshire? 'Huguenot' and 'Smyrna' had promising reverberations of connections with the Jays.[50] A few pages from the book were online. Thinking I'd see Dr Jay mentioned as a physician, I was surprised to find him identified as the schoolteacher of young James and his brother. The source was also online: letters from the boys were held among the Morier family papers at Balliol College Archives.[51] I looked at Johnston's book in the British Library. Isaac, a merchant of Swiss extraction, and his Dutch wife Clara had brought their sons Jack (aged nine) and James (aged five) to London from Smyrna (modern-day Izmir in Turkey) for their education in 1788. Johnston says that the boys were unhappy at their first school in Greenwich, and so 'he installed them in a more suitable establishment in Andover, run by the Reverend Dr Samuel Jay and his wife'. But part of his next statement is wrong and he gives no source: 'Jay had been Anglican chaplain in Smyrna, where he had left a son.'[52] As our research had confirmed, Dr Jay was a physician by profession, had been an elder in the Protestant French church, and was certainly not an ordained clergyman in the Church of England, nor, as far as I know, did he live in Smyrna at any period between residence in the Netherlands and then Hampshire, though he might have visited. However, his wife Mary's brother, William Enslie, had been in Smyrna since 1754 and worked in partnership with merchant David Van Lennep, father of Clara Morier née Van Lennep.[53] Clara's young brother Peter (aged nine) accompanied his nephews Jack and James to Dr Jay's house in Andover.

Mary Jay's brother, the merchant William Enslie, is mentioned in Rev. Steven's book that Eliza may have contributed to, *History of the Scottish Church, Rotterdam*. He is among the list of Rev. Enslie's children that I referred to above: 'William, a merchant of Smyrna. He could fluently converse in Turkish and modern Greek; was never married, and died at Constantinople, July, 1794.'[54] Rev. Steven doesn't mention a son of Dr Jay at Smyrna, but, as I was to discover in the Balliol Archives, Dr Jay's eldest son, also Samuel, was indeed there, presumably working under his uncle, William Enslie, and, from reading the schoolboys' letters, was a close friend of the Morier and Van Lennep families.[55] Sam Jay junior was to die only two years after his uncle William, in his late twenties, having moved back to Rotterdam.[56] The families were therefore close business colleagues in Turkey.

Smyrna, on the Aegean Sea, was the largest port in the Ottoman Empire and the principal centre of trade operated by Europeans. William Makepeace Thackeray travelled there in 1844 and wrote a description (under one of his pseudonyms, Michael Angelo Titmarsh) in *Notes of a Journey from Cornhill to Grand Cairo*:

> boats with real Turks on board came up to the ship. There lay the town with minarets and cypresses, domes and castles; great guns were firing off, and the blood-red flag of the Sultan flaring over the fort ever since sunrise; woods and mountains came down to the gulfs edge, and as you looked at them with the telescope, there peeped out of the general mass a score of pleasant episodes of Eastern life – there were cottages with quaint roofs; silent cool kiosks, where the chief of the eunuchs brings down the ladies of the harem. I saw Hassan, the fisherman, getting his nets; and Ali Baba going off with his donkey to the great forest for wood. Smith [a fellow passenger] looked at these wonders quite unmoved; and I was quite surprised at his apathy; but he had been at Smyrna before. A man only sees the miracle once; though you yearn after it ever so, it won't come again. I saw nothing of Ali Baba and Hassan the next time we came to Smyrna, and had some doubts (recollecting the badness of the inn) about landing at all.[57]

I booked myself into the archives at St Cross Church in Oxford one cold February day in 2016. Was there any more information in the letters about Dr Jay and his wife Mary? Most researchers know the feeling: the train journey, usually starting in the early hours, clutching your laptop or, in my case, pencils, digital camera and paper. The hope, after hours of going through the contents of boxes and folders, maybe fading until you photocopy one possible document – and that is your only reward for a long day's search. But then, one day, you go off with the same pessimistic-realistic expectations, though always hopeful, and to your astonishment you find treasure. Box 1, that I'd asked to see, contained fifty-two letters dating to 1788–91, but not only from the Morier and Van Lennep schoolchildren – there were also letters from Eliza's grandparents Dr Jay and Mary, unlisted in the catalogue. As well as being a physician and a church elder, Dr Jay was a schoolteacher, as was his wife. They took pupils into their home in Andover in the 1780s, just as Jane Austen's father took in pupils at his rectory from at least the 1770s, just fifteen miles to the east at Steventon. It is not impossible that the families met; even quite possible that Eliza's father John as a teenager had, maybe at a picnic, been forced to be pleasant to a ten-year-old Jane Austen – fifteen miles is not so far when there are families of a similar set, similar occupations and education. What is curious for the future, is that a young man in Kent, whom Jane Austen mentioned in a letter to her sister Cassandra as having caught her heart (my words), was the same man who, many years later, sponsored Eliza's husband Evan Jenkins to his living at the Chapel Royal in Brussels. It was a small world – and that story will be told in a later chapter.

Johnston's account of the Moriers' time at Andover, and his extracts from the letters, are brief, not surprising in what is a dual biography: it is also about James's elder brother Jack (John Philip Morier), a diplomat. He was private secretary to Lord Elgin (of marbles fame or notoriety) at the embassy at Constantinople, and was then sent on a secret mission to Egypt in 1799, where he was imprisoned by the French, but released with a warning never to return. This was followed by appointments in the Morea and Albania, Washington DC, Latin America and finally Dresden.[58] He is the main letter-writer in the collection, at first in French until his English improves; his uncle Peter Van Lennep (the same age) often writes his letter to his sister – Jack's mother – on another page of the folded paper; and finally there are a couple of additions by little James after Mary Jay has taught him to write.

I sat in the delightful little church of St Cross with the pile of letters in front of me, surrounded by bookcases, which helped warm the archives. Helpfully the letters had mostly been put into date order (but not the very last ones, which was at first a puzzle). Considering that Dr Jay was not mentioned in the catalogue, the second letter bowled me over. It was a letter from him to Isaac Morier, South Audley Street, London, who was about to return to Smyrna, and dated from

Andover, 21 January 1788. Obviously Morier had just left the three boys with Dr Jay, and returned to his wife (heavily pregnant, or had just given birth) and other children:

> I hope you had an agreeable & safe journey home & that you met Mrs Morier & your sweet little family in good Health, as for the Dear Boys you left with me, I can with Pleasure assure you they are quite cheerful & Happy & have gone thro all their little Occupations this day exceeding well, they all send Love & Duty to their Dear Parents & desire me to tell you they are highly delighted with their Situation & you & your Lady may rest assured that nothing on our Part shall be wanting to forward their Improvement & treat them with the same Tenderness as if they were our own Children. I take ?the freedom to trouble you with a Letter for Sam [the Jays' eldest son in Smyrna] & Mrs Jay joins me in Hearty Wishes for your safe & speedy arrival at Smyrna where we beg you will give our best respects to good Mr Van Lenneps family & kindest love to our Brother William [Enslie] & to Dear Sam.[59]

It is written in a wonderfully curly hand, with the 'd' in the first 'had' sweeping back with a great flourish over the 'you'. Today it reads rather alarmingly saccharine, and I would be immediately on my guard whether my sons had been in floods of tears ever since their father had left them. But in the 1780s it was probably just the right kind of letter to reassure, especially Mrs Morier, that the children were fine, even though there had probably been tears.

There is then a letter from Mary Jay to Mrs Morier, written only four days later, again giving reassurance. She had obviously just received an anxious letter from Clara Morier, still worrying about her children and young brother. Mary Jay's letter is revealing about the kind and gentle schooling young children could be given. Like her husband's letter it is written in English. Mary Jay explains that though she speaks French well, she feels her written French is not adequate. She continues:

> I beg you will consider My Dear Madam, you have not Placed your Confidence in Strangers, but in Friends, who are Particularly connected with you and your worthy and amiable family, from whom my Dear Sam has received the most kind and friendly treatment [in Smyrna], of which both his Parents and he will ever retain the most lively and gratefull

remembrance, and which we are truly Happy to repay in some degree, by every tender attention to your Dear youths, who Indeed are in the highest degree amiable, and docile, and the Doctor begs me to assure you, that he will exert his utmost Endeavors to Promote their Improvement, which will be attended with great Pleasure, as he finds them <u>Possessed of an ambition for learning</u>. So I beg my Dear Madam that you will make your self as easy as their absence from you will Permit, in the firm Persuasion, that your sweet Boys will be treated as tenderly as our own Children, yet <u>not with any foolish Indulgences</u>, which might Prevent their Progress in their learning; as <u>for Corrections we have none</u>, but if at any time they Commit any trifling fault, (which all Children will sometimes do) my Husband only Punishes them, by depriving them of some little Pleasure, and on the other hand when their good Behaviour deserves it, he rewards them by Indulging them in what they like.[60]

The underlining may be Clara's, marking the phrases that were most important to her. It was so exciting for me to handle Dr Samuel and Mary's letters (my four times great-grandparents). Of course the letters are written to the parents of their pupils, and need to display their competency and care, and hide what the parents don't need to know. Whether the boys were as 'docile' as Mary says is perhaps unlikely. But their avowed method of 'carrot' or 'no carrot', without any sticks, is admirable. But how the boys were actually treated lies in what the boys write; Dr Jay assures Mrs Morier that he does not interfere at all[61] – but it looks like Mrs Morier has questioned this since son Jack writes to her in September (in English):

Doctor Jay told me to tell you that all the letters that I wrote you in French and English was intierly by myself, he never tells me what to write but only he corects afterwards the blunders that there is. James thanks you very much for the ink-stand that you are a going to send him. I hope that my Dear Papa will be glad to receive this English letter.[62]

(Dr Jay didn't correct those blunders, however!)

As for what kind of school this is, it seems to consist of just a few boys welcomed into the family home, who are encouraged to call them Mama and Papa. Young Jack mentions two or three others who arrive at various times, including one from Persia and a seventeen-year-old from Russia; and Dr Jay enquires about the possibility of another pupil from Mrs Morier.[63] Why did they take pupils in?

Perhaps he was not earning enough money as a physician (which seems unlikely given his education and background, but not impossible); or maybe he and Mary simply loved teaching, and their sons had left home. It seems that pupils arrived through word of mouth (no advertisements have been found): young Jack says that Dr Jay's son Sam in Smyrna had wanted them to come to his parents for their education.[64] There are visiting teachers: a music master, a dance master and a master for writing and numbers,[65] with Dr Jay presumably teaching English, Latin and French, and maybe geography and history, and Mary Jay teaching the youngest, such as little James – in a letter from Jack to his mother in April he writes that five-year-old James can now spell English words of two syllables and has learnt them by heart, and 'Madame Jay est bien content de lui'.[66] And in a note from Dr Jay in English to Isaac Morier in Smyrna in October, he writes:

> the young folks are in perfect Health & continue to give me Satisfaction. Mrs Jay has great credit with her sweet little pupil James who now reads very prettily & is a great favorite with us all.[67]

Nine-year-old Jack recounts a typical day in a letter to his father in February 1788 (in French). First, after washing, he works on his Latin grammar, while Peter works on his English and French (apparently because there is only one Latin grammar):

> At 9 o'clock we have breakfast, after breakfast we read a bit of the Bible, after that we play until 10.30, then we return to studying again until noon [when] the writing and numbers master arrives, after which we have lunch at 2.30, after lunch we return to studying until 5 o'clock. We then have tea, then do a bit of geography. On Sunday we go to church. After church we learn our catechism.[68]

That is a long day, presumably little James is not also working such long hours. It seems they all attend the Anglican church in Andover, even though both Mary and Dr Samuel have Presbyterian backgrounds, but it was fluid whether to 'conform' or not: both, after all, were Protestant Churches.

The schoolboys have a few books, either bought by their father, or by their uncle, Captain Waldegrave (second son of Earl Waldegrave, and married to Clara Morier's sister),[69] or provided by Dr Jay: Latin and French dictionaries; a painting book; English and Roman history books; four volumes of the *Children's Friend*, two volumes of the *Arabian Nights*. In July, Jack describes to his mother, in French, one of the English books they have been encouraged to buy:

> For example, there is a little girl who doesn't do what she is told, and when she eats she fills her mouth so much so that, one day, you think she is going to die: that's a good lesson for James because sometimes he fills his mouth so much that he can't swallow. These books are also good for James to read [... and in English:] the title of the book is Little Stories for Little Folks.[70]

If Jack sounds weary about his lessons in the following letter to his father, in December 1788, there is also music and dancing. After thanking his father (in French) for silk stockings, he writes in English:

> I go on with French Latin and English every day of my life and with a little history. I begun some days ago to play upon the violin and I like it a great deal better than the harpsicord. My dear Papa, James learns french and he can read it a little. My dear Mama was so extreemly glad to see how he was improved in every thing and he can write so prettily [...] God be thankd James has had a few chilblains this year but nothing like last years.[71]

There are also frequent extra-curricular activities: Jack says that they have seen a 'comedie', which 'nous a bien se amuzé'.[72] Andover was a major stopping place for stagecoaches, and a busy hub; it is not known where they saw the play, maybe it was a pantomime or harlequinade staged by a touring theatre company in a hired hall. A display board in the Andover museum (in a Georgian house that the Jays would have known) states that the first theatre opened only in 1803. They are taken to several fairs, at one of which: 'Mr Jay showed us a magic lantern which had lots of funny things that made us laugh.' And at another they see a tiger, monkeys, a hyena and a clever horse: 'You ask the horse how many pennies there are in a shilling and it beats on the ground with its hoof how many there are.' In the same letter Jack mentions that Dr Jay has a camera obscura in his house: 'one can see objects so clearly and distinctly', he enthuses.[73] In October they were taken to the largest fair in England: Weyhill, three miles west of Andover, which Jack loved, where he bought a little knife for himself, and a pretty mirror for Mrs Jay, and saw lots of wild animals.[74] Alas, Weyhill Fair ended in the 1950s. I looked for the site, taking the bus from Andover, and saw a rather unhappy pub on the dismal A road, amid arable fields with no memory of the hubbub of a fair.

The Jays' garden in Andover receives many mentions: in April, Jack writes that when the weather is good they play there every day; they even had their tea and breakfast outside, just as they do at their home in Turkey. And in June: 'You would be astonished to see how full the garden is with flowers, apples, strawberries, gooseberries, and all sorts of good things.' A few weeks later he writes: 'It was such beautiful weather on Monday that we had lunch in the arbour [...] almost every day we eat strawberries [...] peas and excellent salads' (the last seems rather startling from a nine-year-old boy). Jack and Peter later mention plums and apricots and 'Mr and Madame Jay always have the goodness to give us fruit every day and sometimes raspberries with milk and bread for supper [...] I love Mr and Madame Jay as if they were our Papa and Mama because they have so many good things for us.'[75] Their father Isaac Morier has sent the Jays melon seeds from Turkey (in March), which were presumably planted in a greenhouse, and harvested in July.[76] Is Dr Jay recreating his memories of the Hortus Botanicus in Leiden?

Their lush garden and the mention of little James's chilblains remind me of the description of Mrs Goddard's school in Jane Austen's *Emma* (published about thirty years later in 1816). The school in Highbury in Surrey 'was reckoned a particularly healthy spot: she had an ample house and garden, gave the children plenty of wholesome food, let them run about a great deal in the summer, and in winter dressed their chilblains with her own hands'.[77]

Having a physician as a headmaster is also a reassurance for the parents. Dr Jay writes in French to Mrs Morier in June, who it seems is worried about the health of her nine-year-old brother Peter after a short holiday in London: 'In relation to dear Peter we made the same observation on his return here [...] He looked pale and unhealthy but since he has been back with us he has been perfectly well. Eating, drinking and sleeping well. He has a little cough and my wife made a tisane for him.'[78] He later writes that he has hired little horses (*Petits Chevaux*) for the boys 'which are very gentle [*fort doux*]' and the boys (presumably Jack and Peter) can ride as a reward for good behaviour. He assures her that they will not be allowed to go out on their own. He has even organized the eighteenth-century equivalent of a school photo – he has commissioned miniatures of the boys, at Mr Morier's request, at only eight shillings each.[79] Unfortunately, we find out in a later letter from him that Mrs Morier didn't like the portraits since they didn't resemble her sons or brother at all. But Dr Jay sends them anyway to Isaac Morier in Smyrna. He assures her on a different topic that little James has a good disposition for dance and that he is quite old enough to start learning.[80] I discern great tact with a somewhat difficult mother here. Jack tells her about games they play – shuttlecock, which they have played often with Dr Jay, and cricket – the bats and balls are presents from their uncle Captain Waldegrave.[81]

Then in what sounds a blissful year of schooling in the Eden that was Andover, the serpent enters Paradise, the shadow falls. It is also the harbinger of tragedy for the Jays. On 28 December, Dr Jay writes to Mrs Morier in French about the death of her and Peter's brother George:

> I have communicated with as much tenderness as possible to your dear sons and brother [Peter] the fatal news that we feared to receive by each courier. They all burst into torrents of tears, which relieved them much, and we mixed our tears with theirs […] a son so dear at the flower of his age! […] you need to appear tranquil with your dear sister even though your heart is stricken with grief [*navré de douleur*], but in the name of God may it be possible that she does not know this fatal blow […] because the consequences promise to be dangerous to the utmost degree [sister Cornelia Waldegrave had just given birth]. – My dear wife as well as myself join sincerely in your grief and we hope that the fatigues of body and spirit that you have suffered will not harm your precious health. – I presume that the boys will assume mourning, but I will await your reply on this subject. – Adieu my dear Madam, may the good Lord comfort you [*Le Bon Dieu vous Console*].[82]

There are far fewer letters that survive for 1789. The very last letter from Dr Jay is in June, accompanying a letter from Jack to his father in Smyrna, both in English:

> As my Dear Friend Jack has left me room to add a few lines I most chearfully embrace the opportunity to assure you how happy both my Dear Wife & I are at the thoughts of having the pleasure of seeing you here again towards the latter end of the year to ?residing in this Country with your amiable Lady & sweet little family. You will I am sure shed tears of Joy on seeing your Dear Boys & Brother in Law & finding how much they are grown & improved since you left them, they daily, I assure you, endear themselves more & more to us. We have enjoyed the Satisfaction of embracing our Dear worthy friend Coco [another Van Lennep brother] who spent ten days with us which passed away like so many hours in chatting about our much esteemed Smyrna friends […] He was] quite delighted with England and our

charming Country about Andover, the heather was delightful [...] Pray give our kind love to our Dear Sam whom I hope you still continue to favor with your good Counsels & friendship, which I assure you he sets the highest value on [...] My Page being full I have only to add Mrs Jays love.[83]

That is the last letter of his that has survived in the archive. There is so much affection, which I feel is genuine.

There is one letter from young Jack in August 1789 to his mother, in French, about a turbot safely received.[84] The next letter is not until 16 February 1790, in French: in the middle of his ink-faded, one-page letter, he mentions, almost in passing:

Mr Jay sends his greetings and you wouldn't believe what a comfort it is for him to have his son here [*et vous ne sauriez croire quelle consolation que c'est pour lui qu'il a son fils ici*].

I stopped and breathed hard here before rereading that short letter in French with faded ink. Peter adds in his part of the letter a brief clarification, also in French: 'Mr John Jay arrived in Andover this morning.' In a letter a few weeks later, Jack writes to his father: 'Mr Jay et son fils vous saluent' ('Mr Jay and his son greet you').[85] Mrs Jay has disappeared.

The registration of her death notes that Mary Jay died on 2 February; she was in her late forties. From young Jack's letter it seems that their nineteen-year-old second son, John, had come over from Rotterdam to support his father. He missed the funeral (on 7 February) by nine days. I was utterly stilled, sitting in the little cold church in Oxford that February over two hundred years later, having pieced together what had happened, after sorting out the last three letters, which were in the wrong order in the pile. It reminded me of Tom Stoppard's *Rosencrantz and Guildenstern are Dead*, where in the foreground the two men chat and toss coins, while in the background you see glimpses of the tragedy, largely happening offstage. As a physician, Dr Jay's expertise was in curing people, but he hadn't been able to save his wife, and he had to cope with the schoolboys in the house. It seems his wife's sister, Janet, lived with them, as Jack mentions Miss Enslie accompanying him on the harpsichord, and presumably she was of help.[86] His son John is summoned, and this is John Jay's first entrance in this book's drama – appearing, like Hamlet, fleetingly in the background in the boys' letters. (Miss Janet Enslie will appear again in the next chapter; she possibly never cared for her nephew John, or took a dislike to him later.) And how strange that John will find himself in the same situation, almost thirty years later, with daughter Eliza maybe to comfort him. And then it will be Eliza's turn to be comforted, almost thirty years after that: and always there are the schoolboys in the foreground, getting on with their lives as they pen a letter to their mother.

There is one final letter in the Balliol box from young Jack to his father that appears almost brutal, it is dated about two years later. The boys are still receiving their education in Andover, but this time it is not 'Mr and Mrs Jay send their love' but 'Mr & Mrs Eisdell desire their kind Respects to you'. It is telling about the relationships, and so sad: respects from one set of teachers; love from the other.[87]

It seems that after his wife's death Dr Jay moved to live with (Huguenot descendant) Fontaine relations in Salisbury. He didn't long outlive his wife Mary, dying in 1793, only three years later. They were both buried in Andover, where a plaque was erected for them in St Mary's Church.[88] The Norman church was demolished by the Victorians and replaced with a larger building. When I visited Andover, I was told the plaque might be in the crypt, which had been part of the chancel of the Norman church, but, alas, the crypt was locked that day and I presumed that it no longer existed. Over a year later I emailed the church asking about it, with little hope, but received a reply the same day, with a photo. The small plaque and its wording are very simple: 'Here lies the body of Mary Jay wife of Samuel Jay M.D. obiit Febr 2d 1790 aged 47. Samuel Jay M.D. obiit Novr 30th 1793 aged 57'. His short death notice has been found in one newspaper: 'At Salisbury, Dr. Jay, formerly a physician of eminence at Andover.'[89] I think he was also a good and caring schoolteacher.

* * *

But the story doesn't end there. When I was finalizing this chapter, I emailed Marcia Watson about the books that our ancestor Dr Jay had obtained for Dr Skene at Aberdeen University. When sending me scans of the letters from Dr Jay to Dr Skene, Marcia also sent me an eighteenth-century note that mentioned Dr Jay. I read it with growing astonishment: it was the kind of note that was written when the person that you called on, whom you hadn't met before, was out or indisposed, but it crammed in two names linked fast to the Scottish Enlightenment, as well as one renowned scholar who was a friend of Handel, one 'nobleman' and one Dr Jay of Andover. I emailed back fast: what is this, where from? Marcia had found the note in the Hampshire Archives (via the online hub) and mentioned it in a *Dalwood Newsletter* article (June 2018) that, being busy, I had merely filed for the future without reading.

The bald facts are that the note was written on 27 June 1777 by Andrew Dalziel, Greek Professor at Edinburgh University (1742–1806). He has called at the house in the Cathedral Close at Salisbury of the renowned James Harris (1709–80), to 'pay his respects' to the author of *Hermes* 'that admirable work [...] studied at Edinburgh by the students of Greek & Latin', but 'is extremely sorry to find that he is indisposed'. He would have brought with him a letter of introduction from Lord Monboddo (1714–99), but he hadn't realized that he would find himself in Salisbury. Dalziel is accompanying a young nobleman from Scotland and, the eye-opener for me, they are on their way 'to spend a few months in study, in the house of Dr. Jay, Physician at Andover, Hants'.[90] Mr Dalziel will call again, and it is possible that he and Harris (and the nobleman) did indeed meet up.

The Enlightenment historian may well now be interested to learn about Eliza's grandfather Dr Samuel Jay; for the unenlightened among us: Andrew Dalziel (or Dalzel) was a Scottish classical scholar of humble origins. He was picked out as a bright youngster and sent to the University of Edinburgh as a potential minister. However, he instead became a private tutor to the aristocratic family of Lauderdale in Dunbar, east of Edinburgh, giving a progressive education to James, Viscount Maitland, later eighth Earl of Lauderdale, and his younger brother Thomas. James seems the likeliest candidate as 'the nobleman' staying with Dr Jay and his family as he was eighteen in June 1777. Two years previously he had spent a term at Trinity College, Oxford and then in 1777 went to Glasgow University, so a few months' stay with Dr Jay in the summer of that year fits well. But to be suitable as a host, Dr Jay must have been as formidably interesting a physician or scientist as anything Oxford or Glasgow could offer: Maitland had not been brought to Dr Jay's to enjoy the melons. In fact, as a graduate of the great university of Leiden, Jay probably had much more to impart than Oxford: Dalziel commented that 'very little study goes on at Oxford except among a few book-worms that shut themselves up, and do not associate with others'. He later remarked that 'dissipation, idleness, drinking, and gambling' are learned at English universities, which 'are huge masses of magnificence and form, but ill calculated to promote the cause of science or of liberal inquiry'.[91]

Maitland later went into Parliament, voting frequently against the abolition of the slave trade; he became radicalized in Revolutionary France, and, naming himself 'Citizen', he took to wearing Jacobin costume. He later focused on writing about the economy. 'Long dismissed as eccentric, his contribution to economic theory has more recently been acknowledged.'[92] Surely he would have been an entertaining teenage guest, with forthright opinions, around the Jays' dinner table in Andover.

Dalziel had been appointed joint professor of Greek at Edinburgh in 1772, and became sole professor in 1779; he was later to help found the Royal Society of Edinburgh.[93] The man he had left the note for in Salisbury, James Harris, was a musical patron, a Member of Parliament, a philosopher, a librettist and passionate admirer of Handel, who visited him in Salisbury in 1739. The author Fanny Burney liked Harris 'amazingly'.[94] It is possible that James Harris knew Dr Jay, as Harris's son (1746–1820; later first Earl of Malmesbury), a diplomat, studied for a year at Leiden University; he was there a few years after Dr Jay had left, but a fellow alumnus Dutch-speaker in the neighbourhood would have been welcome at the rather grand Harris family home.[95] Finally, the very short James Burnett, Lord Monboddo, judge, philosopher, anthropologist, who would have given Dalziel a letter of introduction to Harris – his fascinating biography can be read elsewhere since, as far as I know, he wasn't entertained by Dr Samuel and Mary Jay in Andover, though he certainly was by his friend James Boswell and Dr Johnson.

* * *

More notes and letters may come online to amplify Dr Jay's contribution to the age of the enlightenment, but I value the school letters of the late 1780s that tell of those few years in Andover. In her book about Ted Hughes and Sylvia Plath, *Silent Woman*, the American writer Janet Malcolm comments on a packet of letters she has been given to read:

> Letters are the great fixative of experience. Time erodes feeling. Time creates indifference. Letters prove to us that we once cared. They are the fossils of feeling. This is why biographers prize them so: they are biography's only conduit to unmediated experience. Everything else the biographer touches is stale, hashed over, told and retold, dubious, unauthentic, suspect. Only when he reads a subject's letters does the biographer feel he has come fully into his presence, and only when he quotes from the letters does he share with his readers his sense of life retrieved.[96]

The letters from Dr Samuel and Mary Jay and the schoolboys retrieve lives during a short space of two years, over two hundred years ago, fixed like a silent movie, though in colour. They are in the garden at Andover, where it is always summer: there is Mary sitting in the arbour with five-year-old James, guiding his pencil; Jack and Peter smashing at shuttlecocks with Dr Jay. There are ripe melons in the greenhouse and always strawberries for tea.

Six

Eliza

Moving On

Between 1780 and 1813 [...] the Netherlands was despoiled of its colonies, routed at sea, invaded four times (twice unsuccessfully); driven to the edge of bankruptcy; and finally forced to drain the dregs of its misfortune by becoming mere departments of the French Empire.

– Simon Schama, *Patriots and Liberators*[1]

In the 1780s, Eliza's father John Jay, then a teenager, moved to Rotterdam from the family home in Andover to learn the mercantile trade from his mother's Enslie brothers.[2] All three sons of Dr Samuel and Mary Jay became merchants: the eldest, Sam, joined his uncle William in Smyrna for a few years, as told in the last chapter. Teenage John was taken under the wing of his uncle John Enslie, who was also his godfather, and who operated between Scotland and Rotterdam.[3] The youngest son, William, may have accompanied his brother John to Rotterdam; he was just a year younger and there is no mention of him in the Morier letters I read. Another maternal uncle, James Enslie, was also a merchant in Rotterdam, and they may have lived with him or Uncle John. Uncle James's eldest daughter Johanna was later to become John Jay's second wife.

When the teenaged John moved to Rotterdam, the Republic of the United Provinces was embroiled in the 'Patriot Revolt' (1781–7): self-styled 'Patriots' were roughly democrats who wanted 'liberty' and more representation, and to limit the powers of the Stadtholder, the utterly inept William V, Prince of Orange;

they were backed (or so they thought) by the Ancien Régime in France. On the other side were the Orangists, who often vacillated, but had some backing from Prussia and especially from Great Britain.[4] James Harris the younger, now Sir James, who made a brief appearance in my last chapter – the Dutch-speaking son of the music patron in Salisbury for whom Professor Dalziel had left a note – was now British envoy-extraordinary at The Hague. Simon Schama states that the formidably talented Harris 'engineered the defeat of the Patriot revolution',[5] especially through British subsidies (or bribes), though it was the unexpected folly of the Patriots in detaining Princess Wilhelmina, the Stadtholder's wife – who wore the trousers in their relationship – that spurred the new Prussian king, who happened to be her brother, to invade in 1787 and restore William V. So when John returned to Andover, too late for his mother's funeral in 1790, he hadn't come from a country embroiled in a bloody civil war, which had been threatened; but it was a lull before the French/Dutch storm, and William V was to be the very last Stadtholder.[6]

It sounds interesting learning to become a merchant, but it was probably deadly dull most of the time. Boys learnt the trade in the counting house, where they spent years with ledgers and invoices. Schoolboys Jack Morier and Peter Van Lennep knew that this was their destiny. Jack wrote to his father Isaac in November 1788 (when he was ten): 'I hope I shall be able to come and help you in your countinghouse in two or three years hence,' and Peter wrote to his parents in Smyrna (in French): 'I will do all I can to learn in order to return to Smyrna and work in the counting house like my brothers.'[7] It was fascinating to find an advertisement placed by John Jay in his early forties (in 1812), when he turned to teaching, after his merchant adventures had come to a halt. He had set up a school in Essex – 'A New Institution for Commercial Education' – as an alternative to 'spending several years in a counting-house, in order to learn the routine of business, which is generally attended with much inconvenience, expence, and loss of time'. It is impossible to know if his experience of the counting house, with his uncle, had been poor and a bit of a drudge, or whether he knew of others' experiences and was offering the ideal alternative:

It is the object of this SEMINARY to lead the Pupil through a regular Course of Instruction, pecularly [sic] adapted to the Commercial line of life, by directing his attention to the English and Foreign Languages (particularly French, German, and Spanish), Geography, Political Economy, Commercial Law, Arithmetic, and Italian Book-keeping, and instructing him in all the practical forms and daily occupations attendant on the various branches of actual business, both inland and foreign; as also in the origin and qualities of the principal articles of Merchandize; while at the same time the study of the Latin Language, History, Mathematics, the Belles Letters, and other useful and ornamental branches of Learning, will be strictly attended to, in order that the pupils may be enabled to enter into any other profession with honour and advantage, should they not be disposed to pursue their mercantile views. It is therefore hoped that the young persons who are educated in this Institution may unite the endowments of the Gentleman and the Scholar, with the regular commercial habits and professional information of the enlightened merchant.[8]

The advertisement continues with the superiority of this kind of education as opposed to a boy going into a counting house. It is interesting that Dutch is not one of the languages (perhaps because under French occupation the Dutch had sunk so far) and that he uses the phrase 'enlightened merchant' – a fully rounded education was promised, maybe in case the continuing French Wars, the embargoes and naval blockades made parents wary of investing in their sons learning the mercantile trade, or their sons turned out to be useless at arithmetic and modern languages.

* * *

Going back twenty years: when John Jay's counting-house drudgery was completed – perhaps when he was twenty-one, in 1791 – he and his uncle John Enslie were both admitted to the Arbroath Burgess Roll in Angus, Scotland, as partners in an import and export business.[9] Arbroath is on the North Sea, on the east coast of Scotland, about fifty miles south of Aberdeen, where his future father-in-law (Alexander Livingston, who had died in Rotterdam in 1783) had been provost forty years earlier. Arbroath was a major centre of industry for the import of flax, jute and hemp and the making of sailcoth, which was a highly lucrative business during the French Wars. Although John may have travelled frequently to Scotland, it seems that he continued to live in Rotterdam, since Rev. Steven records him as a deacon of the Scottish church there from 1788 to 1798.[10]

In August 1796, John married Provost Livingston's heiress daughter Helen, Eliza's mother, in Rotterdam. Helen was then eighteen; John twenty-six. His father had known the Livingston family and presumably John had met Helen when he moved to Rotterdam to live with an uncle in the 1780s. There may have been fewer than a couple of hundred Scots in Rotterdam at the time of their wedding. Rev. Steven states that a list made in 1795 consisted of 320 worshippers, but that many left after the French invasion. Helen would have few memories of her elderly father, who died when she was five, but she had soon acquired a stepfather. Her mother, née Elizabeth Hardie, was a wealthy widow, with three children under the age of eight, when she married Rev. Alexander Layel in 1785, pastor of the Scottish church in Rotterdam. They were both in their forties. They had a daughter, Isabella, who was to marry John Jay's younger brother William, as his second wife. Layel was a native of Melrose and had studied at Edinburgh University, where he was a distinguished scholar of Hebrew; he had served previously at the church in Dordrecht. Rather alarmingly, Rev. Steven in his book about the church in Rotterdam states that Layel 'was a student of prophecy' and published a pamphlet about the downfall of the Turkish dynasty. But to balance this perhaps mild eccentricity, Layel was passionate about sacred music, a 'much neglected branch of public worship', Rev. Steven says, and the Scottish church became celebrated for its music during Layel's tenure in Rotterdam, which lasted almost twenty-six years.[11] Surely he encouraged his Livingston stepchildren to play instruments and to sing.

Layel died, aged fifty-seven, one month before the marriage of his step-daughter Helen to John Jay. That year also saw the death of John's elder brother Sam. But if I thought that at least Helen had a mother to help her through the start of married life, research has uncovered a sad story.[12] A year after Elizabeth's second husband, Rev. Layel, died, her new son-in-law, 'Citizen' John Jay, was appointed co-curator of her affairs. The document stated that it was 'taking from her all power, authority and faculty to dispose of her goods, to alienate, mortgage or charge the same', and 'prohibiting all and every person or persons to deal or make any bargains with the said Elizabeth Hardy wid. Alexander Layell, to credit or trust her for anything'. Elizabeth was fifty-three. Various documents refer to her insanity and she was placed in a home for insane women in Delft in 1798, ten miles north of Rotterdam. The owners of the home stated in 1822, when Elizabeth was still there, that they cared for women 'whose intellectual powers are not in proper order or are unsuitable for sociable society due to circumstances like melancholy, gloomy ideas, persistent or temporary deviation from the state of reason'. It seems that women were locked up for depression or dementia. What kind of mental illness Elizabeth had is unknowable, and whether her children visited her. She didn't die until her late seventies in 1824, all four of her children having moved to Scotland or England many years before.

* * *

The reference to 'Citizen' John Jay is a reminder that the Netherlands – now renamed the Batavian Republic (referring to Dutch ancestors, the Germanic tribe of the Batavi) – had been invaded by Revolutionary France in 1795. William Hague, in his biography of Pitt the Younger, the then British Prime Minister, describes it neatly: 'Amsterdam fell on 20 January: at the end of the month the icebound Dutch fleet became the first ships in the history of warfare to surrender to a force of cavalry.'[13] The Patriots – those exiled in France and those who had stayed despite the repressive measures against them – had longed for the French to help liberate their country, and then to let them get on with governing it. Simon Schama comments that they were asking from their French liberators 'an altruism bordering on the saintly, a quality conspicuous by its absence from French strategy'. The Stadtholder, Prince William V, fled from The Hague to England with his family in January, and, as Schama states, into 'historical obloquy', dying in 1806.[14] But there was no oblivion in exile for his family: his son was to return in 1813, becoming King William I, and founder of the present Dutch monarchy, two years later.

At first the French did let the Dutch get on with trying to govern themselves – albeit with 10,000 French troops billeted among them[15] – but after three years of failing to get a constitution approved by Dutch voters, French patience snapped. A new, tougher ambassador, Charles Delacroix, arrived in December 1797 – although this may also have been to get him out of the way since Foreign Minister Talleyrand and Mme Delacroix were allegedly having an affair and she was noticeably pregnant (with Eugène Delacroix, that supreme Romantic artist, born in April 1798).[16] Ambassador Delacroix encouraged the radical Dutch coup of January 1798, which finally produced a (democratic) constitution in April, but which was followed, in June, by a counter-coup. The Batavian Republic, and then Commonwealth, was to last only another eight years, when Louis Bonaparte, Napoleon's brother, was reluctantly offered the crown of 'Holland' by the Dutch.

* * *

Nine months after the marriage of John Jay and Helen Livingston their first child was born into the political and economic chaos of Rotterdam. Eliza arrived on 19 May 1797 and was baptized in the Scottish church. Rev. Steven comments, writing about thirty years later, that the 'Scottish Church experienced, at the hands of the French authorities, no hardships but such as were then common to others'.[17] But in the 1790s, the French authorities still stood on the sidelines. The Dutch Revolution was fairly bloodless, but the Scots and English who remained had to keep their heads down. British soldiers evacuating the country in 1795 turned into 'gangs of pillaging bandits' and one Orangist declared that 'all Dutchmen heartily loathed the British, who had "ruined our manufactures, devastated our trade and dragged us into a ruinous war"'. This was followed by the Dutch disaster at the Battle of Camperdown in October 1797, when the entire fleet was destroyed or captured by the British. The Scots residents also had to contribute to the enormous 'indemnity' – 100 million guilders – demanded by the French for 'liberating' the country. The Netherlands was in crisis, and trade crippled because of the British blockade.[18]

But John Jay's decision – and probably his opportunity – to move to Scotland with his wife Helen and newborn daughter was possibly because of the death of his uncle and partner in Arbroath, John Enslie, in October 1798, in Glasgow. John Jay was an executor of the will as well as inheriting money. As co-curator of his 'lunatic' mother-in-law, he was maybe able to use her money too, as well as his wife's fortune. It is not known when exactly the Jays left Rotterdam, but their second daughter, Mary, was born in Glasgow in February 1799, the month Uncle John Enslie's will was proved (Mary was to die, aged thirteen, in Edmonton, Middlesex).[19] John and his younger brother William set up an import and export business, John Jay & Co., with William staying in Rotterdam.[20] By June 1800, John Jay's family were in Edinburgh: their third child, and first son, Samuel, was born there. I wonder if the family felt the relief that I do that they were out of the chaos of the Batavian Republic, with its constant changes of name and personnel, its devastated economy and high taxes. And I could now follow in the Jay family's footsteps to Edinburgh and the port of Leith, where they would settle for the next ten years.

* * *

I have no hard evidence, but I am convinced that the Jays knew Walter Scott and his French wife Charlotte in Edinburgh. Scott and Charlotte had married in December 1797 and moved first to 50 George Street in the New Town; after their first child was stillborn they moved a few streets away to 19 Castle Street, and by December 1801 to 39 Castle Street.[21] When I arrived by train in Edinburgh after my trip to foggy Aberdeen I was clutching a list of addresses where the Jays had been living or working. The very first (in 1801) was 5 North Charlotte Street, downhill from Charlotte Square, four minutes' walk from where the Scotts were living that year. Scott, Charlotte (née Charpentier) and John Jay were the same age – born in 1770 or 1771, so just turned thirty at this time. Charlotte Scott and Helen Jay almost kept pace with their production of babies – Charlotte having four surviving children by 1806; Helen having six. John Sutherland, in his biography of Scott, describes Mrs Scott as 'worldly, foreign, London-fashionably-dressed'. She began a salon in her home, and he adds: 'The open-house hospitality which all commentators note as a feature of Abbotsford began with Charlotte's regime at 50 George Street. One of the very few facts which we know about the Charpentier household in Lyons where she was brought up was that many interesting strangers seem to have dropped in. So too did people drop in on the Scotts in the New Town.'[22] The wealthy Helen and John Jay would surely have been 'interesting', with their Scottish, Dutch and Huguenot connections, their experiences in Rotterdam and perhaps their fluent French, which would have been welcome to Charlotte. Also, Scott's maternal grandfather had studied at Leiden, as had John Jay's father. At the time of his marriage, Scott was an advocate (barrister) earning low fees, but in 1799 he became sheriff-depute (principal judge) for Selkirkshire and had a better income. By the early 1800s he had published a few translations from German and was now working on his great project, *Minstrelsy of the Scottish Border*, published in 1802, which has been called 'the most exciting collection of ballads ever to appear'.[23] There is no family story that three-year-old Eliza was patted on the head by Walter Scott. But it is not improbable that she played with the Scott children, and, as the eldest, bossed them around.

New Town in Edinburgh – the Georgian grid running between Princes Street and Queen Street, north of the castle – had been conceived in the seventeenth century to provide better housing for the middle and upper classes than the squashed, increasingly slummy, old part of Edinburgh. The houses next door to the Jays at 5 North Charlotte Street (named after George III's wife) are now listed, dated to 1790. No. 5 seems also to be Georgian, though it looks a bit of an architectural hybrid, but on the top floor there are views of the Firth of Forth. Now divided into flats, with a sandwich shop rammed onto its frontage, no. 5 was presumably then a modern three-storeyed house, with basement and attic. Helen and John Jay stayed there about two years, since their fourth child, John Livingston (who later rose unspectacularly through clerkships at Greenwich Hospital), was born at 'Lixmount' 'in this Parish' in August 1802, according to the parish register of North Leith. But there is a puzzle as regards the date (see below).

Lixmount. There is a legend that when the Catholic Queen Mary Tudor was dying in 1558, she said that Calais would be found engraved on her heart, because the English had lost the town in France after two hundred years. If there was one place engraved on John Jay's heart – and also daughter Eliza's – it was surely Lixmount. But to find Lixmount I first needed to walk a couple of miles north-east to North Leith to find my B&B and drop my rucksack off. After leaving Princes Street, with its huge monument to Walter Scott, I ticked off another place John Jay had inhabited, probably as an office – Gayfield Square. It is a lovely square – calming green sward in its centre – of neoclassical houses and tenements off the (now) hideous, traffic-polluted Leith Walk. Some of the houses were built in 1807; only three or so years later, John Jay and his brother William were listed as merchants here. I walked on to my B&B and to the harbour of North Leith. Leith was the pre-eminent port of Scotland, the marine gateway to the capital Edinburgh, until Glasgow overtook it because of its better sailing route to America. There is now a Michelin-starred restaurant by the gloriously named Water of Leith, a pub in the fifteenth-century King's Wark, a bistro in the seventeenth-century Signal Tower, and the Vaults for the storage of wine are now the headquarters of the Scotch Malt Whisky Society. When John Jay arrived to run his merchant business from here around 1799 there were plans in place to build docks next to the harbour. The future looked so promising.

My first aim down at the harbour was to look for the remains of St Ninian's Church. For some bizarre reason, five of Eliza's siblings were all baptized in a lump here, in October 1805. It is a mystery why a deacon of the Rotterdam Scottish church had not had his children, except for his eldest, Eliza, baptized until now – aged between two months and six years. The church had been demolished but the lovely bell tower of the manse that adjoined the church remains. It is Dutch in style, dating to 1675, and rather beautiful, with a blue belfry, the blue matching the sky on the June day that I saw it. St Ninian's on Quayside was the parish church for North Leith until it was replaced by a larger church in 1816 a few streets away, after the Jays had left. The architectural practice that restored and inhabits the remains was so uninterested in my little story that I left clutching only a short leaflet of their heroic endeavours of restoration as I was shown out of the door. More notable members of the church were the Gladstone family. Thomas Gladstones, the grandfather of William Ewart Gladstone, the Prime Minister, was a merchant in Leith. (The family later dropped the 's'.) Thomas (1732–1809) may well have known the Jays. His eldest son, John, was a few years older than John Jay, born in 1764. He served an apprenticeship in the counting house of the Edinburgh Roperie and Sailcloth Company in Leith, from the age of thirteen, but moved to Liverpool in the 1780s and made his first fortune from American tobacco and grain, thereafter acquiring sugar estates in the West Indies, worked by hundreds of slaves.[24] The minister who baptized the Jay children may have been Dr Johnston, 'who was always lovingly and familiarly spoken of, especially by the fisherfolk of Newhaven [...] as the "bonnie Dr. Johnston," from his handsome appearance and refined and courteous manner'. He was apparently minister for fifty-nine years, from 1765 to 1824.[25]

As I walked on, I could see that one address on my list – Elbe Street, hard by the docks – must have been where the Jays had a warehouse. I now needed to walk west along the Firth of Forth to find Trinity, the district where 'Lixmount' had been, trying to avoid the horrendous modern road along the coast, which can be done for a short stretch by walking along the cobbles through the old village of Newhaven. The district of Trinity is now a much sought-after place to live. Lixmount Avenue and Lixmount Gardens, perched on a leafy hill, are the only signs that Lixmount House was once here.[26] There are views of the glistening Firth of Forth to the north and the high mound of Arthur's Seat in Holyrood Park to the south. Early twentieth-century terraced houses line an avenue where the house once stood; in John Jay's time, country houses with large gardens stretched along East Trinity Road. It was a district for the rich. On one map of 1804 in the National Library of Scotland the house and extensive grounds of Lixmount are shown, with the annotation 'Jay Esq.' On the map, fields stretch down the hill north to the Firth, with the occasional villa dotted here and there. Next door to Lixmount in 1804 was Mr Menzies' house and (much smaller) grounds, and further west was the villa of 'Sir Henry Moncrief'. This was presumably Sir Henry Moncrieff-Wellwood, eighth baronet of Tullibole and minister of St Cuthbert's Church, at the west end of Princes Street. To the south the boundary to the Jays' grounds was marked by the Anchorfield Burn.[27] For most of her childhood, until she was in her early teens, Eliza had a privileged upbringing, with surely a governess, a pony, walks on Leith Sands and the excitement of watching the annual horse race there, the awesome sights and sounds of the noisy, busy harbour, with sailing ships from St Petersburg, Jamaica or Copenhagen unloading their cargo, and prize ships (seized from the enemy) and goods being auctioned;[28] there was tea and music with Great-Aunt Janet Enslie – last seen in the 1780s playing the harpsichord in Andover but later living in Leith – and trips into Edinburgh, to the shops, the botanic garden, the castle, and to see Shakespeare at the Theatre Royal (managed by Walter Scott from 1809).

I knew that Lixmount House had been built in 1793 by George Andrew, 'writer' of Edinburgh, a law-agent or attorney.[29] (Walter Scott's father was Writer to the Signet, 'a distinguished legal corporation of solicitors', the top tier in Scotland.[30]) On my return home, I discovered an article on the internet, 'Lixmount House and its People' by Rosemary Philip, published in the *Scottish*

Genealogist in 2017.[31] I enthusiastically badgered the society to please send me the issue. When I tore open the envelope I feared the worst, that there would be little if any mention of the Jays. I was stunned that I was wrong, and that Philip provided a few more details I hadn't known, but I later discovered that all the research on John Jay had been done by my colleague Marcia Watson, who receives no acknowledgement. In the article there is a contemporary drawing of what was obviously a lovely house, with a round tower in the centre of its cream façade, reminiscent of those at Holyrood Palace. The sketch of the house had been located over three hundred miles away at Charlecote Park near Stratford-upon-Avon. In the time of lockdown, my travails to get a copy of the sketch were somewhat tortuous, but culminated in wonderful generosity, alluded to in my Acknowledgements. It felt important to show the sketch in its frame, and as the last image in my book.

Having already sensed that Lixmount House had been special for some of Eliza's family, it was interesting to learn that it had been named 'Lix' by George Andrew (1740–1819) for nostalgic reasons. His second wife Catherine was the daughter of Hugh Campbell, '9th of Lix', though Lix lands, in Glen Dochart, had been forfeited in 1745.[32] I turned to the internet for Glen Dochart: the river runs between Killin and Crianlarich, now in the Loch Lomond and Trossachs National Park – and I suddenly had a vision of a welcome ice cream I had in a heatwave, because as any trail walker in Scotland will know, Crianlarich is about two-thirds along the West Highland Way as you backpack to Fort William. It was very hot at the end of May 2012, and during my glorious solo walk I saw on my map that the little town of Crianlarich was only fifteen minutes downhill through the trees, so down I went. Then I puffed up again, satisfied and happily ice-creamed. Since Lixmount was named after an estate along that glen, I was glad that there was a shared sense from different generations of love for the Scottish countryside. And surely during the two years that Charlotte Brontë visited the Jenkins home, Eliza's nostalgic memories of her childhood in Edinburgh were mentioned. After Charlotte visited Edinburgh in July 1850, she wrote, 'who indeed that has once seen Edinburgh, with its couchant crag-lion, but must see it again in dreams waking or sleeping'.[33] Perhaps as Eliza did.

George Andrew got into financial difficulties and had to give up Lixmount. It was advertised for sale in 1800, eventually being bought by John Jay in August 1803 for about £3,000.[34] And therein lies the puzzle I mentioned above, since his second son, John Livingston, was recorded in the baptism register of North Leith as born at Lixmount in August 1802. But the solution is simple: the house was advertised to be let, furnished or unfurnished, in 1800 after it failed to sell. The last advertisement was on 19 January 1801:

> The house of Lixmount, near Newhaven, which may be entered to immediately.
>
> The house will suit a large family, is pleasantly situated; and, besides proper offices, there is an excellent garden, and three adjoining inclosures in grass, which the possessor can have access to.
>
> For particulars apply to Joseph Cauvin, writer to the signet; and Mr Williamson, at Trinity Mains, will show the premisses.[35]

So the Jays probably rented the house in 1801 before buying it two years later.

Younger brother William Jay moved to Scotland to join John around 1804, after the death of his first wife, bringing his daughter with him. Perhaps John Jay & Co. thereafter used an agent in Rotterdam. William married Helen's half-sister Isabella Layel and the couple were living in 'Lixmount Cottage' in March 1809 when their son was born. The baby died in August at 'Summer Lodge' in Trinity. Both Summer Lodge and Lixmount Cottage are mentioned in the advertisement for the sale of Lixmount in September 1811:[36]

> The house and grounds of Lixmount, with the Offices, Garden, &c. pleasantly situated upon the lands of Trinity Mains, within two miles of Edinburgh, one mile of Leith, and a quarter of a mile of the Frith [sic] of Forth.
>
> The house, which commands very extensive views, and is surrounded with a lawn and shrubbery, consists of a dining-room, drawing-room, library, five bed-rooms (three of which have dressing closets, kitchen, laundry, servants hall, house-keeper's room, cellars and other conveniences.
>
> The grounds consist of about nine English acres one of which is contained in the garden, the north side whereof is fenced with a wall 15 feet high, covered with fruit trees of the best kinds and qualities. The premises are plentifully supplied with water, from several pump-wells in different parts of the grounds, as also from a rivulet, which forms the boundary to the south.
>
> This villa, from its beautiful situation, and the many advantages it unites, is well worthy attention, so desirable a residence being seldom to be met with.

Estate-agent speak has hardly changed in over two hundred years. The advertisement continues:

> Also to be sold, Summer Lodge and Lixmount Cottage; two small Houses adjoining the above property, each of which has a small Green, and is capable of accommodating a genteel family.

An advertisement in the *Scotsman* some thirty years later also mentions 'excellent Stables, Coach-House, and Coachman's House'.[37]

From a few notices found in the *Caledonian Mercury* of November and December 1808, I know that the brothers imported flax and raffia from Gothenburg (across the North Sea in Sweden, which had many Dutch and Scottish settlers) and Riga (on the Baltic, now in Latvia, but then part of the Russian Empire).[38] Presumably the flax and raffia were intended for the hugely successful Edinburgh Roperie and Sailcloth Company, established in 1750 in Leith, where Prime Minister Gladstone's father had worked as a boy.[39] John Jay & Co. also imported '38 casks ashes' from Riga, and exported casks of refined sugar to Gothenburg.[40] There was a sugar-refining business in Breadalbane Street, Leith, producing, in its heyday, 250 tons of refined sugar every week. The ash was presumably soda ash, used for making glass: the glass-bottle trade was another major industry, suitably located in Salamander Street, which was a few minutes from the Jays' warehouse in Elbe Street.[41]

John Jay & Co. therefore seem to have been involved in most of the major industries in Leith. One other lucrative trade at this time, that they may not have been involved in, was that of shipping prisoners to be slaves in the plantations in America and the West Indies. It seems that there was a good supply from Edinburgh. The trade paid so well that people were sometimes kidnapped, well known from the story of David Balfour in *Kidnapped* (set in 1751; published in 1886) by Robert Louis Stevenson, who is knocked on the head during a visit to a ship with his rascally uncle and intended to be sold as a slave in the Carolinas (luckily Scottish fog intervenes). Having delivered their prisoners, the ships would return laden with sugar cane, tobacco and beaver fur. The bulk of the trade that arrived in Leith, however, came from the Baltic during the French Wars, where there were fewer enemy ships and privateers.[42] By 1809, John Jay was a highly successful merchant and was admitted to the Edinburgh Burgess Roll.

Then it all went wrong. In 1810 he was taken to court for not paying debts; there had been several cases of litigation before, but this time it was particularly serious.[43] One piece of ill fortune can be told in some detail. Around the summer of 1809, John Jay & Co., Merchants in Leith, hired a shipmaster, Frederick Andreas Kelting, to deliver a cargo of 51 casks of tallow, 92 tons of hemp and 8 tons of flax to Leith from Riga. The cargo, which cost over £8,000, had been paid for and the Jay brothers expected Kelting to deliver it before the winter set in (November is about the last month before ice prevents safe sailing), and to join a convoy, with an armed vessel protecting merchant ships against privateers.

The *Caledonian Mercury* reports that convoys were indeed arriving in Leith from the Baltic that November.[44] Kelting's ship the *Adelaide*, however, stopped in Karlskrona in south-east Sweden for the winter instead of sailing on. We don't know why. Maybe the shipmaster was being ultra cautious as the weather closed in, or his ship was damaged and needed repairs, or perhaps something murky was going on. The ship was sighted in early January, and John Jay & Co. expected it any day. Meanwhile it's possible that the people who had been interested in buying the goods had changed their minds because of the delay or that the price had tumbled. But John Jay found one merchant who agreed to buy the cargo, and John endorsed the bill of lading – that is, the receipt from the ship's captain agreeing to do the job – to this merchant, Mr Duncan of Glasgow. John was handing over all the goods and, importantly for what happened over ten years later, the cost of hiring the ship – the freight – to Duncan. John was only to receive in return two-thirds of the money that he had originally paid, and that was not enough to prevent Jay & Co. being taken to court and made bankrupt (sequestered) in 1810; Duncan also went bankrupt. The *Adelaide* finally turned up in Leith in June 1810, having taken well over six months from Riga, rather than a few weeks. The Jay brothers had wanted to take action against shipmaster Kelting but the trustees working for their creditors advised against it – in hindsight this looks like the wrong advice. The Jays agreed to pay their creditors a composition, which was accepted, 'and the two partners of the House were left to follow such occupations as might procure their subsistence'. It was also agreed by the court that Mr Duncan was responsible for paying the freight. However, this was not to be the end of the story.

Whatever was going on in John Jay's case, it was a very difficult time for most merchants and manufacturers. In November 1806, Napoleon had issued his Berlin Decree, forbidding British imports into any European country controlled by France. The British had retaliated by issuing a series of Orders in Council that further damaged British trade. Although canny merchants found loopholes, many businesses suffered. In her novel *Shirley*, set in 1811–12, Charlotte Brontë describes the devastating effect these restrictions placed on her half-Belgian mill-owner Robert Gérard Moore: 'Men like Yorke and Moore – and there were thousands whom the war placed where it placed them, shuddering on the verge of bankruptcy – insisted on peace with the energy of desperation.'[45]

In her book *In These Times*, Jenny Uglow describes the situation in 1809–10 which might have directly impacted on John Jay:

> When the French retook Stralsund, on the Baltic coast of Germany, in 1809, they seized six hundred neutral vessels full of British goods and confiscated most of the cargoes; the following year, British warehouses were seized and burnt in the Netherlands and Italy. At the same time the rates of exchange became increasingly unfavourable, leaving Britain on the edge of a serious depression. In the summer of 1810 twenty provincial banks failed, and six in London. A loss of confidence, intensified by a poor harvest and the threat of more shortages, affected stocks, trade and industry.[46]

Indeed, in the Court of Session judgment, the representor for the Jays remarks that they 'suffered in the distresses of the Country in 1810'. John Jay was certainly not alone in his troubles. In 1812 the famous poet Anna Laetitia Barbauld published a highly controversial anti-war poem, *Eighteen Hundred and Eleven*, in which she portrayed the despair of the merchants caused by the war:

> No more on crowded mart or busy street
> Friends, meeting friends, with cheerful hurry greet;
> Sad, on the ground thy princely merchants bend
> Their altered looks, and evil days portend (ll. 55–8)

William McCarthy, her most recent editor, comments in his notes on these lines that 'the lists of "Bankrupts" in the *European Magazine* in the second half of 1810 are at least twice as long as those for 1808–9', and that in September 1810, the financier Abraham Goldsmid, one of London's richest men, shot himself dead because of his debts.[47]

Lixmount was taken over by the trustees on behalf of the creditors and bought in 1812 by another merchant, Thomas Williamson (1756–1838), who later added his wife's surname of Ramsay to the family name. A fascinating discovery by Rosemary Philip in her article is that Lixmount is in the background of an oil portrait of his son, 'Lieutenant' George Williamson Ramsay 'of Lixmont', by the French artist Charles-Achille d'Hardiviller, a pupil of David. The house is identical to that in the sketch at Charlecote. George inherited Lixmount in 1838,[48] and the portrait must date to then since he died in 1841 and d'Hardiviller around 1840. The portrait was sold at Christie's in 2006 and its whereabouts are unknown, but it is on the internet. What is curious is that his father's company had professional links with the shipmaster Captain Kelting, which would surface again in 1821, as I shall discuss below. I find something odd and rather disturbing in this whole affair.

In 1810, along with countless others at this period, John Jay had his house and assets seized and had to somehow start again. The Jays left Scotland for England. The motto of Leith is 'Persevere', and he did. But Lixmount wasn't forgotten: fifteen years later, after the marriage of Eliza to Evan Jenkins, someone (the father of the bride?) sent notice of it to Edinburgh: 'At the house of his Excellency the British Ambassador, at Brussels, the Rev. E. Jenkins, B.A. of Trinity College, Cambridge, to Eliza, eldest daughter of John Jay, Esq. formerly of Lixmount, near Edinburgh'.[49] The publication was *The Edinburgh Annual Register*, owned by Sir Walter Scott.

* * *

From the time you left me, our friends say I have altered completely – am not the same person [...] Our bodies every seven years are completely fresh-materiald – seven years ago it was not this hand that clench'd itself against Hammond

– John Keats, letter to the George Keatses, September 1819[50]

John Keats is remembering – to his brother and sister-in-law in America – his ghastly time as an apprentice to Thomas Hammond, apothecary and surgeon of Edmonton, Middlesex, from August 1810, when he was fourteen. Some readers may raise an eyebrow at my segue from Walter Scott to John Keats. It also reminds me of a wonderful quote by Richard Altick in *Lives and Letters* about a 'frantically eccentric' biography of Emily Brontë by Romer Wilson in 1928, who 'listed among her "References" Michelangelo's "David," the complete works of Nietzsche and Dostoevsky, Joyce's *Ulysses*, and the later quartets of Beethoven'.[51] But this is exactly the village (Edmonton), and the month (August 1810), that it is known that the Jays were after they left Scotland.

Helen Jay's younger sister Margaret née Livingston and her merchant husband James Bowden had first leased a house in Edmonton, about nine miles north of the City of London, in about 1806. It was countryside, ideal for a growing family, and easily commutable to London by horse or stagecoach. Like Helen and John Jay, Margaret and James Bowden had married in Rotterdam, where their first two children were born. By 1810, when Helen and her family arrived in Edmonton after the long journey from Leith, the Bowdens were living at Bury Hall, a villa that was a ten-minute walk up the road from the village of Edmonton. Margaret was then in her early thirties, and had recently buried her two eldest children at the parish church of All Saints in Church Street: James in 1809 (aged nine) and Alexander Livingston in May 1810 (also aged nine). So far surviving were a further five children aged between one and seven years, and in June 1810 Margaret was pregnant again. If her younger children were some distraction from her grief, the arrival of her sister Helen with her six children – even in the awful circumstances of a husband made bankrupt – must have been welcome, and a shoulder to cry on about the deaths of her boys. Perhaps brother Alexander Livingston also paid a visit after his return from Martinique and before heading off with his regiment to fight the French in Portugal. Helen Jay was also pregnant, and gave birth to her last child on 19 August in Edmonton – a daughter, Janet (also known as Jenny or Jen, who was later to live in Greenwich with her brother and maybe envy her siblings for memories of a Scotland she had never known). It is not known if the Jays stayed at Bury Hall – from the one photo I have found it was only two storeys high as opposed to Lixmount's three storeys and it would have been a squash – but if not, perhaps they rented a house nearby before their move to nearby Woodford, where they were living in May 1812. The parish register of baptisms at Edmonton states that Janet's parents were 'John and Helen of Lixmount near Edinburgh'. They were as yet unsettled in England.

The thirteen-year-old Eliza must have been a great help with her young Bowden cousins as well as her siblings, disrupted by the move south. But surely she was miserable to have left all that she knew – the fruit trees in the garden, the view of the sea from her bedroom window, the rides on the beach. She and younger sister Mary (then eleven) would know something huge and awful had happened, whereas their siblings – Samuel at ten, John aged eight, Margaret (Meg) aged six and William just five – saw the long sail down to London on the packet and the encounter with their cousins as a huge adventure. But worse than leaving friends and the only home you remember was to happen over the next two years.

The apothecary and surgeon in Edmonton, who surely would have attended the dying Bowden boys, and the illnesses and deaths to come, was Thomas Hammond. And it is thanks to John Keats's letter, quoted above, and Keats's biographers that we know about him. In summer 1806, Keats's widowed grandmother Alice Jennings moved to an end-terrace house in Church Street, Edmonton, near Dr Hammond's fine large house and the parish church of All Saints.[52] It was here that from the age of ten Keats was to revel in the fields and streams of Edmonton during school holidays from the progressive Clarke's Academy at Enfield, just two miles away, with his brothers and sister. After his father's fatal fall from a horse when Keats was eight, and his increasingly alcoholic mother's hasty remarriage to a much younger man, the stable element in his life was his grandmother Alice, a northerner from Lancashire.

Keats's mother Frances reappeared in 1809 when she moved into her mother's house in Church Street, separated from her young husband. She was ill. Her brother, who had taken part in the Battle of Camperdown, had died the year before, of tuberculosis, and now Frances had a persistent cough:

> Beside her bed were bottles of brandy, and the opium Dr Hammond provided: during the Christmas holiday Keats would let nobody administer her medicine but himself, trusting to this and Hammond's regime of bleeding and cupping to draw off disease. He prepared her meals and read novels to her. At night he kept vigil in his grandfather's great chair, listening to the rattle of her breathing.[53]

She died in March 1810, aged thirty-five, when Keats was back at school. As a distraction from his misery he began translating the whole of Virgil's *Aeneid*. In the summer, when Keats was fourteen, grandmother Alice and his guardians decided on a medical career for him and apprenticed him to the family's doctor, Thomas Hammond, who 'belonged to the remarkable dynasty of apothecaries and surgeons descended from John Hammond, parish surgeon at Edmonton'.[54] Keats moved into a small room above the surgery and dispensary next to Hammond's house in Church Street, a few yards from his grandmother's, once the two hundred guineas had been paid – the money came from the trust fund he was to inherit when he came of age. He would learn to roll pills, make up medicines, clean the leech jars and the cupping sets for Dr Hammond to take to patients. Soon he would learn how to dress wounds, fix fractures and help with difficult births.

The news of the arrival of the Bowdens' Scottish relatives at Bury Hall would have passed around the village, with ever-active rumour spreading about the reason for their arrival. As seemingly wealthy relatives of the family at Bury Hall, they would be welcome additions to Dr Hammond's list of patients. Perhaps he attended at Janet Jay's birth on 19 August, accompanied by his new fourteen-year-old apprentice. The relationship between Keats and Hammond soured rapidly as Hammond treated the boy as a servant rather than a pupil. There is an account of Hammond calling on the schoolmaster's wife, leaving Keats outside with the carriage, 'listlessly holding the reins, leaning back immovably', and on another occasion, waiting with the horse, 'his head sunken forward in a brown study'.[55] In spring the next year, a joyous event for the Jays was followed by tragedy at Bury Hall: Helen's sister Margaret gave birth to another daughter, Anne, in March but the baby died three weeks later, and in November 1811 Margaret died. She was thirty-three.[56] Helen and daughter Eliza had their hands full with caring for the five Bowden children and distraught husband. One of the children, Alfred, then aged four, seems to have had mental problems, since his father's will leaves him extra money because 'it has pleased God to afflict [him] with a disease which may and probably will prevent him from earning a comfortable subsistence'.

Dr Hammond's carriage would have been often at Bury Hall, and no doubt Eliza noticed the sturdy, unhappy apprentice, eighteen months older than her, with his fine brown, tousled hair and the secret clench of the fist, the angry spark in the eye, when Hammond gave him an order. And surely Keats noticed the fair-haired Scottish girl who had to help her mother care for her dying aunt and had to look out for eleven younger children (siblings and cousins). Of course there were nursemaids and servants, and Bowden relatives, but Eliza must have grown up fast at this unhappy time. Keats may have noticed too that Eliza's sister Mary had an ominous cough. Eliza may have accompanied her mother to the dispensary for pills and opium for Aunt Margaret and her sister, and also seen Keats at All Saints on Sundays, where her aunt and baby cousin were buried that year. Maybe there were sympathetic smiles between the teenagers, both battling in what Keats called this 'space of life between':

> The imagination of a boy is healthy, and the mature imagination of a man is healthy; but there is a space of life between, in which the soul is in a ferment, the character undecided, the way of life uncertain[57]

Eliza's world surely fell apart when her sister Mary died in May 1812, aged thirteen. Perhaps it was in her sister's memory that she named her second daughter Mary almost twenty years later, but, alas, the name was jinxed. I can only guess that sister Mary had tuberculosis, and that most of her Bowden cousins and her aunt also died of the disease: of the five Bowden cousins who were alive when their mother Margaret died, Helen would die aged five, William aged sixteen, Alfred aged seventeen, John aged twenty. Only one of them, Margaret (born in 1806), lived on, leaving a memorably nasty will as regards one of her first cousin Eliza Jenkins's sons. James Bowden married again and had a further five children, one of whom was to know Thackeray. Both the nasty will and the encounter with Thackeray are for another chapter.

When Eliza's sister Mary died in 1812, the parish register states that her parents were living in Woodford. Yet Mary was buried at All Saints, Church Street, Edmonton, near Hammond's surgery. Perhaps Dr Hammond and Keats were at the funeral; maybe they had tried to treat her with bleeding, blistering and pills. The Jays may have only just moved to Woodford and knew the minister at All Saints Edmonton better than the minister at their new church, and probably it was felt right that Mary Jay should lie near her aunt and Bowden cousins.

In 1812 the 'life between' teenagers moved on. In the autumn, Keats was released early from his hated apprenticeship and the Jays were settled in Woodford.[58] In his early forties, John Jay had established himself in a new career. It is possible that Eliza later learned that Hammond's apprentice became a poet: in 1848, almost thirty years after Keats's death, Richard Monckton Milnes published his biography in which he mentions Keats being apprenticed to Hammond in Edmonton, though without the unhappy details.[59]

* * *

John Jay had found a suitable house for the family and a school five miles east from Edmonton, across the river Lea, at Woodford Wells in Essex. Like Edmonton it was 'healthy' countryside (always important for a school, whether true or not), on the fringes of Epping Forest, and it was also only nine miles north of London, with stagecoaches thundering past. It was reported to the Court of Session in Edinburgh that he had set up 'a Mercantile Academy in which his great knowledge of mercantile affairs has enabled him to acquire some little money by the most severe of all Labours, the instruction of youth'.[60] He thus had a sense of humour – maybe a sign of his bullish perseverance – or maybe it was penned by his attorney in Edinburgh trying, ultimately unsuccessfully, to humour the judge. I quoted above from John Jay's advertisement in July 1812 that announced the opening of the school: 'A New Institution for Commercial Education […] in a fine healthy situation'.

The house that he leased – which he bought two years later – was Prospect House. Woodford then consisted of four hamlets – three strung along the High Road, the fourth to the east by the bridge across the river Roding – surrounded by numerous mansions. It was where, for centuries, rich City of London merchants had acquired their country estates for the air, the nearness to London and the hunting in Epping Forest; others rented a house for the summer. There is an extraordinary statistic that in 1762 there were 178 houses, of which 156 were mansions.[61] Cricket was played on The Green from the early eighteenth century, and there were several inns.

Prospect House was 'a large and attractively positioned mansion with a wonderful view', built in the 1770s, near the 'wells' at the top of the High Road on the fringes of Epping Forest; once fashionable, the wells had fallen into disuse for their medicinal properties in the late eighteenth century. The first floor of the house was raised above a basement storey, with 'a curved sweep of steps leading up to a pedimental front door'.[62] According to an advertisement in 1818, it had seven bedrooms, two parlours, a coach house and stable and a small garden.[63] In an advertisement five years earlier, John Jay states that 'a Suite of Apartments is fitted up for Studies, Counting House, Sample-room, Library, &c'.[64] In April 1814, he announces that the school is for 'all ages', which seems to be spreading the net rather wide, and that there are 'extensive buildings', so perhaps the coach house was in use too.[65]

The Victoria County History states (in 1973) that the house had 'disappeared'. I emailed Woodford Historical Society to see if they had anything about the house and how I might find where it had been. I had a quick reply from John Lovell of the society inviting me to phone him, which ended up with him generously meeting me at Woodford tube station and driving me around on a fascinating personally guided tour. Apparently I was one of several John had guided who were hunting for family links in Woodford, including, especially, Americans and Australians. The place had brimmed with lawyers and merchants from Scotland, and Quakers had been abundant. We drove to the site of Prospect House and he gave me a photocopied auction leaflet dating from 1919: 'Lot 1: A Fine Old Mansion: Standing back from the main road from London to Epping, close to and overlooking Woodford Green [...] It was formerly distinguished as Prospect Hall, but has been divided into two spacious residences known as "The Outlook" and "Montclair", each having very delightful gardens the whole forming a first-class building site.'[66]

How could a bankrupt acquire such a house? In 1814, John's brother William reported to the creditors' trustees in Scotland that he and John could only pay 2s 2½d in the pound (with help from friends).[67] But, undaunted, it seems that John bought the house for £1,575 by taking out several mortgages and borrowing £3,000 from a friend, William Whitmore (godfather to his last son William). Then he leased the house to his aunt Janet in Scotland (she of the harpsichord), to his bankrupt brother William and to two others in Scotland. And then he mortgaged the house to the same people the next day (in August 1814).[68] He agreed to pay interest to them twice a year, confident that his school would be a success. For me, alarm bells are jangling, but at this period perhaps this type of transaction was not unusual. Becky Sharp, now Mrs Rawdon Crawley, in Thackeray's *Vanity Fair* might well just smile knowingly. Thackeray's chapter 36 (set not long after the Battle of Waterloo) is titled 'How to live well on nothing a year'. He gives an example of a ('Jenkins') family that *Punch* (the magazine he wrote for) loved to satirize:

> I suppose there is no man in this Vanity Fair of ours so little observant as not to think sometimes about the worldly affairs of his acquaintances, or so extremely charitable as not to wonder how his neighbour Jones or his neighbour Smith can make both ends meet at the end of the year. With the utmost regard for the family, for instance [...], I cannot but own that the appearance of the Jenkinses in the Park, in the large barouche with the grenadier-footmen, will surprise and mystify me to my dying day; for though I know the equipage is only jobbed, and all the Jenkins people are on board wages, yet those three men and the carriage must represent an expense of six hundred a year at the very least. And then there are the splendid dinners; the two boys at Eton; the prize governess and masters for the girls; the trip abroad [...] Who, I say, with the most good-natured feelings in the world, can help wondering how the Jenkinses make out matters? [...] How is it that he has not been outlawed long since, and that he ever came back (as he did to the surprise of everybody) last year from Boulogne?

Boulogne was, like Brussels after the end of the Napoleonic Wars, the place to flee to from your creditors. Thackeray later sums up: 'The truth is, that by economy and good management – by a sparing use of ready money and by paying scarcely anybody – people can manage, for a time at least.'[69]

How could John Jay hope to attract enough pupils so quickly? Of course he had contacts in the merchant community, not least his bereaved brother-in-law James Bowden. An auction for the contents of Prospect House in June 1821 lists sixty school beds and bedding 'in excellent condition'.[70] I wonder if some of those sixty beds had never been slept in. But there were pupils because we know that there were masters, though I read some of the advertisements with a pinch of salt: 'Masters resident in the house for the following branches, viz., the Classics, – the English, French, Spanish, Portuguese, German and Dutch languages; Mathematics, Book-keeping, Writing, and Arithmetic; and a regular course of Lectures on Chemistry'.[71] That might only mean himself and one or two other resident masters, and another coming in daily to give the lectures, though in 1814 he announced there were six resident masters – but it's hard to imagine where they all slept. But we do have the names of three. Charles Henry Peters is known because he died at the age of twenty-two in 1816 ('Teacher at Mr Jay's school'). Also, a book was dedicated to John Jay in 1820 by John Hefford, 'formerly professor in the Commercial College, Woodford'. It is entitled *Crestyphon, a Theban Tale: and the Vandal Robbery, a Carthaginian Tale*. They appear to be original short stories.[72] Three years earlier, the mathematics teacher George Carey published *A Complete System of Theoretical and Mercantile Arithmetic*, with a fulsome dedication to his headmaster:

> To John Jay, Esq.
> Principal of the Commercial Institution, Woodford
> There is no person to whom I can with greater propriety inscribe this Work, than to you, Sir. The distinguished situation you have held in the commercial world, both in this Country and on the Continent, combined with the liberal course of mercantile instruction, to which you have since devoted your time and abilities, eminently qualify you to appreciate the claims of such a production to the patronage of the friends of the useful sciences, and to give a sanction to its object, that of contributing to the diffusion of a correct knowledge of that branch of science, to the cultivation and improvement of which your attention is at present so laudably and successfully devoted.
>
> The utility of the institution established by you, and conducted under your auspices, in which a regular and enlightened system of education is carried on, has been widely and deservedly acknowledged.[73]

That is an impressive dedication, but I was still sceptical about the success of the school.

I looked through the 570 pages of Carey's textbook. It begins with the basics of arithmetic: addition, subtraction; goes on to vulgar and decimal fractions and logarithms; then commercial arithmetic (e.g. multiplication of money, commission, partnership); explaining stocks, annuities, marine insurance, foreign exchange – and as far as I could see always explaining clearly, giving a few rules, then examples and finally exercises.

Here is one of the exercises:

An insurance was effected on 150 tons of hemp, at £52. per ton, from St. Petersburgh to London, at 6 guineas per cent, to return £3 per cent for convoy and arrival; of this quantity insured, 50 tons were shipped on board a vessel, which was completely lost, and 80 tons arrived safe, by a vessel which sailed with convoy the whole of the voyage; the remaining 20 tons were not shipped. Required the whole cost of the *insurance*; the net proceeds of the *loss*; the net amount the assured would receive credit for, from his agent; the amount of the return of premium, for short interest; for convoy and arrival; and the return per cent.[74]

The example could have been provided by John Jay. I give the answer in my notes for those keen to try. Though neither John Jay's eldest sons Samuel nor John were to go into trade, one chapter in Carey's book of what he taught at the school in Woodford, 'Annuities on Lives', will become of particular relevance for Samuel. As usual Carey explains it clearly: 'Life Annuities are payments made, at regular periods, during the life of one or more persons. The value of these for any proposed life, or lives, depends on two circumstances; the *interest* of money, and the *probability* of the *duration* of the proposed life, or lives.' He proceeds to explain tables of mortality and the probability of living to any proposed age – vital for life insurance today as well as then.[75]

Carey even cheekily uses for one exercise the names Jay and Bowden – he must have known John Jay's relations by marriage: 'What balance is due on the following account, 1st January, 1816, with interest? Dr. Mr. John Jay his Account Current with W. Bowden. 1815.'[76] Interestingly he also includes exercises on bankruptcy: 'Suppose a bankrupt's effects amount to £1739. 13s. 8½d., what dividend would fall to each of the following creditors, in proportion to their respective claims.'[77] It seems for him at this time that bankruptcy was normal, as indeed it probably was.

So why am I dubious about the success of the school when John Jay had a master of the calibre of Carey? Because the house was advertised to be let in December 1817 and August 1818, and there seem to be no advertisements for the school during the first six months of 1819. Something had happened. Mathematics teacher Carey left: he set up his own school in January 1819, but that lasted only a couple of years.[78] There were a few advertisements inserted by John Jay after mid-1819, but he sold the house in June 1821, which I will come to below.

Carey's book changed my mind about John Jay, not only about his school at Woodford, but about his previous career as a merchant. No, he didn't write the book, but he employed someone who did, and who obviously admired him. Most of what was in Carey's book John Jay would have learned as a teenager, and been part of his daily life in Arbroath, Leith or Rotterdam – the complicated business of insurance, discounts, exchange rates. He had a wealth of knowledge to impart and for a while it seems to have gone well. But maybe there was too much competition from other schools, and he had no experience of running a large school; or maybe he couldn't resist speculating as a merchant once again and got his fingers burnt. It's odd because what his school was offering seems increasingly popular. In 1791 Oundle Grammar School, founded in the sixteenth century and eighty miles north of Woodford, had no pupils; but the next year the new headmaster added geography, surveying and merchants' accounting to studies of the classics, and the school revived, with forty-five pupils.[79]

What was life like for Eliza? She had lost her Scottish friends and above all her closest sister. As at Lixmount, they were surrounded by wealthy families, but it seems unlikely that a bankrupt (the news would have spread) schoolmaster (likewise undesirable) and his family were welcome at some of them. Their nearest neighbour lived at Monkhams – Brice Pearse, who married Charlotte Raikes of Woodford in 1796.[80] He was an army clothier based in the City. After the British government abolished slavery in 1833 (over twenty years after the abolishment of the British slave trade) he was compensated over £15,000 for 841 slaves on his four estates in Jamaica.[81] He had Snakes Lane (which linked the bridge over the Roding to Woodford) moved from his estate so that he could demolish the houses that were there and build a new mansion. In return he gave £1,000 to the parish for the new workhouse (the poor had to be kept somewhere). He died leaving £100,000.[82] I rather hope that the Jays were personae non gratae at his mansion. (Though I equally hope that Eliza posed that famous question uttered by Fanny Price in Austen's *Mansfield Park*.[83])

* * *

In 1818 Eliza turned twenty-one. She had probably spent many of the previous years helping her mother with the schoolboys, teaching the little ones, though if the house was let, they would have had to stay somewhere else that winter and spring. The country was in a parlous state: the year before, the Prince Regent (the future George IV) had been attacked on his way to opening Parliament, Habeas Corpus had been suspended, and the heir but one to the throne, Princess Charlotte, had died in childbirth, to the great distress of her husband, Prince Leopold, and of the general public. But if the Jays were in Woodford for Eliza's birthday, at least the air was cleaner than in London. Sara Hutchinson wrote to William Wordsworth's teenage daughter Dora from where the Wordsworths were staying in London, in January 1818, that she 'could not see the Houses on the other side of the street – the fog is not only thick but of a yellow color and makes one as dirty as smoke'.[84] I hope Eliza was able to dance on her birthday in May at the Assembly Rooms at the White Hart inn at Woodford Bridge, or ride in Epping Forest, but nothing is known, and they may have stayed with relatives somewhere – in Rotterdam? Or maybe with her mother's brother, the Peninsular War hero, one-armed Alexander Livingston, and his wife, the Scottish baronet's daughter, in Berkshire or Somerset. From the 1836 letter I quoted from above, it seems that Eliza's younger sister Margaret (younger by about five years) might have stayed with her aunt Jane for some time.[85]

However, what *is* known is that her father John Jay was somehow able to send his eldest son to Oxford University in 1818, when Samuel was eighteen, and then, after gaining his BA, to the Inns of Court, where he was called to the Bar in 1826. An education at Oxford and training to be a lawyer at Lincoln's Inn in London were extremely expensive. Eliza's younger brother Samuel was to spend most of his long life (he died in 1881 in London) as a hardworking barrister. Perhaps the exile from Scotland when he was ten had affected him, turning him into a studious striver, albeit one who loved horse racing.

Samuel was admitted commoner at Oriel College on 17 February 1818 and matriculated on the same day, but he presumably started his course in October that year along with most of the other students.[86] 'Commoner' meant that, at one end of the scale, he wasn't a nobleman, nor, at the other end of the scale, had he been granted an exhibition, and he was paying the standard amount of fees, the equivalent of a 'pensioner' at Cambridge. He is noted in the Oxford alumni record as son of John, Esquire, 'of Edinburgh'. That might well be a sign that his childhood home – and indeed where he was born – dominated in his mind, or maybe still in his father's. The fees would be around £200 per annum, and the rule of thumb is to add two noughts for a modern-day equivalent. He had also paid a 'caution' (money deposited as security for his good conduct) of £30. Then there would be other living expenses: including books and furniture, and to his bed maker and for his laundry. Oriel was one of the oldest colleges, founded in the fourteenth century, and if it had been a bit sleepy in the eighteenth century, it was now intellectually the foremost college in Oxford, brimming with new ideas and men who were to shape profoundly the Victorian age that was to come.[87] There were only about eighteen undergraduates a year at this time, and it was 'eminently a gentlemen's college'.[88] In the same year as Samuel was Charles Wood, who got a first in classics and mathematics; he was Chancellor of the Exchequer in 1846–52 and has been called 'the strongest secretary of state [for India] between 1858 and Indian independence'; he was made first Viscount Halifax in 1866.[89] It is possible that Samuel's father had squirrelled money away that should have gone to creditors in order to send his son to Oxford and then Lincoln's Inn. I wondered whether Samuel was desperate to have a stable career (at huge expense) because his father's career as a merchant had failed so badly, but he was obviously bright.

This is where George Carey's arithmetic book illuminated for me what had shaped Samuel's choice of career, because the same day that I studied the book I received a few details of what kind of barrister Samuel became, and it suddenly all made sense. John Jay's son specialized in conveyancing as a barrister. When he was thirty he was involved in a case at the Court of King's Bench, Westminster, Taylor *v.* Street and Others, acting for the plaintiff. He needed to be adroit at understanding mortgages, securities and bonds, and be trusted by the jury and the judge.[90] Under his guidance, the plaintiff won. Over ten years later, in an 1842 advertisement, Samuel Jay is listed as 'Conveyancing Counsel' for Western Life Assurance Society, Westminster; and in 1869, just before he turned seventy, as Director for London and Provincial Law Assurance Society, 21 Fleet Street (albeit one of twenty-three directors).[91] His education at his father's school in Woodford – doing the exercises on probability of death for annuities and acquiring a thorough knowledge of commercial arithmetic – was far more useful than studying classics at Oxford. But of course the contacts made at Oxford, the having been there, would have been absolutely vital. It is not therefore surprising to find mentioned in the Wyndham letters his love of shooting, and that he even at one time owned a racehorse.[92]

It was necessary for his son Samuel's career that John Jay included the classics in his school for that is what Samuel needed in order to be accepted at Oxford or Cambridge. His father had not been to university, though he would have studied Latin. The classics teacher that John employed would have been important, and this was probably a clergyman who might have been at Oxford and encouraged Samuel to aim at the top college. Eliza surely visited her younger brother at Oriel. Oxford is about seventy miles west of Woodford, and they would perhaps stay at an inn on the High. But it was extraordinary in their family's history: for a long-established Presbyterian, Dissenting family, this was the first time one of them had been to Oxford or Cambridge. Like his father in Andover, John Jay probably attended the Anglican church in Woodford Green, putting his years as a Presbyterian deacon in Rotterdam aside, and son Samuel would accept the Thirty-Nine Articles of the Church of England in order to be enrolled for his degree. Times were changing.

There are just two letters from Samuel in the Wyndham collection in Australia, written many years later to his sister Margaret whom he hadn't seen for almost forty years. He apologizes that he hadn't written for a long time, and that he wishes he had a pension to retire upon (he was then sixty-five), and in his next letter he writes that work is so uncertain for barristers, 'dependent on attorneys', adding, 'People are obliged to fight a hard battle in this country in whatever pursuit they may engage, but particularly in my profession.'[93] But that can also be read, between the lines, as: I am very comfortably well off, but you have numerous children, and I am not a soft touch. He had two daughters, and at his death in 1881 he left a personal estate worth £16,742 16s 8d. Add two noughts to that. His father, John Jay, had educated him wisely and well.

* * *

In 1820, Samuel's studies would have been enlivened by gossip about one of the new Oriel Fellows – Hartley Coleridge, the poet's son, who was four years older than Samuel. Hartley, when he was just sixteen months, was addressed by his father in that moving poem 'Frost at Midnight' (1798):

> Dear Babe, that sleepest cradled by my side,
> Whose gentle breathings, heard in this deep calm,
> Fill up the interspersèd vacancies
> And momentary pauses of the thought!
> My babe so beautiful! it thrills my heart
> With tender gladness, thus to look at thee,
> And think that thou shalt learn far other lore,
> And in far other scenes![94]

I had forgotten when I used the image of 'Calais' engraved on the heart as regards Lixmount that Coleridge had used it about his son Hartley, as quoted by Richard Holmes (maybe its poignancy had burred itself onto my heart): Coleridge wrote in a letter in 1829, 'What Queen Mary said, on the loss of our last stronghold in France – that if her heart were opened, Calais would be found written at the Core – I might say of my poor dear Hartley.'[95] He was writing after his son's brutal rejection of him. The signs of Hartley's unhappiness and eccentricity can be found in a pivotal episode at Oriel College, maybe witnessed by some of the students, Samuel Jay among them. In 1819, Coleridge was hugely proud that Hartley had been elected a Probationary Fellow of Oriel and told all his friends how superior Hartley had been to all the other candidates. Hartley's school at Ambleside had a holiday in his honour. As Holmes writes: 'The child of "Frost at Midnight" had proved their finest alumnus.'[96] But in June 1820 the happiness was shattered. Hartley's Fellowship was not being renewed by Oriel because of his 'drunkenness, irregular behaviour, and keeping low company'.[97] I wonder what Samuel Jay and the other undergraduates had observed: that Hartley did indeed drink too much? Or that he was unfairly picked upon, because he was a bit 'odd', when everybody drank? Hartley disappeared, with rumours that he had run away to America. Coleridge was utterly distraught (especially, probably, because he had fled Cambridge as a student years before). He tried to get his son reinstated and bombarded Fellows at Oriel with letters, which culminated with his confrontation with the Provost of Oriel in October. Unfortunately Oriel College was unusual in Oxford for its austere moral tone. At Samuel Jay's and Hartley Coleridge's college were the formidable trio of John Keble, John Henry Newman and Thomas Arnold. All Fellows at that time. Holmes remarks brilliantly that Hartley 'had fallen among saints, and they were unsparing in their righteousness'.[98] S.T. Coleridge arrived at Oriel on 15 October (a week before his forty-eighth birthday) for the confrontation. Student heads must have popped out of library and study windows as the news spread around the small college that the famous author of *The Rime of the Ancient Mariner* was among them, about to have it out with the provost. The provost was urbane but firm: Hartley did not return. Samuel Jay carried on with his studies, gaining a respectable, if not scintillating, third in the classics that was sufficient for his purposes.

* * *

John Jay's aunt Janet Enslie came down from Scotland and actually died at Prospect House on 18 February 1820, the year also of the death of Edward Duke of Kent (the future Queen Victoria's father) and six days later of his father, King George III, after a reign of sixty years. Perhaps after John Jay part-mortgaged the house to her, Aunt Janet travelled down from Edinburgh to see it, or maybe John Jay was not paying her the interest he had pledged. She had made a will in 1815, adding a codicil in 1816, a couple of years after the mortgaging, in which

John Jay, son of her sister Mary, is strikingly absent. But his brother, William Jay, 'merchant in Leith', is an executor. She leaves large sums (£500 or £400) to nephews and nieces by her brother James, and there are legacies too for William's wife Isabella and his daughter by his first marriage (£200 each). There is also £50 for her goddaughter (and great-niece) Janet to buy a watch and chain (she was the youngest Jay child, then aged six; it sounds a bizarre legacy). In the codicil she adds £15 each to John's wife Helen and her other great-nieces Eliza and Margaret 'all of Woodford Wells Essex', 'as a trifling token of my regard and regret it is not in my power to leave them a more substantial proof of my esteem': she leaves well over £2,000 and doesn't have it in her power to give John Jay's family a bit more? The residue of her estate, including property in Princes Street, Edinburgh, went to a niece by her brother James; there is no mention of her share in Prospect House. Her visit to Woodford, therefore, after writing such a will, may not have been a friendly one – she was in her eighty-fourth year and it is a long way to travel at that age.[99] Even if she decided that the money she had given John Jay for the house was his legacy, she still gave only £15 to his wife (as an afterthought), while giving £200 to his brother William's wife.

John Jay was now planning on selling the house he had bought with such complicated mortgages only six years before. The man who was interested was William Mellish, a wealthy victualler to the navy. His father had been a wholesale butcher at Smithfield market, who had bought land on the Isle of Dogs, in the East End of London, to fatten the cattle.[100] After his death in 1777 his sons Peter and William took over. They also had a shipbuilding business in Shadwell Dock on the Thames. It seems much of their money was first made during the American War of Independence (1775–83) when they contracted with the British Victualling Board to supply cattle and oxen. During the French Wars they were the monopoly suppliers of live cattle, which were driven to Deptford for slaughter and processing; they also cured meat at Shadwell Dock. Enormous sums were involved; for example, in 1813 William Mellish (his brother Peter died some years before) was paid £412,120 for his supplies of oxen and beef. It is not known what his profit was, but when he died in 1833 he left a fortune thought to be three million pounds. His heiress daughter married Richard Butler, the second Earl of Glengall, a year later. A guide on the internet to the 'Butler Trail of Cahir' (near Kilkenny in south-east Ireland) states that the earl managed to make himself bankrupt despite the vast fortune his wife brought him.

According to the Woodford Historical Society, William Mellish lived at Harts House, a newly rebuilt mansion almost opposite Prospect House; if so, then maybe he was adding John Jay's house to his Woodford portfolio.[101] He does sound to be a highly competent businessman. The auction of the contents of Prospect House took place on 2 and 3 July 1821, with a viewing on Saturday 30 June. The advertisement states that 'the Commercial Institution [...] has been removed to the Continent'.[102] Other than the sixty school beds, mentioned above, it is interesting to see what objects the family had possessed and were now giving up. Obviously they wouldn't want to take across the Channel household furniture even if it was 'genteel', nor dairy and brewing utensils, nor the mangle; and 'secretary bookcases, celleret sideboards [for wine bottles], sofa, set of dining tables' would be too bulky. But it sounds like money from the auction was needed – by the Jays or by Mellish – because also on the list are philosophical instruments, a pair of twenty-four-inch globes and a 'library of books': surely these would be needed in the new school? And were the family tired of the 'set of proof prints, by Holloway, from the Cartoons of Raphael, and a beautiful Italian ditto, (the Last Supper) in elegant gilt frames'? Thomas Holloway (1748–1827) was a London engraver who began work in 1800 on a folio edition of the cartoons by Raphael then at Windsor Castle.[103] Four plates had been completed by 1820, so the prints in the Jays' house had only just been bought or given as a gift. Apparently there was little demand for the Raphael engravings, so maybe they were better sold, perhaps at a loss. Finally, the four-wheel chaise, horse and harness also had to go. Not a two-horse family, then.

Just two days after the auction another advertisement appeared in *The Times*:

> Institut Britannique, Brussels, formerly the Commercial Institution at Woodford in Essex. – This establishment has been removed to the vicinity of the City of Brussels, in order to facilitate the acquisition of the foreign languages, a large commodious house, with suitable premises, having been fitted up in an elevated airy situation.[104]

The name of the school was different but the type of school was the same, 'uniting all the advantages of literary and commercial education', though a special emphasis now is on the 'comforts of British accommodation' – reassuring parents about British-style beds and breakfasts? Classes would start less than a month later, on Wednesday 1 August. Junior pupils below the age of twelve would be charged forty guineas, older pupils fifty. But also 'Gentlemen wishing to finish their education by a few months residence on the continent will be received as Parlour Boarders or Seniors, under very liberal regulations, adapted to their more advanced age, and to gentlemanly habits of life, at 100 guineas per annum.' The net is cast wide as before. Pupils would also be escorted to Brussels.

* * *

It seems such an orderly move: sometime between the last advertisement for the school in Woodford on 1 February and the one for the auction on 20 June 1821, the Jays had decided to move; the sale of the house in Woodford was progressing, and they had found a good house in Brussels: six years after the final defeat of Napoleon, Europe was now open for business. But I have niggles: Aunt Janet coming all the way from Edinburgh in her eighties and leaving John out of her will; Mellish agreeing to take on 'overdue interest payments' as part of buying the house (deducting them from the purchase price);[105] and Brussels was a favourite city to escape to if you had financial difficulties. But perhaps the family's move was not as suddenly traumatic as Anthony Trollope's about ten years later.

In his autobiography, Trollope describes what happened in March 1834 when the family were living on their failing farm in Harrow. His father, an unsuccessful barrister, summoned the nineteen-year-old to drive him in the gig to London. 'It was not till we had started that he told me that I was to put him on board the Ostend boat. This I did, driving him through the city down to the docks.' When Trollope got home, he discovered that the house had been taken over by the sheriff's officers – the bailiffs had arrived: 'a scene of devastation was in progress, which still was not without its amusement':

> My mother [the author Frances Trollope], through her various troubles, had contrived to keep a certain number of pretty-pretties which were dear to her heart. They were not much, for in those days the ornamentation of houses was not lavish as it is now; but there was some china, and a little glass, a few books, and a very moderate supply of household silver. These things, and things like them, were being carried down surreptitiously, through a gap between the two gardens, on to the premises of our friend Colonel Grant. My two sisters, then sixteen and seventeen, and the Grant girls, who were just younger, were the chief marauders. To such forces I was happy to add myself for any enterprise, and between us we cheated the creditors to the extent of our powers [...] I still own a few books that were thus purloined.[106]

The Trollope family followed father to Bruges in Belgium (and Anthony will appear again in my narrative). Hopefully Eliza, aged twenty-four in May 1821, managed to keep a few precious things from going to auction. If she had been miserable at leaving her home at Lixmount, I would think that, unmarried and getting on in age, she was excited to leave England for a new start.

The advertisements that John Jay penned for British newspapers unravelled some mysteries that I had puzzled over for years, but it was what was happening in Edinburgh in 1821 that finally made sense of their move – or rather their escape – abroad.

* * *

The settlement the Jay brothers had agreed to pay their creditors in Scotland in 1810 had seemingly wound up that unhappy business.[107] But shipmaster Kelting had not gone quietly. The 1810 judgment had been that merchant Mr Duncan was responsible for paying Kelting the balance of the freight – the cost of hiring his ship. But Duncan had gone bankrupt and a loophole had been found whereby it was deemed, eleven years later by the Lord Ordinary, Lord Pitmilly, that John Jay and his brother William were still responsible for the balance, which, with interest, was now £4,000 – perhaps half a million in today's money. On 18 January 1822 the Lord Ordinary judged on behalf of Captain Kelting, with seemingly no questions asked as to why he had delayed bringing the cargo for over six months. But no doubt John Jay had been well advised by his Scottish friends to flee to the Continent some time before this: otherwise everything he had earned in eleven years would have been seized, his family made destitute, himself imprisoned. Without examining other cases before Lord Pitmilly and the Edinburgh Court of Session it is impossible to say whether the pernickety letter of the law was applied unfairly in John Jay's case, but what I find murky is that the agents acting for Captain Kelting were the same people who bought Lixmount in 1812 after John had moved to England as a bankrupt – Ramsay Williamson & Co., run by Thomas Williamson.[108] That the loophole was found and that John Jay was hounded over eleven more years may have been a personal vendetta against an initially successful merchant who was perceived as an outsider. Conspiracy theories are usually unhinged, but this one is certainly possible. If over the years I had been a bit ambivalent about John Jay, I now find his resilience fabulously impressive. He started yet again.

So the Jays fled to Brussels, where more tragedy was to befall. But I must turn back to where I left Evan Jenkins in Wales. Somehow, he had to get to Cambridge and then to Brussels to meet Eliza Jay. How?

Seven

Cambridge

'I was the Dreamer, they the Dream'

I was the Dreamer, they the Dream; I roamed
Delighted, through the motley spectacle;
Gowns grave or gaudy, Doctors, Students, Streets,
Lamps, Gateways, Flocks of Churches, Courts and Towers:
Strange transformation for a mountain Youth,
A northern Villager.

– William Wordsworth, *The Prelude*,
'Book Three: Residence at Cambridge',
ll. 28–33[1]

The 'northern Villager' Wordsworth arrived at St John's College, Cambridge, next door to Trinity College, in October 1787, aged seventeen. From his rooms he could see Trinity: he heard its 'loquacious' clock striking every quarter hour, night and day, and the 'pealing' sound of that college's organ:

And, from my Bedroom, I in moonlight nights
Could see, right opposite, a few yards off,
The Antechapel, where the Statue stood
Of Newton, with his Prism and silent Face.

(ll. 56–9)

Wordsworth's excitement on arriving at Cambridge did not last. He early felt 'A feeling that I was not for that hour, / Nor for that place' (ll. 80–1). Isaac Newton is maybe Trinity College's most famous graduate (admitted in 1661), but when Evan Jenkins arrived, thirty-one years after Wordsworth, the most famous recent student at Trinity was George Gordon, Lord Byron (accompanied by his bear), who was variously there between 1805 and 1807 and had become famous overnight with *Childe Harold* in 1812. He was currently in Italy, scandal and rumour whirling around the very mention of his name. The early nineteenth-century Fellows would be astounded that a full-size, white marble statue of Byron (shown seated and tuning in to his Muse) now dominates the college's elegant, late seventeenth-century Wren Library. That was where I was headed in 2014 to see the college admissions book and try to sort out why Evan had been entered in it as aged '20' – thus supplying the wrong birth year for all Brontë publications – when the ordination papers, and much else besides, had him as definitely twenty-three when he was admitted.

There are conflicting contemporary accounts about the University of Cambridge at this time, and since the colleges were different in the way they were run, and the students could have totally different experiences depending on their class/rank and studious (or not) inclinations, it is not hard to see why. Added to this are the numerous changes that took place in the late eighteenth and nineteenth centuries, so that a student in 1818 would have a different experience from one in 1828, one example being the introduction of the Classical Tripos in 1822 by the Master of Trinity, Christopher Wordsworth, brother of the poet.[2] However, in Evan Jenkins's final year (1822), the university written examinations in the Senate House for BA were on what might generally be called mathematics.

There are also misleading secondary accounts that can muddy the waters. In William Hague's biography of William Pitt the Younger (Prime Minister 1783–1801 and 1804–6) he notes that Pitt 'took his Master of Arts degree without an examination, as he was entitled to do as the son of a nobleman'.[3] Hague, former Foreign Secretary and now in the House of Lords, was at Magdalen College, Oxford in 1979–82. He knows that an Oxbridge graduate has never done an examination for their MA. As long as we are alive, are not divorced or in prison (I think those were the rules), we pay a few guineas to acquire it after three years from being made BA. As a New Yorker at Trinity College, Charles Astor Bristed, of the extremely wealthy Astor family, comments about his time there in the 1840s: 'the M.A. degree can be obtained by anyone who has taken a B.A. on paying a certain sum and performing some trifling ceremonies'.[4] In the nineteenth century you had to attend in person; in my day at Oxford (1970s) the postal service was sufficient. Hague, however, is perfectly correct that a nobleman could *acquire* an MA without doing any examinations at all during his years at Cambridge (if he stayed the necessary number of terms). Thackeray comments in his *Book of Snobs* on this 'absurd and monstrous' custom: 'Because a lad is a lord, the University gives him a degree at the end of two years which another is seven in acquiring. Because he is a lord, he has no call to go through an examination.'[5] The university calendar listed the types of noblemen who were entitled to an honorary degree 'at two years standing'. This included 'Persons related to the King's Majesty by consanguinity or affinity; provided they be also honorable'.[6]

In this chapter I focus on contemporary accounts of Trinity and Cambridge. They range from an angry mathematical village 'genius' (Atkinson, whom I call the 'angry wrangler') to an urbane New Yorker (Bristed) and an intense poet (Tennyson, with his snake). Formidable Thackeray will also comment, who arrived at Trinity in 1829, though he stayed for only five terms.[7] Somehow a tenant farmer's son from Cardiganshire, Evan Jenkins, is one of them, forever a Trinity man.

First, our New Yorker will explain what Cambridge was like two decades after Evan arrived:

> Imagine the most irregular town that *can* be imagined, streets of the very crookedest kind, twisting about like those in a nightmare, and not unfrequently bringing you back to the same point you started from [...] The houses are low and antique; sometimes their upper stories project out into and over the narrow pathway, making it still narrower; and their lower stories are usually occupied as shops – tailors and booksellers being the predominant varieties. Every now and then your road passes over a muddy little river, not larger than a tolerable canal, which rambles through and about the town in all sorts of ways, so that in *whatever* direction you walk from *any* point, you are pretty sure to come to a bridge before long, such is the town of Cambridge – the *bridge* over the *Cam*.
>
> Among these narrow, ugly, and dirty streets, are tumbled in, as it were at random [...] some of the most beautiful academical buildings in the world.[8]

Among the beautiful academical buildings were the two largest and richest colleges, Trinity and St John's, with maybe eighty to one hundred freshmen a year each at this time; the others were known as 'small' colleges. The Wren Library at

Trinity and how new students registered at Trinity College on their arrival needs to be explained by a contemporary. Who better than John Martin F. Wright, well known later in debtors' prisons, as our guide? His book was written anonymously by 'A Trinity-Man', but later attributed to him. There is only one John Wright at Trinity College who fits. This one was admitted as a sizar in 1813, aged twenty. (My guides will try to explain sizar below.) He was born in Frampton in Lincolnshire, went to school at King's Lynn in Norfolk, and obtained his BA in 1819. Such is the brief, dry record in *Alumni Cantabrigienses*. Wright himself says in his book that he started at Trinity in October 1815 and was from the north of England, but in keeping with his desire to remain anonymous he seems to have been making that up.[9] However, he certainly started at Trinity only a few years before Evan Jenkins arrived, and they might have been acquaintances. John Martin Frederick Wright married Mary Anne Moriarty in 1825 in London and two years later published *Alma Mater; or, Seven Years at the University of Cambridge*.[10] It seems he had already started a life in and out of debtors' prisons. The Court for Relief of Insolvent Debtors in June 1829 (when Wright was in his thirties) announced that his case was to be heard in July at the Court House at Cambridge, and that previously he had been at the King's Bench Prison in Surrey (now South London, twice) and was currently at the Gaol in Cambridge. He was a gentleman, a private tutor and 'author of some mathematical works'.[11] His woes do not end there. In 1835 and 1839 he again came before the court for debt.[12] It gets worse: in September 1841, now in his forties, his five children were baptized in a batch in Lambeth, South London. He is noted as a 'graduate of Cambridge'. His abode is: workhouse.[13] I haven't been able to trace him further, but I doubt if his end was happy.

In his 1827 Cambridge book, Wright remembers better times. The book is far from dry: it is often amusing, sometimes flippant and very helpful (if you feel like trusting him, and I think I do, some of the time, since he quotes from *Othello* in his Preface, which is disarming), though he sometimes thinks he is funnier than he actually is (or maybe that is the passing of time and changes in humour). It is also a defence of Cambridge University, in spite of his later troubles:

> after the maturest consideration, the best service I can render the public, and my own particular Alma Mater, appears to be, a full and frank avowal of my own experience whilst under her protection. I, too, as the Reader will perceive, have been one of the disappointed; but still will I speak honestly, and 'Nothing extenuate, nor set down aught in malice.'[14]

He then simply asks students, parents and guardians to 'take me as their guide [...] This is all I ask.'

In the first decades of the nineteenth century, four or five hundred freshmen arrived at Cambridge University in October.[15] Unless you were a nobleman or a rich 'fellow commoner' with estates to inherit, neither of whom needed a degree, the men were supposed to be in residence for three years (three terms each year), plus Michaelmas (autumn) term in their fourth year in which they revised, and a final term in January in which they sat for their final examinations – which were increasingly paper examinations rather than oral. They all studied the same main subjects: classics and mathematics. At Trinity their names were sent in gradually during the year before October, and they were approved and 'admitted' – their names being written down into the register, in date order of 'admittance', ready for the student to arrive in the autumn and fill in further details. So, how, Mr Wright, do students register at Trinity?

Wright has a letter of introduction to a senior soph (a third-year man; soph is an abbreviation of sophister, derived from Greek) who shows him around. He takes Wright to the Wren Library to complete his entry in the register. Wright likes the look of the library, 'a magnificent and superb structure in the Grecian style, built by sir Christopher Wren [...] supported by a long colonnade of arches and pillars, [which] form a most agreeable as well as useful promenade, in wet or otherwise disagreeable weather, for the whole University' near the 'slowly-winding Cam'.[16] He rhapsodizes about the lawns, the enchanting chestnut and lime trees and the bridges over the river, getting in a quote from *A Midsummer Night's Dream*. That view hasn't changed; it is his description of the interior of the library that now sounds weird. The marble floor reminds him of a boa-constrictor (possibly a good effect), and the stained glass displaying Isaac Newton, Francis Bacon and 'a lion or two' has exquisite colours but overall is in bad taste, though he is impressed by the thousands of books and manuscripts. But also on display are 'costumes of savage nations, their warlike implements, musical instruments, stuffed crocodiles, dried men's hands, and a pickled mummy or two'.[17] Some might regret their later disappearance or repatriation, and he doesn't mention the stuffed zebra.[18] Then Wright's third-year companion introduces him to the librarian who is in charge of the admissions book:

'[...] my friend here, being a *First-Year Man*, and but just arrived, as you may see, may as well enter his name in your list for the year.' My guide having thus introduced me, the sub-librarian produced a large ledger-looking book, in which are written the names and former residences, at full length, of all Freshmen, their fathers, and schoolmasters, as also their own ages. If the reader be curious after such knowledge, he or *she* may learn my age, and other particulars, by reference to this same book, wherein it is stated that in the month of February 1815 I was nineteen. Prodigious![19]

The exact same 'large ledger-looking book' is what I looked at in the Wren Library. The pages of the register are divided into eleven columns across verso and recto; the handwriting shows that the librarian entered the date the student was admitted (that is 'accepted', usually by post), his 'rank' (or in order of fees being paid: nobleman, fellow commoner, pensioner, sizar) and his name; the student (on arrival in October) fills in his father's name and, in the next column, place of birth/residence, and on the recto the county, his school and its county, and his (school)master's name; then comes his age (at admittance, that is, not in October); and finally the librarian wrote his tutor's name: in 1817–18 at Trinity the students were divided between Mr Hustler, Mr Brown and (occasionally) Professor Monk, probably mainly at random. (More on tutors later: it meant something different then.) As regards 'rank', there is one instance in the admissions book of 'prince' (admitted September 1818), but HRH the Duke of Sussex didn't turn up it seems and it is rather bewildering since the only Duke of Sussex (Augustus Frederick, ninth child of George III) was in his mid-forties then. It is an oddity, or a prank?

I have not yet stated who inserted the age of the candidate, which we know from Wright's account is the age of 'admittance' not that in October. It looks from the handwriting in the register that it was inserted by the student. In a few cases the student didn't arrive: for example, Edward Armytage was admitted on 9 July 1818 as a pensioner; his admittance date, name and tutor have been written in by the librarian, but all the other columns are blank since he failed to show. What is clear is that in Evan's case his age certainly looks like '20', but the '0' has been inked in heavily. Whatever was put there, presumably '23', by Evan, was possibly thought later by the librarian to be wrong since it is an unusual age to start at Cambridge (most students 'admitted' were seventeen, eighteen or at the most twenty). Maybe it was originally written so faintly that the librarian inked over the figure '3' to make it a clearer '0'. But where was this mature student, actually aged twenty-three, before he went to Trinity? And why Trinity? Why Cambridge?

* * *

I did a search of the Cambridge alumni database (ACAD) just for the word 'ystrad'. Before Evan, the only student who had gone to Cambridge from the school at Ystrad Meurig was in 1771, almost fifty years before, and he had gone to Gonville and Caius College at the age of twenty-five. If I could find out where Evan was between school and Cambridge maybe I might also find the man who recommended him to go to Trinity. For many months I investigated frustrating cul-de-sacs: did he stay at school as a teacher? Did he teach privately or somewhere else in Wales? What about Chelsea where his brother David had taught? Or he might have joined his brother in Yorkshire. I could find nothing and there was no clue in his ordination papers. But then over a year later, a discovery was made: the National Library of Wales in Aberystwyth had a letter written by an 'E. Jenkins, Brussels' in 1823.[20] I scrambled to order it. It was an utterly wonderful find that took my breath away, but most of its contents will be explored later. For now what was striking was one phrase, in beautifully clear handwriting – and yes, it was by my great-great-grandfather Evan – 'my best friend the Revd. Peter Felix', who was apparently in London. The name Felix rang a bell. I just sat there thinking Felix, Felix, and a memory of something I had read about Chelsea during David's time there leapt into my mind. I frantically searched through notebooks, computer files, archfiles, the internet: got it. *The Survey of London*, published in 1913, under 'Cheyne House, Upper Cheyne Row: Historical Notes', stated: 'Cheyne House, during the end of the 18th century and the first half of the 19th, was a school, and is marked on Thompson's map as "Cheyne House Academy." Faulkner says it was carried on in 1829 by Dr. Felix, and formerly by Mr. Edwards.'

That 1829 date is wrong; it was over a decade earlier. Peter Felix's elder brother Rev. David Felix took over Mr Edwards's school in Chelsea, where David Jenkins had taught, and if Peter Felix was Evan's 'best friend' – presumably a schoolfellow at Ystrad Meurig – then could Evan have gone to teach at the same school in Chelsea that David had? The National Library in Wales had documents relating to Peter Felix, but I was in London and a visit looked unlikely for a few weeks. But meanwhile I found that there were more things to look at in Cambridge: I needed to see the university calendars of the period when Evan was there (only one of which seemed to be online) and I had found out from Adam Green, the Assistant Archivist at the Wren Library, that Evan Jenkins was grouped in the fifth class for his college examinations in 1819 and 1821, though his name was missing in 1820. It meant little: not being in the first or second class wasn't great, but fifth? How appalling was that? I needed to see the Head Lecturer's book that he referred to.

February 2016 saw me again at the Wren Library at Trinity. Cambridge was freezing. The library was icy. Wearing all my walkers' layers, I tucked myself at a desk behind the back of white marble Byron still invoking his Muse, and the Head Lecturer's book was brought to me. Almost as welcome, a radiator was all mine, to stop me from freezing to death on the boa-constrictor, black and white marble floor. I have never been provided with my very own radiator in a library before – it was warming, in more than one sense – well, mostly in the very obvious sense. Frankly, since students in Evan's day had to do their final examinations in January, in the freezing Senate House, it is a mystery how any survived, let alone became wranglers (the very best). The Astronomer Royal Sir George Biddell Airy comments that in the cold January of 1823 no fire was allowed during their BA exams and it was a 'severe time', but he did become senior wrangler.[21] He was in the year below Evan and was also a sizar.

In the Trinity College Head Lecturer's book was a 'List of the Undergraduates examined May 27–28 – 31st – June 1–2 1819', with columns of surnames under 'Sophs', 'Junr Sophs' and 'Freshmen'. In Evan's column, sixty-eight freshmen sat their first-year college examinations, and a further three were 'aegrotat' (ill). My rough count in the admissions book of those who had arrived in October 1818 had come to over one hundred, though another list produced only about eighty, but even so, there were a large number who had dropped out, didn't need to do exams, had died or gone to another college, or even escaped to Oxford once they found the heavy emphasis on mathematics at Cambridge uncongenial. William Wordsworth was persuaded that his eldest son John would not be able to cope with Cambridge mathematics, and in 1823 he sent him to New College, Oxford.[22] (John Wordsworth will appear again in my book.)

One of the drop-outs was William Wilberforce's eldest son, also William. The great evangelical MP who spent decades trying to end the British slave trade, finally succeeding in 1807, had an eldest son who couldn't cope with the temptations at Cambridge. William the elder had been at St John's College in the 1770s. A few pages after Evan's entry in the admissions book is that of William Wilberforce the younger, admitted to Trinity on 26 June 1817 as a pensioner: residence Clapham (London); schooling private under Rev. M. Preston; aged eighteen. His tutor was Mr Brown. William Hague in his biography of Wilberforce the elder says that the son dissipated his father's allowance at Trinity and was taken advantage of by students who liked using his money and 'tarnishing the Wilberforce reputation'. In 1819 Wilberforce senior was annoyed that his son had bought yet another horse. He cancelled his allowance to teach him a lesson, but one Sunday in March 1819 son William got very drunk, he:

forced his presence on friends who were 'piously disposed', ignored the fact that the body of one of his good friends was lying in the neighbouring set of rooms awaiting the funeral the next day, and then told lies about the whole incident afterwards. It would have been difficult to come up with a set of misdemeanours more offensive to his father, and William found himself removed from Cambridge, with Wilberforce noting with some anguish in his diary, 'O my poor Willm. How strange he can make so miserable those who love him best and whom really he loves.'[23]

The pressures on young men at Cambridge were immense. There was peer pressure to spend money, gamble, strut about, whore and go to the races. If you were unfortunate enough to have a famous father, particularly one who was so morally renowned as William Wilberforce, your fate was probably sealed unless you were particularly strong and independent, or had a set of friends from school, but, alas, the young man had been privately educated. Wilberforce's other sons went to Oriel College, Oxford. And whether they were tougher, or Oriel was a stronghold of virtue (which we know in Hartley Coleridge's case it seems to have been), they succeeded when William at Cambridge had not. We will meet another of Wilberforce's sons ('Soapy Sam', the bishop) in a later chapter.

I was eager to see the next page in the Head Lecturer's book: where the freshmen were placed in classes according to their results. I was relieved that Evan's fifth class wasn't at the bottom – there was also a sixth class. In the first class was a well-known name, Macaulay. The startlingly precocious Thomas Babington Macaulay, the future historian, was six years younger than Evan. He was an insatiable reader; Thackeray remarked that Macaulay read 'twenty books to write a sentence'.[24] But Macaulay, brilliant at classics, disliked mathematics, and over the next two years he slipped down to third class and then fourth; in 1822 he withdrew from the university mathematics examination and had to leave with a plain BA, without honours.[25] But he sits in resplendent white marble in the college chapel, clutching one of his books and looking knowingly clever. Tennyson sits next to him, looking poetically avuncular and aged – rather different from when he arrived at Trinity in the late 1820s. They are a rather intimidating marble duo.

Evan's name is missing in the list for the second-year examinations. In the third-year (senior soph) examinations in 1821 he was again in the fifth class, but this time undergraduates were grouped into eight classes, so that was a definite improvement in the rankings, and there were only fifteen men above him. 'Mr' Heneage (unlike most of the students he is 'Mr') managed only seventh class: George

Fieschi Heneage had been to Eton and was to become a Member of Parliament and sheriff of Lincolnshire. His home was Hainton Hill in Lincolnshire, which is now grade 1 listed, and had been the country seat of the Heneage family since the thirteenth century.[26] Evan's future brother-in-law George Wyndham had been to Harrow School, and arrived a year after Evan. His home was Dinton House (now called Philipps House) in Wiltshire, which is also listed. In his second-year examination in 1821 George was classed sixth; and likewise sixth for his 1822 examinations. I think Evan, whose one-room farmhouse is not listed, can hold his head high, as can Ystrad Meurig. But maybe George Wyndham was spending too much time playing cricket: he was a co-founder (with his schoolfriend Charles Oxenden) of the Cambridge University Cricket Club in 1820.[27]

I handed back the Head Lecturer's book with some satisfaction, but I was no nearer knowing why Evan had come to Trinity or Cambridge. I explained my frustration to Jonathan Smith, the archivist, who was sitting with his own personal heater at the end of the long library by the door. Suddenly he stood up. I think it was a lightbulb moment. 'Go back to the table,' he said. I walked back to Byron and my radiator, expectant. It is always useful to ask 'is there anything else?' of an archivist/librarian. Jonathan Smith reappeared with a bundle of files and put them on my table. Inside were numerous pieces of paper, most of them with spike holes (I could imagine the admission slips arriving in the library and being put on the spike, before being entered into the admissions book). Now it was the hair standing on the back of my neck moment: these were the actual admission slips from 1817–18, with the accepted undergraduate's name on, jotted down by one of the tutors of Trinity, in Latin; for example:

Trin: Coll: Cant. Jan 14th. 1818
Johannes Hampden Thelwall, a Magistro Copley A.M. examinatus, admissus est Sisator hujus Collegii
    J. Brown Tutor
    A. Sedgwick. Dept. Dean [signed also by two others]
[John Hampden Thelwall, examined by Mr Copley MA, admitted to be a sizar at this college]

Thelwall was admitted aged twenty after private tuition in Derbyshire. He received his BA in 1823 and became rector of Oving in Buckinghamshire until his death in the 1870s. It wasn't only sizars who were examined privately, so were pensioners (those who paid the standard fees): Richard ('Ricardus') Wellesley

Rothman was 'Examinatus et approbatus' by a Mr Sumner, and was admitted 'Pensionarius' on 24 November 1817 at the age of nineteen. Rothman was born at Chowringhee, Calcutta and went to Westminster School, gaining his BA in 1823 and becoming a Fellow. Another pensioner was examined and approved 'a nobis' – 'by us', perhaps meaning Mr Hustler, his future tutor. My guides will comment on how they were examined below, but it seems that some kind of personal examination was conducted by Trinity graduates or Fellows (usually ordained ones), or if the student didn't know any, then he would be examined in the college. But if you had the money or the pedigree, you were not examined: the admissions slip for The Honourable Henry Scott Stopford simply reads (3 November 1817) that he 'Requests to be admitted a Fellow-Commoner of the Dean's Table', signed by J.D. Hustler, Tutor. Stopford arrived aged twenty; he was the fifth son of the Earl of Courtown, grandson of the third Duke of Buccleuch; he was ordained and became Archdeacon of Leighlin in Ireland. He acquired his MA in 1819 without actually doing a BA: his name doesn't appear on any of the Trinity College examination lists. It was indeed a strange world of reading and non-reading men – about which more below.

And then I found the admission slip for Evan:

Coll. Trin. Decris 29th 1817

Evan Jenkins, examinatus et approbatus a Mr Allen, admissus est Sisator.

It was signed by J.D. Hustler, Tutor, the Senior Dean William Judgson, Professor Monk and the then Master of Trinity, William Mansel, Bishop of Bristol. Evan had been 'examined and approved by Mr Allen'. Who was Allen? I didn't have long to find out. Archivist Jonathan Smith came back again with a list of three Allens who had been at Trinity: 'It's probably this one,' he said, pointing to the top name: Joseph Allen. I hadn't mentioned anything about Chelsea, but what immediately leapt out at me was 'V. of Battersea, Surrey, 1808–29'. Battersea, a walk across the bridge from Chelsea. There was no point looking at the other two Allens, who were vicars in Norfolk. I had found the man who had influenced Evan to go to Cambridge, and changed his life.

* * *

Rev. Joseph Allen (born in 1770 in Manchester) was clever enough at mathematics to be seventh wrangler at Cambridge in the final examinations for BA in 1792 and Fellow of Trinity the following year; he was to become Bishop of Ely in 1836. An obituary about him in 1845 is startlingly malignant:

[He] passed his school and college life without attracting much attention at the places of his education, or bringing down upon his head either the reproaches, the jealousy, or the admiration of his contemporaries [...] [H]is name will not descend to posterity in connexion with any great public services or any remarkable sacrifice of personal convenience or advantage.

The obituary ends a little more kindly: 'the right rev prelate quitted this world, leaving behind him a reputation not so brilliant as to excite envy, but quite sufficient to secure respect'.[28]

But the obituarist is right that 'a far greater advantage' than obtaining a Fellowship was Allen's appointment as tutor to Viscount Althorp, the eldest son of the second Earl Spencer, possibly in 1798, when John Charles Spencer was sixteen.[29] Certainly from that appointment all Allen's future wealth and (not quite glittering) career resulted. Earl Spencer held the living of Battersea and presented it to Allen in 1806 along with a prebendal stall in Westminster Abbey, which provided him with £1,500 a year. He later also acquired the living of St Bride's in the City of London, which, the obituarist notes sarcastically, meant that in 1829 this 'pluralist' had an income of £2,000 a year, 'almost enough for a bishop'. What was even more fortunate was that his former pupil went into politics and became one of the leaders of the Whigs: 'Mitres, crosiers, and all the ensigns of episcopal authority, naturally presented themselves to the imaginations of the learned persons who had superintended the education of the Whig nobility,' and indeed Allen was made Bishop of Bristol in 1834, before moving to Ely.

But if the reader is snarling alongside the obituarist, there is another, very different picture. Viscount Althorp had an appalling childhood. His mother, née Lavinia Bingham, was controlling and brutal.[30] He had a 'Gothic childhood which included drunken servants, extended periods of parental desertion, and ferocious verbal abuse', a childhood that 'permanently maimed' him. He was sent to Harrow School at the age of eight but was withdrawn when he was sixteen as his father was not satisfied with the education he was being given. It is perhaps then that Joseph Allen was appointed the boy's private tutor, to prepare him for Cambridge.[31] Apparently Allen's role was significant: 'The don was sensitive to the fragile nature of Althorp's emotional development [...] He succeeded in nurturing Althorp's intellectual curiosity and deepening religious faith, tempering both with a gentle worldliness.' Althorp was to become one of the great reforming Whigs, decisively steering the 'Great' Reform Act of 1832 through the Commons and abolishing slavery in the British Empire a year later.

In 1817, Rev. Joseph Allen made an impact on another young man, from a completely different background, Evan Jenkins. Allen was then in his late forties, the glories of bishoprics and a seat in the House of Lords still in the future, but living comfortably in London with his wife and two young sons. He must have seen something in the young Welshman that impressed him, and presumably it was Allen who dissuaded Evan from going straight into orders as his elder brother David had done. Allen's father had started the first bank in Manchester in 1771 (Byrom, Allen, Sedgwick and Place) but the same year that Allen started as a pensioner at Trinity College his father was made bankrupt. It doesn't seem to have affected his son's time at Trinity, but perhaps the experience made Joseph Allen sensitive to the pecuniary difficulties of others, and he was able to persuade Evan that even with little money, the 'motley spectacle' of Cambridge was not out of the question. As a former wrangler, Allen maybe helped Evan with his mathematics; and in December 1817 he examined him satisfactorily and wrote to Trinity requesting that Evan should be admitted as a sizar the following October. I now wanted to find out if Evan had been teaching at the Felix school in Chelsea. I needed to go back to Aberystwyth to see the Felix files.

* * *

The school in Chelsea advertised on 4 January 1814; like John Jay's in Woodford, it was offering book-keeping as well as the classics:

> Education in the Classics, Mathematics, and Arithmetic, including Book-Keeping (by Single and Double Entry) at Mr. Felix's School, late Mr. Edwards, Upper Cheyne-row, Chelsea. Mr. F. a Member of the University of Cambridge, and of considerable experience in his profession, is assisted by two of his brothers, educated, like himself, in every possible study of the Greek and Latin Classics, with other Sciences, at a reputable public school [presumably Ystrad Meurig] [...] The House is airy and commodious, with extensive grounds of recreation, in an open situation. The Young Gentlemen's domestic comforts have Mrs. F.'s immediate attention.[32]

David Felix has gone one up on John Jay's advertisements by mentioning his wife, which would attract the young gentlemen's mothers. He was also taking over a school, not starting from scratch. The school could accommodate fifty boarders, at forty guineas per annum. Rev. David was a 24-year-man at Trinity Hall, Cambridge (from 1821; a 'small' college) while his brother Rev. Peter was a ten-year-man at Trinity (from 1820, when his friend Evan was in his second year).

My guides really let me down here. Our occasional prisoner John Wright attempts to explain:

> Ten-Year-Men are so called because being admitted at college late in life [mature students], the Bishop immediately ordains them with the proviso that they reside at certain periods in the University, keep their names on the Boards, and keep certain Exercises in the Divinity Schools during ten years; or perhaps it is otherwise derived.[33]

That is not helpful! But he could have copied from the printed university calendar: a ten-year-man is aiming for a Bachelor in Divinity degree (BD). The man must be over twenty-four and reside in (any) college for three terms in his ninth and tenth years. His exercises (examinations) consist of 'one act', 'two opponencies, a clerum, and an English sermon'.[34] The BA man also does acts and opponencies, or instead does 'what is termed huddling'. In line with Wright's occasional flippancy, I merely state here that I will either explain some of these, or may not.[35]

Interestingly, according to the *Alumni Cantabrigienses* database, Lewis Jones, who was a pupil at Ystrad Meurig, became a ten-year-man at Trinity College in 1821, the year he was ordained priest, and while Evan was there. He was appointed Vicar at Almondbury, West Yorkshire, about fifteen miles south of Pudsey, in 1823, so he presumably knew both Evan and David, and perhaps he had been encouraged by Evan to become a ten-year-man. Another ten-year-man I am curious about in the database is Charles Williamson. His details are brief. He was admitted sizar at St John's College in 1816, born in Bengal, India, around 1792. He became chaplain at Smyrna in 1817, and died at Samos in Greece in 1820 (when he was presumably in his late twenties). So far, so typical of a missionary. The odd thing is that he left money for a scholarship to St John's for students from Ystrad Meurig. The only pupil of that school he might possibly have met at Cambridge was Evan.

* * *

March 2016, and I was back in my seat at the National Library of Wales to see the Felix folders. It was a strange preamble for what I was about to do: walk all the way from Machynlleth to Conwy through Snowdonia, over ninety miles, as my son's guinea pig, testing out his newly created Snowdonia Way.[36] Charlotte Brontë and Arthur Nicholls spent the first night of their honeymoon in Conwy, on 29 June 1854.[37] Charlotte mentions one drive they took from Llanberis, at the foot of Snowdon, to Beddgelert, which 'surpassed anything I remember of the English Lakes'. It is possible that they stayed at the Goat Hotel in Beddgelert.[38] I arrived there in the dusk, freezing cold and dripping wet, never wanting to walk ever again. Numerous heaters to put my wet layers on, and a hot supper and wine, rallied me hugely.

Peter Felix's folders were catalogued under Roberts & Evans (solicitors). There were about eleven folders and I waded, ever more wearily, through all of them, my fingers getting blacker and blacker. It seemed that everything had been kept: numerous accounts, all muddled together, from the parish of St Luke, Chelsea for 'amendment and preservation of the highways', church rates, water rents, and stuff from Llanilar, a village in Cardiganshire where Peter was vicar. One interesting item was a memorandum from Chelsea dated 13 January 1822 in which Rev. John Rush (who had signed David Jenkins's testimonial in 1810) agreed that Rev. Peter Felix would 'assist in the Duty of Chelsea Parish for One Year' for £63. Peter was to do 'half the Duty every Sunday & the occasional Duties to be performed during the rest of the week to be equally divided'.[39] It seems that both his curate, Peter Felix, and John Rush were pluralists.

In another folder I found a letter from Rev. Peter Felix dated 1831, from 5 Markham Place, King's Road, Chelsea, to an unnamed man concerning his possible curacy at John Rush's living: 'I think you may almost consider yourself the future curate of Hartwell. I have this morning recommended you in the strongest terms to my worthy friend Mr Rush.' That is how it worked: connections, recommendations. Peter Felix was living in Markham Place in 1829 when he subscribed to Thomas Faulkner's guidebook to Chelsea.[40] In another folder I unearthed a reference to his elder brother David's death at Chelsea in July 1829 (he was forty-nine and was buried at St Luke's). In the very last folder I found a piece of paper headed 'Peter Felix's Acct. with D. Felix', dated 1817.[41] Maybe Evan Jenkins had finally made an appearance.

The Account is a list of monies gone out in the left-hand column on various dates between 1814 and 1820, and in the right-hand column monies coming in: £661 9d going out, £624 10s 6d coming in. What had caught my eye was the item of money going out above the entry 'To Hughes's Salary 20.0.0': it read 'To Jenkin Evans 4.8.0' in July 1817, when Evan Jenkins was presumably in Chelsea. 'Jenkin' was fine because of the fluidity of Welsh surnames, but 'Evans' was odd. Even if Rev. David Felix rather than Peter Felix had written the account, he surely knew Evan well and wouldn't distort his name. I had to dismiss it. In Evan's 1823 letter from Brussels to David Richards in Wales (the same man who had witnessed his father's will), Evan writes about Richards's son finding work as a teacher in London: 'I was sorry to find that fewer situations were vacant last Christmas [1822] than in any year since I first came to England.' I am certain that Evan was teaching in London before going to Cambridge, but whether at a school or privately has not been discovered.

Rev. Peter Felix was about the same age as Evan. He died in 1861 at his parish in Llanilar (or, rather, one of his parishes, as he also held the living of Easton Neston in Northamptonshire), about ten miles north of Evan's childhood home; it seems that after his brother's death in Chelsea in 1829, Peter, then in his mid-thirties, moved back to Cardiganshire. His only child – a daughter, Eliza Ann – died at the age of only a few weeks and was buried in Chelsea in 1826. According to the obituary of Peter in the *Aberystwith Observer* in 1861, he had been in Llanilar for thirty years, and given free education to the poor.[42] But what is slightly startling is that 'England and the West Indies were the spheres of his labour' before he moved back to Wales. You think you have the gist of someone's life after just a few details, and then something, here the West Indies, is thrown into the mix, presumably in connection with missionary or anti-slavery work. I have only guessed that he knew Evan from school at Ystrad Meurig, but maybe it is confirmed by the obituarist: 'The burial service in the church was read by the Rev. L. Evans, master of the Ystradmeurig Grammar School.' As Evan's best friend almost forty years before, what can it tell us about Evan? '[I]n him the poor of the parish have lost a kind benefactor. He was always ready with outstretching hand to relieve their wants, and that without distinction in party or creed. He was of a truly christian and benevolent spirit.' Peter's sermons were 'evangelical, doctrinal, and practical'. And 'His life was a pattern of the minister, the christian, and the gentleman.' About twenty-two ministers followed his coffin. One has to read sceptically between the lines of a eulogy, but the 'twenty-two ministers' is astounding. Peter Felix's haphazard nature of dealing with bills and payments, as shown by his Account around 1820, is surely a minor misdeed – exasperating to his older brother – but perfectly acceptable in the context of the life of a good man, who maybe valued the friendship of another good man, Evan Jenkins.

* * *

I can therefore only guess, but on good grounds, that Evan was teaching in London from about 1814, when he was twenty, until October 1818, when he arrived for his first term at Cambridge. Presuming he was in Chelsea, he might have encountered the Stevenson family. Indeed, his elder brother David might have also. Some readers may not recognize the name Elizabeth Cleghorn

Stevenson, born in Chelsea in 1810, but most will know her authorial name as Mrs Gaskell. But before I try to unravel a possible Stevenson acquaintanceship with the Jenkins brothers in Chelsea, I must go back a few years to Edinburgh, where the names of two men, already met with in previous chapters, crop up in a way that might be considered too coincidental in a novel.

Elizabeth Gaskell's father William Stevenson gave up teaching the classics as a young man when he decided it was useless for the modern world. He published a pamphlet, *Remarks on the Very Inferior Utility of Classical Learning*, in 1796, and took over a farm near Edinburgh with his new wife Elizabeth. But after poor harvests they moved into the Old Town in 1801 and let lodgings to students. William became editor of the monthly *Scots Magazine* in 1803, one of whose contributors was a lawyer – Walter Scott. If the Jay family knew Walter Scott, as I consider likely, then John and Helen Jay, Eliza's parents, could have known the Stevensons. If the reader thinks my hypotheses are stretching it a bit, then the next man who makes a reappearance could be just another coincidence, or could be a clue to close links between the Jays of Lixmount and the Stevensons: William Stevenson was asked to become private secretary to none other than the man who had stayed in John Jay's father's house in Andover for a month in 1777. This was the eccentric James Maitland, eighth Earl of Lauderdale. In 1806 Maitland was in his forties and about to be made Governor-General of India. The proposed appointment was greeted with hostility and did not go ahead, but meanwhile the Stevensons had moved to Chelsea in expectation of William receiving the post of private secretary. However, Maitland did not let William down: he found him a job as keeper of the records at the Treasury and he stayed in Chelsea for the rest of his life.[43]

When I first read Jenny Uglow's biography of Elizabeth Gaskell the name Maitland meant absolutely nothing. But the digitalization of that note left by Professor Dalziel in Salisbury emphatically connected the eighth Earl of Lauderdale with the Jay family. It was like a scene in a detective series where photos are pinned on the board and gradually lines of connection appear between seemingly totally unconnected people. Were either Eliza or Mrs Gaskell aware of the possible connection between their families when they met in Brussels in May 1856? As Jenny Uglow remarks, Mrs Gaskell had a 'burrowing curiosity' and Victorians busily talked about each other, so the short conversation as reported in the biography of Charlotte Brontë may well be simply the relevant anecdote from a much longer chat.[44] One interesting detail about her father that Mrs Gaskell might have known, is that before his marriage William Stevenson had gone to

Bruges as tutor to an English student, returning to England in 1793 when war broke out between England and France. Bruges is north-west of Brussels, on the way to Ostend, where Eliza often took her family on holiday, and she would know the town well. They would have much to talk about.

William Stevenson was a prolific writer, ranging from agriculture, naval history and political economy to a life of William Caxton. He would have been a well-known name in Chelsea circles in David's time there (1807–10) and later Evan's, and a well-known face, which was disfigured by 'a severe leprous complaint'.[45] The future writer Elizabeth, their eighth child, was born on 29 September 1810 in Lindsey Row, now Cheyne Walk on the Thames Embankment (there is a plaque on the house), a few yards from the Old Church where David had his 'Si Quis' announced in June that year. The family then moved to nearby 3 Beaufort Row (now demolished), but Elizabeth's mother was ill and died aged forty in October 1811. The baby Elizabeth and her brother John, then thirteen, were the only surviving children. The baby was taken in by her maternal aunt in Knutsford, Cheshire – which became the fictional Cranford – making lengthy visits to Chelsea to stay with her father and his new wife.[46] Her visits were often miserable, as she wrote in a letter years later:

> Long ago I lived in Chelsea occasionally[,] with my father and stepmother, and *very, very* unhappy I used to be; and if it had not been for the beautiful, grand river, which was an inexplicable comfort to me [...] I think my child's heart would have broken.[47]

The family were nonconformist Unitarians, but Elizabeth's half-sister Catherine was baptized in the Old Church at Chelsea in June 1817, and her father William's funeral was held at the new parish church of St Luke's in 1829, so they possibly attended services at the Old Church. Indeed Elizabeth often went to an Anglican church in later life.[48] Evan Jenkins may have noticed an unhappy little girl tucked into one of the high-walled pews with a stepmother who disliked her. I find it so strange but enchanting that this child would one day, fifty years later, mention this dark-haired young Welshman in one of the most famous biographies ever written, and refer to his elder brother (without name) who may have had fierce arguments with her father about the utility of a classical education. Could even William Stevenson's anecdotes about his time as a private tutor in Belgium have lodged themselves in Evan's mind? Only connect.

* * *

In June 1817, Evan's older sister Mary married Moses Roderick of Llangeitho (the Methodist village down the hill) at the Llanbadarn Odwyn church, a few fields from her home at Penycastell. She was seven months pregnant. As I mentioned in an earlier chapter, she was able to sign her name in the register; Moses made his mark. There is a huge gulf between the world her brothers lived in – Evan possibly teaching the classics in London; David with his Anglican congregation in Yorkshire – and her rural, Methodist, Welsh life. David did not go to Wales to marry them; the couple were married by the curate, Dan. Lewis. Nor did either brother witness the wedding – witnesses were Peter Davies and Stephen Evans (probably relatives), both of whom signed their names. Surely Evan went to Wales to see his mother and sister when he could, but maybe June was term time. Perhaps David's duties in Yorkshire and his two young children made the journey too difficult – these were Harriet born in 1814 and Joseph two years later, both of whom would know the Brontës. But the absence of David's name in particular makes me wonder if he disapproved of the marriage.

At the time of their wedding, Mary and Moses were about twenty-eight; their first son, Evan, was baptized two months later – perhaps brother Evan was there and was a godfather. The marriage had been by banns, not by any hurried licence: her pregnancy at marriage wasn't unusual in Cardiganshire.[49] Moses was prominent in the Calvinistic Methodist chapel of Llwynpiod down the lane on the Roman road, but David had grown up in this Methodist stronghold, thus Methodism seems unlikely to have been the problem. Perhaps it was that Moses was illiterate, and that Mary's £50 'dowry' in David's eyes had been thrown away on someone unworthy of her. And I sense that a huge gulf had opened up between the highly educated brothers and their sister and her husband. The name Roderick doesn't crop up in any of my family records, whereas the connection between David's and Evan's families lasted into the twentieth century. Mary and Moses stayed on at Penycastell, farming, and had six more children. Some descendants left Wales, moving to England, South Africa and Wisconsin, and it seems that the family only finally left their tenanted farmhouse about a hundred years after their ancestor, farmer Evan Jenkins, had died there around 1806. Both Mary and Moses have prominent gravestones outside the little church of Llanbadarn Odwyn with its wonderful Scots pines, above the Vale of Aeron.

* * *

Cambridge, start of term, Saturday 10 October 1818.[50] The excitement at arriving at university was often followed by disillusionment, then as now:

> The man who has expended four years within the walls of this University, has either attended to her peculiar studies, and acquired knowledge which is useless; or he has not, and he departs more ignorant than he came.[51]

So wrote Solomon Atkinson, some nine years after he was admitted to Cambridge, in an anonymous article. Yet this angry wrangler, who was at Trinity for some of the same years as Evan, had 'started with a heart full of glee and joyous anticipation for the great seat of learning and science',[52] and he came top in the final university examinations. As senior wrangler, maybe he expected the prizes of life to fall into his lap; when they didn't he became angry. As a mature student, Evan may have been more realistic about what he intended to get out of Cambridge. But Atkinson's experience is useful as he came from a similarly poor background, and faced Evan across the sizars' dinner table at Trinity, though his account is often weirdly melodramatic and vituperative – perhaps he needed the money and that is what the *London Magazine and Review* wanted (and one wonders how much the editor rewrote his piece to create a bit of sensationalism).

Atkinson claims that he was the son of a 'Cumbrian peasant' and proceeds to vilify his parents by stating that they took on a farm and 'expended their little means in mismanaging it', and that only his grandfather understood his desire for education and gave him some money. He comes across as thoroughly nasty, arrogant and selfish. What is more interesting is how he got into Cambridge. And here comes more melodrama: he describes the jobs he had to do on the farm in italics, poor soul: 'tending sheep, *herding* cattle [...] *hoeing* turnips' while reading Virgil, Xenophon and Euclid. Why does his life remind me of a sketch in *Monty Python's Flying Circus*? With his grandfather's money (£100) promised, he needed to get in contact with someone from Cambridge. But where in this 'remote and barbarous district' could he find such a man? He discovered that the Dean of Carlisle, Dr Isaac Milner, was the man, as he was also President of Queens' College, Cambridge. (In my ear I can hear Thomas De Quincey snorting with laughter – see below.)

So Atkinson, well aware how 'rude and untutored' he is, decides to walk twenty miles to see Dr Milner, and it is obviously through 'rain and hail and snow' with a specific north-easterly wind. Dr Milner, who had been admitted as a sizar in 1770 to Cambridge, and became senior wrangler, is luckily in Carlisle rather than in Cambridge, his head wrapped in a turban; he is reposing on a sofa. Atkinson is grilled on what he has read in Latin and Greek, and answers satisfactorily about Virgil, Horace and the Greek Testament, and is then asked if he knows anything of mathematics, especially knowledge of Euclid, which was important for Cambridge:

> 'Can you demonstrate the forty-seventh proposition?' I was lost. I had read Euclid, I knew it thoroughly; but had never considered it expedient to know the propositions by number. He immediately recollected himself, 'I should have given you the enunciation, – I mean the proposition about the square of the hypothenuse.' I forthwith scrawled the diagram on a slip of paper, and went through the proposition. This was 'very satisfactory, very good, very good indeed.' And so we went on for a very considerable length of time. He then opened the question of my finances.[53]

Atkinson had wanted to go to one of the large colleges, Trinity or St John's, but Dr Milner persuaded him to go to his own college, Queens'. Then Milner 'wrote to Mr. Barnes, the senior tutor, stating in substance that he had examined me, found me competent, and desiring him without delay to admit me a Sizar'. And that is maybe exactly how Evan went to Trinity: perhaps he likewise saw Rev. Allen only the once for his examination and recommendation. We may never know. Except that *someone* had influenced him about Cambridge. As for Atkinson, in his second year at Queens' he migrated a short walk along the Cam to Trinity the same year that Evan arrived (apparently because there was a better chance of getting a Fellowship at Trinity since the Queens' quota for his county was full).

Thomas De Quincey laughing? Maybe, because he naughtily outed Dr Milner, Dean of Carlisle (1750–1820), as an opium eater in his *Confessions*, along with Milner's erstwhile pupil William Wilberforce. He has a long footnote about Dean Milner in one edition of his bestselling book. The footnote is fairly tedious about Milner's church pluralism and sympathies, but ends that as 'an opium-eater, Dean Milner was understood to be a strenuous wrestler with the physical necessity that coerced him into this habit. From several quarters I have heard that his daily *ration* was 34 grains (or about 850 drops of laudanum), divided into four portions, and administered to him at regular intervals of six hours by a confidential valet.'[54] Isaac's elder brother, Joseph Milner, was the great teacher at Hull grammar school to whom William Wilberforce was indebted for his education; Isaac was briefly an usher in his brother's school, even though he had had to leave school at twelve.[55] But Isaac Milner was hugely more than these anecdotes: he was a chemist who corresponded with Joseph Priestley, an evangelist and the converter of William Wilberforce, an author, anti-slave-trader, professor of mathematics; he was also very large in size, had an 'astonishing intellect' and a 'peculiar lifestyle': he enjoyed running naked through the garden at Queens'.[56]

* * *

> A sizar at a Cambridge college [...] has not pleasant days, or used not to have them half a century ago [1830s]; but his position was recognised, and the misery was measured.

So wrote Anthony Trollope in his *Autobiography*. He failed on several occasions to get a scholarship or sizarship to Oxbridge in the early 1830s and is here comparing his misery as a 'sizar' at fashionable Harrow School – we might call him a scholarship boy, on charity. He continues: 'What right had a wretched farmer's boy, reeking from a dunghill, to sit next to the sons of peers, – or much worse still, next to the sons of big tradesmen who had made their ten thousand a-year?'[57] He exaggerates the dunghill though not the misery, but was he accurate that being a sizar at Cambridge in Evan's time could be a degrading experience?

A guide to Cambridge in 1804 states that 'sizars are generally men of inferior fortune, though frequently by their merit they succeed to the highest honors in the University. Most of our Church Dignatories have been of this order.'[58] But surely they were *always* 'of inferior fortune'. *The Cambridge University Calendar* for 1822 gives some of the reduced fees that sizars paid. For example, the 'caution' money paid on admission to his tutor at a man's college was £15 for a pensioner, £10 for a sizar. A nobleman provided instead valuable plate. Quarterly tuition was £2 10s for a pensioner, 15s for a sizar. Matriculation fees were £1 10s and 15s respectively. Various benefactions were divided among sizars at Trinity College, and also noblemen and fellow commoners paid sizars a few guineas each quarter.[59] How that worked is not explained. A further complication is that some sizars were 'foundation sizars', who had begun paying their fees in advance and were thus entitled to rooms and other 'perks' (a room in college was indeed a perk; some undergraduates had to live in lodgings in the town, at least at the beginning). I have found no list of who was and was not a foundation sizar, but the *Cambridge University Calendar* lists forty-three undergraduates who were sizars at Trinity in 1822, including Evan Jenkins.[60] If it might be slightly demoralizing to receive the crumbs (or guineas) from the rich men's tables, then on the other hand the sizars had strength and solidarity in their numbers.

Twenty years later, the New Yorker Charles Bristed commented that sizars in former times 'waited on the Fellows at dinner, but this practice has long been abolished'. He was admitted as a (rich) fellow commoner, who dined with the

Fellows, and knew the practice in the 1840s. The only difference between sizars and 'others' that he mentions was that sizars dined later in the hall.[61] This was true in Evan's day, as a contemporary confirms: George Biddell Airy, later Astronomer Royal. Sitting with Evan at the Trinity sizars' dinner table were two future senior wranglers – Atkinson ('the angry wrangler') and Airy. Both were helped into Cambridge by an extraordinary man who had an equally extraordinary brother, and both sets of brothers were intimately acquainted with William Wilberforce. In Atkinson's case it was the formidably clever educationists, the Milner brothers. In Airy's it was the great anti-slave traders, the Clarkson brothers.

George Biddell Airy (1801–92) was from an old family who had subsided under hardships in the previous century. His father was a self-educated man who rose from farm labourer to collector of excise, finally moving to Essex in 1810, when his eldest son George was eight. He lost his job and they lived in comparative poverty, but he managed to maintain his son's school education.[62] Airy junior went to school at Colchester and frequently spent holidays with his maternal uncle at Playford, a village near Ipswich in Suffolk. His uncle not only had a good library, with books on optics, chemistry, modern poets and Scott's Waverley novels, but his neighbours from around 1816 were the renowned, indefatigable slavery abolitionist Thomas Clarkson (1760–1846) and his wife Catherine, who had become a close friend of William Wordsworth's sister Dorothy when the Clarksons had lived near Ullswater in the Lake District. After the abolition of the British slave trade in 1807, Wordsworth wrote a sonnet in praise of Clarkson, who, like him, had attended St John's College, Cambridge, though some eight years previously (Clarkson almost overlapped with Wilberforce at St John's). When the Clarksons moved south to Playford Hall, Thomas, now in his fifties, was busy with his mainly Quaker colleagues on the next prong of abolition – ending the slave trade internationally.[63]

In George Biddell Airy's *Autobiography*, edited posthumously by his son Wilfrid (published in 1896), Airy comments that his schoolmaster had recommended he go on to college (Oxford or Cambridge), but when his father found out it would cost £200 a year, the idea was dropped. But his uncle did not give up: in about 1816 he asked Thomas Clarkson to examine the teenaged Airy on his classical knowledge; as Airy remembers: 'he did so, I think, twice. He also gave some better information about the probable expenses &c. at College. The result was a strong recommendation by my uncle [...] that I should be sent to Cambridge, and this was adopted by my father.' Obviously Clarkson had told Airy's father about sizarships and possible exhibitions and prizes. Thereafter Airy progressed rapidly in mathematics, usually from his own reading as his teacher couldn't keep up; he also spent time at school translating from the *Aeneid* and *Iliad*, and, his son Wilfrid comments endearingly, he 'read through the whole of Sophocles *very carefully*'.[64]

Since we are spending a little time with Airy, it is helpful to know what he looked like. There is a photograph of him taken in 1864, in his early sixties.[65] He is sitting, but from a clue about his 'middle height' I would guess he was around five foot eight inches; sandy haired and lean, bony, not unhandsome. He holds his spectacles in his left hand (he was astigmatic and made several of his own); his eyes look sharply intelligent as he looks to the side and he has a wide (sensual?) mouth. In looks only, I might cast the film actor Steve McQueen to play him. I have digressed a little; he and Evan Jenkins knew each other at Trinity, but whether on nodding terms, or whether he visited the Jenkinses in Brussels, I don't know, but Airy's impressively wide interests, his independence of thought, liberalism, courtesy, professionalism and gift for friendship (as reported by his son) make me hope they might have been more than nodding acquaintances in chapel and hall at Trinity.

Thomas Clarkson suggested to the family that young Airy should go to St Peter's College (Peterhouse), Cambridge, but then Clarkson told a friend of his about Airy, who urged that the young man should go instead to Trinity. And in our spider's web of connections at this period, Clarkson's friend is James D. Hustler, tutor at Trinity College, who was also Evan's tutor. And so it was settled, and Hustler had bagged a future senior wrangler in the battle between the colleges. Airy was examined privately in 1819, in the company of Clarkson, by an MA of Trinity, Rev. Rogers, who lived nearby, 'and I was entered on Mr Hustler's side as Sizar of Trinity College'.[66] He arrived at Trinity on 18 October 1819 with letters of introduction to various Fellows of Trinity, including the geologist Professor Sedgwick. Young Airy's precocious skill in mathematics had preceded him. There is nothing obvious to suggest that being a sizar affected him – perhaps because he was too clever, or maybe discrimination was negligible. But there is a hint: one difference was dinner time in hall. In talking about his afternoons he merely states at first:

> At 2 or a little sooner I went out for a long walk, usually 4 or 5 miles into the country: sometimes if I found companions I rowed on the Cam [...] A little before 4 I returned, and at 4 went to College Hall. After dinner I lounged till evening chapel time, ½ past 5, and returning about 6 I then had tea.

Then I read quietly, usually a classical subject, till 11; and I never, even in the times when I might seem most severely pressed, sat up later.

However, later he adds: 'The Sizars dined after all the rest; their dinner usually began soon after 4.'[67] Bristed, twenty years later, is clear: sizars dine 'after the Fellows on the remains of their table'.[68] Eating separately perhaps niggled Airy – note that he says about sizars 'their dinner', not 'our'. Psychologically it is not surprising: dining after the 'great ones' had eaten must have rankled. But if that was the only college discrimination between ordinary students (that is, pensioners – I shall ignore fellow commoners and the odd nobleman) and the poor sizars on 'charity' then it was better at Trinity than at some of the smaller colleges. Angry wrangler Atkinson confirms that the 'degrading duties and services' that sizars used to perform are 'now abolished at Cambridge', but in the small colleges the sizars had to wear 'a paltry kind of gown, which I am sure no parish clerk or beadle in the kingdom would put on', whereas at Trinity everyone wore purple fustian. He gives an anecdote about Dean (opium-eater) Isaac Milner, President of Queens' College. When Milner was a sizar at Queens' in the 1770s he had to ring the chapel bell in the morning and serve the first dish to the Fellows at dinner:

> Happening one day to scatter on the floor of the hall the tureen of soup which was to regale the Fellows, he is said to have exclaimed, in reply to some sharp rebuke, 'By G— but when I get into power I will do away with this nuisance.' 'When I get into power' was the subject of many a burst of laughter over the bottle. They could not see, under his rough dialect and unpolished manners, the future President of the College.[69]

* * *

It is time to rejoin our guide, future jailbird Wright, for a tour of the 'magnificent glories' of Trinity. The grand entrance is the King's Gate, on Trinity Street. The brown and cream battlemented gate is of three storeys, with slender turrets on either side. Above the arched wooden doors stands a statue of the founder of the college (in 1546), Henry VIII, wielding a wooden chair leg instead of a sceptre (an old student prank). Wright is enthusiastic that here is where Isaac Newton had his observatory. Unfortunately, he says, it had recently been barbarously destroyed. Through the gate extends the Great Court, its paths and green lawns, 'which is certainly romantic in the extreme, from the dimensions, aided by the turrets, pinnacles, and embattlements which are lavished upon the venerable stone buildings in ample profusion'. On the right stands the 'stately gothic pile' of the college chapel, and the ante-chapel, whose organ he was longing to hear. Ahead is the magnificent seventeenth-century hall. But there is a slight delay as the Master's servant has been sent to reprimand Wright for wearing trousers instead of breeches and gaiters.

In Wright's day the hall could seat 400–500 on benches at tables placed end to end, just as today. Only at the high table, elevated on a dais, where sat the Fellows, noblemen, fellow commoners and their guests, was there one chair for the vice-master. Wainscoting around the hall gives it a warmth that was vital in the cold winter months, supplemented by candles on the tables, and a fireplace. The ceiling soars high with its glorious hammerbeam roof; the tall windows have much heraldic glass: both the roof and many of the windows remain from Evan's and Wright's day. Wright has returned after his reprimand; he was threatened with being 'put out of sizings and commons', that is, banned for a while from ordering extra food from the kitchen and from eating in hall, but he pleaded successfully. He points to the portraits of Newton and Bacon above the high table at the far end, and the portraits of 'the illustrious dead' on the wainscoting. Although a sizar, he describes dinner in hall with the whole throng of undergraduates:

> I had played a good knife and fork into a defunct cod's head, and limb of a bullock, and had somewhat diminished the pies, puddings, jellies, *blue*mange (as the squint-eyed waitress behind me for years pronounced it), and trifle [...] The conversation on this occasion, at the upper ends of the tables, where sat the seniors of the several species of flat-caps, was doubtless very superior; for it seemed to excite great merriment amongst all who heard it – and it may also be reasonably inferred that these elder brothers should strive to lord it over the youngsters.[70]

As a freshman he kept quiet, and was obviously well fed, especially as the day he describes was a Saint's Day or Fast Day. Next stop, the chapel.

If we expected the experience at chapel to be a solemn religious experience, Wright's description of a service sounds exactly like getting by mistake onto a school bus: 'there is not one man who goes to *pray*'. Chapel was compulsory for a certain number of morning (at 7 a.m.) and evening services, or, as Wright says, '"There is no compulsion" in this Chapel-going, "only you must"'. Punishment for not going might be learning by heart a satire by Juvenal or a section of Homer 'and, in short, to do so many disagreeables, that the very recollection of them makes my pen drop'.[71] The undergraduate's name was pricked on a list with a pin during the service. Some who wanted a lie in after a night of hard reading or a bit of debauchery might bribe the markers – the men with the pins. The students sat in long choir stalls facing each other along the length of the chapel, and Wright enjoys many pages of describing the whispered conversations that took place, from discussing a lecture or the amount of claret drunk the night before, to boasting about fights with the townsmen or passing on gossip about Fellows. On his first visit he notices that the men arriving are all wearing surplices, since it is a Fast day; he is quickly lent one that is far too long, but apart from a few stumbles in it, he is saved from embarrassment. It seems to have been a great joke among the senior years when a freshman wore a surplice at a non-surplice service, and vice versa. But Wright is delighted at the sight of the surpliced: 'The chapel was thronged to excess [...] and the spectacle, presenting in long parallel lines, one rising above another, the select youth of Britain, pure and unspotted (at least in appearance) as their angelic vests, was to me, at first sight, as it were, a peep into Heaven.'[72] And then the 'fine undulating swells of the organ (the best perhaps in the kingdom)' sounds, and he is transported. It surely entranced Evan Jenkins, too: in 1840 his congregation subscribed to the cost of a wonderful new organ for the Chapel Royal, which the Brontë sisters heard, and perhaps especially Emily loved.[73]

* * *

Evan arrived at the porter's lodge of Trinity in October 1818, no doubt with a letter of introduction from Rev. Allen to his new tutor, Mr Hustler. James Devereux Hustler had also been admitted as a sizar; he became third wrangler in 1806 and, according to Airy, gave the third-year lectures in mathematics. He wrote a book on *The Elements of the Conic Sections* (1820) and was, in addition, a good classicist, having won the second Chancellor's Classical medal in 1806. Hustler was just ten years older than Evan; he had been ordained priest in 1809 after becoming a Fellow. He was to leave Trinity a year after Evan graduated in order to marry, and acquired a church living (or two) in Suffolk.[74] I can find nothing colourful about him, except that the place he is buried (in 1849) – Euston, Suffolk – is a green and gorgeous village. His brother William was a Fellow at Jesus College, and was the tutor of Evan's friend William Branwhite Clarke, whom we shall meet later in Brussels. Since Clarke was younger and at a different college, if they met at Cambridge rather than later it might have been through the Hustler brothers. Tutors were little involved in the academic lives of those undergraduates admitted 'on their side', they dealt with money, fees, and awarded exhibitions in the gift of the college. Angry wrangler Atkinson turns his venom on a tutor at Queens':

Mr. K—g [...] graduated some five or six years ago. He was Senior Wrangler, and took that degree with higher distinction than perhaps any other man ever did. He *might* have been one of the first mathematicians of Europe: he *is* the tutor of a college. His extraordinary powers of acquisition, the energy of his mind, and the vigour of his temperament, are wholly employed in making up college bills, arranging college squabbles, and looking after the morals of Freshmen. His knowledge of mathematical science *was* most extensive, and his mastery over it complete. At present the game of whist is his favourite study [...] The man that might have rescued the name of English science from contempt is fast approaching the honours of a three-bottle man in a tippling college, and of the best whist player in a gambling University.[75]

Perhaps we should move swiftly on to the lectures in the first year. Oh dear, Atkinson is muttering away now about the lectures, he was 'wretchedly disappointed': college lectures 'are in general little more than a kind of desultory conversation, – meagre, unconnected, and barren', they are 'universally voted a *bore*'.[76] I shall let him mutter on. Wright knew Atkinson and of his criticisms in the popular press, and hit back: Atkinson, Wright writes, was 'gifted with as vigorous an intellect as any I ever fell in with, and yet as to the imaginative, inventive faculties, as barren as the desert [...] any thing original, whether in the Classics or Mathematics from him, were a forlorn hope [...] So much for Solomon.'[77] Touché.

* * *

Wright, admitted sizar, lived first in lodgings in King's Street, near Christ's College; there was no room at Trinity and his father could afford the expense. But in July 1814 Sheath's Bank in Boston, Lincolnshire failed and the owners were made bankrupt, their ships put up for auction.[78] It wasn't the only bank to fail and many people were ruined; Wright says that his father's finances had become exhausted by that bank failure and that his tutor offered him free rooms in college that hadn't been assigned to anyone because they were so dilapidated. There was 'no paper to the walls, no doors' and Wright refused the first offered rooms as he couldn't afford to decorate and fit them up. But there was also one tiny, six-sided room in a turret of the Great Court which Wright grabbed at, as there was no alternative. Byron had had rooms on the same staircase and Wright says that he kept his 'immense' bear in the same hexagonal turret room.[79] The legend, and the bear, may have grown over a decade – Fiona MacCarthy in her biography of

Byron thinks that the bear was probably small and instead lived in the stables. Wright obviously loved his little turret, where he entertained a squash of friends, and held impromptu concerts with fiddle and flute.[80]

Another sizar, George Airy, also started in lodgings, this time in Bridge Street, slightly nearer Trinity than Wright's first lodgings. When impecunious Atkinson migrated from Queens' to Trinity he also had to live in town for the first year; he was only able to pay for his accommodation by taking on a pupil.[81] Pensioners also might first live in lodgings – Macaulay lived in Jesus Lane, near Jesus College. When he moved into rooms at college he hoped that the mattress would be dry and that he wouldn't be eaten by rats, so maybe lodgings were sometimes preferable if you could afford them.[82] Samuel Taylor Coleridge might agree. Coleridge, just turned sixty, stayed with a friend at Trinity for a scientific conference in 1833. He noted that his bed was 'as near as I can describe it a couple of sacks full of potatoes tied together [...] Truly I lay down at night a man, and arose in the morning a bruise.'[83]

A decade after Airy, Alfred Tennyson and his brother Charles were admitted as pensioners at Trinity; their elder brother Frederick was at St John's. The shy younger brothers also first lived in lodgings.[84] In April 1828, a few months after he arrived, Alfred wrote to his aunt:

> I am sitting owl-like and solitary in my rooms (nothing between me and the stars but a stratum of tiles). The hoof of the steed, the roll of the wheel, the shouts of drunken Gown, and drunken Town come up from below with a sea-like murmur. I wish to Heaven I had Prince Hussain's fairy carpet to transport me along the deeps of air to your coteries [...] What a pity it is that the golden days of Faerie are over! What a misery not to be able to consolidate our gossamer dreams into reality! When, my dearest Aunt, may I hope to see you again? I know not how it is, but I feel isolated here in the midst of society. The country is so disgustingly level, the revelry of the place so monotonous, the studies of the University so uninteresting, so much matter of fact. None but dry-headed, calculating, angular little gentlemen can take much delight in them.[85]

In Christopher Ricks's biography of Tennyson he comments on this letter that there 'is something blasé about such drawling dissatisfaction', which seems to me to miss Tennyson's mood utterly.[86] Many twenty-first-century undergraduates might well recognize in Tennyson's words their own depression and isolation during their first months at university. It seems that until he met his soulmate, Arthur Hallam, about a year later, Tennyson was lonely and unhappy. He longs to see his aunt, but is certainly not homesick for his home. His mother had died a few years before, and though his elder brother had been sent to Eton and acquired friends, the younger brothers had been taught by their violent, alcoholic father. Forty years before Tennyson's arrival at Trinity, there was a homesick new undergraduate at neighbouring St John's, who later remembered that 'from the first crude days / Of settling-time in this my new abode, / Not seldom I had melancholy thoughts, / From personal and family regards'. Wordsworth.[87] A feeling of depression, deflation, after the first excitement of arriving at college is familiar over the centuries.

Since Evan had presumably been working in London for some years and was about five years older than Tennyson or Wordsworth when they arrived at Cambridge, I doubt if he felt homesick. But perhaps he was also lonely at first, being so much older. Thackeray's historical novel *The History of Henry Esmond* is set in the early eighteenth century. Henry goes to Trinity College – for once Thackeray doesn't disguise the name:

> But he had the ill-fortune to be older by a couple of years than most of his fellow-students; and by his previous solitary mode of bringing up, the circumstances of his life, and the peculiar thoughtfulness and melancholy that had naturally engendered, he was, in a great measure, cut off from the society of comrades who were much younger and higher-spirited than he [...] When the lads used to assemble in their *grèges* [college slang for 'groups'] in hall, Harry found himself alone in the midst of that little flock of boys.[88]

But Thackeray doesn't leave us feeling too sorry for Harry for long. Frankly Harry was being oversensitive, his own pride and vanity were at fault: if you go around looking glum, most people will avoid you.

I couldn't establish from my guides' experiences whether Evan would have lived in college when he first arrived, though when a room became available he might be able to move in. From Wright's story it does seem that the tutor would not have let a student pay for lodgings if they really couldn't afford it. But it is possible that if Evan had to live outside college that he was paying for it by teaching.

* * *

All Trinity freshmen had to attend the mathematical lecture given, in Wright's time, by Mr Brown at 9 a.m., followed at 10 a.m. by the Greek lecture given by Professor Monk. These were not lectures as we might know them today. Wright is vivid in his recollections: 'After chapel I had scarcely time to breakfast before St. Mary's [the university church] struck nine – the hour for the Mathematical Lecture. Palpitating at all points, I "wended my way" to the Lecture-room, which presently received about a hundred of us.'[89] In chapel and hall the men were segregated according to their 'rank', but here they sat 'indiscriminately'. The lecturer stood on a rostrum and the students were supplied with pens, ink and paper. 'Mr. Brown very learnedly inquired of us, one by one, if we knew our own names.' (I think that if he had gone to Cambridge 150 years later, Wright might have been a member of Footlights.) 'The first gentleman addressed, foreseeing that the portentous question was about to be popped to him, turned pale as ashes, and with some difficulty pronounced the word most familiar to him.' Mr Brown inquires if they had brought with them a case of mathematical instruments: eager students produce their cases. Mr Brown smiles and tells them to put them away and not bring them again, as he presumes they can all draw a straight line and a circle. He sends them away early, telling them to prepare the first book of Euclid's *Elements*, on which he will ask them questions. 'Very good. Good morning, gentlemen.' He is an encouraging, friendly teacher, constantly reassuring with his 'very good'. At the second lecture he summarizes: 'Step by step, gentlemen, we hence shall climb successively, as by a tower of Babel, the several rounds of Geometry, of Algebra, of the Analytics generally, of Mechanics, and Optics, winding our way to the topmost pinnacle – Astronomy.' Wright made this speech up: he remarks that Brown 'either did, or did not deliver this speech'. But it was the gist. No wonder the lecturer was referred to affectionately as Johnny Brown.[90]

The students all trotted back at ten, on the first morning, to Professor Monk's lecture on Greek, in the room above the mathematics lecture room. He also dismissed them early, telling them to prepare Aeschylus' *Seven Against Thebes* for the next morning. Professor Monk was always thus addressed. 'Stiff and formal to a degree,' Wright says, 'he could never relax into a smile, much less could he endure anything bordering upon jocularity, however pleasant might be the subject of his lectures, or admit the slightest familiarity from these grown-up gentlemen.' But Wright did learn much from his lectures, and Monk kindly lent him books and examination papers, even though Wright was at first so scared of being picked out to construe that he kept his head down in an 'obscure part of the room' to avoid the derision of his fellow students if he got something horribly wrong.[91] Of course, there were the show-offs as well as the ones who hid like Wright; and those with great memories but no understanding: it is very familiar.

Gradually, as the terms proceeded, the division between 'reading men' and 'non-reading men' emerged as the latter didn't prepare for class or couldn't keep up and began to stop attending, even though Mr Brown tried to help the really thick (or non-mathematically minded) students.[92] At St John's College, the mix of students is similar. Wordsworth describes the students at lectures in *The Prelude*: 'Of College labours, of the Lecturer's Room, / All studded round, as thick as chairs could stand, / With loyal Students, faithful to their books, / Half-and-half Idlers, hardy Recusants, / And honest Dunces'.[93] The non-reading men would aim to just get a pass at BA, without honours, and might gravitate to cards, gambling, boating, novel-reading, horse racing at Newmarket, cricket, tennis or billiards, and of course drinking and giving wine parties; but these 'gay-men', as Wright calls them, might not only 'ruin themselves and their parents' but also seduce reading men into leading a more frivolous life, and run up huge debts.[94] Wright says that he was only once so enticed in his first term by drinking too much wine. And yet we know what happened to him later – debtors' prison – and can only wonder what happened. Twenty years later, Bristed is flippant about drinking: 'There is indeed a tradition that a total-abstinence society was once established in Cambridge, and that in three years it increased to two members,' but as a member of the rich Astor family he had little understanding of the fear of debt.[95] A major problem at Cambridge was tradesmen giving any student in a gown easy credit. The temptation to buy books, prints for their walls, good furniture and wine, even, as Thackeray says, 'those shirt-studs and pins which the jewellers would persist on thrusting into our artless bosoms',[96] and to be presented with a staggering bill later, was immense. Angry wrangler Atkinson found trying to live on his small resources a 'distressing problem': 'The first term I paid my tutor's bill; the second I fell into arrear; the third I fell still farther into arrear.' He incurred debts with the bookseller, tailor and other tradesmen; he had to pay for meals (only dinner in hall was free) and gradually lost his fear of paying by credit:

It is thus that many a hapless victim of inexperience and cupidity is rendered miserable for life. His Cambridge debts hang on him like an incubus, break up his spirits, and baffle his best exertions […] it is folly to condemn the extravagance of youth, when there is every thing to stimulate, and nothing to control.[97]

Coleridge went to Jesus College in 1791 when he was nineteen, where, Holmes comments, he ran up 'disastrous debts' while 'flirting with drink, whores, and suicide'. His rooms were cold and damp and he furnished them on credit which he could ill afford, and kept a cat there, which was cheaper. He piled up more debts on books, violin lessons and prostitutes, as well as occasional opium, so that by 1793 he owed the huge sum of almost £150. In despair, unable to control his spending, he ran away to enlist in the army. When he was rescued by his brother George, Coleridge reflected that 'To real Happiness I bade adieu from the moment, I received my first Tutor's Bill'.[98]

* * *

Since Evan scraped into only fifth class in his first-year examinations, I wanted to know what subjects he had to write on, but in Wright's first year the May/June college examination was cancelled because of fever that had spread through Cambridge. Airy merely mentions that classics dominated the mathematics component, and that he was not only in the first class, but came top of the first class. Possibly the freshmen were examined on some of the classical authors Airy was told to prepare before October: Euripides' *Hippolytus*, the third book of Thucydides' *History of the Peloponnesian War*, the second Philippic of Cicero (criticism of Mark Antony, after the murder of Julius Caesar), and in mathematics Euclid.[99] The second Philippic is Cicero's most famous denunciation of Antony ('You are a drink-sodden, sex-ridden wretch'), and these authors were standard fare in schools, and maybe even taught by Evan.[100] Surely he should have been higher than fifth.

The only explanation that makes sense to me is that Evan may have been teaching at the same time. My family memory is that his grandson (my grandfather), John Card Jenkins the younger, taught while doing his degree at Cambridge, and it may have also applied to Evan. After Macaulay took his BA the same year as Evan, he stayed at Cambridge to prepare to take the Fellowship exam and took on two pupils aged thirteen and fifteen, earning 100 guineas over nine months.[101]

In his 1823 letter from Brussels, Evan remarks that he has almost paid off his debts incurred in Cambridge – that is, only a year after graduation, and maybe another sign that he was earning an income at Cambridge and not able to work on the examination texts as much as he would have liked. What is also clear from this period is how widespread the quasi-acceptable system of private tutoring was to help students through their studies and to prepare for exams. This might be provided by undergraduates, by those studying to acquire a Fellowship, even by Fellows, lecturers and exam moderators. Sizars generally paid less for private tuition, but it was another lot of money to find, and maybe Evan simply couldn't afford it, or didn't have the time.

* * *

At the end of the first term of his second year (1819–20) Evan received his certificate (a handwritten slip of paper) for attending the Norrisian lectures: 'Mr. E. Jenkins of Trinity College has attended the lectures of the Norrisian Professor', signed 'St John's College T. Calvert. Norr: Prof:', dated 16 December 1819.[102] Thomas Calvert, née Jackson, had been admitted sizar at St John's in 1792, and was fourth wrangler five years later; he was Norrisian Professor of Divinity 1815–24. St John's College isn't where the lectures were held, which was in the University or 'Public' Library, near the Senate House and King's College Chapel, and luckily for sizars the lectures were 'free'.[103] Bishops required this certificate in order to ordain a man. In his book on Cambridge, published in 1815, Rev. Latham Wainewright, who took his BA in 1802 as a student at Emmanuel College, stated that these were a 'most useful series of lectures' which looked into the 'evidences of revealed religion', and the history and proof of Christian, especially Anglican, doctrines.[104]

Wright, however, says that he managed to attend only about fifteen of the minimum twenty-five lectures 'in the room under the front of the University library': 'these grew so tiresome to me, being read out of a book, Pearson on the Creed [...] and there being so much irreverance and disorderly conduct amongst the students, that for the life of me I could not get through the course'. And what he describes belies any notion that these certificates were of any value in producing a responsible clergymen:

> The gay-men as well as the reading-men being obliged every day at twelve to go to the Professor's table to drop their card, we had all sorts of such scenes as might be expected from a host of dissipated impatient young fellows caring nor more for the lecturer or lectures than they did for bishop Pearson or the creed. It was an every-day trick with them, to contrive to bolt in at the same moment with a dozen or two of the more sedate students, throw their cards upon the table, and then in the crowd slip out at the door, and thus run off to resume their amusements. Many times have I seen them in their extreme desire to escape the bore, as they called it, of being detained an hour, creep out on all-fours, the Professor being a man of such small altitude, that the wags thus became eclipsed by the table.[105]

Such certificates were therefore as useless as college testimonials. American Charles Astor Bristed, whose father was an Episcopal clergyman, argues that college testimonials resulted in the 'admission of improper characters into the Church' because the testimonials simply reflected that a man had attended the proper number of chapel services: 'I have known men who at a pretty advanced stage of their Undergraduate course committed open acts of profligacy and disorder [...] but whose testimonials were not thereby forfeited or suspended.'[106] Over half of all Oxbridge graduates, until the 1840s, were ordained; and in the Victorian period the clergy was the largest profession,[107] so most of those who sneaked out of the divinity lectures became clergymen. Incidentally, the Norrisian prizeman for 1821 – for writing the best essay on a sacred subject – was William Trollope of Pembroke College (a cousin of Anthony), who could also have known Evan at Cambridge. He was to marry the sister of geologist Rev. William Branwhite Clarke and will appear again in a later chapter.[108]

The divinity lectures were not the only source of religious or biblical knowledge. Professor Monk's lectures in the second year included the New Testament in Greek. Wright describes a viva-voce examination on the Bible, with the examiner questioning the undergraduate: '"Can you tell me, Mr. L., who was king of Israel when Jonas was in the whale's belly?" – "The Prince of Wales," said Lynam, which being delivered instanter, disconcerted the examiner, and gave to the former a character for repartee at least equal to that of the latter.'[109] Lynam – later a preacher – obviously had great comic timing.

There was also a written college examination at the end of the second year on their study of the Gospel of St Luke. Wright provides an example of the paper; out of eighteen (often very lengthy) questions only two could be answered without having to translate or know Greek, for example: 'Give a very short abstract of the history of the Hebrew nation, from the calling of Abraham to the time of Alexander the Great [...] noticing any persons or circumstances that you know to be mentioned by any ancient Greek writer.' Also examined was 'moral philosophy', which was based largely on Paley's writings. For example 'What is *Revenge*? Show that it is prohibited both by Reason and by Scripture'; 'What are our duties towards our inferior and dependents? Show the futility of the pretences by which some people excuse themselves from giving to the poor'; and the rather interesting 'Explain the guilt, the inefficacy, and the absurdity of Duelling.'[110] Of course one admires the tenor of the second question, but the questions are telling the students what they should think: there is no room for argument or for thinking outside the box. The questions, and no doubt the course of lectures, must have been intellectually stultifying.

William Paley (1743–1805) had been a sizar at Christ's College and graduated as senior wrangler in 1763, later becoming a Fellow. For a few years Paley taught the course on the Greek Testament, ethics and metaphysics, compiling his own notes on ethics, which he published in 1785 as *The Principles of Moral and Political Philosophy*, which became a textbook at Cambridge. After numerous church appointments, he wrote, among many other works, what has been called a 'masterpiece of Christian apologetics': *A View of the Evidences of Christianity* (1794), which became a standard book for those seeking to be ordained, and required reading at Cambridge into the twentieth century. He had been a popular teacher at Cambridge, never dry; his writings have been described as 'natural and easy', and he had a sense of humour, once being accused of 'almost perpetual jests', which the solemn and pompous declared weakened his literary reputation. His recommending students at Cambridge to compose one sermon and steal five might have raised a laugh, but would have been helpful to those anxious about one of the burdensome tasks of a clergyman.[111] His work *Natural Theology* (1802) is well known for the argument from design – if you look at the mechanism of a watch you must infer there was a watchmaker, and thus if you observe nature you must infer there was a creator. He dismissed evolutionary theory (this was about fifty years before Darwin's lightning flash of a book *On the Origin of Species*), which may have produced dilemmas for the increasing numbers of clergymen, reared on Paley, actively working in the field of geology, such as Evan's friend Rev. William Branwhite Clarke of Jesus College, who has been called the father of Australian geology. Clarke was also a correspondent of Professor Adam Sedgwick of Trinity, whom I will touch on below.

* * *

There were various extra-curricular lectures on offer to students. In the printed Cambridge University calendar of 1822, there is a list of university professors and lecturers, from political economy to music, Arabic to casuistry, mineralogy to natural and experimental philosophy (the term 'philosophy' was gradually renamed 'science', and those who studied it 'scientists'), and physic and pathology.[112] A 'lecturer' didn't always mean that 'lectures' might be on offer, nor that the professor knew much about his subject. Paley had been made Hebrew lecturer in the 1760s, but it is possible that he knew not a word of the language.[113] But this was beginning to change in the nineteenth century. Bishop John Kaye, senior wrangler in 1804, Regius Professor of Divinity from 1816, revived the public lectures after a lapse of over a century. He gave a course of lectures on the Church Fathers, whose writings had been rarely studied previously.[114] The Professor of Arabic, who was also well qualified, was Samuel Lee. He has been called one of the greatest linguists of the nineteenth century. At twelve he was apprenticed to a carpenter in Shropshire. One day he was working in a house with a good library and was found reading the books in his lunch hour. He taught himself Latin, Greek and Hebrew, and progressed to learning Chaldee, Syriac, Persian, Hindustani and possibly another eleven languages. The Church Missionary Society and Isaac Milner brought him to Queens' College, Cambridge. He learned the mathematics required in two weeks and gained his BA in 1818 at the age of thirty-five. He was fast-tracked to MA by royal mandate in order to be made Professor of Arabic a year later.[115] Evan might have gone to his course of lectures to learn some Arabic, about the Qur'an and 'of such other books on the history, customs, or science of the Arabs, as the class may be prepared to receive'. It sounds as if Professor Lee knew that most of his students would not be able to keep up. However, the Professor of Astronomy, William Lax, did not give any lectures, according to the 1822 Calendar when Lax was sixty, though he had a small observatory at his vicarage in Hertfordshire.[116]

One man who knew only a little about his subject when he was made Professor of Geology in 1818 was Adam Sedgwick – he had been to some lectures on mineralogy. I want to explore him a little since I can only confirm two or three friends of Evan that were at Cambridge, and one was Clarke the geologist. Did they meet at Sedgwick's lectures? If so, did these three ordained men reconcile strata and fossils with the creation of the world by a 'watchmaker' or with evolution? There is a summary of the progress of geology at Cambridge in the Calendar, from the foundation of the professorship in 1727.[117] A large number of fossils had been acquired, but were housed poorly. Sedgwick had provided more fossils, gave a course of lectures, and encouraged 'scientific' members of the university to discover and donate more, but a proper museum *must* be made available, he writes. George Biddell Airy arrived at Cambridge with a letter of introduction to Sedgwick, attended his lectures and became a lifelong friend.[118]

Adam Sedgwick was nine years older than Evan, born in Dent in the Yorkshire Dales (later shoved into the county of Cumbria) in 1785, son of the local vicar. He went a few miles north-west to Sedbergh school when he was sixteen (Wordsworth's eldest son John was sent to the same school twenty years later).[119] Recently it took me three hours to walk along the Dales Way between Dent and Sedbergh through a gorgeous green landscape, along the river Dee then up and down a hill. There is a sizeable plaque to Sedgwick in Dent which expands on the

Dent fault. Sedbergh School, founded in the sixteenth century, throngs with pupils still, of both sexes now. Sedgwick entered Trinity College as a sizar in 1804. It is interesting how many of the students I have named were sizars; there were of course some clever pensioners, and even rumours of a clever nobleman.

Sedgwick looks rather Byronic in his 1832 portrait by Thomas Phillips, who painted many scientists, poets and explorers, though Sedgwick is wearing an academical gown and high dark cravat, rather than a Romantic open-necked white shirt or exotic Albanian dress. Byron was indeed Phillips's most famous sitter (in 1813). In his late 1860s' carte-de-visite, however, Sedgwick reminds me of Yoda in *Star Wars*.[120] The *ODNB* writer calls the young Sedgwick 'unsophisticated, untravelled, and uncouth' when he first arrived at Cambridge. He graduated as fifth wrangler in 1808, then acquired a Fellowship. Despite ill health, he was elected as the Woodwardian Professor of Geology, based apparently on his connections and general ability, which post he held for fifty-five years, and which required that he remain a bachelor. He was to be dynamic in his field studies and his collecting and it must have been exciting to attend his university lectures only a few years into his professorship when he was only in his thirties. In 1831 he took the young Charles Darwin – who had arrived at Christ's College in January 1828 – with him on a field trip to North Wales. Darwin had learnt a bit about geology at Edinburgh University; at Cambridge he succumbed to the usual temptations, he 'ran up bills, drank, rode, and gambled', and admired Paley's *Evidences of Christianity*. But he also enjoyed the extra-curricular lectures and field trips with the young botany professor, John Stevens Henslow. After North Wales, Henslow offered him a passage on the *Beagle* – the turning point in Darwin's life. It is often the extra-curricular activities, and the contacts made, rather than the formal course at university that could affect a young man's future. Professor Sedgwick, an evangelical, was angry when he read *On the Origin of Species* in 1859 – he vehemently disapproved of evolution and natural selection – but he and Darwin remained friendly.[121]

* * *

Evan may have gone to the geology lectures, but angry wrangler Atkinson doesn't seem to have. He sweepingly dismisses all lecturers and professors as 'a degenerate and pigmy race' and won't comment on 'the peculiarities or worthlessness of their pursuits', though he thinks Herbert Marsh, the Lady Margaret's Professor of Divinity, is an 'ornament to this University' and he grudgingly likes the Professor of Modern History and his lectures.[122] Atkinson nowhere comments on one of the most famous men at that time in Cambridge, Rev. Charles Simeon (1759–1836).

> Every body knows that at Trinity Church, Cambridge, there has been, evangelizing the gownsmen for the last half century, a great saint called Simeon.[123]

So comments jailbird Wright. Simeon was converted to a more evangelical Christianity at King's College in the late 1770s and 1780s. Apparently he was so ugly that at Eton he was nicknamed 'Chin Simeon'. He was made vicar of Holy Trinity Church in 1782, a short walk from Trinity College, to the fury of the congregation, the churchwardens, and undergraduates – who disrupted his sermons, but he survived there for fifty-four years. His preaching focused on the evangelical message of the salvation of individual souls, rather than the usual emphasis on morals. By 1818, the year of Evan's arrival at Cambridge, undergraduates were flocking to hear him, and there was standing room only. Simeon gave classes on sermon composition and how to project the voice, and from 1812 he began weekly 'conversation classes' in his rooms at King's. Macaulay, who heard him preach, commented that Simeon's influence in England was far greater than that of any bishop.[124] Surely Evan knew him and his sermons.

Simeon is one of the topics of conversation in Wright's overheard whispered chats in chapel, this time between two non-reading senior sophs (third-year men): 'The gay old cushion-thumper was amusing himself with leaping over the ditches. He's as good a horseman as a preacher, and that's saying much for his jockeyship; for much as he's sneered at for his works of supererogation – for his evangelization, he's the most powerful expositor and advocate I have ever heard.' This third-year man has obviously succumbed: 'All his actions [...] his benefactions, public and private, of every kind, most nobly illustrate the doctrines which he promulgates [...] on this account, if ever I go to church [...] I go to Simeon's.' His friend, though, is wary of the students who follow Simeon: 'I am too honest for the hypocrites. I fancy I see myself at old Simeon's Bitch Levee. I should cut a pretty figure, with my lingo, amongst these saints.' His friend agrees: 'much as I like old Simeon, the Simeonites I hate indiscriminately, as I do all serpents'.[125] 'Bitch Levee' – another term for Simeon's conversation classes. Apparently, Wright, says, the conversation on religious topics in Simeon's rooms often turned to discuss the news or literature. Simeon was also active in the Church Missionary Society. He organized a subscription for the poor during the corn famine of 1788, and a later master of Jesus' College was told when he went up to Cambridge that Simeon could be seen either in his stables with the horses 'or by the sick bed of his parishioners'.[126]

* * *

The university examinations for the degree of BA in the Senate House every January were fraught. One difference from today was that undergraduates were divided into different classes according to their ability in mathematics, and given different questions. Wright describes one man who was a gifted classicist but had no head for mathematics:

> At his examination for B.A. the Moderator, having previously determined to give him his degree for his classical acquirements, laid before him a small scrap of paper, and without requiring him to solve any particular question, said, 'I will thank you, Mr. B., to write out upon that piece of paper all the mathematics you know.' The paper [...] nearly remained a blank.[127]

Evan's final exams started on Monday 14 January 1822 (the first Monday of Lent term) and lasted for five days. I can only guess that he had been grouped into the fifth and sixth classes. If so, he started in the afternoon, and the moderator was Rev. Temple Chevallier, a Fellow and tutor at Catharine Hall – now St Catharine's College – who was to become a noted astronomer. He was the same age as Evan, and had been second wrangler the year before Evan arrived at Cambridge. Evan's youngest son, John Card Jenkins (who didn't escort the Brontë sisters when he was a child), married the daughter of Temple's first cousin in 1865. Was there friendship between the families dating back to Evan's time at Cambridge?

Wright describes the atmosphere at a college examination, which must have been dramatically heightened for the BA examination: 'The utmost anxiety is depicted upon the countenances of the Reading-Men [those going for honours]. Some you see entering the hall with a handful of the *very best pens*, although there is an ample supply upon every table, so fearful are they lest a moment should be lost in mending the same.' Others are 'writhing with the anticipation', and the 'gay-men', who have done little preparation, 'languish and look sad [...] and look foolish with their hands in their pockets'. Perhaps many had nightmares for years about the final university examination. Wright described those aiming to be wranglers as 'cadaverous other-world looking beings [...] for which they are committing a slow sort of suicide'.[128]

* * *

In later life, Baron Macaulay looked back on his time at Trinity, with only slight regrets about having flunked mathematics:

If a man brings away from Cambridge self-knowledge, accuracy of mind, and habits of strong intellectual exertion, he has gained more than if he had made a display of showy superficial Etonian scholarship [...] After all, what a man does at Cambridge is, in itself, nothing. If he makes a poor figure in life, his having been Senior Wrangler or University scholar is never mentioned but with derision. If he makes a distinguished figure, his early honours merge in those of a later date.[129]

Later in life, the successful Macaulay could shrug his shoulders at not having become senior wrangler, or any wrangler at all, with his ordinary BA. In his historical novel *Henry Esmond*, Thackeray depicted the poet, essayist, politician, founder of the famous *Spectator*, Joseph Addison (1672–1719) – a classicist like Macaulay – in a threadbare coat in a dark chamber, reminiscing to Henry Esmond about his time as an undergraduate at Magdalen College, Oxford:

'When I came out of Oxford into the world, my patrons promised me great things; and you see where their promises have landed me, in a lodging up two pair of stairs, with a sixpenny dinner from the cook's shop [...] I came out of the lap of Alma Mater, puffed up with her praises of me, and thinking to make a figure in the world with the parts and learning which had got me no small name in our college. The world is the ocean, and Isis and Charwell are but little drops, of which the sea takes no account. My reputation ended a mile beyond Maudlin Tower.'[130]

Evan Jenkins left Cambridge in 1822 with his testimonial, his Norrisian certificate and his BA. But he left with more than that: he was established as a gentleman, a graduate of Trinity College, Cambridge. He had made contacts, and maybe someone said: would you like to go to Brussels for a while as a tutor?

The reader may like to know what happened to the angry wrangler Solomon Atkinson. He went to Lincoln's Inn, became a barrister and wrote several books on conveyancing.[131] In this spider's web of connections, he surely knew Evan's future brother-in-law Samuel Jay, who was called to the Bar at Lincoln's Inn just a year before Atkinson.

Eight

Belgium, 1814–1823

'C'est le feu!'

Belgium! name unromantic and unpoetic, yet name that whenever uttered has in my ear a sound, in my heart an echo, such as no other assemblage of syllables, however sweet or classic, can produce.

– Charlotte Brontë, *The Professor*[1]

So declares William Crimsworth, Charlotte's unprepossessing hero in her first novel that no one wanted to publish in her lifetime. Crimsworth falls in love in Brussels and looks back at his time there with the romantic flush that love suffuses a place with. It is partly autobiographical, though Charlotte's love for her married teacher, M. Constantin Heger, was unrequited. In Brussels Eliza Jay also fell in love, and maybe that is why she never wanted to leave what her brother John called 'that horrid place'. John had the opposite experience there, but that is for another chapter.

The history of the southern part of the Low Countries that became modern Belgium is even knottier to untangle than the northern part that is now the Netherlands. It is probably advisable to skip some fifteen hundred years from Julius Caesar's Gallia Belgica to the Habsburgs. Premature deaths and a paucity of offspring led to the whole of the Low Countries becoming part of the Habsburg Empire at the end of the fifteenth century; the lands were known as the Spanish Netherlands when the ruler was also King of Spain. The Dutch in the northern provinces broke into revolt against King Philip II of Spain some twenty years before he sent the Armada against England. It is the period of Verdi's soaring, magnificent opera *Don Carlos* (1867/84), in which the Marquis of Posa urges Philip's son, Don Carlos, to save the people of Flanders – 'L'ora suonò; / te chiama il popolo fiammingo! / Soccorrer tu lo dêi; / ti fa suo salvator!' – though unfortunately in real life Don Carlos was 'an epileptic cripple [and] also a viciously sadistic madman'.[2] After eighty years the Dutch finally achieved independence in 1648.

It gets complicated in the south, but after the War of the Spanish Succession, the Spanish Netherlands were given to Austria in 1714, and thus became known, unimaginatively, as the Austrian Netherlands. Both the Habsburg Empress Maria Theresa (d. 1780) and her son Joseph II (d. 1790), brother of Marie Antoinette, brought reforms and some modernization to the country, despite the occasional chaos of revolt. That brings us up to the French Revolution and yet more invasions by the French (Louis XIV had bombarded Brussels into ruins in 1695) – leading to occupation in 1795, and the bloody suppression of an uprising three years later. Napoleon ordered the old city walls to be demolished, gradually to be replaced by wide leafy boulevards, now replaced by a noisy ring road. I rather prefer Napoleon as town planner.

October 1813 saw Napoleon's crushing defeat at the Battle of Leipzig that followed the calamitous Retreat from Moscow. It was the start of the endgame. In March 1814, Paris capitulated to the Allies. In April, Wellington's forces took Toulouse in southern France. The military historian Richard Holmes describes Wellington entering the city to find 'Napoleon's statue lying smashed on the ground and workmen chipping imperial iconography from public buildings':

> [Wellington] was to give a dinner at the prefecture that evening, and was dressing when Colonel Frederick Ponsonby galloped in from Bordeaux with extraordinary news: Napoleon had abdicated. 'You don't say so, upon my honour! Hurrah!' Wellington, still in his shirtsleeves, spun round on his heel, snapping his fingers like a schoolboy.[3]

The Allies meeting in Paris began their work on redistributing Napoleon's empire – a little prematurely – and discussing what on earth to do with the former Austrian Netherlands. Easy really, they had never governed themselves, so amalgamate the country with the Dutch north to form the United Kingdom of the Netherlands. No one, it seems, worried unduly about uniting Dutch Reformed Protestants with French-speaking Catholics under a Dutch Protestant king.

* * *

In May 1814, London-born George Griffin Stonestreet, new Chaplain to the Forces, arrived in Brussels. He was thirty-two and a Cambridge graduate, ordained priest in 1806.[4] He also had pretensions as a poet: in November 1813 there is an advertisement for his poem 'in three cantos', *Fairlight Rock*, and in preparation was his epic poem on the Battle of Hastings.[5] According to the Clergy database he was Rector of Honeychurch in Devon and curate at Ewhurst in Sussex. One might conjure up unreasonable deductions about excessive pluralism if we just had the database, but wonderfully he wrote a journal about his appointment as Chaplain to the Forces (written some time after the events), from March 1814 to 1816.[6] He has a place in my story since he began Anglican worship at the Chapel Royal, rue du Musée – where Evan was to officiate for over twenty years, and where the Brontë sisters worshipped.

The 1914 *Almanack of the Church of the Resurrection* in Brussels mentions Rev. Stonestreet as the first of the Anglican chaplains.[7] I have known that page most of my life as it was pasted in a great-aunt's album. About a decade after Evan's death, his two sons battled to build a church solely for Anglicans – previously they had shared with Belgian, German or Dutch Protestants – and their Church of the Resurrection in the rue de Stassart became the Anglican successor to the Chapel Royal in 1874. The *Almanack* dates the founding of an Anglican chaplaincy under Stonestreet to 1815, the year of the Battle of Waterloo, but Stonestreet had arrived a year earlier. His story is a fascinating one of ambition, competition and that great word 'interest' (with the meaning 'influence due to personal connection'): his story shows how a young clergyman in Evan's day might try to get preferment.

Stonestreet describes how, one day in 1813, he rode to the coastal town of Hastings from his curacy at Ewhurst in Sussex. He met an acquaintance from his college at Cambridge and invited him to stay. The college friend had just resigned his post as a chaplain to the forces as he had come into a legacy. 'He spoke so favourably of the various advantages accruing to such appointments, that I began to turn it in my own mind, how far my interest [my connections] might serve me, to procure one.'[8] Stonestreet doesn't list what these 'advantages' might be, but they include prize money and making new, useful contacts for future preferment. Obviously the little living he held in Devon and his curacy in Sussex were not remunerative enough, nor a good stepping stone for an ambitious man. Stonestreet thinks through all his acquaintances: which one might be useful? He settles eventually on someone who had married the sister of the Secretary of War, Lord Palmerston, and writes to him. Alas, this acquaintance merely tells him to write to the Chaplain General, Rev. John Owen – it seems he has no interest (influence) at all. But it would not do to write such a letter to someone he has never met: Stonestreet needs a reference from someone the Chaplain General might know. So he writes to the Archdeacon of London, Joseph Holden Pott, with whom he has previously corresponded, requesting him to report on his eligibility. It works: Stonestreet is offered a chaplain's commission, but he has to give up his living and curacy and get over the Channel quickly since peace negotiations are ongoing and the post may disappear. The Chaplain General tells Stonestreet that he has won 'a considerable prize in the lottery of life', especially as there were a dozen other applicants, 'many of them of high character'.[9] Maybe Stonestreet's clever use of Archdeacon Pott, closely connected with the new Bishop of London William Howley, rather than his being 'more fit for our Service' than the other candidates, swung it for him. Probably the Chaplain General felt that the archdeacon (and the bishop) was a useful person to do a good turn for. I again think of Eliza's remark in a later letter that her husband Evan 'is very backwards in going forwards'.[10] Perhaps the delay between graduating and getting his first post as a clergyman, and also staying in Brussels all his life, may be partly explained not just by Evan's humble (or proud) Welsh background, but by his dislike of using acquaintances in this way. But I feel that Eliza would act just as Stonestreet did. What is also important in Stonestreet's account is how he dashes around, before leaving England, acquiring letters of introduction. Although almost thirty years earlier, it is an important corrective, which I will discuss later, for the anachronistic and made-up stories about the Jenkins family meeting the Brontës on their arrival in Brussels.

Stonestreet was based wherever his troops were. In May 1814 he was in Antwerp, but he began to officiate when he could for the few English residents in Brussels. In an 1816 letter to the Bishop of London, he says that when he went to Brussels that May there were eight families who were in need of Anglican worship and that he had 'procure[d] for their use a very convenient chapel'.[11] He implies in a letter to a friend, dated from Brussels on 2 February 1815, that he has officiated, without remuneration, in Brussels for English residents since at least May 1814 ('for more than nine months'). He also says that he is angling to be attached officially to the current ambassador, Sir Charles Stuart, as 'I should [...] prefer remaining on the Continent, as my acquaintance is daily increasing and improving. The Hereditary Prince [22-year-old 'Slender Billy', from 1840 William II, King of the Netherlands] pays me more and more attention.' Stonestreet was concerned for his future as the troops started disbanding and there would be little need for a chaplain to the forces. He writes that he is 'in possession of the Chapel Royal'. He reports in another letter in February 1815 that he has started a school in Brussels, which the Duchess of Richmond had shown an interest in. But in March he writes: 'We are quite as much astonished with the recent convulsion of the political world, as you can be.'[12] Napoleon had escaped from Elba.

* * *

In March 1815, the (recently created) Duke of Wellington was in Vienna at the peace negotiations, having taken the place of his close friend the Foreign Secretary Lord Castlereagh, who had gone to London for the new Parliamentary session.[13] Wellington had been appointed ambassador to Paris the year before, but the atmosphere in the city was volatile, with rumours of attempts to kill him. So the Prime Minister, Lord Liverpool, was keen to get him out of France. Wellington was getting ready to go out hunting one morning when the news reached him of the escape of Napoleon from Elba. He was appointed commander-in-chief of the British forces in the Netherlands, and apparently Tsar Alexander told him: 'It is for you to save the world again.'[14] The Iron Duke as Superman, which rather sidelines the Prussian Marshal Blücher. The tsar was described by a former foreign secretary as a 'silly vain fellow', and Alexander might have meant it sarcastically.[15] The new duke arrived in Brussels on 4 April. On Sunday 18 June, Waterloo was Wellington's – and Napoleon's – very last battle.

> No more firing was heard at Brussels – the pursuit rolled miles away. Darkness came down on the field and city; and Amelia was praying for George, who was lying on his face, dead, with a bullet through his heart.[16]

Around 50,000 French and Allied soldiers were killed or wounded. After Thackeray has stunned his readers with the totally unexpected death of George Osborne, he wickedly insets two chapters in Vanity Fair territory with Becky and Miss Crawley, before resuming with chapter xxxv, 'Widow and Mother', and the anguish of those who wait for news: 'after the announcement of the victories came the list of the wounded and the slain. Who can tell the dread with which that catalogue was opened and read! [...] the great news coming of the battles in Flanders, and the feelings of exultation and gratitude, bereavement and sickening dismay'.[17] One of the places that the wounded were taken to was the seventeenth-century Church of the Augustines. A guidebook writer on Brussels (there were to be almost as many guidebooks as battlefield tourists and trophy hunters in the years to come), J.B. Romberg, comments in 1824 that the church had been used for Protestant worship 'since the entrance of the allied armies' and that after the Battle of Waterloo 'a considerable number of wounded soldiers were there deposited'.[18] Along with the Chapel Royal, it was to be an important church for the Anglicans – and for Evan Jenkins – until the Revolution of 1830.

* * *

Stonestreet's use of the Chapel Royal wasn't continuous, partly because he was not always stationed near Brussels; but he says in a letter two months before the Battle of Waterloo that 'I have given up my duty at the Chapel Royal because the English families behaved very shabbily about the expenses.'[19] Yet a year later he was still keen at establishing himself as the chaplain at Brussels, and he writes to his friend on 22 March 1816 that 'my chapel has been going on sadly':

> For three months the duty was entirely discontinued. At length three Clergymen there agreed to take it among them, to read prayers, and occasionally to preach. A committee was nominated to superintend a sub-scription, but this has failed so lamentably that they have been obliged to give up their singing, their organist, and their clerk. To give the finish to this state of things, the whole duty devolves after next Sunday upon one of these three now remaining, and he has a dropsy on the chest which prevents his officiating!
>
> In the mean time the congregation is every day increasing. Brussels is become perfectly an English Town, and the Duke of Kent arrived after me only a few hours to take up his residence for the next three years in that beautiful city.[20]

Three days before this letter to a friend, Stonestreet wrote his long account to William Howley, Bishop of London, about the Church of England congregation in Brussels, in which he suggested how money might be raised from the British or Dutch government (the English inhabitants were not confident, or keen, about finding money for a stipend or for other expenses among themselves) and how he would like the post.[21] Money was not forthcoming and by June Stonestreet had given up on Brussels. But by October a committee for the Chapel Royal had been established. It was going to be fraught, angry, verging on violence. Two dukes were involved (one royal), and two (or three) combative clergymen. As for George Griffin Stonestreet – he went home: he found the wife he wanted (the daughter of a merchant), became a prebendary at Lincoln Cathedral and acquired a fine country house (or two) before his death at the age of seventy-five.[22]

* * *

I was nervous when I first visited the Chapel Royal in Brussels in 2014 – the Église Protestante de Bruxelles: Chapelle Royale. I had been puzzled about why on its website there was a list of 'Pasteurs d'hier' from 1804 to 2011 with no mention of the Jenkins dynasty (Evan and two of his sons held services there) or any other Anglican clergyman. Maybe I had got the wrong city, or it had all been made up. I emailed the Chapel Royal and got a reply just a few days before I set off: someone would meet me there with 'information about the Jenkins'. It was exciting, but ominous.

That Sunday morning in February I was entranced by the loveliness of the cobbled Place Royale in the upper town, perched wide, quiet and high above the old city: on one side the grandiose royal palace and the park that features in the opium-fuelled night wanderings in Charlotte Brontë's *Villette*, stretching north to the rue de la Loi where stood the British Embassy where so many marriages took place.[23] On another side squats the vast, painting-crammed Musées des Beaux Arts. The eighteenth-century neoclassical chapel is down a short lane and through a discreet door in a white, curved stone building of pilasters, stone foliage and high windows – and there was 'deep, blue air' above and around me.[24] It is part of the palace built by the Austrian Governor, Charles of Lorraine (d. 1780). The chapel itself is classically gorgeous and unshowy: proud pillars with Ionic capitals, chandeliers, red velvety seating and a graceful cast-iron-enclosed gallery above. Or perhaps that isn't 'unshowy', but it is simple in comparison with some of the baroque churches in Brussels. I sat through the French service, understanding barely anything. I was trying to imagine my ancestors here – Welsh Evan with a congregation that a few times included the future Prince Consort, Albert, and his brother; and frequently attended by Albert's uncle, the solemn, rather darkly handsome King of the Belgians, Leopold. Or little Charlotte Brontë squinting at the pulpit, having mislaid her spectacles, always observing and ready to criticize, or Emily entranced by the sound of the splendid new organ, dreaming of her moors.

I was welcomed so courteously after the service by Mme Jacqueline Charade, who had prepared photocopies of their few records about the Jenkinses. There weren't many. It seems that some documents that ought to be in the Chapel Royal had been 'borrowed' and never returned by an eminent researcher who had recently died. But apart from one letter by Evan about the new organ, it is unlikely that much else emanating from the Anglicans had been in their archives.[25] I importantly learnt from her what should have been obvious, that the Anglicans, starting with Rev. Stonestreet, had rented their time in the chapel from the indigenous Protestants, who had been allowed the use of the chapel only about a decade before. For the Belgians, the British, understandably, weren't an important part of their Protestant history in a very Catholic country.

After Stonestreet's departure, the start of the more permanent Anglican occupancy of the Chapel Royal is joyously unedifying, as related in the next section.

* * *

The Battle for the Anglican Chaplaincy
Brussels, 1817–18

Dramatis Personae

In the royal corner:

Rev. Dr Thomas Prince (b. c.1788), *graduate of Wadham College, Oxford University, ordained priest 1812, former royal chaplain to the Prince Regent, 'not quite right in his mind'* [26]

Supported by:

HRH Prince Edward, Duke of Kent and Strathearn (b. 1767), *army general, fifth child of George III, future father of Queen Victoria, sometimes a harsh, unsuccessful disciplinarian*

Madame de Saint-Laurent, *the Duke of Kent's long-term companion*

Rev. E.C. Willoughby, *chaplain at the Chapel Royal 1816–17, 'turned out for Drunkenness & other Immoralities', won't hand over the Register* [27]

Princess Charlotte (1796–6 Nov. 1817), *heir but one to the throne*

A motley collection of British residents

In the noble corner:

Rev. George Hornby (b. 1790), *graduate of Brasenose College, Oxford University, nephew to the Earl of Derby, ordained priest 1817* [28]

Supported by:

Charles Lennox, 4th Duke of Richmond (b. 1764), *cricketer, army general, sometime duellist*

Charlotte, Duchess of Richmond (b. 1768), *famous ball giver (dancing, not cricket)*

Hon. Colonel Thomas Parker (b. 1763), *Chairman of the Church Committee, son* of the 3rd Earl of Macclesfield, future 5th Earl

Sir Richard Borough, Bart (b. 1756), *member of the Church Committee*

Richard Le Poer Trench, 2nd Earl of Clancarty (b. 1767), *Irish Protestant, Ambassador to the United Kingdom of the Netherlands until 1823, appointed by Castlereagh*

Michael Marlow, *President of St John's College, Oxford*

Fairly impartial, fairly powerless and not in Brussels:

William Howley, Bishop of London, 1813–28 (b. 1766), *Archbishop of Canterbury 1828–48, one-time tutor to the Prince of Orange, 'a very little cadaverous jaundiced man, with a peculiar cast in his eye [... with] much the look & manner of a Dissenter',*[29] *famously was to announce to Victoria at 5 a.m. on 20 June 1837 that she was now Queen*

The two wives/partners do not appear in the letters to the Bishop of London, but I have opted to place them on the side of their husband/partner's candidate; they are colourful characters and I am sure they had something to say. As for the ungainly, imprudent Princess Charlotte – the Prince Regent's only heir, and married to Prince Leopold in May 1816, 'the best of all those I have seen', she said of her future husband – apparently she was an admirer of Dr Prince, but she was shortly to die in childbirth.[30] I will attempt to trace the story of what was called a decade later 'one of the most violent disputes on record' through the letters from the aggrieved parties in the Lambeth Palace Archives.[31]

* * *

On Thursday 24 October 1816, according to the later printed agreement, 'The British inhabitants of the City of Bruxelles, desirous of establishing on a due and permanent plan, the regular Celebration of Divine Worship in the Royal Chapel, according to the ritual of the Church of England, assembled' and a group of 'Noblemen and Gentlemen were requested to form Themselves into a Committee'.[32] It was probably more chaotic and informal than that and one wonders if Rev. Stonestreet would recognize this printed summary as accurate, though by now he had probably departed to pastures new. Heading the list is the Earl of Clancarty, the ambassador to the King of the Netherlands, who had to move between the two capital cities: The Hague and Brussels. After him in the list is the Duke of Richmond. It also includes Hon. Col. Parker, Sir Richard Borough and thirteen other (gentle)men. Note that HRH the Duke of Kent is not on the committee, though he had arrived in Brussels some seven months previously. Stonestreet mentions in his last letter in the Lambeth Archive, dated 23 September 1816, that the duke had been at Stuttgart but was expected back in Brussels 'about the middle' of October.[33] Decisions and wording were made extraordinarily rapidly by the Church Committee meeting at the Chapel Royal, under the chairmanship of Col. Parker: in just two weeks everything had been agreed, including the rents by subscribers for pews or chairs (twenty francs a year for heads of families and 'grown Persons attached to them') and where the servants are placed (in the gallery, with the schoolchildren and public, or downstairs on benches). The Brontë sisters would therefore have to stand in the gallery as members of the public, for free, or buy a ticket at the door for one franc, and have a chair downstairs in the main body of the chapel (though it is likely that the Jenkinses gave them tickets).[34] The subscribers had to bring their ticket with them showing the number of their seat: coloured red for those right of the aisle, blue on the left. There is no information on what you do if you lose your ticket or it is eaten by the dog.

Out of the income derived from subscribers and 'accidental visitors' the committee will need to pay the rent for the chapel, fire and chairs (500 francs a year); the fees for the clerk and vergers, the organist (six francs per duty) and organ blower; and for advertising. This doesn't leave much for the salary of the clergyman, whom they recommend should receive twenty louis (gold coins, i.e. 400 francs = £16) per quarter, though he will get additional money from surplice fees (duties such as marriages and burials) and Easter offerings (a yearly tip from the congregation). Finally only those who subscribe can vote in the ballot for the clergyman.

What is obviously different on the Continent was that the clergyman was selected by the subscribers, the wealthier members of the congregation, not as in England and Wales by whoever owned the living, whether the lady of the manor (*Pride and Prejudice*) or your father (*Mansfield Park*). One hopeful clergyman didn't understand this. He wrote to the Bishop of London only a week after the Church Committee met in October to ask how he could put his name forward; he was currently in Brussels visiting a relation. Does he go through the Duke of Kent or the embassy to get a recommendation to the committee?[35] We do not have Howley's reply to Rev. Back but I presume he says that he has no power in the matter. Presumably the best advice would be to find out the names of the members of the committee and try to get a letter of introduction to at least one of them; ambassadors had little to do with chaplaincies in an official capacity, and European congregations were only loosely under the control of the Bishop of London until later in the century.[36] By November 1816, the committee had elected Rev. E.C. Willoughby on a one year's contract.[37]

What is curious is that in the letter files for Bishop Howley there is a draft letter to Rev. T. Prince, who seems to have enquired about being chaplain in Brussels as far back as January 1816. The bishop replied that he had no jurisdiction there and no advice to give. The date is faint but the letter is placed at the front of the 'Brussels' section, immediately before Rev. Stonestreet's long report of 19 March 1816.[38] From his obituary we learn that Thomas Prince had been tutor to the sons of the Duke of Brunswick, brother of Caroline, the divisive wife of the Prince Regent, from the time of his ordination in 1811. But the duke died at Quatre Bras, just prior to the Battle of Waterloo; Rev. Prince was replaced by a German tutor and needed a new job. Thomas Prince was rather unlucky in the deaths of his patrons, but, after angering various people in Oxford, he was taken under the wing of the Prince Regent's brother, the Duke of Kent, who invited him to Brussels to be chaplain there.[39] We don't have the date, but it seems to have been of huge annoyance to the committee, who had found their own candidate to replace Willoughby, who had proved unsatisfactory – Rev. Hornby, who had been ordained priest in Oxford on 1 June.

It is not until autumn 1817 that we know what happened next: Rev. George Hornby gave a statement about 'what passed in the Vestry room of the Chapel Royal' on 7 October. Involved were Rev. Willoughby, who had not had his contract renewed, Rev. Prince and Colonel Parker. Hornby reports that he had been requested to do divine service by the committee, and

> having expressed to the Hon. the Col. Parker, the Chairman, his fears of interruption from Mr Prince & his determination to avoid all altercation with that Gentleman was requested by Col. Parker to call him in case of such an occurrence. During the time of preparation in the robing room, Mr Prince entered in Company with another person. (Mr Hornby supposed it to be Mr Willoughby). He very loudly stated it to be an indecent thing for any clergyman to assume the Duty of Mr Willoughby, or any part of it, without that Gentleman's assent (having himself done so some Sundays before) and added addressing himself to Mr Willoughby, 'if you do not do duty yourself, I shall insist on reading prayers.' Col. Parker entered, in consequence of a message having been sent to him at the moment Mr Prince was preparing to take the Surplice, then held by the Clerk, & seeing what was going on, exclaimed, 'No. Mr Prince, that cannot be.' interposing himself between the Clerk & Mr Prince. Upon which Mr Prince snapped his fingers in Col. Parkers face several times, saying, 'I don't care

that for you', Col. P— said 'recollect Sir I beg who you are & where you are'. Mr Prince replied, 'I think I ought to know Church matters as well as you.' He then turned on his heel & continued to back himself upon Col. Parker evidently thrusting himself very offensively upon him. Col. Parker kept him off with the palms of his hands out spread, saying, at the same time 'Mr Prince take care.' Mr Prince immediately turned round & addressing those present exclaiming 'take notice Gentlemen', then turning to Col. P said you have struck me sir, you have struck me several times – Upon this Col. Parker said 'Sir you are beneath me.' to which Mr Prince answer'd, 'only in as much as I am somewhat shorter than yourself.' Further conversation [illegible word] between Mr Willoughby & Mr Prince, Mr Hornby having once said 'Mr Prince for Gods sake [illegible word] & consider your character as a Clergyman,' he replied 'Mr Hornby you are very impertinent in daring to speak to me at all.' Mr Willoughby then intimating his intention of doing duty himself which Col. Parker declined and the Rev. E Back was in consequence requested to undertake it.

This must be the Rev. Back who wrote to the bishop over a year before. Hornby is then questioned by the Church Committee:

Question: Had Mr Prince the Surplice on?
Answer: Certainly not.
Question by Col. Parker: Do you conceive I tore it off his back?
Answer: Certainly not.
[...]
Question: Do you recollect that Mr Prince seized the surplice when I interposed, & said 'I cannot allow that'?
Answer: He certainly attempted to seize it but did not touch it.[40]

The pecking order at this period is fascinating and often amusing. Thomas Prince was the son of the chaplain at Magdalen College, Oxford. So how he can presume to lord it over a nephew of the Earl of Derby and the Hon. Col. Parker is odd. He may not have known who Hornby was, but to be aggressive to an older, military man who was the son of a nobleman and chairman of the Church Committee is startling.[41] And why was he supporting Rev. Willoughby in this aggressive way? Willoughby had been appointed the previous October or November, so his year's contract had not yet run out. Perhaps Rev. Prince had the backing of the Duke of Kent. Unfortunately the letters in the archive are sometimes too faint to be legible.[42]

The next item in the archive is a copy of a letter from Rev. Prince to Sir Richard Borough, dated almost two months later (29 November 1817). It is more or less a threatening letter – I expect no less from Rev. Prince now. It seems that Willoughby had departed, other than performing occasional duties, and there was an ongoing 'unhappy contest' between Prince and Hornby for the chaplaincy.[43] According to Prince, Sir Richard at one point said he was neutral and would like both candidates to share the post. But now, Prince fumes, he has favoured the other candidate and 'foul aspersions' are doing the rounds at a time when a certain 'noble family' are away (the Duke of Kent and Madame presumably). It has also been spread around that Prince 'had written a rude and vulgar letter', which is false and he will give a statement to the public unless Sir Richard puts the record straight. This is just the start of an icily insulting correspondence, all copied to the Bishop of London a month later by Sir Richard. It contains gems, such as Prince's lofty comment (?13 December) that Sir Richard's 'mode of argumentation reminds Mr P. of the complaints little Children make to their Parents who have <u>apparently</u> failed of performing their promise to give them gew-gaws & bons-bons'. He also refers to the incident in the vestry:

> Sir R.B. seems to be as free with his tongue as a friend of his with his hands – so it is these Men of the World imagine they may deal with a Clergyman as they please because his profession precludes him from avenging himself – otherwise he is convinced that neither Col. P. would have had the courage to <u>strike</u> him nor Sir R.B. to call him a <u>liar</u>.

But it works both ways: Colonel Parker must have itched to challenge Prince to a duel, but Prince is protected by his cloth. Sir Richard replies to Prince on 15 December remarking on the latter's 'evasive and puerile tenor'. Prince ends the correspondence three days later by returning a note to him from Sir Richard in a 'blank cover'. Chairman Col. Parker writes to the bishop the same day (18 December), giving his summary of what he knows so far:

> [The committee] hired a place for Worship, and a Mr Willoughby was Chosen Chaplain, for <u>One</u> year [...] Our Chaplain not turning out so well [...] the Committee rather preferred to take advantage of the appointment being only for <u>One year</u> than to formally dismiss him, he having a large

family. We now wish to appoint for the year coming Rev. George Hornby, nephew to Lord Derby [...] but Mr Willoughby refuses to give up the register.

Two days later Sir Richard sent copies of his correspondence with Rev. Prince to the bishop as a precaution 'as [Prince] may endeavour to obtain the sanction of your authority, for obtaining possession of our Church-Register, of which I consider him to be unworthy'.

Meanwhile Rev. Hornby had written to Michael Marlow, the President of St John's College, Oxford (previously Vice Chancellor), to intervene. Bishop Howley had been Regius Professor of Divinity at Oxford before being appointed Bishop of London, so the two knew each other. Marlow writes that 'I believe I told you of Mr Hornby's wish to obtain the Chaplainship at Brussels. He went over & was supported by almost all the important families there':

> But his opponent, Mr Prince, whose strange & violent Conduct contrasted with the high Character with which he set out ?indicates him not quite right in his mind, has gained a numerous tho not very respectable party, and the congregation is likely to be divided into two.

Marlow also reports that the committee are looking for a new building since the Dutch won't let them rent the Chapel Royal on the same terms. He is also concerned about the register: 'which register the late Chaplain, who has been turned out for Drunkenness & other Immoralities, refuses to give up'. He says that Rev. Prince talks of hiring a building, perhaps with a Dissenting minister: 'it is supposed that he will through the interest of H.R.H. the Duke of Kent, to whom he was first recommended, apply to your Lordship for the Custody of the Register'. The bishop replies that he cannot intervene,[44] though he seeks advice from someone who knows Rev. Prince, who is astonished at Prince's letters to the baronet.[45]

This convoluted quarrel culminates in an unexpected way: there is a general meeting of British residents at Brussels (presumably just the subscribers, over a hundred of them), under the chairmanship of the Duke of Kent (certainly not neutral), at the Hôtel d'Angleterre on 1 January 1818, the candidates being absent, who resolve that Rev. Prince and Rev. Hornby should be joint chaplains. But Rev. Hornby is 'nowhere to be found'; when he is found he refuses the post. Prince triumphantly, and pompously, reports to the bishop that he has been elected and that he has the register. But that is not the end of the affair. We learn from Prince's obituary (and a letter by him in the Lambeth Archives, which refers to his 'cruel and implacable enemies' as late as September 1818) that the King of the United Netherlands intervened, who offered Rev. Prince use of the royal family's church in Brussels – the Church of the Augustines – sharing it with the Dutch Protestants. It is this church that Evan will be attached to when he is ordained in 1825, and I will describe it then.

And Hornby? The power struggle – between the royal Duke of Kent and the cricketing, duelling Duke of Richmond – actually resulted in Hornby as chaplain at the Chapel Royal and to the British Embassy in 1818.[46] It may be that King William put pressure on the Chapel Royal Protestants to offer better terms to the Anglicans. The death of Princess Charlotte in November 1817 eliminated the main protagonist in the struggle: the Duke of Kent was called on (some might say bribed – he was always in debt) to quit his rented house near the Place Royale in Brussels and abandon Madame – who had been his partner for almost thirty years – to marry the sister of the bereaved Prince Leopold and produce an heir, Victoria.[47] The Duke of Richmond was summoned away to be Governor General of British North America in 1818, where he died in agony of rabies a year later, but his legacy of Lord's cricket ground lives on, scene of a different type of power struggle, though some not so different from the incident in the vestry.

Rev. Willoughby's name appears twice in the register of the Chapel Royal, Brussels in 1821, so he was still around and called upon.[48] Rev. Prince left Brussels a few years after the contest for the chaplaincy: he found another patron in the Countess of Athlone, at The Hague, where he ran a school. He returned to England in 1825 because of his health, dying five years later in his early forties, his obituarist wishing he had been less 'irritable'. And he indeed took the register with him: it surfaced at an auction in December 1862 in Leicester Square, London and was sent to the ambassador in Brussels, Lord Howard de Walden, in early 1863. It was presumed that it had been sold as part of Rev. Prince's library. After over a hundred years in Brussels it was moved to Leuven with the other Anglican registers. When I studied it in the reading room there, I wondered if Rev. Prince's ghost would irritably snatch it back.[49]

* * *

Eliza Jay and her family arrived in Brussels in early July 1821 for their next new life.[50] Eliza was twenty-four; siblings John Livingston almost nineteen, Margaret seventeen, William fifteen. Samuel was working hard at Oxford, though no doubt also going off with friends to the races and shooting parties. I wonder if the family would recognize Thackeray's description of Brussels as 'one of the gayest and most brilliant little capitals in Europe [...] a rare old city, with strange costumes and wonderful architecture'.[51] Perhaps they admired the Grand-Place in the Old Town, defiantly rebuilt after Louis XIV destroyed many of the medieval buildings, to make it the 'most beautiful square in the world', according to Victor Hugo, who first saw it in the 1830s.[52] The Jays had left behind economic and social crises in Britain, such as the horror of the Peterloo Massacre two years before, and John Jay's own money problems. Thackeray comments: 'When a man, under pecuniary difficulties, disappears from among his usual friends and equals, – dives out of sight, as it were, from the flock of birds in which he is accustomed to sail, it is wonderful at what strange and distant nooks he comes up again for breath.'[53] But Brussels was no longer strange for the British: it was *the* place to visit or reside in. The Duke of Kent may have departed (dying, less than a year after his daughter's birth, in 1820), but his elder brother, now King George IV, was about to visit.[54] Tourists, pilgrims, writers were flocking to Brussels to see the site of the Battle of Waterloo, about ten miles south. Walter Scott hurried there in the summer of 1815, his first ever trip outside Britain.[55] The new Poet Laureate Robert Southey was also keen to see the battlefield and arrived that autumn. He was horrified to see human bones that had been dug up by pigs or dogs, but believed that right had triumphed.[56] In a poem published shortly after, he writes about the suffering and deaths of the British soldiers: 'Only the British traveller bends his way / To see them on that unfrequented shore, / and as a mournful feeling blends with pride, / Remembers those who fought, and those who died.' Byron arrived for a short stay in spring 1816 after fleeing England, never to return. He stayed in rue Ducale near the British Embassy, and worked on the third canto of *Childe Harold's Pilgrimage* which is influenced by the Battle of Waterloo and his angry belief that it was a calamity, not a victory.

William and Mary Wordsworth with his sister Dorothy and friends arrived on 15 July 1820 on their way to William's beloved Alps, via the battlefield.[57] In her journal the excited Dorothy describes their arrival:

> I was rouzed from sleep at the gates of *Brussels*. The man who demanded our passports had the impudence to ask for money [...] W., with grumbling, presented *two sous*. Light and shade very solemn upon the drawbridge. Passing through a heavy gate-way, we entered the City, and drove through street after street, with a pleasure wholly new to us. Garlands of fresh boughs and flowers, in festoons, hung on each side; and the great height

of the houses, especially in the narrow streets, (lighted as they were) gave a beautiful effect to the exhibition [...] We stopped at the Hotel *de Belle Vue* in the *Place Royale*, which looked like a square of palaces. It was past 11 o'clock [...]

    After breakfast, proceeded through the park, (a very large open space with shady walks, statues, fountains, pools, arbours, and seats, and surrounded by palaces and fine houses) to the Cathedral.[58]

Alas, they went to Mass at the Cathedral of St Gudule and not to the Chapel Royal.

    A year, later, on 5 July 1821, John Jay's advertisement appeared in *The Times* for his 'Institut Britannique' in Brussels.[59] The school was at first presumably where their home was – on the 'Boulevard opposite to the Porte de Louvain', now known as Place Madou, north-east of the park, in the district of Saint-Josse-ten-Noode. We know the address of their home from the register for burials of the Chapel Royal: Eliza's mother Helen died, aged forty-four, on 30 November 1821, only five months after arriving in Brussels.[60] John Jay is described as 'school master' in the Chapel Royal register. Their son Samuel is mentioned in the *Actes des Décès* and had presumably hurried to Brussels from Oxford. Then Eliza's youngest brother, William, died five months later, aged sixteen, in Ixelles.[61] The family had moved a short way south after Helen's death. The promise of a new life in Brussels had turned into a nightmare. Helen and William were buried in the Protestant cemetery outside the Porte de Louvain, which the Brontë sisters came to know in their own sad times, and Charlotte to describe in *The Professor*:

I turned up a by-path to the right. I had not followed it far ere it brought me, as I expected, into the fields, amidst which, just before me, stretched a long and lofty white wall enclosing, as it seemed from the foliage showing above, some thickly planted nursery of yew and cypress [...] – the gates were open. I pushed one leaf back – rain had rusted its hinges, for it groaned dolefully as they revolved. Thick planting embowered the entrance. Passing up the avenue, I saw objects on each hand which, in their own mute language of inscription and sign, explained clearly to what abode I had made my way [...] Hither people of many kindreds, tongues, and nations had brought their dead for interment; and here, on pages of stone, of marble, and of brass, were written names, dates, last tributes of pomp or love, in English, in French, in German, and Latin.[62]

When the cemetery was closed many decades later, and the bodies of the Jenkins family were moved to the Evere cemetery, Helen and her youngest son were left behind; their remains lie under the modern development.[63] Like his father, John Jay had lost his wife and had to keep a school going. But it seems that there was not just Eliza, his eldest daughter, to take on Helen's duties; his first cousin Johanna Enslie, in her early forties, daughter of his uncle James, may have been living with them at the time or moved in to help when Helen was ill. She and John Jay married a year later, in Rotterdam.

The officiating minister at the Chapel Royal was then Charlton Lane – Rev. Hornby seems to have moved away in 1820; his last marriage at the British Embassy was in October 1819.[64] But before Rev. Lane, the register gives the names of a great-great-grandson of Daniel Defoe (Henry Defoe Baker) and Whitworth Russell.[65] Rev. Russell, son of a baronet, committed suicide when he was Inspector of Prisons in England – he shot himself in the boardroom at Millbank penitentiary in Westminster in 1847. Rev. Lane stayed only about a year in Brussels. He had been admitted sizar at Trinity College, Cambridge in 1815, and migrated to Jesus College, getting his BA in 1820, so it is possible that Evan knew him.[66] He was ordained priest in 1821 and was in his early twenties when he officiated at the funeral of Eliza's mother Helen. It is possible also that Charlton Lane worked in John Jay's school: the next advertisement for the school in September 1821 says that the 'Classical Department' is 'conducted by a Clergyman of the Church of England'[67] – Lane had started officiating at the Chapel Royal by July so it might be him. But he, or a different clergyman, had left the school by July 1823 since the advertisement in that month merely states that the school was 'under the direction of a member of the Church of England' – John Jay, just by attending services at the Chapel Royal, could call himself that and he obviously thought it was a useful selling point.[68] Whether these priests didn't want to stay long, or whether the subscribers were dissatisfied with them and didn't extend their yearly contract, is not known. Charlton Lane next appears in the Clergy database as a curate in Lambeth, Surrey, in 1824. His obituary in 1875 states that he had also been chaplain to the embassy at Brussels, just as Rev. Hornby had been. The obituarist says that he was 'very popular as a preacher, especially in South London' and was attached to the 'old Evangelical school', as David Jenkins was.[69]

The next clergyman to arrive at the Chapel Royal stayed more than a year – Rev. Streynsham Master MA, an Oxford graduate in his fifties – and Evan would come to know him well: Rev. Master read out Evan's 'Si Quis' in the Chapel Royal in February 1825, describing himself on the document sent to the Bishop of London, verifying Evan's suitability to be ordained, as 'Chaplain to the British Residents in Brussels'.[70] He came from a dynasty of rectors of Croston in Lancashire, a village on the river Yarrow. His great-uncle, Dr Streynsham Master, had married the heiress and daughter of the Rev. Dr William Pilkington, who was rector there for fifty-two years from 1703, and not only inherited the parish but also the patronage of the living.[71] Our Streynsham Master (1766–1864) succeeded to the parish in 1798 on the death of his father but got into financial difficulties in 1820, 'which caused a good deal of unpleasantness and trouble at the time. In consequence of this he had to leave the country, and acted as British chaplain at Ghent and Brussels.'[72] The 1914 *Almanack of the Church of the Resurrection* dates his arrival at the Chapel Royal to 1822, taking over from Charlton Lane.

Rev. Master seems to have been a great success as chaplain. When he finally returned to England and his parish in Croston, around May 1826, after four years in Brussels, his parishioners expressed 'the strongest regret at his departure, and return him their thanks for the excellent tenor of his ministry as their pastor, and for his attention to his flock, and the charitable, benevolent, and affectionate demeanour of Mrs. Master and himself, which will leave with them a lasting impression of affectionate regard for him and his family'. The Roman Catholic English also signed a 'testimonial of their esteem for his character'. Both Protestants and Catholics combined to present him with a piece of plate 'as a memorial of their sincere regard, affection, and respect for him'.[73] Charlotte Brontë's comment in *The Professor* that some of Crimsworth's pupils in Brussels were 'daughters chiefly of broken adventurers, whom debt or dishonour had driven from their own country'[74] seems a bit harsh if applied to Rev. Streynsham Master, hoping that he did eventually pay his creditors something, but life was different twenty years later. His wife, Elizabeth, was a daughter of Sir John Parker Mosley, Bart, a Manchester hatter.[75] Sir John's direct descendant, the sixth baronet, was Sir Oswald Mosley (1896–1980), founder of the British Union of Fascists.

* * *

On 4 May 1822, Evan Jenkins received his BA at Cambridge. It seems likely that he almost immediately went to Brussels because in his deacon ordination bundle is a testimonial, dated 3 May 1825, stating that Streynsham Master and another clergyman had known Evan 'for the space of nearly three years'. This other clergyman, William Henry Holworthy, Chaplain to the British Embassy, would be significant for Evan's future. It is not likely that Evan had met Holworthy or Master before Brussels. So what led him to Brussels? It is possible that coming from a poor Welsh background he had few clerical connections and he struggled to find a title for orders. His brother David was now well established in West Yorkshire, and might find a curacy there for him, but maybe Evan was not as evangelically zealous, or even not sure about taking orders. So like many other graduates in his position he decided to teach for a while, and Brussels was cheaper to live in than London. He worked either as a private tutor to a British family or in a school there, but I don't think it was at first in his future father-in-law's school, because of the wording of the advertisement I mentioned above dating to July 1823 – probably over a year after Evan's arrival in Brussels – which merely states that subjects include 'the Greek and Latin Classics taught on the Eton Plan so as to prepare young Gentlemen for the English Public Schools and Universities'. If you had a Cambridge graduate on your staff, you would sell it loudly – and that is exactly what John Jay does in January 1824, right at the start of the ad: 'BRUSSELS BRITISH INSTITUTION.– The Classical Department is under direction of a Graduate of the University of Cambridge'.[76]

* * *

There is another clue to what was happening for Evan during his first year and a half after graduating: it is the 1823 letter from Brussels that I have already mentioned. It was written on 26 March to David Richards of Glanywern near Lampeter, Cardiganshire, friend of the family, who had witnessed his father's will almost twenty years before. I had been sent the scan, but I really needed to go and see it in Aberystwyth.[77] It folds over into a tiny size that would fit into the palm of your hand when posted. It came all the way across the Channel to a farmhouse by the river Aeron in mid-Wales, along muddy spring tracks, and was never thrown out, perhaps because David Richards was so proud of the little boy who had lost his father. It starts:

My dear Sir,

Ever since my return here at the beginning of last month I have been daily expecting a letter from your son John whom I left in London in good health and spirits – your last communication, inclosed in his letter, I only received a few hours previous to my leaving England – the bustle attendant on the commencement of a long journey put it out of my power to reply to it that day; and I have delayed writing till now in expectation of receiving some satisfactory intelligence respecting your son's proceedings. As he has not yet written to me according to his promise, I can only hope that he has succeeded in procuring a Situation in England, and has lost my address here which I gave him at our last interview.

I chewed over every word: so Evan had returned to Brussels in early February 1823 after a visit to London (and Wales?). He had been trying to help the son find a teaching job and he writes that the son has good qualifications, though his English needs improving, 'which of course is the case with us all when we first leave Wales'. Evan continues:

> Experience in teaching likewise goes a great way with most Schoolmasters. His age, his appearance, and steadiness of character were universally approved. I felt great pleasure in giving him every hint which I thought might be useful. I am only sorry it was out of my power to remain any longer in England and do more for him.

Evan then mentions that the son should see his 'best friend the Revd. Peter Felix', as mentioned above, and gives further encouraging words: 'He must not despair, as he is sure in the end to do well. I was sorry to find that fewer situations were vacant last Christmas than in any year since I first came to England.' So it seems that Evan had been in England/Wales since maybe December. Evan then gives advice about David Richards's other son Thomas, 'you may depend that whatever interest I have shall be exerted in his behalf'. That important word 'interest'. Then it turns wonderfully personal:

> As to myself, thanks be to the Almighty, I ?never was in better health and spirits in my life, & succeed here much better than I at first expected. I begin to make up for the heavy expences incurred at Cambridge. It is my intention in a very short time to forward to my uncle at Carmarthen a sufficient sum to pay the whole of my poor Mother's debts, including of course what is due to yourself. I am sorry they should have been so long unpaid.

Such riches for a researcher in a few sentences. My immediate reaction was: he's met Eliza Jay! Then that he knows that her father is keen for Evan to work in his school. But also maybe he has been told that a title for orders might come up – as a deacon assisting Rev. Holworthy in the King's Church, or Rev. Master in the Chapel Royal. He's paying off his student debts really quickly, so perhaps he's getting a good salary from a British family to prepare their son for Cambridge. In his PS he mentions that letters should be sent 'direct to me at the Hotel d'Angleterre, Brussels'.

In *Villette*, Lucy Snowe is offered a 'handsome sum – thrice my present salary' to be a private governess/companion to Paulina and live with her and her father, now a count, at their 'great' hotel in Villette/Brussels. Lucy – just like Charlotte Brontë no doubt – would prefer to sew shirts and starve.[78] Maybe Charlotte heard Evan mentioning his first experiences in Brussels over the dinner table. The Hôtel d'Angleterre, in fashionable rue de la Madelaine, where the Duke of Kent had chaired the meeting of the British residents in 1818, heads the list of the chief inns in Brussels in an 1823 guidebook.[79] It was a short walk from the Place Royale and the park. It was hardly a hotel where a mere schoolteacher would stay; nor likely that they would take kindly to his request to pick up his post from them. The Hôtel was redeveloped as the Salle de la Société de la Grande Harmonie, where Charlotte attended a 'grand concert' on 24 October 1843, which may feature in *Villette*.[80] A conversation at the Jenkinses' house about the duet from Bellini's *Norma* or Handel's *Rinaldo* could easily turn to Evan reminiscing about when the concert hall was a splendid hotel, where Napoleon had stayed in February 1798, and where maybe Evan had lived for a while as a private tutor.[81]

Finally the phrase 'my poor Mother's debts' struck me. It sounded as if she had died, perhaps recently, and had struggled. I have not identified the uncle at Carmarthen: he was probably Evan's mother's brother, and Davies is too common a surname without any other information. But it might be possible to find out what happened to Elizabeth Jenkins if she had died around this time – that is, if she had stayed in the same parish of Llanbadarn Odwyn and had not remarried. My research colleague Marcia had sent me a list of deaths in the parish after 1813. The only people who had died at 'Pencastell' between 1820 and 1854 were men, including Elizabeth's son-in-law Moses Roderick. With Evan's reference to his 'poor' mother giving a possible death date around 1822–3, coupled with a fairly lengthy trip to England/Wales that winter, and his parents' marriage bond of November 1785, I was looking for an Elizabeth Jenkins born around 1760. I stared with disbelief at the perfect match on the list, which I had merely glanced at with my usual scepticism before: Elizabeth Jenkins, aged sixty-two, born 1760, died 1822. But the deceased's abode was 'Pantyboidy'. It also had the date of her burial: 19 December. It couldn't fit more perfectly with Evan leaving Brussels for a few months and his mention of Christmas in London. But where was 'Pantyboidy'? It might mean 'bridge of' something, so it could be near a river. I studied the modern OS map, sweeping left from the rivers Brennig and Teifi, past the Sarn Helen Roman road and onto the Methodist village of Llangeitho on the river

Aeron. There were several names beginning with 'Pont'. My eye skimmed upriver and – I found it. I couldn't believe it: there was a Pantbeudy Hall. It was so near a match, surely that was the place where she had died. It was less than a mile from Elizabeth's old home of Penycastell. And immediately I remembered standing on the hill looking down towards that same house by the Afon Aeron, having lost the footpath to Llangeitho. I can't claim that family memory had made me pause there: probably it had been simply that I knew the footpath I wanted didn't lead down a trackless meadow with grazing sheep. But I won't discount it. This was once a pagan land.

I looked back at the list of deaths: two more Jenkinses had died at 'Pantyboidy' and I suddenly noticed their dates of death and some feeling of horror and sadness crept up on me: because less than a month before Elizabeth's death a man called John Jenkins had died there, aged thirty-seven. The next year, in 1823 (no month is given), Magdalen Jenkins died, aged only twenty-six. And listed below her was another Magdalen Jenkins, aged two – who had died at somewhere called Penbryn... (the transcriber had found it hard to decipher). I haven't been able to work out the exact relationship with Elizabeth or Evan, but surely John and Magdalen were husband and wife, and little Magdalen, who had died in 1825, after being taken in by relatives, was their daughter. The dates suggested that the elder Magdalen had died in childbirth.

Did Evan get back in time before his mother died, or in time for her burial under the high damp grass by the little white church? Surely he stood by that Scots pine with the view of the Vale of Aeron and said goodbye to the mother who had struggled so hard to see him through his education at Ystrad Meurig, and was so utterly proud to see it had been worth it when he visited her from Cambridge. I just wanted to give her a hug and say something in stumbling Welsh. And maybe this little Welsh woman would have looked up bemusedly at her giant of a three times great-granddaughter and thought ... No, let her think on, as long as she invites me into her lilting house to sit for a while by the fire.[82]

Like Eliza's mother Helen in Brussels, Evan's mother Elizabeth has no headstone, no trace in the grass where she lies. Evan returned to Brussels – and to the life that was holding out such promise, including a young woman who cared for him. Perhaps in that ancient December-dark churchyard he stood looking at the darkening valley below, the bare-branched trees swaying powerlessly in the wind and the rain, and also said goodbye to Wales.

Nine

Yorkshire and Brussels, 1824–1825

School, Death and Marriage

'Oh, dear papa, how quiet and plain all the girls at Lowood look! with their hair combed behind their ears, and their long pinafores, and those little holland pockets outside their frocks, they are almost like poor people's children!'

– Charlotte Brontë, *Jane Eyre*[1]

Lowood School, one of the most famous schools in literature, was soon discovered to be based on the Clergy Daughters' School at Cowan Bridge, Lancashire. Until I read Juliet Barker's book on the Brontës, I had not known that Harriet, the daughter of Rev. David Jenkins, was at the school in the mid-1820s with four of the Brontë sisters.[2] No one before had researched the Jenkins family, and any tiny bit about them was usually made up by Gérin in the 1960s, and slavishly copied. It has therefore not been noticed that when Charlotte and Emily met the Jenkinses' eldest son, fifteen-year-old Edward, in 1842 in Brussels that he was the first cousin of their schoolfriend – they had a real connection. Nor did I know, when I was made to read *Jane Eyre* at school, that some chapters were describing (with literary licence) the school experience of a relative of mine.

In an earlier chapter I left David Jenkins and Patrick Brontë around 1813, both starting married life with their own livings as clergymen. On 21 June 1814, David was licensed as perpetual curate of the chapel at ease in Pudsey, aged twenty-seven, but he and his wife Harriet had probably been living in Pudsey for some time, perhaps after their marriage in July 1813. They would surely visit David's friend Patrick and his new wife Maria in Hartshead and then Thornton, both about eight miles away. The young women might compare notes on their pregnancies, their worries and the extraordinary achievements of their new babies. Patrick and Maria's first child, Maria, was baptized at Hartshead on 23 April 1814; David and Harriet's first child, Harriet, was born on 15 July and baptized in 'the Chapelry of Pudsey in the Parish of Calverley' on 24 August by J. Wardle (probably Joseph), curate of Gildersome, four miles south of Pudsey.[3] David performed all the other baptisms: there were six in August.

The parish church of Calverley is three miles north of Pudsey. Whereas Pudsey has now been largely swallowed by the urban sprawl that extends from Leeds, Calverley is still a compact large village near the river Aire, surrounded by hilly golf courses, woods and farms. The little chapel at Pudsey was in existence in the fourteenth century when John de Pudsey was the minister.[4] It stood on the site of the World War I cenotaph, erected in 1922. A long-standing grievance was that Pudsey people had to pay tithes, and later money, to both the church at Calverley and to their chapel, and pay double fees for baptisms and burials: to the minister at Calverley as well as to their own incumbent. Just as for Patrick Brontë, David Jenkins faced continuing ill will about unfair parish rates.

Pudsey was a small wool-manufacturing town in the early seventeenth century when one of its most famous ministers arrived – the Puritan Elkanah Wales (1588–1669), a fitting name for one of David's predecessors, though he was a native Yorkshireman. He went to Trinity College, Cambridge and came to Pudsey chapel in about 1615. He was renowned for his powerful preaching, one young member of his congregation commenting, 'I have known Mr. Wales spend six to eight hours preaching and praying and rarely go out of the pulpit [...] O what confession of sin did we make, what prayers and tears and wrestling with God were in that place of weepers.'[5] He was a principled man since he not only got into trouble with the authorities before the Civil Wars, but during the Commonwealth Oliver Cromwell warned a colleague that Wales was about to preach against the government. Yet Wales was supported by his fellow Yorkshireman Sir Thomas, Lord Fairfax, one of the true heroes of history. Wales's real troubles came after the restoration of Charles II: Wales refused to assent to the new 1662 Prayer Book. The chapel door was locked against him, which he broke open, and he continued preaching illegally. But he was then banished from living in Pudsey and neighbours ransacked his house. He continued to preach privately, and died in his eighties in Leeds; it was considered too provocative to bury him in Pudsey.[6] I wonder if David knew of him and admired Wales's zeal and integrity.

The chapel was rebuilt under David Jenkins's predecessor, William Howorth, who arrived in his early thirties in 1767.[7] As David himself noted in the burial register, William Howorth was for forty-seven years the perpetual curate at Pudsey. Howorth probably moved the two-decker pulpit to the south wall, giving it far more significance than the communion table at the east wall: preaching then was far more important than giving the sacraments. The clerk would read the service on the lower deck; the incumbent deliver the sermon on the upper deck. The chapel was sixty feet by thirty feet, slightly smaller than a singles tennis court, and could seat about four hundred people. Passers-by could peer down through the windows at the worshippers since the floor lay below the level of the road. There was a gallery along the north and west sides, where the singers were stationed, and an organ was installed in 1792. Howorth's annual income was around £200 by the time David arrived, a not unsizeable amount, and Howorth had built a new kitchen in the 1780s, changing the old kitchen into another sitting room. The parsonage was floored with flagstones and had no cellar, so was probably damp – I wonder whether the newly married Harriet Jenkins eyed it with pleasure or with dismay.

An unnamed minister came to help with the services when Howorth was in his seventies. 'He apparently breathed new life into the chapel, the Moravians [a Dissenting sect] noticing a hurtful tendency in many of their Pudsey congregation to be induced out of curiosity to go to that place of worship pretty frequently. Amongst those attracted by Mr. Howarth's new assistant was the Bramley textile entrepreneur, Joseph Rogerson, who in 1812 walked over to Pudsey to enjoy a very good sermon.'[8] Since we now know that David Jenkins was involved at the chapel in Pudsey from 1812, that 'very good sermon' may have been given by the young David.

* * *

In 1814 David had the church lands revalued and relet at a higher price, and later had the new burial ground he had acquired walled at the town's expense; he also repaired a building to create a Sunday school.[9] Harriet gave birth to their second child and first son, Joseph Walker Jenkins, on 31 October 1816, whom Charlotte Brontë would know, and describe to a friend, rather nastily, as an 'unclerical little Welsh pony' almost thirty years later after listening to his sermon when he was visiting his relatives in Brussels.[10] Joseph went to St Bees Theological College in

Cumberland, the first independent college for the training of Church of England clergymen, which was much cheaper than Cambridge or Oxford. Joseph stayed closely in touch with his cousins in Brussels; after his death his daughter Mina moved to live there, and she was living with or near two of Evan and Eliza's grandchildren in Leicester when she died in 1926. My mother remembered an 'Aunt' Mina, who was her father's godmother, but not that they were second cousins, nor who Mina's parents were: it is not something one enquires about at the age of seven.

The year 1818 saw not only the arrival of another son for David and Harriet, whom they called David and who was to die in his twenties, but the hugely important Church Building Act, known as the Million Act, which provided a million pounds for the building of new churches, especially for new centres of population in the industrial North.[11] Many Anglican churches were full and there were not enough free seats for the poor, who were going instead to Nonconformist chapels. As Frances Knight observes, middle-class Anglicans 'made an explicit link between church-going and the disciplined behaviour that they wished to instil in the lower orders. If there were more churches with free seats, they reasoned, working people would fill them and learn to be moral.' Above all it would lead to fewer illegitimate births, and thus less poverty and less misery.[12] Whether David Jenkins accepted the strange logic that chapel-going produced more illegitimate births (maybe he thought of his sister, though she had married in time), he was one of the first to apply for a grant. The site of the newly acquired burial ground, elevated above the town, was ideal. The Archbishop of York, Edward Venables-Vernon (he changed his surname later to Harcourt), wrote to the Church Commissioners that 'I am not aware that there is any part of my Diocese in which an additional Church is more wanted than at Pudsey [...] [S]o great is the present Distress in that District from want of adequate employment [...] that no assistance is to be expected from the inhabitants themselves.'[13]

It was agreed to build a church that could seat 2,000, which finally cost the huge amount of £13,360. The architect chosen was Thomas Taylor (1777/8–1826); he was also an artist who exhibited landscapes at the Royal Academy.[14] He set up an architectural office in Leeds in 1811 and created an influential new style of Gothic churches. He had trained under James Wyatt, who was largely responsible for the Gothic revival, designing Fonthill Abbey in Wiltshire (1796–1812) and Belvoir Castle in Leicestershire (1801–13). Taylor probably drew medieval buildings and details for Wyatt, thus gaining experience of the true spirit of the Gothic style that classically trained architects didn't possess. David Jenkins certainly knew Taylor's new Gothic church at Liversedge (1812–16), less than two miles from the church at Hartshead, where he had assisted Patrick Brontë, and he knew Rev. Hammond Roberson (1757–1841) who had commissioned the church and paid for it himself. Roberson was the inspiration behind the creation of the warlike clergyman Rev. Matthew Helstone in Charlotte Brontë's *Shirley* and, like him, was an indomitable foe of the Luddites.[15] Like Patrick Brontë and David, Roberson had been a curate at Dewsbury, and then minister at Hartshead, Patrick's predecessor but one – his portrait hangs in the vestry at Hartshead church next to Patrick Brontë's and there is also a painting of him in the Parsonage Museum in Haworth. It is probable that David and his church-building committee went to view the church when it opened, were impressed, and commissioned Taylor to design their new church in Pudsey, which was to be named St Lawrence's.

The church at Liversedge 'was a remarkably scholarly Gothic essay, carefully detailed and with a long chancel [… it was] the country's first serious Gothic church of the nineteenth century', and where it seems Taylor chose to be buried.[16] The Archbishop of York approved of Taylor's style for the churches he designed as 'perfect examples of what we need'.[17] The first stone at Pudsey was laid on 19 July 1821 by David, who by then had two more children: Thomas, born in 1819 who died less than a year later; and Elizabeth, born six weeks before the stone laying, presumably named after his mother. I wonder if she saw the new baby – perhaps not, as Cardiganshire was so far away, but David must have written to tell her of her latest grandchild. Daughter Elizabeth later married Erasmus Lloyd, a 'gentleman' of Cashel, Ireland, in 1848, and was in close touch with the Jenkins family in Brussels: she was godmother to a granddaughter of Evan and Eliza, Margaret Wilhelmina, in 1877.[18]

The digging contractors had to excavate twelve feet beneath where the tower was to stand in order to remove a seam of coal. Bramley Fell gritstone – a sandstone from around Leeds, used for building nearby Kirkstall Abbey in the twelfth century – was transported in wagons to the site. It seems that Westmorland slate was also used, and one slater in his early twenties, from Bowness in Windermere, fell to his death on 6 April 1823.[19] The church is impressively immense and dominates the landscape. The churchwarden who kindly showed me around in April 2014, Doug Whiteley, commented on the powerful statement this building must have made to the community about the Church of England. Inside it has been altered many times but retains most of its high, plain-glass, Georgian windows that perhaps David liked at Dewsbury. There are galleries on three sides, where the singers perched, and a peal of eight bells was commissioned, which required the employment of a bell-ringer to instruct volunteers. Whiteley remarked on how 'formidable' David Jenkins must have been, not only in overseeing the build but in his preaching, since the pulpit seems to have had no canopy to help his voice reach his huge congregation.

But if fellow clergymen were envious, and the people of Pudsey awed, the consecration of St Lawrence Church on 30 August 1824 came a few months after tragedy for David: his wife Harriet died on 17 April, aged thirty-six. What should have been his year of triumph must have left him utterly bereft, and perhaps only organizing the completion and consecration of the church helped him. His wife may have had a lingering illness after the birth of their last child Susannah in April 1823, or perhaps tuberculosis. Their eldest daughter Harriet was sent to the Clergy Daughters' School at Cowan Bridge on 4 March 1824, six weeks before her mother died, aged ten. But before I accompany little Harriet to Cowan Bridge, I will go with David to the consecration of his church.

* * *

Edward Venables-Vernon, Archbishop of York, was then in his mid-sixties and from a privileged background as the Derbyshire-born son of a baron, and grandson of a viscount. He was a Fellow of All Souls, Oxford and married the daughter of a marquess. He was appointed to his first bishopric (Carlisle) in his early thirties since his father-in-law was Lord Privy Seal in the government of William Pitt the Younger. But he was scrupulous in attending to his duties, benevolent and a good family man.[20] He was made Archbishop of York in 1808 but almost refused it since he was so keen on hunting. His friends eventually advised that he could keep on hunting as long as he didn't shout.[21] He also loved sacred music and was involved with the Society for Ancient Music. He was one of the council who advised Queen Charlotte when George III was incapacitated and was often at Windsor between 1811 and 1818. Apparently, the day after consecrating David's new church in Pudsey he was at Haworth consecrating Patrick Brontë's new burial ground,[22] so if Patrick had not been able to attend David's ceremony he would have heard about it from the archbishop, and been maybe a bit envious of what his former young colleague had achieved. But surely only for an instant: he would know of David's bereavement and empathize; Patrick had lost his wife Maria to cancer three years before. Both men were now widowers, Patrick with six children, and David with five, all under the age of eleven.

The 'fine Gothic Church' was consecrated on Monday 30 August 1824 by the archbishop:

The morning was ushered in by the ringing of bells and other demonstrations of joy, and a flag was hoisted upon the south west pinnacle of the steeple. At an early part of the day, the influx of the company of the first respectability, was very considerable. At a little past eleven o'clock the Archbishop, accompanied by the Chancellor of the Diocese, and his Chaplain, arrived at the south entrance of the church-yard, where they were met by the Rev. Samuel Redhead, Vicar of Calverley, the Rev. D. Jenkins, Incumbent of Pudsey and a great number of the neighbouring Clergy.[23]

The archbishop then went to robe in the vestry, and the public – over two thousand of them – were allowed into the church. The archbishop and clergy processed down the aisle, repeating Psalm 24, beginning 'The earth is the Lord's, and the fulness thereof; the world, and they that dwell therein.' David sat on a chair by the pulpit while the chancellor read the deed of consecration, which the archbishop signed. The service of the day was read, the archbishop reciting the Nicene Creed, then Psalm 100 was sung: 'Make a joyful noise unto the Lord, all ye lands' accompanied by 'a band of music'. David then 'delivered an appropriate and impressive discourse' from 1 Chronicles 22:1, which delightfully begins 'Then David said, This is the house of the Lord God, and this is the altar of the burnt offering for Israel. And David commanded to gather together the strangers that were in the land of Israel: and he set masons to hew wrought stones to build the house of God.' After three years of building, the deaths of a labourer and of his wife, I can sense how immensely proud and moved he must have been. The archbishop closed the ceremony with a prayer, the band played 'Luther's Hymn' – possibly 'A mighty fortress is our God' – and the audience filed out. He left Pudsey around three to consecrate a churchyard in Bierley, about four miles away.

Unfortunately, however, all was not well with the acoustics of the new church. The archbishop wrote to the Church Commissioners that the building was too high: 'had the roofs been lower [...] there still would have been ample space and the Reader and the Preacher [David] might have been heard with less exertion'.[24] Having to shout the sermon was not the only problem: the pews were uncomfortable, and the white walls, high plain-glass windows and vast size of the space were a shock after the small, familiar old chapel, and some people wanted to have both as places of Anglican worship. Then there was the quarrel about ownership of the pews; David lost income as many were not taken up, and the free seats did not bring in many of the 'lower orders'. He also faced a continuing battle to separate Pudsey from Calverley, which no vicar at Calverley would agree to since he would lose a large part of his income. There must have been times when David was depressed and unsure about building his new church, and now he had no partner to confide in. But he did have his younger brother. Evan certainly saw the new church in 1825 (see below), and he may have been able to come to the consecration the year before.

* * *

Ten-year-old Harriet Jenkins – the same age as Jane Eyre – is number fourteen in the register of the newly opened Clergy Daughters' School at Cowan Bridge in Lancashire.[25] She arrived on Thursday 4 March 1824 after travelling fifty miles from Pudsey. The register must have been compiled as an after-thought since the girl who is number thirteen, Elizabeth Dawson, aged eleven, arrived later, in April, and was expelled in October 'for repeated ill conduct'. Number fifteen, Mary Anne Hillyerd, aged ten, arrived earlier than Harriet, on 12 February, from even further away in Lincolnshire. It may be just a coincidence that Jane Eyre's friend, other than Helen Burns, is the older Mary Ann Wilson. The register is also inconsistent in the details it gives. For example it does not say when Mary Anne or Harriet left the school – perhaps they stayed for many years, as Jane Eyre was to do at Lowood. But it is interesting to compare what it says about Harriet's 'Acquirements on entering' with those of Maria Brontë (also aged ten), who arrived in July with her younger sister Elizabeth, though they had both spent some time at a boarding school in Wakefield and it is not known if Harriet had previously been to school. Maria's entry reads:

> Reads tolerably – Writes pretty well – Ciphers a little – Works very badly – Knows a little of Grammar, very little of Geography & History. Has made some progress in reading French but knows nothing of the language grammatically[26]

'Works' meant sewing; 'Ciphers' was arithmetic. That is impressive compared to the comments on Harriet:

> Reads badly – Writes none – Ciphers none – Works but little – Knows nothing of Grammar, Geography, History or Accomplishments.

'Accomplishments' usually meant music, drawing and French. It seems unlikely that the daughter of a classicist was really such a dunce; maybe she was terrified when assessed, upset when her father left her so far from home, and worried about her ill mother. The register also notes, however, under 'General Remarks' the one word 'Music', so it sounds as if Harriet had one accomplishment that elevated her above the rank of the total dunces. What is also interesting is that under the column 'For what educated' is the word 'Governess', as it was for Maria, Charlotte and Emily Brontë (though not Elizabeth).[27] We might be alarmed, anachronistically, at the low expectations of such an education, but the advertisement for the school implies that this was a high expectation: 'If a more liberal education is required for any who may be sent to be educated as teachers and governesses, an extra charge will probably be made.' The advertisement also states that sixty pupils will be accommodated eventually, that it should open in January and be 'ready to receive the whole number proposed, in March or April'. Every 'effort will be made to confine the benefits of the school to the really *necessitous* clergy'.[28] What it also states is that 'It were indeed to be wished, that the clergy could be relieved from the necessity of accepting such aid', that is, it is appalling that some clergy have so little income that they are forced to rely on charity for educating their children. The list of those giving donations and/or giving an annual subscription included William Wilberforce and Rev. Charles Simeon, whom surely Evan had known at Cambridge, as had Patrick Brontë.[29]

It seems that both Maria and Elizabeth Brontë were supposed to start at the same time as Harriet (they should have gone in the spring but they were still recovering from whooping cough and measles)[30] and probable that David and Patrick had discussed the school. Later, Charlotte arrived there in August (aged eight) and Emily in November (aged six). Since Maria and Elizabeth are numbered seventeenth and eighteenth in the register, the two eldest Brontë sisters would have known Harriet well, especially if they had met beforehand. It seems that Maria showed signs of tuberculosis that December; Patrick was only told that she was ill in February 1825 and took her home at once, but she died that May. That same month Elizabeth became ill, along with many of the other girls. The doctor recommended that the healthier girls should be sent to Silverdale on Morecambe Bay for the sea air, while Elizabeth was sent home. Next day, Patrick went to Silverdale and took both Charlotte and Emily home for good; they were with Elizabeth when she died two weeks later.[31] Harriet survived less than a decade. She died in November 1834 aged twenty.

No letters have been found between Patrick and David, and I wonder if the trauma at their children's school changed their relationship. Illness and death are often not handled well and it is frequent to ostracize a friend if they are bereaved, or take wrongly a friend's attempt to empathize. Patrick might have been angry that David's daughter was not ill. It strikes me how close they once were and yet Charlotte knew nothing of the Jenkins family when she was thinking of going to Brussels. If there was a rupture rather than just a drifting away, then it surely happened because of the school at Cowan Bridge.

* * *

It is time to return to Brussels and Evan's exciting prospects. In 2017, Marcia and I were bouncing ideas off each other about when John Jay had started his school in Brussels and whether Evan went to teach there straight after graduating or not, and we were getting nowhere. Then an excited email arrived from Perth in Western Australia: 'Did you hear me yelling "I've found it, Monica"?' Researchers who trawl through online newspapers will know the unremitting length of time it can take – when keywords that you have guessed must be there produce either nothing at all or thousands of entries, and missing are words at the end of lines that have been hyphenated. Marcia had found an advertisement for John Jay's school in Brussels for July 1825 (which did not mention his name or exactly where the school was) and thought it might also refer to Evan. Gradually she found more ads – dating from 1812 for the school in Essex, up to 1827. I slotted them into my timeline and began examining the wording in comparison with the items in Evan's ordination bundles. The story started to make perfect sense.

By 6 January 1824 'a Graduate of the University of Cambridge' was in charge of the classical department, and that graduate was Evan. The ad describes John Jay as 'an experienced Merchant, who was at the head of a Mercantile House in Rotterdam and in Leith for many years', and he was in charge of the 'Commercial Branches' of the school.[32] Then at the latest in early autumn, Rev. Holworthy, chaplain to the embassy at The Hague and Brussels, offered Evan a title for orders as his curate in Brussels, because on 18 September, Fellows of Trinity College, Cambridge wrote a flourishing testimonial addressed to the Bishop of London:

> Whereas Evan Jenkins Bachelor of Arts of this College (who was admitted 22nd December 1817 and took the degree of Bachelor of Arts 4th May 1822) intends to offer himself to the Bishop for the holy office of Deacon and has requested of us a Testimonial for that purpose We the Vice Master and Senior Fellows of this College whose names are underwritten Do testify that the said Evan Jenkins did during his residence with us apply himself to good and useful learning and live soberly and regularly amongst us and that to the best of our knowledge he never held or maintained any doctrine or tenet contrary to the Church of England as by Law established.

The testimonial is sealed, and signed by the Vice Chancellor and seven Senior Fellows.[33]

Evan presumably had taken with him to Brussels the note signed by the Norrisian professor to confirm he had attended the correct number of lectures, since that is also in his deacon ordination bundle, but he didn't have confirmation of his age and baptism. It is interesting that David went all the way to Cardiganshire that September to copy it out from the register. Could Evan not trust his sister Mary to do it? Or perhaps David had volunteered as he wanted to visit the family. The odd thing was that it didn't arrive in Brussels for over a year. On 9 May 1825 Evan sent his testimonials to Bishop Howley but had to apologize that he couldn't enclose his certificate of baptism 'which by some mistake or other has not yet been received. Mr. Jenkins will deliver in person to his Lordship's Secretary on his arrival in London in course of the ensuing week.' But he wasn't able to do that either – the certificate signed by David is instead in his priest ordination bundle, together with a letter from Evan about it dated 10 November 1825. Perhaps the first one had been lost in the post; maybe David had made a copy and sent it again. The bishop was obviously not fussed, and perhaps it was a vital curacy to fill. But Evan wasn't ordained deacon until the end of May 1825, that is eight months after his Trinity College testimonial. Why the delay?

Rev. William Holworthy must have been keen to have Evan as his curate; he could perhaps have got a 'ready-made' curate, already ordained, but a stipend of £40 wasn't much and Evan had his teaching job. Holworthy's great-great-grandmother Elizabeth Desborough had inherited Elsworth manor house, a few miles from Cambridge. In 1697 she married Matthew Holworthy of a London merchant family. They left the manor to the illegitimate son, Samuel (d. 1765), of their daughter Susannah by her eldest sister's husband (I wonder what story lies behind that). Samuel's son was our William Holworthy's father, Rev. Matthew Holworthy, a graduate of Cambridge and Rector of Elsworth from 1791. By then the manor was heavily mortgaged and Matthew agreed to sell it in 1824.[34] That must have been devastating for his son. William was born at Elsworth in 1792, so he was two years older than Evan. He matriculated at Clare College, Cambridge in 1816, but seems to have stayed only a term – if that – since he was offered a title for orders and ordained deacon in December, and priest six months later, having acquired a living at Earlham with Bowthorpe in Norfolk on the death of the incumbent in September 1817. He also acquired two posts as stipendiary curate.

It seems probable that his father took William out of Cambridge – where he had been admitted pensioner – because of his financial difficulties, and used his contacts to get his son the living and the two curacies even though he had barely spent any time at Cambridge, let alone graduated. But less than seven months later, William was described as 'Vicar of Earlham, and Chaplain to the British Embassy at the Hague' when he married Sarah Churchill, daughter of the Rector of Blickling in Norfolk, on 2 April 1818.[35] The salary as embassy chaplain was obviously good enough for him to employ a curate at Earlham and support a wife.

As I mentioned above, Rev. Stonestreet had tried to get himself made chaplain to the then ambassador in 1815, Sir Charles Stuart. But Stuart was discouraging: Stonestreet writes that Stuart 'says that Ambassadors have no allowance for Chaplains: that when they accompany Embassies, it is on terms of private acquaintance. Of this I do not believe one word.' Stonestreet had also commented earlier, 'Contrary to custom the late Ambassador Lord Clancarty, had no Chaplain.'[36] The Earl of Clancarty was reappointed as ambassador in 1816, though the decision to appoint Holworthy as chaplain may have been made by the Minister Plenipotentiary at the Court of the Netherlands, George William Chad.[37] Clancarty's accounts during his time in The Hague are known, since in 1822 Parliament demanded to know how the huge sums provided for diplomatic salaries were actually spent. Clancarty provided detailed lists which showed that, before he took up his post, his manager had reckoned that £500 per annum would be needed for the chaplain and secretary. Raymond A. Jones in his book on the diplomatic service states that 'after 1818' £300 was paid by Clancarty to the chaplain.[38] That is a good amount contrasted with the £40 a year that Holworthy was offering Evan.[39]

From a letter Holworthy wrote to the Bishop of London, it appears that the reason he needed a curate was the constant removal of the Court between The Hague and Brussels, and he was concerned that his Brussels congregation were left without a chaplain when he was at The Hague.[40] It may also have been because by July 1824 he had four children under the age of six, and his wife could no longer face the constant upheaval or his prolonged absences.[41]

* * *

Holworthy was based in Brussels at the baroque Church of the Augustines, which evidence suggests the irritable Rev. Prince had first used for Anglican services in 1818. It was also known as the King's Church, since King William and his family attended Dutch services there after he became King of the United Netherlands. The *temple des Augustins* was built for Augustinian monks in the seventeenth century, on the site of the modern Place de Brouckère and the bus station, and near the early nineteenth-century neoclassical Théâtre royal de la Monnaie. After the 1830 revolution the church was used for exhibitions and concerts – Liszt and Berlioz were there in 1842 – and for prize-givings of the Conservatoire Royale and the Athenée Royale at which Charlotte's teacher M. Heger delivered speeches, giving a copy of one of them to Emily.[42] The church was demolished in the last years of the nineteenth century because it blocked the traffic along the new boulevard, but its 1642 façade was rebuilt at the front of the église de la Trinité in the Ixelles area of Brussels.[43] A plaque on the imposing black wood door states that the church was built by Franquart. Jacob Franquart (d. 1651) was a painter, court architect and copper-plate engraver, born in Brussels or Antwerp. The plaque is wonderfully defiant and proud: the church was 'sauvee grace a la paroisse de la Trinite qui en fit l'acquisition et la reedifia pierre par pierre' – the parish rebuilt it stone by stone. I was glad they had been so bullish and felt rather sentimental when I saw it one May afternoon in 2015. The interior had been smashed into rubble in the late nineteenth century and the façade is now in a completely different place, but this was the church where Evan had started his life as a clergyman, in a building that whispered with memories of Catholic monks. The façade and its new church are only a minute's walk from where my other Brussels family, the Hodsons, lived from the 1890s onwards. Constance Hodson was to marry Evan and Eliza's grandson in 1913.[44]

* * *

I noted above the delay that occurred between Evan receiving his testimonial from Trinity College in September 1824 and his ordination as deacon at St James's Palace in London in May 1825. It may be that the bishop wanted to be certain that Evan was being offered a genuine job and that the small figure of £40 was adequate and guaranteed – Evan was being got very cheaply. Frances Knight considers what might have concerned the bishop:

> As the competition for titles had intensified at the beginning of the century, so the climate had become ripe for the exploitation of potential curates by unscrupulous incumbents or their agents. It was not unusual for such people to offer a title for orders with a nominal or non-existent stipend [...] Although the Stipendiary Curates' Act (1813) [and] the Consolidated Act (1817) [...] had outlawed such proceedings, the evidence suggests that plenty of incumbents were prepared to enter into secret, illegal agreements with desperate potential curates.[45]

Also Evan might have wanted more time to prepare his New Testament Greek, doctrinal and scriptural knowledge ready for the examination in London. But the five months between his Trinity College testimonial and the 'Si Quis' in February seems long. Perhaps the main reason for the delay was the change of ambassadors at The Hague in 1823/4: this would have an effect on Rev. Holworthy as well as on the man he wanted as his curate.

* * *

I met Murder on the way
He had a mask like Castlereagh –

– Shelley, 'The Mask of Anarchy'

Shelley's poem was written in Italy soon after the 'Peterloo' Massacre of 16 August 1819, when unarmed men and women, including a child, were killed by volunteer forces and soldiers – some who had fought at Waterloo, hence 'Peterloo' – at a peaceful protest meeting for Parliamentary reform at St Peter's Field outside Manchester. Shelley's reaction is understandable, but the lines are vicious and unfair. Castlereagh was not directly involved – he was Foreign Secretary and Leader of the House of Commons – but as the government spokesman in the Commons (the Prime Minister sat in the Lords) he had to justify the Manchester magistrates' use of yeomanry and Hussars. Following unrest elsewhere in the North, the government introduced the repressive 'Six Acts', which has been likened by one historian to the South African Apartheid government's measures after the Sharpeville Massacre in 1960.[46] Castlereagh became immensely unpopular, yet he had been an indefatigable and supremely skilful Foreign Secretary (from 1812) in bringing an end to the long years of war and in deftly negotiating the peace. Leigh Hunt didn't publish what Richard Holmes has called 'the greatest poem of political protest ever written in English' until after Shelley's death, probably fearful of another imprisonment.[47]

As Foreign Secretary, Robert Stewart, Viscount Castlereagh (b. 1769), chose ambassadors, and for important postings these were often friends whom he could trust. The Earl of Clancarty, also Irish-born, was a close friend, and returned to The Hague in 1816/17; he would thus have approved of the appointment of Rev. Holworthy as chaplain. The unbearable workload that Castlereagh faced, and the death of his father, contributed to his mental breakdown in 1822: on 12 August he committed suicide by slitting his throat with a penknife; he was just fifty-three.[48]

His natural successor as Foreign Secretary was George Canning (1770–1827), who had served in the post over a decade before, and had even been challenged to a duel by Castlereagh in 1809. Canning had never fired a pistol in his life and was shot in the thigh.[49] Canning had a very different background to his Irish-titled predecessor, though both his parents were also Irish Protestants; his mother became an actress after his father died, which became an embarrassment for him and a handy taunt for others. (The taunt against his sometime colleague/ sometime adversary Castlereagh was that he and his wife couldn't produce children – the same fatuous taunt directed at a female Prime Minister in the twenty-first century. Byron even compared Castlereagh unfavourably with his Don Juan.[50]) Canning was the only man without a title to be Foreign Secretary until 1924.[51] If the handsome, courteous Castlereagh was sometimes drawling and dull in his speeches and despatches, Canning, a brilliant classicist, was a lightning rod of eloquence, oratory and humour, and he was a populist. However, the writer and painter William Hazlitt, one-time friend of Coleridge and Wordsworth, derided Canning's eloquence in his *The Spirit of the Age* (1824): 'Beneath the broad and gilded chandelier that throws its light upon "the nation's Great Divan," Mr. Canning piles the lofty harangue, high over-arched with metaphor, dazzling with epithets, sparkling with jests – take it out of doors, or examine it by the light of common sense, and it is not more than a paltry string of sophisms, of trite truisms, and sorry buffooneries [...] Truth, liberty, justice, humanity, war or peace, civilization or barbarism, are things of little consequence, except for him to make speeches upon them.'[52]

Important for this story is that Canning chose his friends to be ambassadors even more than Castlereagh had done, and he got to work on that in 1823. One man he wanted to get rid of was Castlereagh's friend Clancarty as ambassador in the Netherlands, who was forced to retire that December.[53] Then Canning had to arrange the posting of two of his personal friends, Sir Charles Bagot and Lord Granville, which was tricky when Sir Charles Stuart – Castlereagh's appointment in Paris, and whom we have already met in connection with Rev. Stonestreet – could not be recalled, it had been agreed, until King Louis XVIII's death: at the age of sixty-eight Louis was obese and had gout and gangrene, but he lingered on.

Oxford-educated Sir Charles Bagot (1781–1843) will be important for the beginning of Evan and Eliza's story. He was a long-time friend of Foreign Secretary George Canning, and was currently ambassador at one of the most important postings, St Petersburg. But he wrote to Canning that he couldn't afford to have his nine children educated in England while he remained in Russia trying to finance two homes; he asked for a 'demotion' to The Hague, which would be nearer to his children. He wrote that he couldn't have his children educated in Russia for moral reasons, as well as the climate. He was a professional diplomat, having worked as under-secretary at the Foreign Office in 1807, where he had met Canning, and he had successfully served in Washington in 1815–19.[54] Canning was sympathetic, but he wanted to get his other trusted friend Lord Granville to Paris, where Sir Charles Stuart was being obdurate, so Granville was posted 'pro tem' as ambassador to the Netherlands in February 1824. Finally Louis XVIII died on 16 September 1824, and Canning could move his ambassadorial chess-men. Stuart was recalled from Paris; but he made such a fuss that Bagot's move to the Netherlands became a problem with both King George IV and the Prime Minister, Lord Liverpool. Canning soothed King George into acquiescence about Bagot.[55] And meanwhile the 'little people' – Holworthy and Evan – had to wait; for both, their futures were at stake, especially Evan's.

Sir Charles Bagot finally arrived at The Hague in the autumn of 1824, possibly on 9 November. There survives a list of expenses for officials in the United Netherlands which includes, for Bagot: 'for post-office charges, salary of the paid attaché, and of the chaplain to the embassy, and extra allowance for house rent, in consequence of the double residence of the Court at Brussels and at the Hague, from the 9th November to the 31st of December 1824 222 7 6'.[56] I can only speculate, but approving of Holworthy as his chaplain and of his chaplain's plans for a curate might have taken a while: it was the least of his duties. For Evan, his life hung in the balance as he went on with his classical teaching at John Jay's school, wondering if he would ever be ordained. But obviously the go-ahead – and the guarantee for the tiny amount of £40 a year (which presumably Holworthy had to pay out of his salary) – was given. On 27 February 1825, Rev. Streynsham Master read out the 'Si Quis' in the Chapel Royal and Rev. William Holworthy read it out in the 'King's Church of St. Augustine':

> Notice is hereby given that Evan Jenkins, Bachelor of Arts, of Trinity College, Cambridge, and now resident in this City, intends to offer himself a Candidate for the Holy Office of Deacon at the ensuing Ordination of the Lord Bishop of London, and if any person knows any just cause or impediment for which he ought not to be admitted into Holy Orders, he is now to declare the same or to signify the same forthwith to the Bishop of London.[57]

I don't know whether it is unusual to read a 'Si Quis' in two churches simulta-neously: presumably it had been agreed that Evan would sometimes take Rev. Master's place in the Chapel Royal. No one in the congregation objected: they all approved of Evan as Holworthy's curate. I hope John Jay opened a bottle of claret for him that Sunday evening, and maybe Eliza's heavily pregnant stepmother Johanna celebrated with a cup of tea – she gave birth only a few days later. Did Evan now propose to Eliza formally? No doubt John Jay gave his consent with delight: an ordained son-in-law was good; a mere schoolteacher was not.

* * *

Yet there were still delays as they waited for the bishop's next ordination in London. It wasn't until 3 May that Holworthy and Master wrote their testimonial to the bishop: 'We […] do testify and make known that Evan Jenkins Bachelor of Arts nominated to serve in the Church of Saint Augustines in Brussels' had 'been personally known to us for the space of nearly three years', and Holworthy added a note to the bishop confirming that Evan would be given a yearly stipend of £40, 'and I hereby declare that I do not fraudulently give this certificate to entitle the said Evan Jenkins to receive Holy Orders but with a real intention to employ him in my said Church'.[58]

Finally, on Sunday 29 May 1825, Evan Jenkins BA was ordained deacon at the sixteenth-century Chapel Royal, St James's Palace in central London by William Howley, Bishop of London, along with thirty-seven other men.[59] Fifteen years later, Queen Victoria and Prince Albert were married there, both of whom Evan was to meet. It surely must be one of the most atmospheric places to be ordained, both exciting and moving, redolent of hundreds of years of history since the time of Henry VIII. The Bishop's Act Book correctly has Evan's age as thirty, but wrongly Oxford – 'Oxon' – instead of Cambridge. Thankfully the clerk got his university right when he was ordained priest.

Evan perhaps lodged with his friend Peter Felix in Chelsea. It may have been a long stay in England since on 3 July Evan was in Pudsey with his brother David: Evan officiated at the baptism there of Samuel, son of Joshua and Hannah Armitage. It was surely the first he had done and he must have been grateful, if nervous, to have some practice with his brother looking on. I'd like to think that Eliza was with him and met David; but as yet unmarried, Eliza would have needed a female companion – possibly her younger sister Margaret went with her.[60] In perhaps their absence, Streynsham Master baptized John's and stepmother Johanna Jay's daughter Lucy-Hermione on 7 July at the Chapel Royal in Brussels, who was to die in France aged only six. But everything now was so bright for the Jays. On 4 July, Eliza's younger brother John Livingston Jay was admitted as a pensioner at Gonville and Caius College, Cambridge, and on 11 July, John Jay put in another advertisement for his school – the ad that Marcia had excitedly found – and this time 'The Classical Department [is] under the direction of a Clergyman of the Church of England, a Graduate of the University of Cambridge'.[61] This was definitely Evan. Eleven days later, Evan and Eliza were married.

* * *

The marriage took place on Friday 22 July 1825:

> I hereby certify that Evan Jenkins Clerk, of Aberystwith in the County of Cardigan in South Wales, now residing in Brussels, Bachelor, and Eliza Jay, Spinster, daughter of John and the late Helen Jay, late of Woodford in the County of Essex, now residing in Brussels, were duly married according to the Rites of the Church of England in the House of his Britannic Majesty's Ambassador at Brussels this twenty second day of July 1825. By me
> W.M. Pierce A.M.
> Officiating Minister

It was witnessed by George Edgcumbe and George Tierney 'Attached to the Embassy'. In addition there is a statement signed by Evan and Eliza that they were of full age, that there was no lawful impediment to their marrying and that they were British subjects. Below their statement, Charles Bagot has written: 'Sworn before me His Britannic Majesty's Ambassador at Brussels', which is witnessed by George Edgcumbe and this time W.H. Holworthy 'Attached to the Embassy'. (The Hon. George Edgcumbe was at Harrow at about the same time as Evan's future brother-in-law George Wyndham.)[62]

To be recognized as lawful, the marriage had to take place at the embassy. In 1825 it was at no. 110 rue de Brabant, 'au parc'.[63] This was the old name for the rue de la Loi, which starts at the north end of the park. After the Revolution of 1830 the embassy was at no. 3 rue Ducale, also on the north side of the park.[64] It seems that the old embassy had been destroyed during the revolution. One guidebook of 1834 states that on the rue de Brabant that ran along one side of the park 'On our right are the black ruins, the walls alone standing, of the *hotel Torrington*, so called from its having been long the residence of the British ambassador of that name. This noble edifice was burned during the combat in the park in 1830. It must be rebuilt in 1834.'[65] No doubt the French translator boasted of his fluent English! He presumably meant that the embassy was about to be rebuilt on the same site, perhaps as the lovely house that now lies on the corner of rue Ducale. George Byng, fourth Viscount Torrington, was Envoy to the Imperial Court at Brussels, 1783–92.[66] I can only imagine that Eliza and Evan were married in an elegant room overlooking the park; he would officiate numerous times at marriages in the new ambassador's house.

The officiating minister, W.M. Pierce, was surely a Cambridge friend of Evan's, since Rev. Holworthy or Rev. Master would have been happy to marry Eliza to the new curate. Evan may also have hoped that brother David could come to Brussels. William Matthews Pierce was admitted sizar at St John's College, Cambridge in July 1817, took his BA a year earlier than Evan and was ordained as deacon that year in Lincoln (1821).[67] He got his first living as priest two years later and after a variety of livings, all in Lincolnshire, he died in his mid-sixties in 1864 after what sounds a straightforward life. But like everyone he had his share of tragedies. After a search through newspapers and censuses, which had only a few bare bones to offer, I found poignant details of his last years: the census of 1851 has him as a visitor to the curate of Belchford with his wife Elizabeth. She is forty-seven, he is fifty-three – he was thus about four years younger than Evan. But I was struck by the 1861 census: William is described as the Incumbent of West Ashby, but he is down as 'Father', whereas his son Francis Rockcliffe Pierce is 'Head' and a 'Landed Proprietor' and the only other inhabitants of the house are seven servants. William's wife has presumably died and he is living in his son's house with no other family. It sounds grim. But a note in a newspaper the next year is sadder: it is an advertisement for creditors and debtors to get in touch with William because his son Francis has died (aged thirty-four).[68] Rev. William died sixteen months after his son.

* * *

On 4 October, Rev. Holworthy wrote to the bishop about his curate, Rev. Jenkins, asking him to be made a priest at the next ordination:

> [Evan Jenkins] informed me your Lordship was kind enough to assure him that upon showing sufficient cause, he would be admitted for Priest's orders at your Lordship's next ordination. To this end allow me to state that I am about to quit Brussels with the Court, for a twelve months residence at the Hague; that I have here a numerous congregation, which certainly ought not to be left so long a time without a Clergyman in full orders; may I trust therefore your Lordship will consider this a sufficient plea to induce your Lordship to deviate from the general rule, in favour of Mr. Jenkins, and that he may be received at the next ordination.[69]

The bishop agreed to fast-track Evan, who was given another testimonial from Rev. Holworthy and Rev. Master. After two months under Rev. Holworthy's wing, he was probably looking forward to being in sole charge, which was almost immediate, since we know from Evan's letter to the bishop that Rev. Holworthy and his family had gone to The Hague on 18 October. With this letter of 10 November, Evan enclosed, finally, his certificate of baptism from brother David. He also put in a request as regards the ordination in London in December:

> Having undertaken the whole of the duty at the King's Church during Mr. Holworthy's absence I should wish to be away from Brussels for as short a time as possible. I shall therefore consider a great favour if you will have the kindness to inform me on what day the Examination of the Candidates for Priest's Orders is to take place, as I think, by timing it well, I may only be obliged to be absent from my duties here one Sunday.[70]

Written on the front cover of the priest's bundle is 'Did not attend examination', so perhaps a date could not be found that would enable Evan to miss only one Sunday service, or the bishop just waived it in Evan's case – maybe he had been suitably impressed by Evan at his examination only six months before, or a congregation doing without a priest in the lead up to Christmas was a serious matter for Bishop Howley.

On Sunday 18 December 1825, Evan attended the priest's ordination at Fulham Palace, the bishop's residence just outside London. A palace on the Thames sounds suitably grand, but parts of it were in a woeful condition. The rather splendid chapel that visitors can view now was not built until 1866, and the Tudor red-brick courtyard was partly in ruins. The eighteenth-century extension, with its high windows looking out onto extensive grounds leading to the river, would have been elegant and impressive, but the 'hall' used as the chapel for ordinations is small and could fit twice into the great hall that Evan knew at Trinity College. But maybe Evan hardly noticed – to be made priest was moving, exciting, nerve-wracking – especially as he would be concerned about the packet back to Antwerp in stormy December weather. There were seven other men from Cambridge ordained priest alongside him, and one from Oxford (if the clerk is to be believed – he manages to spell Evan as 'Evans', but he gets his university right this time), as well as seven men labelled 'Literate' and 'Colonial'.[71] Evan possibly again stayed with his friend Peter Felix, as Chelsea is just three miles east, towards London, along the river. Evan must have been thrilled and maybe daunted. His trip to Brussels to pay off his Cambridge debts had led, in three years, to ordination and to marriage, and in less than seven months he was to become a father. Perhaps his concern about leaving his Brussels congregation for more than one Sunday was not the only reason he wanted to head back home fast.

* * *

One incredibly useful piece of information in Evan's letter to the bishop of 10 November was that he gave his address as 'Glacis de Namur', that is, on the boulevard near the Porte de Namur in Ixelles – on the other side of the former city walls that were gradually being levelled around Brussels. He was living somewhere along the modern Boulevard de Waterloo ring road, a short distance from the Royal Palace. This is where John Jay's school was, according to the Almanac of 1828,[72] and where Evan and Eliza were living after their marriage, though probably with hopes of renting somewhere of their own to get away from Eliza's stepmother and a noisy baby (Eliza's half-sister) and prepare for their own baby. I wonder also if Evan soon began to think how long he could stay on in a predominantly commercial school run by his father-in-law which, in a Dutch advertisement, mentioned Latin as only one of the languages, and which didn't mention that it was taught by a Cambridge graduate and clergyman since no Dutch parent would be particularly interested in that.[73]

It is impossible to tell if the school was getting enough pupils, despite the claims of the advertisements that it had (or could accommodate) fifty or more pupils. Eliza's brother John Livingston Jay had been admitted, as I mentioned above, to Gonville and Caius College, Cambridge in July of that year, but below his name in the register are five blank lines.[74] It seems clear that he didn't show up. John Livingston is recorded as a clerk at Greenwich Hospital that year, but he might have started there in 1823, as he retired at the age of sixty-three (b. 1802) after forty-two years and four months' service.[75] It could be that his father's school wasn't doing well and he didn't have the money to send his second son to Cambridge, or that John Livingston changed his mind – the only point in going to Cambridge for him would be to become a clergyman or a lawyer, and maybe he found the work of a clerk more congenial and less stressful.

But if Eliza's pregnancy was one exciting piece of news for the family, at the end of that year younger sister Margaret met someone who would change her life in a more extreme fashion. When the Jay family arrived in 1821, it is probable that Margaret, at seventeen, attended school to hone her accomplishments, such as languages, music and drawing, and make friends with English girls sent to Brussels to get that extra bit of polish before entering the marriage market. Her granddaughter Charlotte May Wright, whose memoirs contain the usual Chinese whispers of family history, wrote that 'Grandmama was very beautiful and charming. Her son met an old gentleman in Sydney, who told him he remembered his mother as a noted beauty in Brussels. She was very French in many ways. She and my mother conversed in French. I remember being rather horrified as a little girl, when a travelling French scientist came to Dalwood [Margaret's home in the Hunter Valley], seeing Grandmama turn into a vivacious Frenchwoman, talking French and gesticulating.'[76]

A letter in the archives in New South Wales, written over sixty years later by Margaret's sister-in-law, is our source for how Margaret met her husband George Wyndham. At Christmas 1825, Margaret, shortly to turn twenty-two, was in Rome with the Taylor family. There was widowed Hannah Taylor, her son Samuel and his new wife Mary née Still (then twenty-three), Hannah's daughter Mary (aged twenty-one) and the bride's brother, the newly ordained John Still. With them was 'her friend & schoolfellow Miss Jay'. It is ambiguous which Mary the 'her' refers to.[77] The Taylors had acquired their wealth in the cotton industry and lived in Moston, near Manchester. The Stills lived in Wiltshire. Rev. John Still, the patriarch, who did not accompany them, was prebendary at Salisbury Cathedral, and was well enough off to send his son to Harrow and then Oxford. It is sometimes thought that the unmarried Mary Taylor from Manchester was the schoolfriend, as there are a few letters from her to Margaret in the archives, and none from Mary Taylor née Still. In 1849 the unmarried Mary wrote to Margaret remarking that she had last seen her almost twenty-three years ago (implying in 1826 at the end of the grand tour), and that the lock of hair that Margaret had sent her was just as black and silky as then.[78] My instinct is that had she been a schoolfriend in Brussels she might have thought back instead to the time when she first met Margaret, and there are no reminiscences of Brussels in her few letters. There is also evidence that she was 'delicate' (though she lived into her nineties) and may never have been abroad before 1825.[79] The newly married Taylors, however, lived in Brussels for a while: Mary Taylor née Still gave birth there to her son Samuel in June 1826; the registration was witnessed by John Livingston Jay, who was presumably on holiday from his job in Greenwich.[80] It is possible that Mary Still and her younger sister Eliza were at a boarding school in Brussels in the early 1820s, anticipating two other pairs of sisters twenty years later.

George Wyndham, of Dinton House in Wiltshire, was travelling abroad to research wine-making a few years after graduation from Trinity College, Cambridge. He was laid low with a fever in Malta and was advised to leave the island. In Rome he was again ill but on Christmas Day he went for a walk with his stick in the sunshine to the Pincian Hill, with its beautiful walks and trees, recently commissioned by Napoleon. He knew no one in Rome and was thinking wistfully of the family gathering at home, according to his sister, when he was hailed by 'a cheery voice asking "if he saw George Wyndham or was it the ghost of George Wyndham"'. It was his schoolfriend from Harrow, John Still. It doesn't seem that the fateful meeting between George and Margaret took place on the romantic Pincian Hill: George was taken back to the hotel to meet the rest of the touring party.

> The whole party were most kind to my invalid brother & he afterwards saw them every day, explored all that was to be seen in that ancient city, & when the Taylors went to Naples he followed them & also joined their party part of the way homewards – but left them before they reached Switzerland [and] was then engaged to marry Margaret Jay if her Father consented.

I imagine that John Jay was more than willing to give his consent (and especially Margaret's stepmother), as that left only teenage Janet at home. It is possible that Margaret arrived back in Brussels around March 1826. George wasn't a total stranger: Margaret's brother Samuel Jay knew John Still's brother at Lincoln's Inn, as well as Samuel Taylor there.[81] Also Evan had been at Trinity College the same time as George, though he was unlikely to have known him well. Evan married the couple, a year later, in the ambassador's residence on 26 April 1827. Their sworn statement was signed by the ambassador, Charles Bagot. Four months later, Margaret and George Wyndham sailed to Australia from Plymouth; Eliza and Margaret were never to see each other again. But Margaret's descendants kept letters, and because of that we have fascinating and often moving glimpses into Eliza's life that will be explored in later chapters.

* * *

A few hours after I thought I had ended this chapter, something struck me about the pairs of sisters at school in Brussels in the 1820s and 1840s. I had typed up my notebooks containing jottings of four years of research and was trying to think of the keyword. I found what I was looking for. I whizzed to my timeline to check two dates: they were just what I wanted – that is, it suddenly dawned on me that the school that Eliza's younger sister Margaret had attended with Mary Still, and probably also Eliza Still, may have been the same school that the Brontë sisters' friends Mary and Martha Taylor had attended, and that Charlotte had wanted to join them at, except that it was too expensive. It was surely the Château de Koekelberg. My exploration of this school must wait for a later chapter.

Ten

Evan Embattled, 1826–1829

The Button-maker's Grandson and the Scottish Bishop

The 'grandson' and 'bishop' arrived as irritants in Evan Jenkins's life at the end of this period. The grandson's epithet has been provided by Lord Byron. The 'bishop' was frankly rather dubious, and maybe Thackeray agreed. Charlotte Brontë encountered the 'grandson', though the reader will search in vain for his name in any of the biographies about her.

* * *

On 31 January 1826, the ambassador to the United Netherlands, Sir Charles Bagot, received a despatch in code from his friend George Canning, the Foreign Secretary. Britain had just signed a trade treaty with France, but agreement on trade with the Netherlands was foundering. Bagot and the second secretary George Tierney were unable to decipher the despatch, so they asked for more codes. They spent all night deciphering it, only to discover that it was in rhyme: 'In matter of commerce the fault of the Dutch, / Is offering too little and asking too much. / The French are with equal advantage content. / So we clap on Dutch bottoms just 20 per cent.' Bagot was amused.[1] There is a glimpse of the man Charles Bagot in the memoirs of the Irish journalist and novelist Thomas Colley Grattan (1791–1864). Grattan was a distant cousin of the Duke of Wellington, and thus of Bagot's wife, Mary Charlotte Anne Wellesley-Pole, who was a niece of the duke. In 1827 Grattan had persuaded the great actor Edmund Kean to star in his play *Ben Nazir, the Saracen* at Drury Lane. It is probable that the mercury the by-now dissipated Kean was taking to cure his syphilis affected his ability to remember lines. He broke down on the first night, which rather killed the play.[2]

Financial difficulties forced Grattan to move to Brussels with his family, where he remained (apart from a short period during the revolution) until the end of the 1830s.

Grattan's memoirs, *Beaten Paths, and those who trod them* (1862), is a collection of essays and sketches about people he had met, places he had been to and events he had witnessed. In June 1828, for example, Grattan was invited by his Scottish neighbour, Pryse Lockhart Gordon (who had shown Byron around the battlefield of Waterloo in 1816), to meet two poets who were passing through Brussels – Wordsworth and Coleridge. The pair, now in their fifties, had finally ended their long period of estrangement, and this time Wordsworth had brought his daughter, 23-year-old Dora, to Europe.[3] 'I had pictured [Coleridge] a giant in look and a tyrant in talk,' writes Grattan. 'But Coleridge was neither. He was about five feet five inches in height, of a full and lazy appearance but not actually stout [...] His face was extremely handsome, its expression placid and benevolent [...] He seemed to breathe in words.' But Wordsworth 'was a perfect antithesis to Coleridge – tall, wiry, harsh in features, coarse in figure, inelegant in looks [...] He more resembled a mountain farmer than a "lake poet". His whole air was unrefined and unprepossessing.'[4] So much for Wordsworth!

Grattan's memories of Sir Charles Bagot (1781–1843) are warm, but fuzzy. After a period of illness in Brussels after his first arrival there, Grattan was invited to dinner by the ambassador, then in his late forties, and Lady Bagot. 'Even to this moment I have a cheering recollection of that pleasant day, when, relieved from the long confinement of a sick room, I seemed once more entering the world of social fellowship, and joining a circle of friendly acquaintances [...] From that day, in the spring of 1829, to the last on which I saw him in the Government House at Kingston, in Upper Canada, in the summer of 1842, I received continued proofs of kindness and friendship from that most generous-hearted and least-intolerant of public men.'[5] He writes that he would like to describe more of his relations with Sir Charles, but his book is not 'a series of biographies'. Alas. But I think Grattan's few words explain wonderfully well why Eliza and Evan gave their son, born on 7 July 1826, the first name of Charles.[6] Charles Bagot is the only one with that name that I can find, and it suddenly seemed an obvious choice. Presumably Sir Charles was one of the godfathers when the baby was baptized in December by Rev. Holworthy. It might look like a bit of upstart social climbing to name a son after a baronet, but perhaps instead Evan and Eliza named him after a man who had become a family friend. My mother often said that the Jenkins family had been promised a legacy if they named a son 'Card', as Evan and Eliza were to do later, but that it never appeared. But I wonder if the legacy might have been hoped for from Sir Charles Bagot. However, he was to leave Brussels in 1831 after the revolution (his patron and friend George Canning had died four years before), and his appointment as Governor-in-Chief of British North America ten years later took him a long way from his Brussels godson, who is not mentioned in his will. Evan and Eliza's eldest son was never known as Charles; he was always called by his second name, Edward (often shortened to Ned). So my hunt for a possible godfather named Edward began. Could it be a family name or was it another new friend in Brussels? Their first son's godmother was Margaret Bowden, Eliza's first cousin and the only member of the family of eight children, whom John Keats encountered in Edmonton, to survive beyond the age of twenty, as I described above. At least Margaret mentioned her godson in her will of 1865, although she was brutal in it about one of his brothers.

* * *

Although Evan's title for orders was as curate at the Church of the Augustines in the lower town, deputizing for Rev. Holworthy, this changed early in 1826. Rev. Streynsham Master, who had won affection from his congregation at the Chapel Royal, had gone home to Croston, Lancashire by May 1826. His last signature in the register of baptisms and burials as he signs off 'for the year 1825' is on 2 January 1826, and he sent a copy to London, to be kept 'in the Registry of Doctors Commons', on 4 February.[7] Perhaps negotiations with his creditors in England were now settled and he was no longer in danger of being arrested. His family returned home some time between February and May. That obviously meant a shuffling of duties for Holworthy and Evan. After Rev. Prince had absconded with the original register, there was a new register for the two churches used by British residents, which again does not name the church the ministers officiated at. Evan's first baptism was on 19 February 1826; his first burial on 2 March. His first marriage (at the embassy) was in June. That year, in Brussels, Evan performed thirteen baptisms; Holworthy performed four (in November and December). There is a letter in the Lincolnshire Archives from Rev. Richard Waldo Sibthorp, dated 28 August 1826, as he did a mini-tour of the Continent, who is clear that both churches were in use. Lytton Strachey had fun with him in his *Eminent Victorians* of 1918; Sibthorp got off lightly. Sibthorp's story reflects the religious uncertainties and dramatic shifts in Britain, the pendulum swinging between at one extreme evangelicalism and the zeal of a Methodist to, on the other, Roman Catholicism, sometimes in the same person: Cardinal Newman is a good example; Sibthorp another.

Sibthorp – there is a mezzotint of him with a long nose, heavy black eyebrows and kindly, sloping eyes in the National Portrait Gallery – was born in 1792 near Lincoln, the youngest son of its MP, Colonel Humphry Waldo Sibthorp. He was thus two years older than Evan and in his early thirties when he visited Brussels. He had matriculated at Oxford in 1809; two years later he tried to become a Roman Catholic in Wolverhampton, when they were still subject to discrimination. A brother brought him back 'under police surveillance and chancery order'. He was ordained as an Anglican in 1815, and was apparently enthusiastically evangelical in his preaching; by 1825 he was recognized as 'one of the leaders of the London evangelicals'.[8] It is perhaps for that reason that Evan, or Rev. Holworthy, invited him to preach at the Church of the Augustines in Brussels a year later. He wrote to his sister, in Arundel, Sussex, on 28 August 1826 that Brussels 'is the handsomest city I have been in yet'. He stayed in the splendid Hôtel de Bellevue in the Place Royale 'on the top of the hill, overlooking the city & the park':

> I preached yesterday at the Dutch Church which is lent to the English in the middle of the day: there is also another English congregation in the French protestant Church at 2 in the afternoon: & both are well attended. It is full indeed of English – many as residents.

He dined that day at the table d'hôte. With a new baby, Evan and Eliza might have apologized that they couldn't entertain Rev. Sibthorp. He adds that 'The King [King William I of the Netherlands] & Royal family tolerably popular:- & a very great contrast in many respects to France: where all seems ready for an explosion.' He is about to see the battlefield at Waterloo and comments: 'The Place Royale in which our hotel is situated was filled with the wounded, brought from the field of battle: & the blood actually ran down the gutters of the street leading to the lower town.' Possibly Evan and Eliza were relieved that they couldn't invite Sibthorp to dinner, since he ends his letter eulogizing England: 'I come back more satisfied with my native country than ever: & I hope more sensible of the blessing of being an Englishman [...] I shall not again visit the continent: it is a sort of travelling which does not suit my taste altogether.'[9] The last thing you want from a guest is a comment on how ghastly it is where you live.

Fifteen years later, having resided at Magdalen College as a Fellow and then at a living on the Isle of Wight, Sibthorp became a Roman Catholic priest, to the consternation of many. A few years later he returned to the established church, but in the 1860s became a Roman Catholic again. He had a Catholic requiem mass at his funeral in 1879, but had insisted that the Anglican service was read at his grave. If Prime Minister Gladstone thought of him as a 'holy man', Lytton Strachey was amused.[10] In his description of Cardinal Newman's change from Anglican orders to Roman Catholic priest under the influence of the Oxford Movement in 1845, Strachey mentions 'unhappy Mr Sibthorpe [sic], who subsequently changed his mind, and returned to the Church of his fathers, and then – perhaps it was only natural – changed his mind again'.[11] Strachey is entertaining, but hardly fair to a man who struggled to find the church he could wholly commit to. It is fascinating that Sibthorp says in his letter to his sister that on the Continent he felt like 'a fish out of water' – he surely felt like that in his religious life as well, and perhaps Evan might have found him fascinating to talk to. Interestingly, Sir Charles Bagot's younger brother, diffident, nervous Richard, became Bishop of Oxford in 1829 and was to be heavily embroiled in the Oxford Movement and the move towards Roman Catholicism among the Anglican clergy.

* * *

On 22 December 1826, Evan received a letter from the 'lessees' of the Chapel Royal – the British residents who formed the committee. He was still teaching at his father-in-law's school on the Boulevard de Namur, Eliza was pregnant again, and for much of the year he had been flitting back and forth between the two Anglican congregations at the King's Church in the lower town and the Chapel Royal in the upper town, but now his life as a clergyman might be settled at one church:

> As the Chaplaincy of the Chapel Royal will be at our disposal on the 1st of January next, it is with great pleasure that we offer it to you, both as a proof of our approval of the satisfactory manner you discharged the duties in the Chapel, during the absence of the Revd. Mr. Holworthy, & that we are convinced that we could not name any one to that appointment who would be more agreeable to the congregation.
>
> It is necessary to inform you, that we rent the chapel, only from year to year, & that your appointment must only be considered for one year.[12]

In the event, Evan was to preside at the Chapel Royal for twenty-two years, until his untimely death. It seems that after Streynsham Master's return to England, Rev. Holworthy had taken charge of both congregations, with Evan probably doing double duty on Sundays when he was away. And he had got his reward. Five men signed their names below the letter. Alongside the name E. Taylor someone has added in brackets '(Brother of Lt.gen. Sir Herbert Taylor)'. The letter survives as a copy made by Evan of the one he received in 1826, which he sent to the Archbishop of Canterbury in September 1829 – more of which later.

Jane Austen, who had died only nine years before, would know the name E. Taylor of Brussels, and perhaps remember him with a wistful smile. In September 1796, when she was twenty, she wrote to her elder sister Cassandra while she was staying in Kent:

> We went by Bifrons, & I contemplated with a melancholy pleasure, the abode of Him, on whom I once fondly doated.[13]

Four years later Austen wrote, 'I hope it is true that Edward Taylor is to marry his cousin Charlotte. Those beautiful dark Eyes will then adorn another Generation at least in all their purity.'[14] Edward's dark eyes or Charlotte's? Maybe deliberately ambiguous. Edward Taylor (1774–1843) of Bifrons, Patrixbourne, near Canterbury, instead married Louisa Beckingham of Bourne Park in 1802.[15] Probably Jane and Cassandra had met the Taylor family in summer 1794 when they visited their brother at Rowling House, also in Kent.

The reader may have noticed that I have discovered an Edward. There are no Edwards in the Jenkins, Davies, Jay or Livingston families, as far as I know. This could be the man. If my great-great-uncle was named after this Edward, at that time on the committee of the Chapel Royal, whom a teenaged Jane Austen 'doated' on, then I am more than content. There is a bit about Edward Taylor, and a few letters from him, in his younger brother's memoirs.[16] Their father, Rev. Edward Taylor, had inherited Bifrons Park in Kent, which had been bought by the Taylors in 1694. Edward's younger brother, eventually Lieutenant-General Sir Herbert, is described on the title-page as 'at various stages in his career [...] private secretary to King George III., to Queen Charlotte, and to King William IV.' No wonder someone, maybe in the Bishop of London's employ, noted that 'E. Taylor' was the 'brother of'; younger brother Herbert has rather nice eyes too in his frontispiece.

In 1780 their father, Rev. Taylor, moved the family to Brussels, partly for reasons of economy, and partly for his eight children's education. 'An attempt was made by my father to send my brother and me to a day school at Brussels, but our pockets being picked by our school-fellows, the visit was not repeated.'[17] Herbert and Edward's mother died in Brussels, and Rev. Taylor moved the family to Heidelberg and then Carlsruhe. The children were not only learning German and French, but were childhood friends of the future wives of the King of Bavaria, Tsar Alexander I of Russia, the King of Sweden and the Prince of Brunswick. They went back to England in 1788 for about a year, returning to the Continent to reside mainly in Italy for another three years. Herbert read avidly, as perhaps did Edward, and music was very important to the family. No wonder the eighteen-year-old Jane Austen was captivated by such a well-travelled young man. Edward went to Merton College, Oxford in autumn 1793 when he was nineteen. The annual buttery books show that he was resident until the end of June the following year, so presumably Jane Austen met him that summer at the end of his first year at Oxford. But he seems to have dropped out sometime after this, not completing his degree. His name was crossed out in the buttery book in March 1799.[18] He was MP for Canterbury from 1807 to 1812, having been urged to stand alongside John Baker, a wealthy billiard and whist player, who usually voted with the Whig opposition. Taylor was regarded as of uncertain views and had an inconspicuous time in Parliament. He decided not to fight his seat in 1812 because of the expense, but he might have won. He perhaps preferred the time he spent in various yeomanry bodies, becoming Major of the East Kent yeomanry in 1820.[19]

On 4 July 1828, Edward's other brother, Sir Brook Taylor – British Minister in Berlin – wrote to their brother Sir Herbert mentioning Edward's decision to sell Bifrons: 'I confess that from [Edward's] statement I considered him as over-sanguine. Nothing could, however, be more proper than Herbert's answer to his father, expressing his regret at the necessity of parting with the old family estate, but showing his readiness to enter into any arrangement which may contribute to the comfort and happiness of his parents.'[20] Herbert was Edward's eldest son. Like Rev. Holworthy's father, possibly Edward Taylor didn't have the money to keep the large house and estate going, especially as he also had his wife's country house only a few miles away. That year Bifrons was rented to the widowed Lady Byron and her twelve-year-old daughter Ada (Augusta), later Countess of Lovelace and computer pioneer. Two years later Edward Taylor sold Bifrons to Henry, first Marquess Conyngham, former Lord Steward of the Household to King George IV, whose wife, Elizabeth, 'the Vice Queen', was the king's last mistress. She had an ongoing feud with Castlereagh's wife, Lady Emily, which may have also contributed to his breakdown. Lady Conyngham died at the age of ninety-two at Bifrons as late as 1861, persona non grata to Queen Victoria.[21] The house was demolished in 1945: another disastrous loss of a country house that had witnessed so much within its walls.[22] Edward Taylor died in Dover in 1843 aged sixty-eight.

* * *

In February 1826, numerous newspapers delighted in a scandal that had just
erupted at Harrow School, a few miles north of London:

> The town of Harrow has lately been thrown into the utmost state of
> consternation, owing to the sudden disappearance and unforeseen
> defalcation of Mr. Mark Drury, the second master of the school, and who
> has been above 40 years in the Harrow establishment; and also of his son,
> Mr. John Drury, another master of the school; both of whom quitted the
> town by night, leaving enormous debts behind them; but they have since
> been arrested, and are both at present in prison.[23]

The correspondent got the son's name wrong – he was Oxford graduate Rev.
William James Joseph Drury (1791–1878), and he was to be a huge presence in
Brussels (certainly in physical size) for the next fifty years. He was then aged
thirty-four. His father, Rev. Mark, was the younger brother of the former
headmaster Rev. Dr Joseph Drury, and a graduate of Trinity College, Cambridge;
he was in his mid-sixties: 'popular, affable, and lazy, a sought-after tutor and
housemaster, most noted for his massive bulk which made it necessary for him
to have a specially huge chair constructed to fit his size', says one historian.[24]
The newspaper correspondent added, perhaps exaggerating, that they had left
debts of around £40,000, including £2,700 owed to a butcher, that many of the
tradespeople were ruined, and that their servants had been left with wages unpaid.
'The young gentlemen of the school under their care, as masters, and of course
residing in their houses, returned home to their friends on the first disclosure of
the event', but had now mostly gone back to school. He added: 'The townspeople
now begin to wonder how the Drurys could have obtained so much credit [...]
but their astonishment comes too late.' It also seems that 'both the father and son
lived at a most extravagant rate, and played very high at whist'. The amount of
their debts, even if exaggerated, is staggering. Another journalist, in the *Morning
Herald*, inflated the amount owed to a butcher to nearly £7,000. A rival at a
Manchester newspaper commented on this report with incredulity: 'They must
have eaten cattle whole.'[25] Whether father and son went to prison is not known;
there is another newspaper report, of 2 March, that the Home Secretary stepped
in: 'we have heard of an instance of kindheartedness on the part of Mr. Peel,
which does him great honour, on the score of humanity, as well as of gratitude
to the establishment whence he derived his education. We understand that the
Home Secretary, immediately on learning the state of their affairs, sent 200*l.* to

Messrs. Drury; and that, on hearing of their arrest, he took such measures as were in his power to prevent both the unfortunate Gentlemen from undergoing the humiliation, and suffering the inconvenience of an immediate incarceration.'[26] How much of that is true is not known; I presume this Devizes journalist copied his report from a London newspaper.

Robert Peel, the future Prime Minister, had resided as a pupil at Mark Drury's house at Harrow between 1801 and 1804. Lord Byron was at Harrow the same time, and was just two weeks older than Peel; they were in the fourth form together, though Byron lived in a different house – mostly at the headmaster's son Henry's house. There is a well-known anecdote that on Speech Day in July 1804, when Byron and Peel were sixteen, they acted in an extract from Virgil's *Aeneid*: Peel played Turnus – Aeneas' rival in Italy, while the lame Byron played King Latinus (because he could sit throughout).[27] I'm curious to know what happened to the lad who played the starring role of Aeneas. Twenty or so years later, Robert Peel could certainly afford to help the Druries and their creditors, and the Druries were lucky in that Peel was Home Secretary at this time – he was out of office for a while after Prime Minister Lord Liverpool's stroke in February 1827. But Peel did write at one point that 'I would not send my boys [to Harrow ...] unless [...] it is better conducted now than it was when I misspent my time there.'[28]

If Peel did help, then it may have been because of good memories of his housemaster Mark and of Mark's son William, who was just three years younger than Peel and Byron (pronounced by everyone as Birron). The Devizes journalist commented that the Druries 'are not so unpopular as may be supposed', and that they had 'many good-hearted traits and amiable qualities'. Byron said he hated Harrow until the last year and a half, but despite a quarrel with Henry Drury, his housemaster – William Drury's first cousin – they stayed friends till the end of Byron's life.[29] Anthony Trollope hated the whole time he was at Harrow (which he attended twice), but since he wasn't there until almost twenty years later, I will let him, and his mother Frances Trollope, fume and laugh about the Druries and Harrow – and its treatment of Byron's daughter – in a later chapter.

The Drury family practically owned Harrow School from the time Joseph (1751–1834) was made Head in 1785. He soon appointed his brother, 'the portly and popular' Mark, to the staff.[30] Under this headmaster, despite the fact that he had had to withdraw from Trinity College, Cambridge after only a few terms, five future Prime Ministers were educated: Perceval, Goderich, Peel, Aberdeen and Palmerston. In his biography of Robert Peel, the politician Douglas Hurd, an old boy of Eton, remarks that he once spoke at a festival at Harrow, and knowing that more old Etonians than old Harrovians had become Prime Minister, he remarked dryly how convenient it was for Harrow to be able to list all their Prime Ministers on just one sheet of paper. He seems to have enjoyed the hissing he received.[31] A recent historian of the school says of this family-run affair by the Druries:

> When, announcing his own retirement in 1804, Joseph Drury advised the governors to appoint Mark to succeed him, Harrow displayed a remarkable dynastic spectacle. The Head and Under Masters were brothers; the senior master was the Head's brother-in-law; the Head's eldest son was a master, tutor, and housemaster; and the Head of School was Charles Drury, the Head Master's third son.[32]

The Head of School three years later was Mark's son William Drury, later of Brussels, and a thorn in Evan Jenkins's side.[33]

The club-footed, fatherless Lord Byron, eventually enjoying his time at Harrow, partly thanks to passionate friendships with other boys, claimed that he was one of the leaders who championed Joseph Drury's younger brother Mark as the next headmaster in 1805. This is despite the fact that Byron once called Mark Drury 'this upstart Son of a Button maker'.[34] Opinions differ on how much of a leader Byron was. At school, Byron could be disruptive and a bully, according to some – his way of coping with his lameness and lamentable childhood, no doubt. His mother despaired that she couldn't get him back to school one term, but the Druries were patient. That could be why Byron was vehemently against an outsider, Rev. Dr George Butler, being appointed as Head instead of Mark Drury. I have mentioned Dr Butler before as a son of the successful schoolmaster Rev. Butler in Chelsea when David Jenkins was a teacher of Greek and Latin at a neighbouring school. Fiona MacCarthy describes Byron's actions in 1805 against Dr Butler as a 'vendetta', and that he was 'the leader of the party' opposing Butler's appointment; she says he did not lead a gunpowder plot against him, as one legend has it, though he penned antagonistic posters. She adds that he 'was the ringleader when Dr Butler's desk was dragged into the middle of the School House and set on fire' and wrote nasty poems about the man, as he was to do later about Castlereagh after his suicide. However, Christopher Tyerman concludes that the 1805 rebellion against the new head was a myth, 'it never happened'.[35]

Tyerman also states that Dr Joseph Drury retired a very rich man, and that his brother Mark probably earned £1,500 a year just from his boarders. 'Harrow School under Dr Drury was big business, generating huge profits, the chief and direct beneficiaries of which were the masters.' He compares that with a 'substantial merchant' who might earn £2,500 a year.[36] But father and son were maybe not so financially incompetent: numbers of pupils plummeted under Butler and in 1825 there was a stock-market crash.[37] It is not clear when exactly they turned up in Brussels or what happened to William's wife and his six children, aged in 1826 between one and nine. All I have is a newspaper report of the death of his first wife Anna Frances Drury née Taylor in 1827 in Hastings, Sussex. If William had had to flee to the Continent it may be that his wife was left in England. William married again as early as November 1828, in Brussels, and had a further ten children.[38] He was obviously a man of large appetites.

* * *

One day, in August 2017, not thinking of William Drury at all, I decided to do a blitz on the *Oxford Dictionary of National Biography*, searching for just the word 'Brussels'. I was looking for anyone who might have been at John Jay's school in Brussels in the 1820s (and thus maybe also taught by Evan). I presumed it might be a fairly hopeless task. There were 1,148 results. Since I had asked for birthdate order I was able to whittle out a fair number. But then I had to go through about seventy of them, though easily weeding out King Leopold I, the Duke of Kent and Karl Marx. A few articles remained that needed careful reading – and I was hoping for published memoirs in the references, not, please, a manuscript in an archive that had never been transcribed and might take time and travel. One man looked promising: Charles Mackay, born in Perth, Scotland, 'poet and writer' (1812–89). The *ODNB* article stated: 'Charles Mackay's father settled comfortably in Brussels, where his half pay [as a bandmaster in the Royal Artillery] stretched further than in Britain and he could augment it by language teaching (his pupils included the sons of the prince of Orange) [...] Charles joined his father in Brussels, where he went to a school in the boulevard de Namur.'[39] The right place! But how many schools were in that boulevard and when exactly? Mackay had published his memoirs. I ordered them at the British Library – there were two sets of memoirs in four volumes – though I feared that Mackay might be as vague about his school as the *ODNB* writer.

I found it! Charles Mackay, in *Through the Long Day*, wrote:

On the attainment of my fourteenth year, I was transferred to my father's care in Brussels, and was placed at school on the Boulevard de Namur, under the care of a Mr. Jay, who was afterwards succeeded by the Rev. Dr. Drury. Under their superintendence I made but slight progress in Greek and

Latin, though I rapidly became proficient in French and German, and, in less than a twelvemonth, was able to speak and write in the former languages as fluently and correctly as in English.[40]

It should be easy to establish exactly when Mackay was at John Jay's school and when William Drury (Mackay was mistaken, he was not a 'Dr') took over. But Mackay was confused about the year he was born. The *ODNB* article states that Mackay thought he was born in March 1814 instead of 1812, but agrees that he was fourteen when he went to John Jay's school in Brussels. That would mean that Mackay went to the school in 1826 and that William Drury took over the school around 1828 – since Mackay says he was there for two years.[41] But I needed another verification of those dates. After his time at school, Mackay worked in Brussels as private secretary to William Cockerill, an expat Lancashire inventor and engineer. One day Cockerill's physician paid a visit with a 'fresh handsome-looking' Irishman, a young medical student who was on his way to attend a German university, by the name of Charles Lever: the future novelist, prolific and popular, but largely forgotten today. That visit seems to confirm the year that Mackay left school: 1828. Charles Lever was to return to live and work in Brussels, and will appear in a later chapter.[42] As for Mackay, he returned to London in 1832 and became a journalist, beating Thackeray to the post of subeditor at the *Morning Chronicle*; he wrote verse, song lyrics, history, a novel and essays; he became editor of the *Glasgow Argus*, later joined the *Illustrated London News* and was the *Times*'s correspondent during the American Civil War. He was also the father of the famous novelist 'Marie Corelli' (Mary Mackay). Frankly he was a rather impressive alumnus of the Brussels school of John Jay/ William Drury and Evan Jenkins.

It seems from the Belgian almanacs that survive that Evan and his father-in-law John Jay parted professional ways in late 1827. Evan had started at the Chapel Royal formally in January 1827. In June an advertisement for John Jay's school still implied that Evan was teaching on the boulevard de Namur (and thus teaching Latin and Greek to the not quite eager Charles Mackay, who preferred modern languages).[43] But the *Almanach royal de la cour* of 1828 (and thus referring to the year before) has Evan and John Jay running different boarding schools (*pensionnats*): 'Jay, au glacis, hors de la porte de Namur' and 'Jenkins, nouvelle rue d'Orange, hors de la porte de Namur'. In June 1827 there is an advertisement for a house to be let with a beautiful garden in Ixelles, 'habitée par M. Jenkins'.[44] This is perhaps the first house that Evan and Eliza had rented; I would guess that with their second child arriving they needed a bigger house and that Evan wanted to leave his teaching job and take pupils into his own house instead, to focus on what he could do best: teach Latin and Greek and maybe Cambridge mathematics and divinity. John Jay seems to have put his last advertisements for his commercial school in the Dutch newspapers this year: the last found is for 20 November 1827.[45] Putting all these elements together, it could be that William Drury's arrival, fleeing from his creditors, meant that Evan could leave his father-in-law's school (there was a useful replacement in Drury) and that John Jay could retire (after teaching for a while in the school, Drury presumably indicated that he would like to take it over). William Drury wasn't a thorn in Evan's side as regards the school, it was over what Drury did next: and Evan Jenkins, the Bishop of London, the Archbishop of Canterbury, the King of the Netherlands and the Foreign Secretary, the Earl of Aberdeen, were all involved.

* * *

This puzzling piece appeared in a London newspaper on 30 January 1829:

> Brussels, Jan. 27 – His Majesty [William I] having authorized the opening of the church of the Anglican Confession, built at Brussels, in Orange-street, on the site of the ancient Orangery, it was consecrated last Sunday morning at 11 o'clock. The Rev. Mr. Drury, Pastor of the church, which is dedicated to St. George, delivered a very fine Sermon, which was listened to with the greatest attention by a numerous congregation. The Architect has made the best use of the room that he had to dispose of, and from 400 to 500 persons may be accommodated. The whole is very simple and elegant.[46]

The reason for the bafflement is that the interim Brussels Chargé d'Affaires, Thomas Cartwright, sent a despatch to the Foreign Secretary, the fourth Earl of Aberdeen, on 11 *September* (over seven months later) saying that the chapel 'was consecrated *last week* by Bishop Luscombe', the 'Scottish Bishop' of my subtitle. On the same day, Evan wrote to the new Archbishop of Canterbury, William Howley (the man who had ordained him when Bishop of London), about Luscombe's 'late visit to Brussels' and about 'the *recent* consecration' of St George's.[47] A bishop is normally needed to consecrate a place of Anglican worship and in the January notice there is no mention of who performed the consecration, which may have been penned by Drury himself, inflating the few people who came to his unorthodox opening of his (unconsecrated) chapel into a 'numerous congregation'. Also, where could a man, who owed thousands of pounds to creditors in England, find the money to hire it? The chapel was just a stone's throw from where Evan presided at the Chapel Royal, also in the former palace of Charles of Lorraine, and now within the modern Bibliothèque Royale de Belgique: how could Evan not have noticed until September? I discovered at the archives in Leuven that Drury had bought two large, clasped ledgers, one for burials and one for baptisms; inside the burials ledger he wrote 'St. George's. Brussels. rue de l'Orangerie'. The first burial he recorded was on 26 May 1829; the first baptism as early as 8 September 1828.[48] Such offices would bring in useful income.

Drury had been ordained deacon by the Bishop of Norwich in 1818, when he was twenty-seven, and not made priest until five years later, by the Bishop of London. The only appointment in the modern Clergy database is misleading and incorrect: that is, to the 'Royal Chapel' in Brussels on 3 September 1829, though the source also has 'St George's Church'.[49] Who called this chapel a 'Royal Chapel'? It certainly wasn't. King William and his family went to the King's Church when they were in Brussels, that is, the Church of the Augustines, where Evan had started.

Did Drury have any experience as a curate after he was ordained as deacon? He was assistant master at Harrow from 1811 to 1826, so his ordination as deacon could have been one of those fraudulent titles for orders and he never did any duties. Tyerman, in his recent history of Harrow School, says that very little religion was practised then at the school, where it was 'ignored or despised', and gives an ominous quote about the quality of Drury as a clergyman. 'Even the formal motions of faith were degraded', he says, and 'a future bishop of St Andrew's [Charles Wordsworth] received no preparation for his confirmation [in 1824] beyond his tutor, the improvident William Drury, inquiring if he knew his catechism. Holy Communion was unknown.'[50]

Four days after the opening of this new chapel in January, three clergymen (only one in Belgium, the others in Devon and Yorkshire) wrote a letter to Bishop Luscombe, saying that Drury 'nominated as Minister of the British Church (called St. George's Church) in Brussels in the Kingdom of the Netherlands, having been personally known to us for the space of two years last past (to some of us more, to others less) hath, during that time lived piously, soberly, and honestly; [...] and moreover we believe him in our consciences to be a person worthy to be licensed to the Ministry of the said Church.'[51] The first who signed was Rev. William Watson Bolton, 'Licensed Chaplain to British Protestant Church Bruges'; he could only have been licensed by Luscombe, and indeed he was.[52] Bolton was approving of a man who seems to have barely performed the duties of a clergyman previously, who had debts in England of a staggering amount, and whom one or two of these clergymen might have met only once, recently. Drury came from a school, as teacher and pupil, whose culture was often bullying and violent; and where monitors were allowed to cane other pupils – Drury had been made a monitor in 1805 – sometimes causing serious injuries.[53] But perhaps the violence described by Tyerman was exceptional; Charles Wordsworth, who left school in 1825, wrote that he 'left Harrow with intense regret'.[54]

It is time to open another can of worms: who was Bishop Luscombe?

* * *

We can trace Luscombe's role in Europe back to the obdurate diplomat Sir Charles Stuart, whom new Foreign Secretary George Canning was trying to remove from Paris after Castlereagh's suicide in 1822. Sir Charles had reported to the Foreign Office in London, highly critical of the irregularities and morals of some of the Anglican clergymen he had encountered. Canning decided to do something about it. Matthew Henry Thornhill Luscombe was baptized in April 1775 in Exeter, so he was in his mid-fifties when he had a confrontation with 34-year-old Evan in Brussels in September 1829. Like Evan he had gone to Trinity College, Cambridge but soon migrated to St Catharine's, in 1793.[55] He had a curacy in Windsor and then became master of the East India Company's school at Haileybury in Hertfordshire, a famous public school today (it has produced just one Prime Minister, but an impressive one, Clement Attlee). There Luscombe worked alongside Robert Malthus, who had published his influential book *An Essay on the Principle of Population* a few years before. One of Luscombe's pupils was Walter Farquhar Hook (1798–1875), who was to become a pioneering Vicar in Leeds in 1837 – and no doubt well known to David Jenkins and Patrick Brontë – and in 1825 Hook was to be vital to his former teacher Dr Luscombe's role in Europe, which has been called 'a most revolutionary experiment'.[56]

In 1819 Luscombe moved to France, and in 1824 Foreign Secretary Canning appointed him to the chaplaincy at Paris with a superintending role, but he was only a priest. Hook therefore suggested that Luscombe be ordained Bishop by the Scottish Episcopal Church, which took place in 1825 at Stirling, with tacit approval by the Archbishop of Canterbury and Bishop Howley of London. Although Bishops of London had been given some kind of jurisdiction in 1633 over all Anglican congregations outside the dioceses in England, Wales and Ireland, legally it was a fuzzy situation: the bishop only had power if the congregation wanted him to have power; and if the British government had no role in paying a clergyman, then the Bishop of London had no power over him at all, and the government had generally taken a back seat – until Canning.[57] One historian remarks, 'If an episcopal license was issued [to a clergyman abroad], it was regarded by the congregation and perhaps by the priest himself as merely a "matter of courteous reference, or of voluntary submission," rather than as a "spiritual obligation" or "ecclesiastical allegiance.""[58] Some worried about the role in Europe of this new bishop; others thought that as a 'Missionary Bishop' his status was assured. They had not reckoned with the concerned views of several clergymen abroad, nor the nature of the man so promoted.

In spring 1826, Chaplain to the Embassy of the Netherlands Rev. Holworthy wrote to the Bishop of London, William Howley, enquiring about Luscombe. His letter does not survive, but the bishop's reply of 24 April is among diplomat Sir Thomas Cartwright's papers. Howley wrote that Bishop Luscombe could confirm people into the faith, and he could confer orders, but those so ordained 'would not be allowed to officiate in the United Church'.[59] I think one might respond that this is as clear as mud. His successor as Bishop two years later, Blomfield, was to be unsure and inconsistent over the position of this 'Missionary Bishop' in Europe for the next twenty years, and some men whom Luscombe ordained in Europe were persuaded to stop officiating and their baptisms and marriages were not recognized in law.[60] Howley does not mention licences in his letter, which was to create more friction.

As a child, Charles James Blomfield (1786–1857) was studious and precocious, and declared at a very early age that he meant to be a bishop. Anthony Trollope portrayed him as the eldest of Dr Grantly's sons in *The Warden* (1855):

> Charles James was an exact and careful boy; he never committed himself; he well knew how much was expected from the eldest son of the Archdeacon of Barchester, and was therefore mindful not to mix too freely with other boys. He had not the great talents of his younger brothers, but he exceeded them in judgment and propriety of demeanour; his fault, if he had one, was an over-attention to words instead of things; there was a thought too much *finesse* about him, and, as even his father sometimes told him, he was too fond of a compromise.[61]

Blomfield's schoolmaster father refused to send him to Eton, where perhaps his ambition would have been beaten out of him (it was a notoriously brutal school). Whether his father considered the barbarity of Eton in turning down the scholarship is not known, but possible since the boy was sickly. He did very well at Trinity College, Cambridge, some fourteen years before Evan arrived, emerging as third wrangler in 1808 as well as being brilliant at classics, and he was to become an editor of many classical texts. Blomfield married in 1810; five of his six children died in infancy, and his wife died eight years later. His second marriage produced another eleven children. As Bishop of Chester from 1824 until his promotion to London in August 1828, he imposed a strict ordination procedure to raise standards (including minimizing the number of Irish), and was keen on Sunday observance and temperance – presumably he would have disapproved of Evan drinking claret with a parishioner.[62] He was a high churchman, as also was Hook, and presumably Luscombe and William Drury – if the latter had any particular religious inclination at all.

In May 1829, Rev. J. Symons in Boulogne refused to recognize that Bishop Luscombe had any authority over him and his congregation. It is reasonable to assume that Symons had been in touch with colleagues, particularly Holworthy in Brussels and The Hague. Luscombe was sweeping in his condemnation: 'You thus separate yourselves from communion with the Church of England.'[63] Luscombe had arrogance but no power over this congregation and its chosen clergyman. Undaunted, Luscombe moved into Belgium in September, and this is when the fat hit the fire. Holworthy and Evan would have been prepared and resolved on their response. But the new, 'rogue' clergyman, William Drury, had actually asked for a licence from Luscombe as early as January.

Before these autumn events, Evan went to Cambridge for Commencement in July to collect his MA, seven years after graduating. It was perhaps the first time he had been able to get away, or the first time he had enough money for the ceremony. Possibly also he wanted his Master's degree for the fight he knew was ahead. I wonder if he heard the prize poem read out, which was 'Timbuctoo' by an undergraduate called Alfred Tennyson.[64] The author was too nervous or embarrassed to read it at Commencement himself, and got a friend to do so. Tennyson later wanted his blank-verse poem 'to slide quietly off, with all its errors, into forgetfulness' rather than be published.[65] Charles Wordsworth, son of the Master of Trinity College and erstwhile pupil of William Drury at Harrow, wrote to his brother later that year: 'What do you think of Tennyson's Prize poem ("Timbuctoo")? If such an exercise had been sent up at Oxford, the author would have had a better chance of being rusticated, with the view of his passing a few months at a Lunatic Asylum, than of obtaining the prize.'[66]

Collecting his degree would have been a good opportunity for Evan to discuss Bishop Luscombe with friends and Fellows. He may also have visited Rev. Peter Felix in Chelsea, whose brother David would die that month. Eliza maybe went to the seaside at Ostend with the children – Edward just turned three, Helen almost two, Alexander Livingston three months – for a blissful rest, paddling and making sandcastles.

I think that Evan had been emboldened by talking the situation over in England to make a stand against Bishop Luscombe on Sunday 6 September. There are three letters in the Lambeth Palace Archive – two from Evan, one from Thomas Cartwright at the embassy – all dated 11 September 1829. Evan's letters were to the Bishop of London, Blomfield, and to the Archbishop of Canterbury, Howley; at the same time, Thomas Cartwright, Chargé d'Affaires in Brussels, wrote to the Foreign Secretary the Earl of Aberdeen. It was surely coordinated between them. What probably had happened was that Bishop Luscombe had stormed off to the embassy after the Sunday dispute, which is described below, and that Evan was asked by Cartwright to give his version of events, and agree on what they should do. Cartwright's letter to Lord Aberdeen explains succinctly what happened (his letter was then copied to the Bishop of London). But first some character sketches.

One problem I have with the stunning portraits by Sir Thomas Lawrence (1769–1830) is that sometimes the sitter is so beautiful or handsome, and if you look at a photograph of the sitter in old age it's hard to work out how that person managed to disintegrate so much. But Lawrence's aim was to make a more beautiful reality. Compare the portrait of George Hamilton Gordon, fourth Earl of Aberdeen, by his friend Lawrence, with the photograph of him just before his death, some years after he resigned as Prime Minister, defeated by the disaster of the Crimean War.[67] The unfinished portrait of 1829/30 was one of Lawrence's last paintings. It was described as having 'an air of courteous suavity'.[68] The dark good looks of this fascinating politician are a joy, and although statesmanlike, he has a Byronic air: he was not only a cousin of Lord Byron, but had also spent time as a young man doing archaeology in Greece, looking for the site of Troy and attempting to buy some friezes from the Parthenon, but was forestalled by Lord Elgin. Yet when he sat for this portrait, at the time of the tussle in Brussels, when he was Foreign Secretary and in his mid-forties, he had lost not only the wife he had married for love, Catherine, but all three of their daughters whom he adored – the last to die was only five months before the Brussels incident, aged twenty; probably all died from tuberculosis.[69] You would never guess that from the portrait.

The Earl of Aberdeen was a Presbyterian north of the border, and Anglican south of it. He became Foreign Secretary in Wellington's administration in May 1828 during the last stages of the Greek War of Independence, for which his cousin had died four years before, and he was still in post when the Belgian Revolution broke out in 1830. He was more sympathetic to Greek nationalism than to Belgian independence, but in 1829 he had to deal with the problem, created by a predecessor at the Foreign Office, George Canning, that was destabilizing the clergy on the Continent.

Thomas Cartwright the diplomat gets just one paragraph in *ODNB*. He was the same age as Evan, so in his mid-thirties, and an Oxford graduate. He had gone to The Hague and Brussels after seven years in Munich, and would move on in 1830 to Frankfurt and then Stockholm; so in 1829 when he had to deal with the Anglican spat, in the absence of the ambassador Bagot, he was experienced. He was married to the daughter of Count von Sandizell of Bavaria, and had young children.[70] I am sure that Eliza Jenkins frequently visited the wife of the Chargé d'Affaires, with baby and toddlers in tow. Eliza would not let Luscombe win this battle, but she and Evan must have been worried.

This is how Cartwright described what had happened a few days before to the Earl of Aberdeen at the Foreign Office:

> Bishop Luscombe, who holds the appointment of chaplain to His Majesty's Embassy at Paris, came here the end of last week to administer Confirmation, when some circumstances occurred touching the authority and Episcopal character of that Clergyman, which I think necessary to make known to Your Lordship, as I understand they are about to be laid before His Grace, the Archbishop of Canterbury.

Presumably it had been agreed between Cartwright and Evan that the latter would write to the archbishop.

> On account of the number of English residents at Brussels, there are now three churches, where services are performed every Sunday, according to the Rites of the Established Church:
> 1st the King's Church, where Mr. Holworthy the chaplain of the Embassy officiates; 2nd the Chapel Royal, where services have been performed nearly five years [an exaggeration] by Mr. Jenkins; – and lastly a Building which has lately been turned into a Chapel, and which was consecrated last week by Bishop Luscombe, under the name of St. George's

chapel, where duty is performed by Mr. Drury.

When Mr. Holworthy and Mr. Jenkins saw Bishop Luscombe for the first time after his arrival here, the latter expressed a desire that they should receive licences from him, which these Gentlemen declined, as they conceived that it was not necessary in order to officiate here, that they should have any licence, and much less from Bishop Luscombe, whose only title or character they believed to be that of a Missionary Bishop of the Church of Scotland. Not believing therefore, that Bishop Luscombe had any Episcopal Authority beyond what they chose to allow him, they thus refused respectfully to receive his licence, and upon their expressing their resolution to that effect, at that interview he did not press the subject further.

On Friday, he consecrated Mr. Drury's chapel, which has been the subject of much surprize here, because the Building is not freehold, but only rented on a lease of 9 years, and may at the expiration of that term be turned to any use whatever, at the will of the Proprietor.

On the Saturday, Bishop Luscombe confirmed several Persons in the King's Church, assisted by Mr. Holworthy, Mr. Jenkins and Mr. Drury, and on Sunday last he preached a Sermon in the same Church.

He had also intimated to Mr. Jenkins, that he would afterwards administer the Sacrament at the Chapel Royal, but when that Gentleman went to Bishop Luscombe, a quarter of an hour before the time fixed for the commencement of the Service, for the purpose of conducting him to the Chapel, the Bishop asked Mr. Jenkins whether he meant to accept his licence, which the latter again declined, and Bishop Luscombe then told him, that as by not accepting his licence, he refused to acknowledge his jurisdiction, he should not administer the Sacrament in his Chapel.

Mr. Jenkins told Bishop Luscombe that he could not conscientiously take the licence, as he did not understand what jurisdiction he had, and the Bishop, in consequence, persisted in his resolution and did not officiate in the Chapel Royal.

Mr. Jenkins refused the licence, because in common with the general opinion, he believes Bishop Luscombe to have assumed an authority and power which he does not really possess; for though he offers the licence in the name of the Bishop of London, it is not clear in what light he can do so. The Bishop of London's jurisdiction being understood not to extend into these Countries, and Bishop Luscombe's Episcopal character being only that of a Missionary Bishop of the Church of Scotland. – Mr. Jenkins and Mr. Holworthy considering therefore, that Bishop Luscombe was going beyond his power, and had no right to force the licence upon them, declined accepting them on the grounds above stated, and Mr. Jenkins conceiving that, he has been unfairly treated by Bishop Luscombe, means to carry this case to the knowledge of the Archbishop of Canterbury, for the purpose of obtaining his Grace's opinion, – whether the Clergymen of the Established Church resident in this Country, are under the jurisdiction of Bishop Luscombe, who is at present believed generally to have no Authority at all.

Mr. Jenkins was appointed to the Chapel Royal by the lessees, who are Gentlemen of the highest respectability. – He was ordained by His Grace the Archbishop, when Bishop of London, and on that occasion was informed, that for the purposes of officiating in this Country, a licence was unnecessary.[71]

The Earl of Aberdeen sent a copy of this despatch to the Bishop of London, Blomfield. Evan, in his letter of 11 September to the bishop, writes that when he was ordained in 1825, he had 'been then told that it would not be necessary for me to have a licence, in order to officiate to a congregation of British subjects in the Kingdom of the Netherlands' and that he had considered it his duty to 'respectfully' decline the Luscombe licence. But Evan must have been worried, as he adds that he has sent his letters of Orders and a copy of the letter appointing him to the Chapel Royal to the archbishop. Also, 'I can with safety refer your Lordship for any additional information respecting my character as a Clergyman of the Established Church to His Excellency Sir Charles Bagot, H.B.M. Ambassador at this Court, who is now in England, & in whose family I have been called to officiate during the absence of the Chaplain to the Embassy.' To underline his character as a clergyman, he signs off as 'E. Jenkins M.A. of Trinity College, Cambridge & Chaplain of the Chapel Royal at Brussels'.[72] It's a 'don't take me lightly' letter, which many of us will recognize after a conflict at work, but he may have been shaking when writing it.

In his letter written on the same day to Archbishop Howley, however, Evan adds a damning point about the worrying nature of St George's Chapel:

I think it likewise my duty to inform your Grace, that I could not conscientiously attend at the recent consecration of a place of worship for the use of a small portion only of the British Residents – the consecration of this building was, according to my view of the subject, irregular, for the following reasons: – that it is attached to a private house, the property of a Catholic (having been recently used as a stable belonging to that house); that it is only held on a lease of a very few years & consequently liable to be appropriated to some other purpose at the expiration of that period. The ceremony of consecrating such a place must, in my humble opinion, have impressed foreigners with very indifferent and erroneous ideas of the dignity of the Episcopal office in England, & cannot fail proving injurious to the interests of the Protestant Religion, in the midst of a Catholic population.

Evan's combination of 'Catholic' and 'stable' is designed to shock, surely, rather than what he believed, since the Chapel Royal and the Church of the Augustines had once been Catholic. But he is under attack by Luscombe and gets his thrust in first. He adds another point: 'Of the three English Clergymen of the Established Church now officiating at Brussels, the Revd. W. Drury, late of Harrow [...] is the only one who has accepted Bishop Luscombe's licence.' Evan may be hoping the archbishop will remember the scandal at Harrow just three years before. He then writes that he certainly accepted that Bishop Luscombe could confirm: 'I took considerable pains to prepare the youngest part of my congregation for receiving the Rite of Confirmation at his hands on Saturday last' (unlike some clergymen, one might add). Finally he gives his account of what happened on the Sunday, and for the first time underlines a word – Evan is angry:

> Wishing to pay due respect to the office which Dr. Luscombe holds in the Church of Christ, as well as to his appointment of Chaplain to the British Embassy at Paris, I was induced to ask him if he would have any objection to officiate in my chapel on the Sunday following, to which proposal he readily assented and pledged himself <u>unconditionally</u> to take a part in the administration of the Sacrament. Every thing was arranged to that effect; but on my waiting upon him at the King's Church where he had preached, for the purpose of conducting him to my chapel, a few minutes only before the commencement of the Service he positively refused to fulfil his promise unless I agreed on the spot to receive his licence & thereby acknowledge his jurisdiction which I felt it my duty to decline.[73]

Having marshalled all his arguments so clearly and confidently in a four-page letter to the man who had ordained him, Evan doesn't need to hammer home that he is an alumnus of Trinity College, Cambridge: just his new 'M.A.' will do. But now he has to wait. In the event it took six weeks, and despite Evan's seeming confidence, he must have felt anxious whether his arguments would be accepted, and maybe whether he had wrongly bypassed the Bishop of London in writing to the archbishop as well.

It was not until 29 October that Bishop Blomfield wrote a reply to the Earl of Aberdeen.[74] He says that he had written some months before to Bishop Luscombe 'reminding him that he had no jurisdiction over English Clergymen officiating abroad', but if the clergyman was partly paid by the government then it was customary for the Bishop of London to license him. He had indeed authorized Luscombe to license 'in my name' any English clergymen who were willing to receive it. 'I have since been informed that he has made an indiscreet use of this conditional authority' – presumably referring to Evan. Luscombe 'informs me […] that Mr. Jenkins is the only instance in which any objection has been made', which was untrue, since Holworthy had objected, as had Rev. Symons in Boulogne. Blomfield also regards the consecration of St George's Chapel as 'ill advised'. He is sorry that Bishop Luscombe 'has gone so far as to confer Holy Orders upon 1 or 2 persons whose anomalous character had produced some confusion'. On the other hand, some control of clergymen abroad was needed, 'some of whom have disgraced our Church'. Aberdeen was at a loss to know what to do.[75] Probably that same day, Bishop Blomfield wrote to Evan: 'I am sorry that any unpleasantness should have taken place between you & Bishop Luscombe. He has undoubtedly no jurisdiction over you; nor have I.' He then repeats what he had written to Lord Aberdeen, that Luscombe could license in the name of the Bishop of London any clergyman who thought it proper. 'But of this every Clergyman must judge for himself.' He adds that 'the consecration of a place of worship under the circumstances mentioned in your letter [to the archbishop] ought not to have taken place.'[76] Evan had won his point, but the chapel and its pastor, Drury, remained – for the time being, as did the bully Luscombe.

In August 1836, 25-year-old Thackeray was married at the British Embassy in Paris to Isabella Shawe by Bishop Luscombe.[77] I don't believe it was just to add a note of realism in his 1840 novella, *A Shabby Genteel Story*, that the Paris clergyman is called Bishop Luscombe. It is a satirical story about the lower middle classes with a sprinkling of dissolute toffs. The couple the fictional Luscombe marries are a Cockney bearded 'hartist' named 'Andrea' Fitch, fond of striking attitudes, who has been hiding in a boarding house in Margate, and the elderly 'immense fat' widow who has chased him all the way from Rome. At the wedding are Earl and Countess Crabs, General Sir Rice Curry and Miss Runt.[78] A respected clergyman would not want to be in such company. Anthony Trollope's elder brother Thomas Adolphus later encountered Luscombe in Paris: he was 'pompous and very *bishopy*' and gave 'a very stupid sermon'.[79] It may be that Thackeray was getting his own back: having lost all the family money, he and Isabella were poor and it could be that Luscombe behaved arrogantly to them in a way that riled Thackeray.

* * *

Evan adhered stubbornly to his right not to be licensed for another five years. It was not until March 1835 that he accepted a licence from the Bishop of London. This was possibly because of two events that were about to occur. In June, King Leopold distinguished Evan by making him his honorary chaplain: the first Anglican clergyman so honoured in Belgium (it is possible that Evan knew about this some months beforehand as it might have to be discussed with the government and the Bishop of London). Then in September, Bishop Blomfield went to Brussels and confirmed about seventy young people at the Chapel Royal, and Evan took him on a tour of the sites.[80] Luscombe died in 1846, leaving a situation in north and central Europe of twenty-seven clergy licensed by the Bishop of London; thirteen licensed by Luscombe; and twenty-eight with no licences.[81] It was confusing and divisive, and no doubt a relief when he died. No bishop was appointed to replace him.

Eleven

Revolution and a Love Triangle, 1830–1831

Monday, fireworks! Tuesday, illumination! Wednesday, revolution!

– placard in Brussels, August 1830[1]

My guides to the Belgian Revolution of 1830 are three British residents and two American adventurers. There were mob riots, wanton destruction and many deaths; it also involved the very first grand opera, a British butler and the curious tale of the Princess of Orange's stolen jewels.

The revolution that began in Brussels on Wednesday 25 August 1830 was an utterly unexpected success. Charles White, an eyewitness who wrote an account of it in his invaluable two-volume *The Belgic Revolution* (1835), comments that participants were thunderstruck that 'a mere theatre riot' had led to the dissolution of the monarchy, and above all 'national emancipation, for which Belgium had vainly struggled during many centuries'. For 'many centuries' read eighteen centuries, since the time of the Romans.[2] It needed a fair amount of digging to find out about Charles White Esq. – called Captain White in an admiring review of his Belgian book – despite his having also written four novels and a thoroughly researched guide to Constantinople and the Turks.[3] His most successful novel, *Almack's Revisited* (1828), involves a heroine who fortunately turns out not to be the sister of her dead husband; there is a villain who plunges to his death at a waterfall and an appearance by the Duke of Wellington, whose veins flow with 'immortal fire'.[4]

White was born in 1793 in Shropshire, and went to Eton.[5] The laconic description of him in *The Eton School Lists* (published in 1864) states that he was a 'cousin of Sir T. Jones; was in the Coldstream Guards, and lately living in Constantinople'. He actually lived there for a few years in the 1840s, and died in Brussels as Colonel White in 1861, so the register is only twenty years out. Other sources state that he served in the Peninsular campaign under Wellington and then as adjunct to the Duke of Cambridge (tenth child of George III). He married Maria Blackshaw in 1821, to whom he dedicated his book; it seems they had one child, born in Paris, later Lt. Col. Charles Henry White.[6]

What is fascinating about his book about the revolution is not only his often lucid command of complicated events, written immediately afterwards, but also that he was involved in monitoring the armistice between the new 'Belgians' and the Dutch, often with no British government advice. There is also one nice set piece where he rushes to see the new King Leopold when Belgium is in between ambassadors, which I will describe below – though White, always modest about himself, is a bit outdone by the new, elderly British ambassador who arrives at the last minute, leaps onto a horse and saves the day through a hail of bullets. But perhaps even more intriguing is the side White takes: he writes that he has aimed to be even-handed but, unlike the British government and, it seems, most of the British press and public, he is totally sympathetic to the Belgians.

* * *

Captain White states in his Preface (1834/5) that he had 'resided more than four years in Belgium', thus arriving in 1829 or 1830 in his mid-thirties.[7] Whether he knew the Jenkins family and went to the Chapel Royal cannot be deduced, and among a population of maybe 5,000 British residents it is not inevitable that the families encountered each other, though White would know of Rev. Jenkins as one of the three Anglican clergymen in the city.[8] In 1860, according to the Brussels Almanac, White was living at Place de Namur 3, by the Porte de Namur, near the Jay school of the 1820s and the Jenkins home at rue d'Orange of the 1830s (after the defeat of the Orange King William the street name changed speedily). But it is surely probable that he got to know the Jenkinses at some stage since one letter in the Wyndham collection states that Evan and Eliza stayed in Brussels throughout the revolution, when most British had fled. The letter to Eliza's sister Margaret in Australia is from Emma Lane, who may have been a schoolfriend of Margaret's in Brussels. It is dated August 1831, a year after the start of the revolution, and she comments: 'Your sister has we learn been in Brussels during the whole of the time – The English have mostly deserted the place, save the very old inhabitants who are in some degree naturalized.'[9] She also comments that 'we [...] were never very great lovers of Belgium'. Poor Belgium seems to have had very few admirers.

But Captain White was sympathetic to the grievances of the Belgians. A Catholic country of four million had been fused by the Great Powers in 1814 with a country of half that number under a new Dutch Protestant king, William I. The future Belgium was then known only as the Southern Provinces. The Great Powers had needed a strong barrier, a buffer zone, against France, and this was the only solution that made sense to them. The Dutch language was imposed on the Belgians, many of whom spoke French. Representation and employment in government was predominantly and disproportionately Dutch; and blatantly so in the army, which Captain White finds scarcely credible. For example, in the army list for 1830 there were five Dutch Generals but no Belgians; 538 Dutch Lieutenants but a mere 70 Belgians. Taxes were high and regarded as unfair. Trial by jury was abolished, and in June 1830 the supreme court of justice was established at The Hague, so that the monopoly of justice was in the hands of Dutch lawyers, in the Dutch language, one hundred miles north of Brussels.[10] If we find these grievances sound, few others did. Writing in 1842, Rev. William Trollope – an acquaintance or friend of the Jenkinses, a distant cousin of Anthony, and sometime resident in Belgium – declared that although some of the Belgian demands were 'far from unreasonable' there was 'nothing to justify that rancorous hatred and base ingratitude, which led to the separation from Holland'.[11] Yet he admits that 'a more conciliatory tone' should have been adopted by the king and his ministers. But although some concessions were made to redress grievances in the first half of 1830, repression seemed to be the only language the Dutch government understood. This was shown in the totally counterproductive extrajudicial prosecutions of Belgian journalists and writers – measures that would normally only be used in times of open sedition. White comments: 'in defiance of edicts and prosecutions, the press augmented its temerity, and assumed a tone which tended to place the government and country in a state of implacable hostility'. The most influential newspaper was the *Courrier des Pays-Bas* which 'concentrated the revolution in its columns'.[12] Other than combating the press with arbitrary arrests, the Dutch government established a government newspaper, *National*, under the editorship of an Italian, Libry Bagnano, whose vindictiveness and sarcasm towards the Belgians, and servility to the Minister of Justice Van Maanen, made him the most hated man in Brussels, as the events of 25 August were to demonstrate. Throw into this unhappy mix a flourishing centre for the book trade (ironically promoted by the government) – where cheap editions of books banned in France were printed – and encouragement for foreigners to settle, intended to show that the Netherlands was a land of liberty. 'Thus', White comments, 'Brussels became the rendezvous [...] of all the discontented spirits in Europe.'[13]

* * *

The fireworks and illuminations in Brussels quoted in the epigraph to this chapter had been planned for the celebration of the fifty-eighth birthday of King William I on Tuesday 24 August 1830. The idea for revolution on the Wednesday could well have emerged among aggrieved young Belgian lawyers and writers meeting in a tavern with excited Frenchmen eager to spread the euphoria of their three-day revolution in Paris of 27–9 July – the *Trois Glorieuses*. The final Bourbon king, Charles X – yet another brother of the guillotined Louis XVI – had been replaced by his cousin, Louis-Philippe, Duc d'Orléans (then in his mid-fifties; his reign lasted until the Revolution of 1848). French journalists were in the thick of it. When the riots in Paris seemed to be turning into revolution, King Charles was urged to be conciliatory; he chose resistance. Less than a week later he went into exile. The obstinate King William of the Netherlands should have taken note. His eldest son, the Prince of Orange – once 'Slender Billy', who had been rejected as 'a detested Dutchman' by the heir but one to the British throne, Princess Charlotte, in favour of Prince Leopold – was certainly more prepared to grant concessions but had no power. Before I turn to the theatre riot that was decided to be the start of the revolution, the Prince of Orange's relationship with Belgium needs explaining – by Charles White – as well as the curious theft of his wife's jewels.

William, Prince of Orange was about the same age as author Charles White and Evan Jenkins. He was born in December 1792, so he was in his late thirties at the time of the revolution. He had grown up in England and Berlin and served under Wellington in the Peninsular War and, as a totally inexperienced General, at Waterloo, where he was wounded in the shoulder and thus became very popular. In 1816 he married the tsar's sister; although he was bisexual he seems to have preferred relationships with men and was subjected to blackmail. Captain White of course does not mention his homosexuality in his book, but certainly hints at serial philandering which resulted in many 'domestic discussions' with the Princess of Orange. The family lived in their palace at Brussels, which the prince much preferred to the gloom of the Dutch Court and arguments with his father. He loved the gay life of the city and was generally popular, but his lavish expenditure and indiscretions did not make him universally respected.

Now for the strange tale of the princess's jewels. From October 1829, many column inches in newspapers were filled with the theft:

> Stolen from the palace of his Royal Highness the Prince of Orange, at Brussels, 15 very large brilliants set in gold net work, and 10 chalons set in silver, marked 'A.'; a large bouquet, composed of a rose, a jonquille, two fleurs-de-lis, and small flowers in brilliants, enclosed in a knot of rubies [...] a bracelet, containing a portrait of the Emperor Paul and the Empress Marie, set in hair and diamonds, with the eye of Providence; a malachite bracelet, with turquoise, rubies, and brilliants in flower – motto *'Ne m'oubliez pas'*.[14]

The list goes on. A week later, the *Morning Post* carried a piece sent from Brussels:

> The theft of the diamonds continues to be the subject of general conversation, and the most curious rumours are circulated. However, not only have the diamonds been taken, but also a number of papers, amongst which was the will of the Empress, mother of the Princess.
>
> It is asserted that the square of glass was not cut on the outside, but on the inside, which shows that the thief must have got out at the aperture he had made, and he must have entered by another way; most likely during the day he had let himself be locked up in the palace [...] It was easy to obtain a knowledge of the palace, which request is always granted, but only during the absence of the Prince and Princess.
>
> It was natural enough to suspect the servants; foot marks were noticed in the garden, and all the boots and shoes of the palace were tried to see if the size corresponded with the marks, but none were found that did.[15]

One might remark that checking the servants' shoes was rather futile: why would a servant need to cut the window in order to get out of the palace? I would use the stairs. But it is the 'curious rumours' that are intriguing. Captain White makes this 'mysterious and unhappy event' even more bizarre when he adds that it 'contributed in the highest degree to injure the Prince of Orange in public opinion' – the prince, not the princess – and likens it to the affair of Marie Antoinette and the diamond necklace over forty years earlier. The French queen had had no involvement in the murky story of fraud and an expensive diamond necklace, but few believed her, and it added to her reputation for extravagance and frivolity, which damaged her – and the French monarchy – disastrously. White adds about the Prince of Orange: 'it was impossible to adopt any judicial steps to dissipate the mystery, or to relieve the prince from the odious and improbable imputations so virulently cast upon him by his enemies, and so confidently believed by the credulous public'. He tantalizes further:

> That His Royal Highness may have been extravagant; that he may have been injudicious in the selection of some of his private and confidential friends; that his domestic happiness may now and then have been clouded, may be true; but to suppose, for one moment, that he directly or indirectly participated in a burglarious attack on his own palace, or in the plunder of his own wife, was a monstrous supposition that every generous heart ought to have spurned with indignation. That this robbery was adroitly executed, that the size of the footmarks in the garden, and other coincidences, unfortunately cast strong suspicions on an innocent, but unpopular individual, known to enjoy the prince's favour is possible.[16]

White defends the prince, rather lamely, saying he didn't need money, and he cannot resist later in his book somewhat disingenuously relating what 'calumniators' were asserting about the prince, 'that he was an undutiful son, a faithless husband, a bad father, a vile midnight robber'.[17] One man was later charged with the theft and most of the jewels were recovered, but the rumours about the prince never went away – perhaps not just stealing from his own wife, perhaps not just about attempted fraud, but about male lovers – and 'gross' graffiti appeared on the palace walls.[18]

* * *

The great festival announced by King William to be held in Brussels in the summer of 1830 was to include for the first time an exhibition of national industry. If the Dutch king was soon to be found lacking one ounce of political sagacity, his laudable efforts and interest lay in industry and commerce. Crowds from Europe flocked to his second capital for horse races, fêtes, balls and the promised fireworks. Gold medals would be awarded to the best works of industry and art. The retired English industrialist William Cockerill and his sons had promised machines from their renowned factories near Liège, the *Morning Post* announced, and 'Mr. Cooper, a young English artist of this city, is also to enter the lists with his pencil – a bold enterprise in the land of Rubens and Teniers – but, judging from the *on dits* regarding his vast and exquisite production, a landscape view, we may hope he will snatch a laurel for his country in that particular department, in which of late years she has suffered them to wither on her brow.'[19] William Cockerill's teenage secretary Charles Mackay is another of my eyewitnesses to the revolution, as is the artist Thomas Sidney Cooper. Both were writing many decades after the events and their memories had probably morphed after constant retellings, but their anecdotes are illuminating and personal.

By the time Cooper wrote his memoirs, in 1891, he was in his late eighties and a Royal Academician, famous for his paintings of bulls, cows and sheep, and there are wonderful snow scenes and paintings of wild goats in Snowdonia. Cooper was born in Canterbury in the middle of the Napoleonic Wars; he had no memory of his father, who abandoned the family when he was about five. But Cooper was resilient: he had an obsession for drawing and a knack of meeting useful men that made splendid anecdotes. As a child all he had to draw on was his school slate. One day, while he was drawing the cathedral, an artist came to look at what he was doing. On hearing that the child had no money for pencils or paper, the artist said he was going home to London and donated his remaining pencils and paper to the boy. Unfortunately the boy could not afford a knife to cut the pencils. He spotted a priest and approached him, asking if he had a knife. The priest obliged, cut all twelve for him, and walked on. The boy was told by an amazed onlooker: 'That was the Archbishop of Canterbury.' Young Sidney was not impressed: 'I only knew that he cut my pencils.'[20]

A few years later he acquired a job as scene-painter to a theatrical troupe touring Kent. While sitting on the beach making water-colours of the cliffs to give him ideas for the scenery for a production of *The Battle of Hastings*, a man stopped to look and asked if he was doing them for sale. Cooper explained to him about the production: 'Scenery for the theatre?' 'Oh, indeed!' and walked on. Cooper adds that 'he had the most wonderful pair of eyes I had ever seen – they were most piercing, most searching, and, at the same time, most kind'.[21] It was the famous actor Edmund Kean, in Hastings for the benefit of his health. Though, strangely, Cooper tells us, he offered his services to the troupe for one night of his famous Shylock.

At twenty Cooper moved in with his uncle, a Dissenting minister, in London and succeeded in getting into the Royal Academy as a student; but what follows is odd, since he was immediately thrown out by his uncle and had to return to Canterbury, his dreams shattered. A few years later, in the summer of 1827, he decided to try his luck as a painter on the Continent. After crossing 'on an express boat' from Dover to Calais for 2s 6d, he headed for Brussels.[22] He eventually found himself in demand as a portrait painter and drawing teacher, and two years later married Charlotte Pearson, the daughter of a professor of mathematics. They were married at the house of the British ambassador by Rev. Holworthy, 'Chaplain to H.B.M. Embassy'.[23] It is likely that Cooper and his wife went to Holworthy's services at the Church of the Augustines since he says that they held open house 'after morning service' on Sundays to exhibit his latest paintings.[24] Evan Jenkins's services at the Chapel Royal were then at 2 o'clock in the afternoon.[25]

Cooper is adamant that there was a conspiracy afoot in Brussels in the summer of 1830. The community in Brussels watched events in France with anxiety and there was much discussion among the distinguished Belgian families whom Cooper knew: 'I did not know by name all the gentlemen that I met at the houses of my pupils, nor did I understand everything that was said; but I made out sufficient to be certain that a deep and well-laid plot, leading to an extensively organized revolution, was being planned at Brussels, Liège, Ghent, and Antwerp [...] My friend Verböckhoven was, I grieve to state, a terrible revolutionist, and was mixed up with the most virulent of the party.' Cooper says that his friend had just painted a large picture for the Prince of Orange, who was delighted and presented him with a beautiful, bejewelled sword, but Verböckhoven exclaimed: 'ce sabre qu'il ma donné pour cadeau, mais cette bagatelle! Jolie que ce soit, je la tournerai contre lui' ('this sword that he gave me as a present, this bit of trumpery. Despite its prettiness I will turn it against him').[26] Cooper was horrified. But he was obviously not too concerned, since he and his wife had determined to go to England for a visit to his family at the end of July 1830, despite the volatile atmosphere, and leaving their two-week-old daughter in Brussels with his wife's family. Charlotte was then aged twenty, seven years younger than her husband, and perhaps the family (one of the most respectable of British residents) decided that she needed a break and employing a wet nurse was regarded as normal.[27]

In Brussels on the evening of Tuesday 24 August, Captain White reports that crowds roamed the streets singing patriotic songs, and windows were smashed. Either he observed, or it was related to him, that at one point a large body of young men of a better class were leading the mob.[28] Placards announced 'revolution' for the next day, and graffiti promised 'Death to the Dutch'. The fireworks were postponed (the weather was given as an excuse) but strangely not the performance of Daniel Auber's *Muette de Portici* at the Théâtre de la Monnaie which was widely rumoured to be a signal for the uprising.[29] 'The Dumb Girl of Portici', also known as *Masaniello*, had premiered in Paris in 1828. It is in five acts, with the mute title role played by a dancer. It has been called the first 'grand opera', with its large orchestra, chorus and stage effects. It is loosely based on an uprising in Naples in the seventeenth century. The mute, Fenella, has been seduced and abandoned by the viceroy's son. Her brother, Masaniello, a fisherman, calls his companions to arms. In the next act, the people revolt and are victorious, but Masaniello is appalled by the cruelty and wants only liberty and he is crowned King of Naples (the plot is somewhat complex). Masaniello is poisoned but rallies to combat the returning, ousted noblemen, ultimately unsuccessfully. Vesuvius erupts, he dies and his mute sister plunges to her death. Richard Wagner later found it riveting.

Young Charles Mackay – former pupil at John Jay and William Drury's school – decided to see it that night of Wednesday 25th with his father. His father was a fierce loyalist of the Dutch king and had apparently taught the Prince of Orange's sons English; Charles, however, was sympathetic to the Belgian cause. Did they go out of curiosity about the rumours of an uprising or because they wanted to see the opera? They possibly had misplaced confidence in the authorities quelling any disturbances. 'The crowd in the Place de la Monnaie', Charles writes, 'half an hour before the opening of the doors, was vast and uproarious. It was with the utmost difficulty that my father and I obtained entrance to the pit, where there was only standing room.'[30] The overture was greeted with huge excitement, and several times the audience sprang to their feet 'as if by one simultaneous impulse, and cheered and waved their handkerchiefs, and stamped, and roared, and gesticulated as if they had been a congregation of madmen and madwomen – the women, perhaps, being the maddest of all'. As the curtain finally descended, someone in the boxes, a woman or a student, waved the French tricolour flag. The audience shouted, then sang the *Marseillaise* and rushed out of the theatre. He and his father were trapped among the crowd and heard someone yell, 'Chez Libri Bagnano!' – the hated government newspaper editor. His shop in the rue Montagne de la Cour, near the Place Royale, was smashed to pieces, though Bagnano escaped.[31] Next, the mansion of the equally hated Minister of Justice, Van Maanen, was set on fire. The king's palace was protected by troops, which the mob decided not to attempt, instead ransacking gunsmiths' shops. Charles Mackay also says that in the morning he witnessed the royal coat of arms being daubed over everywhere it could be found, and even a bootmaker was forced by an armed crowd of youths to take down the board displaying his name because it proclaimed that he was M. Leroy ('king').[32] What Captain White finds incomprehensible is the lethargy of the garrison in not putting down the riot or stopping the destruction of property. He also comments that the decided French tone at the start of the riots finally yielded to the cry of 'Vive les Belges'.[33] The next day, influential citizens gathered at the barracks to take over the policing of the city and a burgher guard was formed. After a few days, some tranquillity was achieved by the citizens – not by the troops. If this was a 'riot', a month was to pass before the riot turned into a 'revolution'.

* * *

The painter Thomas Sidney Cooper and his wife Charlotte read in the London newspapers about the August riots in Brussels and neighbouring villages with horror, and hurried home: 'on reaching Brussels we found the whole town in a deplorable state. The diligence put us down at the Rue de la Madeleine, and in order to get to our house in the Rue d'Abricot [near the church of St Gudule] we had to pass over thirty or forty barricades, with porters carrying our luggage.' The porters sound impressive. Cooper continues:

> This was neither an easy nor an agreeable matter, challenged as we were by every armed brute we came across, who thought no more of one's life than if it had been worth but a penny or a *sou*. Evidence of the *émeute* [riots] met us at every step – lawlessness, destruction of property, and an utter disregard of order pervaded the place; and we met several bands of armed men (not soldiers) crying out: 'Vive la patrie!' and 'À bas les Hollondais!' etc.
>
> By dint of struggles, and an expenditure of breath, as well as of money, we eventually reached our home, where we were thankful to find our baby safe and well.[34]

He learned that his wife's brother, George, had been badly wounded (by whom or how, he doesn't say). He visited him in hospital, surrounded 'by others groaning in pain and dying'. George died some time later.

British residents were terrified, White says, and began an exodus: some to Antwerp, others to France, or to the packets at Ostend and on to Britain. Those who stayed armed themselves and their servants to protect their houses and families. Wild rumours of atrocities spread.[35] And yet, it seems, Evan and Eliza stayed. By this time they had four children under the age of five: Edward (four), Helen (three), Alexander (one) and Mary Jane Wilhelmina (four months) – her third name surely in honour of the Dutch queen. They also possibly had a few schoolchildren under their charge. In rue d'Orange – now rue d'Edimbourg – on the country side of the largely demolished city wall by the Porte de Namur, they were perhaps relatively safe from the maraudings of rioters, however drunk some of the rioters got. Evan would surely know his duty to his remaining flock: to rally or comfort them at church services in the Chapel Royal, and to attend the calls of any Protestant English who were sick or dying, like George Pearson.

One of the British who left was the wealthy, elderly William Cockerill with his secretary, young Charles Mackay. As soon as he heard that the king, in The Hague, was sending a large force to Brussels, he resolved to go to his son's home in Aix-la-Chapelle/Aachen, over the border in Germany. Rioting had spread, and a mob had ransacked his son's house, but being a very rich man his son rented an even larger mansion, and the King of Prussia acted firmly in restoring order.[36] In contrast, Captain White is astonished at the ineptitude of King William of the United Netherlands and his ministers after the August riots. The Belgian patriots had fortuitously picked the right time to have a revolution: the Duke of Wellington, then Prime Minister, now believed strongly in a policy of non-interference in European affairs, as long as Britain was not affected. He had allowed the July revolution in Paris to proceed, and he and his successors in government had no desire to interfere in the Low Countries, even though he had been one of those responsible for cobbling the two Netherlands together as a buffer zone in 1814. Wellington's object was to avoid another European war, and there were enough problems at home with the reformist agitation and the huge national debt. Another piece of luck was that the other European powers were busy with their own problems, and from November the biggest danger – Russia – was embroiled in the Polish uprising, so the tsar was unable to help his sister, the Princess of Orange.[37]

The forces under the Prince of Orange and his younger brother Prince Frederick arrived at Vilvoorde on 31 August, about six miles north of Brussels. Prince William had quarrelled with his father about the need to be conciliatory; the prince had no desire to use force, and had been given no powers by his mulish father than that of listening to the deputation from Brussels and reporting back to The Hague. Captain White comments that Frederick was the complete antithesis to his brother: cold, reserved, a good administrator with no 'military genius' – frankly he was an utterly useless military strategist, as events were to prove.[38] The Prince of Orange bravely entered Brussels with just his own staff for talks, which were futile. Despite the rumours and vile graffiti, the leading citizens offered him the leadership of a separate Belgium, but he refused and returned to The Hague. It was the last time a member of the Orange family would reside in that palace.[39]

The Hague government procrastinated, deluded that the Great Powers would come to help. It was decided to hold an extraordinary session of parliament in mid-September. Meanwhile in Brussels, tradespeople were beginning to feel the effects of the flight of the British inhabitants, of wealthy Belgian nobles and the Court; but on 12 September the theatre reopened and markets resumed.[40] Thomas Sidney Cooper was so reassured that order was restored that he went to Amsterdam to make a drawing of the king's palace – a commission from the king himself – little knowing that his journey back would become a nightmare.

At the extraordinary session at The Hague in September, it was eventually decided that no concessions were to be made and that force must be used. The Belgian representatives returned home in disgust. The intransigence of the Hague government led one Belgian deputy to proclaim: 'Belgians, be prepared for combat or slavery.' In Brussels, trees were hewn down in the boulevards, the barricades were strengthened, and volunteers and adventurers began arriving, but six pieces of artillery against an approaching army of 13,000, under Prince Frederick, were hopeless odds, and most only had paving stones to fight off the army.[41] The endgame had arrived.

* * *

Prince Frederick believed that he would receive a warm welcome from citizens longing for a restoration of order. The plan, according to Captain White's source – which all of Brussels seemed to know beforehand – was for the main attack to enter the city on 23 September by the Porte de Schaerbeek and sweep south to the park and the palaces (the king's and the Prince of Orange's). After taking the upper town, any resistance could then be mopped up: it should take a mere five hours. But instead of Prince Frederick being met with shouts of loyalty at the gate, his column was greeted with a volley of musketry from the nearby barricades and houses. His troops managed to get into the rue Royale and to the shelter of the park, but with much loss of life.[42] However, the royal troops now occupied the two royal palaces and held all the ramparts and boulevards between the Gates of Schaerbeek and Namur, some being stationed at the end of the rue d'Orange where the Jenkinses lived. But then, inexplicably, they stopped. 'It was evident [to the royal troops]', White writes, 'that the populace, though forced to abandon the gates, were resolved to dispute every inch of ground, and to fight from room to room, from house to house.'[43] Again their intelligence was utterly deluded: most of the rebels fled or were hiding in cellars. White is damning in his criticism:

> so many fatal errors were committed [by Prince Frederick], that it is a matter of difficulty to discover a single instance undeserving of censure. Never was a good game so fearfully mismanaged by the players, and never were the

lives of brave men so wantonly exposed through the unskilful tactic of their commanders [...] The whole responsibility of the failure must rest, not with the soldiery, but with the chiefs.[44]

For four days the royal troops were trapped in the park and the two palaces, harassed by fire from surrounding windows and roofs, with no orders, while Prince Frederick attempted negotiations with an emboldened provisional government, or whoever was in charge. And here Captain White is at his most exasperated: no attempt was made by the royal troops to take an adjacent building and stop the firing; no trenches were dug to protect the men, who instead had to use the carcasses of their dead horses. And yet at night, Brussels rebels went to bed.[45] It is time for the two American adventurers to appear.

* * *

In 1831 a pamphlet of forty-odd pages was published in London, entitled *Adventures of Two Americans in the Siege of Brussels, September, 1830. By One of Them.*[46] The author is clearly Augustus Hardin Beaumont (1798–1838), since his elder brother Arthur was wounded on the first day of the four-day siege and the rest of the narrative must come from Augustus.[47] If one scene at a barricade is reminiscent of that in Victor Hugo's *Les Misérables* (published in 1862), many rebels, Augustus says, just ran away, or got drunk, but it didn't put the brothers off. It seems to have made them even more radical, despite the confusion, the chaos and the lack of any leadership that they could fight under.

Augustus Beaumont was the second of three brothers born in New York. Their father (a doctor in the British army during the American Revolution) and Irish mother died when they were young and they went to live with an aunt in Jamaica. Elder brother Arthur was sent to study at Oxford; younger brother Edmund to do a medical degree in Edinburgh. When Augustus was working as a lawyer's clerk, he protested at the hanging of a coloured woman, was imprisoned for sixteen days and successfully sued the deputy marshal. With the proceeds he began life as a journalist. In 1826 he was sent to England by the planters to campaign for compensation for when slavery was abolished. On his return to Jamaica he took part in colonial politics, licensing the first ever black man as a preacher and removing disabilities from the Jews. Possibly just after the French July revolution in 1830 he and brother Arthur went to Paris to join the National Guard, but on 20 September they journeyed to Brussels in a diligence coach to join in the fight for liberty there. The diligence driver made them and a Belgian medical student – who was rushing home to take part in the promised fighting –

get out near Halle and walk the final few miles, as he didn't want his vehicle to be broken up to become part of a barricade.

On Wednesday 22nd the brothers bought a musket each and went to volunteer at the Hôtel de Ville in the Grand-Place, which Augustus describes as 'abandoned by all the authorities'.[48] His style is flippant and mocking, in total contrast to Captain White's sober narrative. They were told to join the corps led by the owner of their hotel, but he seemed to be in hiding. That evening they went to the Porte de Schaerbeek to volunteer their services, but they found a group of dispirited people – the 'Vulgar Rabble' – who felt abandoned as their leaders had run away. 'It appeared that nothing was to be done that night but grumble.[49] They were roused the next morning (23 September) by the sound of cannon and encountered their first Dutch – lying dead in the street. Augustus's mocking style lapses. 'A Belgian woman kicked the slaughtered foe, calling them *Cochons*. The whole sight was sickening.'[50] Arthur offered to lead a 'half-armed rabble' to make a stand against the approaching cavalry; but on hearing the horses' hoofs most fled, and Arthur was left with only his brother, a young French boy and a Belgian, so they ran to a barricade. Belgian women turned loose powder into cartridges and threw them from the windows, which enabled the rebels to force the king's troops to flee back to the park. However, a lot of free beer and schnapps was being distributed and in the confusion some Belgians shot each other. Despite their bravery at the barricade, Augustus says that 'fifty determined men could have entered the town in the direction where the Brothers fought, without meeting serious resistance from more than half a dozen'.[51]

When the brothers got to the Place Royale 'they saw no enemy, but they were told they were in the Park; they looked but saw only trees. The Dutch it appeared were hid in a deep hollow in the Park, which effectually covered them from any fire but that of bombs or rockets, and these the Belgians did not possess.' Arthur was shot in the leg: 'I've got it, *Vive la liberté*.' He was carried to a temporary hospital at his hotel accompanied by a cheering crowd and 'the pain of his protracted cure was alleviated by the friendship which it conciliated to him of some of the most amiable ladies of Brussels'.[52]

On Friday 24 September, Augustus went back to the Place Royale, where he found the rebels firing at the trees in the park. 'He aided them some time in this work of arboricide, but consider[ed] it a pity to waste so much powder and ball.'[53] And, just like Captain White, he marvels at what on earth the king's troops were up to against the leaderless revolutionaries. He is certain that if Prince Frederick had started to bombard the town:

the Citizens would have run away, leaving their cannon and muskets to take care of themselves. As each man fought how, and when he pleased – eating his breakfast, then going a Dutchman-shooting – then returning to dinner – then out again for a little more sport – afterward to the tavern to boast his exploits, tell how many he had killed, eaten, &c. &c.[54] and then to bed, it may be easily conceived that the Citizen's Posts were often slenderly guarded [...] At the best of times, and when the spirits of Beer, Patriotism, and Schnaps were most powerful, there was not a position of the Patriots which would have stood one demonstration of the Bayonet.[55]

There were plans to surrender the town, but Prince Frederick pre-empted them: at midnight on Sunday 26th his troops evacuated the park and Brussels; Augustus can only use the baffled adjective '*extra-extraordinary* evacuation'. He is equally scathing of the provisional government whom he says crept back when it was safe: 'People of Brussels, who fought your battle? the very lowest orders, aided and commanded by foreigners, especially Frenchmen.'[56]

Arthur had recovered from his leg wound by spring 1831 and became involved with radical French groups and street riots in France in 1834, for which he was imprisoned and sentenced to transportation, but probably released in 1837. Augustus made himself unpopular in Jamaica after his return and left for England in 1835. He possibly joined revolutionary groups in Spain for a while, but he is remembered for the radical newspaper he founded in Newcastle upon Tyne, advocating universal suffrage for men and the nationalization of the railways, and for his contribution to the rise of the Chartist movement. He died aged thirty-nine in January 1838 as he prepared to go to Canada to join the rebellion there.

* * *

On 27 September the bells rang out in Brussels as its people rejoiced in their improbable victory. 'The doom of the dynasty was sealed,' comments White at the close of volume one of his narrative.[57] He says that the carnage and destruction in the upper town fuelled hatred against the Dutch and especially Prince Frederick:

In the park, the statues, trees, gates, and ornaments were shattered or defaced; the walks, alleys, and hollows, were strewed with fragments of fire-arms, gun-carriages, uniforms, and military equipments. Here, the mangled bodies of dead horses obstructed the path; there, lay a still palpitating, half-stripped, unburied corpse; and there again, a dozen others, barely covered by a few handfuls of earth or leaves. Here, ensanguined or discoloured streaks marked the trace where some wounded victim had dragged himself from the scene of combat; while there, deep indentures in the sand, and dark coagulated pools, covered by myriads of insects, indicated the spots where other gallant men had made their last death struggle.

He describes neighbouring houses 'spangled with shot', broken window glass, splintered doors, 'brains on the walls, and blood on the floors'. The discordant shouts of armed volunteers 'were only hushed as they encountered the funeral convoy of some fallen comrade, on its way to the general receptable of the killed, in the Place des Martyres'.[58]

If the Jenkinses really did stay through these four days, it must have been terrifying, not least the noise: their house was only a ten-minute walk from the park. Young Charles Mackay was sent back to Brussels from Germany by his employer Mr Cockerill to find out if his mansion 'on the Boulevards' was still intact. He found that over a hundred Dutch troops had been installed in the house; they had drunk all the wine and spirits in the cellar; smashed mirrors, chandeliers and pictures, and 'in the most outrageous manner defiled the beds, and even the tables and chairs, refusing, with disgusting malice, to make use of the conveniences which every well-constructed house affords', that is, there was shit and urine everywhere.[59]

Arriving only twelve years after these events, Charlotte Brontë would have heard much about the revolution, so her short paragraph as Lucy Snowe begins her opiate-fuelled walk into the park at night seems curious and detached: 'In past days there had been, said history, an awful crisis in the fate of Labassecour, involving I know not what peril to the rights and liberties of her gallant citizens.' She, or rather Lucy, continues:

Rumours of wars, there had been, if not wars themselves; a kind of struggling in the streets – a bustle – a running to and fro, some rearing of barricades, some burgher-rioting, some calling out of troops, much interchange of brick-bats, and even a little of shot. Tradition held that patriots had fallen: in the old Basse-Ville was shown an enclosure, solemnly built in and set apart, holding, it was said, the sacred bones of martyrs. Be this as it may, a certain day in the year was still kept as a festival in honour of the said patriots and martyrs of somewhat apocryphal memory –[60]

Belgium has become the fairy-tale country of Labassecour, 'a land of enchantment' as seen in a dream. After the deaths of Emily, Branwell and Anne, perhaps Charlotte Brontë is turning from the pain of too much reality, and there are echoes of Byron's account in *Childe Harold* of the Battle of Waterloo: 'Ah! then and there was hurrying to and fro, / And gathering tears, and tremblings of distress'.[61]

* * *

I left the painter Thomas Sidney Cooper going off to Amsterdam to do his sketches in August or early September. As soon as he heard of the advance of the royal troops towards Brussels he tried to hurry back. Three thousand Dutch troops were drawn up between Antwerp and Brussels, temporarily delaying his journey south; he found a diligence going south-east to Leuven, where he was again stopped by troops. He then started walking, the sounds of gunfire and cannon getting louder the more he progressed towards the city. Stopped again by soldiers, he was escorted to an inn, wet through, muddy and exhausted, but he climbed out of a window and walked as far as Tervuren, only a few miles east of Brussels. He was frantically worried about what had happened to his family inside the city. Much later he wrote in his memoirs of what happened next:

> The firing had entirely ceased, and meeting a young man, of whom I asked an explanation of this circumstance, he told me that there was a truce, and that as people were leaving the town, I could have passed in had I been at the gate [the Porte de Namur, near where the Jenkinses lived]. He had been in the artillery, and had lost an arm; and he said that he would get me in the next morning if I would go with him, to which I gladly assented. I then sought some rest, which I sorely needed.
>
> The morning came, and, as soon as I had eaten some breakfast, I set out with my one-armed guide. We had walked about three miles, when we met two men. One of them stopped and addressed me, asking if my name was Cooper. I asked why, in great surprise, not having the remotest idea who the man was.
>
> 'I suppose you don't recollect me,' he said; 'I am butler to the Hon. Mr. Freke, and you are the gentleman that teaches drawing to the young ladies.'
>
> 'Yes, that is quite right,' I replied; 'but have you come from Brussels now?'
>
> He said: 'The family left last night, sir, and so did your wife and child, but we all had to get over the town wall. The soldiers helped us over on shutters and doors that had been knocked off by the cannonading.'[62]

It seems that Cooper got back to Brussels on the second day of the siege on 24 September. He doesn't say exactly where his wife's family's house was, but it was possibly near the Porte de Louvain, about fifteen minutes' walk north from the Jenkinses' home in the rue d'Orange. Perhaps Cooper's account of trying to get to his parents-in-law's house tells us of the Jenkinses' experience. 'We got as far as the ponds of Etterbeek, which lie outside the town, between the Porte de Namur and the Porte de Louvain, and having no arms, we were allowed to pass on unmolested; but we had not gone much farther, when we saw several people running towards us. They were frightened by a trooper, who was firing his carbine at the windows of some houses.' The trooper was drunk and was disposed of in one of the ponds. Cooper was then reunited with his wife and child and her family. She told him 'how the officers, as well as the soldiers, helped the women over the barricades and walls by heaping up doors, shutters and debris of every description – even the bodies of dead horses!'[63] They had no food, but he managed to find some, and he had to also feed the dragoons posted in their house. 'Being outside the gates, we were safe from shot and cannon-balls. The sentry only fired on those who carried arms, or tried to enter the town; but we could hear the fearful struggle that was going on inside, and see some of the effects of the awful slaughter.' The 'cavalry could not act against the barricades', 'the army could make no headway against the *bourgeoisie*', and carts full of wounded and dead passed their house.[64] He then notes that on 26 September, Prince Frederick finding it impossible to take the town of Brussels, marched his army back to Antwerp. The gates were thrown open and the Coopers returned to their house near the rue Royale:

> What a sight met our eyes as we entered the town, literally walking on glass, the shattered remains of windows from the houses, which were all terribly battered by the cannon-balls and shot, some quite in ruins, with their roofs broken up, their doors and windows wrenched off, to assist in the formation of barricades. The roads were torn up for the same purpose, carts and waggons overturned, and the whole place presented a deplorable spectacle.[65]

For Cooper, 'all was dreariness and desolation', many of his acquaintances had been killed, and most of his pupils had left Brussels.[66] He decided to leave, and returned to England in spring 1831.

* * *

> We shall have Prince Leopold for our King. A ?serious discussion took
> place in Congress yesterday when they met in secret but one of the
> Members told Mr Taylor that they had nearly come to fisty cuffs in
> debating
>
> – Eliza Jenkins to William Branwhite Clarke, 1 July 1831[67]

It must have been with huge relief that Eliza was able to pass on the news to her
and Evan's friend Rev. Clarke. This is the earliest of Eliza's letters and for the first
time I could hear her voice and read her handwriting. But the hope of a final end
to disorder and uncertainty was still a fragile thing: subsequent events might have
ended Leopold's reign after less than a month.

Not many weeks after the rapid departure of Prince Frederick, the authority
of the self-elected provisional government was recognized throughout Belgium,
and in November by the British government, and the Brabant tricolour flew from
every tower and spire. This Belgian government – comprising writers, journalists
and lawyers with no parliamentary experience – was not united on what kind of
country they wanted: some were keen on an independent kingdom under the
Prince of Orange; others wanted reunion with France; a few were republicans.
On 10 November an elected National Congress assembled in Brussels to decide
the matter. Most of Europe would have been happy with a member of the Nassau
house as king, and for a long time the British government favoured the Prince
of Orange. However, although the Congress voted that the country should
be an independent, constitutional monarchy, it also agreed that the Orange
Nassau family should be 'excluded in perpetuity from all power in Belgium'.[68]
In December the Conference of the five Great Powers, sitting in London, invited
the provisional government to send commissioners to discuss independence, and
so began the arduous discussions and a succession of protocols going backwards
and forwards between London and Brussels – rather reminiscent of the time I am
writing.

Captain White describes the first months of 1831 in Brussels as dominated
by the fear of civil war, of plots and disorder; factories and shops were closed,
causing a large increase in unemployment, the poorest managing only because of
charity; grass grew in the squares, and public walks were abandoned: the wealthy
and the tourists stayed away.[69] The provisional government resolved to elect a
sovereign to prevent anarchy. Numerous names were put forward, mostly without
the knowledge of the actual candidate, including those of Lafayette, the hero of
the American and French Revolutions, then in his seventies, and of the Pope.

1 The author at the graves of Evan and Eliza Jenkins (left) and their son Edward (right), Brussels City Cemetery in Evere, February 2014.

2 The 'very white' church of St Padarn: Llanbadarn Odwyn church, Ceredigion.

3 Rev. John Williams, headmaster of Ystrad Meurig
school from 1777 to 1818.

4 Canolfan Edward Richard, Ystrad Meurig: the restored school, built 1812, with a
modern extension, and the nineteenth-century church under which Edward Richard
lies buried. The tomb of Rev. John Williams lies within the railed enclosure.

5 Impossibly educated labourers confound nineteenth-century
school inspectors on their way to Ystrad Meurig school
(Noel Ford, 2012). This is a different version of the story.

6 Chelsea Old Church in 1788, about twenty years before
David Jenkins arrived.

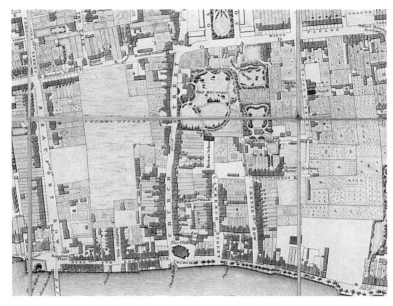

7 F.P. Thompson's map of Chelsea (1836). David's school, Cheyne House Academy, is just right of centre. The Old Church lies by the Thames, south of the Rectory, which stretches to the King's Road. Battersea Bridge is to the left.

REVᴰ DAVID JENKINS
INCUMBENT OF ALL S·S CHAPEL 1814-1824
& OF ST LAWRENCE CHURCH 1824-1854.

8 Rev. David Jenkins, incumbent of Pudsey St Lawrence (c.1850), once a close colleague of Patrick Brontë.

9 Provost Alexander Livingston of Countesswells (c.1750), Eliza Jenkins's grandfather.

10 Eliza Jenkins and daughter Helen (c.1860), perhaps in the garden of 14 rue des Champs Elysées, Brussels, where Mrs Gaskell visited them in 1856.

11 The distinctive bell tower of St Ninian's Church and Manse, North Leith.
Five of Eliza's siblings were baptized here in a batch in 1805.

12 Margaret Wyndham née Jay (1860s),
Eliza's younger sister, who emigrated to
Australia in 1827. The explorer Ludwig
Leichhardt wrote admiringly of her when
she was younger.

13 François Gailliard's painting of 1886
depicts the Church of the Augustines
before it was demolished and the façade
moved. It was known as the King's
Church, or the Dutch Church.

14 An early twentieth-century postcard showing the Chapel Royal, Brussels in the upper town. The entrance is the third door on the right of the curved part of the former palace.

15 Interior view of the eighteenth-century Chapel Royal, Brussels, with the pulpit and gallery (2014).

16 William, Prince of Orange ('Slender Billy') confronted by the rebels in Brussels in summer 1830 as he arrives to mediate between them and the government in The Hague.

17 King Leopold I of the Belgians, painted when he was about seventy (1860–1).
He died a few years later. Evan Jenkins was his first honorary chaplain,
appointed in 1835. Princess Victoria wrote to her uncle Leopold,
'my love for you exceeds all that words can express'.

18 The Place Royale in the upper town and the Roman Catholic church of
St Jacques-sur-Coudenberg, outside which King Leopold was inaugurated in July
1831. Charlotte Brontë compared the elegant worshippers going to *salut* there with the
abysmally dressed British residents coming out of the Chapel Royal, on the other side
of the Place, in *The Professor*. The arches on the right led to the
Porte de Namur and the Jenkins home.

19 The Isabelle Quarter in 1843: the pensionnat and its garden.
The rue Royale and park were up the steps to the left.
The Chapel Royal was beyond the end of the road (not shown).

20 George Richmond, *Portrait of Charlotte Brontë* (1850).

21 Samuel Laurence, *Portrait of Elizabeth Gaskell* (1854).

22 Edward Jenkins, when he was about forty (1865).

23 Edward Jenkins, family and friends, probably in the rue des Champs Elysées (before 1873).

List of former Chaplains.

who officiated in : (1) The Church of the Augustins,
(2) The Chapel Royal,
(3) The Church of the Resurrection,
from the Battle of Waterloo to the year 1911.

J Stonestreet.	1815 ⎱ Chaplains to
R. W. Tunney	1816 ⎰ the Forces
E. C Willoughby	1816-1818
T. Prince	1818-1822
(a) G. Hornby.	1818-1820
Henry D. Baker.	1820-1821
Whitworth Russell.	1821
Charlton Lane	1821-1822
(a) Streynsham Master.	1822-1826
(a) W. Holworthy	1826-1829
(b) Evan Jenkins.	1825-1849
M. J. Blacker.	1850-1856

(a) Chaplain to H. B. M Embassy.
(b) Chaplain to H. M. King Leopold I.

C. E. JENKINS, M.A.,
1856-1873.

J. C. JENKINS, M.A.,
1873-1894.

24 Edward and his younger brother John Card Jenkins in the
Almanack of the Church of the Resurrection.

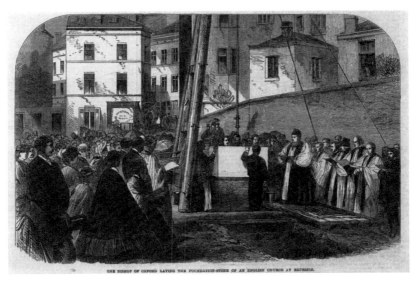

25 Engraving of the laying of the stone for the unbuilt Church of the Resurrection, from a photograph by Ghémar (1864). The Bishop of Oxford, 'Soapy Sam' Wilberforce, is accompanied by Edward and John Card Jenkins (immediately on his left) and the tall William Drury. Eliza's daughter Helen may be depicted on the other side of the trench.

26 Sketch of Lixmount House, near Edinburgh, Eliza's childhood home in the early nineteenth century. It is now at Charlecote Park in Warwickshire.

One German prince even advertised himself by pasting up handbills.[70] One of the favourites was the new King of France's second son, the Duc de Nemours, who was only sixteen; he was elected by one vote. But the Belgian Congress had not reckoned on the views of the French king: in February, Louis-Philippe refused to accept the Belgian crown for his son. An interim regent was installed, and by April, the election of Prince Leopold was being considered seriously.

* * *

The more one knows him, the more one values him. His conduct is perfect. Always quiet, always circumspect, he will never be elated by prosperity, or cast down by adversity. He sees everything in its true light [...] In a word, he is judicious, clever, and thoroughly good.

– Baron Hardenbroek on Prince Leopold in March 1816[71]

On 2 May 1816, Leopold of Coburg, the eighth child of a minor German prince, married the most eligible heiress in Europe. He was twenty-five; Princess Charlotte was twenty. The Duchy of Saxe-Coburg-Saalfeld was small and obscure, but its ruling family were to marry outstandingly well among the royal and aristocratic families of Europe. One of Leopold's sisters was married to the tsar's brother (albeit unhappily), and from the age of six Leopold was an officer in the Russian army, though it is unlikely that he was involved in any fighting until he was in his twenties. There is a delightful story that he was seduced in Paris by Empress Josephine's daughter Hortense when he was seventeen. She was seven years older and, at the time, Queen of Holland during the short reign of Napoleon's brother Louis, whom she detested. But I am more impressed that he met Napoleon in 1808, who wanted him to become his aide-de-camp. France had overrun Coburg, and Leopold had been sent on a diplomatic mission to save the duchy.[72] Six years later, in 1814, Leopold was part of the victorious tsar's army as the Allies entered Paris, and Napoleon was despatched to Elba.

That year, Princess Charlotte broke off her engagement with William, Prince of Orange and fell for Prince Frederick of Prussia. But when the latter rebuffed her, her thoughts turned to Leopold, whom she had met in London during the Allied celebrations for the (first) defeat of Napoleon in 1814. London had been so full of sovereigns and grandees that this fairly impecunious minor prince was lodged on the second floor of a grocer's shop in Marylebone High Street – a fashionable shopping street near Oxford Street now, but perhaps hardly suitable for a decorated, and eligible, soldier-prince in the tsar's entourage who was presented to the heiress apparent by another of Tsar Alexander's sisters. Charlotte longed to be free of her father, the Prince Regent, and wrote about Leopold: 'I know that worse off, more unhappy & wretched I cannot be than I am now, & after all if I end by marrying Prince L., I marry the best of all those I have seen, & that is some satisfaction.'[73] I remarked earlier that, in Leopold, Charlotte met her Colonel Brandon, or even her Professor Higgins. Where she was wild, talkative, prone to laughing too much, Leopold was grave, studious, more interested in reading, drawing, music and botany than field sports. 'He cannot be called Handsome', wrote one observer, 'but he is a good-looking man, and well made, and about 5 feet 10 inches high. His countenance is rather severe, but He is spoken of as being good-humoured.' Another added that Charlotte 'looked up to her husband with the most perfect respect, and he deserved it all. His influence over her was unbounded, though the exercise of it was of the gentlest kind.' Leopold called her 'an amiable and glorious little woman'.[74] 'Glorious' is a wonderfully revealing adjective: he was happy, and so was she. Nine months after the wedding Charlotte wrote: 'It is quite certain that he is the only being in the world who would have suited me and who could have made me happy and a good woman.'[75]

The couple moved to Claremont House near Esher in Surrey to enjoy a private married life; it was to last a mere eighteen months. In November 1817, after two miscarriages, Charlotte endured a fifty-hour labour, giving birth to a stillborn son. A few hours later she was dead, no doubt aided by the doctor, who starved and bled her. Leopold's friend Baron Stockmar wrote: 'we went to the chamber of death; kneeling by the bed, he kissed her cold hands, and then raising himself up, he pressed me to him and said, "I am now quite desolate. Promise me never to leave me."'[76] Much of the country went into sincere, stunned mourning. At the funeral Leopold stood 'pale, emaciated, and drooping'; Stockmar commented that Leopold 'is convinced that no feeling of happiness can ever again enter his heart'.[77]

Over twenty years later, Charlotte Brontë probably saw King Leopold at a concert in Brussels; she transforms it in *Villette* to Lucy Snowe's observations of the King of Labassecour, but it is unmistakably Leopold, 'a man of fifty, a little bowed, a little gray':

> at first the strong hieroglyphics graven as with iron stylet on his brow, round his eyes, beside his mouth, puzzled and baffled instinct. Ere long, however, if I did not *know*, at least I *felt*, the meaning of those characters written without hand. There sat a silent sufferer – a nervous, melancholy man.

Lucy/Charlotte sees him haunted by the spectre of 'Hypochondria' – which we might call melancholia, depression, today – 'she freezes the blood in his heart, and beclouds the light in his eye'.[78] Charlotte too had known that feeling, that despair. She continues:

> Some might say it was the foreign crown pressing the King's brows which bent them to that peculiar and painful fold; some might quote the effects of early bereavement. Something there might be of both these; but these as embittered by that darkest foe of humanity – constitutional melancholy.

In *Villette*, Lucy watches the elite of resident foreigners, including a party from the British Embassy, enter the concert hall. Among them, in Brussels, were probably the Jenkins family. Surely they took Charlotte with them. With her poor eyesight, she was sitting close enough to observe the king's face.[79]

At the age of twenty-six, the bereaved Leopold was given Claremont and its beautiful grounds for life and retained the large annual grant awarded on his marriage (not without sniping from the press and some parliamentarians). He had become a British citizen and, though born a Lutheran, was a communicant of the Church of England. But if one member of this extraordinary Saxe-Coburg family had failed to provide an heir for the British people, another would. Three middle-aged brothers of the Prince Regent resolved to do their duty and marry to save the Hanoverian dynasty, including the Duke of Clarence – the future 'sailor king' William IV (1830–7) – and his younger brother, Edward, Duke of Kent, who forsook Brussels and the heartbroken Madame de St Laurent to marry Leopold's older, widowed sister, Victoria Mary Louisa, in 1818. No doubt Leopold was instrumental in arranging the match, the first of many he was to encourage. Princess Alexandrina Victoria was born at Kensington Palace in May 1819, the Duke of Kent dying only eight months later. But whether Leopold was to become the uncle of a queen depended on whether the future sailor king William and his new wife Adelaide could produce children: two daughters died swiftly, and there were two miscarriages. During the 1820s it was becoming clear that the heir presumptive was Leopold's niece. Later, Queen Victoria was to remember her visits to Uncle Leopold at 'dear Claremont' as the 'brightest epoch of my otherwise rather melancholy childhood'.[80] At the age of seventeen she wrote to him, 'no creature on earth loves you more dearly, or has a higher sense of admiration for you, than I have [...] my love for you exceeds all that words can express; it is innate in me, for from my earliest years the name of Uncle was the dearest I knew, the word Uncle, alone, meant no other but you!'[81]

* * *

For much of his father-in-law George IV's reign (1820–30) Leopold travelled abroad. He had been in an impossible situation in that his mother-in-law, Queen Caroline, was the detested, estranged wife of the king and he had unfortunately paid her a visit, to the king's fury. Leopold kept out of the way of his dysfunctional, unpleasant in-laws, returning occasionally to Claremont or his London home at Marlborough House. There were mistresses, but they, and Society, found the serious prince 'heavy work'; frankly, Society found him tedious.[82] But there must have been some who enjoyed talking quietly with Leopold about art, history or literature, even novels, and who found the frivolities and gossip of Society tedious. In 1828 he met a young German actress, Caroline (Karoline) Bauer, a cousin of Baron Stockmar, who encouraged their liaison. As Joanna Richardson paraphrases: 'Here [Stockmar said] was a prince to be saved from disillusion and misery, from the series of stupid and soul-destroying love-affairs with which he had attempted "to beguile the everlasting *ennui*".'[83] Immediately one thinks of the character of Eugene Onegin, whom Pushkin was creating at just this time. It is likely that Leopold read the verse novel (he was fluent in Russian).[84] The vibrant, youthful Caroline reminded the weary prince of Charlotte, and he had Caroline (and her mother) installed in a house in Regent's Park. Caroline later described him looking like 'a musty, bookish fogey and an old bachelor in his fifties than a prince in the life and spirits of thirty-eight'. According to Caroline, her relationship with Leopold was a dreary non-event, as his first attraction had almost immediately died. She returned to her acting career, never seeing him again.[85]

Meanwhile the appealing prospect of the crown of Greece intrigued the romantic imagination of Leopold. Whether Caroline's embittered memoirs contain a fair portrait of Leopold at this time, he certainly needed a job. Leopold's name had been put forward as the first King of Greece for several years, though bitterly opposed by George IV. He eventually declined the throne in May 1830. He wrote:

> When the undersigned entertained the idea of becoming the sovereign of Greece, it was in the hope of being recognized *freely* and unanimously by the Greek nation, and of being welcomed by it as the friend who would compensate it for its long and heroic struggle, by the security of its territory and the establishment of its independence on a permanent and honourable basis. It is with the most profound regret that the undersigned sees these hopes deceived.[86]

Some said that King George's illness (he died that June) had focused Leopold's mind instead on becoming the power behind the British throne once Victoria was crowned. The future William IV was elderly and asthmatic, and a regency needed to be set up if William died before Victoria was eighteen. But it is more likely that the conditions, especially regarding the borders of the new country, that Leopold demanded of the British government and the Allied powers were not met. In 1862 he wrote that he regretted that the romance of a Greek crown had not materialized and, enigmatically, 'If I had taken command of things in England in 1830, many things would have happened differently.'[87] Would the next offer of a throne fail in the same way?

* * *

On 12 April 1831, our historian, Captain Charles White, passed on privately to Leopold's equerry that the Belgian Congress were interested in his views on becoming the Belgian sovereign. The diplomat who was the official British liaison between Brussels and London, Lord John Ponsonby, couldn't start the negotiations formally. Leopold was careful in his response, he 'strictly abstained from giving any authority to the exertions that were being made in his favour' but he learned what he needed to hear: above all, that most deputies would vote for him and, mindful of his Protestant faith, that the Catholic clergy and leading laity were in favour.[88] A Belgian deputation was sent to discuss the details with him personally in London. Leopold had not only read the new constitution carefully and followed the wording of the protocols that were going to and fro, he had no doubt been studying the history of the Austrian Netherlands. One problem was Luxembourg: the new Belgium claimed it as part of their territory; the Great Powers disagreed. Concessions were needed on both sides before Leopold could accept. On 4 June, the Belgian deputies voted by a majority of forty-four to proclaim Leopold as King of the Belgians. Lord Ponsonby 'deemed it expedient to dispatch a confidential person to communicate this important intelligence' to Leopold, then at Claremont, and the British government.[89] White doesn't mention who this trusted person was, but Théodore Juste, writing his *Memoirs* of Leopold in 1868, says that it was Captain White himself.[90] Perhaps the detail that White supplies – 'The prince [… was] apprised of the honour conferred on him at an early hour on the 6th' – confirms the identification. Leopold 'manifested deep emotion [...] on being assured that the dissentient votes were political – not personal'.[91] He had enemies at home and abroad, but Captain White was one of Leopold's admirers:

Not a shilling was expended in gaining over the people; not a single article was inserted in the journals; nor was recourse had to any of the various artifices of songs, busts and portraits, that had been employed on previous occasions by the supporters of other combinations. The selection of Prince Leopold was founded on political and moral grounds of the highest order [...] History does not furnish an example of the election of a sovereign, so utterly devoid of all intrigue [...] as that of Leopold.[92]

But Leopold had accepted only conditionally. The formal Belgian deputation arrived back in Brussels on 27 June to put the election of Leopold and his conditions to the final vote: that the Congress should accept the eighteen articles laid out by the Conference of the Great Powers in London, which largely involved the territory that was to form part of the new Belgian kingdom. There was violent opposition in some quarters: 'Irresolution and tumult reigned within the chambers [of Congress], riot and distrust without; plots and conspiracies were actively carried on.'[93] There were threats against deputies and inflammatory graffiti. Finally one brave deputy rose to propose the adoption of the eighteen articles: Mr Van Snick of Mons. 'To follow the nine days' debates that ensued, would be to retrace scenes of disorder and uproar never exceeded in any legislative assembly,' comments White, who may have sat in the gallery and been deafened by 'the most appalling yells' as the voices of moderation were drowned out. But finally a division was demanded, and on 9 July 'Van Snick's proposition was carried by a majority of 126 to 70 votes'.[94] The capital, White says, was overjoyed. The deal was done. A relieved deputation left for London and it was announced that Leopold would arrive in the country on 17 July.

* * *

'We shall have Prince Leopold for our King.' I quoted above from a letter that Eliza wrote to Rev. Clarke on 1 July 1831. Her excitement was surely matched by mine when I was told that there were two letters from Eliza and three from Evan in the State Library of New South Wales in Sydney, as well as one from Eliza's brother John Livingston Jay, written in 1830–1. My cousin Marcia had come across the familiar name John Livingston Jay in the archive, which puzzled her: what was the English brother of her ancestor doing in the archive of the pioneering Australian geologist William B. Clarke (1798–1878)? She ordered the letter and also those listed in the catalogue as written by people called Jenkins, not knowing if they referred to the Brussels Jenkins. She then found their names mentioned in a biography of Clarke.[95] It turned out that John Livingston Jay and Clarke were rivals: the 'love triangle' of my chapter title. The great biographer Richard Holmes describes his curiosity about scientists in the Romantic period: 'Did the Romantic men of science ("men in white coats") have inner emotional lives comparable in intensity to those of the poets [...]?'[96] It led him to write his celebrated book *The Age of Wonder* (2008). Clarke doesn't feature in Holmes's book, but he could have. He was a poet as well as a geologist, and on the basis of his entanglement with Miss Sophia Barker of Brazil, Brussels and London in 1830–1 – as traced through the letters in the Sydney Archive – his inner emotional life was certainly turbulent at the time. But what was so intriguing about these letters were the glimpses I had of how life was going for the Jenkinses just after the revolution and strong clues to their personalities. But how had they met Rev. Clarke?

William Clarke was born in East Bergholt in Suffolk, some twenty years after John Constable, who referred to him in letters as 'little Billy Clarke'. Constable had once helped Clarke's blind father, who was the headmaster of the Free School, and it is obvious from a letter Clarke wrote to Constable in 1833 that he greatly admired the artist, which few people in England did.[97] Clarke attended Dedham Grammar School, as Constable had done, and was admitted to Jesus College, Cambridge in 1817 as a pensioner, even though his family seems to have been fairly poor. Although four years younger than Evan Jenkins, and at a different college, it may be that they met as undergraduates. Clarke's tutor was William Hustler, the brother of Evan's tutor. There are clues in the letters that Clarke was not a recent acquaintance: in her letter of 1 July 1831 Eliza addresses him as 'My dear Friend'; and Evan's tone is familiar and joking, as to someone he had known for a long time. But the puzzle is: why are there no other letters before or after 1831? I shall speculate below.

While at Cambridge, Clarke published his first volume of poetry (four more were to come) but, more importantly for his future career, met Edward Daniel Clarke (probably not a relation), who lectured on mineralogy, and Adam Sedgwick, the Professor of Geology, with whom he was to correspond for many years. Clarke went on several geological expeditions in Britain before he took his BA degree in 1821, a year before Evan. He was ordained deacon at Norwich Cathedral that year, becoming curate in East Bergholt three years later. His geological expeditions spread to Europe, and in 1826 he was elected a Fellow of the Geological Society of London. In 1829, on his father's death, he took over the headmastership of the Free School in East Bergholt.[98] It is a year after this that he enters my story. He had made geological explorations in the Netherlands since 1826 and it seems that he stayed with the Jenkinses: in her letter of 26 July 1831, Eliza mentions that 'you will find your room ready here as usual'.

* * *

Was Miss Sophia Barker an unprincipled minx or the pathetic prisoner of her stepfather and mother? She was supposedly an heiress to £17,500 – around two million pounds today. Her father Thomas had been a merchant who had died, aged forty, in Rio de Janeiro in 1812. He left a widow, Frances, and two children – John, born in 1807 who died nine years later, and Sophia, born around 1810. Another daughter was born after her father's death, and died in Brazil a few months later. Thomas Barker had died in the house of James Gill, who married Barker's widow. They had two sons – James Sebastian (b. 1814) and Francis Turner (b. c.1818) – both born in Brazil. By 1830 the Gill family had moved to or near Brussels. According to a letter from Evan to Clarke, the Gill brothers boarded at the Jenkins home school in rue d'Orange: James aged about sixteen; Francis twelve. Rev. Clarke possibly met the Gills and Sophia in 1830 through the Jenkinses. Eliza's youngest sister Janet was also a close friend of Sophia – perhaps they had attended school together; both were around twenty at the time. Janet seems to have been floating between her siblings: staying with Eliza in Brussels, Samuel in London, John Livingston in Greenwich – he had been a clerk there for about five years and was now in his late twenties. Her father John Jay and his second wife and daughter had left Brussels, perhaps moving to Boulogne in France, and Janet also probably stayed with them.[99]

By Christmas 1830, William Clarke, then in his early thirties, had proposed and been accepted by Sophia and her family.[100] But while he was staying with Evan and Eliza he received a letter from Eliza's brother, John Livingston Jay. It was dated 24 December 1830, from the Royal Hospital, Greenwich, and noted as received (by Clarke?) on 31 December. It opens:

> Sir,
> The nature of the present communication induces me to wave all ceremony, &, without further preface, to introduce myself to you as the brother-in-law of your friend Mr. Jenkins: convinced from your character that whether or not the Lady who is the object of this letter, Miss Barker, be sincere in the declarations she has made you will be the first to acknowledge that, in thus addressing you, I am only doing an act of justice to all parties.
>
> Happening to visit Brussels in April last, I had the opportunity of meeting Miss Barker on a very familiar footing in consequence of her being the intimate friend of my sister Janet. She was in the habit of relating to us the misery she endured at home, I pitied her, & became strongly attached

to her; I, as well as those in her confidence, having every reason to suppose our affection mutual. Both Mr. & Mrs. Gill however, were so hostile to me, that, from the very day of my arrival, all intercourse between Miss Barker, & my Sister & myself, was prohibited, and, after the first fortnight of my stay, so rigidly was this injunction enforced, (Mr Gill accompanying Miss Barker in all her walks, even after dinner, so contrary to his usual habits) that I could never afterwards enjoy the pleasure of her society. We then had recourse to signs, but, altho' during the remainder of my visit we daily met at the window, we failed in rendering them intelligible. In this state of the affair I was obliged to quit Brussels.

My Sister returned to that City in November, & Miss Barker, in the only interview they could have, informed her, that an intercepted letter had led to a discovery, & that her Mother then exacted a promise that she would marry the Man she approved: hinting that person to be yourself – Miss Barker declared she had not the slightest regard for you but the contrary, never having met you except in a formal manner, that her attachment for me continued altho' very base means had been resorted to, to undermine it; & that you were courting her thro' the Gills, the whole being a plan of Mr Gills – but so completely was she in his power, that even in such a matter, on which her future happiness so much depended, she had no alternative, however distressing to her feelings, than silent submission.[101]

John Livingston Jay had possibly come to Brussels for the birth of his niece, Mary Jane Wilhelmina (b. 14 April), Eliza and Evan's fourth child. His chronology is not clear in that he says he had heard Miss Barker's tales of woe, he implies often, and was attracted to her, yet he was prohibited from visiting her at her home immediately, as was his sister Janet. Whether it was the case that John and Janet were told they were 'prohibited' or that when they next visited they were not allowed into the house to see Sophia, it does seem to be very controlling behaviour on the part of her stepfather and mother. It is a muddled account: did John meet her only once? If so, is this quite the thing to write to her new fiancé in this way? Perhaps he comes across as muddled since he was emotionally distraught.

John was hardly an eligible suitor for an heiress: he was a clerk (albeit with very clear handwriting and admirable punctuation); whereas William Clarke was an ordained Cambridge graduate with a promising background of published scientific papers. The Gills' preference seems understandable. But to ban not only

Revolution and a Love Triangle, 1830–1831

the sister and brother of the British chaplain's wife, but the relatives of their sons' headmaster, sounds an awkward proceeding in a small expat community. John cannot understand Sophia's deserting him for Clarke, unless she is obeying her parents. And, he continues, both Sophia's confidante Miss Stather and his sister Janet have confirmed that Sophia prefers him to Clarke. Miss Stather's name will be significant. She has told John that if Sophia could choose her husband 'she would select me'. Without this intelligence and the memory of Sophia's encouragement and affection, he would have 'endeavoured to forget the person who could thus so wantonly lacerate my feelings'. The rub is, he writes: is Miss Barker sincere in her expressed feelings for himself, or insincere? 'If insincere, after conduct so inexcusable [...] I trust I shall have little difficulty in effacing the recollection of such a being from my mind.' We do not know if Clarke replied. He carried on with the engagement. But he kept the letter. Poor John – he remained a bachelor until he was in his fifties, his wife dying just three years later. Maybe it was a bitter memory of Sophia that caused him to describe Brussels as 'that horrid place' in a letter to his sister Margaret in 1840, and to add that 'the greatest evil attending residence on the Continent is the few friends (useful ones) made by a family'.[102]

The next letter from a member of the Jenkins or Jay family among the Clarke papers in Sydney is that from Eliza to Clarke in East Bergholt, Suffolk (no house name or street) on Friday 1 July 1831. The letter is crossed so that six pages are crammed onto three, which largely baffles legibility until you gradually learn to focus on one horizontal line, trying not to be distracted by the vertical lines running through it. On page four, where the address and postmarks appear, Eliza has even crossed in narrow columns either side of the postmarks, so that you have to turn the paper round and round trying to work out which bit to read next, only to discover (if you have scans) that you have to print out the page and fold it as Eliza did in order to connect up lines. Several authors commented on this marvel. In Jane Austen's *Emma* (1816), Emma visits Miss Bates, who has received a letter from her niece Jane Fairfax and insists on reading it out: 'but, first of all, I really must, in justice to Jane, apologise for her writing so short a letter – only two pages, you see – hardly two – and in general she fills the whole paper and crosses half. My mother often wonders that I can make it out so well. She often says, when the letter is first opened, "Well, Hetty, now I think you will be put to it to make out all that chequer-work".'[103] Thankfully Emma is able to escape the ordeal of being read a crossed letter.

By July, Clarke had resigned his headmastership in East Bergholt and rented or bought a cottage in Rydal in the Lake District in preparation for his marriage. He was also in the process of selling the house in East Bergholt where he and his mother lived and he had received several affectionate letters from Sophia.[104] Eliza's letter begins:

> My dear Friend,
> Mr Jenkins having several letters to write today fears he will not have time to write to you himself, and therefore deputes me to tell you that he arrived here safely on Tuesday morning [28 June], at 8 o'clock, after a very tempestuous passage from Dover to Ostend. The letters you sent by him he delivered unto the hands of those to whom they were addressed[105]

I pause here because it is interesting that Evan arrived back in Brussels one day later than the deputies, who were bringing back Prince Leopold's conditional acceptance of the crown. Even if he had been escorting a few pupils to England for the summer holidays, it is quite possible that Evan had carried a confidential letter from the embassy to the government in London, or even to Leopold, and had taken letters back to Brussels not just from his friend William Clarke: hence having no time that day to write to Clarke?

The next two pages are mostly filled (horizontally) with advice for Clarke's sister on what to wear for the wedding: that it would be better for her to buy clothes in Brussels, since everything is made so badly and is so expensive in England. She adds about the current fashion that 'the dresses are made entirely without trimming on any part of them and the bonnets of all shapes but little trimmed & rather small'. I think it's plausible that, over a decade later, Eliza had a hand in smartening up Charlotte and Emily. Friend Ellen Nussey commented that 'none of the Brontës understood dress with its right and simple advantages, till Charlotte and Emily had been in Brussels; they then began to perceive the elegance of a well-fitting garment made with simplicity and neatness'.[106] Eliza then adds that she hasn't had a chance to see Miss Barker to 'speak to her on the subject of your letter to me': which, alas, we remain ignorant of. Finally she turns to her exciting news, as quoted above (horizontally and vertically):

> So you see after all we shall have Prince Leopold for our King. A ?serious discussion took place in Congress yesterday when they met in secret but one of the Members told Mr Taylor that they had nearly come to fisty cuffs in

debating as to whether or not they should accept the Prince on the terms he offers himself. Only 39 protested against the proposition which the Deputies brought over (and no doubt you have seen a copy of) so that we are sanguine as to the result.

Eliza then discusses the opposition members who that day, in the public debate, will try to prevent the affair being settled 'á l'aimable [by mutual consent]', but the people seem set against further trouble, and she expects the troublemakers to be driven out of Brussels. She adds plaintively: 'What would I not give to have an end to all the turmoil, the anxiety it occasions is extremely trying to body and mind. Fain would I hope we are near the end of our troubles.' By 9 July the opposition had risen from thirty-nine to seventy, as mentioned above – so perhaps Eliza's optimism was slightly misplaced; it is possible that many members were frightened off by the abuse directed at them. The Jenkinses are obviously well informed: Mr Taylor – probably Edward Taylor, whom Jane Austen had 'doated' on – had already reported to them what had happened in the Congress only the night before. I also think that this slight reference confirms my conjecture that Evan and Eliza's eldest son was named Edward after him and that he was a close family friend, and possibly one of the godfathers of their son.

Eliza's letter continues with the affairs of their home school – despite the turmoil they still had pupils: 'We received a letter from Steward and his father yesterday. The latter is greatly pleased with his son's improvement, and expresses himself in the most flattering terms, which fully compensates for the trouble we have had with him.' But she is anxious and needs Clarke to help to send them pupils. 'I don't expect James fils to return & hate vacant places. Do therefore your best to fill up the gap, and if you succeed my spouse will gladly go to England to fetch him but says he cannot afford to undertake the journey on an uncertainty.'

I could feel Eliza's energy bounding off the letter, on which every space is used. She even passes on gossip in two PS's squeezed in by the postmarks. This is a woman in her mid-thirties with four small children and schoolboys to look after, who must surely adore social occasions as she is never at a loss to discuss anything from politics to rumours of the latest marriage, encouraging William Clarke to get them pupils and happy to spend hours with one of his sisters buying a dress and bonnet for the wedding (especially more cheaply – Eliza keeps a sharp eye on money).

Two weeks later, on 15 July, Evan wrote to Clarke. I immediately sensed that he was more laid back than Eliza:

> My dear Clarke,
>
> Many thanks for your endeavour to secure me your late pupil Smyth. If his uncle should make up his mind to send him, we shall of course receive him with pleasure: if not, his place will no doubt be filled by another. Where have you been & what have you been doing since you wrote last? Somebody told me this morning that you have been confined to your bed for ten days by 'la Grippe'. Is it so? You say nothing about it in my letter & I did not deny it to that person. What a bore that you are not to be here before the 1st August. Just the time I shall re-commence fagging [working hard: i.e. the school term starts then]. Why <u>can</u> you stay away for so long a time?[107]

That is the confident, friendly drawl of a Cambridge graduate in his late thirties. Or maybe a man who hides anxiety, which I doubt Eliza would. A few sentences later, Evan mentions the courageous member of Congress who initiated the debate on accepting Prince Leopold's conditions (the eighteen articles), whom Clarke presumably knew from his geological forays on the border of Belgium and France:

> Pray what think you now of your friend Van Snick? Has he not acted his part nobly? He <u>will</u> bring in the King without fail on Tuesday next [19 July]. Sa Majesté will pass Saturday night at Calais – Sunday night at Ostend – Monday night at Ghent & will make his public entry into Brussels the following day. His inauguration will take place in front of the Church in the Place Royal. They are already preparing the woodwork. All agitation has at length subsided & the Propagandists have either been consigned to the Amigo here or unceremoniously conducted beyond the frontiers. – all I hope will now end well.

Captain White writes in a footnote on François Van Snick that 'this courageous deputy fell a victim to the cholera in 1834, at Ghent, where he was appointed to high judicial functions'.[108] The Amigo was a prison near the Grand-Place, now a hotel.[109]

Evan asks Clarke to hire a cassock for him at 'Webb the Robe-maker' in Holywell Street (near the Strand in London) so that he can have it copied in Brussels more cheaply, and buy a 'decent cover' for a sermon at Rivingtons, the publisher and bookseller. He also needs 'a copy of the long prayer, the bidding prayer, in use at Cambridge'. But, alas, that 'I will tell you my reasons for these things when you arrive.' The bidding prayer was said at Cambridge before the sermon. Perhaps Evan wanted to look smart when he officiated at a church service for the new king.

On the evening of 19 July Leopold arrived at his royal palace in Laeken near Brussels 'amidst the glare of a thousand torches, the shouts and acclamations of the multitude, and the roaring of artillery', Captain White recounts.[110] On the 21st he rode to the Place Royale on horseback as church bells rang and a multitude cheered and waved banners:

> Here, upon an elevated platform, splendidly decorated with national and royal emblems, Leopold was received by the regent, the members of congress, and the various constituted authorities; while dense masses of the people filled the square, the windows, and the house-tops, rending the air with joyful acclamations. The whole together formed an animating and splendid spectacle. After a short pause, the regent addressed the royal stranger in an impressive speech, and terminated by resigning his authority into the hands of congress. The prince then rose, and replied in brief but impressive language; and the constitution having been read aloud by one of the attendant secretaries, a salute of a hundred and one guns announced that the prescribed oaths had been taken and that Leopold was inaugurated king.[111]

Evan had presided for over four years at the chapel nearby; he and Eliza surely had seats among the foreign dignitaries to watch the ceremony, but, alas, there is no letter that describes the scene from their point of view.

Unfortunately 19 July turned out to be a disastrous date for William Clarke. He had moved his mother and a sister to Hackney, London and auctioned the contents of their East Bergholt home. But all was not going well: he had been receiving prevaricating letters about the marriage settlement. Had Gill mismanaged his stepdaughter's money or even taken some of it? Impatient at the delay, he wrote to Gill voicing his suspicions: 'I have only one object in view, her deliverance from a state of unhappiness.'

> Situated as she is in the midst of connexions who are anxious to manage her concerns as much for their own future advantage as for her present benefit – young and unsuspicious and open to advice from all quarters provided that advice comes clothed in the guise of friendship – I have felt for her in a way which a sense of conscientious integrity fully allows.[112]

As Dr Thorne comments in the eponymous novel by Anthony Trollope: 'I think that if I were much in love with a young lady I should not write such a letter as that to her father', and especially not to her stepfather.[113] Eliza wrote to Clarke on 26 July urging him to come to Brussels 'immediately':[114]

> I had not long received your letter yesterday, when an opportunity occurred of seeing Miss B– <u>alone</u>, a circumstance which I immediately availed myself of to <u>hint</u> your wishes to her. We were soon however interrupted in our tête à tête, & I had only just time to discover that Mr & Mrs G– are tampering with her to your disadvantage […] you should by all means come to Brussels <u>immediately</u>. I am convinced they have succeeded in deceiving her, and are endeavouring to persuade her now that the interest you take in her affairs is only on account of her money. – Your presence will I doubt not set all to rights for to tell you the truth she is certainly much hurt at some thing you have done or written, which I cannot find out as I scarce see her alone or hear anything new but what you write on the subject.

The Gills, who had favoured Clarke, had now turned against him: was he asking too many awkward questions about the money? Or had his letter seriously offended Mr Gill and Sophia? Eliza adds a heartfelt moment of empathy for Clarke having left his home. Surely she is thinking of Lixmount: 'I perfectly (from sad experience) enter into your feelings regarding your leaving Bergholt – nothing is more trying than leaving a place where we have been <u>born</u> and <u>bred</u>.' She says that no British ambassador had yet been appointed although the Belgian ambassador, Van de Weyer, had already gone to London. And then she adds what will be pertinent for Evan's future:

> The Dutch or German Consistory are doing their utmost to induce the king to attend their service but nothing has yet transpired as to which Church he will attend. My spouse (who is very backwards in going forwards) has had a good word spoken <u>for his</u> by Sir H. Taylor but I cannot say I am, or he indeed, very anxious as to the result. His Majesty is enthusiastically (beyond all description) received all over Belgium, & is already very popular here.

'Sir H. Taylor' is the 'doated'-on Edward Taylor's younger brother, Lieutenant-General Sir Herbert, private secretary to the new king William IV. I don't believe Eliza for one moment that she wasn't 'anxious' as to whether King Leopold attended Anglican services at the Chapel Royal. The phrase in brackets about 'backwards in going forwards' gives it away: Eliza is excited; Evan is being frustratingly laid back and not pushing the possibility, but he was maybe thrilled at the prospect, and hid it well. Eliza (of course) adds a PS: 'We passed a long day at Tervuren on Edwards birthday and thoughts of old times.' It was their eldest son's fifth birthday on 7 July 1831. One imagines a picnic and a long sunny day in the garden of a friend's chateau that hadn't been burnt down in the revolution. We learn no more about that day. It made me think of Richard Holmes's beautifully felt comment in *Footsteps* on his experience as he searched for Shelley. I suddenly identified with his poignant image, shut out from the magic circle. Yet this time it was *my* family, who didn't know me. Holmes writes:

> Indeed I came to suspect that there is something frequently comic about the trailing figure of the biographer: a sort of tramp permanently knocking at the kitchen window and secretly hoping he might be invited in for supper.[115]

Six days after Eliza's letter, Evan wrote urgently on 'Monday Evening' to Clarke, who had not yet arrived in Brussels.[116] The letter is addressed to the care of Mrs Wilson in rue St Joseph in Ostend: presumably where Clarke would spend the night after arriving at the port, before taking the long journey by diligence coach to Brussels (it is a distance of seventy miles; when the railroad opened in 1838 it took five hours by the much quicker train).[117] Evan had gone to the rue de la Madelaine that evening (near the Grand-Place) to meet the diligences from Ostend on the off-chance of meeting Clarke 'as I hoped that the tenor of my wife's letter would have induced you to leave London without delay'. It is clear that the Jenkinses have not had a reply to Eliza's letter as Evan repeats that Clarke's letter to Gill 'has given mortal offence & I dread to think how matters will end'. It seems that the urgency of Evan's letter is to prevent Clarke and his sister going straight to the Gills: 'your sister's going there is entirely out of the question. You had better therefore bring her here direct & to occupy your bed' while Clarke stays in a hotel (Evan's pupils had arrived back for the new term a few days before, so there was only one bedroom available). It may be that Clarke was delayed by being quarantined: one newspaper reported that 'No passenger is allowed to land at Ostend from England until a strict inquiry has been made by the proper Officers as to the cholera.'[118] We also learn from Evan's letter that Eliza had managed to have the interrupted tête à tête with Sophia at the Jenkinses' home:

You have already been informed of our suspicions that tampering was going on. This day week the old man dined with us [on 25 July; Gill was about sixty], & with two or three more sat on drinking my Claret till ½ past 11 o'clock!! Madelle [mademoiselle: Sophia Barker] came in the Evening, & appeared rather queer, & it was then that my better half took occasion to hint to her your wishes which were but coldly listened to. Things remained in statu quo till Friday [29 July]. Half an hour before I was going out to dine the old man requested an interview with me which I granted. To my unutterable surprise he attacked me about your letter & raved like a mad bull, cried like a baby, & terminated this pathetic scene by saying that 'although he had nothing to say against me individually, all intercourse between the female members of our families must cease'. In the Evening he sent me a note commencing 'Sir' announcing his determination of removing his sons 'in consequence of what had passed between us in the morning'. As nothing <u>had</u> passed relative to the boys, I kicked at this & demanded a quarter's pay according to our original assessment, which he refuses. Today I have another letter from him on the same subject enclosing your two despatches to himself & Miss B. unopened!! Hers in an envelope re-directed to you <u>in her own handwriting</u>. These I immediately returned to the old sinner, since which time we have heard nothing. Of Miss B.'s feelings on the occasion we are totally ignorant, as she has sent us no explanation of this extraordinary conduct. All we know is that she was at a Ball given by Mrs. Lowe, dancing till 2 o'clock on Sunday morning. We had declined the invitation a fortnight before. I must not forget to tell you a part of our conversation on Friday. Old G. wished me to write to you by that day's post (but it was too late) that 'he would never exchange a word with you as long as he lived – that you should never set foot within his door – that he would deliver Miss B. to her friends in England & wash his hands of the whole affair & that the marriage might take place there if all the parties were agreeable'. These things I think it right you should know before you arrive in order that you may have time to consider what steps to take on your arrival here. After this exposé can we be surprised at any thing that has been done or may hereafter occur? So far as the removal of the boys is concerned, the old Buffer will find himself in the wrong box. The loss is very trivial in any point of view, but I am determined he shall pay the uttermost farthing. My avocat [lawyer] shall be at work in a very few days or perhaps in a few hours: I have got in his own handwriting that, he 'has no fault to find with my Establishment' – that is quite sufficient for my purpose: – We must bring these old Bashaws to their senses.

That is such a strong letter, and in such idiomatic English that one forgets that English is Evan's second language. Buffer and Bashaw – meaning respectively a contemptuously regarded 'fellow' and a haughty grandee: Evan simply won't accept the man's behaviour and seems to have already approached his lawyer. Evan constantly comes across in his letters as a strong-minded man, aware of his standing and his rights. It's a crossed letter – crossing letters was not just a female habit – so some words get tangled up with those crossing them. Evan obviously is impassioned and needs to let it all out, including that Eliza has now been banned from seeing Sophia. That is presumably because Sophia has passed on to her mother and/or stepfather that Eliza had given her a message from Clarke – her fiancé! It is getting clear what Evan is now beginning to think about the minx/victim who has stayed out late at a ball when she is engaged to his friend.

I am also heartily relieved that Evan was a wine drinker – a 'cakes and ale' man. In Anthony Trollope's *Framley Parsonage* (1861) the hero, Mark Robarts, considers what type of clergyman he wants to be:

> he would not be known as a denouncer of dancing or of card-tables, of theatres or of novel-reading [...] Cake and ale would still be popular, and ginger be hot in the mouth,[119] let him preach ever so; – let him be never so solemn a hermit; but a bright face, a true trusting heart, a strong arm, and a humble mind, might do much in teaching those around him that men may be gay and yet not profligate, that women may be devout and yet not dead to the world.[120]

I think I am getting to know Evan and I find similarities in my own character – and I don't just mean enjoying wine, but the refusal to grovel – which may cost Evan the loss of two pupils. When he lost his father at a young age he had to grow up quickly. With his elder brother David away in London, the twelve-year-old became the man of the family, no doubt combining work on the farm with long rides or walks to school and late nights studying.

Evan adds finally that 'Brussels begins to be itself again. The King returns from his tour on Thursday [4 August].' But the day after this letter was written, on 2 August, the Dutch invaded Belgium. The end of Clarke and Sophia's story must wait.

* * *

Never was a country surprised in a situation so utterly defenceless; never was victory more certain, or more easily obtained.[121]

Captain Charles White describes grimly the rotten state of the Belgian army that King Leopold had inherited: 'The gangrene of insubordination and confusion had penetrated to the very marrow.' It would be no match for the remodelled Dutch army of almost 80,000 under the Prince of Orange. But, yet again, Captain White is baffled at the slow progress of the Dutch troops 'who moved with a degree of drowsy precaution utterly inconsistent with the object of the operation'. With a bit more vigour the Dutch could have taken Brussels on 7 August.[122]

King Leopold was in Liège, sixty miles east of Brussels, when news of the advance of the Dutch army reached him. He at once despatched a message to Paris to request military assistance. But his Belgian government, unaware how inept their army was, declared that requesting French help was derogatory to the national honour. In the absence of a British ambassador, Captain White took on the role of hastening to Leopold to implore him not to ask for French assistance. Leopold, however, replied that his request was 'contingent, not absolute', that is, only in case of need.[123] In his less than two weeks as king, Leopold had inspected his troops and knew how hopelessly inadequate they were. Against the wishes of the Belgian government, he had made a wise move in approaching the French, and it would save his throne.

On 4 August Leopold issued a proclamation appealing to the courage of the nation. Brussels filled with volunteers loudly demanding to fight the Dutch, which White comments was 'more detrimental than beneficial to the defence of the country'.[124] The Dutch army advanced on Leuven (Louvain), just sixteen miles east of Brussels. 'To describe the confusion that reigned at Louvain at this moment would be as difficult as to account for the tardy advance of the Dutch,' White comments. The undisciplined Belgian volunteers were causing chaos.[125] But White is full of admiration for Leopold during the battle or skirmishes that followed. Many Belgians deserted and his force was completely outnumbered:

> It was in vain that he multiplied himself in every direction, and performed the united duties of king, general, and subaltern. The odds were too powerful, the discouragement too great. Flight or surrender were the only alternatives. His situation was most critical; but the inertness of his opponents saved him. Had the Prince of Orange availed himself of his numerous and brilliant cavalry [...] had he not been shackled by the drowsy routine of Dutch tactics – neither the king nor a man of his army ought to have escaped.[126]

Fortunately also for Leopold the British arrived, or rather Lord William Russell (army officer turned diplomat) with a flag of truce and a letter from the new British ambassador, Sir Robert Adair, who had arrived in Brussels on the 9th.[127] The letter demanded a suspension of arms and warned the prince that the French advanced guard had reached Brussels (on 12 August). But the Prince of Orange's troops continued to advance. White continues:

> Finding that Lord William Russell had failed in the principal object of his mission, and that not a moment should be lost in relieving Leopold from his hazardous position, Sir Robert Adair determined to proceed in person towards the prince [of Orange]. Hastily throwing himself across the first horse he could procure, the veteran diplomatist galloped through the confused masses which encumbered the streets and suburbs of the city, and reckless of all personal danger, gallantly traversed the fire of the contending parties, who utterly regardless of the flag of truce, borne by the ambassador's attendant, continued a sharp but irregular combat.[128]

Sir Robert – who was then in his late sixties, and considered by Edward Taylor to be 'considerably *passé*'[129] – reached the Prince of Orange and insisted on a suspension of hostilities. The prince assented on condition that the Belgians evacuate Leuven and surrender it to the Dutch. However, the French had moved quickly, and on 13 August the French army of the north began to escort the Dutch back to the frontier. But the Dutch felt triumphant; the new Belgians humiliated. The invasion was over; for the time being Leopold had kept his throne, and Belgium its independence – but only just. The least glimmer of hope that Edward Taylor held on to (writing to his brother on 23 September) was that he was 'much inclined to think we shall not have a renewal of the war this winter'.[130]

* * *

Meanwhile the affairs of the heart were not going well. Clarke and one of his sisters finally arrived in Brussels – Sarah, wife of Rev. William Trollope from whose book on Belgium I quoted above.[131] But the bird had flown: Sophia had been taken by her stepfather to London, to stay with her uncle John Barker. Clarke finally managed to see Sophia in London, which he thought went well, but the next day she returned the engagement ring, referring to his 'very offensive letter of 19 July'. Clarke turned to his Cambridge friend and brother-in-law, Rev. Trollope, who seems to have made matters worse. He wrote to Sophia's uncle on 7 September, that 'Mr. Clarke's feelings have been so hurt at the reply which Miss Barker has given to the letter he addressed to her on Sunday that he is utterly incapable of acting for himself.'[132] Trollope, having read the correspondence between Mr Gill, Clarke and Sophia, is 'fully impressed with the idea that it was never till recently the intention of Miss Barker to abandon her engagement. Mr. Clarke himself is so completely persuaded that she is acting under influence that his affection for her is undiminished.' But Trollope writes that in order to vindicate Clarke's character and make reparation it is necessary 'to bring the matter immediately to a judicial issue'. He adds that Clarke had told him that Sophia had said she would marry him 'if her friends did not urge her to the contrary'. Trollope offers himself as a peacemaker, but then repeats his threat: 'I shall be obliged for an immediate answer as the affair will be shortly put into professional hands.' This was a huge mistake. Sophia's uncle replied quickly that he would be ready to meet Trollope, but then he read the letter again and penned a longer letter:

> I regret exceedingly the peremptory and threatening tenor of all the communications which have been received from your family since Miss Barker has been in England, for this mode of proceeding must have been prejudicial to their wishes, if they are or were desirous that she should marry your brother, for I can scarcely imagine that Mr. Clarke, or any man of feeling, would accept for a wife, a lady offered up as a victim to appease his family.[133]

He refers to Clarke's fatal letter of 19 July which appears to say that Sophia would have to give up all connections with her family after marriage, so that 'if Miss Barker becomes one of your family, she must not look for happiness'. He assures Trollope that if Clarke hadn't written that letter then the whole of her property 'would at this time have been in Mr. Clarke's possession'. Referring to the threats of a court case, Barker writes: 'It is for your family to consider how far this exposure in a judicial court, (which you threaten) would add to your Mother's tranquillity.' And then, interestingly, he seems to refer to the letter that Eliza's brother John Livingston Jay had written to Clarke in December about Sophia preferring him:

> you may judge what I felt in Mr. Clarke's shewing me on Sunday last, a letter he had received some months since, strongly reflecting on the conduct of my niece, which appeared to have been worn into pieces by frequent perusal, and to be still carefully treasured up – If this letter had been shewn to me, to be assigned as a cause for breaking off the acquaintance with Miss

Barker, I might have admitted its validity; and on the other hand I should consider that this, coupled with some remarks which were made at the interview, would fully justify Miss Barker in acting in the same manner; for if happiness is to be reflected in the marriage state, each party must be free from suspicion.

So John Livingston's letter really had worried Clarke. Sophia's uncle believes that it is actually Clarke who wants to end the engagement: 'I will tell you candidly,' he continues to Trollope, 'that after one of my interviews with Mr. Clarke, I mentioned to Miss Barker that it seemed to me that Mr. Clarke was not desirous of the marriage, and that I thought it not improbable that something might occur to break it off, provided he could secure remuneration for any loss he had sustained.' John Barker ends his letter:

> you must be interested in the happiness of Mr. Clarke, as I am in that of the only daughter of a beloved brother, and convinced, as I am, from a general view of all the circumstances that happiness could not now result from an union between these parties, (and this state of the case originating in the act of your brother, which possibly might have been averted by conciliation and kindness, but not by threatenings and revilings) I am of opinion that our joint advice should be that no marriage should take place – and I think it would ill become me to recommend my niece to offer herself as a propitiatory sacrifice, when there at present appears neither esteem nor affection.

There is a draft letter in the Clarke papers in which Clarke rebuts the points in Barker's letter.[134] It includes extracts from letters that Sophia had sent to him, stressing how much she was treated like a child and kept a prisoner, and how she looked forward to seeing him and his sister in August. Clarke is arguing in his draft that she needs rescuing and loves him, but that she is under pressure from her family. The draft also includes extracts concerning the numerous delays in sorting out the marriage settlement, and that a legal friend had suspicions. Clarke had given up his headmastership and his curacy, and he describes himself as 'harassed, fatigued, unwell, irritated'. In another draft letter he states that the events have 'blighted my prospects in life'.[135] A few days before these drafts, he had written to Evan in Brussels, whose reply is the last from him in the Clarke papers. Clarke's letters to Evan had probably been full of despair for his future, with no job and no money:

My dear Clarke,

I am, as usual, in the midst of bustle & confusion & will not therefore attempt <u>replying</u> to either of your letters. I only write a few lines, for the purpose of offering you my sincere & heartfelt congratulations on the termination of your correspondence with that weak, silly, & unprincipled girl. I might add many other & worse terms, which your own feelings & experience will naturally suggest. You have indeed had a most lucky escape. May God preserve you from falling into such a snare again! Do not regret any hopes you may have sustained; for had you lost every [sic] you possessed in the world, <u>your honour and senses excepted</u>, I should have still considered you a most fortunate man in coming off as you did. If you ask my advice about bringing the matter into a court of law, I would say, decidedly not. Threaten the parties as much as you like, & pocket, sans façon [without fuss], any thing you may get out of them, but let not your name be mixed in a court of justice, with that of the horrid crew. So far as I have been able to learn, every body here takes your part, & I feel confident that, if the worthless young woman were to show her face in Brussels, no notice would be taken of her by any respectable person. Recollect what Dr. Gough said to me respecting G— & his family, & I am sure you will bless your stars for being again free, your honour untarnished. On no account make yourself uneasy about the future. The world is all before you. You have talents, you have kind friends, & most respectable connexions. Why should you for one moment entertain a doubt of succeeding agreeably to your wishes whenever you may choose to put your shoulders to the wheel? I trust I need not say that we & all your friends in Brussels will be delighted to see you whenever you may think proper to pay us a visit. How gay you must have been at the time of the coronation. Every thing here is much the same as when you left. King Leopold is becoming more popular every day. Baron Stockmar is just returned from England, & I hope in a few days to go & pay my respects to His Majesty. I must now close or I shall be too late. My wife & the children unite in kindest regards to your mother & sister.

& I remain

Yours ever sincerely

E.J.[136]

(The coronation was that of King William IV on 8 September 1831, who had succeeded his brother George IV. Presumably Clarke had mentioned it in one of his letters: as a Fellow of the Geological Society he may have taken part in the coronation procession.)

I think Evan is being too harsh about Sophia Barker, but one has to think about the context of two hundred years ago: a young woman (especially an heiress) had to be protected for the marriage market; nothing must damage her reputation. Sophia was controlled by her guardians (her mother and stepfather) and then would be handed over to a husband, with whom she had barely exchanged a word in private. She had not been allowed to talk or walk with John Livingston Jay, whom she liked, and was handed over to William Clarke, whom it seems she did grow fond of. But he had offended her and her family by his letter of 19 July. If she appeared cold or 'queer' to Eliza and Evan, it could be that they misread her, just as Jane Bennet's feelings for Bingley were totally misread by Darcy as indifference.[137] Sophia's going to the ball could also be misread: neither Eliza nor Evan were actually there.

But Evan is so kindly and encouraging to his friend, who must have sounded so depressed. When we are down we all need someone to write and say 'You have talents, you have kind friends' and come and visit us. And the mention of his four children (all under the age of six) all passing on their 'kindest regards' is lovely. I also enjoy the airy comment that he will go and see King Leopold 'in a few days' – no rush: Clarke may have taken part in the coronation procession of one king; Evan is going to pop in to the palace to see another king (it is written so unpompously, but I get a glimpse of a friendly rivalry). As friends, Clarke and Evan complemented each other: the former highly emotional, passionate – for geology, for Sophia – impulsive, bellicose, a poet and a scientist; the latter displaying the calmness of an older man to his younger friend, generous and caring in his comments designed to hearten a depressed man who despaired about his future. What a pity Clarke didn't keep other letters from Evan or Eliza. I shall explore that briefly below.

* * *

On the rebound, or maybe even in defiance, Clarke married Maria Moreton Stather less than four months later, in January 1832 – the one-time companion or friend of Sophia Barker. Or maybe, as Charles Lever writes in his novel *Harry Lorrequer*: 'at no time is a man so prone to fall in love as immediately after his being jilted'.[138] Maybe Maria had done her bit to damage his relationship with Sophia – an uncharitable thought, but surely quite common for women in the desperate marriage market when middle-class women had so few options. Clarke was given the living of a church in Dorset and then, six years later, in 1839, emigrated to

Australia. Maria went back to Europe three years later with their three children, not returning for fourteen years.[139] Clarke's geological discoveries, his travels, his correspondence with scientists, including Charles Darwin, and his renown as 'the father of Australian geology', as well as his constant poverty, are for another book. 'His large correspondence, preserved in the Mitchell Library, Sydney, represents a major archival source on Australia's nineteenth-century science.'[140] It also includes, rather strangely, personal letters about his doomed wooing of Sophia Barker that he took with him 10,000 miles to New South Wales, accompanied by his wife and children. I think he did so because he was much in love with Sophia (or thought he was) and he couldn't bear to destroy any of the correspondence, however painful some of it was. If he had just been after her money, it is unlikely he would have kept the letters; instead he had been profoundly hurt. Did his wife Maria know that he kept Sophia's affectionate letters?

Why are there no letters from Evan or Eliza before or after this period of his unhappy love affair? Perhaps Evan's harsh description of Sophia in his last letter had offended Clarke. But the kindliness of the rest of it surely wouldn't lead Clarke to reject his friends in Brussels? One explanation is maybe that other letters from Brussels were just weeded out as he prepared his archive for scientific posterity. But friendship can break over the slightest of misunderstandings: something said, or something not said. And love is blind: Clarke believed Sophia loved him as he loved her; he believed she had been 'tampered' with. Perhaps he longed for Evan to write instead: I am sure she loves you; she is a lovely girl; be patient. Instead Evan damned her, which was probably with the best of intentions, but maybe at the cost of his friendship with Clarke.

As for Sophia Barker, I have found no trace of her in later life because it is not an uncommon name. I think she was a victim, desperate to escape her cloistered life, but in return she wanted affection from a potential husband, not someone who seemed keen on her money. I hope she found a caring partner.

Twelve

Chaplain to the King

In February 1832 a wealthy, Liverpool-born Oxford graduate arrived in Brussels with his elder brother on a continental tour. He wrote in his diary:

> Having seen in the coffee room announcements of two English services, we set out in the morning for one, and, to our annoyance, found the church was now shut, only just in time to enable us, after another long hunt, to come in for part of Mr. Drury's sermon at the other, in the Rue de l'Orangerie.
>
> Congregation small – but it is to be expected, according to the accounts we hear, that the English have almost all been driven out of Brussels by the Revolution – Communicants about 22. – Returned in the afternoon – congregation miserable: and *this* cannot be accounted for by any reason equally unexceptionable [...] Brussels is exceedingly full of beggars and great indigence is stated to prevail.[1]

Alas, future Prime Minister William Ewart Gladstone, then aged twenty-two, did not go to the Jenkins chapel. The first church the brothers went to in the morning was surely the Church of the Augustines – the King's Church – in the lower town, Evan Jenkins's church before his move to the Chapel Royal. The phrase 'now shut' would fit this church, formerly attended by the King of the Netherlands, which during the revolution in September 1830 was damaged by excited revolutionaries and saved from being destroyed by its being used as a hospital.[2] It may be that the coffee-room announcement was in error in omitting the Chapel Royal, or that Gladstone had misunderstood the slightly muddling description of Anglican services in the 1832 Almanac which had not been updated: 'L'office anglican est célébré par le reverend M. Hollworthy, à midi, dans le temple dit *des Augustins*; par le reverend M. Jenkins, au temple de l'église française et allemande, rue du Musée à 2 heures; et dans le temple rue de l'Orangerie, par le reverend M. Drury, à 11 et à 3 heures.' The notice could be understood as meaning that M. Jenkins's service was in French and German. Alas, therefore, I cannot conjure up in my mind a conversation about Leith between Eliza and the young man who was to become one of the most influential politicians of the nineteenth century.

Two years later, the 1834 Almanac comments that the Church of the Augustines, 'which for a long time was used for the Calvinist Reformed religion, is now closed and its upkeep is perhaps neglected'. Now only Reverends Jenkins and Drury are listed as giving Anglican services.[3] Presumably Rev. Holworthy stayed as chaplain to the embassy in The Hague before moving back to England, where he is listed as a rector in Norfolk from 1836, dying only two years later in his mid-forties.[4]

Gladstone was from an evangelical family and a regular communicant all his life: hence, no doubt, his counting the number at Drury's service who took holy communion. At this period a very small percentage of an Anglican congregation received the sacrament of bread and wine regularly, which was rarely offered weekly.[5] Almost forty years later, as Prime Minister, Gladstone arranged a treaty with France and Prussia by which Britain would co-operate with one of those countries if the other invaded neutral Belgium. 'His statement on it to the Commons on 8 August 1870 was the basis for Britain's declaration of war in August 1914.'[6]

* * *

'My dearest Love', King Leopold wrote to his thirteen-year-old niece Victoria on 31 August 1832:

> You told me you wished to have a description of your new Aunt [...] she is highly informed and very clever; she speaks and writes English, German and Italian; she speaks English very well indeed. In short, my dear Love, you see that I may well recommend her as an example for all young ladies, being Princesses or not.
>
> [...] She is about Feodore's height [Victoria's half-sister], her hair very fair, light blue eyes, of a very gentle, intelligent and kind expression. A Bourbon nose and small mouth. The figure is much like Feodore's but

rather less stout. She rides very well, which she proved to my great alarm the other day, by keeping her seat though a horse of mine ran away with her full speed for at least half a mile. What she does particularly well is dancing. Music unfortunately she is not very fond of, though she plays on the harp; I believe there is some idleness in the case.[7]

Leopold's letter is obviously teaching his niece how to behave even while supposedly describing his new wife, who was only seven years older than Victoria: Don't be idle! Appreciate music! He continues: 'There exists already great confidence and affection between us; she is desirous of doing everything that can contribute to my happiness, and I study whatever can make her happy and contented.' (This reads as advice on how Victoria should behave once she is married, but not the less truthful for that.)

On 9 August 1832, Leopold had made an astute political marriage with the eldest daughter of the new French king Louis-Philippe. Louise-Marie d'Orléans was born in 1812 when her father had been in exile for nineteen years. His experiences during exile from 1793 are a fascinating epic of travel that reads like a novel – teaching under an assumed name in Reichenau; living in a village in Lapland; in the United States for several years, where he met George Washington and Alexander Hamilton; a year in Cuba, from where he was expelled; forming a friendship with Victoria's father the Duke of Kent in Canada; and then to Middlesex, teaching mathematics and geography at Great Ealing School,[8] where perhaps he taught John Henry (later Cardinal) Newman. Finally in 1809, in his mid-thirties, he married Princess Marie-Amélie of Naples and Sicily, niece of Queen Marie Antoinette. Louise was their second child, born in Palermo, Sicily. Three years later the family returned to France, during the reign of Louis-Philippe's cousin Louis XVIII.

When Louise married King Leopold she was twenty, half her husband's age. They had known each other since she was a child, but she had found him 'indifferent, as indifferent as a passer-by in the street'. She wrote to a friend just after the wedding: 'On Monday, I think, I shall be leaving France and all that is dear to me, and my only compensation will be the hope of a happiness that I still do not feel or understand. Pity me, pray for me, though I am calm and resigned, for I have done my duty […] the present is sad, solemn and cruel. I feel all dizzy and overwhelmed.' The wedding had taken place in Compiègne, fifty miles north of Paris; they arrived at the palace at Laeken on 16 August where crowds had gathered to welcome her. Louise's fears were diminishing. 'I am perfectly at ease with him,' she wrote to her mother. 'I talk to him about everything [...] I am perfectly content with his feelings and his moral and political principles, which are exactly the same as my own; and you could have no idea of his kindness to me.'[9]

A few days later the new queen entered her capital of Brussels. The streets, lined with Lancers, Cuirassiers and Civic Horse Guards, were crowded. Trees bore the French and Belgian colours and some houses displayed tapestries depicting the 'Belgic Lion and the Gallic Cock'. Two batteries of artillery announced the arrival of the procession in Brussels, which had left the palace at Laeken, about four miles away, at half-past twelve. 'The Royal pair were in an open caleche. The King was in a General's uniform, and wore all his orders; the Queen sat on his right hand, and was dressed with elegant simplicity in white, wearing diamonds, but not in profusion. They were cheered with the loudest and most loyal acclamations.' The couple then appeared on the balcony of the palace. 'The square before the Palace, and the whole of the Park, were completely covered with people.'[10] The king then descended and reviewed his troops on horseback. August 19 was a Sunday and Eliza Jenkins was six months pregnant with their fifth child, but surely Evan would have taken his schoolboys to watch the procession and the appearance on the balcony, maybe also taking his two eldest children, Edward and Helen, aged six and five. Perhaps he had moved the time of his normal two o'clock service because of the expected crowds.

Ambassadors arrived at the palace to give their congratulations, and in the evening the royal couple went to the theatre. It is fascinating that the performance was *La Muette de Portici* – the very same grand opera that had kicked off the revolution. Surely that was a deliberate choice by the Belgians' new king.

> The whole of the boxes and galleries were filled with ladies, officers, and principal citizens. Their Majesties were received on their entrance into their box with a burst of applause, which was repeated when they retired after the fourth act [...] The King and Queen then rode through the town, which was brilliantly illuminated. Many transparencies were displayed, showing the loyalty and attachment of the people to their King, and their satisfaction on the occasion of his marriage. Fireworks were constantly let off, and universal gaiety reigned throughout the evening.[11]

There is nothing like a royal wedding to produce gaiety (and clichés from a newspaper writer, who resolutely ignores detractors such as the Orangists). Another writer commented, in surprise, that the opera had been chosen 'with strange discretion'; and on the royal couple leaving before the last act of the opera: 'Leopold, perhaps, thought it not delicate to remain and witness the *fusilade* of the revolutioners.'[12] (Though, frankly, it is a very long opera and maybe he wanted to spare his young wife the eruption of Vesuvius and several deaths, especially if she had already seen it in Paris.) The writer also found a frisson in that Queen Louise looked to him (or her?) a bit like Princess Charlotte, 'the hair of the two ladies having been dressed much after the same fashion, with curls at each side of the forehead, a bandeau of diamonds, and a plume of not very high ostrich feathers'. Slightly tactless.

Their life at Laeken was quiet and domestic. Louise wrote a month later that 'The King, his dog and I are alone in the palace. I go to bed late, and get up late. At ten o'clock I hear Mass.' Servants don't count, nor the lady who read to her, who had recommended the Pensionnat Heger to Eliza. They had a daily walk or ride, then she read and he worked. 'On ordinary days, we dine alone, but quite often we have people to dinner. On these days, after dinner, I sit with the ladies and talk to them as I embroider.'[13] A few miles north of Brussels, the palace of Laeken is surrounded by a large, beautiful park. Apparently Napoleon had stayed there with Josephine in 1804. The original late eighteenth-century palace was partly destroyed by fire in 1890 and rebuilt; it is still the private residence of the royal family. Occasionally Leopold and Louise resided in the palace in Brussels, where their daily schedule, Louise wrote, 'is disarranged'.[14] It is not known when Leopold started to attend Evan's Anglican service at the Chapel Royal. One historian states that he went to a church service 'on average, three Sundays a month, sometimes to L'Eglise du Musée [the Chapel Royal], but most often in his private chapel'.[15] Surely Leopold attended Evan's service whenever he was staying at the palace in Brussels, just around the corner, and got to know Evan well, who would sometimes have dined at the palace, with Eliza chatting to the queen over embroidery while the men talked over the wine. By the end of the year Queen Louise was pregnant, giving birth to a son on 24 July 1833. Leopold must have been terrified as he waited for the birth, and remembered vividly the trauma and deaths over a decade before, but all seemed well.

* * *

Some eight months before the birth of the Prince Royal, Eliza gave birth to her fifth child, a son, on 12 November 1832. He was named simply Evan, after his father and grandfather. It is possible that by then the name of the road where they lived had been changed from rue d'Orange to a more suitable Belgian name: rue Léopold. It is that name in the 1834 Almanac, and they were living at nos. 65 and

66, 'hors la porte de Namur'. But I was shocked to discover that Rev. William Drury was listed in the same Almanac as 'aumônier de l'ambassade d'Angleterre'. Clearly I am biased, but Evan had deputed for Rev. Holworthy as chaplain to the embassy and Evan was now the senior Anglican clergyman, so how had Drury swung it? I looked at the Almanac for the previous year: Drury was also listed as chaplain, which applied to the year 1832. Had he pounced with his Harrow connections when the new ambassador arrived?

Sir Robert Adair had made his memorable start as ambassador in August 1831 when the old man had grabbed a horse and stopped the Prince of Orange from advancing on Brussels. Edward Taylor was unimpressed by him, wishing instead that his own brother had been appointed to this 'troublesome post'. Taylor had tried to let his house to Sir Robert for six months, 'and should have been satisfied with £200, which should have included a winter's provision of wood and coals, but Sir R. was already in treaty for a house in the Park, very inferior to this, which he is to pay £40 a month for, and will be obliged to hire rooms elsewhere for his servants'.[16] The Irish writer Thomas Colley Grattan – who had entertained Coleridge and Wordsworth, and was a close friend of Sir Charles Bagot – gives a clue as to the choice of Drury. But first, Sir Robert's background is worth a look.

Robert Adair (1763–1855) was the son of a sergeant-surgeon to George III, and went to Westminster School and the University of Göttingen. Before he was twenty he became a close friend of Charles James Fox (1749–1806), the larger than life Whig politician who called George III 'Satan', while the king, in turn, thought him beyond morality and the debaucher of his son, the future George IV. Fox was indeed notorious for his gambling and womanizing, but he was a great orator in Parliament – when he attended – and had a huge gift for friendship (as well as continuing hatred for the king and Prime Minister William Pitt). Adair was sent by Fox to St Petersburg in 1791 to resolve a dispute (in Russia's favour), which some believed was deliberately aimed against Pitt's policy.[17] Adair was a Whig Member of Parliament between 1799 and 1812, and made an unfortunate marriage to a French woman known as 'Talleyrand's spy'. Denied office because of this, though the couple separated, he was sent by Fox to Vienna, and later by Canning to the Constantinople embassy for a short while. Foreign Secretary Lord Palmerston picked Adair to go on a special mission to Brussels in 1831, perhaps because he was also a Whig and Adair seemed a safe pair of old hands. The *ODNB* writer claims that Adair was successful on this supposedly temporary mission, and he was granted a huge pension; but Grattan, who knew him, was scathing. Although Adair was 'very active and energetic in the exercise of his functions [and] kept a hospitable table':

> On several occasions he certainly made great mistakes in his estimate of individuals. He was obstinate, prejudiced, and old-fashioned. His leaning was always towards the banished dynasty. The House of Orange and its pretensions had in him a staunch but not very judicious supporter; and it was difficult at times for the Government he was accredited to, to tolerate his avowed sympathy with the one it replaced. But the main-spring of the national movements, the regulator of all, King Leopold in fact, was never at fault. He took the true measure of all the men he had to deal with, and managed the whole with a judgment and skill that brought the most discordant elements into harmony. And thus Sir Robert Adair was kept from doing much mischief.[18]

A likely reason that Evan was not made chaplain to the embassy, therefore, was that King Leopold attended Evan's chapel, but the British ambassador sympathized with the king's enemies, the Orangists.

In early April 1834 there were serious disturbances in Brussels. Renewed hostilities with the Dutch were often likely as no peace treaty had been signed, since King William proved obdurate, or dignified and firm, depending on whose side you were on (and many in Britain were sympathetic to the Netherlands). On the evening of Sunday 6 April, according to the *Courrier Belge*, translated and published in the *Morning Post*, 'there was some disturbance, and at the breaking up of the Theatre there were loud demands that the play of the *Muette* should be substituted for that of *Faust*.'[19] (I do hope that the composer was getting royalties every time *Muette de Portici* was performed in Brussels.)

> About sixty persons collected in the Place de Monnaie, about the tree of liberty, and the mob was soon increased considerably by the idle and the curious. The youth and the workmen, who had formed the circle, after singing patriotic songs, went off towards the Rue de l'Eveque, where they stopped before a house which is the place of meeting of a society recently formed [the Orange Society]. Very soon the windows were demolished by stones, the mob crying out, 'Down with the Orangeists, down with the club of the enemies of the people!'

Some of the mob invaded the building and smashed mirrors, the newspaper report states, but were dispersed when a small guard arrived. However, the mob then went on to gut other houses belonging to wealthy Orangists. In Théodore Juste's *Memoirs* of Leopold I he states that Sir Robert Adair 'having with indignation witnessed these acts of violence which disturbed the quiet of Sunday, repaired to the palace, and told the king what he had seen'.[20] I wonder if he grabbed a passing horse. The newspaper takes up the story:

> Towards half-past eleven o'clock, at the time when the quarter of the Park was filled with the lower order of people, and other idlers, the King left the Palace on horseback, escorted by four or five officers of the Staff. He rode through the Rue Ducale, preceded and followed by an immense crowd, who made the air resound with cries of 'Vive Leopold,' 'Down with the Orangeists,' 'Death to the Dutch.' [...] The King was very pale and was much affected. He several times attempted to speak to the people, but his words, drowned as they were by the tumult and the cries of 'Vive Leopold,' were not audible.

But after his return to the palace the violence continued. The newspaper report ends: 'The *Muette de Portici* is to be played this evening at the Grand Theatre. It is stated in the playbills in large characters that this piece is given "by request."'

What is fascinating are Edward Taylor's comments on the events in two letters. On 11 April he wrote to his brother Sir Herbert that there was 'no doubt that during the latter part of the last week the military were all tamper'd with (the garrison consisting of 3000 men) and they were bribed to act as they did on Sunday last – that is, to offer no resistance to the destruction of the houses of the obnoxious persons among the Orangists, under the assurance that they would only be rendering service to their country and their King by punishing their enemies.'[21] He adds that it was unfortunate that Leopold was advised (by Adair?) to show himself to the crowd before other troops arrived. He then implicates Orangist sympathizer Adair in the disturbances, knowing that this will reach the ear of King William IV and the government, and perhaps hoping that Ambassador Adair will be censored for his actions:

> There is no doubt, however, that the Orangists have by their conduct during the whole of last winter brought this punishment upon themselves; and they have been particularly encouraged by the English [Adair], Austrian, and

Prussian Ministers who were always in their houses and present when the King and the Government were grossly abused, and when the party went even so far as to express a wish that the young Prince should die when he was lately ill.

It is but justice to Sir George Hamilton to say, that as soon as he found how treasonable they all were, he ceased to go to their houses.

Sir George Hamilton was Secretary to the Embassy and was to become the ambassador, but not until a year later. There is obviously a huge division in the British Embassy, if not open antagonism. Edward Taylor goes for the kill:

The Prince de Ligne, Madame de L—, and some others were received in Sir R. A[dair]'s house during the riots, and instead of being there in private, they exhibited themselves with impudence at the windows; and the conversation at dinner before the servants was calculated to give the greatest offence to the people.

Did Taylor have an informer in Adair's house? Was he there? He finishes his letter by saying that he is worried for his property (because of Orangists taking revenge, or simply because of lawlessness spreading?). He must have discussed the riot with Leopold, because four days later Taylor writes to his sister-in-law, asking her to pass on to his brother that King Leopold 'has desired me to write him a detailed account of the late deplorable events here, and to explain how we have been surprised by a sudden disturbance after such a long period of profound peace and quietness'.[22]

I find this fascinating: the King of the Belgians has asked an Englishman with no official position to write a report. The rest of his letter on this subject needs to be copied here:

The first part I have already done [written a detailed account], and as to the latter – it should be understood that when the King went out of his Palace, it was with the intention of putting a stop to the destruction which was going on.

At first this seems like a non sequitur: the 'explain how we have been surprised' is countered with his emphasis that the king went out to *stop* the destruction. But Taylor knows the rumours and that the British press had had a field day in spreading the belief that Leopold went out of the palace that night to *encourage* the mob against his Orangist enemies. It would certainly have looked like that as he was cheered by the rioters.[23] What a tightrope Leopold had to walk. And was the British ambassador Adair one of those involved in undermining Leopold, despite his government's supposed policy of propping Leopold up? Politics was as devious then as it is now. There were many in England who hated Leopold. One correspondent to the *Morning Post*, referring to the ransacking of the Orangists' houses, wrote: 'Let us look to Belgium, and what see we there? We see the doctrines of Liberalism in the ascendant – we see a good King [William I of the Netherlands] driven out and a money-getting adventurer placed on his throne.'[24] The letter is anonymous but could well have been written by a Mr 'Disgusted of Tunbridge Wells' for whom Liberalism was a dirty word, as Socialism can be today.

Hence maybe why Leopold asked a respected English gentleman, Edward Taylor, to write a report, knowing also how close his brother Sir Herbert was to the centre of power in London. In his letter, Taylor continues:

Unfortunately [King Leopold] was deceived when he supposed he could order the troops to act. That power was by law only vested in the Burgomaster and Magistrates; and it was only after a meeting of the Council, and the necessity of immediately acting, that it was decided to act contrary to the law.

A great number of persons have during the last few days been taken up – many of respectable families, and people of commerce – many strangers also have been sent out of the Kingdom.

Sir R. A[dair] told me the King had sent for him yesterday, and they had a long explanation. Sir R. recommended the King to assume more spirit, and even to threaten to abdicate if he was not invested with greater powers.

The King promised to do so.

I met at Sir R's house the Prussian and Austrian Ministers, the Duc d'Arenberg, and some Orangists. The King's private secretary complained to me in the morning of the encouragement given during the whole winter by those three Ministers to the Orangists, and particularly by the Austrian, who is supposed to have been personally abusive of the King and Queen.

Sir Robert Adair sounds an arrogant, devious nuisance; and, like Jane Austen, I rather like Edward Taylor. But my book is not about the diplomatic machinations that were going on at the time, nor how Lord Palmerston reacted to support

Leopold and the fragile new country, but instead to set the Jenkins family in context and discover their friends. I have no doubt that Edward Taylor spoke to Evan, and perhaps Eliza, about his report and what he had learned. But if the effect of the anti-Orangist riots simmered down eventually, what did not end well was the illness of Leopold and Louise's baby son, whom the Orangists wanted to die.

* * *

God knows if there be any hope.

> – King Leopold to M. Le Hon
> (Belgian envoy in Paris), 13 May 1834[25]

The bulletins about the poor health of the little Prince Royal, Louis-Philippe, began to appear in March, when the baby was eight months old. The announcement is oddly coupled in some newspapers with a report that King Leopold had sent 1,000 francs to Paganini after the concert he gave in Brussels on 15 March.[26] Suffering from syphilis and tuberculosis, Paganini stopped giving concerts six months later; the musical Leopold loved his extraordinary violin playing.

As regards his ailing baby son, Leopold wrote on 13 May that Doctor Clark 'found the child so reduced and so weak that it is impossible to answer for the future':

> The saddest part of it is that he was such a strong, fine child, and that, had he been some peasant's son, he would probably be fresh and healthy now; but, thanks to timidity and ignorance, inflammation of the mucous membrane has been allowed to set in. At the beginning of the year the most ordinary care would have sufficed – now, God knows if there be any hope.[27]

The baby died, aged nine months, three days later. I wonder if Leopold was thinking of the appalling care given to Princess Charlotte when he wrote the words 'timidity and ignorance' and 'ordinary care'. The bulletins on 16 May, issued from the palace at Laeken, read: '9 o'clock, p.m. The Prince Royal, who was yesterday in pretty good health, had a relapse last night, which puts him in the greatest danger.' And two hours later: 'The fits increased, convulsions succeeded. The Prince Royal expired at thirty-five minutes past ten o'clock at night.'[28] It is hard to imagine Leopold's grief. 'He is crushed and afflicted,' said a witness to his suffering, 'to a degree which would touch the hardest heart.'[29] However, I imagine that callous Orangists cheered. But if this was the second darkest period in Leopold's life, at least his wife was well and young, and in the summer she was pregnant again.

* * *

It is time to lighten the mood and return to Rev. William Drury and his new assistant teacher, a nineteen-year-old called Anthony Trollope. There is a moment in this anecdote that hums like an electric wire, connecting all the literature of the nineteenth century – from Byron, Shelley and Mary Godwin/Shelley at the beginning, through the Trollopes, all the way to Henry James at the end. And in the middle are situated the vast Druries (vast in corporeal size) and the Jenkinses. People sometimes talk of six degrees of separation by which we could pass on a message to anyone else in the world through at the most five people. I like to link to the past with the idea of handshakes. In his Preface to 'The Aspern Papers', published in 1888, Henry James commented:

> I delight in a palpable imaginable *visitable* past – in the nearer distances and the clearer mysteries, the marks and signs of a world we may reach over to as by making a long arm we grasp an object at the other end of our own table [...] That, to my imagination, is the past fragrant of all, or of almost all, the poetry of the thing outlived and lost and gone, and yet in which the precious element of closeness, telling so of connexions but tasting so of differences, remains appreciable.[30]

Because of my Jenkins ancestors I can shake Charlotte Brontë's hand with just two intermediaries, and because of the longevity of William Drury, who baptized five of Evan and Eliza's grandchildren, I can shake hands with Anthony Trollope and touch a fingertip with the aristocratic Byron with again just two intermediaries: both are almost palpable at the end of my table when I reach out my arm. The 'fragrant' past is so near. But I digress. I need to get back to Anthony at nineteen and what he did in Brussels, and explain the involvement of Henry James via one of Byron's mistresses and a poignant little coffin.

In a previous chapter I quoted from Anthony Trollope's autobiography about driving his father to the London docks to flee from debts and escape to a new life in Bruges in 1834, but Anthony's resourceful, ever-active mother Frances (Fanny) had tried in an extraordinary way before then to rescue the family finances. Leaving teenage Anthony at Winchester College, and then back at Harrow School because his college bills hadn't been paid, she had sailed to America (in 1827) with three of her children, first to a swamp in Tennessee and then to Cincinnati, Ohio, where she set up a shopping mall. She returned penniless, and after a bad bout of malaria, in 1831.[31] But, and it's an enormous but, she came back with material for a book. *Domestic Manners of the Americans*, published in 1832, was a sensation to those who had believed in America as a shining light of democracy and equality. Mrs Trollope controversially, and often with wicked humour, criticized Americans, who 'are most lamentably deficient in every feeling of honour and integrity' because of their treatment of the Indian tribes, and she found abhorrent their frequent spitting.[32] But despite her success and new fame, her earnings were not enough to prevent her husband's debts accumulating, and thus their flight to Belgium.

Before their flight, in 1833, Fanny had toured Belgium and Western Germany to write another travel book, and it is probable that the family went to Bruges because of her liking for the town and for the people she had been introduced to there.[33] In Brussels she had dined with the British Minister (Adair?, with 'elegant hospitality and pleasing manners') and was introduced to quirky people and places such as the mint and a mansion containing a collection of dead sparrows 'nailed into every imaginable vagary of form – stars, crescents, crosses, all packed close together with such cautious economy of space, that thousands and thousands of little twitterers must have been sacrificed to make up the show'. Her guide to the mint and the collection of dead birds was 'Mr. C. W****, a lively and intelligent Englishman, well known, I believe, in the literary world, and a resident of long standing in Brussels. His obliging attentions to us were particularly acceptable, as he was quite *au fait* of every thing best worth being seen and heard.'[34] This was surely Captain Charles White. What he and Fanny Trollope really thought of the crucified birds is hard to detect. Sometimes we are comforted in finding the past familiar; sometimes we enjoy the frisson that it is strange. I am paraphrasing Henry James here, and it is the same with our travel to foreign countries.[35] It was good copy for a travel book, and both knew it.

In Bruges, Fanny Trollope balanced her writing with caring for a sick husband and children (the latter because of tuberculosis), and Anthony was promised (bizarrely when one looks at his later career) a commission in the Austrian cavalry if he learned French and German. Fanny had possibly renewed acquaintance with the Druries on her travel trip, so it was easy to write later to William Drury enquiring about a position for Anthony. Probably a reply came back that Rev. Drury would welcome young Anthony as classical usher (assistant teacher, teaching Latin and Greek) for a year, and in return Anthony would be taught French and German.

Eliza's father John Jay had sold his school on the Glacis or boulevard de Namur around 1828 to William Drury, and it was to this same school that Anthony Trollope went in 1834, possibly in August, for the start of the school term. It was just around the corner from where Evan and Eliza were living, in the rue d'Orange – now rue Léopold – and despite Evan's past irritation with William Drury for his unorthodox licence from Bishop Luscombe, and the dubious establishment of a chapel near the Chapel Royal, I have no doubt that the Druries and Jenkinses saw each other frequently. In one of his letters to William Branwhite Clarke in 1831, Evan had suggested he go to a hotel 'by Drury's' – implying that Clarke knew where the Druries lived and had their school, and maybe even had dined there – and I have little doubt that, in turn, young Anthony met the Jenkinses.[36] Anthony Trollope has, alas, only a little to say in his *Autobiography* about his time in Brussels, which lasted a much shorter time than he had anticipated:

> Mr Drury had been one of the masters at Harrow when I went there at seven years old [...] my heart still sinks within me as I reflect that any one should have intrusted to me the tuition of thirty boys. I can only hope that those boys went there to learn French, and that their parents were not particular as to their classical acquirements. I remember that on two occasions I was sent to take the school out for a walk; but that after the second attempt Mrs Drury declared that the boys' clothes would not stand any further experiments of that kind.[37]

Probably he communicated his unhappiness to his mother Fanny in Bruges, who worked on her connections, and Anthony was offered a post-office clerkship in London. But other than the amusing anecdote about his six weeks with the Druries in Brussels, at the school Eliza's father had started, it is the poem of his mother's that Anthony took there and showed William Drury that sets that wire thrumming.

A thirty-two-page manuscript, all in Anthony Trollope's handwriting, was given to the University of Illinois library in 1953. Twenty years later, N. John Hall published an edition of the poems in the manuscript (there are four; three are by unknown authors). The manuscript is titled by Trollope 'Salmagundi – *aliena*, 1834' (salmagundi is a dish of a mixture of meats, a hodgepodge). On the title-sheet he identifies one of the poems as 'My mother's lines on the burial of Lord Byron's illegitimate daughter'. It is a 500-line satire on the Harrow church vestry meeting in 1822 to decide on Byron's request for his daughter

Allegra's burial, and what is also fascinating is that Anthony Trollope added many footnotes, not only on the quality of the verse but also on the characters depicted, including William Drury, and he states in it that he showed some of the verses to Drury.

The short life of Allegra Byron is a sad one, but it casts a hugely favourable light on Shelley (if not so much on Byron), whose role in the little girl's life seems to have made him grow up. When I read Richard Holmes's biography it was at this point that I first liked Shelley. Allegra's mother, Claire (originally Mary Jane) Clairmont, was the stepsister of Shelley's second wife, Mary Godwin. Mary was the daughter of Mary Wollstonecraft and William Godwin, the political philosopher and novelist; Claire was the daughter of his second wife and a few months younger than Mary. It was discovered recently that Claire was the illegitimate daughter of John Lethbridge of Sandhill Park, Somerset, who was made a baronet in 1804, and her surname 'Clairmont' was made up by her mother. Lethbridge was married, and in his fifties, when Claire was born.[38]

In July 1814, Shelley, aged twenty-one and still married to Harriet, eloped to the Continent with sixteen-year-old Mary – and Claire went too. Holmes comments that Shelley's relationship with Claire was 'perhaps the kindest and most successful of all his relationships with the opposite sex'.[39] They returned to London that September and the three lived together for a while, often to Mary's irritation. The volatile, lively Claire was completely unlike the intellectual Mary. There is no direct evidence that Shelley and Claire had sexual relations, but it is probable. In March 1816, Claire, then eighteen, began what Holmes calls her 'invasion, storm and capture of Byron', who was then twenty-eight and separated from his wife and in a scandalous relationship with his half-sister Augusta.[40] Claire and Byron frequently met in his private rooms at Drury Lane Theatre. In April Byron fled England, heading for Geneva, and Claire gave chase – in the company of Shelley, Mary and their baby son. Shelley and his tribe arrived ten days before Byron – who had stopped in the rue Ducale and viewed the battlefield of Waterloo – and Claire engineered the famous first meeting of the poets on the shore of the lake. Later Byron wrote to Augusta: 'I was not in love, nor have any love left for any, but I could not exactly play the stoic with a woman who had scrambled eight hundred miles to unphilosophize me.'[41] The poets got on so well that Byron, with his travelling companion Dr Polidori, rented Villa Diodati on the southern shore of the lake, while Shelley took the chalet below it. Claire slipped up to Byron's villa when she could and she was probably already pregnant from their encounters in England; although Byron queried the paternity briefly, he did accept that the child was his and not Shelley's. It was here that Mary conceived the idea for *Frankenstein*.

Byron became increasingly irritated and bored by Claire, and Shelley generously offered to look after her and the child until Byron sent for it. At the end of August the Shelley tribe returned to England, and Allegra (Byron's choice for her name) was born secretly in Bath in January 1817. Two months later the tribe moved to Marlow, on the Thames. There is a plaque on the wall of their cottage stating that Shelley and Mary (now his wife, after the suicide of Harriet) had lived there, but there is no mention on it of Claire and Byron's daughter, who was passed off as the child of a friend. By the end of March 1818, they had moved to Italy and the unhappy Claire sent her daughter to Byron in Venice in April, where he was living at his immoral and wildest worst. Byron refused to see Claire ever again and it was Shelley who worked hard and diplomatically to enable Claire to see her daughter that summer and autumn, but it was at a great cost, because his own baby daughter died, perhaps because he had forced Mary to travel to meet them.

In 1821, when Allegra was four, Byron placed her in a convent at Bagnacavallo, near where he was living in Ravenna. The 'air is good', he wrote, and 'she will, at least, have her learning advanced, and her morals and religion inculcated'.[42] Byron had also left her a large amount of money in his will. Shelley visited the little girl that summer. It was the last time he saw her. Dark haired and blue eyed, she chattered in Italian of baby Jesus, Paradise and angels, and asked to see her father and mother – she was not referring to Claire, whom she had forgotten, but probably to Byron's current mistress, Teresa Guiccioli. It doesn't seem that Byron visited her. Allegra died, maybe of typhus fever, the following April at the age of five; three months later Shelley drowned.

Teresa told Byron of Allegra's death. "'I understand,' said he, – "it is enough, say no more." A mortal paleness spread itself over his face, his strength failed him, and he sunk into a seat [...] He remained immoveable in the same attitude for an hour, and no consolation which I endeavoured to afford him seemed to reach his ears.'[43] He allowed Claire to have a miniature of her daughter and a lock of hair, and resolved on burying Allegra at the church in Harrow, through the help of his publisher John Murray. It is at this point that Fanny Trollope's satiric poem begins, with the arrival of the small coffin at the flustered Murray's door in Albemarle Street. But it is the description of the church vestry meeting that must have led Anthony Trollope to copy it and show some of it to William Drury in Brussels. The bone of contention was not the actual burial, but Byron's wish to have an inscription on the church wall by her grave: 'In memory of Allegra, daughter of G.G. Lord Byron, who died at Bagnacavallo, in Italy, April 20th, 1822, aged five years and three months. "I shall go to her, but she shall not return to me." 2d Samuel, xii. 23.'[44] He also wished Henry (Harry) Drury, William Drury's cousin, to take the funeral service. What he hadn't reckoned on was the nature of the current incumbent of Harrow church: Rev. Joseph William Cunningham. But first, Fanny Trollope describes the Harrow schoolmasters arriving at the vestry, including William Drury, who was then in his early thirties:

> With careless smile, loud jocund William near,
>> He recked but little what they were about,
> Till hints he heard, which roused a sudden fear,
>> That the affair might make a serious rout
> Among the school boys' parents far and near,
>> On which his virtue too began to sprout,
> And in his turn he made a short oration
>> On laws, religion and our prosperous nation.

Anthony Trollope comments in his footnote that

> Jocund William and his father Mark Drury were obliged to run away from their creditors at Harrow a short time after this was written. They now live at Brussels where William has a church and a school. Speaking of these two prize clergymen [presumably meaning 'prize' ironically as in 'prize fools'], and Mark's nephew – Harry [...] the same poet says in allusion to their size

> 'If he and his uncle and cousin
>> Who payed but two pence in the pound
> Were weighed against any two dozen
>> They'd soon find their way to the ground.'

> Arthur Drury, William's brother, my old master at Sunbury is larger than either – well may it be said that he made a short oration, for at that time he stuttered so much, that he could not have made a long one, altho he sometimes preached.[45]

(Anthony had spent two miserable years at Sunbury School before going to Winchester.) Fanny Trollope lampoons a fat, cheerful William Drury as a coward who worries that parents will withdraw their children from the school and they will lose money, and in a separate four lines (surely written some time later) alludes to the little money they were paying their creditors. It seems unlikely that Anthony wrote the footnote in Drury's house in Brussels: a bit risky. The villain of the poem, Rev. Cunningham, then appears. Anthony damns him: 'a man almost worshipped by the low church at Harrow, very unpopular with the gentry, and much feared by the poor – a most despicable hypocrite'. Fanny has Cunningham say:

> 'What now demands your most mature advice
> Is, whether o'er the ashes of the dead
> I should consent to place at any price
> A stone on which the child's name may be read.
> *May it not lead the school boys into vice?'*

Anthony comments in his footnote incredulously: 'This question was actually asked – and the reason given for not putting up a tablet to the memory of Allegra, Lord Byron's natural daughter, in Harrow Church, was for fear it should teach the boys to get bastards.'[46] Rev. Cunningham even wonders if Byron is making this request 'chiefly to vex me / Because he knows my spotless purity'.[47] As Anthony states, the Harrow vestry refused to allow any tablet that mentioned Allegra to be erected 'for fear of injuring the boys' chastity – of course the Drurys had nothing to do with it'. I think he sincerely means that the Druries weren't involved in the decision, especially as in his next footnote he says he showed the lines about the masters to William Drury.[48] Perhaps they were also shown to William's father Mark – he didn't die until July 1835 in his mid-seventies. Whatever the shortcomings of the pair, better to be 'prize' clergymen than sanctimonious hypocrites.

Rev. Cunningham wrote an appalling letter to publisher John Murray. It is so unctuously self-righteous that I want to punch him. Fanny Trollope used him for her portrayal of the fraudulently pious Rev. Cartwright in *The Vicar of Wrexhill*, which I described above. Writing about the wording for the tablet, Cunningham says to Murray: 'whatever [Lord Byron] may wish in the moment of his distress about the loss of this child, he will afterwards regret that he should have taken pains to proclaim to the world what he will not, I am sure, consider as honourable to his name. And if this be probable, then it appears to me the office of a true friend not to suffer him to commit himself but to allow his mind an opportunity of calm deliberation. I feel constrained to say that the inscription he proposed will be felt by every man of refined taste, to say nothing of sound morals, to be an offence against taste and propriety [...] I would entreat, however, that should you think it right to introduce my name into any statement made to Lord Byron, you will not do it without assuring him of my unwillingness to oppose the smallest obstacle to his wishes, or give the slightest pain to his mind. The injury which, in my judgment, he is from day to day inflicting upon society is no justification for measures of retaliation and unkindness.'[49] Even though Byron did neglect his child somewhat, it is to his credit that he acknowledged Allegra as his, and supported her financially, especially when Claire's real father only eventually and grudgingly acknowledged her as his to lawyers. It is unlikely that Claire ever knew about him.

Byron died at Missolonghi two years later. Claire Clairmont lived on, surviving Byron by over fifty years, and her stepsister Mary Shelley by almost thirty. For the last twenty years of her life, having worked as a governess and never married, she lived in Florence, dying, aged eighty, in 1879. A niece with an illegitimate child came to live with her. It is here that Henry James adds his note to the thrumming wire I mentioned, because he heard an account of her last years and based his short story 'The Aspern Papers' on the events, changing the names and nationalities (to American) and relocating the story to Venice. In Florence in 1886 Henry James was told that an American named Silsbee had rented rooms in Claire's house in the hope of getting hold of papers that related to Byron and Shelley.[50] Silsbee didn't succeed, just as James's unnamed narrator doesn't succeed: the niece burns all the letters after he rejects her. James's depiction of the aged Juliana/Claire is frightening in its intensity – she is a demonic Miss Havisham. In his Preface, James reflects on the fact that he had previously been in Florence when Claire was still alive:

> The thrill of learning that she had 'overlapped', and by so much, and the wonder of my having doubtless at several earlier seasons passed again and again, all unknowing, the door of her house, where she sat above, within call and in her habit as she lived, these things gave me all I wanted.

As a writer, he prefers that Claire remained to him 'preciously unseen', that the charm lay in this 'final scene of the rich dim Shelley drama played out in the very theatre of our own "modernity"'.[51]

For me, the 'overlapper' is jocund William Drury at his school in Brussels – a huge physical, incongruous link between limping schoolboy Byron and floundering usher Anthony Trollope. The latter comments in his autobiography in amazement that Drury 'is now, after an interval of fifty-three years, even yet officiating as clergyman at that place'.[52] And while Trollope was working on his autobiography onboard ship as he crossed the Atlantic in 1875, a fellow passenger observed Trollope in 'communion with the muse'. It was, of course, Henry James.[53]

* * *

On 10 February 1835, 'our own correspondent' in the *Morning Chronicle* waxed furiously on the incompetence of the Brussels Senate (the upper or first chamber), which was threatening to revoke the grant of 10,000 francs (£400) given to the English churches in Brussels: 'To talk of refusing so small a sum [...] from motives of economy would be absurd.' Even if it was four times as much, he wrote, it would be well worth it because it would attract more English to reside in the town. The correspondent continues:

> It may not be irrelevant to observe, that Brussels has hitherto been fortunate in this respect, having two English churches – the one administered by the Rev. E. Jenkins, one of the most amiable and respected members of the Established Church, and the other by the Rev. W. Drury, whose attainments as a scholar are well known to the classic world. Both these gentlemen are at the heads of establishments for the education of a limited number of pupils. The emoluments arising from these establishments enable them to offer the services of their ministry gratuitously; for the precarious receipts derived from voluntary contributions, or the hire of pews and seats, are barely sufficient to pay the ordinary expenses of the churches.[54]

Evan is highly praised for his character, while William Drury knows Latin well! The writer may have struggled to find something to say about Drury: there is no evidence that he had any particular skill in the classics apart from what he had acquired at Harrow and during his undergraduate years at Oxford. His employment of Anthony Trollope, with no university background and little knowledge of Latin and Greek despite years of schooling, doesn't speak highly of the quality of the teaching at Drury's school in Brussels.

'Amiable' was a stronger word than its meaning now of having a friendly disposition that makes someone liked. For Jane Austen it was an important word to express a true gentleman (or woman), aware of his (or her) responsibilities to other people. In *Emma*, Mr Knightley draws out its meaning in relation to Frank Churchill, whom he suspects (quite rightly) of deceit, and whom Emma has just called 'amiable':

> 'No, Emma, your amiable young man can be amiable only in French, not in English. He may be very "aimable," have very good manners, and be very agreeable; but he can have no English delicacy towards the feelings of other people: nothing really amiable about him.'[55]

I don't know if the £40 per annum that Evan had been paid had been withdrawn – perhaps there were so few English after the revolution that the subscribers could no longer afford it – but he was still paid for weddings, baptisms and funerals. However cheerful Evan and Eliza sometimes appeared in their letters to Clarke, money must have been tight. But 1835 was to be a year of changes and a high honour. First, however, there were a few interesting visitors to Brussels that spring, whom the Jenkinses may well have met.

In 1834 an Act had been passed to create railroads in Belgium, a project in which Leopold had taken an active interest. It was only the second country in Europe, after Britain, to build railroads and locomotives, and the first to be run by the state. The self-educated, extraordinarily talented engineer George Stephenson and his son Robert, then in his early thirties, were asked by Leopold to advise on the creation of the railroad system. The Stephensons' engine the *Rocket* had inaugurated the railway age in Britain in 1830. In May 1835 they came for the opening of the first stretch from Brussels to Malines (Mechelen). In Julian Barnes's *Flaubert's Parrot* he has a short chapter entitled 'The Train-spotter's Guide to Flaubert'. Flaubert 'belonged to the first railway generation in France; and he hated the invention': 'I get so fed up on a train that after five minutes I'm howling with boredom. Passengers think it's a neglected dog; not at all, it's M. Flaubert, sighing.' Flaubert said in 1843 that railways were 'the third most boring subject imaginable' after an arsenic poisoner and the death of the Duc d'Orléans – killed in 1842 in a carriage accident. (Hardly boring to Louise, the Queen of the Belgians, his sister.) Even in the mid-1830s, at the start of their introduction in Europe, the teenage Flaubert found railways one of the misdeeds of modern civilization.[56] One visitor to Brussels in 1835 found the opening of the first railway in Belgium both comical and awesome. This was the then famous author Captain (Frederick) Marryat (1792–1848).

London-born Marryat had begun his eventful naval career aged fourteen, and published his first naval adventure novel in 1829, which was a great literary and financial success. Later he began writing children's books, *The Children of the New Forest* (1847) being his most famous. Set during the Civil Wars in England in the 1640s, it reads quaintly and stiffly now, but even if you feel like strangling the children, he is a good storyteller and you want to know what happens to them, and it must have inspired a lot of children to want to live in a cottage, keep pigs and chickens, capture wild cows and shoot stags. Marryat took his wife and children on a trip to the Continent in April 1835, later publishing his diary. But first the itinerary needed to be discussed with friends: 'If you go to Bruges, you will find it very dull [...] but you'll meet Mrs. Trollope there – now Brussels is very little farther, and is a delightful place.'[57] On 5 May he joined the crowds in Brussels for the inauguration of the railroad: 'three steam tugs, whose names are the Stephenson, the Arrow, and the Elephant, are to drag to Malines and back again in the presence of his majesty, all his majesty's ministers, all the ambassadors who choose to go, all the heads of the departments, and every body else who can produce a satisfactory yellow ticket, which will warrant their getting into one of the thirty-three omnibuses, diligences, or cars, which are attached to the said three steam tugs'. (Reading that I suddenly get an earworm of Sondheim's 'Another hundred people got off of the train' from *Company*.) Marryat had got hold of a yellow ticket:

In one rich meadow I beheld a crowd of Roman Catholic priests, who looked at the trains in such a manner as if they thought that they were 'heretical and damnable,' and that the Chemin de *Fer* was nothing but the Chemin *d'Enfer*. At Malines we all got out, walked to a stone pillar, where a speech was made to the sound of martial music, and we all got in again. And then to show the power of his engines, Mr. [George] Stephenson attached all the cars, omnibuses, and diligences together, and directed the Elephant to take us back without assistance from the other two engines [...] And Mr. Stephenson having succeeded in bringing back in safety his decorated cars, has been *decorée* himself, and is now a Chevalier de l'Ordre Leopold [...] It is impossible to contemplate any steam-engine, without feeling wonder and admiration at the ingenuity of man; but this feeling is raised to a degree of awe when you look at a locomotive engine.

Marryat loved it: 'It was a brilliant affair.'[58]

* * *

Engineer George Stephenson was not the only Briton honoured that year. On 18 June the king signed a royal decree:

Léopold, Roi des Belges,

A TOUS PRÉSENS ET A VENIR, SALUT:

Voulant donner un témoignage de Notre estime et de

Notre satisfaction au Révérend M. Evan Jenkins

Avons arrêté & Arrêtons

Le Révérend M. Evan Jenkins est nommé

Notre Chapelain honoraire

[…]

Donné à Laeken le 18 Juin 1835

Signé Léopold

'Wanting to give testimony of our esteem and our satisfaction [...] the Reverend Mr Evan Jenkins is named our honorary chaplain.' From his birth on a run-down farm in Cardiganshire to chaplain to a king in forty years, Evan had achieved something extraordinary, and I think there was something about him, his character, that made people respect and like him, and trust him, as King Leopold did. Somehow the copy of the decree presented to Evan survived upheavals of moving house several times, then to England across the water at the end of the century, and through the hands of several generations to get to me: it had been folded up and tucked into various drawers – apparently a brilliant way to preserve it – but is now framed (with museum glass) and hanging on a wall in Wales. I hope Evan would be pleased. Leopold of course had Belgian chaplains, and an Anglican honorary chaplain in Ostend from 1840, but Evan was the first Anglican chaplain to be appointed.[59] As I mentioned earlier, it was possibly because of this royal decree that Evan had finally accepted the licence from Charles Blomfield, the Bishop of London, who came to Brussels on Friday 25 September to confirm young people in the Chapel Royal. Evan took him to see various monuments, an exhibition of the products of industry and the museum, perhaps accompanied by Eliza.[60] It must have been a rather quick sightseeing tour since the confirmations were at 11 and the bishop left for Antwerp at 2 p.m.

It is possible that after Sir Robert Adair finally left for England in July that Evan at last became chaplain to the embassy, though the first mention that

I found is in an 1839 guidebook and the first notice in the Brussels Almanac is in 1840.[61] In November 1835, Sir George Hamilton Seymour was promoted from secretary of the legation to ambassador, and he was to remain in that post for eleven years. The situation in the new kingdom was stabilizing, no doubt aided by Queen Louise giving birth to a healthy son, Leopold, in April 1835. Sir George's actual new title in November 1835 was envoy-extraordinary and minister-plenipotentiary to the Belgian Court. Having been in Brussels since 1831, he was a familiar face and had stood his ground three years later when Sir Robert Adair was hobnobbing with Leopold's enemies who sympathized with the Orange Nassau claim to Belgium. Edward Taylor had not been particularly impressed by Sir George in 1831: 'Sir George H. does not give me the idea of a man of ability, but he is very gentlemanlike and good tempered.'[62]

Sir George (1797–1880) was a few years younger than Evan, and was the eldest son of Lord George Seymour; and grandson of the first Marquess of Hertford on his father's side, and of the Canon of Windsor, Rev. George Hamilton, on his mother's. After Eton and Oxford his whole career was as a diplomat, starting at The Hague when he was nineteen.[63] He became private secretary to Lord Castlereagh in January 1822, when the latter was starting to suffer from the acute paranoia that led to his suicide in August. Four days before Castlereagh's death, Sir George had noticed 'something so melancholy and dejected in his manner', and the young man in his mid-twenties had tried to lighten his chief's spirits, to no avail. Castlereagh's death must have been devastating for him.[64] After postings in Italy, Germany and Constantinople he married Gertrude Brand, daughter of Lord Dacre, in July 1831, and they and their children must have been well known to the Jenkinses. He is also called Sir Hamilton, or Sir H. Seymour, but that is easy compared with his attaché, who was Sir Henry Bulwer (1801–72), and listed in the *ODNB* with his later title as (William) Henry Lytton Earle Bulwer, Baron Dalling and Bulwer, and who was elder brother of the author Edward George Earle Lytton Bulwer Lytton. Prodigious! I think I will risk calling the ambassador to the Belgians from 1835 Seymour for short. I rather like him, because much later, in 1850, the Parliamentary Select Committee on Official Salaries decided to look at diplomatic service salaries. One of the few diplomats examined was Seymour. In reply to the question 'Is it the custom of the profession to entertain the foreign diplomatic body?', he replied, 'Certainly I consider that giving dinners is an essential part of diplomacy; I have no hesitation in saying so. I have no idea of a man being a good diplomatist who does not give good dinners.' I would consider that to be the correct response, but apparently Seymour's reply made him a laughing stock and damaged the reputation of the diplomatic service.[65]

There is one short letter from Seymour to Evan (dated 1 July 1836) in Henry Bulwer's archive in Norfolk, since it was a copy made by Bulwer. It is a reassurance to Evan about who was allowed to conduct marriages at the embassy (the ambassador's house): 'Sir I have the honor to inform you that it is not my intention for the future to allow the celebration of any marriages at my house except such as should be solemnized by yourself or Mr Drury, or such clergymen as shall be specially recommended for that purpose by you. It may be proper to acquaint you that I have notified this purpose to the Foreign Office.'[66] Evan seems to be pulling rank as the senior Anglican clergyman in Brussels, and although Seymour is agreeing that Rev. Drury can also conduct marriages, only Evan can recommend other clergymen to do so. I get the impression of Welshman Evan not only as a stickler for the rules and dignity of the Church of England, especially as he was now Anglican chaplain to the king, but responsibly concerned for the legality of marriages – whether due to the couple's age and whether proper consent had been given and that there were no impediments – which might have been neglected in the embassy under Adair. Perhaps this letter also signals that Evan was now chaplain to the embassy.

* * *

In June 1836 two German princes, nephews to King Leopold, arrived in Brussels to further their education for ten months: eighteen-year-old Ernst and sixteen-year-old Albert. Their uncle introduced them to scientists, politicians and painters, and in his *Memoirs* Ernst recalls that they were taught English by none other than 'Lord Byron's former playmate, the clergyman Mr Drury, who was himself a poet, and gave stimulating lectures on English Literature.' A totally unexpected revelation. Perhaps Evan's Welsh accent ruled him out from teaching the princes English, but I wonder if he gave lectures on Welsh history and poetry. It is likely that William Drury exaggerated his playmateship with the older Byron, but fascinating that he was keen on English literature, whereas I can find so little trace of the Jenkinses' interest. One book is mentioned in a letter to Eliza's sister Margaret in Australia in 1830: John Galt's just published *Life of Byron*, one of the first biographies of Byron. But it was being sent to her husband George Wyndham, not to her, and not because he may have been especially keen on Byron – despite George having also been at Harrow and Trinity College, Cambridge – but perhaps because he had been a travelling companion of Galt's to Canada for a few months in 1826–7.[67] The only book that passed on in my family from this period was a French–English dictionary given to the teenaged Edward Jenkins in 1839 by a lady from Gateshead.

Prince Ernst also singles out among the Englishmen he met in Brussels Sir Henry Lytton Bulwer, then in his mid-thirties, 'who, then just beginning his career as a Diplomate, was in Brussels as Secretary to the Legation, and who was sent thence immediately to Constantinople, where he found more room to exercise his great talents.'[68] Bulwer was at Harrow School and briefly at Trinity, Cambridge, and no doubt knew William Drury at Harrow, and perhaps had met Evan at Cambridge, but that seems unlikely since he was then only interested in horses and gambling. It is hard to escape Byron in this chapter because he crops up again as Bulwer's hero. As a young man Bulwer had wanted to follow Byron to fight in Greece, but instead he was embroiled in the dubious raising of money for the war of independence and was rescued in 1824, suffering from malaria, by the British consul in Smyrna.[69] It is possible that while Ernst loved the anecdotes about Byron, the younger Albert was studiously working on mathematics and political economy, as directed by his uncle.

Leopold was already planning for Albert to marry Victoria. The couple had met that May in England and it had gone even better than maybe Leopold dared to hope, despite King William IV having invited the Prince of Orange and his sons at the same time to thwart Leopold's dynastic plans. Victoria wrote to her uncle Leopold on 7 June 1836: 'I must thank you, my beloved Uncle, for the prospect of *great* happiness you have contributed to give me, in the person of dear Albert. Allow me, then, my dearest Uncle, to tell you how delighted I am with him, and how much I like him in every way. He possesses every quality that could be desired to render me perfectly happy. He is so sensible, so kind, and so good, and so amiable too. He has besides, the most pleasing and delightful exterior and appearance you can possibly see.'[70] No doubt Leopold ensured that Albert attended Anglican services at the Chapel Royal and got to know his honorary chaplain, Evan. In a letter to Princess Victoria in November, Leopold exhorts her to 'express your sincere interest for the [established] Church, and that you comprehend its position and count upon its good-will'.[71] It was advice he repeated several more times.

* * *

Drury's school seems to have been failing in 1836, despite his English literature lectures for princes. We know about one of his teachers, Charles Cock, because of a breach of promise action in the English Court of Exchequer on 7 June 1838 that often caused the judge and jury to howl with laughter.[72] In 1834, Cock ('a deuced awkward name', he admits in one of his letters) was teaching at Oundle School in Northamptonshire, aged about twenty. His excruciatingly long and amorous letters to a milliner, Miss Cecilia Abbott of Warwickshire, were read out in court: these often spoke of his throbbing breast and their kissing, as well as directions to burn his letters. His savvy girlfriend didn't. Cock was possibly a drawing master. In one letter he writes: 'I received an answer from the school-agent, in London, saying that there were no situations near London, but he could get me one at any time in France, for 5*l.* or 10*l.*' Cock longed to go to France, but ended up in Belgium in 1835 where he was teaching at Drury's school and living in lodgings.

In September he writes that Drury 'has only twenty-six boys at present, but expects more'. Cock is learning German and giving English lessons and hoping to teach more, and he has one drawing pupil. He asks Cecilia to address letters to him at 'Rev. W. Drury's, Brussels' because he changes lodgings often. Drury's residence is so well known that he doesn't need a street. The court learns that the defendant, Cock, is now cooling towards Cecilia, as his next letter is not until December 1835 and he asks her again to burn his letters; he also comments that 'Drury has paid me pretty regularly lately; I can complain of nothing now but the bill.' His next letter is dated 6 January 1836 and he says that the long interval is because of the change of ambassador, 'the new one being averse to the ancient system of franking', which has disappointed 'most of the resident English'. Seymour has put his foot down about expats getting free postage. Cock has been skating on the canal and going to the opera, and adds that 'Mr. Drury has fixed the end of this month as the period of my leaving him, but I expect to remain longer, as he cannot well do without me, and certainly he cannot get another at present.' This implies that Drury cannot afford to pay Cock. In February, Cock writes that Drury owes him £6 as well as the bill he mentioned before.

In May, Cock writes that 'Mr. Drury is very tiresome. After we had all three stopped away three days, in which time he came after me three times, we returned to ask for our money, and he paid us all a little, and promised the rest soon.' It sounds as if three teachers had not been paid, and that they maybe constituted the whole teaching body at the school and had gone on strike. By October 1836, Cock had returned to England and ends the relationship by addressing Cecilia as 'Madam'; he writes: 'I solemnly declare I would rather sacrifice liberty, friends, nay, life itself, than be forced into an alliance with a person whose want of education quite disgusts me. I might have spared my mother the trouble of writing [...] had your letter been intelligibly spelt or grammatically expressed.' He confesses that he had met another woman in Brussels (a widow whom he subsequently married) and he is prepared to fight a duel. After much loud laughter in court, it seems to have been agreed that Cecilia had had a lucky escape, and she was awarded £100 in damages.

It looks like Drury's extra pupils did not appear, as in October 1836 his school was seized by bailiffs. In a Belgian newspaper there is a notice headed: 'For sale, by compulsory purchase'.[73] The list includes a house in Ixelles at no. 110 ('now 138') rue du Champ-de-Mars (presumably the new name for Glacis de Namur) occupied by William Drury, containing cellars, a ground floor with three shuttered windows, two storeys and an attic. Behind the house is a courtyard, a stable or shed and two latrines. A second house, in rue Neuve, was also part lived in by Drury. The houses shared a water pump. Drury and his large family (he had about ten children in 1836) moved to rue de l'Orangerie, where his chapel was, and he began teaching privately. It looks as if the Jenkinses helped because the advertisement in *The Times* about his taking pupils mentions that details are obtainable from Mr R. Valpy, Red Lion passage, Fleet Street, who was Eliza's relation by marriage. Her aunt had died when Keats was having a ghastly time as an apprentice in Edmonton, and the widowed James Bowden married Clara Wylde, whose sister was married to Abraham Valpy, a classicist and prolific publisher. One of their daughters knew Thackeray and will be mentioned below. One former pupil of Drury, Thomas Murray-Prior, emigrated to Sydney in 1839 and worked at Eliza's sister Margaret's home at Dalwood, New South Wales, and travelled to Moreton Bay with the explorer Ludwig Leichhardt, who had described Margaret in glowing detail.[74] It seems that the Druries and Jenkinses were now close friends, but I wonder if the latter were somewhat appalled that more babies kept arriving in the impoverished Drury household.

* * *

An Anglo-Irish Protestant doctor arrived in 1837 to enliven the Brussels social scene. Charles Lever had passed through the city in 1828, seeming to confirm the date when young Charles Mackay had left the Jay/Drury school. Referring to his brilliantly funny conversation, Anthony Trollope said he was 'an astounding producer of good things'.[75] Lever was born in Dublin in 1806. Before or after university in Germany (the timeline is obscure) he travelled to Canada and apparently lived with an Indian tribe, escaping eventually to Quebec and home with a canoe, which he used on the canals in Dublin.[76] I found a copy of his first novel, *Harry Lorrequer* (serialized from 1837; published in book form 1839), which he began in Ireland and finished in Brussels. I do like Harry and thus I like the author. Harry is a charming Irish subaltern who has a knack of getting into scrapes, including two duels and being mistaken for the composer Meyerbeer. He is also renowned in his battalion as an amateur actor (playing Othello) and is splendid when drunk. We follow him from Ireland to the Continent as he, sort of, tries to follow the travels of the girl he loves, though he gets distracted a lot, and he knows he has a hopeless chance since he is the poor nephew of a rich uncle, and her family keep moving on. Lever writes so felicitously that you do hope he gets the girl in the end, and you are rewarded with a joyous proposal (if a man leaps from a windowsill twenty feet above ground to propose, who could resist?).

In the novel Lever gives a humorous account of two people trying to get a passport from the French consul in London. The consulate in Poland Street is crowded with those who, 'totally ignorant of French, insisted upon interlarding their demands with an occasional stray phrase, making a kind of tesselated pavement of tongues, which would have shamed Babel'. A mustachioed 'gentleman' wearing primrose gloves demands in a high voice from the aged, bewigged Frenchman a passport:

> 'Je suis – j'ai – that is, donnez-moi passport.'
> 'Where do you go?' replied the Consul.
> 'Calai.'
> 'Comment, diable, speak Inglis, an I understan you as besser. Your name?'
> 'Lorraine Snaggs, gentilhomme.'
> 'What age have you? – how old?'
> 'Twenty-two.'
> 'C'est ça,' said the old Consul, flinging the passport across the table with the air of a man who thoroughly comprehended the applicant's pretension to the designation of gentilhomme Anglais.

However, the next applicant is a pretty young woman and the consul is all gallantry:

> '[…] What old, ma belle?'
> 'Nineteen, sir, in June.'
> 'And are you alone, quite, eh?'
> 'No, sir, my little girl.'
> 'Ah! your leetel girl – c'est fort bien – je m'aperçois; and your name?'
> 'Fanny Linwood, sir.'

'C'est fini, ma chère, – Mademoiselle Fanny Linwood,' said the old man, as he wrote down the name.

'Oh, sir, I beg your pardon, but you have put me down Mademoiselle, and – and – you see, sir, I have my little girl.'

'Ah! c'est égal, mam'selle, they don't mind these things in France. Au plaisir de vous voir – adieu.'

'They don't mind these things in France,' said I to myself, repeating the old Consul's phrase, which I could not help feeling as a whole chapter on his nation.[77]

Possibly Charles Lever overheard these exchanges. He set his novel about twenty years previously, just after the Battle of Waterloo, and perhaps partly he wanted to shock his newly Victorian reader about single parents being accepted as normal in France, but I feel that he also approved of the French attitude. Think of Claire Clairmont having to disown her baby and let Byron take care of it: it wasn't just for the money that he had and that she didn't, but because her reputation as having had an illegitimate baby would destroy any prospects for her future.

I find fascinating that Lever mentions Bishop Luscombe in passing, as prepared to perform the marriage at the British Embassy in Paris of Harry's short fat friend Mr O'Leary (who looks like a small fish) and the widowed Mrs Ram, who pursues him across the Continent. I think that if the bishop had had a good reputation he might have been designated instead as Bishop L—, but here is another author who names him within a comic context. Worse, the bishop apparently would require the inflated sum of £10 to marry them.[78] Thackeray met Lever in 1842 in Dublin, but their friendship soured when the former began to mock Lever's characters in his writings.[79] It may be that Thackeray meant his satires as a homage or a tease, but failed to perceive that the public persona of the witty, good-humoured raconteur was in private a sensitive, unconfident man who veered between highs and lows, perhaps due to opium.[80]

Aged thirty, Lever arrived in Brussels with his pregnant wife Kate and their three-year-old daughter in May 1837. He was desperately in need of a better income and a livelier social scene than he had found as a doctor in the seaside resort of Portstewart in northern Ireland, which shut down once the season was over. Lever had been told that there was an opening for a doctor in Brussels because 'there is but one good English physician in Brussels, and he is constantly in jail for debt'.[81] Lever sensibly made a recce to Brussels in March with letters of introduction to Ambassador Seymour. He seems to have been welcomed with excitement, and the family moved to 16 rue Ducale, in the same road as the embassy, two months later. There is no doubt that the Jenkinses got to know him, as Lever became a close friend of the ambassador and presumably attended the Chapel Royal: since Lever was keen to attract all the best families to be his patients, it seems unlikely that he went to Drury's temporary chapel. They might also meet at 'Saturday soirees at the Embassy, to which we always go, and occasional *petits diners* with the chiefs of the *corps diplomatique*, – very pleasant and lively'.[82]

Alas there is no mention of the Jenkinses in the published letters, but these are selected and abbreviated. He does, however, mention the two Anglican chapels:

> You can form some idea of the extent of the English colony here, on hearing that we have two churches at which service is performed twice on Sundays to large congregations, and that two English newspapers are edited and published here.[83]

Lever needed a *permis* to practise medicine and he was fined for seeing clients before he had taken the exam. But King Leopold intervened and reimbursed the fine, and Lever passed the exam in August. There was another problem, though, affecting his advancement. In December 1837 he writes that he is hoping to be presented at Court soon, but he has not already been presented at St James's.[84] A solution wasn't found until three years later:

> I am about to have a special audience of the king on Friday. My grandeur costs me nearly £50 for a uniform. Do you know, 'I'm Captain in the Derry Militia' and aide-de-camp to somebody! His Majesty has been graciously pleased to move his royal jaws in laughter at something in 'O'Malley,' [Lever's latest novel] and I am to wait upon him while he expounds that same to me in French, – a great bore on many accounts, but an unavoidable one, such requests being very imperative. I am told I shall be asked to dinner, but this I don't calculate on [...] The whole population is skating, and the consumption of schnaps is tremendous.[85]

I am struck again by Leopold's love of novel-reading. Surely the Court, including the Jenkinses, must have been spurred to read the latest novel in order to have something to discuss at palace dinner parties, other than the beastly Dutch and the awesome railroads.

At first Lever was entranced by the social gaiety in Brussels. The family moved to a larger house in the boulevard de l'Observation (where Princes Ernst and Albert had stayed) and gave parties. He calculated that he could entertain fifty people for only £5: 'They all so understand the art of mere chatting that music and dancing would be thought a regular bore [...] the din and clamour of fifty people, talking in about half the tongues of Europe, is about as exciting a scene in a brilliant salon as can be conceived.' He also comments that the 'king himself does everything possible to make his Court agreeable'.[86]

But disillusionment was creeping in, and his debts were increasing: entertaining others was in his lifeblood but it drained away what he earned in medical practice. By August 1839 he was fed up with analysing 'every dirty spring or fetid puddle from Pyrmont to the Pyrenees; and my whole mornings are passed discussing chalybeates and sulphurets with all the scarlet and pimpled faces that Harrogate and Buxton have turned off incurable [...] The English who travel – God bless them! – are an amiable class, and they seldom fail to bring along with them for the journey some family ailment which French wines and high living combine to make troublesome. A constant influx of these pleasant people keeps me here, but if I can manage it I mean to bolt soon.' He continues, more savagely:

> Every *table d'hôte* in this city swarms with the most unlicked cubs of our country, speaking neither German nor French – a few English. They disgust me for the false impression they convey to foreigners of what English gentlemen really are. What they come for, and where they go, I cannot say. It is impossible that they can be escaping for debt, for no one could possibly trust them; and they cannot be swindlers, for swindlers are men of captivating address and prepossessing manners. I rejoice to think that they are poisoned by the living, sent wrong in diligences, cheated by the money-changers, and bullied by the police.[87]

He bolted just over two years later for Ireland and the editorship of the *Dublin University Magazine*, giving up his medical career for that of writing. His stay in Ireland lasted only a few years before he set off for the Continent again, eventually settling in Italy, always poor – despite Charles Dickens's attempts to help, often ill, but always the warmly welcomed, humorous raconteur. Anthony Trollope in his *Autobiography* sums him up:

How shall I speak of my dear old friend Charles Lever, and his rattling, jolly, joyous, swearing Irishmen. Surely never did a sense of vitality come so constantly from a man's pen, nor from man's voice, as from his! [...] Of all the men I have encountered, he was the surest fund of drollery [...] he never monopolised the talk, was never a bore. He would take no more than his own share of the words spoken, and would yet seem to brighten all that was said during the night [...] Lever's novels will not live long – even if they may be said to be alive now, – because it is so.[88]

His novels were indeed forgotten, but everywhere he went he brightened up the room. The Brussels set must have regretted his departure enormously.

* * *

In 1838 Evan and Eliza had to face two family deaths, but there was also another honour from the king.

Eliza's father John Jay and his second wife Johanna had moved to Utrecht in the Netherlands after the death of their daughter in Boulogne in January 1832. I had presumed, even hoped, that in his early sixties John Jay had gone there to retire, in a country that the couple might have found more congenial, with the Dutch language and Protestant churches. But, instead, in the Kromme Nieuwegracht (the fourteenth-century 'curve of the new canal') they set up a school for young ladies.[89] They must have needed the money since Johanna was now in her early fifties. It was a vibrant university town, then as now, with unique split-level canals, where warehouses lined the lower level. Although I got lost trying to get through the ghastly shopping mall out of the station, the medieval centre is enchanting. Their house-school was a mere few minutes from the Domtoren – the Cathedral Tower – which stands high and stranded from the church it once belonged to when in 1674 a hurricane destroyed the nave. The site of their house-school is now on the Canals and Wharves city walk. Utrecht is about one hundred miles north of Brussels; it's a bit nearer than Boulogne, but still a long way from John Jay's nearest grandchildren in Brussels. Perhaps Johanna simply didn't want to be near a stepdaughter with numerous children; perhaps John didn't care too much. It wasn't too far to visit every so often. Maybe, after some research, it seemed a great place to set up a girls' school teaching French and English. Alas, the inspectors' report is poignant regarding John's last attempt at success: there weren't enough young ladies. In 1836 he reported:

For four years, Mrs Jay has run a French and English day and boarding school on the Kromme Nieuwe Gracht. Until the Belgian rebellion [*opstand*], her husband had a school in Brussels. He is an English home teacher at Utrecht. They are already elderly people. The man is very knowledgeable in English and possesses a pleasant way of teaching. She also speaks and writes French and English very well. But her school does not make any progress. I found no more than 14 students and only one ?boarding, although it was arranged on a large scale. There is another pupil from France for French, one from England for English and one from Germany for the High German. Lack of sufficient discipline seems to be the main reason she doesn't have the trust of parents.[90]

Less than two years later, John Jay died in Loenen, aged sixty-eight, some seventy miles east of Utrecht, towards Germany. It seems it was unexpected as the house was an inn. His nephew, William Jay junior, was one of the witnesses, so perhaps, in January 1838, there had been a Christmas visit to friends or relatives and they were on their way home. Johanna Jay disappears from the records; she may have moved back to Rotterdam, near Jay and Enslie relatives.

For years I thought of Eliza's father John Jay as a shadowy figure in the background – as in the schoolboys' letters when the teenage John arrived in Andover to help his father deal with his mother's death. Before I learnt more, it seemed to me that he had fled Scotland and then England after acting irresponsibly. And he had remarried so quickly after the death of Eliza's mother. But the appeal at the Court of Session in Edinburgh in 1821 changed my mind. The Jay brothers had come to an acceptable arrangement with their creditors and John Jay had started a new life, but he was hounded I think unfairly and must have lived with the fear of imprisonment for some time. But he held his nerve and started yet again, in Brussels, only to be faced with the death of his first wife and his youngest son. Apart from his daughter Janet, who took to lying on a sofa in Greenwich, his children were steady and hardworking. It is poignant that he clung to the memory of Lixmount.

One recent article comments as regards his turn to teaching in Woodford, Essex after his Scottish bankruptcy that 'sequestration suggests that his knowledge of mercantile affairs was perhaps not so great'.[91] That is nonsense: as I have shown, the circumstances in 1810 led to numerous merchants failing, and the actions of Captain Kelting and Thomas Williamson appear distinctly dubious. It sounds as if John Jay delighted in his new career and was good at it ('possesses a pleasant way of teaching'). His awful experience of bankruptcy would enable him to pass on invaluable lessons: above all to ensure that a contract with a ship's master was legally tight. He was a good, honest striver.

* * *

In March that year, John Jay's son-in-law Evan Jenkins entered the Freemason Lodge in Brussels of 'Les Amis Philanthropes'. Back in February 2014 when I started my research in Brussels, I had gone to the Chapel Royal rather nervously. The wonderfully helpful Madame Charade had already photocopied for me an article by Dr Hugh Boudin that mentioned Evan. In it Boudin states that the historian of Freemasonry in Belgium, F. Clément, 'maintains that the Sovereign's interest in Belgian Freemasonry showed itself notably in the initiation of several members of his civilian and military households', including Evan Jenkins and his aides-de-camp. Boudin adds: 'Certainly, these affiliations could also be explained as a reaction to the episcopal circular against Freemasonry published in December 1837 [...] E. Jenkins entered the Lodge "Les Amis Philanthropes" on 15 March 1838.'[92] A short article in a religious journal published in Paris in 1839 expands on Evan's fellow Freemasons in Brussels, calling his Lodge 'la royale loge écossaise des amis philantropes'. It says that there were 289 members, which included 28 musicians, 32 painters, 42 merchants, 36 military, 24 lawyers and 1 Protestant minister: Evan Jenkins, chaplain to King Leopold.[93] Evan was now mixing with the most important men in Brussels and it is quite possible that Lucy Snowe's description of Graham Bretton's renown in 'Villette' refers to Evan:

> I often felt amazed at his perfect knowledge of Villette; a knowledge not merely confined to its open streets, but penetrating to all its galleries, salles, and cabinets: of every door which shut in an object worth seeing, of every museum, of every hall, sacred to art or science, he seemed to possess the 'Open! Sesame.'[94]

But if that was the highpoint of 1838 for Evan, life at home was not good: his youngest daughter, Mary Jane Wilhelmina, was ill. It seems that she had caught influenza at the beginning of the previous year when she was six and lingered on for eighteen months – so perhaps she had tuberculosis. Her parents took her to the seaside at Ostend, no doubt hoping for a cure, but she died there in July aged eight years, two months and nineteen days. How cruel the Belgian records can seem with their detailed counting of days.[95] Over fifty years later a piece in *Notes and Queries* described the now abandoned cemetery where the little girl was buried:

Just outside Ostend on the road to Thorout lies a waste piece of land now used as a drying ground for linen and as a playground by the small fry of the neighbourhood. The only remnants of respectability that it has left are two massive gateposts, on which hang the remains of wooden gates [... One headstone is inscribed:] Sacred to the Memory of Mary-Jane Wilhelmina second daughter of The Revd. E. Jenkins, M.A. British Chaplain at Brussels who died at Ostend on the 3rd July 1838 Aged 8 years.[96]

Eliza was surely distraught that her daughter, named after the young sister who had died in Woodford, had died at an even earlier age, and since fathers often have a particular fondness for the youngest it is perhaps not surprising that less than nine months later they had another daughter. Their last child, born on 22 March 1839, was named in the registration of births as Mina Janet ('Mina Jeannette'), presumably after her dead sister and her aunt Janet; she was baptized in Greenwich the following year. Mina was born five years after my great-grandfather John Card, whom they had perhaps intended to be their last.

* * *

Living in Ostend at the time of the little girl's death was a step-cousin of Eliza's, whom they probably met up with: Albinia Jackson Bowden. The Ostend abode is on the banns of her marriage to Rev. William Chave at St Clement Danes, Westminster in January 1839. There are rather strange bits of jigsaw that make up her story.[97] She was the third child of James Bowden and Clara Wylde, whom he married after the death of his first wife, Eliza's maternal aunt, and was baptized in Edmonton in August 1817. I took no notice of her until I was sent an obituary, after her death at the age of ninety-eight in Lausanne, Switzerland, which was headed 'Friend of Thackeray'. The English obituary calls her 'a personal friend of Thackeray', while two French ones call her 'l'amie intime de Thackeray'.[98] A translation as 'intimate friend' sounds a bit racy for a woman just six years younger. I summoned up at the British Library Ray's biography of Thackeray, and his edition of the letters, to find if this obscure woman might turn into an unknown liaison in Thackeray's life. Albinia wasn't mentioned in Ray's biography, but I found her in the index to the edited letters. However, the letters weren't from Thackeray or her, instead she was mentioned in two written by Thackeray's young wife Isabella, the first a brief mention to her mother-in-law on 11 March 1840: 'Did you hear Mr. Chave preach at Marboeuf [in Paris]? he married a charming girl I knew in Paris Albinia Bowden niece of Mrs. Valpy's. He is not <a man> to be liked.' (Mrs Valpy was the wife of the classical scholar and publisher mentioned above in connection with William Drury's notice about taking private pupils.) A week later, Isabella wrote to her sister in Ireland:

> Do you recollect Albinia Bowden? She married a Mr. Chave a clergyman one of the highly evangelical. The Ritchies don't admire him at all[.] They think he has no consideration for his wife of whom they are very fond[.] When she was very large he wanted to drag her up to Paris when the Ritchies interposed and begged he would allow <her> to remain quietly with them; at <the bi>rth she was delivered of a dead ch<ld.> – Charity ought to begin at home.[99]

Thackeray's paternal aunt had married John Ritchie; their home and children had welcomed him among them when he was a lonely boy at school at Charterhouse. Later, after Thackeray had lost over a thousand pounds gambling as a student at Cambridge and then all the family money was lost when an Indian bank failed, he was a frequent visitor at their home in Paris as he struggled in his new poverty to learn art. He met Isabella Shawe in Paris, and despite her Irish mother's forcible dislike of him, they married in 1836. Isabella obviously liked the older Albinia but I wonder if her horror at the actions of Albinia's husband reflects more her own mental troubles than the realities of Albinia's marriage. Later in 1840 Isabella tried to drown herself, and Thackeray was forced to send her to an asylum.

The English obituary of Albinia tells of a remarkable woman: 'She spoke and wrote eleven languages, and at the age of eighty-eight began to master Swedish [... she] remained in touch with the old school of writers in London and Paris to the end. She was the pupil of Jenny Daquin, "the beautiful unknown" of the letters of Prosper Merimee [...] "La grande dame anglaise" was this [sic] oldest inhabitant of Lausanne, where she was extremely popular among rich and poor alike.' She had no children, and it is impossible to learn if her stillborn child was the first of several failed attempts. But what the obituary doesn't mention is her later fostering of a number of children, especially of those whose mothers had died. Her husband was certainly an indefatigable evangelical, serving in Paris, Zurich and Munich, where he died in 1866. Perhaps there is more to Albinia's story that might be uncovered, but whether she knew Thackeray only in Paris in the 1830s, admired his novels and liked to talk about the young man she had known, or whether she had seen him more frequently, may be impossible to discover. That she published her husband's sermons after his death may, or may not, prove that she was a dutiful or even loving wife, or whether he did or did not abuse her, as Isabella Thackeray and the Ritchies feared.

* * *

Towards the end of the 1830s, Evan and Eliza moved to the address the Brontës would know, at 388 Chaussée d'Ixelles, south-east from the Porte de Namur towards the countryside and forest. It was surely a larger house and garden, in a wider road: more suitable not only for a man belonging to the king's circle but to take in more pupils. An English guidebook to Brussels published in 1839 advised that 'for the children of English residents I have no hesitation in strongly recommending the following establishments':

> Viz. that of reverend E. Jenkins, M.A. of Trinity college Cambridge who receives into his family a limited number of pupils to prepare for the public schools, universities, army and navy. His terms are moderate and vary according to the age of the pupil and the instruction required; a prospectus may be had at Mr. Jenkins's house Chaussée d'Ixelles, out of the gate of Namur.

William Drury follows closely behind:

> Also that of the reverend William Drury, son of the reverend doctor Drury of Harrow (the friend of lord Byron), who receives pupils as boarders, and by the day, on very reasonable terms. A prospectus can be obtained at his residence, rue de l'Orangerie.

Byron and Harrow are still Drury's selling points, but he is an 'also': Evan's school comes first. Published only a few years before the Brontë sisters arrived, it would be inexplicable if Charlotte, who loved Byron, did not make sure she met Drury, as I will discuss in a later chapter. Both clergymen are also mentioned by the author of the guidebook as regards their church services: Rev. Jenkins, 'chaplain to the British Embassy', at the Chapel Royal at noon on Sunday, and Rev. Drury in St George's Chapel twice on Sunday, at 11 and 3.[100]

In July 1839, a few months after the birth of Mina, Richard Whately, Archbishop of Dublin, confirmed young people at the Chapel Royal, accompanied by Evan and Drury.[101] The tall thin Whately, tall fat Drury and small Welshman Evan must have made a curious trio. A few years older than Drury and Evan, Whately was intellectual, a prolific writer, brusque and blessedly eccentric. As a tutor at Oxford at the beginning of the nineteenth century he had roamed around wearing a white coat and hat (instead of college cap and gown) accompanied by a white dog whom he encouraged to climb trees. He taught his students while lying on a sofa with one leg hung over the back, and kept herrings in his rooms to cook for breakfast – it is not stated whether the herrings were alive or dead. Maybe his wife cured him of the latter habit, or cured the herrings. On his appointment to the archbishopric in 1831 he remarked that it was 'a call to the helm of a crazy ship in a storm'. He had been Professor of Political Economy and it's a mystery why he was appointed and why he accepted, but he was a strong-minded Christian who rejected both evangelicalism and High-Church Tractarians.[102] Perhaps that indicates that both Evan and Drury were likewise Broad Church. His sermons at the Chapel Royal and at Drury's St George's Church on the following day were surely far from dull. He perhaps stayed at the ambassador's residence, with Evan, Drury and their wives in attendance at dinner. Whately had written a book on whether one could prove the existence of Napoleon, so the conversation might have been lively. Maybe he left Brussels on the new railroad to Ostend, which took about five hours.[103]

The only copy in the British Library of one of the English newspapers in Brussels, the *British Advertiser*, reports the arrival in Ostend of Lord Torrington and Colonel Grey in January 1840.[104] The men were on their way to Germany to escort Prince Albert to England for his wedding to Queen Victoria on 10 February. He was to stay in Brussels en route, where infantry ceremoniously lined the roads leading to the palace, and was expected to attend the court ball on 28 January. No doubt Evan and Eliza attended the ball, but, more significantly, Prince Albert went to Evan's church service, who had surely already made Albert familiar with the form of an Anglican service three years before:

> On Saturday [sic] the 2nd of February, the Duke of Saxe-Coburg and the hereditary Prince [Prince Ernst and his father] attended Divine Service with the king at the Chapel of the Palace; but Prince Albert, accompanied by the British Ambassador, and Lady Seymour, Viscount Torrington, the Hon. Colonel Grey, Mr. Waller the Secretary of the Legation, Mrs. Waller, and Mr. F. Seymour, attended at the English Chapel in the *Rue du Masee* [sic]. Most of the English residents were present at the service, which was performed by the Rev. E. Jenkins, Honorary Chaplain to the King and to the British Embassy.[105]

'Most of the English residents'? You bet! And I wouldn't be surprised if money changed hands for a seat in the chapel to see the prince before one of the weddings of the century. One could say that Prince Albert was formally welcomed into the Church of England and introduced to his new British subjects not only by the ambassador in Brussels, but by a Welsh-born clergyman, a Cardi no less. I'm sure it was carefully thought out by the bride and bridegroom's uncle, King Leopold.

* * *

I quoted briefly from a letter earlier from Eliza's brother John Livingston Jay to their sister Margaret in Australia (written on 8 October 1840), which, in light of the honours shown to Evan and the social set he and Eliza moved among, reads even more curmudgeonly and somewhat weird:

> I do not think that Eliza's continued residence on the Continent, and the society she there meets, have been of any advantage to her, but she is so much attached to that horrid place that willingly she will never quit it. The greatest evil attending residence on the Continent is the few friends (useful ones) made by a family, and the consequent difficulty afterwards in providing for boys.[106]

'Horrid' is a strong word: maybe the memory of Miss Sophia Barker, coupled with the deaths of his mother and his brother William, had completely soured the place for him. Since Eliza's four boys were then aged between five and fourteen, it seems hardly the time to worry about their employment. But I am thinking anachronistically and not of the rigid society that they lived in, where there were limited employment opportunities for 'gentlemen'. John Livingston tells Margaret that he and sister Janet (then aged thirty) were still single: 'such are the hardness of the times, and having had so uphill a ?game during our early years that we are not likely to run into difficulties now. – In this country it is not only the difficulty of living when married, but afterwards of settling a family in the class of society in which they have moved.' It is interesting that his older brother Samuel, the barrister, writes something similar in a letter to Margaret a quarter of a century later: 'Your children are happy in having a pursuit as in this country it is difficult to know what to do with Boys when ready to enter on the world. I congratulate myself on this ground that I have none – I am equally blessed with yourself in my two Daughters.'[107] In Australia, he is perhaps saying, upholding distinctions of class was unnecessary, but in England it was who you knew (your interest) and not merit that prevailed.

In his 1840 letter, John Livingston Jay mentions that the Jenkins family 'were all here [in Greenwich] in the summer. I endeavoured to persuade her to delay her visit until the Children were older and that they might then derive some advantages for the great expense she would incur but she was bent upon the visit and over they came.' I wonder if there were several reasons why Eliza was set on going to Greenwich despite her brother advising otherwise. The first was to have Mina baptized, which she was in the chapel of the Royal Naval Hospital on 2 July. Mina was then fifteen months old and it seems strange that Evan hadn't already baptized his daughter. Presuming that Eliza's sister Janet was indeed to be her godmother, maybe Eliza had wanted Janet to be present in person at the baptism, but Janet would only do it in Greenwich. It is a fabulous chapel to be baptized in: large, neoclassical and highly decorated, set amongst Sir Christopher Wren's resplendent white colonnaded buildings on a curve of the wide Thames. I went on a private 'Huguenot' tour led by Michael Palin's son Will, the conservation director, in 2015. He is so like his father, that it was fitting to the spirit of Monty Python that we ended the tour in an undercroft playing skittles with practice cannonballs.

Or Eliza's determination could have been because of the clergyman, who was Rev. John Kellow Goldney. He had been at St John's College, Cambridge at the same time as Evan and might have been a friend, or a past acquaintance worth cultivating. It is odd that Eliza's brother doesn't mention the baptism, but then he doesn't mention the visit of Queen Victoria and Prince Albert by barge on Saturday 27 June a few days earlier either. The Jenkins family may have witnessed the hurried arrangements to welcome the royal couple, since apparently only a few hours' notice were given, but Victoria, pregnant with her first child, enjoyed her visit and found the soup prepared for the 'veteran tars' 'excellent'. The queen's visit was hardly low key: about a thousand pensioners stood around the grand square, 'the nurses under the colonnades; the girls of the school between the painted hall and chapel behind them [...] A guard of 30 boatswain pensioners, with halberts, were drawn up in front of the north entrance where the Queen landed.'[108] It is also possible that Eliza was presented to the queen that July: perhaps another reason for her decision to bring the whole family over on an expensive trip. Perhaps Evan was carrying private correspondence from King Leopold to his niece and nephew about the king's forthcoming visit in August. How I wish that a letter about Greenwich from Eliza to Margaret had survived or that her younger brother had been a less boring correspondent. In the letter John Livingston refers to his 'bald pate and long phiz [which] tend to add to the respectable age I pass for' – he was thirty-eight.

* * *

In November 1841 a 'grand subscription dinner was given by British residents' in Brussels at the Vauxhall Rooms, in honour of the birth of Victoria and Albert's first son, the future Edward VII. Among the 'gentlemen of distinction' present were various knights and colonels and Reverends Jenkins and Drury, as well as the Irish author Dr Charles Lever, about to return to Ireland to give up medicine for journal editing and writing.[109] Meanwhile, trapped in her inferior status as a governess near Leeds, a job she hated, a young woman was scheming how to get to Brussels to join her friends the Taylors there. One idea was for her father to write to Rev. Evan Jenkins, whom she had recently discovered was the English episcopal clergyman and not the British consul: 'but not yet'. A few weeks later Charlotte Brontë wrote to her friend Ellen: 'Brussels is still my promised land'.[110] Just over two months later she, father Patrick and sister Emily finally crossed the Channel.

Thirteen

The Brontës Come to Brussels, 1842

The Trial of Common Sense

When Dr Samuel Johnson wrote his *Lives of the Poets* in his late sixties (biographies of fifty-two poets in four volumes, published in 1781) he rarely had the time or the means to do new research, but, as the American literary scholar Richard Altick said, 'he refused to be taken in by what purported to be the truth'. Altick continued:

> [Dr Johnson] was the first great man of letters to insist that biographical tradition be put to the trial of Common Sense. Johnson's greatest advantage as a scholar was his profound sense of human frailty. No one was more aware than he of the multifarious sources of error in human report, and the ineradicable tendency men have to stray away from the truth, or even invent it. 'Thus it is that characters are written,' he says [...]: 'we know somewhat, and we imagine the rest.'

Unfortunately few of the biographers of the Brontës have followed Dr Johnson's guidance, sometimes inventing when they had nothing new to say; often copying what a previous biographer has written, paraphrasing or reordering to make it look slightly more original; rarely checking whether the previous biographer whom they were copying had used a trustworthy source, or even a sensible-looking source – or no source at all.

Altick adds that one of Dr Johnson's 'favorite devices was to discredit a hand-me-down "fact" simply by applying the homely test of likelihood'.[1] Altick

356

describes wryly one of these hand-me-down 'facts' in another of his brilliant books: it is the 'Brontë snowstorm' story:

> In a travel book I wrote several years ago, I had occasion to recall the trip that Charlotte and Anne Brontë suddenly resolved to take in July, 1848, to reveal their true identities to their London publisher [...] These were my words: 'After tea, as Charlotte recounted it in a letter, they "walked through a snow-storm to the station" (yes: in July) and took the night train for Leeds and London.'[2]

The word snowstorm did not appear in Mrs Gaskell's account of Charlotte and Anne's trip to London. But in 1900 the relevant letter (from Charlotte to her friend Mary Taylor) – and the weather – was mistranscribed in an edition of the letters, and blindly copied by most subsequent biographers. Winifred Gérin was fooled, writing that 'Born in the West Riding, a snowstorm in July would not have surprised Mary unduly', since 'at those altitudes [rain] has an unseasonable habit of falling as snow'. Really?! An earlier biographer, Mrs Ellis Chadwick (1914), was more acute. Like Gérin, she had also lived in Haworth but seems to have been more observant about Yorkshire weather and more sensible in checking other sources: 'Mrs Gaskell was surely more accurate when she described it as a thunderstorm and not a snowstorm, as it occurred in July.'[3] The American Altick, who fell into the trap himself, writes that he 'was troubled by the July snow in Yorkshire' but 'failed to take the obvious and simple step of checking the newspapers or the meteorological records to verify that almost incredible freak of the weather.' The mistranscription of 'snow-storm' for 'thunderstorm' was only finally corrected in the 1970s.[4]

* * *

Here is another so-called 'fact'. In February 1842, after the Brontës arrived by steam packet at Ostend 'they took the "Diligence", an already out-moded means of conveyance, rather than the recently opened railway from Ostend to Brussels, as appears from Charlotte's accounts of the journey both in *The Professor* and *Villette*.' So says Winifred Gérin in her 1967 biography of Charlotte.[5] Readers who recall my account of Gérin's fabrications in my first chapter may be suitably sceptical. Those attuned to Dr Johnson's trial of common sense may be shaking their heads in disbelief. I turned to Juliet Barker's more recent biography of the family and found something odder: 'As the new railway line between Ostend and Brussels had not yet fully opened, they took the more cumbersome and slower diligence, a public stagecoach which passed through the ancient town of Ghent [...] The long, slow journey of nearly seventy miles would have been a trial.'[6] It is odd because in her footnote Barker says she has assumed that 'Charlotte followed the same arrangements as on her return to Brussels the following year and have taken my description of this first journey from her own account of the second.'[7] I dutifully looked up the letter referred to: Charlotte to her friend Ellen Nussey of 30 January 1843, obviously expecting to see the word diligence. I will quote it:

> I left Leeds for London last Friday at 9 o'clock [...] we had a prosperous & speedy voyage – and landed at Ostend at 9 – next morning I took the train at 12 and reached rue d'Isabelle – at 7 Sunday evening[8]

Train. I can indeed confirm that there was a train from Ostend to Brussels in 1842 as well as 1843: in Alexandre Ferrier de Tourettes's *Handbook for Travellers on the Belgian Rail-Road*, published in 1840, he gives the summer timetable – the train leaves Ostend at 6.30 in the morning and at 12.30 in the afternoon.[9] Likewise Mrs Wemyss Dalrymple in her 1839 guide to Brussels states, 'The railroad from Ostend to Brussels is now open, and the whole journey is performed in 5 hours; the fare is 9 francs.'[10] King Leopold travelled on a special train between Brussels and Ostend on 20 August 1838; returning at night, it crushed two vehicles, killing two people.[11] And Prince Albert travelled on the train on the way to his wedding in February 1840.[12] By 1840 there had already been two suicides on the railway track.[13] The station in Brussels was the Allée Verte, west of the current Brussels-Nord station, near the place de l'Yser.[14] Perhaps a glance at the *London Evening Standard* in April 1840 may convince:

> Brussels via Ostend, in 20 Hours, every Wednesday and Saturday. – The journey from Ostend to Brussels by the Railway is performed in about five hours [...] The General Steam Navigation Company's well-known, rapid, and elegant Steam-yacht [...] Earl of Liverpool, on Saturday, May 2, at Eight a.m., and every Saturday.[15]

The time is confirmed for February 1842 in another advertisement by the company: 'Ostend and Brussels every Wednesday, and Saturday mornings [...] the Earl of Liverpool on Saturdays. Next Wednesday and Saturday, 9th and 12th, at 8 morning.'[16]

Mrs Gaskell doesn't mention how the Brontës and their friend Mary Taylor and one of her brothers got to Brussels. Mary wrote in 1857 to Mrs Gaskell about what she remembered of their arrival: 'I don't know what Charlotte thought of Brussels. We arrived in the dark, and went next morning to our respective schools to see them.'[17] In February it would be dark around 6 p.m. So it seems that this is yet another fabrication by Chadwick and Gérin, confused by Charlotte's fictional accounts of her protagonists arriving in Brussels. In the first-person narrative *The Professor*, written in 1846 and published posthumously, 21-year-old William Crimsworth arrives in Brussels at the latest in the mid-1830s, and he spends perhaps eleven years there. Charlotte has him say, as he travels the road to Brussels: 'I gazed often, and always with delight, from the window of the diligence (these, be it remembered, were not the days of trains and railroads).'[18] In *Villette*, the narrator, Lucy Snowe, looks back at events some half a century before. She says, 'I speak of a time gone by: my hair which till a late period withstood the frosts of time, lies now at last, white under a white cap, like snow beneath snow' – thus Lucy also goes to Brussels/Villette by the lumbering diligence.[19] But our trial of common sense says that the Brontës and Taylors took the train.

Does it matter? Yes. Because all of Gérin's fantasy of the Brontës arriving at midnight and staying at a hotel because it was near the diligence terminus is utterly undermined, as is her whole account up to Patrick taking Charlotte and Emily to their school, which is all Mrs Gaskell has after her account of the Brontës in London. Unfortunately Barker partly copies Gérin for the family's arrival in Brussels and gets muddled about diligences and trains. And it matters because it is interesting about Charlotte Brontë as a writer, that her imagination was more active when contemplating the past of slow horse-drawn carriages than with the present of steam. Maybe she and Flaubert would have had a sparkling conversation about their preference for horse-wheeled travel over the modern, faster, steam engine. Thackeray would have enjoyed joining in their conversation. He writes this in his last novel, *The Adventures of Philip* (1861–2), not long before he died:

> What used you to do in old days, ere railroads were, and when diligences ran? They were slow enough; but they have got to their journey's end somehow. They were tight, hot, dusty, dear, stuffy, and uncomfortable; but, for all that, travelling was good sport sometimes. And if the world would have the kindness to go back for five-and-twenty or thirty years, some of us who have travelled on the Tours and Orleans Railway very comfortably would like to take the diligence journey now.[20]

Perhaps a further indication that the Brontës travelled by train is in Charlotte's account of what William Crimsworth saw in *The Professor* as he travelled by diligence to Brussels: 'Green, reedy swamps; fields fertile but flat, cultivated in patches that made them look like magnified kitchen-gardens; belts of cut trees, formal as pollard willows, skirting the horizon; narrow canals, gliding slow by the roadside; painted Flemish farmhouses; some very dirty hovels; a grey, dead sky; wet road, wet fields, wet house-tops [...] it was through streaming and starless darkness my eye caught the first gleam of the lights of Brussels.'[21] But the problem with diligences, one guidebook tells us, is that although the 'inside passengers are seated completely at their ease [...] the smallness of the windows, and the manner in which the seats are arranged, prevent them from enjoying much view of the country.'[22] I therefore suggest that Charlotte's view of the countryside en route to Brussels, that she imagines William seeing, was from a train, not a diligence, window.

* * *

Now for more fabrications. This is Gérin again:

> The Brontës were fetched from their hotel next morning by Mr. and Mrs. Jenkins (whose home outside the city walls on the Chaussée d'Ixelles was too far out to be reached the previous night) and together they walked the short distance to the Pensionnat Heger. It was Mrs. Jenkins, we are told, who effected the introduction to Madame Heger.[23]

This is either shamelessly dishonest or utterly inept. Actually both. As I mentioned in my first chapter, Gérin adds a footnote here: 'Chadwick: evidence derived from Mrs. Jenkins herself, ch. 15.' Not only would Mrs Chadwick have been a true Infant Prodigy to be already researching her biography of Charlotte and interviewing Mrs Jenkins when Chadwick was a toddler, chapter 15 in Chadwick's book is about the Brontës in London. However, in *chapter 18*, Chadwick writes briefly that 'Mr. Brontë took his daughters to call first on the chaplain [Mr Jenkins], who afterwards accompanied them to the pensionnat of Madame Heger.'[24] There is no source for that, which is invented or based on hearsay, and there is no mention in Chadwick of Mrs Jenkins introducing anyone to anyone. Incidentally, Gérin's comment about the Jenkinses' home being 'too far out to be reached the previous night' is just nonsense – there were numerous hackney coaches (*fiacres*) and cheaper vigilantes, and the reader will find prices listed for a variety of journeys in Mrs Dalrymple's 1839 guide.[25]

Why bother with Chadwick and Gérin? Because the latter is still in print and because her book is copied by all biographers. Here is Juliet Barker a few decades ago: 'The next morning, the English Episcopal clergyman who had assisted them in their choice of school, Mr Jenkins, arrived with his wife at the hotel to escort them there.'[26] That is not only copying but plainly wrong since it was Eliza and not Evan who had found the school – a mistake that Barker is making here yet again.[27] I've no idea why Barker is trying to write Eliza out of the picture or why she misreads 'Mrs' for 'Mr' in Charlotte's letters and Mrs Gaskell's account. And here is a biography published in 2015: 'When they arrived in Brussels on the evening of 15 February, the Brontës were met by Reverend Evan Jenkins, chaplain to the British Embassy and the brother of an old friend of Patrick Brontë from Hartshead days [...] The Pensionnat Heger, where the Jenkinses escorted Patrick Brontë and his daughters on the morning after their arrival in Brussels [...]'.[28]

It is all made up or copied. It is also not clear what day the Brontës and Taylors arrived in Brussels. We have the date of Tuesday 8 February in Emily's diary paper for leaving Haworth;[29] a few days spent in London is confirmed by their travelling companion Mary Taylor; and the likely steam packet leaving London for Ostend was on Saturday 12th. Gérin actually gives a source of Police Registers in Ostend and Brussels for the Brontës' arrival.[30] I was duly sceptical until I read a biography of Patrick Brontë, which transcribed the Brussels police entry: 'Patrick's arrival was recorded by the police under the date [Monday] 14th February 1842. "No. 457. Patrick Bronté – 63 [sic: he was 64 ...] place of issue of Passport: Ostende 13th February 1842; date of arrival: 15th February – name of Hotel: Hollande".'[31] Unfortunately, the authors rather spoil their scholarly credentials by stating: 'After breakfast Jenkins arrived at the hotel.' But it is possible that the Brontës arrived in Brussels on the evening of Monday 14 February and that Patrick registered with the police on the 15th. The Hollande hotel is described in one guidebook as a 'secondary' house 'with comfortable accommodation and moderate charges'.[32] It was located in the rue de la Putterie, according to the Almanacs, which was destroyed in the early twentieth century by the building of the Central Station. The hotel was near the school that Charlotte and Emily were to attend in the rue d'Isabelle, and may have been recommended by the Hegers or by Eliza. For those biographers keen on slowly dragging the Brontës to Brussels by diligence, the hotel was also near where these vehicles docked. But I can't imagine that Mary Taylor and her brother, experienced travellers, would have done anything other than insist on the train. Indeed, the train was three times quicker than a diligence, travelling at eighteen miles per hour or more, and much cheaper.[33]

The late Richard Altick continued to guide my frustrations at biographers copying each other and not thinking or researching: he is here talking about biographers from the 1920s onwards, that is, after Lytton Strachey, who had rescued the craft from the thoughtless, dull compilers, but with some unfortunate consequences:

> In the post-Stracheyan era, biographers who derived the substance of their books from preceding ones, without attempting either to test the received facts or supplement them, remained in the majority, as they always will. They placidly passed on the errors they found in their sources, along with fresh ones bred by their carelessness or their desire to supply silences.

But Altick was optimistic because, 'in the upper reaches of the craft there was a notably intensified spirit of skepticism, which resulted in a ceaseless campaign to purge from the body of biographical knowledge all the myths, biases, unsupported assumptions, misinterpretations, and sheer mistakes that had crept past the unvigilant eyes of earlier biographers.'[34]

I shall do some more purging, therefore, even if it would be presumptuous of me to claim that I'm in the upper reach of this craft. There is no source whatsoever for the Jenkinses meeting the Brontës at their hotel, nor for taking them to the school. Since no one had even researched the Jenkins family it can't even be an intelligent guess by a biographer that Evan or Eliza had done so. But now we know a lot more about them, it is important that I look at the possibility, using the trial of common sense – which involves not only knowing about them, but knowing what was socially likely two hundred years ago. I first turn to Charlotte's letters.

* * *

The young Mary and Martha Taylor met the shy, fourteen-year-old Charlotte at Margaret Wooler's small school, Roe Head, near Mirfield, West Yorkshire in 1831, where she also befriended Ellen Nussey. Mary was ten months younger than Charlotte; the 'calm, well-bred Yorkshire girl' Ellen a year younger; and boisterous Martha three years younger (b. 1819).[35] Despite Charlotte only being at the school for eighteen months, Mary and Ellen were to become lifelong friends and correspondents with her, though Mary destroyed nearly all of Charlotte's letters and our information is largely based on those that Ellen preserved, a number of which were read by Mrs Gaskell. The Taylor girls' father was a cloth manufacturer in Gomersal, just a few miles north of the school, and within walking distance of Ellen's home. The French-speaking Mr Yorke in Charlotte's novel *Shirley* (1849) was based on the well-travelled Joshua Taylor; the elder daughter, the grave, intellectual Rose Yorke, on Mary; and little Jessy on Martha Taylor, whom her father has no idea will die young.[36] After the death of Joshua at the end of 1840, Martha, now twenty-one, was sent to Mme Goussaert's school, the Château de Koekelberg, near Brussels – I will discuss the school, which has been misunderstood and barely researched, below – and Mary travelled on the Continent with one of her brothers. In August 1841, unhappy governess Charlotte tells Ellen of a letter she has received from Mary about the pictures and cathedrals she has seen, plus the embarrassingly expensive presents of a silk scarf and kid gloves from Brussels, 'one of the most splendid capitals of Europe'. Charlotte was now fired with her 'strong wish for wings', as I quoted above.[37] Such a letter might inspire many of us to travel, but Charlotte's longing seems more fired by Martha's experience at the school: 'to see – to know – to learn [...] I was tantalized with the consciousness of faculties unexercised'. Charlotte tells Ellen that she has suppressed her longing and she is still thinking more mundanely about setting up a school with her sisters. But she doesn't let it drop. On 29 September she writes the vital letter to Aunt Branwell about using some of the money her aunt will lend her to spend six months learning languages in Belgium in order to be more successful at establishing a school. In the Margaret Smith edited volume of letters this one comes straight after the August letter to Ellen, and of course many letters in between no longer survive, but we can perhaps piece together a scenario.[38]

Although Charlotte writes that she has discussed with her employers the Whites and 'others' about her plan of going to Brussels, my instinct is that her mention of Mr and Mrs White is designed to convince her aunt, whereas most of her impetus comes from letters written by Mary Taylor. It is in this September letter from Charlotte that there is the first mention of Mrs Jenkins 'the wife of the British Consul', who, with Martha Taylor, would 'be able to secure me a cheap and decent residence and respectable protection' and 'with the assistance of [Martha's] cousins [the Dixons], I should probably in time be introduced to connections far more improving, polished, and cultivated, than any I have yet known'. As I wrote in my first chapter, in her biography Mrs Gaskell changed 'Consul' to 'clergyman', and 'Martha' to her older sister 'Mary'. But it is interesting why Charlotte called Evan the consul, which is an odd mistake. Martha was at the school and there are several ways she would have known that Mrs Jenkins was the wife of the English clergyman and not the consul: she would have attended his services at the Chapel Royal; she would probably have met the Jenkinses at her cousins, the Dixons. There is also a third reason, which I will reveal below. So it is possible that Mary conveyed all this information, taken from her younger sister, to Charlotte and by mistake called Evan the consul because she misunderstood her sister and was not yet at the school or attending church services in Brussels (Mary joined her sister at the school in February 1842). And indeed in a later letter to sister Emily, Charlotte writes: 'Mr. Jenkins I find was mistakenly termed the British Consul at Brussels; he is in fact the English Episcopal clergyman.'[39] Charlotte has possibly had another letter from Mary, correcting her earlier mistake.

What is intriguing is that the name Jenkins means nothing to Charlotte, nor seemingly to Mary Taylor, despite the fact that Evan's brother David had been presiding for almost twenty years over the huge new church at Pudsey, only five miles north of the Taylors' home. But Jenkins is a fairly common name. It is also clear that David Jenkins, despite his once close connection to their father Patrick, was not a familiar name in the Brontë household. Maybe there had been an estrangement between the men after the deaths of the two eldest Brontë girls. So in mentioning 'Mrs Jenkins', Charlotte had no idea that she was the wife of the brother of a once close friend of her father. But it is interesting that Martha (I would guess) had mentioned 'Mrs Jenkins' as a person who would give respectable protection rather than any other woman: she must have known her well and known her as one of the leaders of the British community.

So far, however, Charlotte had not found a school, and Martha's school was too expensive. The letters between Mary and Charlotte must have carried on relentlessly as the former tried to find a cheaper school in Brussels that was suitable for Charlotte and Emily, perhaps via Martha or her Dixon cousins. But September turned into November, and although her aunt had approved of the scheme, no school had been found. Charlotte wrote to Emily, around 7 November, that 'I have written letters but I have received no letters in reply yet. Belgium is a long way off.'[40] Charlotte possibly means that she has written to various schools in Brussels, from addresses sent by Mary or Martha. She suggests that their father should write to Evan Jenkins 'by and bye, but not yet' – this is maybe just to mention from one clergyman to another that his daughters will be in Brussels and ask Evan to take pastoral care of them, but Charlotte merely adds: 'I will give an intimation when this should be done, and also some idea of what had best be said.' Perhaps Charlotte also needs her choice of school to be endorsed by the British chaplain. In Rev. Biber's account of the English Church in Europe, published just a few years later, he quotes one clergyman as saying: 'I would recommend [...] any one wishing to send their children abroad for education, first of all to apply to the resident clergyman. Parents cannot be too particular.'[41] But that is a rather tall order for a busy clergyman in a large town, and surely less necessary for women in their twenties. Finally around 9 December Charlotte writes to Ellen that she has heard 'of a less expensive establishment' than Martha's school in Brussels, perhaps from Martha or Mary.[42] And presumably Charlotte then wrote to that school.

One mystery is in a letter to Ellen dated by Margaret Smith as ?17 December, so only a week later, in which Charlotte thanks Ellen for 'Mr J address'. This was expanded by Smith to 'Mr Jenkins', and noted by her as Evan's address in Brussels. Smith adds that Evan's nephew, David's eldest son, Joseph Walker Jenkins, was a curate at Batley, less than two miles from Ellen's home. If this is a correct identification and expansion – and Joseph was indeed there – then the connection between the Jenkinses of Brussels and of Yorkshire had suddenly been made.[43] So it is possible that in December, Charlotte told her father of her efforts to find a school and about the 'Mrs Jenkins' in Brussels, and Patrick told her that she was the sister-in-law of his colleague all those years ago. Charlotte might have avoided a lot of letter-writing if she had told Patrick many months before. Also, it seems that Martha Taylor knew of the relationship between the Brussels and Yorkshire Jenkinses (see the joint letter of March–April 1842, which I discuss below) and had omitted to explain this to her sister Mary for several months. There was a lack of communication all round.

Mrs Gaskell avoids all the unnecessary letter-writing by Charlotte and the Taylors and cuts straight to the chase: 'At the request of [Evan's] brother – a clergyman [David], living not many miles from Haworth, and an acquaintance of Mr. Brontë's – [Eliza] made much inquiry [about schools in Brussels].'[44]

Patrick would know that David's brother Evan was the clergyman in Brussels. He presumably then wrote to David in Pudsey to ask if Evan might know of any suitable schools. David then wrote to Evan, who handed the job over to Eliza – when you want something done, ask a busy woman. I can't work out why Charlotte would ask Ellen to get hold of Mr J's address. Patrick couldn't possibly write to Evan to ask about schools – it would be presumptuous, even if they had met briefly before. Nor would David's address be needed – Patrick knew he was at Pudsey. Perhaps if 'J' really can be expanded to 'Jenkins' then Charlotte was in an eager flap – thinking of writing to the Jenkinses in Brussels herself if her father didn't do anything about it.

In January, Charlotte was back in Haworth having given up her job as a governess. Around 20 January she wrote to Ellen that her father had heard from 'Mr or rather Mrs Jenkins of the French Schools in Bruxelles – representing them as of an inferior caste in many respects' and that it looked like she and Emily were instead going to Lille in France.[45] Eliza had obviously done her research in December and January into schools that she had known little about before. Charlotte here reinforces my assumption that she and Mary had corresponded about schools in the autumn: 'Mary has been indefatigably kind in providing me with information – she has grudged no labour & scarcely any expenses to that end – Mary's price is above rubies.' But Charlotte was disappointed – Lille was not the promised land. However, the next surviving letter is written to stay-at-home Ellen from Brussels.

Mrs Gaskell fills in what happened, surely as told to her by Eliza: 'at length, after some discouragement in her search, [Eliza] heard of a school which seemed in every respect desirable. There was an English lady, who had long lived in the Orleans family, amidst the various fluctuations of their fortunes, and who, when the Princess Louise was married to King Leopold, accompanied her to Brussels, in the capacity of reader. This lady's granddaughter was receiving her education at the pensionnat of Madame Héger; and so satisfied was the grandmother with the kind of instruction given, that she named the establishment, with high encomiums, to Mrs. Jenkins; and, in consequence, it was decided that, if the terms suited, Miss Brontë and Emily should proceed thither.' Mrs Gaskell then states that Charlotte wrote to the school, and the agreement with Mme Heger was concluded.[46]

Apart from Eliza continuing to enquire about a school among her acquaintances and friends, the point is that she did not know it, hadn't before heard of it and didn't know the Hegers. She merely passed on the recommendation, Charlotte duly wrote, and Mme Heger replied. Not only is it stretching credibility that you would introduce people you had never met to other people you had never met, it is obvious to common sense that neither Evan nor Eliza took the Brontës to the Catholic school. Nor, thus, did they meet them at their hotel. Patrick took his daughters on his own to the school and then went, by himself, to the Jenkinses to stay one night, possibly with a letter of introduction from Evan's brother David, having received an invitation from the Jenkinses for him – and only him – to stay (there was maybe just the one guestroom in termtime). Mrs Gaskell presumably was told by Patrick himself, and by Eliza, that he stayed there one night – some biographers stretch this to more than one night and pile fabrication on fantasy.[47]

* * *

Further, the invention of either Evan or Eliza, or both, meeting the Brontës and taking them to the school is naïve and patronizing – as if a clergyman and his wife, who also ran a school, had such leisure time. The reader may remember

Evan's letter to the geologist Rev. William Branwhite Clarke in 1831 when Evan comments: 'I am, as usual, in the midst of bustle & confusion.'[48] Over ten years later he was no doubt even more stretched. In 1842 Evan was mentioned in yet another book, this time by his friend/acquaintance Rev. William Trollope – Clarke's brother-in-law, who seems to have killed off the final chance for Clarke to win his Sophia. In his book, *Belgium since the Revolution of 1830*, Trollope states:

> The chapel of the ancient palace [the Chapel Royal] is now appropriated to the service of English and German Protestants conjointly. It is a very elegant building; and our fellow-countrymen, under the zealous ministry and courteous attention of the Rev. E. Jenkins, chaplain to the embassy and to King Leopold, have all the religious advantages of their native land.

He tells us of the fate of William Drury's chapel of St George, around the corner, which Evan had been concerned about over ten years before: 'There was also another English Church in the Rue de l'Orangerie, at which the service was performed by the Rev. W. Drury; but, the lease having expired, that gentleman has removed his congregation to the French Methodist Chapel. Is this quite the thing?'[49] In Rev. Biber's first survey of the English Church in Europe of 1845, neither Evan nor William Drury had replied to his questionnaire (there were ninety-nine questions), so just their names were given for Brussels. But in his next edition in 1846, William Drury had found a bit of time (Evan had not, so just his name is given as the minister at the 'Chapelle Royale'). As Rev. Trollope had stated, Drury's services were now at 50 boulevard de l'Observatoire in the Leopold Quarter (a residential area created after the revolution, outside the site of the old walls, east of the park), with services on Sunday at 12.45 and 3.30. Drury claimed a congregation of between 150 and 200, with an average number of thirty receiving communion on the first Sunday of the month. Biber also relates that Drury had officiated at St George's Church for eleven years, 'but the lease having expired, and the revolution intervening, no renewal took place. The present Chapel is used also for the French service.' As the building was private property, Biber or Drury adds, 'tenure is precarious'. 'Sittings are rented by the residents, and visitors' contributions received at the door.'[50] I mention these details because, as I shall argue in my next chapter, Charlotte went to at least one of these services.

Rev. Trollope mentions in his book the English charitable fund, 'which, under the direction of Mr. Jenkins, assisted by a committee of subscribers, is so dispensed as to administer most efficiently to the relief of our necessitous fellow-countrymen, and more especially to supply them with the means of returning home. King Leopold is a willing contributor to this fund, and every Englishman passing through Brussels would do well to think of it.'[51] A contemporary guidebook to Brussels also mentions the charity: 'The fund is under the patronage of the King of the Belgians [...] The British Ambassador is at the head of this excellent charity; and the Rev. E. Jenkins, M.A., Chaplain to the King of the Belgians, is the Honorary Secretary: at his residence every information regarding this institution may be obtained [...] The Committee meet weekly.'[52]

Rev. Trollope later comments that marriages between British subjects could only be legally celebrated in the presence of the ambassador at Brussels 'and their performance is the exclusive privilege of the Rev. E. Jenkins, the chaplain to the embassy'. But that is not true, since William Drury was certainly also officiating, for example at the marriage of Lieutenant Richard Harvey and Carolina-Alithea Walker in the presence of the ambassador, Sir Hamilton Seymour, on 21 August 1842. Drury signed himself as 'Minister of an English Congregation in Brussels'; Evan is instead 'Chaplain to His Majesty King Leopold'.[53] In Drury's registers he had first signed himself as 'Minister of St George's Brussels', but after 10 May 1840 he is 'Officiating Minister', since he is in a new church, shared with Belgian Protestants.[54]

Also, Trollope is not correct about the presence of the ambassador, another British official could instead preside. I remarked above that it needed to be in the ambassador's house and thus that in Charlotte's first novel *The Professor* the marriage between William Crimsworth and Frances was invalid, since they married in 'the Protestant chapel'. Indeed, in his account of the English Church in Europe published in 1845, Rev. Biber remarks that

> by the Act 4 Geo. IV. c.91, there are only three cases in which the English law confers validity upon marriages (both parties being British subjects) solemnized abroad by a clergyman of the Established Church, according to the office of the Book of Common Prayer; viz., when the marriage is so solemnized, 1. in the chapel or house of the British ambassador residing within the country to the court of which he is accredited.

The other two places were in the chapel of a British factory (the trading station of a merchant company) and within the British lines of the army abroad.[55] He also states in his second edition: 'Marriages [in Brussels] between British subjects are solemnized at the house of the British Ambassador.'[56] Several marriages took place when Charlotte was in Brussels, and it seems unlikely that she was unaware that marriages did not take place in the chapel. Maybe it was an imaginative tincture of the past that she wanted to give to Crimsworth's wedding, as with him arriving in Brussels by the old-fashioned diligence.

Finally Rev. Trollope mentions Evan's school:

> Mr. Jenkin's [sic] establishment at Brussels has maintained a high reputation for many years, and the attention which is paid to the domestic comfort, as well as the moral and intellectual improvement of the pupils, is said to be unremitting.[57]

'Unremitting' – Evan certainly did not have time to take several hours off school to do any greeting and escorting. It is interestingly the only school that Rev. Trollope mentions. I hope that Evan and Eliza rewarded him with a good dinner. It is unlikely that Trollope made much money from his book on Belgium or his *Greek Grammar to the New Testament*, nor his various church livings and curacies. In 1849, the family (there were about eleven children) followed his wife Sarah's brother, William Branwhite Clarke, to Australia, but Trollope had difficulty in finding educational employment until 1852, when he started a grammar school in Tasmania, which seems to have failed. Eight years later, at the age of sixty-two, he was declared insolvent, dying a year later, in March 1863, of 'decay of nature'. Sarah had died in 1858 of consumption.[58]

* * *

Sometime towards the end of January or in early February 1842, Evan went to London, presumably with the main task of accompanying some of his schoolboys to Brussels for the new term. He visited or stayed with his brother- and sister-in-law, John Livingston Jay and Janet, in Greenwich, and there is an intriguing letter from Janet (Jenny) to her sister Margaret in Australia which mentions his stay, and which stunned me. It is a folded letter of four pages, crossed heavily. After attempting to read the scan, I was hugely relieved and grateful to receive from Australia a transcription. Dated 15 February 1842, Janet gives an account of their barrister brother Samuel's wedding on 18 January to Maria Spicer, 'daughter of the late Colonel Spicer, of the Mansion, Letherhead [sic; Surrey]'.[59] Eliza's younger brother Sam was now forty-one, nervous and 'so white', Janet relates; Maria was ten years younger and 'shaking all over'. She then adds:

> Jenkins came over lately with letters from Leopold to Victoria & P.A. [Prince
> Albert] – & has hopes of a Stall when one falls Vacant – He would be a lucky
> Man as it would make him rich & only require his presence (shame to say)
> a Month or so in the year – I trust he may succeed – He has the very first &
> best interest any man can possibly have

'Interest', of course, meaning connections. This is in stark contrast to her
lugubrious brother John's comment in a letter I mentioned above: 'I do not
think that Eliza's continued residence on the Continent, and the society she
there meets, have been of any advantage to her.'[60] I have suggested before
that Evan carried private letters between Leopold and his niece and nephew,
and here is the evidence. Leopold had written to Princess Victoria in May
1836 about using messengers of his own for confidential letters.[61] Possibly
every time Evan went to London to collect his pupils he was acting as a
courier for the King of the Belgians, and perhaps also for the ambassador.
On 29 January, Queen Victoria, who was then at Windsor Castle, remarks
in her journal that she had read 'a private letter of Sir H. Seymour's'. Perhaps
Leopold's letter that Evan carried was about Victoria and Albert's planned
visit to Belgium that spring, which had to be postponed to the following
year.[62]

The award of a stall in a cathedral would have been a tremendous prize for
the Jenkinses, even if it was mocked by Jane Austen and especially by Anthony
Trollope. In *Mansfield Park* (1814), Austen disposes of Mary Crawford's brother-
in-law Dr Grant thus:

> Dr. Grant, through an interest on which he had almost ceased to form
> hopes, succeeded to a stall in Westminster, which, as affording an occasion
> for leaving Mansfield, an excuse for residence in London, and an increase
> of income to answer the expenses of the change, was highly acceptable to
> those who went, and those who staid.

She deliciously relates his death 'by three great institutionary dinners in one
week'.[63]

The giving of stalls was often corrupt. In Trollope's *Framley Parsonage*
(1861), the ambitious and naïve young clergyman Mark Robarts gets entangled
with an unscrupulous Member of Parliament, Mr Sowerby, who seeks to entangle
Mark further with the offer of a stall:

'I have just heard that poor little Burslem, the Barsetshire prebendary, is dead. We must all die some day, you know, – as you have told your parishioners from the Framley pulpit more than once, no doubt. The stall must be filled up, and why should not you have it as well as another? It is six hundred a year and a house. Little Burslem had nine, but the good old times are gone [...] The stall will just suit you, – will give you no trouble, improve your position, and give some little assistance towards bed and board, and rack and manger.'[64]

Since Evan's 'interest' were the king of one country and his niece, the queen of another, it is a mystery why Evan didn't receive a stall. Was he perhaps teasing Janet? Or did no suitable stall become vacant before his early death?

In her February letter, Janet then mentions Evan's eldest daughter, now fourteen: 'Helen is taking a piano lesson daily from a first rate Master & will be quite a wonder I do believe – She comes here for her holiday I hope – Eliza is going to her smart parties.' I wonder if the music teacher was the same from whom Emily 'was about to learn the piano – to receive lessons from the best teacher we have in Belgium', as Constantin Heger wrote to Patrick Brontë after she and Charlotte had rushed home in November 1842 on hearing of Aunt Branwell's death. Perhaps Charlotte described the teacher in *Villette*: 'an artistic looking man, bearded, and with long hair, was a noted pianiste, and also the first music teacher in Villette; he attended twice a week at Madame Beck's pensionnat, to give lessons to the few pupils whose parents were rich enough to allow their daughters the privilege of his instructions'.[65]

I can thus make a neat segue to Charlotte Brontë's first surviving letter from Brussels, and to the school (not Mme Heger's) she wrote it from. The justification for my segue will soon become apparent. It is a mystery why it has taken well over a hundred years to make the identification that I shall reveal below.

* * *

Mary Taylor, about to turn twenty-five, had joined her younger sister at the 'Château de Koekelberg' on the day after arriving in Brussels in February 1842. The school was probably the model for the Brettons' continental home, La Terrasse, in *Villette*. It was not until 1972 that the location of this school was discovered – by an Oxford-educated academic teaching in New Zealand, Joan Stevens (1908– 90).[66] Professor Stevens – one of the first women in New Zealand to be awarded that title – had gained her first BA in English and French at the University of Otago in Dunedin, South Island, and continued to Somerville College, Oxford, graduating with first-class honours in English in 1932. In 1947, having returned to New Zealand, she became senior lecturer at Victoria University in Wellington, her special fields being Victorian and New Zealand literature. Charlotte's independently minded friend Mary Taylor had emigrated to New Zealand in 1845 (returning to Yorkshire fifteen years later) and Stevens was curious about Mary's unusual experience overseas 'as a middle-class spinster settler' who was 'articulate, lively, and shrewd'. Stevens soon realized that she couldn't just focus on Mary's letters about New Zealand, but needed the context of the Brontës and the tribal network of families in the West Riding of Yorkshire.[67] (The Taylors and Nusseys were related.) The entry for Stevens in the *Dictionary of New Zealand Biography* states that 'she challenged students to explore topics in thorough detail'. One is therefore confident that, 11,000 miles away in New Zealand, she would not fabricate, and, indeed, in the early 1970s, wanting to know exactly where Mary's school had been in Belgium, she requested two Belgian researchers to delve into the archives.[68] It is rather telling that no biographer had managed it before.

The place Koekelberg had been obvious – it was a commune less than two miles north-west of the centre of Brussels. But what of the school? Winifred Gérin got it totally wrong in her biography a few years earlier, even mentioning as 'fact' the wrong name for the headmistress as 'Miss Evans'.[69] We are in more trustworthy hands with Professor Stevens, even though she got two things wrong, as I shall relate below. First, Stevens identifies the headmistress as Madame Goussaert (the spelling varies), née Catherine Phelps. She was the wife of Norbert Goussaert, sometimes referred to as 'rentier' (that is, living off his own means, implying well off), and they had a son born in 1836 in Koekelberg who died twenty years later at his parents' house, 123 Chaussée de Jette; his mother was described as 'directrice de pensionnat' on the death certificate. By 1875, she was at no. 154 – this is on her husband's death certificate. This was no doubt because of street renumbering after the new boulevard Léopold II cut through the area. Stevens's researchers found a survey of about 1835 which showed that 'Goussart-Phelps' held land *in usufract* which seemed to be located at the junction of the new boulevard and the modern railway where they had a house and garden, the latter to be sliced through by the boulevard. A deed names this house as 'Château de Koekelberg'; it was demolished after 1888, but a painting was made of it by Henri Pauwels the year before. It is a fairly substantial mansion of three storeys and attic, perhaps with a basement, with five windows along the front façade of its uppermost storey, shaded by trees. Stevens states that the actual château had been demolished in 1820 and that 'Madame Goussaert probably chose the name as attractive to the international customers of her ladies' finishing school.'[70] Therein lies her first mistake, so often copied since. It was not a finishing school, as I will explain below, but Stevens was doing some admirable purging in her book and presenting new research. It is time to look at the joint letter of March to April 1842, written at the 'Château', by the Yorkshire trio of Charlotte Brontë and Mary and Martha Taylor to their friend Ellen Nussey marooned in the West Riding.

Mary Taylor starts off the letter on a wet Sunday, probably in March. She hasn't seen Charlotte since their arrival. Mary writes that she is frantically busy drawing, learning German and writing French compositions. It is too wet to go to church, presumably at the Chapel Royal, so she has finally found time to write.[71] She mentions a French girl, a Belgian girl, but 'more English & Germans than French girls'. Among the staff there is an English teacher named Miss Evans, a French music mistress whose husband is a 'broadshouldered man with a tremendous mouth', a drawing master who smells of bad tobacco, a 'french puppy' for a dancing master, a gymnastics master who 'makes strange noises in the back school room' and a Belgian who teaches 'Cosmosgraphy', whom the girls call 'ainsi donc' because of his constant repetition of the phrase, and 'Mr Globes', for obvious reasons. These are the usual subjects that middle- and upper-class parents would expect for their daughters. What is impossible to know is how many pupils there were. I hazard at around twenty to thirty at the most. Compare it to Thackeray's school in *Vanity Fair* on Chiswick Mall (with twenty-four young ladies) in the teens of the nineteenth century (written in the mid-1840s), attended by Miss Amelia Sedley and Becky Sharp, and young ladies' education can be seen as the same in England, at Miss Pinkerton's academy, as at Koekelberg, Belgium, at Mme Goussaert's, but the latter had the advantage of more language teaching (usually: the French teacher was supposed to arrive in December or January and still hadn't). Part of the letter from Thackeray's Miss Pinkerton, accompanying the final account to Amelia's father, reads:

> After her six years' residence at the Mall, I have the honour and happiness of presenting Miss Amelia Sedley to her parents [...] In music, in dancing, in orthography, in every variety of embroidery and needlework, she will be found to have realised her friends' fondest wishes. In geography there is still much to be desired.[72]

On Easter Saturday, 26 March, Charlotte had finally been able to visit her friends (with Emily) and added her bit to the letter: 'You will have heard that we have settled at Brussels instead of Lille – I think we have done well – we have got into a very good school – and are considerably comfortable – just now we are at Kokleberg spending the day with Mary & Martha Taylor – to us such a happy day – for one's blood requires a little warming – it gets cold with living amongst strangers.' Martha Taylor then added another bit on Monday 4 April. This is the part of the joint letter that no one had investigated before and gave me that frisson of 'only connect', so I will set out the beginning of it:

> I am going to add my bit to this to this [sic] newspaper which you are to have sometime but no one knows when. We have had holiday for the last ten days & I don't feel at all inclined to begin lessons again. I am tired of this everlasting German & long for the day after tomorrow when our new French Mistress will come & we shall continue our French – I have the cousin of the Mr Jenkins who took tea with my brother Joe at Brookroyd [Ellen Nussey's home] – sat by me, chattering like a magpie, & hoping it may be true that her cousin will come to Brussels before July. Mary is on the other side of me staring into a german dictionary, & looking as fierce as a tiger.

In her edition of the first volume of Charlotte Brontë's letters, Margaret Smith identifies the 'Mr Jenkins' as 'Probably the Revd Joseph Walker Jenkins, curate to the Revd Andrew Cassels at Batley, near Birstall', David Jenkins's eldest son and Evan's nephew, now in his mid-twenties. I certainly agree. But then there is a weird lacuna in the notes – there is no identification for the cousin of Joseph Jenkins. It is weird because so often when Smith cannot identify someone she notes 'untraced' or 'unidentified'. Another redoubtable scholar, Joan Stevens, has a stab at identification in her book, in a note to a later letter of 30 December 1843, that this 'chattering magpie' is 'Louisa Bright, possibly the cousin of Mr Jenkins mentioned in Letter 2' (the joint letter).[73] It is as if a mist descends over writers as soon as the name Jenkins is mentioned. It is bizarre, because Stevens had surely read Mrs Gaskell's biography of Charlotte. Did it not strike her that the Yorkshire Jenkins might have a cousin in Brussels, called, er, Jenkins?

The Brights were not related to the Jenkinses, nor, may I add – to correct some of what I have read – were the Yorkshire tribe of Nusseys, Taylors or Dixons (unless through David Jenkins's first wife Harriet Walker, which doesn't concern the Jenkinses in Brussels). The Bright family were friends of the Jenkinses, and more will be said on them in a later chapter, and perhaps it was in one respect an unfortunate friendship. But Joseph's cousin, at this supposed 'finishing school', was the fourteen-year-old Helen, Evan and Eliza's eldest daughter. I hope that my segue from the mention of Helen as a 'wonder' to narrate the joint Brontë–Taylor 'newspaper', finished while she was present, will now be understood.

Many writers copy Stevens and describe Mme Goussaert's pensionnat wrongly as a 'finishing school', with its connotation of young ladies learning how to get decorously out of a sports car and prepare for entry into society and marriage; of course that is what these girls were mainly educated for, but the term is totally misleading. The 'Château' was no more a 'finishing school' because it happened to have two women in their twenties as pupils than was Mme Heger's school. Like Miss Pinkerton's academy, it was a school for aspirant bourgeois girls (and aristocrats, when one could get hold of them) of all ages, perhaps from the age of twelve. There is a rather woeful letter from a young lady to her father, not happy that, at nineteen, she is far too old for the school. The letter was written, eleven years after the Taylor–Brontë joint letter, by Theresa Rouse-Boughton, one of the daughters of the widower Sir William, tenth baronet, who resided at Downton Hall near Ludlow in Shropshire. His father, the ninth baronet, had worked for the East India Company, learning Persian in Bengal and aligning himself against Governor-General Warren Hastings. On his return to England he became an MP and married the heiress to the resplendent Downton Hall (the school at Koekelberg might have fitted into a third of it).[74] The ninth baronet is also known as the owner of a remarkable pig – there is a hand-coloured aquatint of 1795 at the Museum of Rural Life in Reading entitled 'A Shropshire Pig'.[75] It looks a splendid beast.

On 13 June 1853, Theresa thanks her father 'for all the excellent advantages you have allowed me during the last ten months [at the school] and I hope when we meet you will be satisfied with the improvement I hope and think I have made in my different studies.' But, she continues:

At the same time I really hope it will not be long before I leave Koekelberg for when you kindly gave me my choice of travelling with you or coming to school I never for one moment imagined you intended me remaining here more than three or four months at longest, for if I had since thought I should have remained here nearly a year I could never have refused travelling with you and coming to school – at my age – in preference. You must not forget that I am now nearly twenty and I assure the remarks the girls have made on my being at school at such an age are far from agreeable – the eldest girls here with the exception of one are but seventeen.[76]

The school would hardly have changed from the Taylors' time – girls of the advanced age of nineteen plus would have been in the minority, while fourteen-year-old Helen Jenkins was one of the normal intake.

The *directrice*/headmistress, Mme Goussaert née Catherine Phelps, was a sister of extraordinary, totally disparate brothers, and was a remarkable woman herself. Apart from Stevens's short account of her, no one has been inclined to research her, but she is relevant to my book and a woman who should be further investigated. I believe that she must have been, of long standing, a friend of the Jenkins and Jay families. My discoveries involve bankruptcy, an influential actor and theatre manager whose performance in *King John* was admired by Queen Victoria, a Vice Chancellor of Cambridge University who was 'a capital hand at frying an omlet', and the Liberator of Argentina, Chile and Peru, the *hombre necesario* of the South American Revolution.

* * *

A drama critic in Leipzig describes Samuel Phelps as King Lear in 1859:

> In the fourth act, the artist reached such effects as only a genius can, chiefly in the scene where his hampered senses return and he recognizes Cordelia. Such moments leave every other portrayal far behind. They belong to the rarest delights which the theatre offers.[77]

The review reminded me vividly of the most memorable Lear I have seen – Donald Sinden for the RSC in 1977 (I can still see him in my mind on the Aldwych stage). Sinden (d. 2014) was a versatile actor in the mould of Phelps, superb at comedic roles as well as tragedy, and both were born near Plymouth in Devon. Samuel Phelps had taken his Sadler's Wells company on a short and not very successful tour of Germany, but his ensemble direction, lack of a prompter and intelligent, psychologically truthful acting were welcomed, and his eighteen-season tenure as manager and actor at Sadler's Wells (1844–62), in an unfashionable part of London, was significant for his productions of most of Shakespeare's plays, deleted of customary excrescences such as singing, dancing witches in *Macbeth*. Born in 1804, he was Catherine Phelps's younger brother. Their youngest brother, Rev. Robert, wrote *An Elementary Treatise on Optics* and became Vice Chancellor of Cambridge University in 1844.

I started by looking at Catherine Goussaert née Phelps's death certificate. It states that she died in her home, on boulevard Léopold II in the commune of Koekelberg, at the age of eighty-nine years, eight months and twenty-five days on

12 August 1884, which gives her birth as November 1794. But I discovered that this was a year out. The person who sent an illiterate labourer and a carpenter to register her death gave them the necessary details that Catherine was born in Stoke Damerel ('Stoke Darmerel, Angleterre') and her parents were Robert Phelps and Ann Turner ('Anne Tuerner'). The register for the parish of Stoke Damerel in Devon, however, notes Catherine's baptism on 22 October 1794 and her birth on 17 November 1793. When Mary and Martha Taylor attended her school, Catherine was in her late forties. What is surprising is that in an advertisement for the school after her retirement, it says that 'this institution was founded in 1815 by Mme Widow Goussaert, née Phelps'.[78] Catherine therefore founded the school when she was about twenty-two. A woman could certainly 'found' a school at that age with a handful of pupils (it surely wasn't at the 'Chateau'), but what was she doing in Brussels at that young age, with a sufficient education but obviously in need of earnings?

After Catherine's birth in Devon, three brothers were born – including future actor Samuel and Cambridge wrangler Robert – and three sisters. Their mother Ann died in 1806, a few months after the birth of Robert, and their father married again. There must have been a serious lack of money in the family for Catherine to turn to teaching and Samuel to the not respectable profession of acting, and Robert entered Cambridge in 1828 as a sizar. Yet the recently revised *ODNB* article on Samuel Phelps refers to their 'affluent father [...] supplier of naval uniforms [who] occupied a significant social position in the town'. It also says, without comment, that Samuel was in London in 1813–14, when he was nine, presumably staying with relatives.[79] Yet knowing that their father's full name was Robert Melliar (or Meliar) Phelps, I quickly found him in the British Newspaper Archive as made bankrupt in 1813. He is described that March as a draper of Plymouth-dock (now Devonport).[80] Although he received his bankrupt's certificate eighteen months later, allowing him to recommence his trading operations, his estate had been surrendered to satisfy creditors, and his social position was crushed. It seems he turned to auctioneering.[81]

Catherine was nineteen when her father was made bankrupt, and her privileged life came to an abrupt end. I was curious as to what had been written about her actor brother's childhood in two books, both published in 1886, eight years after Samuel Phelps's death. One was a 'Memoir' written by an actor friend; the other a 'Life', co-written by a nephew and a theatre critic. The latter starts by saying that Samuel 'inherited the instincts of a gentleman, and throughout the whole of his career he never forgot that he was one' and that he was 'of good family, and, though not what is called college-bred, of good education'.[82] It was obviously very important for his nephew to state that, since actors were still regarded as rather dodgy. It wasn't until Henry Irving's knighthood in 1895 that (some) actors began to be regarded as respectable. Samuel Phelps's main rival, and sometime employer, William Charles Macready (eleven years older than Phelps), had been sent to Rugby School in order to educate him for the Bar or the Church, since his father's profession as actor and theatre manager was not seen as one to emulate. However, the elder Macready ran out of money and the reluctant Macready junior was forced to tread the boards, and longed to give acting a better status.[83]

Phelps's nephew says nothing about the actor's childhood, preferring to emphasize one uncle who was the second husband of the Countess of Antrim and friend of the Duke of Wellington, and his paternal grandfather who was a glove and stocking manufacturer 'on an extensive scale' and lived in the 'Great House' in Pilton, Somerset. He does, however, mention Phelps's father, who in 1804 'kept the principal warehouse in the three towns of Plymouth, Devonport, and Stonehouse for supplying naval officers with their outfits, and was on terms of intimacy with Sir Sidney Smith and other commanders of distinction in the Navy of that period'. I take these intimate friends with a pinch of salt. There is no mention of the death of Phelps's mother when he was two, nor the arrival of a stepmother, but the nephew does mention the death of his father in 1820 when Phelps was sixteen. Phelps went to live with his elder brother, whom I haven't mentioned so far, Peter Turner Phelps, the father of the writer, whom he describes as 'a wine and spirit merchant'. Samuel Phelps was apprenticed by his brother to a printer in Plymouth but crept out of the house to do amateur acting having caught the bug on his visits to London theatres. It is at this point that his nephew mentions, for the only time, Phelps's sisters: 'His sisters, had they known it [about the acting], would, no doubt, have raised objections to his having anything to do with the theatre; but not so his brother.'[84] Is he hammering home that theirs was a respectable, genteel family or was he aware that his aunts really had not approved? Quite possibly both, in that giving up his apprenticeship at seventeen to follow his dream of acting was precarious at best. But that is ironic, since the writer's father, in his more stable profession of 'schoolmaster', was discharged from being an insolvent debtor in 1828, and later made bankrupt as a 'grocer' in 1837.[85] It also seems to be a somewhat dysfunctional family, since the nephew writes that 'His brother heard nothing of him again, after his first arrival [in London], for nearly sixteen years.'[86]

I turned to the *Memoirs* written by Samuel Phelps's friend John Coleman to see if there was any mention of his childhood or of his sister Catherine. The answer is no, except for one remark that is telling: 'On the subject of his early life he was very reticent, merely stating that he was born in 1804, at Plymouth Dock, as Devonport was then called. His father was a prosperous wine merchant, whose sons received their education at Doctor Reed's classical school at Saltash [just over the border in Cornwall].' Wine merchant! Was this Samuel Phelps's fantasy – he would hardly own up to having a bankrupt draper as a father – or a muddle by his younger friend? The author then mentions the Cambridge brother who 'distinguished himself as a mathematician' who 'is still I believe, master of Sidney Sussex College, Cambridge'.[87] Prince Albert met Rev. Robert Phelps, when he was Vice Chancellor, in 1847 (this was his second stint in the post). Victoria wrote in her journal: 'Albert saw Dr Phelps for some time, & was much pleased to find him so very enlightened & intelligent.' A few years later she commented on Samuel Phelps as Hubert in *King John* (Hubert has been despatched to kill the young heir/rival to John's throne): 'Mr Phelps excellent as Hubert de Burgh [...] The scene between Arthur & Hubert, was heartrending.' Though she was damning eight years later: 'The performance of Macbeth, perfectly atrocious, Phelps & Miss Helen Faucit indescribably bad & slow.'[88] Hopefully that didn't erase her memory of his Hubert: his nephew quotes in his book the *Times* review of Phelps in *King John* in 1842: 'the heavings of the heart while he strove to be stern to the innocent child showed the increasing struggle which was going on, till at last all resolved itself into the burst of tears at the words, "I will not touch thine eyes."' I'd be sobbing with the rest of the audience at this point. The nephew adds that 'by command of the Queen he afterwards sat to Sir William Ross for his portrait as Hubert', but unfortunately there is no record of such a miniature in the Royal Archives.[89] A bronze plaque was erected in 1911 outside his home at 8 Canonbury Square, Islington, near Sadler's Wells.

Curiously Queen Victoria doesn't seem to have made a connection between the Phelps of Cambridge and the actor Phelps. Did the Cambridge luminary keep it quiet? His skill at frying omelettes is a noteworthy addition to his listing in *Alumni Cantabrigienses*, which is otherwise not favourable: 'Notorious for his conservatism and belief in the old University customs and regulations.'[90] Perhaps he did indeed keep his close relationship with an acting brother quiet. Did Catherine? The English Heritage website on 'blue plaques' comments that his daughter was barred from admission to a private school because of his profession.

A picture is thus painted of a group of intelligent, independent siblings, who lost their mother when the eldest, Catherine, was thirteen, and had to endure a stepmother, followed by their father losing his money and social position to bankruptcy. They are reminiscent of the Jay siblings. What could Catherine do at nineteen? The options would be teaching in a school or as a governess, or becoming a companion. The reader who knows Charlotte Brontë's *Villette* might here think of the fate of Lucy Snowe, who finds a job after bereavement in her family (we don't know who has died, but she is now on her own) as a carer-companion for Miss Marchmont.

In April 1814, a year after Phelps's bankruptcy, Napoleon abdicated and the Continent was open again. Did Catherine go to Brussels that year as a companion or governess and stay on to teach? Or did she do as 22-year-old Lucy Snowe did after the sudden death of Miss Marchmont: just get on a boat with nowhere definite in mind and find herself first as a governess in a Belgian family and then as a schoolteacher? And could Charlotte Brontë have heard her story? She surely met her when she and Emily spent a day at the school. On 22 October 1828, in the country that was not yet Belgium, Catherine married Norbert Goussaert 'of Brussels'; both were in their mid-thirties – and they were married by Rev. Evan Jenkins, who perhaps knew Catherine and her story well. Catherine is described as 'of Berchem St. Agate, near Brussels' (Sint-Agatha-Berchem). It is now a separate commune/municipality neighbouring Koekelberg, a few miles north-west of Brussels, but before 1842 Sint-Agatha-Berchem included the former hamlet of Koekelberg. It seems to me unlikely that at the time of her marriage she was running her school in the substantial 'Château de Koekelberg'; probably the couple acquired the house and vast garden after their marriage. An advertisement for the school in 1877 also describes its ravishing view.[91] Norbert was well-off: on their civil marriage certificate in the Belgian Archives she is merely a 'teacher', his occupation is 'particulier' ('private') and his newly widowed mother is a rentier (living off her own means).[92] What is curious is that her wrong date of birth is given again here – 17 November 1794 instead of 1793. Did Catherine really not know her actual year of birth, or had she made herself younger for some reason? But her marriage in October 1828 is not the only account of her in Brussels that year; what I found is intriguing, and involves a foray into Napoleonic Spain and South America and an encounter with one of the great men of the nineteenth century – General José de San Martín (1778–1850).

* * *

In Brussels there is a plaque to the South American Liberator General San Martín on a modern building at the corner of rue du Pont Neuf and rue de la Fiancée, where he lived in the 1820s and early 1830s, a couple of minutes' walk from modern-day Waterstones. There is also an equestrian statue of him at the intersection of the avenue de Tervueren and boulevard de la Woluwe, east of the city, since he had first lived in a country house in the commune of Woluwe-Saint-Pierre. The statue is a copy of the one in Buenos Aires.[93] The Liberator had obscure beginnings in an outpost of the Spanish Empire. In a village in Argentina, Yapeyú, on the west bank of the river Uruguay, the youngest son of a Spanish military administrator was born in February 1778.[94] The family moved back to Spain when José de San Martín was six, but the distinction between 'creoles' (Spaniards born in America) and *peninsulares* (the Spanish elite who had been born in Spain) was significant, not only for the grievances felt by the former, but for the later loyalty and career of San Martín. Because of his dark skin there were rumours that his mother was an Indian, but there is no proof. The only employment available for the sons of a mere captain on half-pay was the military, but with no prospect of promotion if you lacked noble blood. San Martín's education in Málaga was rudimentary, yet this is the man who, in his first weeks as Protector of Peru in 1821, was to found a National Library and donate to it six hundred of his own books.[95] He fought in the Peninsular War alongside the British, which for Spain was their War of Independence after Napoleon's invasion. The war can be bracketed by the visceral painting by Goya of the 1808 uprising in Madrid against the French invasion: he focuses on a man in a white shirt, lit by a spotlight, his arms upstretched, aimed at by the rifles of the French.[96] Four years later there is an image in words of the future Duke of Wellington before the Battle of Salamanca: 'watching the French through his telescope, he pounced on the tactical mistake of his opponents marching across his front in an overstretched line, threw his half-finished chicken leg over his shoulder, and shouting "By God, that will do!" leaped on his horse, and rode off to inspire a legendary victory on 22 July 1812, "Wellington's masterpiece".'[97] At the end of Charlotte Brontë's *Shirley* the double wedding of her protagonists takes place shortly after: 'It is August. The bells clash out again, not only through Yorkshire, but through England. From Spain the voice of a trumpet has sounded long; it now waxes louder and louder; it proclaims Salamanca won.'[98]

At the beginning of that year, San Martín returned to the country of his birth with a vision of independence from Spanish rule across South America. His leadership of the army he raised to cross the Andes and take Chile for the patriots in 1817 and his subsequent non-violent seizure of Lima in Peru are legendary. But he had many detractors, and lacked a power base. At the private meeting between him and the aristocratic, younger Simón Bolívar at Guayaquil (now in Ecuador) in July 1822, it seems that San Martín accepted that only Bolívar's forces could finally defeat the Spanish in Peru, and that Bolívar would not do it as a co-liberator. San Martín, knowing how inadequate his own army was, stepped down, leaving the final liberation of Peru to Bolívar, and went to Europe with his young daughter, Mercedes.

San Martín had barely seen his young wife, whom he had left in Buenos Aires, and who had died, nor his daughter, who was now seven. He sent her to a school in Hampstead, North London, while he moved first, in 1824, to a country house near Brussels. He took one trip back to Argentina in November 1828, and this is when it may be that Mercedes moved to a school near Brussels, at the age of twelve. In his English friend General William Miller's memoirs he gives us a passing mention of someone I am sure must be our Catherine Phelps: 'In November, 1828, he once more visited England, having left his daughter at Brussels under the care of Miss Phelps, a highly respectable English lady resident at that place.'[99]

In the biography of San Martín by the late John Lynch, he says something odd: 'Once he had left public life, though he was concerned to obtain a Catholic education for his daughter in exile and he never completely abandoned the practice of religion, his religiosity was not obvious.'[100] This is unsubstantiated: we do not know if the Hampstead school was Catholic, nor if Miss Phelps (married by an Anglican clergyman) became a Catholic. Although in 1828 Brussels was in the Dutch Protestant Kingdom of the Netherlands, there were certainly respectable Catholic schools for girls, but San Martín chose an English woman to oversee his daughter's education. In his 'Rules for my daughter', written three years earlier, he emphasized love of truth, respect for others and toleration for all religions.[101] Perhaps in his interview with Miss Phelps, he found that she endorsed these qualities in her character and her teaching. Interestingly, in Peru, he had valued the educational value of theatre and wanted to remove prejudice from the acting profession.[102] But he could hardly have known, at that stage, of her brother, still acting in the provinces. What did Miss Phelps see as the exiled Liberator, just turned fifty, enquired about his daughter's education at her school? 'He is a tall, erect, well proportioned, handsome man, with a large aquiline nose, thick black hair, and immense bushy dark whiskers extending from ear to ear under the chin; his complexion is deep olive, and his eyes, which are large, prominent, and piercing, are jet black; his whole appearance being highly military. He is thoroughly well bred and unaffectedly simple in his manners; exceedingly cordial and engaging and possessed evidently of great kindliness of disposition: in short, I have never seen any person the enchantment of whose address was more irresistible.'[103] These are not her words, but I would have given him a discount on the spot. In 1828 a portrait was painted of him by the Belgian artist François-Joseph Navez, which shows an immensely dignified man, with such dark, intelligent eyes.[104] Brussels society must have scrambled to meet him: it is likely that the Jenkinses did.

Shortly after the start of the Belgian Revolution, San Martín escaped the turmoil with his daughter and moved to Paris, where, at sixteen, she married an Argentinian. San Martín subsequently moved to Boulogne, where he died aged seventy-two, surrounded by his daughter and granddaughters. His remains were later taken to Buenos Aires and placed in a magnificent tomb that he might not have relished, but to a country and a continent that he had fought so hard for. Curiously, as Protector of Peru, he had searched for a European prince to install as monarch and had considered Leopold of Saxe-Coburg as a likely candidate.[105] I wonder if San Martín felt vindicated as he saw the astute Leopold gradually taking control of the new country of the Belgians, but perhaps he also felt wryly that all that was needed – what he had needed in Peru – was the help of a great power that could supply arms and an adequate army.

* * *

I must leave an honourable man who loved truth to turn to the lame, lazy and shocking fabrication of the 'escorting story' involving 'John and Edward' in 1842, and Gérin's invention of Eliza talking to the supposed Infant Prodigy Mrs Chadwick, as I described in my first chapter. In 2015 I looked at the latest biography of Charlotte Brontë to see if the writer had read my article on the Brussels Brontë Group website which had demolished the anecdote – alas, no, she had copied the old, old story. As I mentioned, the muddled account about the youngest Jenkins boy, seven-year-old John, being on escort duty with women in their twenties was frankly stupid, so it was with no confidence that I turned to whatever the latest biographer had put as a source, if any. I was taken aback; there was something new but it was obvious that she didn't know what she had found. Her sentence 'The Jenkins' sons, John and Edward, never looked forward to escorting the Brontës home, as the walks would inevitably be conducted in a garroted silence' was glossed in her notes as: 'one of the Jenkins's sons described the task of walking CB home as "a purgatorial process [...] from her invincible tactiturnity [sic]", Thomas Westwood to Lady Alwyne Compton, 21 November 1869, *A Literary Friendship: Letters to Lady Alwyne Compton 1869–1881, from Thomas Westwood*, 3.'[106] I wondered where she had got this source from; it thrummed a low chord in my memory of a book I had looked through at the beginning of my research, by Eric Ruijssenaars, which I had bought from him in a restaurant in Brussels, after his talk to the Brussels Brontë Group. In a section on 'The Heger Family', in his *The Pensionnat Revisited*, he notes that 'In the D'Arcy Thompson collection in St. Andrews the text was found of an article on Constantin Heger, originally published in the *Bradford Observer* of 20 November 1914', which he reprints:

> Mr. Thomas Westwood, died in 1888, was secretary [...] of an Anglo-Belgian railway company. He wrote a volume of two hundred pages of letters to Lady Alwyne Compton. Writing in 1869, he says: – [...] 'I came to Brussels twenty years ago, with an appointment that I believed would be of the briefest, and it holds me still [...] But perhaps you will be passing through Brussels? If so, I trust you will allow me to do the honours – the honours of *Villette*, if you please, for I can show you Currer Bell's [Charlotte Brontë's] house, and perhaps, if chance befriend us, M. Paul Emanuel and Madame Beck too.'

After relating that M. Paul (Constantin Heger) was now grey-headed and Madame Beck (Mme Heger) had retired, Westwood calmly flung his bolt of lightning at me:

> 'Our English chaplain here remembers Charlotte Brontë perfectly. She came over with an introduction to his parents, and his province, as a lad, was to escort her back to school, after evenings spent at their house. A purgatorial process, he declares it was, from her invincible taciturnity. He remembers her, too, in the family circle, screwing her chair round by degrees, till her face was to the wall and her back to everybody, as I think Mrs. Gaskell relates.'[107]

Here was finally an authentic memory – by Rev. Edward Jenkins, the chaplain at the Chapel Royal (1856–73), talking to Thomas Westwood about thirty years after the Brontës' stay. Biographers have been so addicted to Mrs Chadwick's garbled hearsay and Gérin's unethical embroidering about the *two* Jenkins sons (always in the wrong age order) and the concoction of the Jenkinses meeting the Brontës at their hotel, and subsequently introducing strangers to other strangers, that they have been blind to Westwood's comment about a letter of introduction and just the *one* escorting son. Ruijssenaars's notes are muddled, but he refers to Juliet Barker's *The Brontës* in which she quotes a few lines from Westwood's letter about Heger. I found the quote and her note – I was indeed on a trail from note to note. Barker gives as the source: 'Mr Westwood to unidentified, 21 Nov 1869–21

Feb 1870: MS 52,298 pp. 3–4, Brown [University].'[108] A rather strange date span for a quote just four lines long, and, as Ruijssenaars states, Barker's quote was not taken from the published book of Westwood's letters but from a manuscript of some kind. To sort this out I first called up the book of Westwood's letters, published in 1914 (hence the newspaper review of the book quoted above), at the British Library before contacting Brown University.[109]

In her Preface, Lady Alwyne Compton, widow of the Bishop of Ely, says that she started corresponding with Thomas Westwood 'about forty years ago' when he was living in Boitsfort near Brussels. She kept the letters in a box until they were seen by her friend Miss Soulsby, who urged their publication. This was Lucy Soulsby, headmistress of the Oxford High School for Girls between 1887 and 1897, who believed that girls should only be educated to become fine wives and mothers, while remaining single herself.[110] In the book of the published letters, Westwood's Belgian widow Rosa writes an introduction about her husband, who had died in 1888. He had come to Brussels in the mid-1840s when he was thirty. As a child he had known Charles Lamb, who was a neighbour, and was encouraged to read the books in Lamb's library and hid under the table listening to Lamb's famous guests, which included Wordsworth. Westwood was long a correspondent of Elizabeth Barrett Browning (letters are in the British Library), and he was sent a portfolio of photographs by Julia Cameron, which he exhibited in Brussels. What Rosa doesn't mention is that her husband was a published poet.[111]

In the published book, the first letter to Lady Alwyne Compton from Thomas Westwood is dated 21 November 1869, in which he offers to do 'the honours of *Villette*' if she comes to Brussels, and in the next paragraph mentions 'our English chaplain', as quoted above. Juliet Barker's quote about Constantin Heger's 'practise with all his wife's most intellectual pupils' is in a later, separate letter of 21 February 1870.[112] Barker's three-month date span, implying a single letter, was therefore inaccurate. I emailed the repository mentioned in her note – Brown University Library, Providence, RI – requesting a digital image of the 1869 letter, the one I was eager to see because of its mention of the chaplain.[113] I wanted to check it against the published letter. What I was sent was peculiar. There were four pages. The first page is headed 'Letter from Mr. Westwood from Brussels. – Nov. 21. 1869' and starts: 'If you are passing through Brussels' and ends on page 2 with 'Madame Beck with wrath'. Page 3 starts with the date 'Feb. 21. 1870' and starts with 'You were interested in the scanty details I gave you of Charlotte Brontë' and ends on page 4 with 'a witty & warm-hearted man'. The handwriting seems to be the same throughout (the word 'Brussels' in the heading and in the body of the text is almost identical). The first two handwritten pages, dated November 1869, contain just half of the published letter – the bits about Charlotte Brontë, the Hegers and the chaplain. The last two handwritten pages, dated February 1870, also contain just an extract from that published letter, again just the bits about Charlotte and Heger.

There are occasional differences between the handwritten copy and the published letters, such as 'You were interested in the scanty details' in the copy; whereas in the published letter it is 'M.B. told me you "were interested" in the scanty details'. In the handwritten copy there is a curious deletion: 'She came over a poor, friendless, reserved, ~~backward~~ \taciturn/ girl'; in the book: 'She came over, a poor, friendless, reserved, taciturn girl'. This is a fascinating crossed-out word that Sherlock Holmes might enjoy: if Westwood is the writer of the copy, was 'backward' a more authentic memory of what Edward had said, which Westwood changed to what he felt was a more anodyne adjective? 'Backward' often then meant 'shy', not intellectually backward, and could be Edward's joking pun as he remembered as a teenager seeing Charlotte turn her back gradually on the person she was speaking to. There will be more on Edward in my next chapter. Westwood's anecdote also suggests that Edward had read Mrs Gaskell's biography; it is probable that the Jenkins family owned a copy.

At first glance I had thought that the handwritten copy in the John Hay Library at Brown University had been made by someone other than the letter-writer, Westwood. I guessed it might be someone copying out extracts from the published book post-1914 and worthless. But in reply to my puzzled query, Tim Engels, Senior Library Specialist at the Brown University Library, said that although he had no details about its provenance, the watermark might be 1873 or 1878.[114] If so, surely it could only have been copied from the original letter sent to Lady Alwyne Compton: so the handwritten copy was possibly written by her or by Westwood – and sent to someone who had learnt of his letters and was maybe writing a book on the Brontës. It is a mystery, but what might be additional evidence for the copy being written before the end of the nineteenth century is the use of the 'long s' as the first letter in a double 's'. I was invited to check the original, but 3,000 miles is a long way to go to check a watermark. However, Juliet Barker's odd note giving a long date span for that one quote is now resolved: in the archives the extracts from the two letters are catalogued together as by Thomas Westwood as author, under the heading 'Letter, 1869, November 21, Brussels, Belgium', and pages 3 and 4 from the February letter could be misunderstood as Westwood's continuation of his letter three months later.

It was a rather tortuous journey, but I had my golden nugget: the Jenkinses' eldest son Edward was the escorter of the Brontë sisters from the age of fifteen, and he had indeed found it 'a purgatorial process' (admittedly there is no mention of Emily in Westwood's account but *Wuthering Heights* had been forgotten). But teenage Edward didn't have to politely endure the taciturn sisters often, as he went to boarding school in England that same year. I wondered why Thomas Westwood didn't draw more out of him about the Brontës, but in the next chapter I will suggest a solution. However, I now had my likely candidate, Thomas Westwood, for passing on the escorting story – the original one, and one that was later muddled, expanded and embroidered – especially with wretched, fanciful dialogue. In a later letter of 1879, Westwood mentions Edward's youngest brother John and one of his sermons, but I will come to that towards the end of my book. Westwood is not complimentary, but he must have sat through hundreds of sermons given by the Jenkins father and sons.

In October 1842, eight months after their arrival in Brussels, two deaths deeply affected Charlotte and Emily Brontë, and a bizarre fabrication confronted me.

* * *

In preparing my last section in this chapter, I was amused to read Eric Ruijssenaars's denunciation of Winifred Gérin as a 'serial liar'.[115] It was good to feel that I wasn't on my own toiling away at some of the irresponsible nonsense she had made up in the 1960s, and relieved to find another 'purger'. I might less dramatically say that Gérin's ego was bigger than her honesty and intelligence. Ruijssenaars and I are both referring to the death of 'bright, dancing, laughing' Martha Taylor, the young woman who had contributed to the 'newspaper' sent to Ellen Nussey, and who, herself a vivacious chatterer, had described fourteen-year-old Helen Jenkins chattering like a magpie.[116] Ruijssenaars writes about what Martha died of; I write here about Gérin's concoction about her funeral in October 1842. I will add, though, that Mrs Gaskell says that Martha's death was sudden: 'in a few days she died', which she might have heard from Martha's sister Mary, and that sounds more likely than Charlotte not hearing about her illness for a fortnight, as so often mentioned. Charlotte's ambiguous phrase in a letter to Ellen on 10 November, quoted below, could suggest that Martha was ill a fortnight, but might actually only apply to Aunt Branwell.[117]

Martha's elder sister Mary wrote to Ellen just over two weeks after her sister's death at the Château de Koekelberg: 'You will have heard by this time the end of poor Martha', but Mary cannot yet put her illness into words:

> A thousand times I have reviewed the minutest circumstances of it but
> I cannot without great difficulty give a regular account of them – There is
> nothing to regret, nothing to recall – not even Martha – She is better where
> she is – But when I recall the sufferings that have purified her my heart
> aches.[118]

Mary was now staying with her cousins the Dixons in the centre of Brussels. At
the end of her letter she asks Ellen to remember her to various people, who seem to
be close friends, such as their previous headmistress Miss Wooler, and including
the Heads – the Anglican Vicar of Birstall and his sister. This is significant for
the falsehood peddled by Gérin, quoted below. On 10 November, about a week
later, Charlotte wrote to Ellen from Haworth, because, having heard of the death
of Aunt Branwell, she and Emily had rushed home:

> Martha Taylor's illness was unknown to me till the day before she died –
> I hastened to Kokleberg the next morning – unconscious that she was in
> great danger – and was told that it was finished, she had died in the night
> […] Mr Weightman's illness was exactly what Martha's was – he was ill the
> same length of time & died in the same manner – Aunts disease was internal
> obstruction. she also was ill a fortnight[119]

Mr Weightman was her father's wonderful, flirtatious curate in Haworth. Charlotte
describes how Mary had nursed her sister, and they had been to Martha's grave.
There is no mention of the funeral, probably because women seldom went to
them and because there was nothing unusual about who officiated. Ruijssenaars's
quarrel with Gérin is because the latter states, baldly, that Martha died of cholera,
as usual with no evidence at all: there were no cases of cholera then in Brussels
and none in the rest of the school. He plausibly suggests instead that Martha
died of appendicitis. My quarrel is with Gérin's next paragraph, which starts: 'As
dissenters the Taylors did not seek burial for her by a clergyman of the Established
Church. Applying to the Belgian Protestant community, her funeral service was
conducted by a Protestant Pastor of the Reformed Church – Chrétien-Henri Vent
– at the Chapel Royal on 14 October.'[120] What is her source for this clergyman?
The reader might cynically suggest a spread of chapters in Mrs Chadwick's book.
No, there is *no* source at all. And there is no evidence that Martha and Mary
were 'dissenters' from the established church. Gérin was perhaps confused by Mrs
Gaskell quoting from Mary Taylor's letter to her in 1856, in which Mary says that

Charlotte, 'a Tory and clergyman's daughter, was always in a minority of one in our house of violent Dissent and Radicalism'.[121] Their father has been described as a Methodist and their mother as a cold Calvinist, and perhaps when they were children they went to chapel.[122] However, there is contradictory evidence: one needs to tread carefully and judiciously to find facts about real people in fiction, especially with a writer as imaginative as Charlotte Brontë. In *Shirley*, the Yorke family are certainly based on the Taylors. The child Jessy – based on Martha Taylor – regales Caroline Helstone with her father's views against the established church, but it is made abundantly clear that the family attend the Anglican church:

> father and mother, while disclaiming community with the Establishment, failed not duly, once on the sacred day, to fill their large pew in Briarfield Church with the whole of their blooming family. Theoretically, Mr Yorke placed all sects and churches on a level. Mrs Yorke awarded the palm to Moravians and Quakers, on account of that crown of humility by these worthies worn. Neither of them were ever known, however, to set foot in a conventicle.[123]

In her surviving letters, after she had read the novel, Mary Taylor nowhere comments on Charlotte turning her family in *Shirley* into Anglican church-goers instead of chapel-goers.[124]

So I will examine this incongruous suggestion that it was a Belgian clergyman, speaking in French – a language which Martha was then 'cracking' her head with at school – instead of an English clergyman officiating at the funeral of an English girl.[125] And what is this curious plural 'Taylors'? As far as we know, Mary Taylor's brothers were not with her. Gérin gives a source for Martha's death, and a source for the cemetery: both of these I have seen. The *Acte de Décès* of the commune of Koekelberg states in French that Martha died on 12 October at 10 o'clock in the evening, aged twenty-three, born at Gomersal. One of the informants was headmistress Catherine's husband, Norbert Goussaert. The source for the cemetery is the funeral register of the Chapel Royal for 14 October: 'Décédée à Molenbeek St. Jean le 12 octobre, Nouveau Cimetière de l'Est 1er quarrée à droit, en face No. 91, Agée [blank] Ans.' No officiating clergyman is listed for any of the funerals on that page, and everyone whose funeral took place in the Chapel Royal was entered in that register – Belgian Protestants *and* Anglicans – including Evan Jenkins in 1849.

Martha and Mary's uncle Abraham Dixon, who lived in Brussels, was a friend of the Jenkins family, as we will see in the next chapter. From Dixon's letters, which I shall quote from there, and his presence at Christmas dinner at the Jenkins home at the end of 1843 (along with Charlotte Brontë), I think we can confidently say that the Dixons were Anglicans and went to Evan's services at the Chapel Royal. Elder sister Mary Taylor was baptized at the Anglican St Peter's Church in Birstall on 29 March 1817; Martha was baptized there on 2 July 1819, both by Rev. William Margetson Heald senior (d. 1837). I have no idea why no one (as far as I know) has found Martha's date of birth, because it is clearly in the church register: 21 May.[126] That is not evidence for later attendance at the Anglican church since, at that date, 'the only legal method of recording a birth was in a parish register, and an Anglican baptism certificate functioned very much as a birth certificate'.[127] I will therefore turn to more evidence.

Mary Taylor was buried in 1893 in the churchyard of the Anglican church of St Mary the Blessed Virgin in Gomersal, West Yorkshire (built in 1851), which I think she might be pleased to learn has currently a female pastor. Her brothers John (d. 1901) and William Waring Taylor (d. 1903) are both buried in the cemetery at Shannon, Otago, New Zealand. Waring had been the first of the family to emigrate, in 1841, and his sister Mary joined him there for some years. Mary wrote to Charlotte with news of Waring's marriage in 1848, which Charlotte passed on to Miss Wooler, saying that his wife, Mary Knox, 'is a Methodist, and very religious: Mary [Taylor] said that she supplied Waring with tracts, and was trying to convert him; she had prevailed on him to accompany her to chapel, but could not induce him to become a teacher in the Sunday School.'[128] She was the niece of Dr Robert Knox, who in 1828 had bought the corpses supplied by the murderers Burke and Hare for his anatomy lectures in Edinburgh.[129] I dashed off an email to my cousin in Australia to ask if she could check if the cemetery record named the brothers' Protestant 'sect', not too confident that it did. It seems it only took Marcia ten minutes to reply with the relevant pages which stated 'Anglican'. So Waring had resisted his wife's pressure to 'convert' and had been Anglican in the 1840s.

Finally I produce three letters. The first is by Tom Dixon, learning German in Brussels and in his early twenties, whose family I have established as members of Evan's congregation at the Chapel Royal. In late April or early May 1842 he wrote to his sister Mary Dixon (who was to become a friend of Charlotte Brontë):

There is nothing new here; the Koekelbergitesses [Mary and Martha Taylor] did not come to Church last Sunday so I can say nothing about them except that on Wednesday last they were all quite well. One of the young ladies [Martha] will go over on the 8th of May.[130]

Martha went to Yorkshire in the spring of 1842, returning to school and her sad end later. But there are two letters that should finally convince that Martha was an Anglican. The first is by Charlotte Brontë herself, written from Haworth two years earlier to their friend Ellen:

will you be so kind as to deliver the enclosed to Martha Taylor – do not go up to Gomersal on purpose with it & do not on any account send – but give it her yourself when you see her at Church[131]

The second is by Martha to Ellen Nussey on 22 June 1842, when Martha was in Leeds:

Now I am going to take a liberty, I propose to myself the pleasure of spending a long day with you whilst I am at Gomersal. I think of going to my Mother's house on Friday if the day be fine, and if not on Monday. If I go on Friday I shall be at church on Sunday, and then I hope I shall see you[132]

This is without doubt the Anglican St Peter's Church in Birstall, which the Nusseys attended – a short walk from the Nussey and Taylor homes, and where the Taylor sisters had been baptized by the vicar, Rev. William M. Heald, to whose son (who succeeded him as vicar) and daughter, Mary Taylor asked to be remembered by, in her letter quoted above.

My very last research trip was to Leuven in Belgium, where the Anglican registers are archived. Hunting for them had been fairly tortuous. A Belgian archivist gave me the reference number for what was obviously Evan's register of marriages, baptisms and burials because of the dates in the catalogue: '[…] Begrafenissen [funerals], 1818–1849', but he then emailed to say it wasn't there. So I leapt on Eurostar. It was there, but Dr Prins was partly right as regards any entry for Martha Taylor in 1842.[133] Evan's burials end on the penultimate page of the register in 1830. On the final page are funerals that took place in 1849, immediately after Evan's death. It would be easy to assume that Evan's register for 1830 onwards had somehow gone missing, and yet his last entry for a marriage is in 1839, and for a baptism in 1841. It seemed somewhat disorganized. He could surely have asked his friend Clarke to buy a new register from Rivingtons in 1830 and bring it to Brussels. Evan's successor at the Chapel Royal, Rev. Blacker, didn't start a new register: there are loose pages for his baptisms, marriages and funerals for the early 1850s which someone tucked into the register. Evan's son Edward was more organized and started a new register in 1856. So either Evan wrote down details of his funerals from 1830 to 1849 on loose pages that have been lost, or he decided not to duplicate the Chapel Royal register, which combines Belgian Protestant and Anglican services. Obviously, Gérin had not consulted or understood Evan's register – nor indeed read *Shirley* carefully – and leapt to the unlikely conclusion that a Belgian had officiated at Martha's funeral. (I was told that there is no separate register for Belgian ministers at the Chapel Royal.)

I think we can be fairly certain that not only did Evan Jenkins officiate at Martha's Anglican funeral – with the male members of the Dixon family present – but that he had been summoned by his long-time friend Catherine Goussaert née Phelps to Martha's bedside and gave her the last rites. It was maybe the young Tom Dixon who came to see Charlotte at her school and break the news to her of his cousin Martha's illness (I would think that Martha's uncle Abraham Dixon and Evan Jenkins stayed with Mary at Martha's bedside), and with the optimism and embarrassment of youth left the impression that it wasn't too serious.

Perhaps we can now restore to her funeral the presence of the clergyman Martha had known – remember the recommendation of Eliza Jenkins as the woman who would provide respectability for Charlotte and Emily, and her 'chattering magpie' schoolfriend Helen – in a language she understood and a rite she knew. (It is also possible that Evan gave religious instruction classes at the school to the Anglican pupils, just as his son Edward was to do in his time at another girls' pensionnat.) Evan's presence would have been a comfort to her cousins and sister. Perhaps Gérin's 'biography', and those that copy her, should be labelled 'warning: contains fiction'. Through her distortions, she hid the reality of the devastation not only for the family, but for Catherine Goussaert's school and the Jenkinses. Did Evan and Eliza take a distraught Helen out of school for a while for fear that what Martha had died of was contagious? Having lost one daughter already, I think they might have. In a letter that Mary Taylor wrote eight months later, she says to Ellen Nussey: 'Martha's death though not from a contagious disorder has exceedingly affected Mde Gaussaert's [sic] school, which I am very sorry for and would gladly repair if I could. Either this or some other cause has so reduced the number of her pupils that she would be glad to take a few on rather reduced terms.'[134] We shall see how the Jenkinses deal with the illness of one of their pupils in a later chapter.

On hearing the news of Aunt Branwell's final illness, Charlotte and Emily hurried (no doubt by train) to Antwerp to catch the boat, though they were too late for the funeral.[135] Everything had changed. Despite M. Heger's plea for the talented piano-playing Miss Emily to return, she decided to stay in Haworth. Charlotte, offered a teaching job by the Hegers in return for more language learning, and excited about the intellectual stimulation she was finding from M. Heger, returned on her own at the end of January 1843. That is for my next chapter. But before I combat more fabrications, I turn to Charlotte's intelligent genius to articulate feeling as she writes of the death of Martha Taylor/Jessy Yorke in *Shirley*. She has described the child Jessy abusing the established church, Wellington and the Prince Regent and ends: 'But, Jessy, I will write about you no more.' And in the astonishing paragraph that follows, Charlotte changes viewpoint and shifts time – from young, fictional Jessy in 1811, to Charlotte herself writing on 'an autumn evening, wet and wild', perhaps in 1848 just after the death of brother Branwell, to her looking back to autumn 1842 and Martha's death, when she made a 'pilgrimage to a grave new-made in a heretic cemetery' in Brussels.[136]

Fourteen

Charlotte Returns to Brussels, 1843

A Faithless-looking Youth, a Welsh Pony
and Possible Forgery

Autumn 2015 was a turning point. I finally discovered from a distant cousin in New South Wales where the 'Wyndham letters' were archived. R. had kindly sent me snippets and the odd letter she had transcribed – some absolutely invaluable and heartrending – but I was in the dark of what else survived of letters from Eliza to her sister Margaret, or from siblings Janet and John Livingston in Greenwich, or of other letters that might simply mention the Jenkinses, and I also needed scans of the originals to check against her transcriptions. Now I was able to write to the University of New England, NSW; and the archivist, Bill Oates, sent me scans of the letters I requested and an Excel catalogue that listed them all (488 in total). There were letters I was curious to see, but it was a guessing game because of the minimal descriptions. 'Folder 41.1' contained items from 'Wyndham, Alward (Son of George)', that is, Margaret Wyndham née Jay's eldest son, Australian nephew of Eliza and Evan, born in 1828. The catalogue noted that these letters were 'Written by Alward but copied to a book. In 1925 the originals were in the possession of William Wyndham of Kulki Vineyard.' The first letter in the folder was dated 12 May 1853 'From Paris to Margaret', the next 'From Dinton to Margaret', another 'From Greenwich to George', dated 3 August 1852. Dinton was the home of his father George's family in Wiltshire. I wondered whether 25-year-old Alward had visited Aunt Eliza in Brussels. I asked for the scans, not knowing what I'd get. When I read what I'd been sent I was staggered: I could hear the family, and even the scratching of Alward's pen.

His description of the Jenkins family in Brussels in May 1853 is so immediate that I feel that I am in the same room. I quoted a bit of it earlier about Eliza, in her mid-fifties, being active but 'shrivelled', but even though he describes the Jenkins family after Rev. Evan's death and living in a different house, eleven years after shy Charlotte and monosyllabic Emily visited, his vivid picture would surely be clearly recognizable to the sisters. Here is chattering magpie Helen, now in her mid-twenties, and Edward, who had surely endured his escorting duties with courteous style; 'stout' then could mean strong or in robust health. Alward mentions also his twenty-year-old cousin Evan (junior), the third son, who had gone out to Australia and was to become a huge worry to his mother and brother Edward at this time of the gold rush; and there is Mina, Evan and Eliza's last child, now fourteen; and John, their fourth son, who was eighteen:

I left Paris on Tuesday the 17th, was detained, waiting for a train 3 hours at Amiens […] My aunt & cousins received me very kindly and do their best to make my stay here agreeable. They pressed me to stay till the end of June but I mean to go on the tenth. Aunt Eliza is very thin & shrivelled – looks aged – but is full of activity & energy. Edward is taller than Evan [junior], stout & well made & I think not at all ill-looking he seems sensible and gentlemanly with plenty of conversation. Helen is very short, but a good figure enough & has a nice looking face enough with a strong likeness to you [his mother Margaret]. She is natural & unaffected and full of liveliness, conversation & fun. Mina is quieter I think, nice looking & a very nice girl. I have left John to the last instead of taking him in his turn. He is much the same height & figure as Edward, I suppose about 5ft 7. very like Evan [junior] in face. He is a good fellow not so talkative as Edward. He is studying for Cambridge, meaning to try for a Fellowship. I have had the sound of the piano in the drawing room in my ears for some minutes – Mina practising – playing rather slowly – but I hear Helen's voice & suddenly the piano <u>races</u> off at such a pace! She plays better than 49 out of 50 that one hears, but sets the time according to the present fashion in Belgium, which is too fast to please me, but the faster she can make anything – at least any waltz go the better she is pleased.[1]

Edward at twenty-six is now the Cambridge-educated man with 'plenty of conversation' – no wonder he had been frustrated when escorting the sisters. And how else could Martha Taylor's 'chattering magpie' Helen, so enthusiastic about her cousin Joseph coming to Brussels, have turned out except as a manic piano player? For so long these people have been ignored. There is a brother missing in the above account, Alexander. I will write about his death and Eliza's grief in another chapter. But now to go back ten years, as Charlotte returns to Brussels on her own – and by *train* from Ostend.

* * *

In her few surviving letters Charlotte does not mention going to the Jenkins home, but we know she was there at Christmas, and surely at other times. Eliza's comment to Mrs Gaskell that she used to invite Charlotte and Emily to spend Sundays and holidays with the family 'until she found that they felt more pain than pleasure from such visits' doesn't mean that she stopped keeping an eye on them, and she would of course see them at church.[2] Not only had Charlotte sold the idea to Aunt Branwell of Mrs Jenkins as respectable protection, but when Patrick stayed with the Jenkinses he surely asked Eliza and Evan to keep a careful watch over his daughters, just as he had asked Mrs Franks to do in 1835 when the girls were at Roe Head. He had asked Mrs Franks to inform him and Aunt Branwell 'if our interference should be requisite' since they were 'unacquainted with the ways of this delusive, and insnaring world'.[3] It is likely, therefore, that Eliza called on Charlotte at the school shortly after she arrived back, just as 'very elegant & ladylike' Mary Dixon did, then in her early thirties, having been told by her cousin Mary Taylor that Charlotte was on her way.[4] Perhaps whenever the Dixons went to the Jenkinses they brought Charlotte with them and teenage Edward's escorting role was no longer needed.

In 1842, Edward had started at Shrewsbury School in Shropshire. New Yorker Charles Bristed, at Trinity College, Cambridge in the 1840s, commented that Shrewsbury had a great reputation, it 'is one of the very first schools that a Freshman hears of in connexion with this Prize or that Scholarship'.

Even Eton does not send up such a proportion of the Cambridge Classics – in fact I doubt if any three schools together do, Eton included. The Shrewsbury men at Cambridge had a reputation for two things particularly, writing Greek Iambics and playing whist; but their general line was minute accuracy of Scholarship [...] In most things they displayed a hard and subtle acuteness, such as one is accustomed to deem a national characteristic of Scots rather than Englishmen: this showed itself in their very relaxations [...] I often watched a table or two of Shrewsbury men before and after supper, and it was singular to see such youths playing nearly as scientifically and quite as silently as the oldest and most experienced hands, never making a gesture of impatience or exultation, or opening their mouths except during the deals [...] Their accurate habits were of great service to them in Mathematics; they seldom read for high degrees, but were always pretty safe to get through or be Senior Optimes as their Classical prospects required.

He adds later: 'Re-examination of the translation papers disclosed some glaring mistakes, but every one makes mistakes, except now and then a Shrewsbury man.'[5]

The school was founded in 1552 by King Edward VI and housed until the 1880s in what is now the Castle Gates public library. Upstairs you can still see the sixth-form room, which was shared by three classes, whose wooden window ledges are adorned with graffiti dating back to the eighteenth century. Mike Morrogh, in the History Department at the modern school, emailed me that Edward was at the school from 1842 to 1846. He was a Praeposter (Prefect) and played cricket for the First XI. He added: 'Unfortunately we don't know when he started – largely because of the inefficiency of the then Headmaster, the great Benjamin Hall Kennedy of *Latin Primer* fame. Kennedy simply did not keep a register of boys entering Shrewsbury during his reign of 1836–66' but 'along with about 30 other boys Jenkins entered the school some time between 20 May 1842 and Christmas 1842'.[6]

I learned my Latin from Dr Kennedy's *Shorter Latin Primer* – I remember lying on the grass at school chanting my way through it; the cover has turned an odd bluey-green over the years. In the boarding houses, Dr Kennedy enabled boys to have a bed of their own – formerly a luxury that was paid for as an extra – and introduced the school cap or mortarboard to deter boys from getting drunk in pubs (it made them too recognizable). He was also keen on treating boys as rational beings, and if one of them did a good piece of work he would stride around the room exclaiming 'Wonderful, wonderful!'[7] I am thrilled about the cricket; at only five feet seven inches I hardly see Edward as a demon bowler, but from cousin Alward's description of him as 'stout' he was of athletic build. He and his youngest brother John founded the Cricket Club in Brussels in the early 1860s and there is a report of an annual match in June 1861: for the 'Champs Elysees Club', Edward took ten wickets, including one caught and bowled; was out for a duck in the first, but scored twelve not out in the second innings. Since he batted at number one, it looks like he was an all-rounder; it is possible that brother John was the wicket-keeper. The Jenkins team beat the town of Brussels.[8]

Edward also rowed at Shrewsbury and at Cambridge, where he was Captain of the Magdalene Boat Club. It is probable that he played football at Shrewsbury, and it is quite possible that he was the first to bring football to Belgium. I like the suggestion that, because of this, the Jenkinses should have a street named after them in Brussels.[9] Apparently, for the history of football in Belgium it is significant that Edward was at Shrewsbury School and then Cambridge, because it was public schoolboys who began to codify the widely varying rules. In 1848, at Cambridge University, two former pupils of Shrewsbury School held a meeting with old boys of Eton and other schools to agree on what has been called the first set of modern rules. Edward went to Cambridge in 1846 and maybe contributed to drawing up the rules, which began to separate association football from rugby. Before then, everyone played according to the rules of his school, which often resulted in dire confusion: the Eton men howling at the Rugby men for handling the ball.[10] It must have been quite funny: one side playing football and the other side rugby.

From the few photographs that there are of Edward in middle age, I think he must have looked most like his father Evan, with a wide Welsh face. Alas, there is no portrait of Rev. Evan: I can only guess what he looked like from Edward's photographs and from the portrait of Evan's brother Rev. David. In contrast, younger brothers Evan junior and John maybe looked more like their mother Eliza, with a slimmer Scottish face. Edward was almost entirely Celtic: half-Welsh and largely half-Scottish. In Margaret Smith's edition of Charlotte's letters, she comments about Charlotte's novel *Villette*, and about who in real life had suggested the characters of John Graham Bretton and his mother: 'John Graham Bretton's boyhood and his early infatuation with Ginevra are largely imaginary creations. His adult appearance, more mature personality, and his relationship with his mother, are recognizably based on George Smith.' (Scottish descendant Smith was Charlotte's publisher.)[11] George Smith actually wrote to Charlotte about 'the discrepancy, the want of perfect harmony between Graham's boyhood and manhood', and she had agreed.[12] I strongly suggest that the sixteen-year-old Graham was not 'imaginary' but was suggested by the teenage Edward. Here is Graham in *Villette*:

> Graham was at that time a handsome, faithless-looking youth of sixteen. I say faithless-looking, not because he was really of a very perfidious disposition, but because the epithet strikes me as proper to describe the fair, Celtic (not Saxon) character of his good looks; his waved light auburn hair, his supple

symmetry, his smile frequent, and destitute neither of fascination nor of subtlety, (in no bad sense.) A spoiled, whimsical boy he was in those days![13]

I cannot tell the colour of Edward's hair from the few photos, but he has a nice open face and warm eyes, and as the eldest son I am sure he was the apple of his parents' eyes, and spoiled – of course. A later description of the adult Graham Bretton also fits Edward well: 'He is a fine-hearted son; his mother's comfort and hope, her pride and pleasure.'[14] When I went to the Brussels Brontë Group talk in 2014, I was asked if any of my ancestors made an appearance in Charlotte Brontë's novels, and I immediately said Edward as the young Bretton. What also struck me in the novel was teenage Graham's relationship with six-year-old Paulina. It may indeed be that Paulina was based partly on Mrs Gaskell's youngest daughter Julia, but she had no brother, so the description in *Villette* could also be a memory of Edward and his youngest sister Mina, whom Charlotte would have last seen when the little girl was four, perhaps rushing to meet Edward on his return from Shrewsbury for the holidays, teased by him and picked up and held high above his head. It may be that the image of Edward and little Mina in Charlotte's memory made her create a tiny, doll-like Paulina. Mina was known as 'Baby': in a letter to Frances Curwen in 1846, when Mina was seven, Eliza writes about a forthcoming wedding: 'Tell your Girls that Baby "Mina["] I ought to say is to be the Brides Maid!!!'[15]

There are delightful scenes between the two at the beginning of *Villette* and I can only suggest that Charlotte observed quietly and closely the relationship between the eldest and the youngest in the Jenkins family. I can only guess, too, that Edward read *Villette* and recognized some of the description, and I think that in being laconic with Thomas Westwood about the purgatory of escorting Charlotte back to school, he was wary, as a busy responsible clergyman, of becoming a tourist attraction for Charlotte's admirers, whom she called the 'curiosity-hunters' who 'come boring to Haworth'.[16] And he might have been aware that writers keen to make a name for themselves would have hounded him or his family. One just has to look at poor Ellen Nussey, who had kept hundreds of Charlotte's letters, used and abused by the hunters; whereas Mary Taylor destroyed nearly all of them and was left in peace.[17] I think here is the key to why my ancestors' acquaintance with the Brontës was kept quiet.

* * *

Eliza's remark to Mrs Gaskell about Charlotte gradually wheeling her chair around as she talked to someone is less interesting than her remark that 'Charlotte was sometimes excited sufficiently to speak eloquently and well – on certain subjects'.[18] This is in contrast to Mary Taylor's comment to Ellen Nussey, that, after visiting Martha's grave in October 1842, Charlotte and Emily had accompanied her back to the Dixons' residence in rue de la Régence: 'We then spent a pleasant evening with my cousins & in presence of my Uncle & Emily one not speaking at all; the other once or twice.'[19] By 'the other' Mary is referring to Charlotte: the incoherence probably reflects Mary's grief after her sister's death.

Mrs Gaskell commented that there was an English family 'where Charlotte soon became a welcome guest, and where, I suspect, she felt herself more at her ease than either at Mrs Jenkins', or the friends [Dixons] whom I have first mentioned'.[20] This was the Wheelwrights, whom I shall discuss shortly, but it is fascinating that at the Jenkins home Charlotte did speak eloquently 'on certain subjects'. There is a clue in her novel *The Professor*. But I wonder if, a bit intimidated by clergyman Evan Jenkins and ever busy Eliza, Charlotte had good arguments with the less intimidating teenage Edward.

Towards the end of Charlotte's first novel *The Professor*, William Crimsworth takes his aristocratic friend Hunsden to meet the half-Swiss, half-English woman he loves in her small apartment in Brussels. It is such an autobiographic novel, in which Charlotte puts herself and Heger into the character of William, whereas Frances is ostensibly a demure and timid Charlotte. Yet Frances surprises Hunsden, and the reader, with a strongly argumentative defence of the Swiss and the English: Hunsden 'had never before heard a lady say "hell" with that uncompromising sort of accent, and the sound pleased him from a lady's lips; he would fain have had Frances to strike the string again, but it was not in her way. The display of eccentric vigour never gave her pleasure, and it only sounded in her voice or flashed in her countenance when extraordinary circumstances – and those generally painful – forced it out of the depths where it burned latent.'[21] And Charlotte has Frances argue in favour of the Duke of Wellington, just as Charlotte surely argued for her hero: 'You speak of Waterloo! Your Wellington ought to have been conquered there, according to Napoleon; but he persevered in spite of the laws of war, and was victorious in defiance of military tactics.'[22] I think we here get the flavour of the occasionally argumentative Charlotte in the Jenkins household while she twisted her chair around, embarrassed at her own vehemence.

* * *

The Jenkins home also included not just the six children but schoolboys, and possibly two resident teachers. There are some lovely letters from the Curwen boys in the 1840s, which I will look at in the next chapter, but it is impossible to say how many schoolboys there were, or what ages. There might be a dozen boarders on average, but it would vary. At the end of *The Professor*, Frances sets up a home school for girls, while her husband William teaches at a college. I wondered if there was any clue as to the Jenkins school in William's description:

> always at nine o'clock I was left – abandoned. She would extricate herself from my arms, quit my side, take her lamp, and be gone. Her mission was upstairs. I have followed her sometimes and watched her. First she opened the door of the *dortoir* (the pupils' chamber), noiselessly she glided up the long room between the two rows of white beds, surveyed all the sleepers. If any were wakeful, especially if any were sad, spoke to them and soothed them, stood some minutes to ascertain that all was safe and tranquil, trimmed the watchlight which burned in the apartment all night, then withdrew, closing the door behind her without sound.[23]

That might describe Eliza as well.

* * *

Charlotte's new acquaintance Dr Thomas Wheelwright was born in Birmingham and qualified as a surgeon or physician in Edinburgh and London. He had a medical practice in Falcon Square, Aldersgate, London when his eldest daughter, Laetitia, was born in May 1828. The ostensible arrival of Dr and Mrs Wheelwright in Brussels in July 1842 was for the education of their five daughters, aged between six and fourteen, who went to Mme Heger's school. (There was a son, Charles, who presumably stayed at school in England, and later emigrated to South Africa.) The family left only a year later, as Charlotte describes forlornly to Ellen in October 1843: 'I had indeed some very kind acquaintances in the family of Dr Wheelwright – but they too are gone now – they left in latter part of August – and I am completely alone.'[24] In 1916, Joseph J. Green wrote an article titled 'The Brontë–Wheelwright Friendship'. He was married to Dr and Mrs Wheelwright's granddaughter.[25] Green wrote that Dr Wheelwright sold his London medical practice and went to Brussels because he was 'afflicted with cataract and consequent failing eyesight' but that he continued to practise his profession. As a blind surgeon?[26] There was one predominant reason for people to suddenly come to Brussels – bankruptcy, and Green refers to it. But it wasn't Dr Wheelwright who had been made bankrupt, instead it was his Nonconformist father-in-law, William Ridge, whose bank in Chichester had failed at the end of 1841. The bank's failure and the numerous newspaper accounts of it, which included suggestions of forgery, perhaps caused the daughter to escape to the Continent with her family, and place her daughters in Mme Heger's school in the holidays, to endure, it seems, being taught piano by Emily Brontë. The youngest, Julia, died at the pensionnat in November 1842.

It seems that Charlotte visited the Wheelwrights several times in their apartment at the Hotel Cluysenaar in the rue Royale in 1843 – the model for Hotel Crécy in *Villette*. The eldest daughter, Laetitia (1828–1911), although twelve years younger than Charlotte, corresponded with her until Charlotte's death, and both Mrs Gaskell and a later biographer, Clement Shorter, corresponded with or met her for their books on Charlotte. One letter from Mrs Gaskell to Laetitia is a reply to the latter's request for an address for Miss Carr in Brussels (undated but probably 1856). Mrs Gaskell can't remember: 'I could find my way to it, but I have forgotten the name of the street (out of Rue des Paroissiens). But Mr. Jenkins, son of the late chaplain, took us to the door where she lived, and his mother would know the exact address. Her direction is Mrs. Jenkins, Champs Elysees, Chaussée d'Ixelles.'[27] This is Edward, on escorting duty again in May 1856, and I imagine that Mrs Gaskell was far chattier than Charlotte (youngest brother John was then at Cambridge University and Evan junior was up to no good in Australia). Green mentions Clement Shorter, and what particularly intrigues me is Shorter's account that the Wheelwrights took Charlotte to services at William Drury's church.

Clement King Shorter (1857–1926) was a Fleet Street editor and journalist, keen on popularizing literature.[28] His portrait in the magazine *Vanity Fair* as 'Men of the Day No. 607' in 1894 shows him bespectacled with a large moustache, brown tousled hair and green tie, definitely a man who could charm old ladies and even old men – though in his case out of their old letters and memories rather than their life savings.[29] In 1896 he published his first book, *Charlotte Brontë and her Circle*. Shorter had met Ellen Nussey seven years previously, saying he was 'very eager to write on the Brontes'.[30] He found Charlotte's widower Arthur Nicholls in Ireland and charmed out of him the letters that he possessed, and he discovered Laetitia Wheelwright by writing 'to all the Wheelwrights in the London Directory. My first effort succeeded, and *the* Miss Wheelwright kindly lent me all the letters that she had preserved.'[31] Margaret Smith describes his 1896 book as 'the most important and substantial work on the Brontës to appear since the *Life* of 1857'.[32] There is no mention of the Jenkins family, but indefatigable Shorter surely tried to reach them. The youngest Jenkins son, Rev. John, had died in 1894 in Brussels, mourned by his parishioners. It would have been easy to trace his surviving sibling – chattering, manic piano-player Helen – and his children, but I can only guess that there was a rebuff or no reply, especially at a time of grief. But from Laetitia Wheelwright he learned that her family had taken Charlotte to Drury's service, now housed in a church in the Leopold Quarter used also by French 'Methodists'; as William Trollope remarked: 'Is this quite the thing?'[33] Shorter writes about Charlotte: 'With the Wheelwright children she sometimes spent the Sunday, and with them she occasionally visited the English Episcopal church which the Wheelwrights attended, and of which the clergyman was a Mr. Drury.'[34] Surely the Wheelwrights would have told her that Drury had been the 'playmate' of Byron at Harrow. I wish we had Charlotte's comment about meeting one of her heroes at second hand. But I regret Shorter's '*a* Mr. Drury'. Is there anything more contemptuous or lazy that a writer can call a person other than the indefinite article before his name? Something similar has been done to Eliza recently: she has been called 'one Mrs Jenkins'.[35]

Gérin states that the funeral for Julia Wheelwright was conducted by Drury – which was indeed the case – but then confuses with saying it was at St George's Chapel, which we know from Rev. Biber and William Trollope was no longer in use.[36] In about 1829, inside the front cover of his church register, Drury had inscribed: 'St George's Brussels / rue de l'Orangerie Sect. 7 No. 21.' but his services were in a different place after 1839.[37] Gérin then adds in a footnote that 'Julia's obituary appeared in the *Journal de Bruxelles*, 21 Nov. 1842' – an obituary for a seven-year-old? It turns out to be simply a list of those who have recently died in the 'Etat-Civil de Bruxelles': '*Décès du 19* [...] J. Wheelwright, âgée de 7 ans, rue Royale'. As Ruijssenaars states, three weeks earlier Julia would have been younger than seven and her name would have been omitted: at the end of the list there are 'Trois enfants au-dessous de 7 ans'.[38]

Why Mrs Gaskell thought that Charlotte would have been more at her ease with the Wheelwrights is not obvious, unless it was Mrs Wheelwright's calm maternal demeanour as opposed to Eliza rushing around running a large household, and the lack of Mrs Dixon in that household; or the preponderance of young girls in the Wheelwright apartment in contrast to the predominantly male-oriented Jenkins and Dixon households.

* * *

There are illuminating letters from Abraham Dixon about the Jenkinses, archived now at the Brontë Parsonage Museum. I felt on somewhat shifting sand investigating Abraham since I kept finding different dates of birth for his sons and daughters, and even the number of daughters he had, but we do have definite dates for his fourth son George (1820–98), who became Liberal Member of Parliament for Birmingham from 1867, a renowned education reformer and a 'moderate Anglican'. Ellen Nussey crossed out many names in the letters received from Charlotte. If indeed Charlotte does name George Dixon in a letter in October 1843, then she surprisingly calls him a 'pretty-looking & pretty behaved young man – apparently constructed without a back-bone – by which I don't allude to his corporeal spine – which is all right enough – but to his character'.[39]

George's father Abraham was born around 1780 in Whitehaven, Cumberland.[40] He married Mary and Martha Taylor's aunt Laetitia in May 1808 in Yorkshire, and their children were born in London and Yorkshire. Aunt Laetitia died at their home in Leeds in March 1842.[41] Their daughter Mary, who befriended Charlotte Brontë, was perhaps their second child, born around 1811, and seems to have been the only surviving daughter in the family by 1843. Abraham senior is described in the *ODNB* as a merchant and inventor in the woollen textile industry. In the *British Advertiser* newspaper for January 1840, he is included with six other men in a 'List of Patents Recently Granted by the Belgian Government': 'Dixon, Abraham, residing at Brussels, Hotel de Gronendael, Rue de la Putterie, a patent of invention for 15 years, for additional improvements in the process of water-proofing cloth, linen, cotton, paper, and other tissues, as well as for sizeing paper of all kinds, for which he obtained patents on the 1st and 29th of last July. – Dec. 27, 1839.'[42] But it doesn't look as if he made any headway with it, because in July 1843 he wrote to his daughter Mary that 'the Belgian Government have declined to use Kyan's process, this is very mortifying after all the trouble and expense which I have had with it' and he is hoping to give up the expensive house in the rue de la Régence as he is worried about money.[43] Irish-born John Howard Kyan (1774–1850) had invented kyanizing – a method of preventing the decay of timber using bichloride of mercury – especially valuable for ships; and had extended this to preserving materials like paper and cloth.[44] I can only presume that Dixon's formula was meant as an improvement on Kyan's. Several of Abraham's sons worked at Rabone Bros. & Co., foreign merchants of Birmingham.[45]

The year before, on 3 June 1842, a few months after the Brontë sisters arrived in Brussels, Abraham wrote to daughter Mary from Ostend, there for his health. The house was near the sea and 'the window being open, you have all the benefit of the sea air without the trouble of going out, which is a great advantage & convenience, particularly to me as I can walk so little' – he was then in his early sixties. When he did manage to get out he walked in the adjoining garden belonging to the king, or on the Digue, 'the finest sea side walk perhaps in the world'. He mentions the increased frequency of steamboats from Dover and London, and Mary's brother Tom learning German in the palace, since his tutor had gone on leave for a few weeks and had handed Tom over to his father, the librarian to King Leopold. He then adds: 'It is probable Mr Jenkins will be in Yorkshire next month on a visit to his Brother at Pudsey, & nephew, the curate to Mr Cassel at Batley.'[46] I think Evan must also have visited Patrick Brontë that July in Haworth to report that Charlotte and Emily were doing well and bring him letters from them. I have no evidence, but when I went again to Haworth in September 2019 I felt certain. I looked out of my window in the Old White Lion Hotel towards the steps leading up to the church as dusk fell, and knew that of course he did. It would be appalling to travel to the West Riding of Yorkshire to see his brother without making the journey to Rev. Brontë, who had stayed in his house in Brussels. Probably Evan stayed a night in the parsonage, while Patrick wrote a letter to his daughters to take back with him. The house is so altered now, but I tried to look at it through Evan's eyes. I liked the idea of Evan there, seeing the view from the top of steep cobbled Main Street with the hills in the distance, hearing the squawks of noisy birds around the old church tower, concerned about the thickening of tombstones below the parsonage and the hard life that Rev. Brontë led in such an unhealthy place. Perhaps they had a stroll onto the moors and talked about their Irish/Welsh childhoods: they had such similar backgrounds which by their learning and fierce determination had taken them both to Cambridge. And if Evan felt concern about the unhealthy and hard life that Patrick was leading, ironically Patrick would outlive Evan by many years.

It is probable that Helen Jenkins's hope that her cousin Joseph would come out in the summer of 1842 was dashed, as from the register of clergymen officiating in the church at Batley there looks very little time for him to have gone to Brussels that summer (he had less than three weeks in between duties), but possibly, staying with brother David in Pudsey, Evan discussed with Joseph about his coming to Brussels in 1843.[47] I would love to have changed places with the maid for one moment and brought in their supper as the two brothers talked about their eldest sons: one ordained, the other starting with such promise at Shrewsbury School. But also talking through their problems. What a long way they had come from Ystrad Meurig and the bogs of mid-Wales. Did they talk in Welsh? Alas, perhaps it was in English now.

Abraham Dixon's next relevant letter is a year later, on 24 July 1843, again to daughter Mary, from which I quoted above:

> Mr Jenkins has been very ill of a brain fever & confined several days to his bed, he was taken ill on the day after his return from London about ten days ago. Mrs Jenkins in consequence came up from Ostend. he is now better & they set off this morning for Ostend, from whence they go again to London, or rather to Greenwich for about a fortnight.[48]

Presumably Evan would have been escorting some of his pupils back to London, while Eliza had rented a house in Ostend for part of the holidays. 'Brain fever' was a catch-all term. Catherine has brain fever in *Wuthering Heights*: 'The doctor [...] signified the threatening danger was, not so much death, as permanent alienation of intellect.'[49] Mrs Gaskell also gives it to her heroine in the short story 'Cousin Phillis' after she has been abandoned by the man she loves and lies at death's door. It was written for Charles Dickens's *Household Words* and he was finally irritated with yet another of Gaskell's deathbed scenes. He wrote to his subeditor, 'I wish to Heaven her people would keep a little firmer on their legs!'[50] Whatever the type of fever that Evan had, it was often considered life-threatening.

I now turn to probably the most nonsensical of biographers' identifications regarding a comment by Charlotte concerning the Jenkins family.

* * *

In August 1843, Charlotte wrote to her friend Ellen and described her astonishment at hearing the voice of someone, familiar to both of them, speaking from the pulpit at the Chapel Royal. But before I turn to this I want to set the scene, with Charlotte's description of William Crimsworth searching for Frances in *The Professor*, who has gone missing from the girls' school he has been teaching at:

> I sought her on Sundays all day long; I sought her on the boulevards, in the Allée Verte, in the Park; I sought her in St Gudule and St Jacques; I sought her in the two Protestant chapels; I attended these latter at the German, French, and English services [...] I stood at the door of each chapel after the service, and waited till every individual had come out, scrutinising every gown draping a slender form.

William fears that Frances has left Brussels:

> on the afternoon of the fourth Sunday I turned from the door of the chapel-royal, which the doorkeeper had just closed and locked, and followed in the wake of the last of the congregation, now dispersed and dispersing over

the square. I had soon outwalked the couples of English gentlemen and ladies. (Gracious goodness! why don't they dress better? My eye is yet filled with visions of the high-flounced, slovenly, and tumbled dresses in costly silk and satin, of the large unbecoming collars in expensive lace, of the ill-cut coats and strangely fashioned pantaloons which every Sunday, at the English service, filled the choirs [mistranscription for chairs?] of the chapel-royal, and after it issuing forth into the square, came into disadvantageous contrast with freshly and trimly attired foreign figures, hastening to attend *salut* at the church of Coburg.) I had passed these pairs of Britons, and the groups of pretty British children, and the British footmen and waiting-maids; I had crossed the Place Royale[51]

It is such a wonderful description: it is as vivid as young Alward's description of the Jenkins home ten years later, because here is Evan's congregation leaving church: Evan is perhaps still in the church with his family, about to leave after a word with his churchwarden. I love Charlotte's perhaps unconscious switch between observing the scene outside the Chapel Royal as her hero William saw it, to Charlotte the author remembering the appalling dress of the English. If she has been criticized for her unfavourable depiction of Belgians, they are certainly better dressed than the Brits as they go to the evening service at the Catholic church.

Now to go inside the Chapel Royal. In a letter to Ellen that summer, Charlotte wrote:

Last Sunday afternoon being at the Chapel Royal in Brussels I was surprised to hear a voice proceed from the pulpit – which instantly brought all Birstal and all Battley before my mind's eye – I could ?see nothing but I certainly thought that unclerical little Welsh pony Jenkins was there – I buoyed up my mind with the expectation of receiving a letter from you but however as I have got none I suppose I must have been mistaken[52]

I was dumbfounded by Smith's note in her edition of the letters identifying this 'unclerical little Welsh pony' as 'The Revd Evan Jenkins, MA, the English episcopal clergyman and "Chaplain to H.M. King Leopold" [...] His Welsh voice would recall that of his nephew, the Revd Joseph Walker Jenkins, curate at Batley.' Smith adds that Charlotte's surprise was because Evan had been ill.[53] Smith is seriously suggesting that after eighteen months of going to Evan's services and to his home, Charlotte is surprised at hearing his voice! It is also so incredibly rude to call Evan that, and 'unclerical'? I found that Mrs Chadwick was just as asinine in 1914. When she mentions that Patrick Brontë had spent one night at the residence of Mr Jenkins, she adds: 'whom Charlotte Brontë afterwards referred to as "that little Welsh pony Jenkins"'. She was perhaps nervous of the word 'unclerical', but certainly didn't use common sense.[54] The 'Mr Jenkins' here was certainly not Evan; it was Joseph Walker Jenkins, his nephew, finally come to Brussels, as is obvious from Charlotte's sentence that follows.

Joseph had been ordained a priest in 1842, and was now twenty-six, just six months younger than Charlotte, and we know from *Shirley* the fun she had in being nasty about curates.[55] In the register for baptisms, marriages and funerals at Batley in the summer of 1843, Joseph's last duty was on Sunday 23 July (a marriage) and his next one not until 3 September. As Charlotte's letter to Ellen on 30 January had shown, one could get to Brussels from Yorkshire with three days of travelling. In her 'unclerical' letter it is clear that Charlotte is talking about the service on 30 July (when Evan was in Greenwich). The letter is dated by Smith as Sunday '6 August, 1843' but that refers to the second part of the letter where Charlotte puts that date. She had obviously started writing the letter a few days earlier. She had heard what she thought was Joseph's voice and immediately hoped that he had brought her a letter from Ellen, but then decides that she must have been mistaken in identifying him: she may only have heard Joseph once or twice before (and she was very short-sighted).

But in the second part of her letter, now definitely dated 6 August, Joseph has come to Charlotte's school:

> Since I wrote the preceding pages Mr Jenkins has called – he brought no <news> 'letter' from you but said you were at Harrogate – and that they could not find the letter you had intended to send – He informed me of two melancholy events.

She mentions just one event: the death of Ellen's sister Sarah. Joseph's curacy at Batley was only a couple of miles from Ellen's home. We know from Abraham Dixon's letter that Evan had become ill around 14 July and had gone to John Livingston and Janet in Greenwich on the 24th for two weeks – presumably knowing that Joseph would arrive in time to take his place at the Chapel Royal on Sundays 30 July and 6 August, or at least give the sermon, as Charlotte's letter suggests (the only use of the pulpit was for the sermon).[56] Joseph possibly then made a trip to Spa, eighty miles east of Brussels, where he was made chaplain the next year and no doubt enjoyed the mineral springs.[57] Possibly Evan pulled strings for him, as the chaplain was appointed by the Belgian government.[58] According to Rev. Biber's book about the English Church on the Continent of 1845, Spa had 'no English poor', and the only resident English were two physicians, 'three or four families of gentry, and a few English grooms in the service of foreigners', but during the season about one thousand visitors arrived. It therefore seems to have been a seasonal job for Joseph: perhaps he went back to Yorkshire in the autumn and helped his father in Pudsey, or assisted Evan in Brussels. But there were temptations. In *Pendennis*, Thackeray mentions Rev. Shamble at a spa town on the Continent as 'an erratic Anglican divine, hired for the season at places of English resort, and addicted to debts, drinking, and even to roulette'.[59]

* * *

That same Sunday in August when Charlotte was finishing her letter to Ellen, William Makepeace Thackeray was rushing by train from Brussels to Antwerp, back to Brussels, then back to Antwerp again. He was trying to gather material for a book on the Low Countries, which was never published, and his pocket-book had been mislaid or stolen. It was finally discovered back in Antwerp, minus the bank notes.[60] At thirty-two, he was desperately earning money from magazine articles under pseudonyms. His wife Isabella had recently been committed to an asylum; his daughters were now living with his mother in Paris. He wanted to write a full-length novel: *Barry Lyndon* started serialization in January the following year. It is curious to think of these two authors just about to start on their serious writing careers momentarily in the same foreign town. Perhaps Charlotte took a walk along the Allée Verte and saw a very tall, bothered Englishman leap on or off a train. Four years later she called him an 'intellectual boa-constrictor', and was thrilled that he had enjoyed *Jane Eyre*.[61]

Thackeray and Charlotte first met in London in 1849, after Charlotte had rather unfortunately dedicated the second edition of *Jane Eyre* to him: unknown to Charlotte, Thackeray was not quite hiding a mad wife in his attic, but a mad wife in an asylum. Rumours spread that 'Currer Bell', the author of *Jane Eyre*, was a former governess to Thackeray's children.[62] As late as 1860 he had to bat away salacious rumours, with humour but exasperation. This exchange, between Thackeray and an American woman, is quoted by Gordon Ray in his biography:

Fair American Visitor: 'Tell me, Mr. Thackeray, is it true, the dreadful story about you and Currer Bell?'

Thackeray: 'Alas, Madam, it is all too true. And the fruits of that unhallowed intimacy were six children. I slew them all with my own hand.'[63]

* * *

In October, Charlotte wrote to Emily:

> You ask about Queen Victoria's visit to Brussels. I saw her for an instant flashing through the Rue Royale in a carriage and six, surrounded by soldiers. She was laughing and talking, very gaily. She looked a little, stout, vivacious Lady [...] The Belgians liked her very well on the whole.[64]

We hear Emily's voice so seldom that it is intriguing that she was interested in what Charlotte had seen of the royal couple. Queen Victoria was twenty-four and by then had three children; she describes driving through the rue Royale: 'The streets were crowded with people on foot, & the "beau monde" were at the windows [...] we were quite broiled by the sun.'[65] The visit to Belgium, postponed from the year before perhaps because of the death of Queen Louise's brother, took place between 13 and 20 September. Victoria spent only one Sunday in Belgium and it is amusing to trace the rivalry of *The Times* and *Morning Post* as their correspondents despatched reports back to London on what happened on Sunday 17th in Ostend, and which clergyman led the service: Rev. Jenkins or Rev. Jessopp (the new Anglican clergyman in Ostend).

The *Morning Post* was second in circulation only to *The Times* and it seems they were the only two British newspapers that had correspondents in Belgium. Later their reports were copied by newspapers throughout the country. In *Barchester Towers* (1857), Anthony Trollope comments, tongue in cheek, on 'The *Jupiter* [*The Times*], that daily paper, which, as we all know, is the only true source of infallibly correct information on all subjects.'[66] The *Morning Post* was more interested in the doings of the fashionable. It has been described as 'the organ of the two most aristocratic classes of English society – of gentlemen, and of persons who are known as gentlemen's gentlemen; of ladies, and of ladies' maids'.[67] In the mid-1840s Thackeray was heartily involved in the *Punch* satires on the newspaper listing the names of guests attending select London parties as if it were news. In revenge, in 1847 – as Thackeray was becoming famous for his serialization of *Vanity Fair* – the newspaper omitted Thackeray's name in their lists.[68]

Both articles in *The Times* and the *Morning Post* about Victoria and Albert's Sunday in Ostend were printed in their newspapers just two days later, on Tuesday

19 September. The writers would have to get their despatches onto a steamboat on the Sunday. In the *Messager de Gand* newspaper of 13 September, the steamboats going from Ostend to London are listed: the only one on Sunday 17th was at 7 in the evening. There was no boat on the Monday.[69] I will quote from both articles so that the reader can decide which article is the more truthful.

The *Morning Post* correspondent waxes lyrical; I think 'our correspondent' may be a woman:

Ostend, Sunday Night.
This morning whilst the sun and the morning mist were striving for the mastery, the sound of a gun was heard booming over the waters, and murdering the sleep of the Ostendese [...] She proved to be her Majesty's ship Grecian, a sixteen-gun brig of war, which has been for a long time on the coast of Africa, and had accompanied the Royal squadron previous to being paid off. Captain Smyth came on shore, and immediately repaired to the palace [...] The delightful sea breeze and the beautiful weather attracted myriads of people to the dyke throughout the day. His Majesty King Leopold was walking about on the pier-head.[70]

The 'palace' was actually a small town house. 'Our Correspondent' is then rude about both Belgians and English, and, after showing off by quoting Milton, continues:

The whole of this day has been devoted by her Majesty to repose, which must have been very necessary after the wild and whirling manner in which her Majesty has been dragged about during the last week. Her Majesty adhered to her invariable custom of strictly observing the duties of the day, and Mr. Jenkins accordingly came over from Brussels and performed the service of our Church in a private apartment of the palace. Mr. Jessop, the clergyman here, had made every preparation for the reception of her Majesty in the Protestant Church, which was festooned with flowers and adorned with evergreens, but in the course of the morning he received a communication from her Majesty, requesting him to perform the service at the palace. With this request he was unable to comply, as he could not neglect his duties at his own church [...] Her Majesty will leave Ostend early to morrow morning for Brussels, where she is expected to arrive at about one o'clock.

If we turn to *The Times*, we find:

> Ostend, Sunday, Sept. 17.
>
> It was reported during the week just closed that our most gracious Sovereign, Prince Albert, His Majesty the King of the Belgians, and the suite of Her Majesty, would attend divine service publicly to-day in the Protestant church of Ostend. For reasons not yet known, this intention, if ever entertained, was abandoned. Divine service has been performed before the Queen, Prince Albert, and Her Majesty's suite and attendants, in the chapel in the Royal residence, by the Rev. Mr. Jessop, of this town. Perhaps the heat of the weather may have had something to do with the Queen's seclusion, for it is so intensely hot that it might not be altogether safe for Her Majesty to take exercise in the open air.

He then goes on with a brief description of a Mass, a discussion of Queen Louise's religious habits (as a Catholic) and a bit about dinner that night. He ends up by saying: 'I am not sure that there remains anything further to be said. If any incident of interest occur this evening requiring to be communicated, I shall add it in a postscript.'[71] Alas, the sub should have deleted that. I know which one is the more entertaining read, but who officiated in Ostend for Queen Victoria and Prince Albert: Jenkins or Jessopp? I first turned to Queen Victoria's Journals. She writes: 'After our breakfast, walked over & visited dear Uncle & my beloved Louise.' Victoria and Albert were staying in an equally small town house nearby. 'Remained with them a little while, & then returned, to write &c. – At 1, a Clergyman held a Service for us downstairs, & afterwards Uncle & Louise came to our luncheon.'[72]

I did so hope that Evan, having carried confidential letters between King Leopold and his nephew and niece, whom he had already met, wasn't described just as 'a Clergyman'. I held my breath for a while until I discovered an irate letter from young Rev. Jessopp (the correspondents got the spelling wrong) to the Editor of the *Morning Post*, written by him a day later:

> Sir – The statement in the *Morning Post* of yesterday (which has this night reached me) relative to what took place here last Sunday, is so much at variance with the facts, that I am sure you will thank me for enabling you to rectify them. Your statement is as follows –

'Her Majesty adhered to her invariable custom of strictly observing the duties of the day, and Mr. Jenkins accordingly came over from Brussels and performed the service of our church.'

Jessopp repeats the article and then states:

> Mr. Jenkins was not in Ostend for one moment during her Majesty's visit.
>
> Her Majesty, with the most considerate kindness to Mr. Jessopp's congregation at Ostend, did not command his attendance until *after* he had performed the morning service at his own church; when he proceeded to her Majesty's private apartments, and again performed it in the presence of her Majesty, his Royal Highness Prince Albert, Lord Liverpool, and her Majesty's suite.
>
> It is untrue that the Protestant church at Ostend was 'festooned with flowers and adorned with evergreens' – there was not the slightest addition to the sober and simple appearance it exhibits on every Sabbath day throughout the year. – I am, Sir, your obedient faithful servant,
>
> John Jessopp, M.A.
> British Chaplain at Ostend, and Chaplain to his Majesty the King of the Belgians.[73]

Alas, it is sometimes true that the more you fabricate the more entertaining your writing is, as the tabloids know well. And so did Thomas Love Peacock, friend of Shelley. In his 1831 satirical novel, *Crotchet Castle*, Rev. Dr Folliott defends Walter Scott's historical novels: 'He has misrepresented every thing, or he would not have been very amusing. Sober truth is but dull matter to the reading rabble.'[74]

The 28-year-old Jessopp had been made an honorary chaplain to the king in September 1842; he didn't stay in Ostend long, but flaunted the title it seems for the rest of his life.[75] Mrs Gaskell possibly disliked clergymen calling Sunday the 'Sabbath'. In her short story 'My Lady Ludlow', Lady Ludlow reprimands the clergyman Mr Gray: 'The Sabbath is the Sabbath, and that's one thing – it is Saturday; and if I keep it, I'm a Jew, which I'm not. And Sunday is Sunday; and that's another thing; and if I keep it, I'm a Christian, which I humbly trust I am.'[76]

I am intrigued by the *Morning Post* correspondent. Her/his article is so fabricated but it might be based on a rumour she had heard: that the senior Anglican clergyman in Belgium, Evan Jenkins, might do a round trip of at least ten hours to do the service in Ostend. Perhaps Prince Albert had requested it initially, having been to his services, but it must have proved rather unreasonable, and discourteous to young Rev. Jessopp. The *Morning Post* correspondent sent her despatch off on the boat not having checked any facts, and was rewarded with copies being made of it as late as the October 1843 edition of *Blackwood's Lady's Magazine*. The dull *Times* correspondent, who had nothing interesting to say, had his piece copied a few times. He wins the prize for truth, but one wonders if he was called on again to be a royal correspondent. Perhaps he complained that he had signed up for real news and a royal tour was just too dull. I am sure, though, that Evan and Eliza saw Victoria and Albert personally on 18 September at the palace in Brussels, while Charlotte looked on with the masses in the street, ever in the shadows, but so self-aware that she was – whether in the characters of Jane Eyre, Lucy Snowe, or even William Crimsworth at the start of *The Professor* when he first goes to his rich brother's house in Yorkshire.

But fifteen years later, Queen Victoria read *Jane Eyre* to Prince Albert: 'We remained up, reading in "Jane Eyre", till ½ p. 11, – quite creepy, from the awful account of what happened the night before the marriage, which was interrupted in the Church.' She read it again in 1880: 'Finished Jane Eyre, which is really a wonderful book, very peculiar in parts, but so powerfully – admirably written, such a fine tone in it, such fine religious feeling, & such beautiful writing. The description of the mysterious maniac's nightly appearances, awfully thrilling, – Mr Rochester's character a very remarkable one, & Jane Eyre's herself, a beautiful one. The end is very touching, when Jane Eyre returns to him, & feeds him blind, with one hand gone from injuries during the fire in his house, which was caused by his mad wife.'[77] She later read *Villette*, 'admirably written & very interesting', and *Shirley*, as well as Mrs Gaskell's biography: 'poor Charlotte Brontë! who was so highly gifted & so good. It is one of the saddest lives one can imagine.'[78] The young woman in the crowd in the rue Royale later touched the queen's heart.

* * *

Charlotte was falling in love with her teacher Constantin Heger, and it was hell, as any woman knows who loves a man who is unattainable. Before her impassioned letters to Heger were published in 1913, it could only be a guess, but Anthony Trollope read *Villette* and knew at once. In his posthumously published autobiography he writes: 'The character of Paul [...] is a wonderful study. She must herself have been in love with some Paul when she wrote the book.'[79] Heger (1809–96) was five years younger than his second wife, Zoë Claire Parent; after their marriage in 1836 they had six children, the last born in 1846. Heger was only seven years older than Charlotte.[80] In *The Professor*, Charlotte portrays Heger in her character William as he teaches Frances, perhaps trying to work out what Heger felt as he taught her, while the directress of the school, Mlle Reuter, looks on, jealously alert:

> I stood a good while behind her [Frances], writing on the margin of her book. I could hardly quit my station or relinquish my occupation. Something retained me bending there, my head very near hers, and my hand near hers too; but the margin of a copybook is not an illimitable space – so, doubtless, the directress thought; and she took occasion to walk past, in order to ascertain by what art I prolonged so disproportionately the period necessary for filling it.[81]

Surely that same sexual tension was felt between Heger and Charlotte – or the latter imagined so, and Mme Heger noticed. The fictional Mlle Reuter dispenses with Frances's services at the school, where she has been teaching lace-mending. By May, Mme Heger had cooled towards Charlotte, who rarely saw Heger now that she was no longer a pupil.[82] And possibly in June, Charlotte speculates on the reason for Mme Heger's new 'mighty distance & reserve', which we can read as that the latter is distrustful of her husband's feelings for Charlotte.[83] This surely is one of the causes for Charlotte's confession to a Catholic priest in St Gudule.[84] In October, Charlotte had told Mme Heger that she wanted to go home, but M. Heger 'having heard of what was in agitation – sent for me the day after – and pronounced with vehemence his decision that I should not leave – I could not at that time have persevered in my intention without exciting him to passion – so I promised to stay a while longer'.[85] 'Passion' is a strong word. Is this really how he dealt with his 'intellectual pupils' as Thomas Westwood commented years later, and that there was 'no illicit affection on his part'?[86] Well, that is what Heger would say to Westwood. But if it was instead a power game with Charlotte, then it is unforgivable – along with his reading of Charlotte's letters to him to Mrs Gaskell.

In December, Charlotte decided to go home, and this time she doesn't mention whether Heger tried to persuade her otherwise.[87] It is possible that a letter from her friend Mary Taylor, then in Germany, finally gave her the courage to go.[88] We know from a letter by Abraham Dixon to his daughter Mary that Charlotte was at the Jenkins home for Christmas dinner. The letter has useful insights into the Jenkinses and a great anecdote about an elderly lovesick man whom Evan forthrightly called 'deranged'.

* * *

On Saturday 30 December, Abraham Dixon wrote to his daughter from Brussels: 'I received your very little short letter dated Ilkley 28 Sep. this I send by Miss Brontë who leaves on Sunday for her home, and does not mean to return.'[89] He writes that he has now an excellent servant, 'recommended by Mrs Jenkins, rather older than Mrs Bloom, she keeps the house particularly neat & clean and is very careful. She is I believe a Scotchwoman a widow without children, tho' she may be Irish I forgot to ask.' This may be connected to Evan's charitable work, with which Eliza is involved: they would know of destitute British people. Dixon also encourages Mary to come to Ostend: although she disliked it when she last visited, that was because of bad weather and no society, but again Mrs Jenkins 'would introduce you to as much & of the best society there, as would be desirable' and she could let the house to Mrs Jenkins and family in the summer: 'Mrs J– would be glad of it, she paid last year for a very inferior house 250 or 300 for a month & says this is worth much more.' He then mentions Catherine Goussaert who 'has gone at this unseasonable season to take a tour in Germany & visit Madame Schmidt & of course Mary Taylor'. Maybe she was also trying to get more pupils, especially after the damaging news about Martha's death a year before.

He then writes about the engagement of Miss Bright, 'the youngest but one', to Sir David Cunynghame, a Scottish baronet, 'not very rich, and about 75 or more years old'. It's the kind of gossip that must have fuelled the conversation of the expat community in Brussels, but driven Charlotte to despair, longing for intelligent conversation with Heger, though she would still have listened. Sir David had rented a house near the Bright's new house, nearly opposite the Jenkins home, in the week before Christmas. 'I dined with him at Mr Jenkins's when he was as gay as a lark, and talking of going the next day to the English Embassy to have the marriage settlement signed: when, oh misére [sic], the very next day Thursday the post brings a letter from the young lady's brother, with such information as caused the match to be entirely broken off, and Mrs Bright and the intended Lady Cunynghame went off on the Sunday following by the steamer from Antwerp to London on their way to her son's house near Ludlow, to be out of the way of the old gentleman.' Her sisters had largely kept at home since but the youngest, Louisa, had dined at the Jenkinses on Christmas Day 'along with Miss Brontë & others with myself'. Sir David had since been confined to bed, but in the evening 'goes to the theatre' and 'during the performance keeps his eyes upon the box where he & his intended sat when last there together, & pays no attention to the performance, thus he has been seen for several nights. Mr J– thinks he is deranged & has written for his son, a Gent of about 50, to come over & look after his disapp. love sick Father.' The parishioners that a clergyman has to deal with! Dixon continues that Evan was never consulted about the affair 'which was very imprudent on the part of Mrs B– who I consider much to blame in this affair'.

We don't know what Mrs Bright's son wrote, but there is evidence that Sir David Cunynghame of Milncraig, apparently widowed twice, had seven living sons. If this is the same man, the prospect of being booted out of her new home at her husband's death by stepsons far older than Miss Bright was suddenly a less glamorous future than her mother had envisaged. Or, did the son write that he had a wife still living? Evan had married one of her children, John Bright, and was to officiate at the marriage of the youngest daughter Louisa to Joseph Lucien Coulbaut in 1846. Mrs Bright, widow of a clergyman in Shropshire, was no doubt as desperate as Jane Austen's Mrs Bennet to get her five daughters off her hands, and she sounds as silly a woman. She remained friends with Eliza, as we shall see in a later chapter. Whether Eliza really liked her, or was just being a splendid clergyman's wife, I cannot tell. Hopefully Mrs Bright's teenage daughter Louisa was less daft at the Christmas dinner that Charlotte attended at the Jenkinses. But at least seventeen-year-old Edward was there after his first year at Shrewsbury. If he was anything like his three-times great-nephew, there would have been some sparkling arguments. I relish so.

* * *

I will end this chapter, and Charlotte's stay in Brussels, with what may be the most ludicrous of inventions, embroidered in later biographies without care or common sense. It is that Madame Heger accompanied Charlotte to the boat at Ostend on 1 January 1844.[90] There are three supposed 'facts' in that sentence. Rebecca Fraser in her biography in 1988 even managed to combine anachronistic illogicality with this fantasy: 'Mme Heger accompanied her, a little grimly, perhaps, all the way in the diligence to the boat at Ostend.'[91] No wonder Mme Heger was grim, since normal people took the train. In her 1960s biography of Charlotte, Gérin has: 'She left Brussels on Monday, 1 January 1844, Madame Heger accompanying her to the boat at Ostend.' She gives no source. But I then came across an article by Eric Ruijssenaars on the Brussels Brontë Group website who had found a source for Mme Heger's rather unbelievable journey with Charlotte from 1951.[92] It came from a granddaughter of the Hegers who talked to Dr Phyllis Bentley over lunch in Brussels; the latter stated: 'Mme. Beckers mentioned that when Charlotte left the Pensionnat Heger finally, Mme. Heger accompanied her to the boat at Ostend.'[93] This is a 'memory' or Chinese whisper over one hundred years later. Indeed, Ruijssenaars states that much of the family information this granddaughter gave to Bentley is untrue. Most of his article discusses a melodramatic concoction in a recent 'biography' but he has his doubts about the diligence in Fraser's book (quite wisely), though largely because Charlotte doesn't mention the transport, and he doubts that Mme Heger accompanied her.

The date of 1 January for leaving Brussels is apparently given by Charlotte herself, who allegedly wrote in a book: 'Given to me by Monsieur Heger on the 1st January 1844, the morning I left Brussels.'[94] It was, at the least, a ten-hour round trip by train to Ostend, but probably much longer. Are these biographers seriously suggesting that a mother of five children – the youngest only eleven months – would go on a journey of this length to accompany a woman she no longer trusted in the cold of New Year's Day? Dr Johnson's trial of common sense says *no*: it is as likely as snow in Yorkshire in July.

Further, we don't even know if Charlotte went to Ostend; I believe she went to Antwerp. The problem is Charlotte's supposed date of Monday 1 January for leaving Brussels, since the packet steamer *Soho* left Antwerp at 11 a.m. on Sundays.[95] And, indeed, Abraham Dixon wrote that she was leaving on Sunday 31 December – and her departure on Sunday would have thus been known to the Jenkins family – and Charlotte had written to Emily that she hoped to be home 'the day after New Year's Day', that is, Tuesday 2 January, which fits with a Sunday boat, not with taking a boat on Tuesday 2nd. In Emily's diary paper in July 1845 she even writes that Charlotte, after staying a year in Brussels, 'came back again on new years day 1844'.[96]

Another problem with Ostend is that the General Steam Navigation Company's boat left Ostend at ten in the evening on Tuesday 2 January; the previous boat was Friday 29 December.[97] Thus she would have had to stay the night there, and then the entire day, and she had very little money, as she mentions to Emily.[98] Who on earth would rationally aim to spend a night and a day in Ostend in January? I wouldn't want to spend such a length of time anywhere, whatever the month, whatever the season, while I was trying to get home.

There were two trains to Ostend: at seven in the morning and three in the afternoon; whereas there were five trains to Antwerp, the relevant one in the morning at 7.45.[99] It took about an hour by railroad to Antwerp.[100] It was by far the most sensible route, frequently followed by the Jenkinses, as I relate in my next chapter: when Charlotte arrived at the station in Antwerp she could probably get straight on the packet. Going to Ostend instead makes no sense at all. And the Antwerp route is the one that she and Emily took in November 1842 on hearing the news of Aunt Branwell's death.[101]

I began to wonder if Charlotte's inscription in the book was a forgery and checked the Brontë Parsonage Museum catalogue online. It wasn't there. I should have put two and two together when I saw that Margaret Smith's source for the book and its inscription – and for taking a boat at Ostend on Tuesday 2 January when her family in Haworth were expecting Charlotte to arrive home that day – was Gérin. Gérin also fabricated that the boat left on 'the morning's tide of Tuesday, 2 January', which is slightly difficult for a packet leaving at ten in the evening.[102] Oh, what a tangled web we weave …

The Curatorial Assistant at the Parsonage Museum replied to my query about the book and her informative emails led to my next trip – back to Haworth. And all for the sake of checking an inscription in a book that wasn't there. What I needed to see were three Sotheby's catalogues of the early twentieth century dealing with Brontë memorabilia sold by the widow of Arthur Nicholls. *Les Fleurs* – with that inscription mentioning 1 January – was auctioned in December 1916, over a year after the death of Rev. Nicholls's second wife, and hasn't been heard of since.

Under the heading 'The Property of the late Mrs. A.B. Nicholls' and 'sold by order of the Executrix' the book was the first lot of fifteen (lot 641):

> Brontë (Charlotte) Les Fleurs de la Poésie française depuis le commencement du XVIᵉ siècle, *half calf, m. e. with MS. inscription on fly-leaf: 'Given to me by Monsieur Heger on the 1st of Jany. 1844, the morning I left Brussels, C. Brontë,' in the latter's autograph*   *Tours*, 1841[103]

The next lot were two volumes of the works of Bernardin de Saint-Pierre, inscribed on the fly-leaf as 'The Gift of Monsieur Heger, Brussels, Augst. 15th 1843' 'in C. Brontë's autograph'. The member of the Brontë Society who attended the sale noted the buyer and the price. In both cases the lots were bought by 'Spencer'. What I found surprising was that the book of poetry had gone for £13 (about £800 today), whereas the two volumes went for much less: only £2 18s. As the National Archives Currency Converter charmingly says, for the cost of the book of verse one could buy a cow in 1915, though it was not enough for a horse. Spencer was the most successful buyer, acquiring eight of these fifteen lots of books, manuscripts and a signet ring; the antiquarian bookseller Maggs bought three; 'Chadwick' – presumably Mrs Chadwick – acquired Emily Brontë's accounts notebook for 12 shillings. The most Spencer paid was £41 (over £2,000) for an atlas that contained sketches by Charlotte and a note by her, dated 'Octbr.

14th, 1843', which starts: 'First Class, I am very cold', and describes a teacher 'who seems a rosy sugar-plum, but I know her to be coloured chalk'. If the inscription by Charlotte stating that it was Heger's gift to her on 1 January was a forgery, the forger had enough specimens of Charlotte's handwriting to copy (if the rest were authentic – and there had been quibbles in previous sales),[104] and she/he could see in Mrs Gaskell's *Life* that Charlotte arrived home on 2 January, but made the wrong calculation that she had left Brussels on the 1st – not having access to times and dates of steam packets for 1843–4. After Charlotte's letters to Heger were published in 1913, they might also have calculated that married Heger giving Charlotte a book of poetry at their last meeting was racy enough to command a good price, which it did. Charlotte might comment: 'this would have been unlike real Life, inconsistent with Truth – at variance with Probability'.[105] And we should trust Charlotte about her leave-taking with M. Heger: In a letter to Ellen, a few weeks after she arrived home, she writes: 'at parting he gave me a sort of diploma certifying my abilities as a teacher – sealed with the seal of the Athenée Royal of which he is professor.' It was dated 29 December 1843, which is probably the last date that she saw him. She may have spent the next day with the Dixons. There is no mention of the gift of a book.[106]

My trip to Haworth had provided no definitive proof of forgery, but it was a gloriously sunny day and I discovered that Haworth is now twinned with Machu Picchu, which was a fittingly surreal end to my trip: at least *that* was not a fabrication.

Fifteen

'Why should we weep or mourn'

Schoolboys and Death

We entreat of you to keep them out of the hearing of the village children so that they may not again adopt their language and which has hitherto been such a drawback to their improvement.

– Eliza Jenkins to Mrs Frances Curwen, Brussels, 6 June [1844][1]

Henry and Alfred Curwen, aged nine and eight respectively, arrived at the Jenkins home school in Brussels in early 1844 from their home in Cumberland. They had travelled on the steam packet *Soho* to Antwerp, armed with 'nice bows and some arrows and a target' which their father had bought for them in London. This was probably the same packet that Charlotte Brontë had used to go home a few weeks before. The Jenkinses knew the packet's captain; Eliza wrote in July to Mrs Curwen when the boys were due to return to Brussels after the summer holidays: 'I will also write a few lines to Captain Whitecombe by whose vessel your sons went over, and you can if you please commit them to his charge, in which case I am sure they will be carefully looked after.' Perhaps Eliza wrote a note to the captain in December 1843 asking him to take courteous care of Miss Brontë. When the boys arrived at Antwerp, usually Evan, Eliza or the English master, William Ayers, met them. Normally Evan escorted them back to England, but in June 1845 he was unable to. Eliza asked friends and then two grown-up pupils to accompany the boys, but they let her down by leaving a week early. So she wrote to Mrs Curwen that the Agent to the Company would escort the boys to Antwerp, where Alfred would be put 'under the surveillance of Mr Bust', whereas Henry is a 'steady fellow' and could travel alone if need be. In June 1846, Henry wrote to his mother that they would probably go on the *Wilberforce* from Antwerp, just as Charlotte and Emily had done in November 1842, 'at one o'clock on Sunday the fourteenth, and we shall perhaps get to Blackwall [on the Thames in East London] about 9. o clock on Monday'. They would then possibly take the train to the new station at Fenchurch Street. There is never a mention of going via Ostend.

The Curwens were an ancient family residing at Workington Hall near the mouth of the river Derwent as it flows into the Irish Sea. The once splendid country house, where Mary Queen of Scots stayed one night on her flight from Scotland, is now a ruin. Although the boys' father, Edward Stanley Curwen, was heir to the lordship of the manor after the death of his brother in 1842, the family's finances were probably as precarious as Edward Taylor's, who had had to give up Bifrons, but their collieries were still being worked and young Alfred writes to his mother from Brussels that he hopes 'no accidents have happened at the coal pits'. The schoolboys' great-grandfather was John Christian (1756–1828), a cousin of the mutineer on the *Bounty* Fletcher Christian, equally famous for having been played by both Clark Gable and Marlon Brando. John Christian added the surname Curwen after his marriage to his heiress cousin Isabella Curwen in 1782. He was a reforming Member of Parliament and progressive agriculturist whose estates and collieries in Cumberland were badly hit by the depression after the Napoleonic Wars.[2] Coleridge came to stay in 1809 to recover from mumps, and convinced Curwen to give him free parliamentary franking for the planning of his newspaper *The Friend*.[3] In 1830, Curwen's granddaughter, Isabella Christian Curwen, married William Wordsworth's eldest son, dullard John, a 'truly respectable Clergyman', Coleridge's son Hartley commented dryly. Wordsworth noted that 'the Father's allowance to his daughter is so liberal as to remove every objection on prudential grounds'.[4] But there was an odd coda to this marriage in the 1840s which has not been properly explored, and which I will touch on below.

The Curwen papers at the Whitehaven, Cumbria Archive include letters from the boys at school in Brussels, and from Eliza to their mother Frances Curwen née Jesse. It seems that Evan wrote about the boys' progress to Mr Curwen, but these letters have not survived – it is possibly typical that it was their mother who hoarded the boys' letters. There is a passport for their father, Edward Stanley Curwen, dated 1836 when he was twenty-five. He had blue eyes, was 5 feet 11 inches tall and described as 'Officier au Service de S.M. Britannique demeurant a Londres'. Two of their children were born in Brussels: Alfred in 1835 and Ella in 1853. Alfred was baptized privately in February 1836 by William Drury, so it is interesting that he later went to the Jenkins school and not to Drury's.[5] A younger son, Edward, who became Canon of Carlisle Cathedral, was taught by Edward Jenkins in the 1850s. In a speech he gave in 1913 he said that Captain Marryat had written *The Dog Fiend or Snarleyyow* (1837) in his parents' house in Brussels. It is a historical novel involving smuggling and a Dutch villain; in fact most of the Dutch in the book are nasty. Canon Curwen may be repeating a faulty family memory about the book, but no doubt his parents knew Marryat and were also friends with Charles Lever.[6]

At first, Eliza's letters to Frances Curwen, who was about thirteen years younger, are not those to a friend, despite mutually helping each other out, such as Eliza organizing their apartment and furniture in the Hôtel de France, rue Royale – 'The food is excellent & only the best company frequent the hotel' – or hunting out the best lace for her. In return, Mrs Curwen offered to buy items for Eliza that were cheaper in England, which Eliza avails herself of, requesting '12 pairs of stout Cotton Stockings for my Daughter. She generally wears Boots as is the custom Abroad, therefore it is not necessary to get very fine ones.' Eliza is notably also the headmaster's wife, and in interpreting her letters it is necessary to remember that she was writing to the wife of an influential man, who could help with recommending the Jenkins school to other families. But after the Curwens stayed in Brussels for several months in autumn and winter 1845–6, the letters turn more gossipy.

Henry and Alfred were difficult to educate in the Jenkins school at first. Apart from their Cumberland dialect and rather horrifying vocabulary that they had picked up from the village children, Alfred had had 'obstinate' fits and 'as yet we have had many difficulties to contend against, which being removed in a great measure we will see our way more clearly, & it will be less labourious to impart instructions, now that they have acquired more attentive habits & got rid almost entirely of the Patois'. But Eliza is more upbeat, or attempting to be more reassuring, in July 1844: 'Poor Boys it has been very uphill work for them as yet, but next half year will be comparatively easy both to them and their teachers.' I wonder if the bows and arrows had finally been confiscated. A year later she combines warm words about the boys with a stern, underlined warning about not spoiling them:

Two such happy faces as Harry & Alfred's it does one good to look at, particularly when you feel that they are <u>as good</u> as their looks and deserving of every indulgence that is <u>reasonable</u>.

We learn from the letters that there was a gardener at the Jenkins home, as Henry refers to 'Mrs cribs the gardeners wife', so presumably there was a sizeable garden, but perhaps not the luscious garden that Eliza's grandparents had in Andover, as the boys never mention it. As for teachers, Henry refers to 'the masters' in March 1846 when he writes asking to be sent 'a prodigious monstrous enormus greate cake as we are going to have a picknick unknown to the masters at Easter the picknick is among the Boys that remain here'. Probably most of the masters lived elsewhere in Brussels and came in daily. Two teachers are named in their letters: Charlotte Morse and William Ayers, who were then in their thirties. It is not known if they were living in the Jenkins house, but it seems likely – certainly in Miss Morse's case – and they surely had met the Brontë sisters. In early March 1844, eight-year-old Alfred wrote to his mother: 'a revolution has taken plase in france on the second of lent the king and queen was to be sean in the museum [...] I fell in some water and Mister Eyres brought me into a house tile some of the boys came to fetch me thir was a grate deal of water [...] P.S. The revolution in france is a false report.' I can imagine poor William Ayers having to dry the boy off, and then correct his letter and teach Alfred the phrase 'a false report'. Indeed, Eliza writes to Mrs Curwen in August 1845 that if their letters are inspected, 'it is owing to their taking them to Mr Ayers and asking him "is it all right?"' But I feel also for the little boy, missing his family, and wonder if he deliberately fell in the water in the hope of gaining attention. But the younger Jenkins children would be playmates, especially John, aged nine in 1844. In one letter written during the school holidays in July 1844, Eliza says: 'My young ones beg to be kindly remembered to their companions.'

In October, older brother Henry reports to his mother that 'Mr earys' took them 'to the town when went ther we saw the place wher all the people that were killed in the reveolution were bruied' and that he can't find his seal, which Miss Morse says she doesn't have. He had previously mentioned that she was looking after his watch. What is a nine-year-old doing with a watch and a seal? In 1847 Alfred was ill. After some days in quarantine with scarlatina in the Jenkins home, Eliza sent him off with Miss Morse for a week to the countryside at Tervuren, eight miles from Brussels. Eliza's letter to Mrs Curwen is a mix of information that Alfred has been ill and immediate reassurance, with the enchanting details that Alfred is 'enjoying himself excessively', wants to stay a month and is keen to bring back a goat. I don't think the goat was allowed to come to school, but some of the schoolboys caught pigeons in June 1846 and, instead of being told to release them, were encouraged to build a cage for them. I bet Mr Cribs, the gardener, muttered about having to look after the birds in the school holidays. Eliza comes across as so good in her role – when she and Evan must have been very worried about Alfred's illness – and so in control. Charlotte Morse was Eliza's invaluable help and her background is unusual.

Charlotte Morse's father was Leonard Becher Morse, who died in Brussels in 1827 in his early sixties. He was educated at Eton and Cambridge: his entry at St John's College in 1781 records that his father lived in Downing Street.[7] There was obviously money in the family. Leonard was called to the Bar in 1789 and was made Principal Deputy Commissary-General of the Army in 1809. His wife, Amelia Cox, died around 1795 after giving him a daughter. But in his will, Leonard left everything in Brussels to Charlotte Brown 'who resides with him', and when she died everything was to be divided between the children of Charlotte Brown, of whom the eldest was our teacher, Charlotte Morse.[8] At the close of sending me these details, my cousin Marcia asked three questions: 'Did the Brown children know their parents weren't married? Did the people of Brussels know that Leonard Morse and Charlotte Brown weren't married? Did the people of Brussels care?' I can't answer for the people of Brussels, but the Jenkinses, I think, didn't care. It may be due to a change in mores between the first decade of the nineteenth century and the 1840s that meant Charlotte Brown could accept her unmarried status, while Jane Eyre flees Rochester in horror after being asked to be his mistress – yet the novel is supposedly set during the early 1800s, and Jane returns to him.[9] Charlotte Brown might even have been the governess to widower Leonard Morse's legitimate daughter.

Perhaps Eliza knew that Charlotte Morse's parentage was not above board, but she employed and trusted her. Contrast this with Eliza's seemingly snobbish comments in letters to Mrs Curwen about various women, such as her ironic mention in April 1847 of the 'fascinating Mrs Loughman' whom Eliza instinctively disliked, and who turned out to be the 'Daughter of a music Seller or Master' (shades of *Vanity Fair*'s Becky here):

Lady Falkener mentioned this at Mrs Lowells dinner table and much amused we were to hear it, often hearing her and her accomplishments cried up to the skies! I shall have some fun with Mrs Campbell on the subject for I told her my opinion of Mrs Loughmans manners & way of expressing herself long ago which Mrs Campbell considered a proof of my want of taste I imagine.

Eliza is concerned about breeding and manners – what makes a gentleman or gentlewoman – and highly amused about a snobbish family 'who made a bosom friend of Mrs. L and her Cousin & who think themselves contaminated by associating with anything less than Nobility, making this discovery!' And she can be delightfully waspish: 'Capt & Mrs Duckett have written to express their thanks for the Embassy Pew with which they appear to be extremely pleased & so I imagine they like to be looked at.'

A year earlier (possibly April 1846) Eliza comes across as wanting to express how well-bred she is. She gossips that

Young Morris made an offer of his hand & heart to Miss Wayne \Mrs Brighams niece/ & that she wd not accept him without his Parents consent which was quite correct. In the innocence of my heart & ignorance I perhaps ought to say of the ideas of the world I exclaimed on hearing this. What a lucky Man he will be to have so clever & excellent a girl for a wife! Knowing the young man to have been a bit of a roué & certainly not capable of keeping out of mischief shd anything happen to his Father whose life is not to be reckoned upon. My exclamation & expressions on this subject very much astonished & differed from those of my informant who looked upon it as a take in [ruse or deceit] on the part of the poor girl & in that light does Papa Morris consider it & having valued his Cub at £25,000 with a less sum he will never receive a Daughter in Law.

Miss Wayne was penniless and thus the young man left Brussels and 'fortunately the Damsel does not take the disappointment to heart'. In another letter, in May 1846, Eliza mentions a widow 'of whom queer reports were abroad which threw her out of Society here a few yrs ago, but she was only in the 2nd Set! She is a good looking Woman & Dresses well which is all I can know of her.' At first that sounds snobbish, as Eliza seems to be crowing that she herself is in the first set of Brussels society, but that is how this rigid society worked: and Eliza has complementary things to say about the widow from all that she is allowed to know of her. After reading Thackeray's *Book of Snobs* (published in book form in 1848), I think he might agree that Eliza appears to like people who are well-bred and well-mannered, and not as a snob would do: approve of them because of who they think their parentage is, or who they are chaplain to, or whether they have a title. And yet, as Thackeray remarks, even the calm philosopher who observes the ghastliness of toadyism can fall prey: 'is there one, I wonder, whose heart would not throb with pleasure if he could be seen walking arm-in-arm with a couple of dukes down Pall Mall? No: it is impossible, in our condition of society, not to be sometimes a Snob.'[10] Thus surely Eliza thrilled at her acquaintance with the King and Queen of the Belgians, and was able, from her lofty perch in the inner circle, to pity them as they walked in Ostend: 'The Palace (as it is called) is in the street 3 minutes walk from our Lodging so we shall see the great folks without running after them – Poor creatures there is no privacy for them here – People beset them so.' She is also amusingly spiky about the other inhabitants of their lodging house in Ostend: 'This house is full of clean & unclean Individuals like Noah's Ark.' Presumably among the 'unclean' were a grumbling Russian family and three 'old Maidens dressed up Lamb fashion!'[11]

Eliza has discovered sentiments in common with Mrs Curwen of Workington Hall – breeding matters; ill manners, coarseness and vulgarity are abhorred. Perhaps the irony is that Eliza's husband Evan was born in a farmhouse in the middle of nowhere. Ah, Eliza might retort, but he was at Cambridge and is a clergyman, so is by definition a gentleman, and she would have thought the same of Patrick Brontë. Miss Morse, born in Chelsea, perhaps knew her lower place because of her doubtful parentage, but was well bred enough to be Eliza's assistant. And woe betide any snobbish parent who objected to Miss Morse. I can happily report that she and Suffolk-born William Ayers married in September 1848, with 22-year-old Edward Jenkins as a witness, and didn't die until their seventies.

It is hard to evaluate how many boys were in the school. In June 1844 Henry comments that 'four or five of my companions will cross with us' from Antwerp to London. But there would have been also day boys, and others going home to elsewhere in Belgium or on the Continent. A year later, Eliza mentions two grown-up pupils, perhaps aged eighteen or nineteen, and a large enough number of pupils going home to England enabling Henry and Alfred to travel half price. Eliza is eager to gather any boys that Mrs Curwen has mentioned as interested in the school and always sounds upbeat. But another archive has a letter from the widowed Mrs Mary Bright in Brussels – who had attempted to marry a daughter to elderly Sir David Cunynghame – to her daughter-in-law, which has been dated to probably February 1846, in which she writes that the Jenkinses 'seem to be doing but <u>little</u> this year & have very few boys in the school, & have not given their usual parties. Mrs. Jenkins looks ill.'[12]

School term started in 1844 on Thursday 1 August, but not all the boys arrived then: 'it will be a fortnight or 3 weeks perhaps ere all our Flock meet together, which we always regret, and look upon such delay as a useless loss of time. I hope therefore that you will dispatch your little boys as soon as possible,' Eliza urged Mrs Curwen in July. But she seems not keen on schoolwork in the holidays: 'Entre nous, I am not sorry they have not been kept to work while at home, for I know by my own Children, that the mind requires rest as well as the body, & over straining the intellect is most injurious to young people, & does not make them more clever in the end.' It is hard to say if Eliza really means that. It sounds like reassurance with a groan that they had not practised their reading and writing. In November that year (or maybe in 1845), Eliza continued to be long-suffering and diplomatic: 'Patience & perseverance will overcome every obstacle,' she writes, as she mentions that the boys cannot read their mother's letter but they are 'working hard with their reading, writing and catechism', or what Henry in December calls 'the cattiscum' and 'we are doing lattin frenish sums writting and dancin we lik it better than we thout'.

There were fun things for the boys when back at school, though there was grind: 'It is so dull here that I have nothing to say,' reported Henry in December 1844. But perhaps as in Eliza's grandfather Dr Samuel Jay's school, the boys were rewarded with treats when they behaved well. In September, Alfred wrote to his mother that they had been to the museum, near Evan's Chapel Royal, and seen the 'armerry' and 'a dead man embarmed'. Mrs Dalrymple's guidebook of 1839 states:

> The Museum contains a fine collection of stuffed birds, dried insects, and curious animals; with some extraordinary specimens of not very satisfactory mummies; one treasure it is the repository of, pro tempore, until it can be suitably disposed of for the benefit of the owner, an egyptian mummy of the first class, the property of Mrs. Belzoni, the amiable and interesting widow of the highly gifted and enterprising traveller of that name.
>
> The armoury is well worth seeing, but as it is not open for public view excepting during the fêtes of September, in consequence of the injury caused to the polished steel by the breath of a crowd, a particular permission must be obtained.
>
> The collection of naval, military, architectural, agricultural and mechanicals models, is rich, simple and easy of comprehension; altogether

the Museum is a great source of amusement without expense, and much time may profitably be employed within it's [sic] walls by young persons.[13]

The boys visited the museum again in January: 'we saw a hippolamus a whale and a ostrig and a egil and a cat to feat higt and a sheep with six legs on his body and to legs on his head & a Zebre and a elapant and a rinosus and a seal'. Mr Ayers seems splendidly progressive in not correcting Alfred's spelling – perhaps pleased that the little boy has remembered all the animals' names. In the summer, when the younger boys went to the botanical gardens – 'the flours smelt so nice' – the older ones went to the races.

What I particularly enjoy in Eliza's letters to Frances Curwen are the wheezes for avoiding customs duty, such as Miss Morse fastening the lace being sent to Mrs Curwen to one of the old shirts. Or the best way to get new stockings for Eliza's daughter into Belgium is to 'roll up one stocking & one Sock together, the latter outside, & not put them all together but in different parts of the Trunk so that the quantity may not attract attention when the Bag is examined'. Eliza would have made a good smuggler, and she passed on her strategies to her sons. In 1855 she wrote to her sister Janet from Ostend: 'As we are Lodged in the house of the Lieut des Douanes he will receive Ed & his Boys on their arrival at Ostend & search (or rather not search) their Boxes – "Co" [her son John's nickname] gave up his keys to him when he came over last time, & the Box was not touched! So much for a friend at Court.' She is certainly a capable woman: she met the Curwen boys in Antwerp in August 1845, and writes to their mother:

> There were so many Passengers (112) on Board the Vessel that it was ¼ before 12 ere I could get the Trunk examined, & had I not gone on board myself and found the Brussels Agent whom I happen to know and who lent his aid in providing the Children's Baggage, we should have been detained much later, as many others were, indeed until the table d'hote dinner was nearly over, for as there is no Convooi to Brussels between 10'h & 4 oclock we were obliged to go to the 'St Antoine' and dine there pour passer le temps, the rain falling in torrents the whole time so that we could not walk about [...] we were not sorry to get to Brussels again which we did about 6 in the Evening.

The elegant hotel St Antoine was in the Place Verte, near the cathedral.[14] I wonder whether Charlotte Brontë, when packing her trunk to come home in December

429

1843, carefully scattered her purchases, as advised by Eliza, to fool the customs inspection.

Finally, there are end-of-year accounts that Eliza sends to Frances Curwen in May 1846. Itemized are stationery, *cahiers*, hair cuts, cloth boots, strong shoes and slippers, medicine and for the tailor – all standard. But what I find glorious is listed in Master H. Curwen's account: '6 Bottles of wine'. However, in the midst of these letters in the archive lies something extraordinary, which is catalogued as 'Letter to Edward S. Curwen in Brussels from his father Henry Curwen concerning infidelity'.[15]

* * *

Edward and Frances (Fanny) Curwen had hoped to come to Brussels to see their two eldest sons during the autumn of 1844. In his letter of 21 October, little Alfred wrote: 'I am very glad that you are coming so soon [...] I hope you can stay with us till the holydays' and he hopes that 'all at Brigham quite well' – referring to his six Wordsworth cousins, all under the age of thirteen, where Rev. John Wordsworth, William Wordsworth's eldest son, and Isabella, their father's sister, lived at the vicarage. But the weather turned cold and by December the boys learned that their parents were not coming and that they would spend Christmas at the Jenkins home. Alfred wrote on 9 December: 'I dare say that I shall pass the Christmas holidays happyly. We are very happy at school.' Eliza had been prepared for their disappointment, and seems to have managed the boys well: 'they are by no means overcome as I really feared'. She had warned the boys, she told Frances, that the cold weather 'might prevent your travelling with such little children'. And she reassures her: 'you need have no regrets on their accounts – We only feel for you to whom the disappointment is cruel indeed.' But next autumn and winter, 1845–6, Edward and Frances were able to stay for several months at the Hôtel de France, and that is where Edward received his father Henry's letter delivering the bombshell about the adultery of his brother-in-law Rev. John.

Three recent biographers deal with this newly rediscovered letter in wildly different ways. Julia Summerscale, in her 2013 biography of a cousin of the Curwens, was the first to bring it to modern attention: she notes that Henry Curwen's letter is briefly and cryptically referred to in a biography of Wordsworth in 1965 by Mary Moorman, in which Moorman states that Rev. John is 'unmercifully abused' in the letter, and that Moorman 'gave no clue to its whereabouts nor any detail of its contents', possibly because Moorman did not even see the letter, wanting nothing to detract from her picture of poor, saintly John and the unreasonably angry Curwens.[16] Summerscale, in contrast, believes the accusations about John, and writes that Isabella had been ill after having had six children, was encouraged to improve her health in Rome and that John brought the children to her in 1845. As she states, their youngest son, aged four, died in December 1845 of a fever, John accused Isabella of causing the boy's death and Isabella 'wrote in despair to her parents [actually her mother] in Cumberland, revealing to them that her husband had been sharing a house in Rome with a sixteen-year-old Italian girl', to whom he had written a pledge that he would marry her on his wife's imminent death. Isabella's father then wrote to his eldest son Edward in Brussels about the matter and told him that both he and William Wordsworth had altered their wills, settling their money on the grandchildren, and that Henry Curwen was aiming to buy the pledge of marriage from the Italian girl. Isabella died in 1848 in Bagni di Lucca, a health resort, and her widower's misconduct remained secret. Henry Curwen's handwriting is sometimes hard to read, but I think I may have deciphered more than Summerscale did, and there are interesting new details. A major issue is that of William Wordsworth's will.

In her 2013 biography of Wordsworth's daughter Dora and Coleridge's daughter Sara, Katie Waldegrave summarizes Summerscale's account and leaps in wildly to state that 'Wordsworth had disinherited his son.' I suggest that she ought to have read the will. He didn't. She blames a letter from Isabella to her sister-in-law Dora for the latter's illness in spring 1845 in Portugal (Dora seems to have been frequently ill for years – she died a year before Isabella, in 1847) and decides that Isabella's letter – which doesn't survive – was about John's mistress. Dora's husband Edward Quillinan (then aged fifty-three) certainly singles out the letter Isabella wrote to Dora from Rome in spring 1845, but Waldegrave's account is not only muddled but wrong.[17] Isabella's letter was sent to Dora's mother, Mary Wordsworth, by Quillinan from Portugal. It almost certainly contained absolutely nothing about infidelity, which Dora possibly never knew about. Indeed, in a letter to her mother about five months later, in October 1845, Dora comments on Isabella and John separating, pitying them both: 'Those poor things in Italy it is impossible not to think of them & impossible for such thoughts not to bring anxiety & sorrow; I feel so <u>very</u> much for John in the separation that is about to take place & which seems to be a <u>necessary</u> one. I dont believe Isabella will care much about it & that is a sort of comfort tho' not a pleasant sort.'[18]

Quillinan refers to plural letters as upsetting Dora, but then complains about 'the most extraordinary one' from Isabella: 'the annoyance of receiving such a production seemed the very torch to fever'. He says that 'the whole tone & spirit of the letter is so strange & disagreeable that if it ought to have been written at all it is not to <u>Dora</u> that it should have been addressed'. But he only mentions three things in Isabella's letter: Isabella has 'lightly accused [Dora] of having "deceived" her' – about what we don't know; there are reflections on a Mrs Harrison; and 'complaints of Mrs. Curwen', Isabella's mother. For Waldegrave to leap from that in her biography to declare that Isabella was 'bitter, cruel' and 'hysterical, accusatory, miserable and confused' is careless and unfounded. From the three things that Quillinan mentions, we could deduce that Isabella sounds isolated and indeed miserable, especially if she had quarrelled with her mother, but 'hysterical, accusatory' and 'confused' etc. certainly cannot be deduced. She could have been turning to Dora for help as her marriage was falling apart: Dora was then forty; Isabella some years younger; the sisters-in-law had known each other for years, perhaps long before Isabella married John in 1830.[19] Quillinan's description of the tone of Isabella's letter is his (male) interpretation, not a fact about its contents. When Quillinan describes some of Isabella's letter as 'indelicate', I am forebodingly reminded of Charlotte Brontë's husband Arthur Nicholls censoring her letters to Ellen Nussey, and Charlotte's comments may be appropriate here:

> Arthur has just been glancing over this note – He thinks I have written too freely about Amelia &c. Men don't seem to understand making letters a vehicle of communication – they always seem to think us incautious. I'm sure I don't think I have said anything rash – however you must <u>burn</u> it when read.[20]

Further, Quillinan is hardly consistent, since his description of Dora having a dramatic relapse because of Isabella's letter is overturned by his final comment that he is not 'in the slightest degree downhearted as to D's improvement' and that she is 'now <u>much better</u>, & <u>up</u>'. The spectre of patriarchal controlling behaviour appears again as he says that Isabella '<u>ought</u> to be informed by her husband in such terms as he may think proper that my wife is not in a state of health to receive such a letter'.[21] Husband John's behaviour to Isabella could well be the motive for her writing an unhappy letter to John's sister; it is somewhat stretching credibility to suggest that Edward is asking his mother-in-law – to tell John – to tell his wife to stop writing to Dora about John's sexual misconduct. Isabella's discovery of John's adultery was probably not made until January 1846, when she wrote to her mother.

In a 2014 biography of Wordsworth, John Worthen merely added a footnote about the letter from Henry Curwen to his son Edward as the only source for John's 'sexual delinquency' and added: 'WW clearly did not believe in Curwen's allegations'.[22] Really? Likewise, in his second edition of *William Wordsworth: A Life* (2020), Stephen Gill added an endnote: 'the evidence against the Curwen allegations is overwhelming', but his evidence rests solely on the apparent good relationship between father and son.[23]

For the first time, I print most of the first half of Henry Curwen's letter, for the reader to decide:[24]

W Hall Jan 30 1846

My dearest Edward

I know how this letter will distress dear Fanny & you, that you come better prepared for it, than I was, as I had no idea of JWs infamous conduct to his unhappy wife & children. Never before now did she utter a word of complaint to your mother, but she at last written to her, & the Doctor also. JW had behaved in the most brutal manner to her, & taken all the children from her, tasked her with having murthered her child, by taking him to Rome – it seems he had been previously living with an Italian girl of 16, under her roof, and making her the companion of his [?illegible words] that he has given her a written promise of marriage, saying that his wife could not live 5 weeks, & that he would settle all his father left him, on her, & her children – Dr D says his character is so blasted in Rome he could not remain there. He actually took all the children from their perhaps dying mother, & when Dr D finding he would do so advised him to go to Pisa, he said no it would be so dull, he would go to Florence [...] You may imagine the state your poor mother is in, she means to set out for Rome, on Monday, & Hammy [Isabella's younger brother Henry?], in your absence, offered at once to go with her [...] The old Poet I know has altered his will, & left all to Isabella's children, out of his \JW/ powers, I have done the same[.] I wrote to the poor old Poet, & sent him for his signature my own letter to JW in which I told him, that if he will not immediately take the 3 children back to their mother at Rome, & then return to England, as his remaining at present in Italy with Isabella was out of the question, I should lay the proof of his infamous conduct, before the Bishops, which would deprive him, of both his livings, & we then, if requisite[,] to obtain a divorce. It is ?my opinion we should get the promise of marriage from the girl, as I believe he has now left her, & she would be willing enough to sell it, & that having it, in our hands[,] we could force him, into restoring her children to Isabella & in Cumberland he must at least conduct himself with common decency.

At first I had wondered if Isabella might have a laudanum addiction that caused paranoia and strange fantasies, but it is Doctor 'D' having written to John Wordsworth that discounts that possibility. This supposed respectable clergyman, the disappointing son of a famous man recently made Poet Laureate, is despicably arrogant as he seems to acknowledge his young mistress and refuse to go to Pisa as it is too 'dull'. And if I have transcribed correctly 'under her roof' – meaning in Isabella's house – then it is even more appalling. It is perhaps not surprising that after Isabella's death, which came two years later in September 1848, John married three more times.[25]

The letter mentions only three children: perhaps these were the youngest three, while the two eldest had remained in Cumberland. Wordsworth's final will was made on 31 August 1847, eighteen months after the revelation of adultery (and less than three years before he died).[26] As Henry Curwen states in his letter, it is possible that Wordsworth did change it in 1846, but then changed it again. The clue that he did believe Henry Curwen might lie in the fact that his younger son William is one of the executors and trustees, not John. However, the preliminary wording for both sons is the same: 'To my eldest Son The Reverend John Wordsworth and his assigns for his life with remainder' and then names John and Isabella's sons. And 'To my said second and only other son William Wordsworth the younger and his assigns for his life with remainder'. Wordsworth also names John and Isabella's daughter Jane, bequeathing her £500 when she comes of age. After his wife Mary's death, his furniture, pictures and books are to be divided equally between sons John and William, but the manuscripts, both published and unpublished, are bequeathed to the trustees. I think therein lies adulterer John's punishment: surely it would have been a crushing blow that his younger brother was named as a trustee and he wasn't, and perhaps Wordsworth carefully named all John and Isabella's children so that there was no chance of John disinheriting those children.

The depression Wordsworth felt in his last years is well documented. Stephen Gill's biography mentions the devastating family deaths, including the grandson in Rome, on which Wordsworth wrote a sonnet in 1846: 'Why should we weep or mourn, Angelic boy, / For such thou wert ere from our sight removed / [...] That beauty is laid low / To moulder in a far-off field of Rome'. Although Henry Curwen asks his son Edward in the letter not to reveal John Wordsworth's conduct to 'any one but Fanny', his wife, it is possible that Edward sought out Rev. Evan Jenkins in confidence. Maybe Eliza knew only of Isabella's ill health: some two months later, in April 1846, she asks Frances Curwen to 'tell me what accounts you have of Mr C's sister who was so ill in Italy'. John's adultery was hushed up; Wordsworth worshippers traduced his daughter-in-law Isabella's character.

Over a decade later, in January 1857, young Henry Curwen, educated by the Jenkinses, celebrated his coming of age at Workington Hall. Old Henry Curwen entertained his tenants who welcomed Lieutenant Henry, his grandson, who had just returned from the Crimea. As one local newspaper reports: 'The "memory of those who have fallen" was drunk in solemn silence. – To the toast of "The Church," the Rev. J. Wordsworth responded, and, speaking of the object of that night's festivity, reminded the meeting that the Curwens traced their pedigree to the Saxon Alfred, and his prayer for the ancient house was "*Esto perpetuâ*". – The Chairman then proposed the health of Henry Curwen, Esq.'[27] John Wordsworth – hypocrite to the last? And young Henry's grandfather – old, widowed Henry Curwen? I can only imagine his thoughts on this occasion with a question mark.

* * *

In her letters to Frances Curwen, Eliza says little about her family, except that in July 1844 they had holidayed in Ghlin and then Spa, no doubt visiting nephew Joseph: 'the country in that direction is most beautiful'. A year later they holidayed in Chaudfontaine, which was even lovelier: 'We have greatly enjoyed our sejour in this retired Village, which tho' within ¼ of an hours drive \per railway/ from Liege is as quiet as if we were 50 miles from a Town. The Country too is beautiful, far more romantic than the Environs of Spa & extremely reasonable as to living, which is a great recommendation to us.'[28] Eliza is certainly not too proud to tell Frances that money is tight – and it must have been also for Mrs Curwen, who was presumably pleased when her boys travelled half price on the steam packet. In her 1845 letter Eliza mentions her son Edward as she sympathizes with Mrs Curwen's boys about to return to school in Brussels: 'Poor Boys they are anticipating the trial of parting from all who are dear to them, in which at this moment I seem truly sympathique, seeing that my good Boy leaves me to return to School tomorrow, & a hard struggle it is to Parents & Children, but must be submitted to patiently.' At nineteen, according to his aunt Janet writing in November 1845, Edward was 'distinguishing himself at Dr Kennedys [Shrewsbury School] but goes soon I believe to College': he started at Cambridge the following year.[29] Janet Jay also mentions Helen, now eighteen, staying with her uncle David Jenkins in Pudsey. I wonder if she paid a visit to the Brontës in Haworth: 18 November 1845 is the date of Charlotte's last surviving letter to Heger; perhaps Helen brought the letter back with her to Brussels. Then Janet mentions Alexander, the Jenkinses' third child, aged sixteen, who 'ought indeed to come to you' in Australia. 'He has weak sight and is ordered to save his eyes and be much in the air but Eliza will <u>never</u> send him I am sure.' Instead Eliza and Evan were thinking of his becoming a clergyman and going to the college at St Bees, where his cousin Joseph had studied, 'as they cannot afford more'. Studying for the law would be too expensive and his eyesight was not good enough for all the copying that was needed, Janet adds. Poor Alexander, he was not destined to become a clergyman. But thankfully, as Mrs Bright reported to her daughter-in-law around that time, Edward gained a scholarship of £60 per annum from Shrewsbury, to help fund his degree at Cambridge.[30]

There is a glimpse of Evan the minister in 1845 other than performing his usual duties of Sunday services, weddings, baptisms and funerals. He was one of several who submitted depositions about the treatment of Protestants in Catholic hospitals, some of whom had been forcibly converted to Catholicism. 'Evan Jenkins, âgé de 50 ans, ministre du culte anglican demeurant à Ixelles' wrote (in French) that he had been in office for around twenty years and that he had always been treated politely when he visited Protestant patients in hospital, except once about eight years before, at the hôpital St.-Jean: he had been called to see a sick man to whom he needed to administer the sacraments. It was evening and the light in the ward wasn't sufficient to read by. Evan asked one of the sisters for a candle, but she kept him waiting and finally said that the Catholic chaplain did not want him to have one. The latter then appeared and told Evan that all the sick people in the hospital belonged to him. 'I was not able to administer the sacraments to the sick man, who died that night; I had to limit myself to saying prayers, kneeling by his bed.'[31] It is an insight into Evan's life as a clergyman that he was on call at all hours, visiting the sick and dying in hospitals and at their homes. Perhaps Charlotte Brontë is thinking of Evan Jenkins when she describes Dr John/Graham Bretton in *Villette*:

> I found, on accompanying him to the Basse-Ville – the poor and crowded quarter of the city – that his errands there were as much those of the philanthropist as the physician. I understood presently that – cheerfully, habitually, and in single-minded unconsciousness of any special merit distinguishing his deeds – he was achieving, amongst a very wretched population, a world of active good. The lower orders liked him well; his poor patients in the hospitals welcomed him with a sort of enthusiasm.[32]

But if there were late-night vigils by the beds of the dying, there were also occasional jollies. In March 1846, Evan and Rev. Drury were at a 'sumptuous' banquet to celebrate the inauguration of a stretch of railroad in Leuven. The *London Evening Standard* correspondent was given many column inches to describe the ceremony – 'detachments of infantry and cavalry, and about 30 labourers with new spades were stationed in front of the Hotel de Ville' – because it was a joint English/Belgian affair. Priests blessed the ground, various gentlemen 'successively turned up some sods', 'tastefully ornamented' pavilions accommodated guests at the site for the station, and there was a ceremonial 'elegant mahogany wheelbarrow'. I wonder whether Reverends Jenkins and Drury stayed long at the ball that followed in the Casino, which lasted until three in the morning, where 'all kinds of refreshments were liberally distributed'. If I had been a sub at the *Evening Standard* I would have longed to call the article: 'Sods Turned Up'. Instead it is titled 'The Louvain, Namur, and Charleroi Railway'.[33]

In early August that year Evan visited his brother David in Pudsey – as we can see from the baptismal register for the church, where Evan officiated twice. Perhaps it was the last time the brothers saw each other. I will now go back a few years to describe David's role in the political turmoil that was still engulfing Britain.

* * *

'The Health of the Rev. David Jenkins, Incumbent of Pudsey.' (Drunk with 9 times 9 and rapturous applause.)[34]

On 17 April 1837, David Jenkins gave a keynote speech to the newly formed Operative Conservative Society at Pudsey, at a dinner held at the Commercial Hotel. Over in Haworth, nineteen-year-old Branwell Brontë was at the forefront of establishing their Operative Conservative Society that January.[35] It was a movement that was sweeping the country, as moderate Whigs and Tories combined to confront what they saw as the dangerous radical reform programme of the Whigs under Lord Melbourne, and defend the constitution in church and state.[36] Most bishops had voted against the Great Reform Bill, but it had received royal assent in 1832. The Act had divided the Yorkshire constituency into its three Ridings, each with two MPs, increased the electorate and required for the first time that voters should be registered annually, although voting still had to be public. One of the impetuses behind the rise of the Conservative associations was to ensure that like-minded potential voters were registered – men who distrusted the government's reliance on Irish Catholic and radical votes and feared the disestablishment of the Church of England. The ill-health of King William IV also focused minds since there would be a general election on his death (he died in June) and currently both West Riding MPs were Liberals.

The leading Tory/Conservative newspaper in Yorkshire, the *Leeds Intelligencer*, covered the speeches in five columns. 'Pudsey, industrious Pudsey, was once considered the strong-hold of Whig-Radicalism;' a journalist wrote excitedly, 'we have known the time when scarcely a man in that [...] extensive and populous village might venture to avow himself attached to Conservative politics without risk of personal violence. But now the tide has turned; the "masses" are becoming convinced that to them Reform is but an empty sound.'[37] Members marched to the dinner 'preceded by a Blue silk flag, inscribed "Protestant Patriots of Pudsey."' David Jenkins began his speech by referring to the current 'times of danger', 'when the ministers of the Church [...] are defamed and traduced, and when attempts are made to overthrow the Church of which we are ministers'. He continued, after cheers:

> With regard to myself I will only say that I am a Conservative, and that I have not been afraid, ever since I came among you, nearly 25 years ago, on all fitting occasions, to avow my principles. (All the company rose and cheered.) I may and have been blamed by some of my brother clergymen for taking so active a part in elections, and on other occasions such as the present, but I have acted from a sense of duty.

He refers to the 'Popish and Protestant Dissenters who make a great tumult in the country' and considers the toast to himself and his fellow clergy 'as intended to convey your approbation of the Church established in this country, and your determination by all the means in your power to maintain the rights and the property which belong to that Church. (Here the company rose and loudly cheered.)' David's following argument rests on the antiquity of the Church, established long before the pope sent Augustine (or Austin, as he calls him) to England in the sixth century:

> I am prepared to prove, from authentic documents and other evidence, that the Christian Religion or the Apostolical Church was introduced into this country in the first century, and that it was introduced by some of the Apostles; and it is proved, I think, by the late learned Dr. Burgess, Bishop

of Salisbury, that St. Paul himself was in this country. This is an important fact; and it is a fact, too, that the Christian Religion was established in this country in the second century, under a prince named Lucius, who was the first Christian prince in the world.

The pride of this Welshman is obvious when he declares that Caerleon in South Wales was one of the first archbishoprics, and that one of the general councils during the first four centuries was held in Wales; 'the Popish religion was a bloody religion from the beginning, and our Church, the Primitive Church, was a protecting Church from the sixth century'.[38] We get the flavour of what David's sermons might have been like as he pulls out the oratorical stops: 'A conspiracy has been formed, an unnatural conspiracy, an unholy conspiracy among those who, differing among themselves on almost all other matters, have joined in attacking the Church; by those who only unite for one object, and that is to destroy the Church.' David would have made a formidable politician. He then turns to church rates, opposed by the Dissenters; it was the big issue of the day, especially in the industrial North, especially in Pudsey. 'I have heard so much on this subject that I am shocked by the hypocrisy and cant which I have witnessed. They say "We will not pay a penny to support the church," while at the same time they receive from Parliament several thousands a year.' He argues that if church rates are abolished 'why may not tithes, and why may not the nobility be deprived and gentry be deprived of their estates'. He finishes by urging his audience to return Conservatives as MPs in the next election, which was met with 'vociferous cheering'.

The radical *Leeds Times* was mocking: 'Among other things, he told them, "It *is proved that St. Paul was in this country.*" St. Paul in Pudsey! [...] We do not wonder, after perusing the roll of the great deeds done in Pudsey as narrated by its erudite chronicler, that it should be looked upon as a place of importance, although we have not been able to trace its whereabout with certainty.' And in another article in the same newspaper a writer referred to 'Parson' Jenkins's 'pure unadulterated nonsense'.[39] In hindsight we may quibble with the argument that reforming church rates would lead to a French-style revolution, but the fear was widespread. At the General Election that year, the Conservative candidate, John Stuart-Wortley, was only narrowly beaten by the incumbent Liberals. But in 1841, Conservatives won both seats as, throughout the country, there was a huge swing to Sir Robert Peel's party, and Lord Melbourne's tottering government was ousted.

In Pudsey the fight by Nonconformists against church rates, and the annual fracas over electing a Nonconformist as one of the churchwardens – who often refused to levy a rate – had been going on since the 1830s. A few months before David's rousing speech, there had been the notorious Pudsey Smiting and Brawling Case. In January 1837, Jonas Proctor and William Clarkson of Pudsey appeared at the Consistory Court in York 'having at a vestry meeting held for the purpose of imposing a church-rate, at which considerable tumult prevailed, smitten in the vestry the minister and the churchwardens'. The men denied that they had struck Mr Jenkins or Mr Farrar, but they were sentenced to imprisonment in York Castle.[40] An 'Inhabitant of Pudsey', a few months later, wrote to the Liberal *Leeds Mercury* to protest:

> The crime alleged against Mr. Clarkson, was that of smiting the Rev. Incumbent in the vestry, at a meeting convened for the purpose of choosing Churchwardens. A motion had been made that all parties, who had not paid their rate, but who were there and prepared to pay, should be allowed to vote. This did not meet the Rev. Chairman's [Jenkins] approbation, and he created a great confusion. The Overseer's Book was produced; Mr. Clarkson, it appeared, had not paid his rate; he immediately tendered the amount to the overseer, and demanded its being recorded as paid. In the mean time Mr. Jenkins had taken the rate-book from the overseer into his hands, and Mr. Clarkson plucked it from him. Mr. Rayner exclaimed 'I saw that.' Mr. Jenkins said 'See, I am insulted.' Here originated this vexatious prosecution [...] Mr. Proctor's crime, it is said, was that of smiting Mr. John Farrar. But some say that no blow was given, and that the crime consisted in Mr. Proctor's exercising his hand with his finger at length, endeavouring to impress what he was saying to Mr. Farrar.[41]

The 'inhabitant' rather over-eggs it, however, by ending that Mr Proctor's 'bereaved wife sighs for her absent husband, and his little ones sorrowfully talk about their imprisoned father in the morning, at noon, and in the evening. Mr. Farrar no doubt is transported at his success. Has no voice yet cried – "Ah! Proctor, thou wretch, I have thee now; thou art my dungeon victim; thy gloomy abode befits thee well: lie, and never more offend my eyes."' Mr Proctor had received just one month's sentence.

By 1844 the *Bradford Observer* had turned the annual Pudsey church-rate fight into a set-piece soap opera as ratepayers objected to various items:

Chairman [Rev. Jenkins]: 'Clerk's wages' –

Hargreaves and others: 'I object!' – 'We object, we object.'

Chairman: 'You can't object to this; it is sanctioned by immemorial usage.'

Chorus of Objectors: 'We object to the beadle's expenses; we shall cut them down!'

Chairman: 'You can't. Cleaning spouts' –

Objectors: 'Unlawful!'

Chairman: 'Ringers.'

Objectors: 'Not lawful! We object.'

Chairman: 'Repairing organ' –

Objectors: 'Object – unlawful!'

Chairman: 'Incidental expenses' –

Objectors: 'We don't like incidental expenses; give us the particulars (hear him! hear him!)'[42]

And so on. David compromised with agreeing to a farthing as the church rate. But however time-consuming affairs in Yorkshire were, he was also involved with fellow Welsh-born clergy about conditions in Wales.

In 1841 it was reported in a Welsh-language newspaper that various clergymen in West Yorkshire had met together in Huddersfield to discuss their native country. Patrick Brontë's friend Rev. William Morgan was at the dinner with David.[43] It is likely that David had been at the double wedding in 1812 of Patrick to Maria Branwell, and William to Maria's cousin Jane Fennell. The main outcome of their talk was a petition to the House of Commons to allow St David's College, Lampeter to grant degrees. It seems extraordinary that twenty years after its founding by Bishop Burgess – the same man who had decided that St Paul had come to England, and who was interestingly English, not Welsh – Wales still had no college that could confer a degree. Similar Welsh nationalism – combining history with mythology – is apparent as in David's speech in Pudsey:

[The petitioners] wish to remind your honourable House, that Wales was at one time the seat of learning, her scholars were known and revered on the continent of Europe, and students came from various parts of the world to receive instruction at Caerlleon on the Usk and Bangor is Coed, at that time the two most renowned seminaries of learning.

> That, since the union of Wales with England, the interests of the
> Principality have been greatly neglected, while privileges of the same kind
> [...] have been granted to Ireland, Scotland, and (besides the Universities of
> Oxford and Cambridge), to London and Durham.[44]

It took another ten years to achieve.

In April 1846, some months before Evan visited his brother, David's only surviving daughter Elizabeth married an Irish 'gentleman', Erasmus Lloyd of Roscommon. David had been a widower for over twenty years; two daughters and a son had died young, so it was perhaps with pleasure and relief that he watched his eldest son Rev. Joseph marry the pair in his huge church at Pudsey. David was obviously proud of his little brother because in the wedding announcement in the newspapers Elizabeth is described as 'niece to the Rev. E. Jenkins, M.A., of Trinity College, Cambridge, and Chaplain to his Majesty the King of the Belgians'.[45] But the next year was darker for David.

In an earlier chapter I mentioned that David's second son, also called David, had died in his twenties. In June 1839, aged just twenty-one, this 'woolsorter' of Bradford had married Mary Ann Gomersal in Birstal; her father was an 'overlooker' and she was unable to sign her name. We know it is David Jenkins's son because he puts his father as a clergyman on the registration of marriage. It seems hardly the occupation or marriage that Rev. Jenkins would have wanted, especially as Mary already had a child, Joseph Gomersal, born in 1836. Perhaps the child was young David's, born when he was eighteen. David died in October 1847 of disease of the liver, according to his death certificate, still a woolsorter. It is such a lowly occupation for the son of a respected clergyman, when surely Rev. Jenkins had so many contacts who could at least give his son a job as a clerk. I can only deduce that father and son had fallen out. I presume David junior had what was later called 'woolsorter's disease', anthrax: death is sudden after infection. But whatever had happened between Rev. Jenkins and his second son, young David and Mary's illegitimate boy was included in Rev. Jenkins's will, equally with the couple's legitimate children. The following year, Rev. David married again, to a widow, Rebecca Rayner. It is possible that he felt able to make a second marriage after the last of his children, Joseph (Charlotte Brontë's 'Welsh pony'), having returned from his stint at Spa in Belgium, married Margaret Eggleston in May that year. Rebecca was surely of help when the awful news came from Brussels in September 1849.

* * *

Acte de décès No. 391

L'an mil huit cent quarante-neuf [...] nous ont déclaré que le Vingt-trois Septembre courant, à six heures du soir, est décédé en cette Commune, en son domicile Chaussée d'Ixelles numéro cent trente-huit, Evan Jenkins, âgé de cinquante-quatre ans, dix mois et treize jours, né à Aberystwith (Pays de Galles, Angleterre), Ministre du Culte Anglican, Chapelain honoraire de Sa Majesté le Roi des Belges, Epouse de Eliza Jay, âgée de quarante-trois ans, sans profession, demeurant même maison, fils de Evan Jenkins et de (nom et prénoms de la mere inconnus aux déclarants). Conjoints décédés.

On 23 September 1849, Evan died at the age of fifty-four at his home, 138 Chaussée d'Ixelles, in the commune of Ixelles.[46] It comes as a shock – there is no warning. But one man had heard Evan was ill and grabbed for a prize, which I will come to below. The two informants who registered Evan's death the next day were Simon Salter, a banker living in Brussels, aged sixty, friend; and William Jackson, aged thirty-four, a shopkeeper living in Ixelles, acquaintance. Jackson's shop was probably the grocer's/wine merchant listed in the Almanac, maybe a minute's walk from the Jenkins house.[47] Through her grief, it might have appealed to Eliza that they had taken nine years off her age. Abroad, Wales is often even today located in England and perhaps that was the registrar's addition. Aberystwyth was the nearest large town to Evan's place of birth, which he had entered in the Cambridge University admissions book: a farmhouse near Tregaron was too difficult to explain. The informants knew his date of birth, but hadn't been given his mother's name ('surname and first names of the mother unknown to the informants'). I had been so frustrated at that, but had finally found Elizabeth Jenkins née Davies in David Jenkins's ordination papers. Evan left no will, and perhaps another clue that Evan's death was sudden is that son Edward was not one of the informants: he was probably in Cambridge for the start of his fourth year at Magdalene College for the two terms of examinations. If twenty-year-old Alexander was at home, maybe he couldn't leave his mother and sisters, or couldn't face it. Evan junior at sixteen, and John at fourteen were too young. Perhaps William Ayers and Charlotte, now Mrs Ayers, took charge of the schoolboys in the confused, distraught house.

No obituary has been found, though there are brief death notices in the Belgian newspapers.[48] Evan may have died of cholera. In Belgium, as in England and France, there was an epidemic during 1848–9. Evan's last duty at a wedding was on 7 June 1849; and in that month he officiated at the funeral of Sergeant-Major Cotton, who had fought at the Battle of Waterloo in the 7th Hussars, and was a famous guide to the battlefield.[49] The *Indépendance Belge* gives statistics for the epidemic in Brussels: in the week that Evan died there were eight deaths at the three hospitals (Saint-Jean, Saint-Pierre and the military hospital). In August there was a total of 163 deaths; since the start of the epidemic 460 deaths.[50] Evan would have visited sick patients to pray and give the last rites, and he may have been infected and died within days. In August, 47-year-old Rev. Thomas Tyrwhitt had visited relations in Brussels. He arrived at The Hague on the 10th, feeling some pain, and 'after about eight hours' suffering from Asiatic cholera' died in the early hours of the 11th, leaving a widow and seven children.[51] One Brussels resident, Anna Maria Calhoun Clemson, had recently moved there with her husband, a diplomat, and their children. She wrote to her father, the American statesman John C. Calhoun, on 12 August: 'We are all very well, but the cholera still reigns in Brussels, & keeps us a little uneasy the disease is everywhere. It is not however worth while leaving the city on that account, as the disease is every where, so we are very prudent, & remain quiet.' Twelve days earlier, her husband Thomas Clemson had written to his father-in-law: 'Cholera is not only in Brussels, but every where in Belgium & I may say in the North of Europe. In Antwerp it is very bad, as also in Liege. It has been worse in Brussels than at present, & the deaths have mainly been confined to the lower classes. Still however persons in high position have been swept away. One of the Queens maids of honour died the other day in Liege after a short illness.' The day after Evan's death, on 24 September, Clemson wrote: 'The cholera has almost disappeared from Brussels whilst it lingers in other parts of the Kingdom with considerable violence.'[52] Perhaps Evan was one of the 'almost'.

There was not only distress in the Jenkins household, but panic. That evening or the next day, Helen, now twenty-two, wrote to the Bishop of London, Charles Blomfield. Having lost her father, the family was potentially destitute. The plan had undoubtedly been that once Edward had graduated and been ordained, he would join his father as assistant chaplain at the Chapel Royal, and help with running the school. But Evan had died a year too early. Helen's letter does not survive, but the copy of Bishop Blomfield's letter, dated 26 September 1849, does. He writes in reply to Eliza, whom he had met in 1835:

I have received with great concern from Miss Jenkins, the sad intelligence of her Father's death. I trust that it may please Him who has laid this affliction upon you, to console you under its weight.

I am sorry that the arrangement which you propose is impracticable. Mr de Coetlogon is not a Clergyman of the Church of England, nor could your Son be appointed Chaplain till he is in <u>Priests</u> orders.[53]

If Edward, now twenty-three, ever needed motivation to work hard, now he needed to work even harder as he had his entire family to support. He probably headed back to Brussels as soon as he heard news of his father's illness, arriving in time for the funeral on Wednesday 26 September. Surely the Chapel Royal was overflowing as Rev. Drury officiated.[54] That was a nice touch. Drury noted the funeral of Evan in his own register. When he baptized Evan's grandchildren he added 'at the Chapel Royal'.[55] He didn't here, but it was certainly in Evan's chapel. Drury had started as an irritant to Evan, but the older man saw the Welshman who became his friend to his rest. I found a note from Evan tucked into Drury's register:

My dear Sir,

I have a very bad cold in the head. Will you have the kindness to inter for me a poor woman's child?

Very truly yours

E Jenkins.

Evan has dated it: 'Saturday Morning 30th Decr'. There are only three years that this could apply to: 1837, 1843 and 1848. I wonder if William Drury kept this note because it was the last he received – in December 1848. It is Evan's last surviving letter. According to the register at the Chapel Royal, Evan was buried in the Protestant cemetery 'de l'Est neuf lettre B', after having been chaplain for over twenty years.

The Jenkins hope must have been that whoever was appointed the new chaplain at the Chapel Royal, the man might not stay long. In early 1850 Edward achieved double honours – he was a respectable Junior Optime in the Mathematics examination, and second class in the Classical Tripos. But the greatest prize came in May when he won a College Fellowship: he would thus be automatically ordained deacon.[56] How proud Evan would have been.

* * *

Before Evan died, a clergyman heard the news of his illness and pounced. Rev. Maxwell Julius Blacker wrote to the Bishop of London; his letter does not survive, so the date is not known, but the copy of the bishop's reply survives, dated 25 September:

> This days Post has brought me intelligence of the death of poor Mr Jenkins. If I should be referred to on the subject of his successor in the Chaplaincy, I shall be prepared to recommend you, but I do not see how I can take the initiative. I should advise you to apply to the British Minister at Brussels.[57]

So the same day that Helen's letter arrived, the bishop replied to Blacker. The unseemly haste on Blacker's part was not untypical. In *Barchester Towers* (1857), Anthony Trollope's oily Rev. Obadiah Slope learns of the illness of the dean. He writes an equally oily letter to an epistolary acquaintance who has the ear of the government:

> You cannot I imagine have yet heard that poor dear old Dr Trefoil has been seized with apoplexy [...] the medical men here have declared that one or two days more must limit the tether of his mortal coil. I sincerely trust that his soul may wing its flight to that haven where it may for ever be at rest and for ever be happy.
>
> The bishop has been speaking to me about the preferment, and he is anxious that it should be conferred on me. I confess that I can hardly venture, at my age, to look for such advancement; but I am so far encouraged by his lordship, that I believe I shall be induced to do so [...]
>
> I know well how deservedly great is your weight with the present government. In any matter touching church preferment you would of course be listened to.[58]

Although the Bishop of London had told Rev. Blacker that he had no influence, Blomfield did write to the ambassador in Brussels – which is just about discernible in the faded letter on microfilm – and Blacker was appointed in December.[59]

Rev. Blacker, son of the late Lieut.-Col. Valentine Blacker, was twenty-seven, and after graduating from Merton College, Oxford, had been ordained priest only that year.[60] How had a curate in Suffolk heard of Evan's illness? All is apparent from a series of marriages: after getting the chaplaincy in Brussels he married Emily Georgina Daveney, whose father lived in Malines, near Brussels. Her sister had married Rev. Pascoe Grenfell Hill in 1846, who was the Anglican chaplain in Antwerp. Another sister was married to a man who lived in Antwerp.[61] Eliza must have been filled with foreboding that the new chaplain was about to have relatives in Belgium and might possibly stay in post for a long time. The future for the Jenkins family was now utterly uncertain.

Sixteen

'between Life & death'

What did Eliza do with a house full of schoolboys after Evan's death? After his father's funeral at the end of September 1849, Edward needed to go back to Cambridge to work for his examinations. I speculated that Edward urged his mother to carry on: the only income they now had came from the schoolboys, they had contracts with specialist teachers and perhaps the assistance of William and Charlotte Ayers – though in the 1854 Almanac he is teaching English in rue d'Edimbourg, where the Jenkinses had once lived. But there is a devastating announcement in a Belgian newspaper in November 1849: 'Vente publique pour cause de décès', showing that Eliza was selling possessions and had obviously closed down the school:

> Fine pieces of mahogany furniture and other items, crystalware, porcelain, kettles, teapots, faience, mattresses, pillows, woollen blankets, books, a clock, living-room carpet [...], curtains, mirrors, iron bedsteads, garden benches and chairs, desks, body and table linen, men and women's clothes, pots and pans, 6 silver spoons and 4 forks, 9 silver coffee spoons, and many other objects.[1]

The advertisement stated that she was selling on behalf of four of her children who were minors, and perhaps that is when the family moved to 14 rue des Champs Elysées. But at least Edward's scholarship from Shrewsbury School to study at Magdalene College, Cambridge was one of the most valuable ones.

A Royal Commission in 1864 reported that Shrewsbury was richly endowed by benefactors and trustees, and that scholarships and exhibitions varied in value between £10 and £63 per annum, so Mrs Bright's mention in her letter of Edward receiving £60 per annum (maybe for four years) is significant. Scholarships, it seems, mainly went to sons of burgesses or natives of Shropshire, so how Edward got it is interesting and maybe unknowable.[2] The Fellowship at Magdalene that he gained in May 1850 was as a Hugh Dennis Bye-Fellow, one of the original Fellowships of the college from the sixteenth century: he was not a full Fellow and did not receive a college living, but there was money.[3] It also meant that he could be ordained without having to find a curacy. Thus on 17 November 1850 he was ordained deacon by the Bishop of Ely, and almost exactly a year later he was ordained priest at Ely Cathedral.[4] Edward's 1851 testimonial states that he had been in Brussels for all of the preceding year.[5] Eliza remarks in a letter that Edward was taking pupils in the summer of 1851; and a short newspaper article in June 1852 confirms that the school had been re-established, and that among his pupils were two young Muslim 'guests' who arrived on the *Louise-Marie* from Africa, and that this boded well for Belgian commerce. However, the apparent bullying of at least one of them by a fellow pupil, Edward Curwen, did not bode so well.[6]

One letter-writer comments that Rev. Edward had stood in for Rev. Blacker at the Chapel Royal sometime in 1851.[7] It is also noted on loose papers tucked into Evan's church register that Edward officiated at three baptisms, in December 1851, in 1852 and 1855.[8] But if Eliza prayed that Blacker would move on, her main worries were the ill health of her second son Alexander, and the departure of her third son Evan to Australia at the start of the gold rush.

* * *

Alexander was last heard of at sixteen with weak eyesight, from his aunt Janet's letter of 1845. There is no record of him in the student's entry books of the theological college of St Bees in Cumberland that had been a possible destination for him.[9] He is next found in the 30 March 1851 census on the Isle of Wight: in Ventnor. Staying at this seaside resort out of season usually meant one thing in the nineteenth century: tuberculosis, then known as phthisis or consumption. Ventnor, on the south-eastern coast, had a microclimate considered particularly beneficial to those with lung disease.[10] In 1830, the village had been discovered to have the ideal climate and protection from the cold of winter by the physician Sir James Clark, who wrote on the influence of climate on health. Invalids flocked to it, encouraged to sit or walk on the beach for hours, to take seawater baths, or even sleep outside. The influx created a haphazard building boom, while residents let out rooms for needful money during the off-season. In the census, Alexander is listed on his own as 'Head', aged twenty-one, in what seems to be one such room, or maybe a pair of rooms, in West End Cottage, Belgrave Road. In the rest of the cottage were a family of nine: it is a daunting reminder of how some people lived – Henry Colenutt, a baker, his wife Charlotte, their six children between the ages of one and eleven, and Charlotte's father Joseph Blake, described as a lodging house proprietor, all squashed into part of one cottage. Perhaps the 'lodging house' that Joseph Blake managed was Alexander's part, with its own front door.

It seems this bit of the cottage was often let to invalids. In October 1852, Robert Henderson Esq., advocate from Edinburgh and youngest son of Robert Henderson of Allan Park, Stirling, died there.[11] Since a Scottish advocate had stayed, who presumably had some money, then the room(s) must have been of a decent standard, though not as grand as staying in The Royal Hotel, opened in 1832, on the other side of the road. What is fascinating is that the altitude invalids chose on the Undercliff was considered vital: the most delicate patients needed a mild, warm, low altitude; those who were more robust should reside on a higher level. The most sheltered part was the Cove and the terraces just above it, and Belgrave Road, about 100 feet above the beach, was considered ideal.[12] I found a cluster of picturesque cottages on Belgrave Road as it joins Zig Zag Road, one of which is called Hope Cottage, built in 1832. Perhaps one of the other surviving cottages was West End Cottage; if not, then it was near. It is ominous that Alexander was staying at an altitude recommended for the most ill.

Alexander also stayed for three weeks with his mother's relatives in Somerset that spring: perhaps this was after Ventnor in April or May. Eliza's first cousin wrote to Margaret Wyndham a few years later that of Eliza's children she had only met John and Alex: 'The latter poor fellow was here for 3 weeks the Spring before he died, & we were very fond of him.'[13] It feels as if Eliza is desperately sending her son to anywhere that had mild country or sea air. The end came in the spa town of Cheltenham that October. Eliza's Brussels friend Mrs Mary Bright was frequently in Cheltenham for the season and may have recommended it. I first read Alexander's death certificate in 2015 and I couldn't believe that he seemed to be on his own again. It took four more years before I was finally able to see all the transcribed Wyndham letters, and I was so relieved that my speculation – that surely Eliza was with her son – was confirmed. It's so hard to imagine what she went through, unless you have been through this yourself.

Cheltenham is an elegant Regency town on the edge of the Cotswolds in Gloucestershire, famed for its mineral springs since the early eighteenth century. It was made fashionable after the visit of George III and the royal family at the end of the century, and the establishment of horse racing a few decades later. Lord Byron had stayed in 1812 to relieve the pain of a kidney stone and commented on the 'very medicinal & sufficiently disgusting' waters at the spa.[14] I was told by the guide, whose tour I went on, that the water made you urinate a lot. Cambridge undergraduate Charles Astor Bristed visited in the 1840s:

> Just at the end of the vacation every one feels it a duty to himself to go *somewhere* for a little while. I went to visit a friend residing near Cheltenham. Mesmerism, the Water Cure, and some other German novelties, had just then possessed the good people in that part of the country, and I was induced to try the prevailing panacea, which I underwent five days – and never before did I fully appreciate the force of the metaphor, *to throw a wet blanket* on anything. Even now it presents a sadly ludicrous spectacle to my mind's eye, as I recall myself helplessly swaddled in seven blankets over a wet sheet, powerless to move hand or foot; or squatted in a sitz bath [...] At the end of the fifth day, the process had to be given up in self-defence, as, in addition to certain physical obstructions, it brought on a lowness of spirits which rendered life a burden to me.

He adds that the system of 'rough-washing' 'will be death to a weak man or a delicate woman'.[15] Did Alexander have to undergo that? I hope not, yet I fear he did.

In October 1851, in the letter mentioned above, Charlotte Starky wrote to Eliza's sister Margaret that she had briefly called on Eliza in Brussels that summer: 'We did not see any of her family, one daughter was in England and a Son also who was gone there for Medical advice and Bayntun [her eldest son, finishing his education in Brussels with Rev. Blacker] has mentioned in his letters that he is now very ill and not expected to recover at Cheltenham and Mrs. Jenkins has gone there to nurse him.'[16] Before I read this letter I had stared at a local newspaper announcement of 13 September 1851 concerning 'Arrivals at the Principal Hotels', Cheltenham, that included 'Mr, Mrs Jenkins, Miss Jenkins' at the George Hotel in the High Street, and found no inspiration of how I could identify them.[17] Maybe that is Eliza arriving with Helen, and could the 'Mr' be Alexander accompanied by his family for a possible cure, or could it be Edward accompanying his mother and sister to visit Alexander? Mrs Bright and two of her daughters are announced as arriving on 4 October, to stay at 17 Imperial Square.[18] It is surely no coincidence that young Alexander was staying at 1 Imperial Square when he died.

Imperial Square is very grand. The cream-coloured curve of listed Georgian terraced houses, of three storeys and basement, faces an enormous garden square. A house next to the one the Bright family rented at no. 17 was recently on sale for almost two million pounds. But no. 1, at the truncated northern end near Pizza Express, looks shabbier. In the 1851 census, no. 1 is divided into two separate units: one set of rooms was lived in by a family of four from Ireland; the head of the other set of rooms was a lodging house keeper, living there with her daughter and a servant. There is no indication in the census of which floors they lived on, but it is logical to suppose that the lodging house keeper lived in the basement, letting out the ground-floor rooms to Eliza and Alexander.

The death certificate states that Alexander Livingston Jenkins died on 25 October 1851, aged twenty-two, of 'Phthisis 2 years certified'. Oddly he is described as a clergyman. Perhaps the informant, Ann Milton, 'Present at Death', residing at '1 Imperial Square Cheltenham', knew that his father was, but didn't know what to put for Alexander. There is an Ann Milton in the 1851 census living in Bath Villas, Cheltenham, a widow described as a cook. It is possible that she had been hired as a nurse to look after Alexander, or was also a resident: though if she had lost her job as a cook, renting a room in Imperial Square sounds unlikely. Nurses needed no training or skills at that time.

Phthisis of two years takes us back to when Evan had died. Did Evan have tuberculosis? Louise, Queen of the Belgians had died of tuberculosis the year before Alexander, aged just thirty-eight. Like Evan, it is said that she often visited poor families in need of charity, and could have been infected there. Charlotte Brontë saw her at a concert and was warm in her description in *Villette*: 'A mild, thoughtful, graceful woman that princess seemed [...] She moved no sovereign, but a lady – kind, loving, elegant.'[19]

Five years after Alexander's death, his youngest sister Mina was dying of tuberculosis. Janet Jay wrote to her sister Margaret concerning Eliza: 'what misery that match brought on poor Eliza for who knows but that another may follow Mina[,] their constitutions are so bad & tho' they seem well enough now a bad cold always tries them much & Helen is delicate too – Thank God you escape such trials!'[20] That is cruel about Eliza's marriage to Evan. But ever-unmarried Janet is writing out of concern for 'miserable' Eliza and of her own sadness for her niece. In the event, 'delicate' Helen was to be the longest lived of all Eliza and Evan's children, dying in her eighties.

On Wednesday 29 October 1851, four days after his death, Alexander was buried at St Mary's new burial ground, which was later closed and is now the Winston Churchill Memorial Gardens. In 2016 I walked along Cheltenham's dingy High Street to the Gardens as the June sky grew darker. It would have been a smarter street in 1851, lined with respectable hotels. At the old cemetery there is a small chapel with incongruously tall Greek Doric columns. Three teenagers lounged in the portico, studying their mobile phones. Clumps of lavender grew on the neat plots of grass from where the headstones had been removed and which were now leaning against the perimeter wall. Suddenly the heavens opened and it poured. It added to the melancholy of my visit – I was probably the first person in the family to go there since Eliza with the coffin of her son. It struck me as I huddled under my umbrella and then returned to the High Street how awful that day had been for Eliza, and even worse – so much worse – to leave her son behind, in a country far away, where she couldn't take flowers or sit and think by his grave. Sending Alexander to Cheltenham Spa had ended in a nightmare. It seems that Eliza was also on her own. A few months later, in January 1852, Eliza wrote to sister Margaret. The previous letters she mentions have not survived, but this one is heartrending enough (it is heavily crossed and some words are not easy to read). Here is the inner Eliza, the rawness of feeling has not been smoothed over:

In two previous letters my dear Sister, I told you of my late affliction, the deepest I have yet experienced, for so far as human nature can be in fact, my dear Alexr was so, & never caused me an anxiety or a painful feeling in his life, & I feel the loss of so good a Child the more – This however is selfishly speaking, for have I not reason to hope that his happiness is secured in a better world than in one so full of trouble as I alas have found this to be, & to see one's Children suffer from care & sorrow as mine have, is far more painful to bear than ones own sorrows deep tho' they may be.

Eliza is worried that her son Evan will read about his brother's death in the newspaper:

Friends who were warmly attached to my dear Son, had his decease inserted in 'the Times' expressive of their deep regret as all who knew him were at his loss, but it is only a Parent can feel what a Mothers anguish is on parting with a Child & seeing him laid in the Grave as I did dear Meg, <u>alone</u> as perhaps no Beggar Woman had to go thro' <u>alone</u> in this World before! The Almighty has spared you so great a trial dear Meg and may He in his Infinite mercy continue to shield your darlings from sickness & death, is my fervent prayer – And now an end to these painful topics wch will [illegible word] persistent in my thoughts do what I will.[21]

She lets the mask fall to a sister she has not seen for over twenty years, then pulls herself together: 'an end'. Life is full of pain, but Eliza *has* to go on. She had perhaps forgotten that Margaret's fourth child had died aged only a few months in 1833.[22]

Was Eliza totally on her own at her son's funeral? There is wisely perceptive writing in Mrs Gaskell's *Cranford* (1853) that is perhaps pertinent. The kindly Captain Brown has been killed by a train. His daughter, Miss Jessie, is obstinately set on going to the funeral by herself. But Miss Jenkyns, who had quarrelled with the captain concerning the merits of Dr Johnson versus Charles Dickens, insists on accompanying her: 'It is not fit for you to go alone. It would be against both propriety and humanity were I to allow it.'

> Miss Jessie seemed as if she did not half like this arrangement; but her obstinacy, if she had any, had been exhausted in her determination to go to the interment. She longed, poor thing! I have no doubt, to cry alone over the grave of the dear father to whom she had been all in all; and to give way, for one little half-hour, uninterrupted by sympathy, and unobserved by friendship. But it was not to be.[23]

Perhaps Mrs Bright offered to accompany Eliza, but she obstinately would not give way and yearned for that 'little half-hour' on her own. In the same letter to her sister Margaret, she shows a formidable resilience as she turns from her grief to discuss the wedding dress material she has sent for Margaret's daughter: 'I wish I cd afford a better proof of my love than such trifles but she must take the will for the Deed.' She also comments on the fashion for dangling velvet bracelets: 'most inconvenient as they get into ones Tea & soup – Nothing but black shall I consider in future but I admire pretty Clothes.' Eliza is a survivor, and she has a house to run.

* * *

By 1853, the remaining Jenkins family were settled at their new rented house at 14 rue des Champs Elysées in Ixelles. The pensionnat is listed in the 1854 Almanac as run by 'Jenkins (V^e)' – Jenkins widow. While Eliza worried about her son Evan in Australia, who had now gone to the Diggings, eldest son Edward was accumulating pupils. It must have been a sizeable house since in 1853 Eliza writes to Margaret that they have a 'houseful of 30 persons!!', and in 1854 that there are '20 Boys from 8 to 18 under our Roof'.[24] The two exclamation marks seem to suggest that there was never such a large number in the old house five minutes' walk away. The thirty people presumably included servants as well – in 1854 she mentions her chef de cuisine, or head housekeeper, and nurse, who had been with the household for nearly fifteen years and twenty years respectively. The couple had married; he 'died of apoplexy suddenly (out of doors) a Year after his Marriage'.[25]

Edward, as a Fellow of Magdalene College, must have been a big attraction to parents of boys in Britain. No. 14 was a new build, and was in a delightfully leafy, much quieter side street than the house the Brontës had visited. Alas, when I walked up and down the road I saw that the original house had been demolished and replaced with a mid-twentieth-century block of flats. There was no doubt a good-sized garden. Somehow, after the blind panic at Evan's death, there was enough money – even though Eliza is often anxious – and a splendid new house, where Eliza was to remain until her death. I wonder if Charlotte Brontë was in contact and knew that golden boy Edward was proving to be a veritable lion: if not, she might have read in the newspapers of his success at Cambridge. But despite now being a priest, as Rev. C.E. Jenkins, would Edward ever have a living of his own?

As mentioned above, Charlotte Starky née Wyndham, one of Australian Margaret's sisters-in-law, had taken her seventeen-year-old son John Bayntun – known as Bayntun in the family – to Brussels in summer 1851 to finish his education with Rev. Blacker, and had called on Eliza briefly just before her departure. It seems to have been the start of a closer relationship between the Wyndham/Starky family in Wiltshire and Eliza's in Brussels. Bayntun's arrival was possibly because he, like Rev. Blacker, had been at Eton. Blacker had even been in the Cricket Eleven that had beaten Harrow at the annual fixture at Lord's in July 1840.[26] It was not a distinguished appearance: he came in at no. 10 'and made 1, when he ran himself out'. In the second innings he added just two to the score, but he made one catch.[27] It is not surprising that Blacker is said to approve of Edward in a letter from another of Margaret's sisters-in-law in January 1852.[28] Maybe the Brussels cricket club started much earlier, with Blacker and Edward in the early 1850s. But I doubt if young Bayntun took part in the cricket: his Australian cousin Alward, who painted that living picture of the Jenkinses at home in 1853, described Bayntun as 'the fattest fellow of 18 I ever saw. Walks no more than he can help & of course has no hard riding at this time of year & yet eats recklessly. He is rather silly in his manner but no doubt will get more sensible as he grows older.'[29] It seems that Bayntun had only spent a year at Eton (1847–8); to send him to Brussels to have one-to-one education with a clergyman sounds unwise. He might have been the only pupil since the newly married Blackers were living in perhaps a small house in rue de la Pépinière – a narrow road off rue de Namur, on the city side of Porte de Namur.[30] But the Jenkins family took him under their wing as much as they could. Bayntun's aunt Ella wrote to her brother George in Australia that Edward Jenkins had befriended young Bayntun, and his mother Charlotte wrote later to Margaret that Eliza 'has been very kind to Bayntun in Brussels', and because of Edward's friendship with Bayntun he had been invited to the family home at Spye Park in Wiltshire (the house was demolished in the 1860s by a new owner). Eliza finishes the story in a letter of February 1853:

[Bayntun] has left Brussels owing to the discomforts of the Clergyman's House in which he was placed – Poor fellow two of the best years of his life have been sadly lost for want of a judicious person to guide him for Bleckor [sic] threw him on his own resources & he had neither a companion nor a fireside to resort to, so that if disposed to mischief he wd have been lost in a City like this – He came to us of an Evening generaly & unless we had company never staid after 10 oClock nor accepted more than his Cup of Tea, & from what we know of him after two years nearly, I am sure much might have been made of him in other hands than those he so unfortunately fell into – All this I cd have told Mrs Starky when she called & introduced her Son to us but I should have been thought <u>interested</u> as Edward was taking Pupils himself, & so held my tongue & the Boy is in a great measure sacrificed <u>thro' delicacy</u> on our part which vexes me to look back to when I see the companions he has formed here among Grooms and Stable Boys who have spoilt his manners as you will perceive when he visits you as he purposes in Summer and on this account we rejoice that he is gone home.[31]

The welcoming kindness of Eliza stands out. Her home was open to lonely members of the extended family, or Brontë sisters. The Blackers might give a different version of events, but the bustle and comfort of the Jenkins home was preferable to the young man. There was a reward because Bayntun's younger brother Andrew came to finish his education after Winchester College with the Jenkinses. In August 1855, Charlotte Starky wrote that her seventeen-year-old second son 'is very much improved both in intellect and manners by Mr. Jenkins, he will return in Septr[.] I hear Mrs Jenkins and her youngest Son and Daughter [John and Mina] are spending their holidays at Ostend,' and that Helen was going to stay at Spye Park soon: 'We all like her so much.' Later she writes to her brother George about Helen, now twenty-eight: 'She spent ten days with us here previously and delighted us all with her playing and singing.'[32]

I can't quite deduce that the teaching of one son by Rev. Blacker and the other son by Edward produced the rather different outcomes for the two young men. Second son Andrew went to Cambridge in 1858 and was ordained three years later. He seems to have been a conscientious clergyman, with the use of just one eye, dying in 1871 aged only thirty-three. His elder brother, the wealthy heir Bayntun, got the bug for breeding horses, which his mother feared would ruin the family, and indeed, in 1858, Bayntun had 'made a sad mess of his property, by his mania for farming and racing, it is gone so fast that his Creditors have taken possession of his property', and he fled to Brussels.[33] In 1864: 'Spye Park is sold; if it is not it soon will be; Bayntun has made a great ass of himself'. Three years later he was made bankrupt.[34] He moved to Australia and died there in 1872, also in his thirties. It is such a stereotypical tale for the nineteenth or eighteenth century: the feckless elder son addicted to horse racing; the responsible younger son who cared for the poor. I think Eliza was playing the innocent in her letter to her sister about Bayntun only drinking cups of tea: in hindsight from his later career (and he got even fatter) I can imagine his visits to the Jenkins household as preparatory to riotious and drunken late nights with 'Stable Boys' in town. Could Edward have made a difference if Bayntun had been put under his care instead of Rev. Blacker's? Maybe.

* * *

Eliza had her own problem son – Evan junior. In April 1851, aged eighteen, he sailed on the *Malacca* for Sydney, to stay with his aunt and uncle on their estate in the Hunter Valley in New South Wales.[35] All we know of what happened after his arrival in August is in letters from Eliza, Janet and their cousin to his aunt Margaret. Young Evan wrote to his mother about the warm and hospitable welcome he received, and Eliza warned Margaret that her son was lacking in confidence and oversensitive: 'He is of (perhaps unfortunately) a very susceptible disposition too much afraid of being officious & forward, & more likely to keep behind even when anxious to give assistance – I shall be glad to hear that he prefers a Bush life, where I am sure more real happiness is to be found, than in Towns & certainly fewer temptations to evil – Cannot he be useful to you in teaching your little ones, of which Evan has had some experience so far as seeing others taught from his Childhood [...] I know full well the pleasure it will afford Evan to feel that he earns the bread he eats, so pray desire him to Instruct his Cousins or do anything else which from sheer ?humility or false modesty he may not offer of himself.'[36] Since letters took several months to reach Australia, it seems a bit late in the day to suggest what young Evan could actually do. Nor had Eliza been told that Evan needed a gun and a saddle, which he had to borrow money to buy when he arrived. I wonder if Evan had ever ridden or used a gun before; maybe a few times with his barrister uncle Samuel in England. A city boy going to Australia was likely to be far more out of his depth than an Australian coming to Europe, as cousin Alward Wyndham did at the same time.

Then something happened. Janet in Greenwich replied to sister Margaret in July:

> As to Evan dear Meg we can only think it must be his queer suspicious temper that made him act so strangely & I am glad to find from Ned (who thinks the same) that his poor Mother is more tranquil on the subject but I am sure till she hears from him she will be very anxious Naturally – I only hope he may have written – Sam was astonished when he heard George had consented to receive him at all & John too is shocked at such a return but truly the poor deluded fellow seems grateful to you & his letters have always been full of your kindness to him I know – He used sometimes at home to accuse his Mother & all of them of not treating him properly & was full of [illegible word] Ned says.[37]

We never learn what Evan did: break something in a temper? But his uncle Samuel's reaction is foreboding for the young man, who it seems had form in outbursts, if that is what it is. I wish the illegible word that Ned (brother Edward) supplied was readable. I've tried to surprise it by suddenly glancing at it, but 'fierceness' is all I can come up with. I don't know if this is classic third son syndrome (if that exists), but a child thinking they are being treated unfairly is common of course.

The problem may have been that the eldest boy Edward was the truly favoured one; the second, Alexander, was perhaps cossetted because of his weak sight and ill health; the last, John ('Co'), was the cherished baby of the family. This didn't leave Evan much of a role.

It gets worse. Evan borrowed the large sum of £10 from his uncle George, didn't repay it, and went to the Diggings. Eliza is arranging for the money to be repaid and 'I am in hopes that if this trial at Gold finding fails, he will be induced to remain Stationery & try to get a little money together to begin something for himself.'³⁸ She adds, anxiously: 'We are still without tidings of Evan, and I beg of you dear Meg whenever you can send me a word about him whenever you write to not to omit this – The dangers to be incurred at "the Diggings" we hear much of, & not a word have we heard of his safety since he sent these, & only one short letter all the while he was at Port Fairy.' The coastal town of Port Fairy is in western Victoria, west of Melbourne, where Evan had had a job he disliked. Eliza feels he must have left it because his employers were 'low people'. A few months later, in summer 1853, Eliza is still desperate for news: 'so miserable to us why Evan leaves us in ignorance so cruelly long – The only pleasure left to me in this World is to know that my children & all those near & dear to me are steady, happy & doing well – Get every information of my Son you can dear Sister, & send me all you gather each time you write to Europe.' She also adds as regards Margaret's imminent grandchild: 'I would rather get a tooth extracted'.³⁹ Unfortunately the letter is torn here and it is not clear if Eliza is thinking of the pain of childbirth, the nine months of being pregnant or even having a baby in the house. But her gist is obvious and I love her forthrightness. While other women might coo at the prospect of a baby, Eliza is frank about the ghastliness of it all. She would not be a dull dinner-party guest, and we shall see her rallying call for the rights of wives below. Eliza was to have six grandchildren who survived infancy, through her youngest son John, but the first was born two years after her death.

It was not until March the following year that Eliza heard from Australia that Evan junior had had a fall, was possibly concussed and deaf in one ear, but he was now back near his uncle and aunt. Meanwhile she was trying to repay Evan's increased debts through her brother John Livingston Jay: 'it is John's fault & not mine if your Husband is not repaid every Centime that has been advanced on Evans account, & which I am repaying to John "at my convenience" as he particularly requested I should – More than a £5 or £10 Note, I have it not in my power to send Evan at once for since October last year, everything has doubled in price, & my incomings being the same as before & uncertain as to amount you see how prudent and economical I must be to make two ends meet.[40] At this time, because of the death of her chef de cuisine, she was doing all the shopping – paying cash upfront, which was cheaper than on credit – and had been ill for a month. What impresses me in her March 1854 letter to sister Margaret is Eliza's belief in the rights of wives:

> I wish I could inspire you with the Belgian feelings in Money matters viz (the Code Napoleon) that one half of a Husbands fortune his Wife has a right to even if she had not a penny of her own when she married – A Belgian wd as soon lock up the Larder from his Wife as his Purse & in most cases she keeps La Caisse [cashbox] – Do we not by our labors of housekeeping &c help to make the money and surely we are entitled to spend our share according to our fancy if we prove to be good Wives & if bad ones then naturally we forfeit this privilege – Consider this in its true light & try to avail yourself of it.

Also, I am sure that Eliza would not let her husband censor her letters.

Despite her resilience, Eliza is constantly the worried and defensive mother as regards her son Evan, especially when she hears he has left yet another job. But she accepts sister Margaret's advice that she must not send Evan any money: presumably to teach him that he must stand on his own two feet. Two years later, Janet was more outspoken to sister Margaret about Evan: 'When shall we hear from Evan. We trust he may not return home to them – I quite expect he will drink himself to death or get murdered in a quarrel.' She adds: 'Eliza told me if you write again to put private outside & then none of them see the part about Evan as only she & Edward know it – Noone had ?surely better chances if he would have been steady only.'[41]

Shortly after, around July 1856, Eliza heard something more shocking about Evan, and of his 'departure':

> I will now avail myself of the next Vessel for Australia to reply to the overpowering & unexpected intelligence, for after a young Man has stood high in the estimation of his Employers (as Evan did) & took out more than the usual Certificates, of probity & trustworthiness, of which they had proof for 2½ yrs viz from the age of 15 to 17½, which Certificates he promised to show you, we were stressed to account for such a change in his principles – Had you seen Evan intoxicated, I suppose I must have believed you, but my

dear Margt it is hard to tell his Mother that her Son has acquired so vicious a propensity, from the heresay of Servts, who not comprehending his <u>excitable</u> nature (the <u>only</u> fault wch I ever had to deplore) attributed <u>to drink</u> what arose from <u>despair</u>, occasioned by his unfortunate speculations, wch would to God he had never entered into. At such a distance as exists between us, it is at the least imprudent (not to say cruel) to repeat a mere report invented by Low persons which cannot be contradicted until the Sting is Left, tho' thank God I do <u>not</u> nor does Edwd credit report from such authority, Knowing as we both do Evan's abhorrence of that vice.

Eliza states that she and Edward will repay the debts, then adds:

That he has been ungrateful towards yourself & family, and distressed & hurt your feelings, no one can deplore more than I do, & to you who know what are a Mothers feelings I need not attempt to describe the addition to my present grief this information you send has brought on me –

I daily expect the Post to bring a letter from Evan, who if he sees 'the Times' of the 23d Augst will be overpowered to read the Death of his favorite Little Mina, to whom he always evinced more than common affection – Shd you know of means to trace him out, have the charity to forward Eds Letter to him wch I will enclose in this.[42]

Evan has obviously been accused of being drunk, but there must be something more than that. Eliza emphasizes his probity: was he also accused of stealing from his employers? Eliza, grieving after the death of her daughter, defends Evan to the last, but was naïve, surely, to think that the son she had last seen five years before hadn't discovered a taste for alcohol. A cousin puts the nail in the coffin: 'Poor Evan is I fear quite lost to his family – she [Eliza] never names him in her Notes, & John [Eliza's youngest son] seldom mentions him to our boy at Cambridge.'[43] That is the last mention of him in the Wyndham letters. In 1857, another cousin of Eliza's, Margaret Bowden – the last-surviving of the Bowden children who had fallen to tuberculosis in Edmonton so many years before – specifically left Evan out of her will: 'If any of the legatees are deceased then their share to go to any issue, in equal share. Except in regard to Evan Jenkins son of the said Eliza Jenkins who I entirely exclude from taking any beneficiary interest under this my Will.'[44] That is cruel, especially if Evan hadn't been able to defend himself. Margaret Bowden didn't die until 1865, after Eliza, so perhaps the latter never knew.

There is no further trace of Evan in Australia. His 'departure' was presumably from the area, and from his employment. If he had left for home it would be pointless for Eliza to write in a letter that would take months to arrive: 'If you discover his whereabouts forward the two sheets of this letter in wch I give all the particulars of dear Minas death.' I found him in the new cemetery at Evere, Brussels. In the file of letters of 1887–8 between his younger brother John and the authorities about moving the family from the old Protestant cemetery he has a separate mention because he died in the commune of Saint-Gilles rather than in Ixelles. His death certificate states that he died at the age of thirty-five on 29 April 1868 at home, at his brother John's new school in rue St-Bernard; he had 'no profession'. The informants were his two surviving brothers, Edward and John. It would be unfair and pointless to speculate about the intervening years. What is interesting is the contrast with a parallel trip, in the reverse direction, made by his cousin Alward Wyndham, who was four years older and on holiday. Eliza found him a 'phenomenon', though she thought Alward viewed Brussels as 'dull and unprofitable'.[45] In London, he got involved with the Catholic Apostolic Church, founded by Rev. Edward Irving, who were expecting the Second Coming. Charlotte Brontë scathingly equated a 'congregation of Irvingites in full exercise of their miraculous gift' to the 'Tongues at Babel'.[46] Alward frequented the Gothic Revival church in Gordon Square, Bloomsbury, and was ordained a deacon before he went home to Australia.[47] The movement died out (literally) in the early twentieth century. In a later generation, one young man might have become a drug-user; another a follower of Hare Krishna – both Evan and Alward were trying to find their own identities in the sink-or-swim world of the mid-nineteenth century. The prodigal son returned to Brussels and was cared for, not only before his early death but after his death, when John ensured that he was moved from the old Protestant cemetery with his parents. Did he return before Eliza's death? I don't know. But I'm certain that she thought about him often and longed for him to come home.

* * *

In Pudsey, in the West Riding of Yorkshire, on 14 August 1854, David Jenkins's long tenure and trials had come to an end:

On Monday last, after a lingering illness, aged 67, the Rev. David Jenkins, 42 years incumbent of Pudsey church.[48]

He seems to have been unable to officiate much in his last years, but his curate stood in for him, and son Joseph when he could. Ruth Strong sums up that David arrived at 'an insignificant little chapel with accommodation for just four hundred. When he died Pudsey had three Sunday schools, two church day schools and a huge new church which it could fill.'[49] His son Joseph had finally found a living in 1849 as the first incumbent of tiny St John's Church in Newton, south-west Herefordshire, in the Marches of Wales. I wonder if his wife Margaret, brought up in industrial West Yorkshire, enjoyed the rural remoteness. I think Joseph must have felt honoured to have been chosen because the tale of its foundation (written by Newton's vicar in 1911) is charming.[50] A local yeoman called John Powell was determined in the 1840s to build a church in Newton since the parish church was four miles away. He enlisted the help of the rector in nearby Turnastone to raise money. The combination of the yeoman's ideas and legwork, and the rector's letter-writing, brought in the needed sums – including from Dowager Queen Adelaide – and they built a church in one of Powell's meadows: 'a full-grown church stood manifest one morning before the wondering, gazing, swimming eyes of as devoted a member of our Apostolic Communion as ever trod in shoes'. It was consecrated by the Bishop of St David's, after Powell had walked seventy miles there to ask him. 'Many months more passed away, and then an able and excellent minister was nominated to the cure, in which he has since laboured to the great benefit and satisfaction of his people.' I am glad for Joseph. I wonder if his Welsh roots helped him get the appointment. He died only six years after his father in 1860, in his forties, but the connection with the Brussels Jenkins continued, since his daughter Mina – Sarah Jane Clara Wilhelmina – born in 1849, lived next door to Edward and his wife in Brussels in the 1870s, and then with or near John's son Rev. Charles Edward Jenkins junior in Leicester.[51] She must be one of the ancient ladies in the wedding photograph of my grandparents in 1913 there, and my mother remembered an 'Aunt Mina' from her childhood, actually cousin, but had no idea of how Mina was related. The Jenkinses took care of each other. There was also a fascinating passing on of the name Wilhelmina – presumably named after the Queen of the Netherlands before the Belgian Revolution – from Mary Jane Wilhelmina, Evan and Eliza's second daughter, who died in 1838 at the age of eight, to their last daughter, to Joseph's daughter, and finally to Evan and Eliza's granddaughter, who died aged twenty-one in 1898. Only Joseph's Mina lived a long life, dying a spinster in her seventies.

* * *

A year after Charlotte Brontë's death in March 1855, Elizabeth Gaskell was hard at work gathering materials for the *Life* of her friend and planning a trip to Brussels. She wrote to her cousin Fanny Holland:

> I can get plenty of grand Brussels introductions from Madame Van der Weyer (Belgian Ambassadress,) but I don't want to be pottered by civility that won't help me on in my object – i.e. getting to know all I can of Miss B's two years in Brussels. When I go I don't quite know yet, – about beginning of May I fancy [...] but what I want are literary & educational introductions, without stating my reason for wanting them; as I want to hear the general opinions of the Hegers, (Beck –) Can you help me to these last?[52]

She adds that she can refer her 'respectability to the Ministre de justice, (head of the Police) in Brussels' as they had already been in contact. 'I mean to make him serviceable, as I find he holds a good position for ascertaining past facts in Brussels.' I so admire her: dogged as a biographer and charmingly deceitful in order to learn the truth ('without stating my reason'). It helped to be a famous author: doors would open. She had probably learnt Eliza's name from Charlotte and her father. In a letter in 1853, Mrs Gaskell mentions that Charlotte had told her of incidents in Brussels, which the former recognized when she read *Villette*.[53] What Charlotte had said about the Jenkins family must have encouraged Mrs Gaskell to visit Mrs Jenkins. I wonder what she wrote to Eliza: that she just wanted a chat about Charlotte? Saying to some people that she was writing a biography might distort what they told her, put them on their guard or encourage them to embroider. Clever woman.

On Friday 6 May, Mrs Gaskell took the night boat from Dover to Ostend. She wrote in a letter the day she left that 'so many other things have gone wrong that I am in despair & can hardly keep from perpetually crying which is partly being so overtired'.[54] Here were two overwrought Elizabeths meeting and I so hope they weren't endlessly polite to each other. Because not only was Eliza worried about son Evan in Australia, but her youngest daughter Mina was dying in another room. Perhaps Mrs Gaskell heard Mina coughing, heard schoolboys talking loudly, the sound of the piano. Maybe Helen came in to refill the teapot from the urn before rushing back to her duties; perhaps Mrs Gaskell also chatted to her. Then Edward escorted Mrs Gaskell to the next person on her list.[55]

It was clear that Eliza's youngest daughter, seventeen-year-old Mina, was dying in early 1856. But before the worst happened, something tremendous did for the Jenkins family: Rev. Blacker resigned from his chaplaincy at the Chapel Royal because of 'ill health'.[56] I may be unfair to Rev. Blacker, but it was a ray of hope for Eliza, though no certainty that Edward would be his replacement. One newspaper announced, in April, that: 'One of the best chaplaincies of Brussels will shortly become vacant by the resignation of the present highly esteemed holder, the Rev. M.J. Blacker. The appointment rests with the Bishop of London, upon the recommendation of the Earl of Clarendon.'[57] Clarendon was the current Foreign Secretary. Gone were the days when the choice rested on votes in the vestry with tempers flaring and a couple of dukes at daggers drawn. I imagine that Eliza had taught Edward not to be backward in coming forward, though Eliza's cousin Jane commented in October that it was 'so unexpected Edward getting the Church'.[58] I would like to ask her: why unexpected? It sounds a shoo-in. But maybe cousin Jane meant that it was unexpected that Blacker had resigned. Perhaps 'ill health' was an excuse for differences with his congregation or with his wife about living in Brussels. The Blacker family moved to Pimlico on the Thames embankment and its smart new terraces, which today is utterly dreary apart from the presence of Tate Britain. In 1858 his entire family died of diphtheria.[59] At first I felt awful when I heard this; then discovered that he married again and had another five children.

Charlotte Starky wrote to her brother George Wyndham in early August 1856: 'Mr. Jenkins paid us a short visit when he was in England. he is very much pleased at being appointed the English Chaplain at Brussels. he gives a very poor a/c of his youngest Sister whom Andy [her son Andrew] says is very ill indeed at times.'[60]

* * *

On 19 August 1856, Janet wrote to sister Margaret: 'My thoughts are always with poor dear Eliza for I fear our pet is now going fast – She keeps her bed half the day & seems to like to talk of her own state so her miserable Mother has to struggle against her feelings as tears distress poor Mina sadly.'[61] She also comments on why she had not been to see her sister: 'they take as many pupils as they can stow away [...] I never could live there as they all live in such a state of excitement & enjoy the schooling which I <u>hate</u>.' Later in the letter Janet adds that Mina has died: 'Poor dear Eliza! She can hardly realize it for the poor pet was able to be carried down stairs to the last – One sigh & all was over & quite conscious of her state – The boys return will be better for poor Eliza & Helen.' On 20 August, Mina was buried in the Protestant cemetery, 'in the Grave of her Father, & near to where our Mother was Interred, out of the Porte Louvain', attended by Eliza and by Mina's siblings Helen, Edward and John.[62] It is sad that although John managed to get his parents and three siblings moved to the new cemetery in 1887–8 there is no mention of his grandmother Helen Jay. Perhaps the concession for Protestant clergymen didn't extend to Eliza's mother, and the Jenkins family could not afford to move her – and maybe Eliza's youngest brother William, also buried there, had been forgotten.

Eliza wrote to Margaret at the end of the month after she had heard of Evan's drunkenness and maybe worse:

> Your first letter (to John) in wch you mention Evans departure was forwarded to me My dear Sister about a month ago; fortunately I was alone, so that my darling Mina was spared the pang of knowing the contents, wch in her state between Life & death she cd not have survived an hour. The last Letter to myself reached me the day after my Sainted Child had breathed her last, which I only particularize to account for a silence wch under less distressing circumstances wd not have been prolonged.[63]

I hope Margaret felt suitably contrite. After dealing with the awful accusations against Evan, Eliza returns to Mina:

> The Cough was fearful to the last, & when I looked distressed she said 'I have no pain dear Mama, as I might have in my Chest' & not an impatient word, or moment of irritation ever proceeded from our Darling during her long trial of two years [...] She asked Helen & me before she went to Bed 'how long she was likely to live', & looked very sad at seeing Helens tears, wch I had long schooled my feelings & swallowed – That night she slept as usual, & coughed less perhaps [...] I was putting on her Cap wch fell off & saw her lips move, but did not hear her say (as Helen says she did) 'Couchez Moi' and all was over.

The daughter who had been conceived after little Mary's death nearly twenty years before was the last bereavement that Eliza had to endure: 'so much do I miss her loving words & ways that I can scarcely live without them, Kind & consoling tho' her Sister & brothers are to make up to me for our darlings Loss'.

* * *

John, the youngest, had started at Magdalene College, Cambridge two years before. It could have been that by stowing all the pupils the family could in

Brussels they were able to pay full fees for him as a pensioner. He gained his BA in 1858, but was not as high-flying academically as older brother Edward as he didn't achieve a Fellowship and was ordained deacon in Peterborough a year later. He was the curate in Roade, a village in Northamptonshire, for a year, ordained priest a year later and returned to Brussels to be assistant chaplain to his brother at the Chapel Royal. In June that year, 1860, Eliza's cousin Jane wrote to Margaret that Janet had been busy: 'the young lady who is engaged to Edwd Jenkins has been staying at Greenwich – they seem much pleased with her'. Edward married Meliora Georgina Tinling on 6 July. Her father was the late Lieut.-Col. Tinling of the Grenadier Guards and it seems Lora, as she was known, had been at school in Brussels when they met. Cousin Jane, however, is gloomy about Eliza: 'the sea air has braced Eliza's nerves – but she is I hear beginning to look old – no wonder for she must be getting on & I am now 51, & I always recollect Eliza many many years older than myself'.[64] Eliza was sixty-four, but she was indeed beginning a decline. 'Poor Eliza seems to rally but she will never I expect be able to use much exertion again, or come to England – she has kind affectionate children around her & seems to have every comfort,' cousin Jane reported in May 1863.[65] However, Eliza did rally for a while, as her children prepared for an important event: not only a mass confirmation by the Bishop of Oxford ('Soapy Sam') in the following spring, but hopefully the laying of the stone for the first solely Anglican church in Brussels.

* * *

In the year 1862 the Revd C.E. Jenkins, then Chaplain, feeling the inconvenience of being tributary to the French and German Protestant community for the use of their Chapel, determined to commence the Building of an Anglican Church.

– *Almanac of the Church of the Resurrection*[66]

This was to prove a fraught undertaking. An 'influential' committee was formed and circulars sent out requesting support and funds. Optimistically they expected a free site from the Brussels municipal authorities, and grants from the English and Belgian governments. That didn't happen, but a site was finally bought at the junction of rue de Drapiers and the boulevard de Waterloo, just outside the city proper and a short walk south-west from Porte de Namur. Land was expensive but the large garden seemed ideal. By allotting the frontage for building plots, and the rear being retained for the site of the church, the cost was reduced.[67] The architect chosen was Robert Jewell Withers (1824–94), who specialized in churches, building or restoring over a hundred in Britain, including in South Wales. The warm red bricks were to come from Antwerp, the stone from quarries in France, marble from Luxembourg. A lavish use of Minton's tiles was promised. It was to be in style an English church so that 'our countrymen, who are expatriated for a time, for educational or other purposes, may enjoy the services of the church of their fatherland the same as at home – a comfort seldom enjoyed abroad'.[68] It must have been exciting planning the look of the church – even in committee – and to create a building just for Anglicans: no sharing any more.

In a letter written to Aunty Janet in Greenwich by Helen in April 1864, Helen says that the architect had arrived from London 'and we are all anxiety to know the Bishop's decision, whether he can lay the first stone or not. We shant know till tonight – I hope to goodness he <u>will</u> do it, as that will repay Edward for all his trouble.' She adds that Aunt Janet will be sent a picture of the church because Withers's sketch is going to be photographed: 'It is so pretty!' But the reason presumably why Janet sent Helen's five letters to Australia was because Eliza was dying. The first letter Helen sent to Janet was on Easter Monday, 28 March. Eliza had been unwell for sometime, 'no appetite, nor inclination to move', then she had a stroke on Easter Monday: 'This morning I was very much alarmed on seeing a tendency to paralysis of one hand & of the tongue, and Dr Lebeau, who has just been, fears that the brain is affected.' Helen adds that her mother 'rambles very much in her talk, & strange to say can hardly express herself in English at all – It seems to be French, as much as we can understand'.[69] So-called foreign accent syndrome can result from a stroke. Poor Helen, now in her mid-thirties, had to cope with Eliza's diarrhoea and weakness, hardly helped by the blister that Dr Lebeau had created on the back of Eliza's neck.

On Friday morning Helen asks her aunt to write a letter to cheer her mother up. 'Poor Mamma is as patient & considerate for us all, and will hardly allow anyone to sit up with her at night. Of course, however, either Sydonie or I is always on the watch.' I haven't found out who Sydonie was. Helen lies on her bed, half dressed, ready to help. Dr Lebeau has just visited and 'says that he does not think she can rally this time – God's will be done!' On Sunday Helen writes: 'It is now a quarter to ten, & she is lying perfectly quiet, having had a cup of arrow-root with a little port-wine in it – and better than tea under the circumstances.' Eliza is also getting crotchety: 'She asked me twice this morning why I <u>moved</u> her medicines, meaning it was that that made her worse – so I don't think her head is quite the thing.' How patient Helen sounds; it is so hard caring for a dying parent. But at least Helen can let her feelings out to Aunt Janet:

How thankful I shall be when Thursday comes, & all the Church affairs, Confirmation [in the margin she writes: 'Tuesday 5th laying the stone of the Church this means'] are over! We want the service & music to be particularly nice, & I cant be present on account of this illness of poor Mamma. & two of my best singers have bad colds, and one useful man, Mr Walsh, has his right hand dreadfully bruised & rendered quite useless for the present, by a large piece of cornice falling on it at the Theatre the other night! So the evening service tonight cannot take place at all, and the rest must go on as it can – Quite a chapter of accidents, is it not. – Mamma asked a few questions yesterday about the Church business, the house, &c, for the first time since last week – otherwise she never speaks unless spoken to, and lies for hours without moving.

She adds later in the letter: 'She is very talkative this afternoon, her eyes very wide open, and extremely indignant with me about her medicine – sure I made mistakes &c – Never mind, it soon passes off.' By Tuesday Helen is more optimistic: 'This morning she had a good cup of cocoa for breakfast, and also ate a little bit of buttered roll, after which she washed & changed her things, got out of bed while the sheets were taken off, and actually <u>walked</u> back from the chair to the bed! Since then she has been perfectly quiet, & just now asked me the hour, & said what a nice rest she had had. All this is somewhat encouraging, is it not?' The confirmation was that afternoon and Helen allows herself to dress for the first time in ten days: 'They want me for the singing.' But her brothers still don't know if the bishop will also lay the first stone for the new church because politically it is difficult: 'Lord Howard [the ambassador] is most kind and wonderfully energetic about it, & promises to do all he can to facilitate matters. The Burgomaster & Ministers are full of fine speeches – May they only act up to them when the time comes!'

Charles Augustus Ellis, sixth Baron Howard de Walden (1799–1868), had taken over from Sir Hamilton Seymour as ambassador, or minister plenipotentiary, at the Belgian Court in 1846. An Eton-educated army man, he had married a daughter of the fourth Duke of Portland, Lady Lucy. It is possible that he felt dealing with Belgians easier than coping with emotional Portuguese, his previous posting.[70] In a letter to Frances Curwen soon after the couple's arrival in Brussels, Eliza had commented: 'People remark that the new Ambassador & his Lady do not look amiable.'[71] That might be code for: I don't find them amiable. But daughter Helen gives a nice pen portrait of Lady Lucy in her next letter to Aunt Janet, her last letter in the archive, as Lord Howard flaps. But first, on Tuesday 5 April, came the confirmation: 'The Confirmation was a beautiful sight,' Helen wrote to Aunt Janet, 'and both the Bishop & his Chaplain said they never saw one better managed – There were 46 girls, all except two, in white with long veils and 28 boys – Edward, Co, Drury and Rowton took part in the service, & the Bishop delivered two addresses, one before & one after the Confirmation – The whole ceremony lasted two hours.' Co was Helen and Edward's youngest brother John; Rev. Rupert Rowton was in his forties, and for a couple of years chaplain for an Anglican congregation in rue Belliard before returning to England.[72] The origins of the Bishop of Oxford's nickname 'Soapy Sam' is unclear. Samuel (1805–73) was the third son of evangelical MP and abolitionist William Wilberforce. In *The Warden* (1855), the first of his Barsetshire novels, Anthony Trollope caricatured the Bishop of London, Charles James Blomfield (d. 1857), as the eldest son of Archdeacon Grantly; in the same book Samuel Wilberforce is portrayed as the youngest son:

> Samuel was the general favourite; and dear little Soapy, as he was familiarly called, was as engaging a child as ever fond mother petted. He was soft and gentle in his manners, and attractive in his speech; the tone of his voice was melody, and every action was a grace; unlike his brothers, he was courteous to all [...] Charles James, though he always spoke of him as his dear brother Samuel, was not slow to say a word against him when opportunity offered. To speak the truth, Samuel was a cunning boy, and those even who loved him best could not but own that for one so young, he was too adroit in choosing his words, and too skilled in modulating his voice.[73]

After an evangelical childhood, Samuel Wilberforce leaned towards high-churchism, but disagreed with the Tractarians and their increasingly Roman Catholic beliefs. It is probable that his 'via media' between low-churchism and the Oxford Movement was that shared by the Jenkins brothers. Wilberforce was vigorous in his actions and travels, and renowned as a great speaker; he was made chaplain at Court by Prince Albert in 1841 but Queen Victoria grew to dislike his high-church views. His reputation today is unfairly based on a 'quarrel' with Thomas Huxley in 1860 about our evolution from apes. His energy and mental acuity seem phenomenal: he once simultaneously dictated four letters to secretaries while penning a fifth himself.[74] The Jenkins household must have been buzzing that in place of Bishop Tait of London, they had secured Soapy Sam. But would the blessing of the foundation stone take place? Helen takes up the story:

In the evening [of Tuesday 5th] there was a dinner at the Embassy, to which Edward went, & it was then finally decided that the Bishop should lay the first stone yesterday at ½ past 3 – Poor Lord Howard was so bullied about it, & was so terrified of compromising his official dignity, that he fairly ran away from the discussions twice, and had to be fetched back again – Lady Howard looked on intensely amused, but said nothing and at last the Bishop put an end to everything by declaring himself quite at Mr Jenkins' service for next day at any hour he liked to fix – You may imagine how happy he came home that night! He & Co sat up till ten, arranging matters, and were hard at work by ½ past 7 yesterday morning sending circulars to all the British residents announcing that the Ceremony would take place at ½ past 3 – I had to collect my choir, and by ½ past two we were all on the ground where a number of people were already assembled. – There was a regular service printed & distributed, and a trench had been dug & filled with masonry, & there was the great stone suspended by a lever all ready – In fact everything was in beautiful order – quite marvellous considering the short notice – Luckily the Architect from London [Withers] was here, & he knew exactly how things ought to be done – Edwd, Co, Drury & Rowton were in their surplices ready to receive the Bishop, but first came Lady Howard in a splendid humour, & was conducted to a place of honour – Crowds of people continued to arrive and exactly at ½ past 3, came the Bishop in his robes, with the regular episcopal velvet cap on, & his handsome order with its broad blue ribbon, followed by his nice old Chaplain. He stood a little higher than we did, & there was a trench between him & our choir, who all stood exactly opposite, with the general crowd behind us. He began by an address, in which he told us among other things that he had thought it admirable to change the proposed name of the Church, as there was already one of the name in Brussels. That was our only disappointment, as we had set our hearts on 'St Mary Magdalene' – However, it could not be helped so he called it the Church of the Resurrection, which he thought appropriate to the season when the stone was laid.

After some prayers and a hymn, a collection was made, then the choir sang the Amens in the same key.

It was a most imposing ceremony, & Ghémar the photographer brought his apparatus & took several views, which I am curious to see – If there is anything good, you shall have a picture – Edward dined with the Bishop at Sir John Keanes, where he is staying, & Co went in the evening – So you see the great business is over at last, and much thankful we all are. – I must not forget to add that the weather was lovely, the brightest sun shining down upon us during the whole time – The only drawback was that neither poor Mamma nor Lora were able to be present – but no happiness is perfect in this world, so we must not expect it – Lady Howard's contribution yesterday was £20! – Today the Bishop confirms at Antwerp, tomorrow at Calais, and on Sunday preaches before the Queen – Hard work, is it not?

The engraving in the *Illustrated London News* shows the ceremony, though I wish I could see the photo; Helen's choir seems to include the man in the surplice, and perhaps that is her in a crinoline in the foreground left. On the other side of the trench, Edward and John stand just behind the bishop, to his left.[75] My great-grandfather John, then aged twenty-nine, looks oddly dandyish – I'm so used to photos of him as an elderly, tired patriarch with a long beard.

In the same letter Helen says that her mother Eliza 'got somewhat into a muddle between the two' – the confirmation and the laying of the stone – but doggedly had stayed alive. And in her confusion Eliza maybe grasped that her family were building a splendid church. Knew that her remaining children were kind and steady. Perhaps she thought back to her first meeting with Evan forty years before: they had achieved something, however hard it had been at times.

Eliza died a month later, on 6 May at two o'clock in the morning, aged sixty-six. No doubt Helen and Sydonie shared watching duties, neither dressing fully nor eating much. The death certificate says she died at no. 14 rue des Champs Elysées, where Mrs Gaskell had visited her.[76] She was 'Directrice d'Institution': no 'sans profession' for her now, thanks to son Edward, one of the informants. Her place of birth is given as Edinburgh: maybe Eliza didn't know that she had been born in Rotterdam; Edinburgh was the place in her heart – and Lixmount.

That church was never built.

Seventeen

Coda

Newspaper corrections can be amusing. In 1869, 'Mr Jenkins, the Anglican minister, who celebrated divine service in Liège for the riflemen, has written to us that he officiated at an improvised pulpit, with a drum for a lectern, according to the custom followed in the English army, where this service is called "the drumhead service." It was therefore an error by our correspondent to say that Mr Jenkins had officiated on horseback.'[1] Edward may have enjoyed that. But after the triumph of the blessing of the foundation stone, subscriptions for his new Anglican church tailed off, work stopped and in 1870 the Franco-Prussian War broke out. It seems that as a result the English had to sell the site for their church. On 18 May 1873, Edward died, worn out it is said 'with anxiety and overwork'.[2] He was forty-seven. There were no children from his marriage to Lora, who had been afflicted with rheumatism but lived into her nineties. My mother remembered as a child in the 1920s being taken to see 'Aunt Lora' in London, an ancient lady wearing an old-fashioned dress.

Edward had put most of his own money into the building of the church, much of which must have come from Eliza's savings as he had left her estate unadministered. The £513 that executors declared should now be repaid to the Jenkins family was refused by them. Instead they 'paid over the whole to the Old English Bank in Brussels as a nucleus of a new Fund with which to carry out the wishes of their deeply lamented relative'. A new site was purchased in the rue de Stassart, a narrow road nearer the Porte de Namur in Ixelles. A foundation stone was laid in November 1873, in memory of Edward. There were still legal difficulties, but a royal decree found in their favour. Subscriptions were not forthcoming and had to be fought and begged for. But the church was finally opened on 15 October 1874, blessed by a finally convinced Bishop of London that all was legal. The article pasted into Edward's register states that: 'all anxiety relating to the tenure of the building was removed, and the use of the Church was secured for ever to the Congregation'. Alas, no. My mother thought the church had been destroyed. I found it in February 2014 and wrote after my visit:

> It was cold and the rain was worsening when I found the church building. In my article for St Bernard's School I wrote that the church had been bombed and nothing remained. It was my mother's (confused) memory. She may have been muddling British wartime memories with the fire on 16 March 1927 that totally destroyed it apart from 'a small bell turret and parts of the walls' (*The Times* account in a great-aunt's album). But it was rebuilt, and in 2013 Roger Cox assured me it was still there! I was astounded. He said it was a shop, then reported back that it was a nightclub. I hovered by the 'church' twice on that rainy Friday afternoon. There was no doorbell. But on my second hover suddenly a man came out and I grabbed his attention. 'My ancestors built this church and I'd love to –'. 'I know,' he replied, mysteriously. At first he wouldn't let me in, then reluctantly let me go inside – though I wasn't allowed to take photos. It was rather overwhelming: this is the church the Jenkins brothers had worked so hard to build and it seemed wonderfully restored (though the dazzling nightclub features were a bit hard to disentangle from the fabric of the building). I didn't have time to ask if the memorial window to Rev. Evan and Eliza Jenkins had survived. I guess I felt ambivalent, but pleased to have had a glimpse.

Poet and railway employee Thomas Westwood attended John's services at the new Church of the Resurrection, though it doesn't sound as if John's sermons kept him riveted. In March 1879, Westwood wrote to Lady Alwyne: 'the next Sunday during a sermon, much of a muchness, I revised my lines, of which I send you another version; and when that cobbling was at an end, my mind wandered away, Heaven knows why or wherefore, from the Rev. John Jenkins (that's our pastor, "whom unmerciful disaster hurries fast, and hurries faster" – for my own part I never overtake him) and the little chapel in the rue de Staddart [sic] to the Cap Martin.' He adds: 'Your story of the village clergyman who sent his congregation to sleep and then fell asleep himself comprehends the perfection of pulpit oratory' and copies out the poem he had finished during the service, which starts:

> There shall be no more sea! Oh! Land of Heaven,
> How shall we front thy glories? We, that come
> From such grey skies – that hear for evermore
> The beating of the wind and of the rain
> On bitter moorlands![3]

I thought back to Emily and Charlotte in the 1840s listening to John's father's sermons in the Chapel Royal when Emily was probably drifting away to think of her moorlands, creating poetry in her mind, while Charlotte studied the Jenkins family – golden Edward, chattering musical Helen, bespectacled Alexander, restless Evan junior, serious little John and sweet Mina. And if the sermons of Jenkins father and sons didn't fire up souls, they created a space for writing. In his letter, Westwood paraphrases from Edgar Allan Poe's 'The Raven' – hopefully he wasn't equating John with the demonic raven whose only word is 'Nevermore'. Perhaps he was thinking of the persona of the poet 'napping'; though if John's sermon really brought to mind the melodrama created by Poe, then I have underestimated Jenkins sermons.

On 19 October 1885, Evan and Eliza's youngest son John completed twenty-five years as the chaplain in Brussels – first as assistant to older brother Edward, then after his brother's death overseeing the building of the new church. He was presented with a beautifully bound book stamped with gold fleurs-de-lis and the Jenkins motto 'Perge sed caute' inscribed on the cover. ('Progress cautiously' – I bet Eliza would have preferred a speedier motto.) Inside there is gorgeous calligraphy: 'To the Reverend John Card Jenkins, M.A. Chaplain of the Church of the Resurrection, Brussels. President of the Council of Administration of the Anglican Church in Brussels. Member of the Central Committee of the Anglican Church in Belgium.' There are warm, flattering words such as: 'The Building and Completion of the Church of the Resurrection, erected in memory of your much lamented brother, the Rev. E. Jenkins, are mainly owing to your unwearying exertions and perseverance, and that under no ordinary difficulties.' There are over four hundred signatures by both British and Americans. In his reply to the address, John, 'who was much affected, thanked those present and all who had signed the address, for this renewed proof of the kindness experienced by his family in Brussels for the last 65 years, which he said, far exceeded his desserts'. He also added that 'he would always consider this beautiful address as the most valuable of his worldly possessions, and he felt confident that his family would look upon it as a precious heirloom in years to come'. That is daunting, as the book has descended to me, and without that newspaper cutting I might not have understood its true value, except that it is beautiful.[4] I am curious as to his dating the arrival of his family in Brussels in 1820, a year before I believe his grandfather John Jay and family arrived. But I think that was a neat date that had fixed in the memory.

Two years later he handed over his school in rue St-Bernard to Ernest Hodson, who was to be my other great-grandfather. Rev. John Card Jenkins died after a long and painful illness in September 1894, aged fifty-nine. Apart from a couple of years from the late 1920s when his eldest son returned to Brussels and the Church of the Resurrection, the long line of Jenkins pastors in Brussels had ended after almost seventy years. John's elder sister Helen, after running a 'pensionnat for demoiselles', left for England with her sister-in-law, widowed Lora. There were no more Jenkinses in Belgium. But the school Evan and Eliza had started in the 1820s – carrying on the spirit of the education by Eliza's parents and grandparents – had a descendant in New York, to where Rev. John's younger son emigrated.

The Jenkins family were largely forgotten. But perhaps my book will show that there was once this family who deserve more – more than fabrication, embroidery and sloppy copying. As Charlotte Brontë wrote, 'The first duty of an Author is – I conceive – a faithful allegiance to Truth.'[5] In September 1841 she had written to Aunt Branwell that in Brussels she hoped to make 'connections far more improving, polished, and cultivated, than any I have yet known'. I can only conjecture on the conversations she heard and joined in with at the Jenkins home over two years. I imagine Eliza talking proudly about her Huguenot and Scottish ancestors, interrupted by portly Drury with another anecdote about young Byron. School prefect Edward leaps in to quote from Byron's third canto of *Childe Harold*, composed nearby only decades before – 'is Earth more free?', and banters with Charlotte about the Battle of Waterloo, before he dashes off to the study to do schoolwork. Evan arrives late after visiting a poor parishioner and unseals a note from the palace. And through the open door is heard the sound of Helen on the piano while a *fiacre* rattles over the stony street.

Notes

Chapter 1: The Search Begins

1. 'And once below a time I lordly had the trees and leaves / Trail with daisies and barley / Down the rivers of the windfall light' – Dylan Thomas, 'Fern Hill' (*The Loud Hill of Wales: Poetry of Place*, selected by Walford Davies (London: J.M. Dent, 1991), p. 85).

2. Richard Holmes, *Footsteps: Adventures of a Romantic Biographer* (London: HarperPress, 2011), p. 143.

3. Julian Barnes, *Flaubert's Parrot* (London: Vintage Books, 2009).

4. Virginia Woolf, *The Waves* (Harmondsworth: Penguin Books, 1964), p. 222.

5. *The Letters of Charlotte Brontë*, Volume One: *1829–1847*, ed. Margaret Smith (Oxford: Clarendon Press, 1995), CB to Ellen Nussey, 7 August 1841, p. 266. All subsequent letters are from Smith's three volumes.

6. CB to Ellen Nussey, 17 October 1841, *Letters* I, p. 270.

7. Elizabeth Gaskell, *The Life of Charlotte Brontë*, ed. Elisabeth Jay (London: Penguin Books, 1997), p. 157. (The name of the editor is an interesting coincidence.) I quote from Mrs Gaskell's 1857 version of the letter to Aunt Branwell, and not the version in Margaret Smith's 1995 edition of Charlotte's letters. The original letter has not been traced. Smith thinks that Mrs Gaskell changed the name to Mary in her published book instead of her younger sister Martha 'as being more likely than Martha to secure a residence' for Charlotte. Martha was at the school in September, while Mary was only visiting (*Letters* I, p. 269 n. 6). Aunt Branwell might not be impressed by the idea of the exuberant 22-year-old Martha offering any kind of assistance, and more reassured by the steadier-seeming Mary. Mary started studying at the school in 1842 (e.g. *Letters* I, p. 280). But neither unmarried girl could offer 'respectable protection', unlike the wife of a clergyman. This section of the letter is muddled, which may be Charlotte's excitement or a careless transcription. Smith also has 'Consul' instead of 'Chaplain' for Rev. Evan

Jenkins, which is probably what was in the original as Charlotte confesses she made a mistake about him in a later letter (*Letters* I, p. 273). In Smith's note on him on the opposite page, three out of the four dates she gives for Evan Jenkins are wrong (p. 269 n. 7). Smith's only note for Mrs Jenkins is that she was the wife of the chaplain (p. 279 n. 4).

8.   Gaskell, *Life*, pp. 157, 161, 162, 176.

9.   Monica Kendall, 'My Grandfather Jack', *St. Bernard's School* (4 East 98th Street, New York, New York, 2000), p. 1.

10.   David J. Jones, *Sexuality and the Gothic Magic Lantern* (Basingstoke: Palgrave Macmillan, 2014), ch. 3.

11.   Brian Bracken, 'The Jenkinses' House in Ixelles', The Brussels Brontë Group: Research (18 November 2010).

12.   My information on Gérin comes from the biography by Helen MacEwan, *Winifred Gérin: Biographer of the Brontës* (Brighton: Sussex Academic Press, 2016).

13.   Leon Edel, *Writing Lives: Principia Biographica* [1959] (New York and London: W.W. Norton & Company, 1984), p. 14.

14.   Winifred Gérin, *Charlotte Brontë: The Evolution of Genius* (Oxford: Oxford University Press, 1969), p. 200. My italics.

15.   Mrs. Ellis H. Chadwick, *In the Footsteps of the Brontes* (London: Sir Isaac Pitman & Sons, 1914), p. 225. She gives no source.

16.   Marriage certificate. Ellis Henry Chadwick was twenty-five. They were married in the Edgeley Wesleyan Chapel.

17.   Information from newspaper death notices, censuses and registration of birth of Percival Miller Chadwick, b. 16 June 1888, Rushton Road, Thornbury, Bradford. Killed in action 22 September 1918 in France.

18.   'Baptisms Solemnized in the Parish Church of Christ Church, Heaton Norris', County of Lancaster, 1861, 'born 27 July 1861', Esther Alice, daughter of John and Nancy Miller, baptized 3 November 1861.

19.   See, for example, Richard D. Altick, *Lives and Letters: A History of Literary Biography in England and America* (Westport, CT: Greenwood Press, 1979), ch. 10, esp. pp. 304–5, 346–7, and 347 n. 4 on certain female biographers of the Brontë sisters who seem to have 'worked in a trance' and whose books should be 'relegated to the crowded shelf of curiosities which the practice of biography has engendered during its prolific history'. See also Edel, *Writing Lives*, p. 16: 'In the biographical process the biographer is, as Desmond MacCarthy said, an artist under oath. To be sure, some artists perjure themselves. It is the task of critics to unmask the perjurors.'

20. The fabricated 'John and Edward' escorting story has been copied from Chadwick and Gérin, with no questioning of its dubious source, by, for example: Margot Peters, *Unquiet Soul: A Biography of Charlotte Brontë* (London: Hodder and Stoughton, 1975), p. 114, no source; Rebecca Fraser, *Charlotte Brontë* (London: Methuen–Mandarin, 1989), p. 170, source: Chadwick; Robert Barnard and Louise Barnard, *A Brontë Encyclopedia* (Oxford: Blackwell, 2007), p. 169: no source; Juliet Barker, *The Brontës* (London: Abacus, 2010), p. 461, source: Chadwick; Claire Harman, *Charlotte Brontë: A Life* (UK: Viking, 2015), pp. 144–5, no source: but she adds a different one that I will discuss in chapter 13.

21. Chadwick, *Footsteps*, pp. 201, 255. Eric Ruijssenaars, *Charlotte Brontë's Promised Land: The Pensionnat Heger and Other Brontë Places in Brussels* (Haworth: The Brontë Society, 2000), has a well-researched discussion about the pensionnat and the Isabelle Quarter, though with the usual errors about the Jenkinses. His dates for the demolition of the pensionnat are on pp. 26–8.

22. Chadwick mentions Frances Wheelwright, whom it appears she met in London (*Footsteps*, p. 201). Frances was eleven when she met the Brontë sisters in Brussels. The Wheelwright family were in Brussels for a year (Joseph J. Green, 'The Bronte–Wheelwright Friendship', *Friends' Quarterly Examiner*, 1916). I discuss the church services that they attended in chapter 14 – a missed opportunity by Brontë biographers for an anecdote about Lord Byron.

23. The de Bassompierre family certainly knew the Jenkinses in the 1890s: there is a cutting in a great-aunt's scrapbook from 1893, in my possession, about a tennis tournament in which both families feature, including pairing up in mixed doubles. See also Brian Bracken, 'Football and the Brussels Brontë Story', *Brussels Brontë Blog* (9 June 2014). Charlotte used the name in *Villette* for Ginevra's uncle and Paulina's father, formerly Mr Home.

24. 'Two Brussels Schoolfellows of Charlotte Brontë', *Brontë Society Transactions*, 5:23 (1913), pp. 25–9, at p. 26; Chadwick, *Footsteps*, p. 228.

25. Monica Kendall, 'Brussels, Brontë, Jenkins: My Great-great-grandparents Rev. Evan and Eliza Jenkins and the Brontës', The Brussels Brontë Group: Research (26 March 2014).

26. Richard Altick, *The Art of Literary Research*, 3rd edn (New York: W.W. Norton, 1981), p. 5.

27. Richard Altick, *The Scholar Adventurers* (Columbus: Ohio State University Press, 1987), p. 87.

Chapter 2: Evan: 'In the sweet shire of Cardigan'

1.   'In the sweet shire of Cardigan' is the first line of Wordsworth's poem 'Simon Lee, the Old Huntsman', published in 1798 in his and Coleridge's *Lyrical Ballads*. Mike Benbough Jackson says that Wordsworth was inspired by meeting an old huntsman in Somerset but chose to set it in Cardiganshire, which stood in those days for 'rusticity and poverty' (*Cardiganshire and the Cardi, c.1760–c.2000* (Cardiff: University of Wales Press, 2011), p. 37).

2.   Smith, ed., *Letters* I, p. 269 n. 7. The first italics are mine.

3.   CCEd, Clergy of the Church of England database, 1540–1835.

4.   Thomas Jackson Calvert, Norrisian Professor of Divinity 1815–24 (source: Faculty of Divinity, University of Cambridge, online).

5.   Monica Kendall, ed., *Miss Cavell Was Shot: The Diaries of Amy Hodson, 1914–1920* (Bristol: SilverWood, 2015).

6.   Ceredigion was the medieval name for this part of South/mid-Wales. It was anglicized as Cardiganshire or the County of Cardigan from around the Tudor period until the 1970s. I will refer to Evan's place of birth as Cardiganshire even when I make research trips into Ceredigion.

7.   Sir Samuel Rush Meyrick (1783–1848), the English antiquarian and historian of armour (and adviser to Sir Walter Scott), stated in his first book that the 'epithet Odwynne, "very white," seems to have been judiciously applied, as it may be seen for some miles off on every side, conspicuously exhibiting a contrast to the green turf beneath it': *The History and Antiquities of the County of Cardigan* (London: Longman, 1810), p. 275. His wife, Mary Parry, came from Cardiganshire and he studied Welsh. One of the subscribers was Rev. John Williams, headmaster of Ystrad Meurig school, p. viii.

8.   British Museum Cotton MS Vespasian A xiv.

9.   *The Mabinogion*, trans. Sioned Davies (Oxford: Oxford University Press, 2008), pp. 108 and 251 note.

10.   The Ceredigion Museum in Aberystwyth is housed in the beautiful Coliseum variety theatre, opened in 1905. It became an independent cinema from 1932 until 1976.

11.   Catherine Hutton, *Reminiscences of a Gentlewoman of the Last Century*, ed. Catherine Hutton Beale (Birmingham: Cornish Brothers, 1891), p. 46 (Birmingham City Archives, MS 3597).

12.   *Nicholson's Cambrian Traveller's Guide* (1840), p. vi.

13.   In his book about Tregaron, Rev. Rees says about the non-Roman fort

(earthwork) marked on the OS map behind Llwynpiod chapel that it was called Castell Odwyn, but gives no other information: Rev. D.C. Rees, *Tregaron: Historical and Antiquarian* (Llandyssul: J.D. Lewis & Sons, Gomerian Press, 1936), p. 72.

14. Quoted in Preface, by A.W. Lawrence, to T.E. Lawrence, *Seven Pillars of Wisdom* (Harmondsworth: Penguin Books, 1962), pp. 19–20. I have enjoyed T.E. Lawrence's remarks to his proofreader since I came across them in the early 1970s, partly because I was striving to be an exacting editor/proofreader and would have loved (and been exasperated by) an author like him.

15. George Eyre Evans, *Cardiganshire: A Personal Survey of Some of its Antiquities, Chapels, Churches, Fonts, Plate, and Registers* (Aberystwyth: Printed at the 'Welsh Gazette' Offices, 1903), pp. 3–4. Hutton, *Reminiscences*, pp. 50–4.

16. Email from Marcia Watson, 9 June 2014.

17. 'By the outbreak of the Great War some 70 per cent of farms in the Principality were of less than 50 acres in size, with only 2 per cent exceeding 300 acres, a pattern which had not changed significantly since the early 1870s' (Richard Moore-Colyer, *Welsh Cattle Drovers: Agriculture and the Welsh Cattle Trade before and during the Nineteenth Century* (Ashbourne: Landmark, 2002), p. 13).

18. John Davies, *A History of Wales*, rev. edn (London: Penguin Books, 2007), p. 324; Jenny Uglow, *In These Times: Living in Britain Through Napoleon's Wars, 1793–1815* (London: Faber & Faber, 2015), p. 459.

19. Taken from Richard Holmes's wonderful description of Samuel Taylor Coleridge as a student: 'Self-dramatising and self-mocking by turns, he was like some brilliant overgrown child, performing ceaseless exhausting parlour games for his elders, and never settling down' (Holmes, *Coleridge: Early Visions* (London: Harper Perennial, 2005), p. 39).

20. Holmes, *Early Visions*, p. 60.

21. Holmes, *Early Visions*, p. 67.

22. J. Hucks, *A Pedestrian Tour through North Wales, in a Series of Letters* [1795], ed. Alun R. Jones and William Tydeman (Cardiff: University of Wales Press, 1979), 2 August 1794, p. 55. Hucks had recently graduated and was trying for a Fellowship; he died of TB in 1800 aged twenty-eight. See the Introduction by Jones and Tydeman. They add: 'By Hucks's reckoning, he had travelled 629 miles from Cambridge to Bristol in just over two months' (p. lxvi). He and Coleridge parted at Llandovery, twenty-five miles south-east of Tregaron, on the border of the Brecon Beacons.

23. Richard Vaughan Yates, 'A tour in Wales' (1805), NLW MS 687B, quoted in Benbough-Jackson, *Cardiganshire and the Cardi*, p. 72.

24. Rev. R.H. Newell, *Letters on the Scenery of Wales* (London: printed for Baldwin, Cradock & Joy, 1821), p. 70. Three-dimensional advice as to where exactly to place your 'easel', now a digital camera, have been erected in the Scottish Cairngorms and South Africa almost two hundred years later so that tourists can take the most 'scenic' shot.

25. Moore-Colyer, *Welsh Cattle Drovers*, e.g. pp. 83, 109.

26. I discovered later that the Cardiganshire Family History Society were doing splendid work on recording legible tombstone names throughout Ceredigion. Beryl Evans, the chairman, said that no booklet was yet available for Llanbadarn Odwyn, but she was able to search the notes that had been made. There were five Jenkins gravestones, only one (John, d. 1832) earlier than the mid-nineteenth century. She dampened any other hopes I had for finding farmer Evan by saying that no burial registers survived for Llanbadarn Odwyn before 1813, nor Bishops' transcripts. But John Jenkins will appear again below.

27. Paul Ferris, *Dylan Thomas: The Biography*, new edn (London: J.M. Dent, 1999), p. 185. Apparently there is a Dylan Thomas Trail in Ceredigion that includes Talsarn, opened by his daughter.

28. My account of Daniel Rowland is based on the article in *ODNB* by Eryn M. White (2004) and Davies, *History of Wales*, pp. 299–305.

29. Davies, *History of Wales*, pp. 299–300.

30. Barker, *The Brontës*, p. 290.

31. Charlotte Brontë, *Shirley* (Ware: Wordsworth Classics, 2009), pp. 98, 101.

32. Barker, *The Brontës*, p. 291.

33. Barker, *The Brontës*, p. 42; Smith, ed., *Letters* I, p. 269 n. 7.

34. Borthwick Institute for Archives, University of York: David Jenkins's ordination papers, Ord.D.1810 and Ord.P.1811.

35. Catherine Hutton, Birmingham City Archives, MS 3597, as on display in Ceredigion Museum, Aberystwyth. Hutton, *Reminiscences*, p. 52 has slightly different wording.

36. Anon., 'A journal, with sketches, of a walking tour from Kington to Aberystwyth and through parts of North Wales, 1828', LIGC/NLW MS 6716D, p. 21, also on display in the Ceredigion Museum, Aberystwyth.

37. George Borrow, *Wild Wales: The People, Language and Scenery* [1862] (London: Century, 1984), pp. 150–1.

38. Thomas De Quincey, *Confessions of an English Opium-Eater*, ed. David Ellis (Ware: Wordsworth, 2009), pp. 58–9. This is the expanded version De Quincey made in 1856.

39. De Quincey, *Confessions*, pp. 99, 105.

40. De Quincey, *Confessions*, p. 106.
41. Davies, *History of Wales*, p. 304.
42. Davies, *History of Wales*, p. 258.
43. Brontë, *Shirley*, p. 5.
44. Anthony Trollope, *Doctor Thorne* (Oxford: Oxford University Press, 2014), p. 25.
45. Methodism and Nonconformism in Wales: 'In 1770, there were only a few districts in Wales in which the majority of worshippers had abandoned the parish church; by 1851, Anglicans were a minority almost everywhere and eight out of ten of the Welsh who attended religious services were opting for the Nonconformist chapel.' Davies, *History of Wales*, p. 310.
46. Elizabeth Gaskell, *Half a Life Time Ago* (London: Dent, 1970), p. 277.
47. For estates in Wales and the Powells of Nanteos I rely on Davies, *History of Wales*, Moore-Colyer, *Welsh Cattle Drovers*, ch. 1, and especially Gerald Morgan, ed., *Nanteos: A Welsh House and Its Families* (Llandysul: Gomer Press, 2001).
48. Davies, *History of Wales*, pp. 222–3.
49. See Morgan, ed., *Nanteos*, chs 1 and 4.
50. Morgan (ed., *Nanteos*) mentions a covenant of 1718, now in the NLW, that lists land belonging to the Nanteos estate, including in Llanbadarn Odwyn, p. 23. In the register of the Land Tax of 1798 'granting an Aid to His Majesty' (held at TNA, Kew), the Powells of Nanteos own only two farms in the parish of Llanbadarn Odwyn, including Penycastell occupied by Evan Jenkins. In contrast, the Earl of Lisburne owns seven; Thomas Johnes of Hafod owns nine, but unusually no single landlord dominates: a further thirteen proprietors own one or two farms or smallholdings each, including Evan's elder brother John. John's land at Glanygors is valued as almost twice that of Penycastell, suggesting that he may have farmed about one hundred acres.
51. Morgan, ed., *Nanteos*, p. 35.
52. Quoted by Caroline Palmer in Morgan, ed., *Nanteos*, p. 53.
53. See Morgan, ed., *Nanteos*, ch. 2.

Chapter 3: Ystrad Meurig: 'Far from the Concourse of Men'

1. Evans, *Cardiganshire*, p. 145.
2. Ystradmeiric is an old-fashioned spelling, rendered today as either Ystradmeurig or Ystrad Meurig for the village and for the former school. I have adopted the two words used for the restored building. However, 'Meiric' is a better guide to its

pronunciation for those with little or no Welsh.

3. David Robinson, ed., *The Cistercian Abbeys of Britain: Far from the Concourse of Men* (London: Batsford with English Heritage, Historic Scotland and Cadw, 1998), p. 176, and p. 11 for the quote. I worked as a publisher with David on his book. We both wanted his subtitle to be the main title, but were overruled. My fond memories of working with David, and his appreciation of my enthusiasm for the book, led me to appropriate the quote as a chapter subtitle.

4. For Richard Amerike see Wikipedia and its references.

5. John Leland quoted in Evans, *Cardiganshire*, p. 33.

6. Richard J. Colyer, *The Teifi: Scenery and Antiquities of a Welsh River* (Llandysul: Gomer Press, 1987), p. 16.

7. Rees, *Tregaron*, p. 76.

8. The story about the impossibly educated Welsh 'labourers' is in the antiquities periodical *Bye-gones* (May 1883), p. 245, digitalized on the NLW website. It was submitted by someone using the name of a sixth-century prince and poet, Llywarch Hen. The writer gives Edward Richard's surname as Richards. I have added paragraphs. D.G. Osborne-Jones, *Edward Richard of Ystradmeurig with the Story of His School and its Associations under its Successive Masters 1734–1934* (Carmarthen: W. Spurrell & Son, 1934), ch. IV, gives another version of the story.

9. I rely for my account of Edward Richard on Osborne-Jones, *Edward Richard*. I am grateful to Paul Westney for giving me a scan of the book on disk as it is not available at the NLW and the only copy at the Ceredigion Archives library in Aberystwyth was missing.

10. Osborne-Jones, *Edward Richard*, p. 10.

11. *Alumni Oxonienses* spells his name as Abraham Richards – another example, with Jenkin and Jenkins, of the fluid nature of Welsh surnames.

12. Quoted in Osborne-Jones, *Edward Richard*, p. 23.

13. For the library I rely on William H. Howells, 'The Library of Edward Richard, Ystradmeurig', *Ceredigion: Journal of the Cardiganshire Antiquarian Society*, 9:3 (1982), pp. 227–44. It was very kindly sent to me by Sarah Roberts of the University of Wales Trinity Saint David, Lampeter. Over three hundred books from the school library are housed in the Ystrad Meurig Collection, Roderic Bowen Library and Archives.

14. I can only presume that David Jenkins attended the same school as his younger brother Evan.

15. Extracts from Edward Richard's will transcribed from a copy at Canolfan Edward Richard Centre, Ystrad Meurig, 2014.

16. Osborne-Jones, *Edward Richard*, p. 30.

17. 'John "Latin" Jones on John Williams', transcribed from a manuscript written by John Jones, Vicar and Headmaster, Ystrad Meurig School, January 1886, given to me by Paul Westney.

18. Osborne-Jones, *Edward Richard*, ch. V, n.p.

19. Again, my main source for Rev. John Williams is Osborne-Jones, *Edward Richard*, but see also *ODNB*.

20. Rev. John Williams's renowned medical nephew was Charles James Blasius Williams, MD (1805–89).

21. The meaning of 'curacy' and 'curate' changed. At the beginning of the nineteenth century it usually meant a clergyman in sole charge of a parish on behalf of a non-resident incumbent. Or it might mean a perpetual curate, a vicar. But gradually it came to mean the assistant to a resident clergyman, such as Arthur Nicholls in relation to Patrick Brontë. This was partly the result of the Pluralities Acts of 1838 and 1850, which reduced the number of non-resident incumbents; and partly because of a shortage of incumbencies from the 1820s. See Frances Knight, *The Nineteenth-Century Church and English Society* (Cambridge: Cambridge University Press. 1998), esp. p. 116.

22. Osborne-Jones, *Edward Richard*, ch. V, note.

23. Osborne-Jones, *Edward Richard*, ch. VII, n.p.

24. My main source is Magnus Magnusson, 'Williams, John (1792–1858)', *ODNB* (2004).

25. Sir Walter Scott, *Journal*, 28 August 1827, cited in *ODNB*.

26. Sir Walter Scott, *The Betrothed* (Edinburgh: Adam and Charles Black, 1886), p. 475 for the 'gibberish'. Scott's novel is a strange story to be inspired by a Welshman presumably proud of his Welsh roots. There is only one Welsh character – in disguise for many chapters – who might be seen as slightly redeeming the Welsh portrayed in this novel, but even so, the Normans produce the true gentlemen, and main villain, though the Flemish come off pretty well, with bourgeois honour intact. The 1886 edition has bizarre engravings of Welsh scenes, such as of Cadair Idris and Devil's Bridge near Aberystwyth, which have nothing whatsoever to do with the story, which takes place on the borders and in Gloucester.

27. Archibald Tait lost five of his young daughters within weeks in 1856 to scarlet fever. Perhaps responding to the compassion felt by many, Lord Palmerston offered Tait 'the most important bishopric in England' within months of the tragedy, even though he had not held a bishopric before. See Peter T. Marsh, 'Tait, Archibald Campbell (1811–1882)', *ODNB* (2008).

28. R.M.J. Jones, rev. Robert V. Smith, 'Hughes, John (1787–1860)', *ODNB* (2004).

29. Osborne-Jones, *Edward Richard*, p. 28.

30. Rees, *Tregaron*, p. 108.

31. Borrow, *Wild Wales*, pp. 26–7. Borrow encounters an over six-foot-tall and powerfully built waggoner as he nears the border with Wales and discovers he is English. "'I suppose,' said I, 'there are few Welshmen such big fellows as yourself.' 'No, Measter,' said the fellow, with a grin, 'there are few Welshmen so big as I, or yourself either, they are small men mostly, Measter, them Welshers, very small men – and yet the fellows can use their hands [in fighting].'" Stephen Gill wonders similarly to me about the size and number of pupils of a school in the 1780s, Hawkshead grammar school, and how it had managed with one hundred pupils in a 'small two-storey building'. Stephen Gill, *William Wordsworth: A Life*, 2nd edn (Oxford: Oxford University Press, 2020), p. 10.

32. Gill, *Wordsworth*, p. 10.

33. Osborne-Jones, *Edward Richard*, ch. VII.

34. George Eliot, *The Mill on the Floss* (Oxford: Oxford University Press, 2015), pp. 9, 14.

35. Eliot, *Mill on the Floss*, pp. 15, 19, 21, 22, 67.

36. Davies, *History of Wales*, pp. 288–9, and the SPCK website.

37. My main sources for the Welsh circulating schools are Geraint H. Jenkins, 'Jones, Griffith [*known as* Griffith Jones Llanddowror] (*bap.* 1684, *d.* 1761)', *ODNB* (2004), and Davies, *History of Wales*, pp. 297–9. See also Eryn M. White, 'Bevan [*née* Vaughan], Bridget [*known as* Madam Bevan] (*bap.* 1698, *d.* 1779)', *ODNB* (2004).

38. Quoted in Davies, *History of Wales*, p. 298.

39. Madam Bevan's death doesn't seem to have finished off the circulating schools. Rev. Rees (in 1936) quotes the vestry book of Tregaron church for 4 November 1811: the 'Welsh Circulating Charity School shall be kept in that part of the Church, between the pulpit and the door for a few weeks, and upon trial finding that sufficient number of children do attend, we agree to hire a house in the town for that purpose. M. Evans, Vicar.' Rees, *Tregaron*, p. 108.

40. Davies, *History of Wales*, p. 290.

41. Hucks, *Pedestrian Tour*, pp. 12–13.

42. Hucks, *Pedestrian Tour*, pp. 14, 13.

43. See Davies, *History of Wales*, pp. 223, 287–8.

44. Hucks, *Pedestrian Tour*, p. 8.

45. Osborne-Jones, *Edward Richard*, ch. V, ch. IV, n.p.

46. 'west, towards the setting sun': this phrase is in the first sentence of the first chapter of Richard Holmes's marvellous biography: *Shelley: The Pursuit* (London: Harper

Perennial, 2005), p. 1. He is my source for Shelley in the following paragraphs.

47. Jane Austen, *Mansfield Park*, ed. Kathryn Sutherland (London: Penguin Books, 2014), p. 86.

48. Quoted in Holmes, *Shelley*, p. 47.

49. Austen, *Mansfield Park*, p. 105.

50. Austen, *Mansfield Park*, p. 184.

Chapter 4: David: Chelsea and Yorkshire, 1807–1813

1. Letter from Patrick Brontë to Thomas Porteus, secretary to the Archbishop of York, Dewsbury, Yorkshire, 6 June 1810, in *The Letters of the Reverend Patrick Brontë*, ed. Dudley Green (Stroud: Nonsuch, 2005), p. 25.

2. William Wordsworth, *Selected Poems*, ed. Stephen Gill (London: Penguin Books, 2004), pp. 150–1; it was composed five years earlier in 1802, but first published in *Poems, in Two Volumes* in 1807.

3. Knight, *Nineteenth-Century Church*, p. 109.

4. Francis Watt, rev. Jonathan Harris, 'Edwards, Thomas (1776/7–1845)', *ODNB* (2004), which calls him a 'legal writer'. He also became a magistrate for the county of Surrey.

5. *London County Council Survey of London*, gen. eds Sir Laurence Gomme and Philip Norman, vol. IV: *The Parish of Chelsea (Part II)* (London: London County Council, Spring Gardens, 1913), pp. 71–2.

6. The old wooden Battersea Bridge was opened in 1771 – an initiative by Earl Spencer, Lord of the Manor of Battersea; oil lamps were placed on one side of the bridge in 1799 and it cost a halfpenny for foot passengers to cross: Thomas Faulkner, *An Historical and Topographical Description of Chelsea and its Environs* (London: Printed by J. Tilling, Chelsea, 1810), pp. 411–13. It was replaced by the modern bridge in 1886–90. James Abbott McNeill Whistler, resident of Chelsea, featured the old bridge in one of his 'Nocturnes': *Nocturne in Blue and Gold: Old Battersea Bridge*, c.1872–5, one of the paintings that were derided by John Ruskin and led to the famous trial which broke Whistler.

7. Faulkner, *Chelsea* (1810), pp. 159–60.

8. *A History of the County of Middlesex*, vol. XII: *Chelsea*, ed. Patricia E.C. Croot, The Victoria History of the Counties of England (Published for the Institute of Historical Research by Boydell & Brewer, 2004), pp. 190–5.

9. Thea Holme, *Chelsea* (London: Hamish Hamilton, 1972), pp. 67–9; Jonathan

Swift, *Journal to Stella*, ed. Abigail Williams (Cambridge: Cambridge University Press, 2013), pp. 208, 217. Apparently 'bloody' in 1711 was not as scandalous an adjective as it was later to become in the play by another Irishman (Shaw's *Pygmalion*).

10. VCH, *Chelsea*, p. 191.

11. Thompson Cooper, rev. Philip Carter, 'Butler, Weeden (1742–1823)', *ODNB* (2004).

12. G.C. Boase, rev. M.C. Curthoys, 'Butler, George (1774–1853)', *ODNB* (2016). Anthony Trollope, *An Autobiography and Other Writings*, ed. Nicholas Shrimpton (Oxford: Oxford University Press, 2016), p. 11: 'he was in the habit of flogging me constantly'.

13. VCH, *Chelsea*, p. 193.

14. H.M. Chichester, rev. Joanne Potier, 'Faulkner, Thomas (1777–1855)', *ODNB* (2007). The article compilers misspell Weeden as Weedon and give him a birthdate different from that in his own *ODNB* article.

15. Faulkner, *Chelsea* (1810), n.p.

16. Nigel Aston, 'North, Brownlow (1741–1820)', *ODNB* (2008).

17. Faulkner, *Chelsea*, vol. 1 (1829), ch. IV, 'Walk the Third', p. 259.

18. Largely using VCH, *Chelsea*, and Holme, *Chelsea*.

19. Ben Weinreb and Christopher Hibbert, eds, *The London Encyclopaedia*, rev. edn (London: Macmillan, 1995), p. 107.

20. Faulkner, *Chelsea* (1810), p. 29.

21. Elizabeth Longford, *Wellington: Pillar of State* (London: Weidenfeld & Nicolson, 1972), p. 127. No source is given.

22. ACAD: Wesley, The Hon. Gerald Valerian.

23. Faulkner, *Chelsea* (1810), p. 42.

24. Seymour Baker House, 'More, Sir Thomas [St Thomas More] (1478–1535)', *ODNB* (2008).

25. Alan Russett and Tom Pocock, *A History of Chelsea Old Church: The Church that Refused to Die* (London: Chelsea Old Church, 2004), p. 88.

26. Faulkner, *Chelsea* (1810), p. 280.

27. Faulkner, *Chelsea* (1810), p. 316.

28. Holme, *Chelsea*, pp. 4, 6, 17–19, 122–3.

29. Bridget Cherry and Nikolaus Pevsner, *London 3: North West*, The Buildings of England (New Haven: Yale University Press, 2002), p. 557.

30. Faulkner, *Chelsea*, vol. 1 (1829), p. 266; VCH, *Chelsea*, 'Lawrence Estate', online; Holme, *Chelsea*, p. 73.

31. Faulkner, *Chelsea* (1810), pp. 400–1.

32. Faulkner, *Chelsea* (1810), p. 263.

33. Faulkner, *Chelsea* (1810), pp. 332–3.

34. *Survey of London: Chelsea*, p. 71.

35. Holme, *Chelsea*, p. 150. The silent room can still be visited.

36. Russett and Pocock, *Chelsea Old Church*, p. 117.

37. Faulkner, *Chelsea* (1810), pp. 446–8.

38. Davies, *History of Wales*, p. 295.

39. See CCEd: Henry Thomas Austen. He was ordained deacon 22 December 1816 to Chawton and after only about two months ordained priest, on 2 March 1817. The living itself was in the gift of Thomas Knight, an uncle, who adopted Henry and Jane's brother Edward: Irene Collins, *Jane Austen and the Clergy* (London: The Hambledon Press, 1993), pp. 3, 18. She explores the numerous clerical connections of the Austen family which made it far easier for the Austen sons and relations to get ordained than the Jenkins brothers (see esp. pp. 25–6); she doesn't comment on how Henry could have been priested so quickly but says his stipend as curate was £50 (p. 63).

40. Jane Austen, *Pride and Prejudice*, ed. James Kinsley (Oxford: Oxford University Press, 2008), p. 52.

41. Austen, *Pride and Prejudice*, pp. 47, 48.

42. Austen, *Pride and Prejudice*, p. 63.

43. Austen, *Pride and Prejudice*, p. 139.

44. Austen, *Pride and Prejudice*, p. 293.

45. I rely primarily on Barker, *The Brontës*, for the facts of Patrick Brontë's career here, though I differ in my interpretation. Dudley Green, *Patrick Brontë: Father of Genius* (Stroud: Nonsuch, 2008) largely copies Barker's account of John Buckworth and Dewsbury, almost word for word.

46. CCEd.

47. Barker, *The Brontës*, p. 19.

48. Barker, *The Brontës*, p. 33.

49. Barker later suggests Buckworth may have indeed promised the living of Hartshead to Patrick Brontë to induce him to accept the curacy of Dewsbury: *The Brontës*, p. 41.

50. Barker, *The Brontës*, p. 41.

51. *Letters of the Reverend Patrick Brontë*, ed. Green, p. 25. Green doesn't mention David Jenkins with reference to this letter, but merely adds who Thomas Porteus was. There is no reference to David in his book; no letters have been found between David and Patrick.

52. Patrick Brontë mentions London as that is presumably where the Archbishop of York was at the time.

53. Neil Adams, Archives Assistant at the Borthwick Institute for Archives, University of York, confirmed to me in an email (26 February 2018) that 'according to the Institution Act Book, the previous General Ordination Ceremony that took place in 1810 was on Sunday the 25th March 1810 so the July ceremony was the earliest summer date on which ordinations took place in that year'.

54. Anon., *Memoir of the Rev. John Buckworth, M.A., Late Vicar of Dewsbury, Yorkshire* (London: Messrs. Hatchard [etc.], 1836), pp. 42, 55, 33.

55. According to David's priest ordination bundle, David arrived at Dewsbury on the same day as his deacon ordination on 15 July 1810: the archbishop's main residence at Bishopthorpe Palace, south of York, is only about thirty miles away.

56. Brontë, *Shirley*, pp. 22–3.

57. In Anglo-Saxon times All Saints, Dewsbury was responsible for a very large parish (most of modern West Yorkshire). This was recognized in recent times and the parish church was re-established as a minster. It is now acknowledged as 'mother church of West Yorkshire'; Richard A. Middleton, *The Church at Dewsbury: A History of the Ancient Parish of Dewsbury and A Mother Church of West Yorkshire*, 3rd edn (Printed by Swiftprint, Huddersfield, available from Dewsbury Minster, 2006).

58. Middleton, *The Church at Dewsbury*, pp. 75–7.

59. Barker, *The Brontës*, p. 37.

60. Middleton, *The Church at Dewsbury*. Another booklet I bought at the minster (Dewsbury Brontë 200 Committee, *Patrick Brontë: His Life and Work in Dewsbury 1809–1811*) states baldly, and wrongly, 'He performed 420 baptisms [...] Whilst at All Saints', Patrick was often left for periods in full charge of the church', p. 13. Accuracy would be appreciated.

61. Buckworth, *Memoir*, pp. 175, 177; his university and date he was licensed as curate from CCEd.

62. Barker, *The Brontës*, p. 37.

63. Buckworth, *Memoir*, p. 188.

64. Buckworth, *Memoir*, pp. 117, 130, 133, 138, 135, 139, 141, 142, 193.

65. See D.W. Bebbington, *Evangelicalism in Modern Britain: A History from the 1730s to the 1980s* (London: Routledge, 1989), esp. ch. 1.

66. Buckworth, *Memoir*, pp. 68, 120–1.

67. Mrs [Frances] Trollope, *The Vicar of Wrexhill*, 3 vols (London: Richard Bentley, 1837), vol. 2, p. 62.

68. Trollope, *Vicar of Wrexhill*, vol. 2, p. 40.

69. Trollope, *Vicar of Wrexhill*, vol. 1, pp. 235–9.

70. The parish was officially Hartshead cum Clifton: the two chapels had been combined in the eighteenth century. The then larger village of Clifton is a mile west of Hartshead.

71. Barker, *The Brontës*, p. 42.

72. David's next marriage in Dewsbury is on 10 September and then not until 26 December (with three marriages on one day).

73. Barker, *The Brontës*, p. 41.

74. CCEd gives the date of 25 July 1811 for David's ordination as priest, but the date on his priest ordination papers is 21 July. And since David performed four(!) marriages in Dewsbury on 25 July, then the CCEd date must be an error.

75. The testimonial for David is dated 13 June 1811, the letter from Buckworth appointing David as curate of Dewsbury is 14 June and his Si Quis on Sunday 16 June.

76. CCEd: John Hall. Hall also helped out in Dewsbury: he performed thirteen marriages at the church there in August, September and October 1812, when, presumably, David Jenkins was on holiday, perhaps on a visit to his mother and siblings in Wales.

77. Starting with Mrs Gaskell in *Life*, p. 161.

78. E.g. see Ruth Strong, *The Story of Pudsey Church* (Pudsey St Lawrence and St Paul Parochial Church Council, 1988).

79. In the Pudsey registers David Jenkins sometimes, later, signs himself as just Curate, which can be confusing, but it was simply an abbreviated form he used for Perpetual Curate.

Chapter 5: Eliza: The Ancestors

1. Wyndham: Jane B. Livingston to Margaret Wyndham, 6 Dowry Parade, Hotwells, Clifton, 29 February 1836. The collection of letters to the Wyndham family in Australia is held at the University of New England (UNE), NSW, Australia.

2. Wyndham: John Livingston Jay to Margaret Wyndham, Greenwich Hospital, 8 October 1840.

3. Wyndham: Eliza Jenkins to Margaret Wyndham, Brussels, 30 March 1854. It is my interpretation that sister Janet lay on a sofa all day. Eliza merely comments: 'From what Jen writes of herself, I fear she will lose the use of her legs poor Girl, & yet no

one can induce her to try a change of place before it is too late – That monotonous Life ruins her health & vexes all her friends, none of whose advances to receive them or to visit herself she will meet – Her back is where she suffers, and I cannot make out what it can be tho when I see her perhaps I shall know more about it.'

4. Wyndham: Jane B. Livingston to Margaret Wyndham, 6 Dowry Parade, Hotwells, Clifton, 29 February 1836.

5. Wyndham: Alward Wyndham to Margaret Wyndham, Brussels, 31 May 1853.

6. '"Co" [John] has Photographed a Wedding Party of Belgian Neighbors each of the guests to have a copy – It is so well done.' Wyndham: Eliza Jenkins to Janet Jay, Ostend, 3 August [1855].

7. Quoted by Marcia Watson in *Dalwood House Newsletter*, no. 100 (March 2018), p. 6, from *The Leichhardt Diaries: Early Travels in Australia during 1842–1844*, ed. Thomas A. Darragh and Roderick J. Fensham (South Brisbane: Queensland Museum, 2013), Diary One, Part 2, p. 86.

8. Marcia Watson, 'In Search of Margaret's Family: Grandmother Elizabeth Hardie', *Dalwood House Newsletter*, no. 102 (September 2018), p. 2.

9. *Dalwood House Newsletter*, no. 68 (March 2009), pp. 7–10; Edwin Brockholst Livingston, *The Livingstons of Callendar and their Principal Cadets: The History of an Old Stirlingshire Family*, new edn (Edinburgh: T & A Constable, at the University Press, 1920).

10. Marcia Watson, 'In Search of Margaret's Family: Helen Jay née Livingston', *Dalwood House Newsletter*, no. 107 (December 2019), pp. 15–17, at p. 17.

11. Collins, *Jane Austen and the Clergy*, p. 167.

12. Austen, *Pride and Prejudice*, pp. 81–2. Mr Collins continues: 'you may assure yourself that no ungenerous reproach shall ever pass my lips when we are married'. It implies that some women were subjected to later reproaches if they brought little or no money into a marriage.

13. Alexandre Dumas, *The Three Musketeers* [no translator credited] (London: Francis Aldor, n.d.), chapters XLVI–XLVII.

14. See Marcia Watson, 'To Be or Not to Be', in *A New Tapestry: Huguenot Families in Australia*, ed. Robert Nash (Newtown: NSW Huguenot Society of Australia, 2015), pp. 166–70 for her research into the family's Huguenot ancestors.

15. Information from the invaluable latest edition and translation (unabridged) by another descendant, Dianne W. Ressinger: *Memoirs of the Reverend Jaques Fontaine 1658–1728*, Huguenot Society n.s. no. 2 (London: The Huguenot Society of Great Britain and Ireland, 1992). Family trees for Eliza's Fontaine ancestors, according to Jaques Fontaine, are in Ressinger's Appendix III: Pedigrees I and IV, but they are

possibly inaccurate, as mentioned in the text below.

16. From a Review of *Memoirs of a Huguenot Family*, ed. Ann Maury (New York, 1853) by Prosper Mérimée, published in *Revue des deux mondes* (Paris, 1 September 1853), quoted and trans. in *Memoirs of Jaques Fontaine*, ed. Ressinger, p. 225.

17. Charlotte Brontë, *Villette* (Oxford: Oxford University Press, 2000), p. 7.

18. *Memoirs of Jaques Fontaine*, p. 28. A similar account, according to Ressinger, also appears in Jean Crespin's *Histoire des Martyrs* (Geneva, 1619).

19. *Memoirs of Jaques Fontaine*, p. 26, and editor's note p. 197.

20. *Memoirs of Jaques Fontaine*, p. 32.

21. *Memoirs of Jaques Fontaine*, p. 30.

22. *Memoirs of Jaques Fontaine*, pp. 119, 30, 119–20.

23. *Memoirs of Jaques Fontaine*, pp. 120–2.

24. *Memoirs of Jaques Fontaine*, pp. 33, 36, 46–8.

25. Information about the Pest House and Pierre Fontaine's conformism from *Memoirs of Jaques Fontaine*, editor's note, pp. 202–3; information about Bunhill Fields from Weinreb and Hibbert, eds, *London Encyclopaedia*, s.v. Bunhill Fields.

26. Watson, 'To Be or Not to Be', p. 167.

27. I call him Peter rather than Pierre partly to differentiate the son from his 'beau' father, and partly because he spent most of his life outside France, mainly in England.

28. Peter des Réaux's biography here is a great example of research by Marcia Watson: she found Petrus des Reaux 'Rupellensis' (i.e. of La Rochelle) in the Saumur Academy records for the 1680s, online, then in 1689 he is described as 'op 't eyland Camvy in Engeland'. The *Acta der Particuliere Synoden van Zuid-Holland 1621–1700* lists him at the Colloquium in London, June 1690, having been sent by his community on Canvey Island: 'Van wegen Canvey-Eilant D. Petrus des Reaux' and explains that he hadn't been a minister for long.

29. Canvey Island and the Dutch: www.canveyisland.org/category/the_dutch_connection, from whom my information about this period on Canvey Island comes.

30. *Memoirs of Jaques Fontaine*, p. 48.

31. See Watson, 'To Be or Not to Be', p. 170, and Marcia Watson, 'In Search of Margaret's Family: Elisabeth des Réaux', *Dalwood House Newsletter*, no. 98 (September 2017).

32. Charlotte May Wright, *Memories of Far Off Days: The Memoirs of Charlotte May Wright 1855–1929*, ed. Peter A. Wright, 2nd edn (privately published, 1988), ch. 1.

33. Watson, 'To Be or Not to Be', p. 166.

34. Clare is on Rev. Samuel Jay's marriage certificate of 1734, in Rotterdam; no registration of his birth or baptism has been found.
35. Watson, 'To Be or Not to Be', p. 170.
36. *Munimenta Alme Universitatis Glasguensis: Records of the University of Glasgow*, vol. 3 (Glasgow, 1854).
37. Revd. William Steven, *The History of the Scottish Church, Rotterdam* (Edinburgh: Waugh & Innes, 1832), pp. 191, 153, 336, 77, 153–4. William Steven was the Presbyterian minister in Rotterdam from 1829.
38. Steven, *History of the Scottish Church*, p. 189.
39. See e.g. Simon Schama, *Patriots and Liberators: Revolution in the Netherlands 1780–1813*, 2nd edn (London: Fontana Press, 1992), pp. 38–9.
40. Steven, *History of the Scottish Church*, p. 287: 'Brussels – Church of England – Previous to the late revolution, it was computed that nearly four thousand British subjects constantly resided in this capital. Besides the ambassador's chapel, there were other two [sic] Episcopal Churches of recent institution, both of which still exist [in 1832], respectively under the ministry of the Rev. E. Jenkins, A. B.; and the Rev. William Drury, M. A.' We will meet William Drury in a later chapter.
41. Steven, *History of the Scottish Church*, p. 191. Perhaps the painting was destroyed during the bombing of Rotterdam in the Second World War.
42. Clarke Papers: Eliza Jenkins to William Branwhite Clarke, Brussels, 26 July 1831.
43. Watson, 'To Be or Not to Be', p. 171; see also Keith L. Sprunger, *Dutch Puritanism: A History of English and Scottish Churches of the Netherlands in the Sixteenth and Seventeenth Centuries* (Leiden: E.J. Brill, 1982), pp. 255–6.
44. Watson, 'To Be or Not to Be', p. 171. See also a revised account in Marcia Watson, 'In Search of Margaret's Family: Doctor Samuel Jay', *Dalwood House Newsletter*, no. 101 (June 2018), pp. 3–6.
45. In the 1760s Dr Jay bought books for the physician Dr David Skene, Dean of Faculty at Marischal College, Aberdeen, who researched (among other interests) medicine, botany and geology. Dr Jay wrote to Dr Skene in October 1769 that he hadn't been able to obtain *Classes plantarum* by Linnaeus, but it might come up at auction. Watson, 'To Be or Not to Be', pp. 171–2. The book was first published in 1738 at his old university town of Leiden. It is not clear whether Dr Jay was acting for profit as a middleman between booksellers in Holland and readers in Scotland, or was simply being helpful. He knew William Kennedy, Professor of Greek at Aberdeen, who was the brother of the Scottish/Rotterdam merchant Alexander Livingston's first wife (Alexander was, as mentioned above, Eliza's maternal grandfather). 'Kennedy used his Dutch contacts to acquire journals and scientific

texts for the college library, as well as books on medicine and natural history for David Skene' (Paul Dukes, *The Universities of Aberdeen and Europe: The First Three Centuries* (Aberdeen: Aberdeen University Press, 1995), p. 138).

46. William Cobbett, *Rural Rides*, ed. Ian Dyck (London: Penguin, 2001), p. 27.

47. Stanley Lane-Poole, rev. Elizabeth Baigent, 'Morier, James Justinian (1782–1849)', *ODNB* (2004).

48. W.M. Thackeray, *Pendennis*, ed. John Sutherland (Oxford: Oxford University Press, 1994), p. 396. Sutherland identifies 'Bedwin Sands' as James Morier: note on p. 1037.

49. W.M. Thackeray, *Vanity Fair*, Intro. and Notes by Carole Jones and Owen Knowle (Ware: Wordsworth, 2001), p. 483. Their note on Bedwin Sands (p. 687), however, says 'a fictitious character, with Thackeray here punning on the fashionable passion for all things from Africa and the East'.

50. Isaac Morier was apparently descended from a de la Fontaine, but this seems to be a different family from Eliza's Fontaine ancestors.

51. Balliol College Oxford Archives, Morier family papers, Class C, Box 1, 1788–92.

52. Henry McKenzie Johnston, *Ottoman and Persian Odysseys: James Morier, Creator of Hajji Baba of Ispahan, and His Brothers* (London: British Academic Press, 1998), p. 8.

53. Watson, 'To Be or Not to Be', p. 172.

54. Steven, *History of the Scottish Church*, p. 191.

55. Balliol: Dr Samuel Jay to Isaac Morier, 21 January 1788, asking him to pass on his love to his brother-in-law William and to 'Dear Sam' when he arrives back in Smyrna.

56. Watson, 'To Be or Not to Be', p. 172.

57. W.M. Thackeray, *Lovel the Widower, Etc.*; [*Notes of a Journey from Cornhill to Grand Cairo*] (London: Collins, [1912]), pp. 226–7. *Notes* was originally published in 1846.

58. Stanley Lane-Poole, rev. H.C.G. Matthew, 'Morier, John Philip (1778–1853)', *ODNB* (2006).

59. Balliol: Dr Samuel Jay to Isaac Morier, Andover, 21 January 1788. In my transcriptions I silently expand the contractions, lower superscripts and add punctuation, sometimes creating a new sentence to aid reading. All translations from French are my own. I have left the original English or French spelling, as far as I can decipher it.

60. Balliol: Mary Jay to Clara Morier, 25 January 1788.

61. Balliol: Jack Morier to his mother, ?22 August 1788; on the same paper, letter from

Dr Jay to her, both in French: 'je puis vous assurer que les lettres sont entierement de leur propre composition sans la moindre assistance de ma part'.

62. Balliol: Jack Morier to his mother, 17 September 1788.

63. Balliol: Jack Morier to his mother, 11 March 1788, with note added by Dr Jay, asking whether she has had a response from Mr Dutens regarding his son coming to them (in French). See also letter of 5 August 1788 and ?22 August 1788 for possible mention of a pupil from 'Perse' (Persia); 3 October 1788: pupil from Russia. This is a truly international household in the middle of the Hampshire countryside.

64. Balliol: Jack Morier to his father, 25 February 1788: 'Je vous prie de dire a Mr Sam Jay [in Smyrna] que nous sommes chez Mr son Pere comme il le desiran tant.'

65. Balliol: Jack Morier to his mother, 12 February 1788.

66. Balliol: Jack Morier to his mother, 16 April 1788.

67. Balliol: Jack Morier to his father, 3 October 1788, with note from Dr Jay.

68. Balliol: Jack Morier to his father, 25 February 1788 (in French).

69. William Waldegrave became first Baron Radstock in 1800 and an admiral in 1802.

70. Balliol: Jack Morier to his mother, ?July 1788. For books, see also, e.g., letters of November 1788 and 27 January 1789.

71. Balliol: Jack Morier to his father, 17 December 1788.

72. Balliol: Jack Morier to his mother, 27 January 1788.

73. Respectively, Balliol: Jack Morier to his mother, 30 February 1788 (magic lantern); 14 May 1788 (all translated).

74. Balliol: Jack Morier to his mother, 7 October 1788.

75. Respectively (all translated), Balliol: Jack to his mother, 29 April 1788; 11 June 1788; 23 June 1788 ('l'excellente Salade'); 22 July 1788 ('tant de bontes pour nous').

76. Balliol: Jack to his mother, 19 March 1788; 22 July 1788.

77. Jane Austen, *Emma*, ed. Mary Lascelles (London: Dent, 1964), pp. 16–17. Chilblains ('engelures') in Morier letters 15 October 1788 and 17 December 1788.

78. Balliol: Dr Jay to Mrs Morier, 13 June 1788 (translated).

79. Balliol: Dr Jay to Mrs Morier (on same paper as letter from Jack), 30 June 1788.

80. Balliol: Dr Jay to Mrs Morier (on same paper as letter from Jack), ?July 1788.

81. Balliol: Jack to his mother, 22 July 1788; 5 August 1788.

82. Balliol: Dr Jay to Mrs Morier, 28 December 1788.

83. Balliol: Jack to his father, with a letter from Dr Jay on the same paper, 4 June 1789.

84. Balliol: Jack to his mother, 12 August 1789.

85. Respectively, Balliol: Jack to his mother, and on the same paper Peter to his sister (Mrs Morier), 16 February 1790; Jack to his father, 9 March 1790 (translated).

86. Balliol: Jack Morier to his father, 3 October 1788.

87. Balliol: Jack to his father, 25 November 1791.

88. Watson, 'To Be or Not to Be', p. 172, where she says, mistakenly, that the plaque has 'disappeared'.

89. Death notice for Dr Samuel Jay: *Bath Chronicle and Weekly Gazette*, 12 December 1793, p. 2.

90. Hampshire Record Office: Malmesbury papers: 9M73/G410, Andrew Dalziel [Dalzel in DNB] (1746–1806), Greek professor at University of Edinburgh, 27 June 1777.

91. Andrew Dalzel, *History of the University of Edinburgh from its Foundation, with a Memoir of the Author*, vol. 1: *Memoir* (Edinburgh: Edmonston and Douglas, 1862), p. 14.

92. Roland Thorne, 'Maitland, James, Eighth Earl of Lauderdale (1759–1839)', *ODNB* (2008).

93. Michael Fry, 'Dalzel [*formerly* Dalziel], Andrew (1742–1806)', *ODNB* (2009).

94. Quoted in Rosemary Dunhill, 'Harris, James (1709–1780)', *ODNB* (2009).

95. H.M. Scott, 'Harris, James, First Earl of Malmesbury', *ODNB* (2009).

96. Janet Malcolm, *The Silent Woman: Sylvia Plath and Ted Hughes* (London: Picador, 1994), p. 110.

Chapter 6: Eliza: Moving On

1. Schama, *Patriots and Liberators*, p. 16.

2. John Jay became a member of the Scottish Church in Rotterdam in 1786 when he was sixteen (Watson, 'To Be or Not to Be', p. 172), but he may have gone to Rotterdam a few years earlier.

3. Watson, 'To Be or Not to Be', p. 172.

4. See Schama, *Patriots and Liberators*, ch. 3.

5. Schama, *Patriots and Liberators*, pp. 106, 2. See also H.M. Scott, 'Harris, James, First Earl of Malmesbury (1746–1820)', *ODNB* (2009).

6. Schama has a wonderful description of William V: 'Physically he was singularly unprepossessing, with pop eyes, fat lips, and a weak chin [...] subject to alternating fits of petulant obstinacy and chronic vacillation and he suffered from the unpleasant malady of spitting bile' (*Patriots and Liberators*, p. 56). Both he and his wife were cousins of George III. Schama provides a helpful list of the several name changes of what we know as the Netherlands: from The Republic of the United Provinces (up to 1795) to The Kingdom of the United Netherlands (which included the Austrian Netherlands,

until the Revolution of 1830 created the separate country of Belgium) (p. xix).

7.   Balliol: Jack Morier to his father, November 1788; Peter Van Lennep to his parents, 22 August 1788 (translated).

8.   Advertisement in *London Courier and Evening Gazette*, Tuesday 21 July 1812.

9.   Watson, 'To Be or Not to Be', p. 172.

10. Steven, *History of the Scottish Church*, p. 370.

11. Steven, *History of the Scottish Church*, pp. 203, 227–8. Also Watson, 'Grandmother Elizabeth Hardie', pp. 2–6.

12. Watson, 'Grandmother Elizabeth Hardie', pp. 3–6.

13. William Hague, *William Pitt the Younger* (London: HarperCollins, 2004), p. 365.

14. Schama, *Patriots and Liberators*, pp. 200, 191.

15. Schama, *Patriots and Liberators*, p. 390.

16. See Schama, *Patriots and Liberators*, ch. 7.

17. Steven, *History of the Scottish Church*, p. 277.

18. Schama, *Patriots and Liberators*, pp. 187, 371–2.

19. Marcia Watson, 'In Search of Margaret's Family: John Jay's School for Boys', *Dalwood House Newsletter,* no. 99 (December 2017), p. 8.

20. Watson, 'To Be or Not to Be', pp. 172–3.

21. David Hewitt, 'Scott, Sir Walter (1771–1832)', *ODNB* (2008).

22. John Sutherland, *The Life of Walter Scott* (Oxford: Blackwell, 1995), p. 69.

23. Hewitt, 'Scott', *ODNB*.

24. H.C.G. Matthew, 'Gladstone [Gladstones], Sir John, First Baronet (1764–1851)', *ODNB* (2016); John Russell, *The Story of Leith* (London: T. Nelson and Sons [1922]), pp. 176–7.

25. Russell, *Story of Leith*, p. 177.

26. I found on the internet ('Lothian Life' website) that there is a plaque to Hans Christian Andersen outside the surgery which stands on the site of the lodge of Lixmount House, since he stayed there in 1847. See also Rosemary Philip, 'Lixmount House and its People', *The Scottish Genealogist* (March 2017), p. 23.

27. National Library of Scotland, 'Old and New Town of Edinburgh and Leith with the proposed docks': Town Plans/Views, 1580–1919, map by John Ainslie, 1804: shelf mark Newman 1028. Details about Sir Henry Moncrieff-Wellwood from Wikipedia.

28. Prize goods auctioned: on 13 August 1804, the *Caledonian Mercury* advertised an auction of prize goods at Leith coffeehouse, cargo of the *Irene* from Archangol (the seaport Arkhangelsk in northern Russia), 'Prize to H.M.S. Amethyst, Alexander Campbell, Esq. commander. Apply to Ramsay, Williamson, & Co. Leith'. The goods included '500 seal skins, 40 white fox skins, 5 bags of martins tails' (p. 1).

29. Lixmount House built by George Andrew, writer: http://canmore.org.uk/event/1037067.

30. Sutherland, *Walter Scott*, p. 6.

31. Philip, 'Lixmount House and its People', pp. 17–29.

32. Philip, 'Lixmount House and its People', p. 18.

33. CB to W.S. Williams, 20 July 1850, *Letters* II, pp. 427–8.

34. Philip, 'Lixmount House and its People', pp. 18–19. The upset price for the house was reduced in the advertisement for its sale on 5 April 1800 in the *Caledonian Mercury*. The type on the advertisement is now faint and hard to read (especially onscreen) but looks like £3,300. However, Philip sees the figure as £2,700 (p. 19).

35. *Caledonian Mercury*, 19 January 1801, p. 1.

36. *Caledonian Mercury*, 26 September 1811, p. 1; Philip, 'Lixmount House and its People', p. 20.

37. Philip, 'Lixmount House and its People', p. 17, quoted from *The Scotsman*, 25 March 1848.

38. *Caledonian Mercury*, 19 and 22 December 1808.

39. Russell, *Story of Leith*, p. 446.

40. *Caledonian Mercury*, 17 November and 19 December 1808.

41. Russell, *Story of Leith*, p. 432.

42. Russell, *Story of Leith*, pp. 372, 400.

43. Watson, 'To Be or Not to Be', p. 173. The account of shipmaster Kelting below is my summary from the judgment of the Court of Session, Edinburgh, 1821–3, CS233-K-3-5/11.

44. *Caledonian Mercury*, 11 and 13 November 1809, p. 3.

45. Brontë, *Shirley*, p. 127.

46. Uglow, *In These Times*, p. 519.

47. Anna Laetitia Barbauld, *Collected Works*, vol. I: *The Poems, Revised*, ed. William McCarthy (Oxford: Oxford University Press, 2019), end note for ll. 47–59 of Poem 131.

48. Philip, 'Lixmount House and its People', pp. 19–22.

49. 'Births, Marriages, &c. Within the Year 1825', *The Edinburgh Annual Register*, vol. 18 (Edinburgh: [Sir Walter Scott], John Ballantyne and Company, 1827), p. 314.

50. John Keats, *Letters*, ed. Robert Gittings (Oxford: Oxford University Press, 1970), p. 322.

51. Altick, *Lives and Letters*, p. 411.

52. Nicholas Roe, *John Keats: A New Life* (New Haven and London: Yale University Press, 2013), p. 33.

53. Roe, *John Keats*, p. 39.

54. Roe, *John Keats*, p. 45.

55. Quoted in Roe, *John Keats*, p. 46.

56. Death of Margaret Bowden on 24 November in *Public Ledger and Daily Advertiser*, 27 November 1811: 'daughter of the late Alexander Livingston, Esq. of Rotterdam, formerly Provost of the City of Aberdeen'.

57. From Keats's Preface to *Endymion*, 1818. Roe, in his biography, picks out the phrase 'space of life between' when writing about Keats's apprenticeship years in Edmonton (*John Keats*, p. 45).

58. See Roe, *John Keats*, p. 47.

59. Richard Monckton Milnes, ed., *Life, Letters and Literary Remains of John Keats*, 2 vols (London: Edward Moxon, 1848), vol. 1, p. 9.

60. Court of Session, Edinburgh: CS233-K-3-5 item 12, quoted in Philip, 'Lixmount House and its People', pp. 19–20.

61. VCH, *A History of the County of Essex*, vol. 6, pp. 338–44, British History Online.

62. J. Elsden Tuffs, *The Story of Wanstead and Woodford: From Roman Times to the Present* (Published by the Author, 1962), p. 66.

63. *The Times*, 29 August 1818, quoted in Watson, 'John Jay's School for Boys', p. 11. See also pp. 15–16 for her account of Prospect House.

64. *London Courier and Evening Gazette*, 7 July 1813, p. 1.

65. *London Courier and Evening Gazette*, 22 April 1814, p. 1.

66. 'Woodford Green Essex: "Harts," "The Outlook," "Montclair"', leaflet from Messrs Hallowes & Carter, Solicitors, 39 Bedford Row, London WC1, et al., in possession of Woodford and District Historical Society [1919]. See also Tuffs, *Story of Woodford*, p. 86.

67. Philip, 'Lixmount House and its People', p. 20.

68. Watson, 'John Jay's School for Boys', p. 9.

69. Thackeray, *Vanity Fair*, pp. 340, 680 n. 438, 481.

70. *The Times*, 20 June 1821, quoted in Watson, 'John Jay's School for Boys', p. 11.

71. Advertisement from 1813, quoted in Watson, 'John Jay's School for Boys', p. 9.

72. Watson, 'John Jay's School for Boys', pp. 9, 10–11. John Hefford, *Crestyphon, a Theban Tale: and the Vandal Robbery, a Carthaginian Tale* (London, 1820).

73. Cited in Watson, 'John Jay's School for Boys', p. 10: George G. Carey's dauntingly full title is *A Complete System of Theoretical and Mercantile Arithmetic. Comprehending a Full View of the Various Rules Necessary in Calculation. with Practical Illustrations of the Most Material Regulations and Transactions that Occur in Commerce. Particularly, Interest, Stocks, Annuities, Marine Insurance, Exchange, &c &c: Compiled for the Use of the Students at the Commercial Institution, Woodford.* (London: Law & Whittaker,

1818), pp. iii–iv (it was actually published in autumn 1817, see *London Courier and Evening Gazette*, 15 October 1817, p. 1). On the title-page Carey describes himself as 'Teacher of Mathematics, Commercial Institution, Woodford; author of "Elements of Astronomy," &c. &c.'

74. Carey, *Complete System*, pp. 339–40. Answers on p. 568, including that the whole cost of the insurance will be £549 18s 0d.

75. Carey, *Complete System*, p. 439.

76. Carey, *Complete System*, p. 260. See also pp. 254, 259, 260, 562 for examples giving the name of John Jay.

77. Carey, *Complete System*, p. 283; see also p. 285.

78. Watson, 'John Jay's School for Boys', p. 11.

79. Rosemary O'Day, *Education and Society 1500–1800: The Social Foundations of Education in Early Modern Britain* (London: Longman, 1982), p. 201.

80. The Raikes were a well-known local family: see Tuffs, *Story of Woodford*, p. 70; also p. 80.

81. Brice Pearse in 'Legacies of British Slave-ownership' website, www.ucl.ac.uk/lbs.

82. See also Tuffs, *Story of Woodford*, pp. 84, 86.

83. Austen, *Mansfield Park*, p. 184: 'Did not you hear me ask him about the slave trade last night?'

84. Sara Hutchinson, *The Letters of Sara Hutchinson from 1800 to 1835*, ed. Kathleen Coburn (London: Routledge & Kegan Paul, 1954), p. 115; cited in Gill, *Wordsworth*, p. 325.

85. Wyndham: Jane B. Livingston to Margaret Wyndham, 6 Dowry Parade, Hotwells, Clifton, 29 February 1836; see my ch. 5. The Ogilvy Livingstons were in Berkshire for the birth of their son George in 1813, but were in Somerset at a later date.

86. *Registrum Orielense*, vol. 2: *1701–1900*, compiled by C.L. Shadwell (London, 1902).

87. Ernest Nicholson, 'Eveleigh and Copleston: The Pre-Eminence of Oriel', in Jeremy Catto, ed., *Oriel College: A History* (Oxford: Oxford University Press, 2013), p. 247.

88. Catto, ed., *Oriel College*, p. 284.

89. David Steele, 'Wood, Charles, First Viscount Halifax (1800–1885)', *ODNB* (2009).

90. 'Court of King's Bench, Westminster', 13 November 1830, Taylor *v.* Street and Others, *Evening Mail*, 12–15 November 1830, p. 7.

91. Western Life Assurance Society, *Globe*, 10 August 1842; London and Provincial Law Assurance Society, *Journal of the Institute of Actuaries and Assurance Magazine*, 15:3 (1869).

92. Wyndham: e.g. Mary Anne Wyndham to George and Margaret Wyndham, Dinton,

13 October 1828 about receiving partridges – presuming Samuel is meant rather than John Livingston Jay; Emma Lane to Margaret Wyndham, Reading, 20 March 1829: 'Your eldest Brother is [...] a great Sportsman, and last June, I was really, from seeing the name in the Circulars at Ascot as owner of one of the race-horses, induced thro' the Gentleman's supposed relationship to you, to bet and lose two pairs of gloves.'

93.   Wyndham: Samuel Jay to Margaret Wyndham, n.d. [1865] and Brighton, 25 October 1865.

94.   Samuel Taylor Coleridge, 'Frost at Midnight', ll. 44–51, in Coleridge, *Selected Poems*, ed. Richard Holmes (London: Penguin Books, 1996), p. 47.

95.   Richard Holmes, *Coleridge: Darker Reflections* (London: Flamingo, 1999), caption to plate between pp. 298 and 299.

96.   Holmes, *Darker Reflections*, p. 496.

97.   Holmes, *Darker Reflections*, p. 511.

98.   Holmes, *Darker Reflections*, p. 514; see his superb and moving account, pp. 511–18.

99.   Death notice for Janet Enslie, *Public Ledger and Daily Advertiser*, 23 February 1810, p. 4.

100. My information about William Mellish comes from Roger Knight and Martin Wilcox, *Sustaining the Fleet, 1793–1815: War, the British Navy and the Contractor State* (Woodbridge: The Boydell Press, 2010), pp. 129–30 and *passim*.

101. Harts House still exists as a care home, near to Mellish Gardens, Woodford, presumably named after William Mellish.

102. *The Times*, 20 June 1821. p. 4.

103. Peter Tomory, 'Holloway, Thomas (1748–1827)', *ODNB* (2004).

104. *The Times*, 5 July 1821.

105. Watson, 'John Jay's School for Boys', p. 11.

106. Trollope, *Autobiography*, pp. 23–4.

107. Details from Court of Session, CS233-K-3-5/11.

108. Philip, 'Lixmount House and its People', p. 19.

Chapter 7: Cambridge: 'I was the Dreamer, they the Dream'

1.   William Wordsworth, *The Prelude*: 'Book Three: Residence at Cambridge' [1805, 1st pub. 1850], in Wordsworth, *Selected Poems*, pp. 218–19.

2.   Christopher Stray, 'A Parochial Anomaly: The Classical Tripos 1822–1900', in Jonathan Smith and Christopher Stray, eds, *Teaching and Learning in Nineteenth-Century Cambridge* (Woodbridge: The Boydell Press, 2001), pp. 31–44.

3.   Hague, *William Pitt the Younger*, p. 28.

4.   Charles Astor Bristed, *Five Years in an English University*, 2nd edn (New York: G.P. Putnam & Co, 1852), p. 243. A graduate of Yale, Bristed (1820–74) was admitted at Trinity over twenty years after Evan Jenkins, so I use his book with caution. Through his mother, Charles was the grandson of the founder of the Astor dynasty, John Jacob Astor. At the latter's death in 1848 he was said to be the richest man in the United States.

5.   W.M. Thackeray, *The Book of Snobs: Sketches of Life and Character etc. etc.*, in *The Works of William Makepeace Thackeray*, vol. IX (London: Smith, Elder & Co., 1894), p. 46.

6.   *The Cambridge University Calendar for the Year 1822* (Cambridge: printed for J. Deighton & Sons, 1822), p. 145.

7.   Tennyson's snake: 'I kept a tame snake in my rooms. I liked to watch his wonderful sinuosities on the carpet.' Quoted in [Hallam Lord Tennyson], *Alfred Lord Tennyson: A Memoir* (London: Macmillan, 1897), p. 41. For Thackeray's five terms: Gordon N. Ray, *Thackeray: The Uses of Adversity, 1811–1846* (London: Oxford University Press, 1955), p. 137.

8.   Bristed, *Five Years in an English University*, p. 1.

9.   [John Martin F. Wright] A Trinity-Man, *Alma Mater; or, Seven Years at the University of Cambridge*, 2 vols (London: Black, Young & Young, 1827), p. 4.

10. LMA: St Andrew, Holborn, London, Marriage register, 21 December 1825; [Wright], *Alma Mater*, p. 4.

11. *Huntingdon, Bedford and Peterborough Gazette*, 27 June 1829. For a short discussion of Wright's mathematical works and the journal he published to help students of mathematics, see Andrew Warwick, 'The Analytical Revolution from Below: Private Teaching and Mathematical Reform in Georgian Cambridge', in Jonathan Smith and Christopher Stray, eds, *Teaching and Learning in Nineteenth-Century Cambridge* (Woodbridge: The Boydell Press, 2001), pp. 5–30, at pp. 27–8. Warwick does not mention his time in prison and workhouse.

12. *Cambridge Chronicle and Journal*, 4 September 1835 and 23 March 1839.

13. LMA: Board of Guardian Records, 1834–1906/Church of England Parish Registers, 1754–1906, Parish register for St Andrew's Holborn, Baptisms, St Mary Lambeth, Surrey, 1841.

14. [Wright], *Alma Mater*, p. vii, from his Preface dated 17 January 1827; quoting Shakespeare, *Othello*, Act 5 sc. 2.

15. [Wright], *Alma Mater*, p. 2.

16. [Wright], *Alma Mater*, pp. 84–5.

17. [Wright], *Alma Mater*, p. 88.

18. The stuffed zebra is mentioned in M. Watson (Printer), *The New Cambridge Guide or a Description of the University, Town, and County of Cambridge* (Cambridge: J. Nicholson, 1804), p. 69.

19. [Wright], *Alma Mater*, p. 89.

20. The discovery was made by Marcia Watson, who told me it looked promising. I might never have found it, buried as it is within 'Letters mainly from John Pugh, Llan-gors vicarage, co. Brecon, to his uncle Evan Richards of Nanthenfoel, and one, 1823, from E. Jenkins, Brussels, to David Richards of Glanywern, Lampeter', in NLW, Letters, 1823–1873, ref. 12-21.

21. Sir George Biddell Airy, *Autobiography*, ed. Wilfrid Airy (Cambridge: at the University Press, 1896), p. 39.

22. Gill, *Wordsworth*, p. 359.

23. William Hague, *William Wilberforce: The Life of the Great Anti-Slave Trade Campaigner* (London: HarperCollins, 2007), p. 468.

24. Quoted in William Thackeray, *The History of Henry Esmond* (London: Penguin, 1985), Introduction by John Sutherland, p. 7.

25. William Thomas, 'Macaulay, Thomas Babington, Baron Macaulay (1800–1859)', *ODNB* (2015).

26. Source for George Fieschi Heneage: Historic England.

27. Don Seton Wilkinson, 'George Wyndham's Dalwood Cricket Team', *Hunter Living Histories*, University of Newcastle (Australia), https://hunterlivinghistories. com/2019/05/07/dalwood-cricket-team/.

28. *Evening Mail*, 19–21 March 1845, p. 6.

29. John Charles, third Earl Spencer, had no issue. Diana, Princess of Wales, was the great-great-granddaughter of his younger brother, the fourth Earl Spencer.

30. Ellis Archer Wasson, 'Spencer, John Charles, Viscount Althorp and Third Earl Spencer (1782–1845)', *ODNB* (2008). The details in this paragraph come from Wasson's article.

31. The sources are unclear: Wasson states that Joseph Allen supervised Viscount Althorp at Trinity College (from 1800), but the obituarist in the *Evening Mail* says he became a private tutor soon after getting his Fellowship in 1793.

32. *Morning Post*, 4 January 1814, p. 1.

33. [Wright], *Alma Mater*, note on p. 125.

34. *Cambridge University Calendar 1822*, p. 144.

35. An 'act' was a disputation on mathematics in Latin: see Airy, *Autobiography*, for acts and opponencies, pp. 35, 40 ff.

36. Alex Kendall, *The Snowdonia Way* (Milnthorpe, Cumbria: Cicerone, 2017).

37. CB to Ellen Nussey, [29 June 1854], *Letters* III, p. 274.

38. CB to Catherine Wooler, 18 July 1854, *Letters* III, pp. 278 and 279 n. 3; Margaret and Robert Cochrane, *My Dear Boy: The Life of Arthur Bell Nicholls BA Husband of Charlotte Brontë* (Beverley: Highgate Publications, 1999), p. 56.

39. NLW: Roberts & Evans, folder R&E 9/1.

40. Faulkner, *Chelsea* (1810), p. ix.

41. NLW: Roberts & Evans, folder R&E 9/3.

42. *Aberystwith Observer*, 16 February 1861, p. 1.

43. Jenny Uglow, *Elizabeth Gaskell: A Habit of Stories* (London: Faber & Faber, 1993), pp. 9–10; Thorne, 'Maitland', *ODNB*.

44. Uglow, *Gaskell*, p. 243.

45. John A.V. Chapple, 'Stevenson, William (*bap.* 1770, *d.* 1829)', *ODNB* (2008).

46. Uglow, *Gaskell*, pp. 12, 20.

47. Quoted in Uglow, *Gaskell*, p. 20.

48. Uglow, *Gaskell*, pp. 35, 147.

49. See Anna Brueton, 'Illegitimacy in South Wales, 1660–1870' (Thesis, University of Leicester, 2015). She writes that there was a custom of 'courting in bed' ('caru yn y gwely'), which was the usual mode of courtship among ordinary people, and marriage was the frequent outcome for pregnancy; see e.g. pp. 30, 37, 141. The writer William Bingley charmingly decided in 1800 that the practice 'originated in the scarcity of fuel, and in the disagreeableness of sitting together in cold weather, without fire': Rev. William Bingley, *A Tour round North Wales, performed During the Summer of 1798*, 2 vols (London: Sold by E. Williams, No. 11 Strand and J. Deighton, Cambridge, 1800), vol. II, p. 228^2. The publisher, Evan Williams, was the brother of Rev. John Williams, headmaster of Ystrad Meurig school. Mary's pregnancy at marriage, however normal for many women in Wales, was possibly rather awkward for her brother David as a clergyman in the Church of England.

50. *The Cambridge University Calendar for the Year 1818* (Cambridge: Printed by J. Hodson for J. Deighton & Sons, 1818), p. vii.

51. [Solomon Atkinson], 'Struggles of a Poor Student through Cambridge by a Senior Wrangler', *London Magazine and Review* (1 April 1825), pp. 491–510, p. 492.

52. [Atkinson], 'Struggles', p. 497. See also more about Solomon Atkinson in A.D.D. Craik, *Mr Hopkins' Men: Cambridge Reform and British Mathematics in the 19th Century* (London: Springer, 2007), pp. 10–14.

53. [Atkinson], 'Struggles', p. 496.

54. De Quincey, *Confessions*, p. 4 and note to pp. 4–6.

55. See Hague, *William Wilberforce*, pp. 5–6. Other sources state that Isaac Milner had to leave school at ten because of his father's death.

56. See Kevin C. Knox, 'Milner, Isaac (1750–1820)', *ODNB* (2004).

57. Trollope, *Autobiography*, p. 15.

58. Watson, *New Cambridge Guide*, p. ix.

59. *Cambridge University Calendar 1822*, pp. 147, 273.

60. *Cambridge University Calendar 1822*, pp. 290–1.

61. Bristed, *Five Years in an English University*, p. 14.

62. Allan Chapman, 'Airy, Sir George Biddell (1801–1892)', *ODNB* (2011); Airy, *Autobiography*, p. 14.

63. Hugh Brogan, 'Clarkson, Thomas (1760–1846)', *ODNB* (2011). Thomas Clarkson's younger brother John left the navy to become his brother's secretary and agent. He was at the forefront of the founding of the colony in Sierra Leone for former American slaves, and was the first governor until he was dismissed in 1793. He ceased to take an active role in the anti-slavery movement, though he seems to have remained passionately interested. The founding of the colony is controversial, but his keen interest in anti-slavery is not.

64. Airy, *Autobiography*, pp. 19, 20. My italics.

65. See Chapman, 'Airy', *ODNB*. Photograph in National Portrait Gallery, by Maull & Polyblank, c.1864.

66. Airy, *Autobiography*, p. 21.

67. Airy, *Autobiography*, pp. 26, 46.

68. Bristed, *Five Years in an English University*, p. 14. According to Airy, the foundation sizars were lucky to have the superb remains from the Fellows' table; whereas the non-foundation sizars were given the same meal as the pensioners had been given. Airy, *Autobiography*, p. 46.

69. [Atkinson], 'Struggles', p. 497.

70. [Wright], *Alma Mater*, pp. 12–13.

71. [Wright], *Alma Mater*, pp. 33, 32.

72. [Wright], *Alma Mater*, p. 21.

73. E.M. Braekman, *Le protestantisme à Bruxelles: Des origines à la mort de Léopold I* (Brussels: Bibliothèque Royale Albert I, 1980), p. 113.

74. ACAD: James Devereux Hustler.

75. [Atkinson], 'Struggles', p. 504.

76. [Atkinson], 'Struggles', p. 501.

77. [Wright], *Alma Mater*, p. 151. See also Craik, *Mr Hopkins' Men*, p. 16.

78. *Stamford Mercury*, 8 July 1814, p. 3 and 9 September 1814, p. 2; [Wright], *Alma Mater*, p. 164.

79. [Wright], *Alma Mater*, pp. 165–7.

80. Fiona MacCarthy, *Byron: Life and Legend* (London: John Murray, 2002), p. 68; [Wright], *Alma Mater*, p. 168.

81. [Atkinson], 'Struggles', p. 506.

82. John Clive, *Thomas Babington Macaulay: The Shaping of the Historian* (London: Secker & Warburg, 1973), pp. 38–9.

83. Quoted in Richard Holmes, *The Age of Wonder: How the Romantic Generation Discovered the Beauty and Terror of Science* (London: HarperPress, 2011), p. 448. A wonderful quote.

84. [Tennyson], *Alfred Lord Tennyson*, p. 34.

85. Quoted in [Tennyson], *Alfred Lord Tennyson*, p. 34; dated 18 April 1828 in *Letters*, 1.23 as cited by Christopher Ricks, 'Tennyson, Alfred, first Baron Tennyson (1809–1892)', *ODNB* (2006).

86. Christopher Ricks, *Tennyson* (London: Macmillan, 1972), p. 30.

87. Wordsworth, *The Prelude*, Book Three, ll. 73–6.

88. Thackeray, *Henry Esmond*, p. 145.

89. [Wright], *Alma Mater*, p. 116.

90. [Wright], *Alma Mater*, pp. 118, 123, 126, 128.

91. [Wright], *Alma Mater*, pp. 127, 141.

92. [Wright], *Alma Mater*, p. 170.

93. Wordsworth, *The Prelude*, Book Three, ll. 60–4.

94. e.g. [Wright], *Alma Mater*, p. 179.

95. Bristed, *Five Years in an English University*, pp. 44–5.

96. Thackeray, *Lovel the Widower*, p. 23.

97. [Atkinson], 'Struggles', pp. 506–8.

98. Holmes, *Early Visions*, pp. 39, 40, 41, 49, 50, 53, 56.

99. Airy, *Autobiography*, pp. 27, 22, 23.

100. Cicero, *Selected Works*, ed. and trans. Michael Grant (Harmondsworth: Penguin, 1971), p. 105.

101. Sir George Otto Trevelyan, *The Life and Letters of Lord Macaulay* (Oxford: Oxford University Press, 1978), p. 100.

102. LMA: Evan Jenkins, Deacon ordination bundle, 1825.

103. *Cambridge University Calendar 1822*, p. 34.

104. Rev. Latham Wainewright, *The Literary and Scientific Pursuits Encouraged and Enforced in the University of Cambridge, Briefly Described and Vindicated* (London, 1815), p. 70.

105. [Wright], *Alma Mater*, pp. 222–3. Pearson on the Creed: *An Exposition of the Creed*, by John Pearson, Bishop of Chester, first printed in 1659; it had reached its twelfth edition in 1741 (Preface to 1877 edition, rev. Rev. E. Burton (Oxford: at the Clarendon Press, 1877), pp. vii, viii).

106. Bristed, *Five Years in an English University*, p. 350.

107. Knight, *Nineteenth-Century Church*, pp. 109, 107, 14; see also p. 111.

108. William Trollope: *Cambridge University Calendar 1822*, 'Addenda et Corrigenda', p. vi.

109. [Wright], *Alma Mater*, p. 239.

110. [Wright], *Alma Mater*, pp. 289–90, 280.

111. All quotes in this paragraph on Paley are from James E. Crimmins, 'Paley, William (1743–1805)', *ODNB* (2008).

112. *Cambridge University Calendar 1822*, pp. 20–44.

113. Crimmins, 'Paley', *ODNB*.

114. *Cambridge University Calendar 1822*, p. 20; ACAD.

115. ACAD, and Thomas Hamilton, rev. John D. Haigh, 'Lee, Samuel (1783–1852)', *ODNB* (2004).

116. ACAD: William Lax.

117. *Cambridge University Calendar 1822*, pp. 31–3.

118. Airy, *Autobiography*, pp. 22, 119.

119. J.A. Secord, 'Sedgwick, Adam (1785–1873)', *ODNB* (2013); Gill, *Wordsworth*, p. 359.

120. William Farren, *Adam Sedgwick*: albumen carte-de-visite, 1867, National Portrait Gallery, London x22397.

121. Secord, 'Sedgwick', *ODNB*; Adrian Desmond, James Moore and Janet Browne, 'Darwin, Charles Robert (1809–1882)', *ODNB* (2015).

122. [Atkinson], 'Struggles', p. 503.

123. [Wright], *Alma Mater*, p. 33.

124. Leonard W. Cowie, 'Simeon, Charles (1759–1836)', *ODNB* (2005).

125. [Wright], *Alma Mater*, pp. 56–8.

126. Quoted in Cowie, 'Simeon', *ODNB*.

127. [Wright], *Alma Mater*, p. 150.

128. [Wright], *Alma Mater*, pp. 229, 57.

129. Quoted in Trevelyan, *Macaulay*, p. 81.

130. Thackeray, *Henry Esmond*, p. 301.

131. Craik, *Mr Hopkins' Men*, p. 13, note 12.

Chapter 8: Belgium, 1814–1823: 'C'est le feu!'

1. Subtitle: *'C'est le feu!'* from Thackeray, *Vanity Fair*, p. 290: 'It's gunfire!' Epigraph: Charlotte Brontë, *The Professor* (Ware: Wordsworth Editions, 2010), p. 39. It was written in 1846 and published posthumously in 1856.

2. Verdi: *Don Carlos* (Four-Act Italian Version, 1882–3), conductor Herbert von Karajan (EMI Records, 1979): Act 1 sc. 1: 'The hour has struck; / the Flemish people call you! / You must help them; / appoint yourself their saviour!', p. 17; Charles Osborne, 'An Introduction to Verdi's "Don Carlos"', p. 6. The 1867 date is the first French production; the 1884 date is that of the first production in Italian.

3. Richard Holmes, *Wellington: The Iron Duke* (London: Harper Perennial, 2007), p. 193, quoting from Elizabeth Longford, *Wellington: The Years of the Sword*, p. 344.

4. ACAD; CCEd. Appointment as Chaplain to the Forces announced in the *Evening Gazette*, 11 April 1814.

5. *Sussex Advertiser*, 29 November 1813, p. 3.

6. BL: Add. MS 61805. Stonestreet's journal and letters have been published as *Recollections of the Scenes of which I Was Witness in the Low Countries & France in the Campaigns of 1814 and 1815 and the Subsequent Occupation of French Flanders: The Journal and Letters of the Reverend George Griffin Stonestreet 1814–16*, ed. Gareth Glover (Godmanchester: Ken Trotman Publishing, 2009), but there are errors in the notes (e.g. n. 1: Stonestreet's previous curacy, Ewhurst, is not in Surrey nor anywhere near Cranleigh; it is in East Sussex, ten miles north of Hastings) and in the transcription. My transcription is thus taken instead from the MS, with folio numbers, adding the ed. Glover page number in brackets.

7. The 1914 *Almanack* is in the LMA. Rev. Stonestreet is listed on p. 13.

8. Stonestreet MS fol. 5 (ed. Glover, p. 5).

9. Stonestreet MS fols 51, 52 (ed. Glover, p. 8).

10. Clarke Papers: Eliza Jenkins to William Branwhite Clarke, Brussels, 26 July 1831.

11. Lambeth: FP Howley 4, fol. 181: Stonestreet to the Bishop of London, Head Quarters Cambray, 19 March 1816.

12. Stonestreet MS fols 57, 60, 61 (ed. Glover, pp. 34, 36).

13. See John Bew, *Castlereagh: The Biography of a Statesman* (London: Quercus, 2014), pp. 387–9.

14. Holmes, *Wellington*, pp. 205–7; quote on p. 208.

15. Alexander I, a 'silly vain fellow', quote by Lord Grey, in Bew, *Castlereagh*, p. 365.

16. Thackeray, *Vanity Fair*, p. 304.

17. Thackeray, *Vanity Fair*, p. 330.

18. J.B. Romberg, *Brussels and its Environs* (Brussels: Printed for B. Le Francq, 1824), p. 61. Regarding 'trophy hunters', Thackeray doesn't hide his distaste at Becky sending to Miss Crawley (to curry favour in her will) 'trophies' from the battlefield, which Miss Crawley was supposed to think came from Becky's husband, her nephew. Becky bought them for 'a few francs, from one of the innumerable pedlars who immediately began to deal in relics of the war' (*Vanity Fair*, p. 307).

19. Stonestreet MS fol. 66 (ed. Glover, p. 49): letter dated 18 April 1815.

20. Stonestreet MS fols 82, 83 (ed. Glover, p. 65): letter dated 22 March 1816. In the event, Prince Edward, Duke of Kent, stayed only two years in Brussels; see below.

21. Lambeth: FP Howley 4, fol. 181: 19 March 1816. There is a different and shorter version of the letter in BL: Add. MS 61805, transcribed in Stonestreet, ed. Glover, pp. 66–7. It is perhaps a copy or first draft by Stonestreet.

22. CCEd; Stonestreet, editor's introduction, ed. Glover, p. 3.

23. Charlotte Brontë made a mistake in *The Professor* that William Crimsworth marries Frances in a 'Protestant chapel' (p. 182): it had to be at the ambassador's residence to be valid, i.e. on British soil.

24. Philip Larkin, 'High Windows': I'm not sure how Larkin suddenly showed up – writing is an odd thing. But maybe his stunning poem is not irrelevant to what I was thinking in Brussels in 2014 as I looked at the Chapel Royal where my ancestors had served as priests for over thirty-five years to a maybe not always receptive congregation. Maybe it is the sudden jolt from his frantically dismissive words about God and the priest to his intake of breath as the verse settles into an adagio: 'And immediately / Rather than words comes the thought of high windows: / The sun-comprehending glass, / And beyond it, the deep blue air, that shows / Nothing, and is nowhere, and is endless.' (Philip Larkin, *The Complete Poems*, ed. Archie Burnett (New York: Farrar, Straus and Giroux, 2012), p. 80.) It thus became an epigraph for my book.

25. Braekman, *Le protestantisme à Bruxelles*: mention of a letter from Evan Jenkins to Rev. Vent, 21 November 1840, contributing 500 francs from the Anglican community to the new organ, p. 113.

26. CCEd; Lambeth: FP Howley 4, fol. 219: Michael Marlow, President of St John's College, Oxford, to the Bishop of London, 23 December 1817.

27. Lambeth: FP Howley 4, fol. 219: Marlow to Bishop.

28. Lancashire, England, Church of England Baptisms, Marriages and Burials, 1538–1812; CCEd.

29. Stonestreet MS fol. 10 (ed. Glover, p. 9).

30. Princess Charlotte's comment on Prince Leopold: quoted in Christopher Hibbert, *George IV: Regent and King 1811–1830* (London: Allen Lane, 1973), p. 92. As a sixteen-year-old she called herself 'imprudent' and interestingly identified with Marianne in Jane Austen's 1811 *Sense and Sensibility*: quoted in Claire Tomalin, *Jane Austen: A Life* (London: Penguin Books, 2000), p. 222. I wonder, on reading Hibbert's account of her, if Princess Charlotte was autistic; and on reading her letter quoted in Tomalin that she found her (albeit younger) Colonel Brandon in Prince Leopold. For Princess Charlotte's support of Rev. Prince, see: Obituary of Rev. Thomas Prince, DD, *Gentleman's Magazine and Historical Chronicle*, May 1830, vol. 100, p. 473.

31. Obituary of Thomas Prince, *Gentleman's Magazine*, May 1830.

32. Lambeth: FP Blomfield 65, fols 80–1. The printed document contains no year; but the reference to their meeting on Saturday 9 November can only be 1816.

33. Stonestreet MS fol. 99 (ed. Glover, p. 77).

34. Chapel Royal seating arrangements: this might have changed between 1816 and 1842; the printed document is in Bishop Blomfield's file (Lambeth: FP Blomfield 65, fols 80–1), who was Bishop of London 1828–56.

35. Lambeth: FP Howley 7, fol. 3, from Rev. ?E.J.W. Back BD, 31 October 1816. I haven't been able to trace Edward Back further.

36. Role of ambassadors and Bishop of London: Sara Slinn, pers. email, 5 August 2014.

37. Kadoc: BE/942855/2062/143: church register showing Rev. Willoughby's first marriage on 12 November 1816 and first burial on 16 November.

38. The correspondence relating to the fracas in the vestry room and the contest for the chaplaincy is mostly in Lambeth: FP Howley 4, fols 189–255.

39. Obituary of Thomas Prince, *Gentleman's Magazine*, May 1830.

40. Surplice: a white linen vestment worn usually over a cassock for the religious part of the church service. The controversy about a clergyman wearing a surplice when he also gave his sermon arose some decades later.

41. Perhaps not so startling: Thomas Prince quarrelled with the examiners at Oxford because they had given him what he said was a corrupted passage in Lucretius, and he walked out. Obituary, *Gentleman's Magazine*, 1830.

42. Rev. Willoughby's first recorded duty (a marriage) was on 12 November 1816: Kadoc: BE/942855/2062/143.

43. Rev. Willoughby's last recorded duty as chaplain at the Chapel Royal was a baptism on 7 December 1817: Kadoc: BE/942855/2062/143.

44. Lambeth: FP Howley 5, fol. 100, 29 December 1817.

45. Lambeth: FP Howley 4, fols 239–41, George Gaskin [Secretary to the Society for the Promotion of Christian Knowledge] to the Bishop of London, 30 December 1817.

46. LMA: Register of Baptisms, Marriages and Deaths, Chapel Royal, Brussels, 1818. The first entry is dated 8 February 1818: the baptism of Caroline Jane, daughter of John and Mary Brown, domestic servant to the Duke of Richmond. 'Performed by George Hornby, Chaplain to the British Embassy'. All baptisms up to the final one on 15 December are performed by Hornby. He likewise performs the marriages (always at the embassy) and funerals. The register is a copy of part of the one now archived in Leuven – Kadoc: BE/942855/2062/144.

47. Many readers will sympathize with the abandoned 'Madame de St Laurent' – Thérèse-Bernardine Mongenet – if they read the biography by Mollie Gillen, *The Prince and His Lady: The Love Story of the Duke of Kent and Madame de St Laurent* (London: Sidgwick & Jackson, 1970). If the duke had stayed contentedly with Madame there would be no Victorian age. I wonder which German princeling would have been dragged in to be king then? Perhaps not so bad a situation at all, if you consider a King Leopold or a King Albert. See Gillen, *The Prince*, p. 211 for their rented house in Brussels. Gillen's thoughtful interpretation of the duke's unhappy abandonment of 'my poor faithful Partner' is plausible: see her ch. 18 'Parting'; and p. 223 for this quote from the Duke of Kent.

48. LMA: Register 1821.

49. Kadoc: BE/942855/2062/143, Register of Baptisms, Marriages and Burials. The earliest entry is a marriage by Rev. Willoughby in the 'Ambassador's house' on 12 November 1816; the last is a marriage by Rev. Prince in July 1822. The account of its discovery at the auction and despatch to Brussels in 1862/3 is inscribed on the register.

50. Stadsarchief Rotterdam: Johanna Jacoba Enslie – marriage certificate, 16 December 1822, where it states that John Jay arrived in Saint-Josse-ten-Noode, Brussels in July 1821, and then moved to Ixelles. I presume they arrived in *early* July because of the date of the advertisement for the school in *The Times* of 5 July 1821.

51. Thackeray, *Vanity Fair*, p. 255.

52. Victor Hugo (1802–85): quote according to *Time Out* guide and various websites; possibly a quote from his journal. The Grand-Place is definitely now one of the loveliest squares in Europe. Hugo's *Les Misérables* was first published in Brussels, and the premiere of a play based on the book, adapted by his son, took place here in 1863.

53. Thackeray, *Pendennis*, p. 804.

54. Hibbert, *George IV*, p. 229. Hibbert says that the Duke of Wellington was King George IV's guide around the battlefield of Waterloo in 1821 and was disgruntled that the king did not ask a single question, but at one point burst into tears.

55. Sutherland, *Walter Scott*, p. 185.

56. W.A. Speck, *Robert Southey: Entire Man of Letters* (London: Yale University Press, 2006), p. 164.

57. Gill, *Wordsworth*, p. 338.

58. Dorothy Wordsworth, *Journal of a Tour on the Continent*, in Dorothy Wordsworth, *The Continental Journals*, Intro. by Helen Boden (Bristol: Thoemmes Press, 1995), p. 24.

59. *The Times*, 5 July 1821; see my ch. 6.

60. LMA: Register for the Chapel Royal, Brussels, 1821; Brabant Méridional, Commune de Saint-Josse-ten-Noode, Registre des Décès, 1821.

61. Watson, 'John Jay's School for Boys', p. 11, source: Brabant Méridional, Commune d'Ixelles, Registre des Décés, 1822, where he is wrongly given as seventeen.

62. Brontë, *Professor*, p. 122.

63. See Helen MacEwan, *Down the Belliard Steps: Discovering the Brontës in Brussels* (Hythe: Brussels Brontë Editions, 2012), pp. 99–100 for the Protestant cemetery.

64. TNA: Foreign Registers and Returns, 1627–1960, RG 33.

65. LMA: Chapel Royal register, 1821; CCEd; ACAD.

66. CCEd; ACAD.

67. *The Courier*, 1 September 1821.

68. *Morning Post*, 10 July 1823.

69. *Morning Post*, 1 June 1875. Knight, *Nineteenth-Century Church*, p. 25.

70. LMA: Evan Jenkins: Deacon ordination bundle.

71. Rev. W.G. Procter, 'The Ancient Parish of Croston: A Historical Retrospect', *Transactions of the Historic Society of Lancashire and Cheshire*, lx (for the year 1908; 1909), pp. 1–34, at p. 25; and Rev. W.G. Procter, 'The Ancient Parish of Croston: A Historical Retrospect Part II', *Transactions of the Historic Society of Lancashire and Cheshire*, lxii (for the year 1910; 1911), pp. 35–58, at p. 51 n. 1.

72. Procter, 'Croston Part II', p. 54.

73. *Lancaster Gazette*, 20 May 1826, p. 1.

74. Brontë, *Professor*, p. 74.

75. Procter, 'Croston Part II', p. 54; Wikipedia, 'Sir Oswald Mosley'.

76. *Morning Post*, 6 January 1824.

77. NLW: Evan Richards Papers: Letters 1823–1873, letters-812; 12-21. They were donated by Mrs Estyn Evans, Belfast, in 1983, so maybe it crossed the Irish Sea and came back again. She will never know how grateful I am. I find it curious that the sheet of paper was slightly torn when Evan wrote on it – he has had to indent four lines to avoid the tear.

78. Brontë, *Villette*, pp. 292, 298.

79. Edmund Boyce, *The Belgian Traveller*, 4th edn (London: Printed for Samuel Leigh, 1823), p. 250.

80. Brontë, *Villette*, ch. 20. Thanks to Sarah Laycock of the Brontë Parsonage Museum for sending me a scan of the concert programme, which is archived there, and included Bellini and Handel. Redevelopment of Hôtel d'Angleterre: Eric Ruijssenaars, 'Mapping the Brussels of the Brontës: The Cultural Places', *Brussels Brontë Blog* (28 April 2018).

81. Napoleon: Paul F. State, *Historical Dictionary of Brussels* (Lanham, MD: The Scarecrow Press, 2004), p. 38.

82. 'Lilting': wonderful Dylan Thomas, 'Fern Hill'. A long time after writing this chapter, I think I finally understood the last line of Thomas's poem, 'Though I sang in my chains like the sea', as I struggled to compose *cynghanedd* (in English) under the eye of the inspirational harpist and teacher Harriet Earis at Plas Tan y Bwlch.

Chapter 9: Yorkshire and Brussels, 1824–1825: School, Death and Marriage

1. Charlotte Brontë, *Jane Eyre*, ed. Q.D. Leavis (London: Penguin, 1985), p. 66.

2. Barker, *The Brontës*, p. 149.

3. West Yorkshire, Church of England Births and Baptisms, 1813–1910.

4. Strong, *Story of Pudsey Church*, p. 1.

5. Joseph Lister, quoted in Strong, *Story of Pudsey Church*, pp. 2–3.

6. Details from Strong, *Story of Pudsey Church*, pp. 2–6.

7. Strong, *Story of Pudsey Church*, pp. 15–17. She spells his name as Howarth. He is both Howorth and Howerth in CCEd, which gives his death on 21 June 1814, which is an error: the church register gives the spelling as Howorth and his burial on 2 June 1814 aged seventy-nine, so he was born around 1735.

8. Strong, *Story of Pudsey Church*, p. 16.

9. Strong, *Story of Pudsey Church*, p. 18.

10. CB to Ellen Nussey, 6 August 1843, *Letters* I, p. 327.

11. Strong, *Story of Pudsey Church*, p. 18; Knight, *Nineteenth-Century Church*, p. 64.

12. Knight, *Nineteenth-Century Church*, p. 63.

13. Quoted in Strong, *Story of Pudsey Church*, p. 18.

14. Christopher Webster, 'Taylor, Thomas (1777/8–1826)', *ODNB* (2014).

15. See Gaskell, *Life*, pp. 83–7; Barker, *The Brontës*, pp. 52–3.

16. Webster, 'Taylor', *ODNB*.

17. Quoted in Webster, 'Taylor', *ODNB*.

18. Jenkins family Bible: family possession.

19. Strong, *Story of Pudsey Church*, p. 19.

20. Nigel Aston, 'Harcourt [*formerly* Venables-Vernon], Edward (1757–1847)', *ODNB* (2008).

21. Quoted in Wikipedia, according to an account by Dean Alford.

22. Barker, *The Brontës*, p. 150, citing *Leeds Mercury*, 4 September 1824, p. 3; this may be an error as I have not been able to find any mention of Haworth.

23. *Leeds Intelligencer*, 2 September 1824, p. 3.

24. Quoted in Strong, *Story of Pudsey Church*, p. 20.

25. Cumbria Archive Centre, Kendal: Clergy Daughters' School, Admissions Register, 1824–39, MS WDS/38/3.

26. Quoted in Barker, *The Brontës*, p. 148. Juliet Barker gives an admirable description of the school.

27. Barker, *The Brontës*, pp. 149, 150, 154.

28. *Cambridge Chronicle and Journal*, 5 December 1823, p. 4; see also Barker, *The Brontës*, pp. 136–7.

29. *Cumberland Pacquet, and Ware's Whitehaven Advertiser*, 8 December 1823, p. 1. I am not sure why Barker calls the list of subscribers 'patrons', which implies more involvement than giving an annual subscription: Barker, *The Brontës*, p. 138.

30. Barker, *The Brontës*, p. 148; Gaskell, *Life*, p. 55.

31. Barker, *The Brontës*, pp. 159–60.

32. *Morning Post*, 6 January 1824.

33. LMA: Evan Jenkins: Deacon ordination bundle 1825.

34. VCH: *Cambridgeshire* (London, 1989): Elsworth: Manors, pp. 307–8 (British History Online).

35. *Norfolk Chronicle*, 11 April 1818, p. 3.

36. Stonestreet, letters, 16 March 1815, Stonestreet MS fol. 62 (ed. Glover, p. 46) and 2 February 1815, Stonestreet MS fol. 57 (ed. Glover, p. 34).

37. Wikipedia: 'List of Diplomats of the United Kingdom to the Netherlands'.

38. TNA: FO 83/10, in Raymond A. Jones, *The British Diplomatic Service 1815–1914* (Gerrards Cross: Colin Smythe, 1983), p. 58.

39. LMA: Evan Jenkins: Deacon ordination bundle.

40. Lambeth: FP Howley 24, fols 78–9, Holworthy to the Bishop of London.

41. Ancestry.co.uk.

42. Ruijssenaars, 'Mapping the Brussels of the Brontës'.

43. Caption to 1870 photograph in Musée de la Ville de Bruxelles, Grand-Place. The plaque on the church door has the date 1620, which seems to be the date when it was designed.

44. See Kendall, *Miss Cavell Was Shot*.

45. Knight, *Nineteenth-Century Church*, p. 108.

46. Robert Reid, *The Peterloo Massacre* (London: Heinemann, 1989), p. 211. See Bew, *Castlereagh*, Part III, ch. 12, for a more nuanced approach.

47. Holmes, *Shelley*, pp. 532, 540.

48. See Bew, *Castlereagh*, Part III, chs 20–1. Bew's biography is a superb reassessment of the politician another historian (Andrew Roberts) has called 'perhaps the greatest of all Britain's Foreign Secretaries': Bew, *Castlereagh*, book jacket puff. Bew suggests that Castlereagh's breakdown may have been the result of tertiary syphilis, acquired as a young man, or even rabies (pp. 555–6).

49. Bew, *Castlereagh*, Part II, ch. 14, esp. p. 261.

50. Byron on Castlereagh: see Bew, *Castlereagh*, Part III, ch. 12, pp. 458–9.

51. Derek Beales, 'Canning, George (1770–1827)', *ODNB* (2014).

52. William Hazlitt, *The Spirit of the Age or Contemporary Portraits*, ed. E.D. Mackerness, 2nd edn (Plymouth: Northcote House, 1991), pp. 183, 185. Great Divan = House of Commons; until the fire of 1834 the Commons held debates in St Stephen's Chapel.

53. See e.g. Jones, *British Diplomatic Service*, p. 34. The last marriage Lord Clancarty presided over in The Hague was on 27 December 1823.

54. Jones, *British Diplomatic Service*, pp. 34–5.

55. Jones, *British Diplomatic Service*, pp. 35–6.

56. Expenses by Sir Charles Bagot: *Estimates and Accounts &c.*, Session 2 February to 31 May 1826, in *Parliamentary Papers*, vol. 20 (London: H.M. Stationery Office, 1827).

57. LMA: Evan Jenkins, Deacon ordination bundle.

58. LMA: Evan Jenkins, Deacon ordination bundle.

59. LMA: Bishop's Act Book, 1825.

60. My instinct, however – or perhaps my reading of novels of this period – is that Eliza didn't go to England at this time, that maybe it was Evan's chance to 'enjoy' his last months as a bachelor with his brother.

61. *London Courier and Evening Gazette*, 11 July 1825, p. 1, and several other newspapers on dates in July and August, including *The Times*.

62. *The Harrow School Register, 1800–1911*, 3rd edn (London: Longmans, Green, and Co., 1911).

63. *Almanach de poche* 1825, p. 49; the same address is in the Almanacs for 1826–30. State, *Historical Dictionary*, says that the 1770s rue de Brabant was renamed rue de la Loi in 1797 (p. 183). But no one seems to have informed the Almanac compilers of the change of name.
64. *Almanach*, Supplement, 1832, p. 93.
65. [A.X. Mauvy], *The Stranger's Guide through Brussels and its Environs* (Brussels: Ad. Wahlen, Printer to the Court, 1834), p. 30, who also gives the 1830s address of the embassy. See also Charles White, *The Belgic Revolution of 1830*, 2 vols (London: Whittaker and Co., 1835), vol. II, pp. 10–11.
66. List of ambassadors and envoys in Wikipedia.
67. Information about Pierce from ACAD, CCEd and Ancestry.co.uk.
68. *Derbyshire Courier*, 7 February 1863, p. 3.
69. Lambeth: FP Howley 24, fol. 78.
70. LMA: Evan Jenkins: Priest ordination bundle, letter to Bishop of London, William Howley, 10 November 1825.
71. LMA: Bishop's Act Book, 1825.
72. *Almanach royal* 1828, p. 435: 'Pensionnats Externes' 'Jay, au glacis, hors de la porte de Namur'.
73. e.g. *Opregte Haarlemsche Courant*, 16 August 1825.
74. Admittance register, Gonville and Caius College, Cambridge, scan of the page kindly sent to me on 5 June 2014.
75. John Livingston Jay is listed as in the Secretary's Office, Greenwich Hospital, in an almanac in 1826: *Watson's, or, Gentleman's and Citizen's Almanack, 1826*. Retirement age in *Parliamentary Papers*, vol. 44 (1867), 'Returns Relating to Greenwich Hospital'.
76. Wright, *Memories*, pp. 12–13. See also Marcia Watson, 'Touring Party of Italy', *Dalwood House Newsletter*, no. 96 (March 2017), p. 6, and www.dalwood.org.au.
77. Wyndham: Charlotte Starky to Fanny Wyndham, 23 February 1888. The whole phrase is: '[John Still] is at Rome with his sister Mrs. Taylor, recently married[,] her husband & Mother-in-law also Miss Taylor & her friend & schoolfellow Miss Jay'. I read it as 'her husband … her friend', that is Mary Taylor née Still's friend.
78. Wyndham: Mary Taylor to Margaret Wyndham, Moston, 12 May 1849.
79. Watson, 'Touring Party of Italy'.
80. Belgium, Brabant, Civil Registration, 1582–1914, Brussels, Geboorten 1826. John Livingston Jay has entered his occupation as 'rentier' (living independently); perhaps he was a little embarrassed about calling himself a clerk.
81. Watson, 'Touring Party of Italy'.

Chapter 10: Evan Embattled, 1826–1829: The Button-maker's Grandson and the Scottish Bishop

1. Peter Dixon, *Canning: Politician and Statesman* (London: Weidenfeld and Nicolson, 1976), pp. 253–4.

2. Peter Thomson, 'Kean, Edmund (1787–1833)', *ODNB* (2015) and G.C. Boase, rev. Norman Vance, 'Grattan, Thomas Colley (1791–1864)', *ODNB* (2004).

3. Thomas Colley Grattan, *Beaten Paths; and those who trod them*, 2 vols (London: Chapman and Hall, 1862), vol. II, ch. IV, 'A Three Days' Tour with Coleridge and Wordsworth', pp. 107–45. Pryse Gordon and Byron: Richard Garnett, rev. Rebecca Mills, 'Gordon, Pryse Lockhart (1762–1845)', *ODNB* (2012).

4. Grattan, *Beaten Paths*, pp. 108–9, 110.

5. Grattan, *Beaten Paths*, pp. 234–5.

6. In the Ixelles register, 'Geboorte Akten', he is given the wonderful names Carolus Eduardus.

7. See LMA: Copy of Register for 1825: 'The above is a faithful Extract from the Register of Baptisms & Burials kept by the Officiating Minister of British Protestants at the Chapel Royal Bruxelles in the Kingdom of the Netherlands for the Year of our Lord one thousand eight hundred & twenty five / as Witness my Hand Streynsham Master A.M. Officiating Minister at the Chapel Royal Bruxelles / Bruxelles January 2d 1826.' It is a partial copy of the register in Leuven: Kadoc: BE/942855/2062/144.

8. Thompson Cooper, rev. Michael Clifton, 'Sibthorp, Richard Waldo (1792–1879)', *ODNB* (2004).

9. Lincolnshire Archives: 3-SIB/1/18: Richard Waldo Sibthorp, Brussels, to his sister Mrs Hawkins, Berkeley House, Little Hampton, Arundel, Sussex.

10. Gladstone quoted in Cooper, 'Sibthorp', *ODNB*.

11. Lytton Strachey, *Eminent Victorians* (Oxford: Oxford University Press, 2003), essay on Cardinal Manning, p. 34.

12. Lambeth: FP Blomfield 65, fol. 87.

13. Jane Austen, *Jane Austen's Letters*, ed. Deirdre Le Faye, 3rd edn (Oxford: Oxford University Press, 1997), p. 10.

14. *Austen's Letters*, 8–9 November 1800, p. 57.

15. *Austen's Letters*, p. 576.

16. Lieut.-Gen. Sir Herbert Taylor, *The Taylor Papers: Being a Record of Certain Reminiscences, Letters, and Journals*, arranged by Ernest Taylor (London: Longmans, Green, and Co., 1913).

17. Taylor, *Taylor Papers*, p. 3.

18. Email from Julian Reid, Archivist, Merton College, Oxford, 21 December 2018. The buttery books are daily accounts of purchases of bread and beer from the college buttery.

19. R.G. Thorne, ed., *The History of Parliament: The House of Commons 1790–1820*, online at www.historyofparliamentonline.org.

20. Taylor, *Taylor Papers*, p. 218. There are pictures of Sir Herbert Taylor and Edward's eldest son Herbert in the National Portrait Gallery, London.

21. K.D. Reynolds, 'Conyngham [*née* Denison], Elizabeth, Marchioness Conyngham (1769–1861)', *ODNB* (2004).

22. B.M. Thomas, 'A History of Bifrons Mansion House', *Archaeologia Cantiana*, 110 (1992), pp. 313–29.

23. *The Times*, 16 February 1826, p. 3. The numerous newspapers that copied the story are available in the BNA. See also Christopher Tyerman, *A History of Harrow School 1324–1991* (Oxford: Oxford University Press, 2000), pp. 199–200.

24. Tyerman, *Harrow School*, p. 176.

25. *Manchester Courier and Lancashire General Advertiser*, 25 February 1826, p. 4.

26. *Devizes and Wiltshire Gazette*, 2 March 1826, p. 2.

27. Tyerman, *Harrow School*, pp. 157–8.

28. Tyerman, *Harrow School*, p. 152, quoting from Norman Gash, *Mr Secretary Peel: The Life of Sir Robert Peel to 1830*, p. 46.

29. N. John Hall, *Salmagundi: Byron, Allegra and the Trollope Family* (Pittsburgh: Beta Phi Mu, 1975), pp. 18–19.

30. Tyerman, *Harrow School*, p. 149. See also S.J. Skedd, 'Drury, Joseph (1751–1834)', *ODNB* (2009).

31. Douglas Hurd, *Robert Peel: A Biography* (London: Phoenix, 2008), p. 9 note.

32. Tyerman, *Harrow School*, p. 149.

33. *Harrow School Register*, pp. 9, 901. William Drury's entry contains huge errors: 'Chaplain of the English Chapel at Brussels and to the King of the Belgians 1829–78'! Not only was there no 'King of the Belgians' until Leopold in 1831, William Drury was not made honorary chaplain until 1862, three years before the king's death and many years after Evan Jenkins's death: who was the only chaplain to the king in Brussels from 1835 to 1849. And of course Drury certainly was never chaplain of '*the* English Chapel'. Other publications copy these errors. Drury made honorary chaplain: e.g. *Liverpool Daily Post*, 15 November 1862, p. 5; *Bell's Weekly Messenger*, 24 November 1862, p. 8.

34. Tyerman, *Harrow School*, p. 155: quoting sixteen-year-old Byron in a letter to his

mother from school, 1–10 May 1804?, in Leslie A. Marchand, ed., *'In My Hot Youth': Byron's Letters and Journals*, vol. I (London: John Murray, 1973), p. 49. Later in the letter Byron comments that Mark Drury's son William is 'no friend of mine', who passed on to his friends that Mark had called Byron a 'Blackguard', 'possibly with a few exaggerations' (p. 50).

35. MacCarthy, *Byron*, p. 42; see also Tyerman, *Harrow School*, p. 165. The Druries protected the often wild Byron; though Dr Drury suggested he should not come back for his final year (p. 32), Byron chose to return: he was not expelled, as he might have been under a different headmaster; on the other hand, as long as the parent was paying, there was no reason to get rid of a pupil. For Byron's nastiness after Castlereagh's suicide see Bew, *Castlereagh*, pp. 547–8.

36. Tyerman, *Harrow School*, pp. 143–4.

37. Tyerman, *Harrow School*, p. 200.

38. *Exeter Flying Post*, 4 October 1827, p. 4.

39. Angus Calder, 'Mackay, Charles (1812–1889)', *ODNB* (2011).

40. Charles Mackay, *Through the Long Day, or, Memorials of a Literary Life during Half a Century*, 2 vols (London: W.H. Allen & Co., 1887), vol. I, p. 17.

41. Mackay, *Through the Long Day*, vol. I, p. 18.

42. Mackay, *Through the Long Day*, vol. I, p. 23. 1828 as the year for Charles Lever in the Netherlands and Germany: in E.S. Tilley, 'Lever, Charles James (1806–1872)', *ODNB* (2004). In another book Charles Mackay thinks he left school at the end of 1829 or early 1830: Charles Mackay, *Forty Years' Recollections of Life, Literature, and Public Affairs from 1830 to 1870*, 2 vols (London: Chapman & Hall, 1877), vol. I, p. 35. But Charles Lever was back in Ireland in spring 1829: Edmund Downey, *Charles Lever: His Life in His Letters*, 2 vols (Edinburgh and London: William Blackwood and Sons, 1906), vol. I, pp. 52, 55. I think Mackay's memory of where he encountered Lever is probably more accurate than his memory for dates.

43. *London Courier and Evening Gazette*, 4 June 1827: 'The Classical Department under the direction of a Clergyman, a graduate of the University of Cambridge'.

44. *Le Courrier des Pays-Bas*, 10 June 1827, p. 4. Also on 13, 20 and 30 June.

45. Watson, 'John Jay's School for Boys', p. 13.

46. *Public Ledger and Daily Advertiser*, 30 January 1829, p. 2.

47. Lambeth: FP Blomfield 65.

48. Kadoc: BE/942855/2062/146. Although catalogued as 'Church of St George', that applies only to the first eleven years of Drury as a clergyman, to 1840. Thereafter he shared a church with Belgian Protestants in the Leopold Quarter.

49. CCEd: William Drury.

50. Tyerman, *Harrow School*, p. 170, referring to Bishop Charles Wordsworth, *Annals of My Early Life 1806–1846* (London: Longmans, Green, and Co, 1891), p. 21. Bishop Charles (1806–92) was a nephew of the poet William Wordsworth; he was a classicist and cricketer, and founder of the Oxford and Cambridge Boat Race. His father was Christopher Wordsworth, who was appointed Master of Trinity College, Cambridge when Evan Jenkins was a student there.

51. Lambeth: FP Blomfield 65, fol. 82: Rev. William Watson Bolton et al. to Bishop Luscombe, 29 January 1829.

52. Steven, *History of the Scottish Church*, p. 287. Rev. Steven notes that Rev. Bolton started at Bruges in 1826, and writes: 'Dr. Luscombe of Paris, who periodically visits, with great acceptance, the British Protestant Congregations in France and the Netherlands, and under whose license Mr. Bolton officiates at Bruges, has, on two different occasions, confirmed numerous young persons in this church [at Bruges].' This sounds like he approved of the bishop, or that he is being circumspect; he never mentions the controversy. The only other reference to Luscombe is on p. 331, where it is mentioned that Luscombe confirmed thirty-one people in Rotterdam in 1826 (and none since).

53. *Harrow School Register*; see Tyerman, *Harrow School*, e.g. pp. 197, 199.

54. Wordsworth, *Annals*, p. 23.

55. J.G. Alger, rev. Ellie Clewlow, 'Luscombe, Matthew Henry Thornhill (*bap.* 1775, *d.* 1846)', *ODNB* (2004).

56. See George Herring, 'Hook, Walter Farquhar (1798–1875)', *ODNB* (2004). For the quote see: John Pinnington, 'Anglican Order in Continental Europe', *Historical Magazine of the Protestant Episcopal Church*, 38:4 (December 1969), pp. 381–92, at p. 383.

57. See Pinnington, 'Anglican Order', *passim*.

58. Pinnington, 'Anglican Order', pp. 381–2.

59. Northamptonshire Record Office: Papers of the Cartwright family of Aynho, C(A) Box 15/95: Bishop Howley to Rev. Holworthy, 24 April 1826. The letter was dated wrongly (as March 1829) in The National Archives.

60. Pinnington, 'Anglican Order', pp. 390–1.

61. Anthony Trollope, *The Warden* (Oxford: Oxford University Press, 2014), p. 62.

62. Arthur Burns, 'Blomfield, Charles James (1786–1857)', *ODNB* (2008).

63. Pinnington, 'Anglican Order', p. 387.

64. [Tennyson], *Alfred Lord Tennyson*, pp. 45–8.

65. Letter from Alfred Tennyson quoted in [Tennyson], *Alfred Lord Tennyson*, p. 45.

66. Quoted in [Tennyson], *Alfred Lord Tennyson*, p. 46.

67. Photograph of the fourth Earl of Aberdeen in the National Portrait Gallery, London. The gallery has fifty portraits and cartoons of him or that include him. I refer here to the carte-de-visite of 1860.

68. *The Spectator*, 8 May 1830, quoted in Michael Levey, *Sir Thomas Lawrence (1769–1830)*, exhibition catalogue, National Portrait Gallery, London (1979–80). The portrait of the Earl of Aberdeen of 1829/30 is in the catalogue, p. 85, as is an even more Byronic portrait of him done about twenty years earlier (p. 48).

69. Muriel E. Chamberlain, 'Gordon, George Hamilton-, fourth earl of Aberdeen (1784–1860)', *ODNB* (2010).

70. T.F. Henderson, 'Cartwright, Sir Thomas (1795–1850)', *ODNB* (2004).

71. Lambeth: FP Blomfield 65, fols 83–98.

72. Lambeth: FP Blomfield 65, fol. 83.

73. Lambeth: FP 65, fols 85–6.

74. Copy in Lambeth: FP 65, fol. 97. I have expanded abbreviations.

75. Pinnington, 'Anglican Order', p. 388.

76. Lambeth: FP Blomfield 65, fol. 98. It is a draft of the letter to Evan, but undated. However, it is the next folio in the file after the letter to the Earl of Aberdeen.

77. Ray, *Thackeray: Uses*, p. 187.

78. W.M. Thackeray, *A Shabby Genteel Story and Other Writings* (London: J.M. Dent, 1993).

79. Thomas Adolphus Trollope, *What I Remember* (Cambridge: Cambridge University Press, 2010), pp. 60, 59; he was in Paris c.1842.

80. LMA: Bishop's Act Book and CCEd; *Journal de La Haye*, 1 October 1835.

81. Pinnington, 'Anglican Order', p. 391.

Chapter 11: Revolution and a Love Triangle, 1830–1831

1. White, *Belgic Revolution*, vol. I, p. 166. White was a Brussels resident at the time of the revolution.

2. White, *Belgic Revolution*, vol. I, pp. 183, 1, 299.

3. *Morning Chronicle*, 14 May 1835, p. 4. Charles White is 'Esq' on his title-page.

4. Quoted in Edward Copeland, *The Silver Fork Novel: Fashionable Fiction in the Age of Reform* (Cambridge: Cambridge University Press, 2012), pp. 226–7.

5. S. Austin Allibone, *Critical Dictionary of English Literature and British and American Authors*, 3 vols (London: Trübner & Co, 1871), vol. III, pp. 2682–3.

6. H.E.C. Stapylton, *The Eton School Lists, from 1791 to 1850*, 2nd edn (London: E.P.

Williams, 1864), p. 50; Charles White's death notice in *Gentleman's Magazine*, December 1861 and *Norfolk Chronicle*, 2 November 1861, p. 7; A Database of Victorian Fiction, 1837–1901, online; Ancestry.co.uk.

7. White, *Belgic Revolution*, vol. I, p. vii.

8. White, *Belgic Revolution*, vol. I, p. 138: the English colony in Brussels amounted to 'nearly 5,000 persons of all classes'.

9. Wyndham: Emma Lane to Margaret Wyndham, Eversley [Hampshire], August 1831.

10. White, *Belgic Revolution*, vol. I, pp. 2, 51, 63, 207.

11. Rev. W. Trollope, *Belgium since the Revolution of 1830: Comprising a Topographical and Antiquarian Description of the Country, and a Review of its Political, Commercial, Literary, Religious, and Social Relations, as Affecting its Present Condition and Future Prospects* (London: How and Parsons, 1842), p. 5.

12. White, *Belgic Revolution*, vol. I, p. 80.

13. White, *Belgic Revolution*, vol. I, pp. 81, 85.

14. *Morning Post*, 10 October 1829, p. 2, copying the notice in the *Police Gazette*.

15. *Morning Post*, 17 October 1829, p. 3.

16. White, *Belgic Revolution*, vol. I, pp. 134–5.

17. White, *Belgic Revolution*, vol. I, p. 246.

18. White, *Belgic Revolution*, vol. I, pp. 134, 135.

19. *Morning Post*, 8 July 1830, p. 3.

20. T. Sidney Cooper, RA, *My Life* (London: Richard Bentley and Son, 1891), pp. 25–6, 28–9.

21. Cooper, *My Life*, p. 46.

22. Cooper, *My Life*, p. 87.

23. On the marriage certificate Cooper signs himself as just Thomas Cooper. It was signed also by Rev. Holworthy and by Thomas Cartwright, His Majesty's Minister Plenipotentiary in the Netherlands. Charlotte died in 1842, aged thirty-one (Cooper, *My Life*, p. 191).

24. Cooper, *My Life*, p. 106.

25. *Almanach royal* 1829; *Almanach du commerce du royaume des Pays-Bas: Bruxelles et ses environs* 1830, p. 40.

26. Cooper, *My Life*, pp. 107–8.

27. See Della Clason Sperling, 'Cooper, Thomas Sidney (1803–1902)', *ODNB* (2008) for Charlotte's year of birth and for their children.

28. White, *Belgic Revolution*, vol. I, p. 173.

29. White, *Belgic Revolution*, vol. I, pp. 166–7, 173.

30. Mackay, *Forty Years' Recollections*, vol. I, p. 49.

31. Mackay, *Forty Years' Recollections*, vol. I, pp. 49–50.

32. Mackay, *Forty Years' Recollections*, vol. I, p. 53.

33. White, *Belgic Revolution*, vol. I, pp. 182–3.

34. Cooper, *My Life*, pp. 109–10.

35. White, *Belgic Revolution*, vol. I, pp. 191–2.

36. Mackay, *Forty Years' Recollections*, vol. I, p. 54.

37. White, *Belgic Revolution*, vol. I, pp. 98–102.

38. White, *Belgic Revolution*, vol. I, pp. 132–3.

39. White, *Belgic Revolution*, vol. I, p. 247. Though perhaps Prince Frederick stayed there in September.

40. White, *Belgic Revolution*, vol. I, pp. 275, 294.

41. White, *Belgic Revolution*, vol. I, pp. 306, 325

42. White, *Belgic Revolution*, vol. I, pp. 332, 339, 347–8.

43. White, *Belgic Revolution*, vol. I, p. 349.

44. White, *Belgic Revolution*, vol. I, p. 343.

45. White, *Belgic Revolution*, vol. I, p. 355.

46. *Adventures of Two Americans in the Siege of Brussels, September, 1830. By One of Them* (Edmund H. Beaumont, Printer, St. Michael's Alley, Cornhill) – it was privately printed under the auspices of their third brother. The BL catalogue erroneously has the published date as 1830, yet the pamphlet states that one of the brothers (Arthur) recovered after his injuries sustained on 23 September after five months, which takes the date of publication to not before the end of February 1831. Also, knowledge of the contenders to the Belgian throne, described in the book, was probably not known until January 1831.

47. Details about the Beaumont brothers' lives come from William H. Maehl, Jr, 'Augustus Hardin Beaumont: Anglo-American Radical (1798–1838)', *International Review of Social History* 14:2 (1969), pp. 237–50. See also the website 'Legacies of British Slave-ownership', https://www.ucl.ac.uk/lbs/person/view/20336.

48. [Beaumont], *Adventures*, p. 8.

49. [Beaumont], *Adventures*, p. 9.

50. [Beaumont], *Adventures*, pp. 12–13.

51. [Beaumont], *Adventures*, p. 16.

52. [Beaumont], *Adventures*, pp. 17, 18, 19.

53. [Beaumont], *Adventures*, p. 20.

54. Maybe quoting Beatrice in Shakespeare, *Much Ado About Nothing*, Act 1 sc. 1.

55. [Beaumont], *Adventures*, p. 22.

56. [Beaumont], *Adventures*, pp. 33, 35.

57. White, *Belgic Revolution*, vol. I, p. 363.

58. White, *Belgic Revolution*, vol. II, pp. 10, 11.

59. Mackay, *Forty Years' Recollections*, p. 57.

60. Brontë, *Villette*, p. 453.

61. Byron, *Childe Harold's Pilgrimage*, Canto III, XXIV.

62. Cooper, *My Life*, pp. 122–3.

63. Cooper, *My Life*, pp. 124–5.

64. Cooper, *My Life*, pp. 126, 127, 128.

65. Cooper, *My Life*, p. 130.

66. Cooper, *My Life*, p. 131.

67. Clarke Papers: Eliza Jenkins to William Branwhite Clarke, Brussels, 1 July 1831.

68. White, *Belgic Revolution*, vol. II, p. 76.

69. White, *Belgic Revolution*, vol. II, pp. 155–7.

70. White, *Belgic Revolution*, vol. II, pp. 167, 168.

71. Baron Hardenbroek, Prince Leopold's Dutch equerry, quoted in Joanna Richardson, *My Dearest Uncle: A Life of Leopold: First King of the Belgians* (London: Jonathan Cape, 1961), p. 37.

72. Richardson, *My Dearest Uncle*, pp. 19–20; Théodore Juste, *Memoirs of Leopold I King of the Belgians*, trans. Robert Black, 2 vols (London, 1868), vol. I, p. 78.

73. Richardson, *My Dearest Uncle*, p. 28.

74. Richardson, *My Dearest Uncle*, pp. 44–5.

75. Richardson, *My Dearest Uncle*, p. 50.

76. Richardson, *My Dearest Uncle*, p. 55.

77. Richardson, *My Dearest Uncle*, pp. 60, 57.

78. Brontë, *Villette*, p. 213.

79. Brontë, *Villette*, pp. 214–15. Lucy/Charlotte were in good seats to be so close to the royal family: I think her specific mention of the British Embassy group means that she went to the concert with the Jenkinses.

80. Queen Victoria's Journals: 16 September 1835; *Letters of Queen Victoria*, 1.14, quoted in Janet L. Polasky, 'Leopold I', *ODNB* (2004).

81. Princess Victoria to the King of the Belgians, 21 November 1836, in *The Letters of Queen Victoria*, ed. A.C. Benson and Lord Esher, 3 vols (London: John Murray, 1908), vol. I: *1837–1843*. Project Gutenberg Ebook, updated 2009, p. 54.

82. Richardson, *My Dearest Uncle*, p. 81.

83. Richardson, *My Dearest Uncle*, p. 86.

84. Leopold's languages and novel-reading in Juste, *Memoirs of Leopold I*, vol. I, p. 30.

85. Richardson, *My Dearest Uncle*, pp. 85, 94–5.

86. Juste, *Memoirs of Leopold I*, vol. I, pp. 118–19.

87. Richardson, *My Dearest Uncle*, p. 99.

88. White, *Belgic Revolution*, vol. II, pp. 267–8.

89. White, *Belgic Revolution*, vol. I, p. 273.

90. Juste, *Memoirs of Leopold I*, vol. I, p. 155.

91. White, *Belgic Revolution*, vol. II, p. 273.

92. White, *Belgic Revolution*, vol. II, p. 275.

93. White, *Belgic Revolution*, vol. II, p. 283.

94. White, *Belgic Revolution*, vol. II, pp. 284, 287.

95. Elena Grainger, *The Remarkable Reverend Clarke: The Life and Times of the Father of Australian Geology* (Oxford: Oxford University Press, 1982).

96. Richard Holmes, *This Long Pursuit: Reflections of a Romantic Biographer* (London: William Collins, 2016), p. 16.

97. Grainger, *Reverend Clarke*, pp. 26, 27.

98. Ann Moyal, 'Clarke, William Branwhite (1798–1878)', *ODNB* (2010). She omits entirely his romantic travails in Brussels.

99. Wyndham: Mary Anne Wyndham to George Wyndham, 10 November 1830; Laetitia Wyndham to Margaret Wyndham, 19 November 1830; Emma Lane to Margaret Wyndham, August 1831.

100. Grainger, *Reverend Clarke*, p. 42.

101. Clarke Papers: John Livingston Jay to William Branwhite Clarke, 24 December 1830.

102. Wyndham: John Livingston Jay to Margaret Wyndham, 8 October 1840.

103. Austen, *Emma*, p. 135.

104. Grainger, *Reverend Clarke*, pp. 42–3.

105. Clarke Papers: Eliza Jenkins to William Branwhite Clarke, 1 July 1831.

106. Nussey in Smith, ed., *Letters* I, Appendix III, p. 603.

107. Clarke Papers: Evan Jenkins to William Branwhite Clarke, 15 July 1831.

108. White, *Belgic Revolution*, vol. II, p. 284 fn.

109. The Amigo prison: [Mauvy], *Stranger's Guide*, states that the Amigo was 'a place of confinement for not more than twenty-four hours; this is the usual place of detention for night disturbances and general misdemeanours' (p. 62).

110. White, *Belgic Revolution*, vol. II, pp. 288–9.

111. White, *Belgic Revolution*, vol. II, p. 289.

112. Grainger, *Reverend Clarke*, p. 45.

113. Trollope, *Doctor Thorne*, p. 142.

114. Clarke Papers: Eliza Jenkins to William Branwhite Clarke, 26 July 1831.

115. Holmes, *Footsteps*, p. 144.

116. Clarke Papers: Evan Jenkins to William Branwhite Clarke, 1 August 1831.

117. Mrs Wemyss Dalrymple, *The Economist's New Brussels Guide* (Brussels, 1839), p. 6.

118. 'Dover, July 31', *Morning Post*, 2 August 1831, p. 3.

119. Shakespeare, *Twelfth Night*, Act 2 sc. 3. It is Sir Toby's riposte to the puritanical steward Malvolio: 'Dost thou think because thou art virtuous there shall be no more cakes and ale?' And Feste/the Clown adds: 'and ginger shall be hot I'th'mouth, too'.

120. Anthony Trollope, *Framley Parsonage* (Oxford: Oxford University Press, 2014), p. 127.

121. White, *Belgic Revolution*, vol. II, p. 310.

122. White, *Belgic Revolution*, vol. II, p. 301.

123. White, *Belgic Revolution*, vol. II, p. 303.

124. White, *Belgic Revolution*, vol. II, p. 309.

125. White, *Belgic Revolution*, vol. II, p. 316.

126. White, *Belgic Revolution*, vol. II, pp. 318–19.

127. Lord William Russell was 'shy, witty, and naturally lazy – his career largely the result of aristocratic jobbery': E.M. Lloyd and Thomas Seccombe, rev. James Falkner, 'Russell, Lord George William (1790–1846)', *ODNB* (2008). But Edward Taylor thought him and 'Mr. Fox' 'very efficient': letter to Sir Herbert Taylor, 23 September 1831, from Brussels, in Taylor, *Taylor Papers*, p. 335. Henry Edward Fox, Adair's attaché, was in his late twenties. He had spent several years wandering around Italy and knew Byron's mistress Teresa Guicciole intimately; Adair was a close family friend: see Jones, *British Diplomatic Service*, pp. 22–3.

128. White, *Belgic Revolution*, vol. II, pp. 319–20.

129. Taylor, *Taylor Papers*, p. 335.

130. Taylor, *Taylor Papers*, p. 335.

131. Grainger, *Reverend Clarke*, p. 45, identifies the sister as Sarah Trollope (he had two other sisters). William Trollope was then teaching at Christ's Hospital, his old school: see ACAD.

132. Clarke Papers: William Trollope to John Barker, Christ's Hospital, 7 September 1831.

133. Clarke Papers: John Barker to William Trollope, 27 Cadogan Place, 11 September 1831.

134. Clarke Papers: William Clarke to John Barker, 14 September 1831, draft.

135. Clarke Papers: William Clarke to Mr Miller (a trustee), 15 September 1831, draft.

136. Clarke Papers: Evan Jenkins to William Branwhite Clarke, 13 September 1831.

137. Austen, *Pride and Prejudice*, p. 151: Darcy's letter to Elizabeth: 'I shall not scruple

to assert, that the serenity of your sister's countenance and air was such, as might have given the most acute observer, a conviction that, however amiable her temper, her heart was not likely to be easily touched.'

138. Charles Lever, *Harry Lorrequer* (London: Chapman and Hall, 1857), p. 183.

139. Grainger, *Reverend Clarke*, pp. 207–8, 214.

140. Moyal, 'Clarke', *ODNB*.

Chapter 12: Chaplain to the King

1. William Gladstone, *The Gladstone Diaries, 1825–1832*, ed. M.R.D. Foot (Oxford: Clarendon Press, 1968), p. 413. Foot's note 3 has the same errors about Drury that I corrected in my chapter 10, note 33.

2. Braekman, *Le protestantisme à Bruxelles*, p. 50. There are many errors in his book about the Anglicans, which I have corrected in this book.

3. *Almanach administratif et industriel de Bruxelles* 1834, p. LIII (my translation), p. 114.

4. William Henry Holworthy: CCED; ACAD. Steven, *History of the Scottish Church*, p. 311: 'At present [1832], the Rev. William H. Holworthy, M.A., chaplain to the British embassy at the Hague, preaches regularly in the old Presbyterian church.'

5. Knight, *Nineteenth-Century Church*, e.g. pp. 35–6, 80–2.

6. H.C.G. Matthew, 'Gladstone, William Ewart (1809–1898)', *ODNB* (2011).

7. The King of the Belgians to the Princess Victoria, Laeken, 31 August 1832, in *Letters of Queen Victoria*, vol. I, pp. 34–5.

8. VCH: *A History of the County of Middlesex*, vol. 7: *Acton, Chiswick, Ealing and Brentford, West Twyford, Willesden*: Ealing and Brentford: Education (London, 1982; online).

9. Quoted in Richardson, *My Dearest Uncle*, pp. 125, 128, 126–7, 127.

10. 'King and Queen of Belgium', *Morning Post*, 25 August 1832, 'Extract of a private letter from Brussels, dated evening of the 19th instant', p. 2.

11. *Morning Post*, 25 August 1832, p. 2.

12. *Bell's New Weekly Messenger*, 26 August 1832, p. 7.

13. Quoted in Richardson, *My Dearest Uncle*, p. 129.

14. Quoted in Richardson, *My Dearest Uncle*, p. 129.

15. Braekman, *Le protestantisme à Bruxelles*, p. 51 (my translation).

16. Taylor, *Taylor Papers*, pp. 335–6 (written September 1831).

17. Leslie Mitchell, 'Fox, Charles James (1749–1806)', *ODNB* (2007); W.P. Courtney, rev. H.C.G. Matthew, 'Adair, Sir Robert (1763–1855)', *ODNB* (2008). The details

of Adair's career are from the latter article.

18. Grattan, *Beaten Paths*, vol. II, p. 237.

19. *Morning Post*, 9 April 1834, p. 2.

20. Juste, *Memoirs of Leopold I*, vol. II, p. 105.

21. Edward Taylor to Sir Herbert Taylor, Friday 11 April 1834, in Taylor, *Taylor Papers*, pp. 362–3.

22. Edward Taylor to Lady Taylor, 15 April 1834, in Taylor, *Taylor Papers*, pp. 363–4.

23. e.g. *London Evening Standard*, 9 April 1834, p. 2.

24. 'ZETA', *Morning Post*, 14 April 1834, p. 3.

25. Quoted in Juste, *Memoirs of Leopold I*, vol. II, p. 104.

26. e.g. *Globe*, 25 March 1834, p. 4.

27. Quoted in Juste, *Memoirs of Leopold I*, vol. II, p. 104.

28. *London Evening Standard*, 20 May 1834, p. 2.

29. Quoted in Juste, *Memoirs of Leopold I*, vol. II, p. 104.

30. Henry James, *The Aspern Papers and Other Tales*, ed. Michael Gorra (London: Penguin Books, 2014), 'Preface', p. 323.

31. Pamela Neville-Sington, 'Trollope [*née* Milton], Frances [Fanny] (1779–1863)', *ODNB* (2008).

32. Frances Milton Trollope, *Domestic Manners of the Americans* (London: Whittaker, Treacher, & Co., 1832), vol. II, pp. 11, 30.

33. Mrs Trollope, *Belgium and Western Germany in 1833* (Paris: Baudry's European Library, 1834).

34. Trollope, *Belgium*, vol. I, pp. 61, 66, 64.

35. James, *Aspern Papers*, 'Preface', p. 323: 'We are divided of course between liking to feel the past strange and liking to feel it familiar; the difficulty is, for intensity, to catch it at the moment when the scales of the balance hang with the right evenness.'

36. Clarke Papers: Evan Jenkins to William Branwhite Clarke, 1 August 1831.

37. Trollope, *Autobiography*, pp. 25–6.

38. V.P. Stafford, 'Claire Clairmont, Mary Jane's Daughter', sites.google.com/site/maryjanesdaughter/home, 25 April 2019, cited in Marion Kingston Stocking, 'Clairmont, Clara Mary Jane [Claire] (1798–1879)', *ODNB* (2014). Stocking comments that Claire Clairmont appears as the character of Stella in Thomas Love Peacock's *Nightmare Abbey* of 1818, but Stella/Celinda seems more likely based on the intellectually fierce Mary Godwin, or at least a hybrid of the two. V.P. Stafford discovered Claire Clairmont's father while researching her family tree in Australia in 2010.

39. Holmes, *Shelley*, p. 242.

40. Holmes, *Shelley*, p. 316.

41. Quoted in Holmes, *Shelley*, p. 325.
42. Quoted in Hall, *Salmagundi*, p. 13.
43. Quoted in Hall, *Salmagundi*, p. 16.
44. Quoted in Hall, *Salmagundi*, p. 21.
45. Hall, *Salmagundi*, pp. 69–70.
46. Hall, *Salmagundi*, pp. 71–2.
47. Hall, *Salmagundi*, p. 73.
48. Hall, *Salmagundi*, p. 75.
49. Quoted in Hall, *Salmagundi*, pp. 22–3.
50. James, *Aspern Papers*, 'Appendix: From the Notebooks' [1887], pp. 317–18.
51. Quoted in James, *Aspern Papers*, 'Preface', pp. 321, 320, 322.
52. Trollope, *Autobiography*, pp. 25–6.
53. Quoted in Trollope, *Autobiography*, 'Introduction', p. vii.
54. *Morning Chronicle*, 16 February 1835, p. 2.
55. Austen, *Emma*, p. 131.
56. Barnes, *Flaubert's Parrot*, p. 108.
57. [Frederick Marryat], 'Diary on the Continent', in *Olla Podrida*, 3 vols (London: Longman, Orme, Brown, Green, & Longmans, 1840), vol. I, p. 11.
58. [Marryat], *Olla Podrida*, vol. I, pp. 50–1, 53, 54–5, 51.
59. H.R. Boudin, 'Le Roi Léopold 1er et less communautés protestantes en Belgique', *Bulletin de la Société d'Histoire du Protestantisme Belge*, ser. 8, no. 9 (1981), p. 252.
60. *Journal de La Haye*, 5 October 1835.
61. Dalrymple, *Brussels Guide*, p. 38.
62. Edward Taylor to Sir Herbert Taylor, Brussels, 23 September 1831, in Taylor, *Taylor Papers*, p. 335.
63. C.A. Harris, rev. Muriel E. Chamberlain, 'Seymour, Sir George Hamilton (1797–1880)', *ODNB* (2008).
64. Bew, *Castlereagh*, p. 554.
65. Jones, *British Diplomatic Service*, pp. 97–8.
66. Norfolk Record Office: BUL 1/15/1-54 561 x 9: copy letter to Rev. E. Jenkins 1836 from Sir George Hamilton Seymour GCG His Britannic Majesty's Envoy Extraordinary and Minister Plenipotentiary in Belgium.
67. Wyndham: Charlotte Wyndham to Margaret Wyndham, 24 November 1830. For John Galt and George Wyndham's trip to Canada, see Marcia Watson, 'Off to Canada in 1826', *Dalwood House Newsletter*, no. 95 (December 2016). George Wyndham decided Canada was too cold for him, and emigrated to Australia in 1827 with his new wife Margaret Jay.

68. Ernst II, *Memoirs of Ernest II, Duke of Saxe-Coburg-Gotha*, translated, 4 vols (London: Remington & Co., 1888), vol. I, p. 74.

69. Muriel E. Chamberlain, 'Bulwer, (William) Henry Lytton Earle, Baron Dalling and Bulwer [*formerly* Sir Henry Bulwer] (1801–72)', *ODNB* (2008).

70. Princess Victoria to the King of the Belgians, 7 June 1836, in *Letters of Queen Victoria*, vol. I, p. 49.

71. The King of the Belgians to the Princess Victoria, Laeken, 11 November 1836, in *Letters of Queen Victoria*, vol. I, p. 52.

72. *Morning Advertiser*, 8 June 1838, pp. 3–4, cited in Marcia Watson, 'What Happened to John Jay's School?', *Dalwood House Newsletter*, no. 100 (March 2018).

73. 'A vendre, par expropriation', *L'Indépendance Belge*, 30 October 1836 (my translations).

74. Advertisement for Drury taking private pupils: *The Times*, 5 September 1837; mention of Thomas Murray-Prior, in Watson, 'What Happened to John Jay's School?' See also Abraham John Valpy's obituary in *The Gentleman's Magazine*, vols 197–8 (February 1855), pp. 204–5, which is copied in W.P. Courtney, rev. Richard Jenkyns, 'Valpy, Abraham John (*bap.* 1786, *d.* 1854)', *ODNB* (2015).

75. Trollope, *Autobiography*, p. 98.

76. Lionel Stevenson, *Dr. Quicksilver: The Life of Charles Lever* (London: Chapman & Hall, 1939), pp. 17–19.

77. Lever, *Harry Lorrequer*, pp. 177–8.

78. Lever, *Harry Lorrequer*, pp. 206, 280.

79. James H. Murphy, *Irish Novelists and the Victorian Age* (Oxford: Oxford University Press, 2011), ch. 4, 'Ruin through Rollicking: Poor Charles Lever', at pp. 76–9.

80. See Stevenson, *Dr. Quicksilver*, e.g. pp. 35–6.

81. Quoted in Stevenson, *Dr. Quicksilver*, p. 57.

82. Charles Lever to Alexander Spencer, Brussels, 7 November 1837, in Downey, *Charles Lever*, vol. I, p. 96.

83. Lever to Spencer, Brussels, November 1837, in Downey, *Charles Lever*, vol. I, p. 98.

84. Lever to Spencer, Brussels, 29 December 1837, in Downey, *Charles Lever*, vol. I, p. 100.

85. Lever to Spencer, Brussels, 28 December 1840, in Downey, *Charles Lever*, vol. I, pp. 141–2. *Charles O'Malley: The Irish Dragoon* began serialization in 1840 in the *Dublin University Magazine* and was not published in book form until 1841, so the king seems to have been reading the magazine.

86. Lever to Spencer, Brussels, December 1838, in Downey, *Charles Lever*, vol. I, p. 108; Lever to Spencer, Brussels, December 1837, in Downey, *Charles Lever*, vol. I, p. 101.

87. Lever to James M'Glashan, 6 August 1839, in Downey, *Charles Lever*, vol. I, pp. 124–5.

88. Trollope, *Autobiography*, p. 157.

89. See Watson, 'John Jay's School for Boys', pp. 13–14.

90. http://www.remery.nl/sm-remery/wijnbeek/Utrech/hwut-01a.html. Translated in Watson, 'John Jay's School for Boys', p. 14, with a few changes by myself – e.g. 'rebellion' for *opstand*, which Marcia translated as 'uprising'. I think the Dutch would be less neutral about the revolution.

91. Philip, 'Lixmount House and its People', p. 20.

92. Boudin, 'Le Roi Léopold 1er et less communautés protestantes', p. 258 (my translation), citing F. Clément, *Histoire de la Franc-Maçonnerie belge au XIXe siècle* (Brussels, 1949), p. 114, note. '1949' may be an error for 1940, since that is the edition I found in Brussels. Part of the note on p. 114 reads: 'La protection royale prend à ce moment une forme plus active, se manifestant par l'initiation du général Prisse, aide de camp du Roi, et du pasteur Jenkins, chapelain de Sa Majesté.'

93. *L'Ami de la religion et du roi: journal ecclésiastique, politique et littéraire*, 7 November 1839 (Paris), pp. 266–7. A later newspaper article says that Evan's son Edward was a 'lowton', the son of a Freemason who has not yet been initiated, and that he was initiated in January 1863: *Journal de Bruxelles: politique, littérature et commerce*, 16 May 1882, p. 2. In the Grand Lodge of England a 'lowton' is known as a 'Lewis'.

94. Brontë, *Villette*, p. 198.

95. In the registration of deaths the little girl is 'Maria Joanna Wilhelmina Jenkins'.

96. 'The Old Cemetery at Ostend', *Notes and Queries* (Oxford: Oxford University Press, 1891), p. 221.

97. See Marcia Watson, 'Making a Difference', *Western Ancestor* (Australia), June 2018, pp. 55–7.

98. *Huddersfield Daily Examiner*, 22 December 1915, p. 4, which erroneously calls her 'Mrs. Albinia Jackson [her middle name] [… who] sometimes wrote under the name of Mrs. "Chave"'. Obituaries in French: *Le Gaulois: littéraire et politique*, 23 December 1915, p. 3; *Le Figaro: journal non politique*, 22 December 1915, p. 4.

99. William Makepeace Thackeray, *The Letters and Private Papers*, ed. Gordon N. Ray, 4 vols (Cambridge, MA: Harvard University Press, 1946), vol. I, pp. 429 (11 March 1840) and 432 (20 March 1840).

100. Dalrymple, *Brussels Guide*, pp. 45, 38.

101. *Morning Post*, 2 August 1839, p. 3.

102. Richard Brent, 'Whately, Richard (1787–1863)', *ODNB* (2014).

103. *Morning Post*, 5 July 1839, p. 1.

104. *British Advertiser* (Pratt's English Library, Place Royale), 22 January 1840, p. 2.

105. 'A Lady', *Anecdotes, personal traits, and characteristic sketches of Victoria the first, brought down to the period of her majesty's marriage with his royal highness Prince Albert of Saxe-Gotha* (London: William Bennett etc., 1840), p. 733. She means Sunday 2 February. Mention of Prince Albert at Rev. Jenkins's service is also in the *London Evening Standard*, 8 February 1840, p. 2 and other newspapers, so presumably the 'Lady' copied the newspaper report.

106. Wyndham: John Livingston Jay to Margaret Wyndham, Greenwich Hospital, 8 October 1840.

107. Wyndham: Samuel Jay to Margaret Wyndham, Brighton, 25 October 1865.

108. *The Times*, 29 June 1840, p. 5; *West Kent Guardian*, 4 July 1840, p. 4; see also Queen Victoria's Journals: 27 June 1840.

109. *Bell's Weekly Messenger*, 29 November 1841, p. 5.

110. CB to Emily J. Brontë, Upperwood House, Rawdon, ?7 November 1841, and to Ellen Nussey, [?9 December 1841], *Letters* I, pp. 273 and 274.

Chapter 13: The Brontës Come to Brussels, 1842: The Trial of Common Sense

1. Altick, *Lives and Letters*, p. 54.

2. Altick, *Art of Literary Research*, p. 23.

3. Gérin, *Charlotte Brontë*, p. 360; Chadwick, *Footsteps*, p. 197.

4. Gaskell, *Life*, p. 269; CB to Mary Taylor, 4 September 1848, *Letters* II, p. 112; Altick, *Art of Literary Research*, pp. 23–4. See also Joan Stevens, ed., *Mary Taylor: Friend of Charlotte Brontë: Letters from New Zealand and Elsewhere* (Auckland and Oxford: Auckland University Press, Oxford University Press, 1972), Appendix E.

5. Gérin, *Charlotte Brontë*, p. 185. Chadwick also says 'diligence': *Footsteps*, p. 223.

6. Barker, *The Brontës*, p. 444.

7. Barker, *The Brontës*, p. 1062 n. 107.

8. CB to Ellen Nussey, 30 January [1843], *Letters* I, p. 308.

9. A. Ferrier de Tourettes, *Handbook for Travellers on the Belgian Rail-Road* (Brussels: Published by the Belgian Company of Booksellers, Hauman and Co., 1840), [appendix] p. 14. Also p. 114 for steamships between London and Ostend.

10. Dalrymple, *Brussels Guide*, p. 6. Also p. 5 for steamships from London to Ostend.

11. Ferrier de Tourettes, *Handbook*, p. 160.

12. 'A Lady', *Anecdotes*, p. 733; *The Times*, 7 February 1840, p. 6. The *British Advertiser*, 22 January 1840, has the times of the first-class train from Brussels to Ostend: 8 a.m. and quarter past 3.

13. Ferrier de Tourettes, *Handbook*, p. 161.

14. First station in Brussels: see Archives de la Ville de Bruxelles: https://archiviris.be/2020/02/23/la-premiere-gare-belge-het-eerste-belgische-station/ and www.garesbelges.be/brux/bruxelles_allee_verte.htm.

15. *London Evening Standard*, 30 April 1840, p. 1.

16. *West Kent Guardian*, 5 February 1842, p. 1.

17. Quoted in Stevens, ed., *Mary Taylor*, p. 165.

18. Brontë, *Professor*, p. 191 for ten years in Brussels after his marriage to Frances (he arrives in February of one year and marries her the following January); p. 40 for 'not the days of trains'. William Crimsworth mentions the statue of General Belliard (d. 1832), above the rue d'Isabelle, which was not erected until 1836, a year after the first railway line from Brussels had opened, though before one could get by train from Ostend to Brussels via Malines (p. 43). Charlotte was not always careful with dates, and Hunsden's letter arriving in an 'envelope' (p. 142) – not invented until 1837 – can be excused as I am being pernickety, and she might echo her pupils and comment 'Tant pis!' (CB in 'Preface: A Word to the "Quarterly"', *Letters* II, p. 242).

19. Brontë, *Villette*, p. 45. See also the final sentence of the book, which also confirms that the story is set in the distant past.

20. W.M. Thackeray, *The Adventures of Philip* [and] *A Shabby Genteel Story* (London: Smith, Elder, & Co., 1900), p. 458.

21. Brontë, *Professor*, p. 40.

22. Francis Coghlan, *Hand-book for European Tourists*, 2nd edn (London: H. Hughes, 1847), p. xxii.

23. Gérin, *Charlotte Brontë*, p. 187.

24. Chadwick, *Footsteps*, p. 223.

25. Dalrymple, *Brussels Guide*, pp. 124–8.

26. Barker, *The Brontës*, p. 445.

27. Barker, *The Brontës*, p. 430: 'Mr Jenkins finally found a school of which he approved in Brussels.'

28. Harman, *Charlotte Brontë*, pp. 138, 139.

29. Emily Brontë's diary paper of 30 July 1845, in *Letters* I, p. 283 n. 2.

30. Gérin, *Charlotte Brontë*, pp. 185, 186.

31. John Lock and Canon W.T. Dixon, *A Man of Sorrow: The Life, Letters and Times of the Rev. Patrick Brontë 1777–1861* (London: Ian Hodgkins & Co., 1979), p. 302.

32. An Old Resident, *A Week in Brussels: The Stranger's Guide to the Capital of Belgium*, 3rd edn (London: Edwards and Hughes, 1846), p. 23. He also mentions that Rev. Jenkins's service was at 2.30 p.m. (p. 24).

33. Old Resident, *A Week in Brussels*, p. 13. William Trollope in 1842, however, says that the 'speed at which the trains travel averages 25 miles per hour; but it has been sometimes accelerated to the rate of 36 miles per hour' (*Belgium since the Revolution*, p. 215).

34. Altick, *Lives and Letters*, pp. 304–5.

35. Ellen Nussey as a 'calm, well-bred Yorkshire girl': CB to W.S. Williams, 3 January 1850, *Letters* II, p. 323.

36. E.g. Smith, ed., *Letters* I, pp. 95–6; see also Stevens, ed., *Mary Taylor*; Brontë, *Shirley*, p. 113.

37. CB to Ellen Nussey, 7 August 1841, *Letters* I, p. 266.

38. CB to Elizabeth Branwell, 29 September 1841, *Letters* I, pp. 268–9.

39. CB to Emily J. Brontë, ?7 November 1841, *Letters* I, p. 273.

40. CB to Emily, ?7 November 1841, *Letters* I, p. 273.

41. Rev. G.E. Biber, ed., *The English Church on the Continent: or, an Account of the Foreign Settlements of the English Church* (London: Francis & John Rivington, 1845), p. 16.

42. CB to Ellen Nussey, ?9 December 1841, *Letters* I, p. 274.

43. CB to Ellen Nussey, [?17 December 1841], *Letters* I, p. 275, and p. 276 n. 2.

44. Gaskell, *Life*, p. 161.

45. CB to Ellen Nussey, [20 January 1842], *Letters* I, p. 278.

46. Gaskell, *Life*, p. 161.

47. Gaskell, *Life*, p. 162.

48. Clarke Papers: Evan Jenkins to William Clarke, 13 September 1831.

49. Trollope, *Belgium since the Revolution*, p. 72.

50. Rev. G.E. Biber, ed., *The English Church on the Continent: or, an Account of the Foreign Settlements of the English Church*, 2nd edn (London: Francis & John Rivington, 1846), p. 46.

51. Trollope, *Belgium since the Revolution*, p. 73. Shirley's charitable fund in *Shirley* may have nothing to do with Evan Jenkins's, but Charlotte Brontë was no doubt aware of it.

52. Old Resident, *A Week in Brussels*, p. 68.

53. Trollope, *Belgium since the Revolution*, p. 264. Marriage performed by William Drury on 21 August 1842, and Evan's title at the marriage of Hon. the Francis George Molyneux with the Lady Georgiana-Jemima Ashburnham on 30 March 1842 in 'the Hotel of Her Britannic Majesty's Envoy Extraordinary and Minister

Plenipotentiary at the Court of Brussels': in UK, Foreign and Overseas Registers of British Subjects, 1628–1969: Belgium.

54. Kadoc: BE/942855/2062/146 1 (Baptisms); Drury's change of title can also be seen in his Burials register on 27 May 1840.

55. Biber, ed., *English Church*, p. 10.

56. Biber, ed., *English Church*, 2nd edn, p. 46.

57. Trollope, *Belgium since the Revolution*, p. 318.

58. See http://anglicanhistory.org/aus/cci/.

59. Wyndham: Janet Jay to Margaret Wyndham, 15 February 1842; *The Times*, 20 January 1842, p. 7.

60. Wyndham: John Livingston Jay to Margaret Wyndham, Greenwich Hospital, 8 October 1840.

61. The King of the Belgians to the Princess Victoria, 13 May 1836, in *Letters of Queen Victoria*, vol. I, p. 47.

62. Queen Victoria's Journals: see 21, 26, 27 February 1842.

63. Austen, *Mansfield Park*, pp. 435–6.

64. Trollope, *Framley Parsonage*, pp. 162–3.

65. Constantin Heger to Revd P. Brontë, 5 November 1842, *Letters* I, p. 300 (translation); Brontë, *Villette*, p. 212.

66. For a short biography of Joan Stevens, see Stuart Johnston, 'Stevens, Joan', *Dictionary of New Zealand Biography* (2000): https://teara.govt.nz/en/biographies/5s44/stevens-joan. It is not surprising to learn from Richard Altick that she was the one who pricked the 'snowstorm in July' story: Altick, *Art of Literary Research*, pp. 23–4.

67. Stevens, ed., *Mary Taylor*, p. v.

68. Stevens, ed., *Mary Taylor*, Appendix D, pp. 172–4.

69. Gérin, *Charlotte Brontë*, p. 203.

70. Stevens, ed., *Mary Taylor*, Appendix D, p. 173. The painting of the school is Stevens's Plate 6, opposite p. 144.

71. Mary and Martha Taylor and CB to Ellen Nussey, March–April 1842, *Letters* I, pp. 280–2.

72. Thackeray, *Vanity Fair*, p. 4.

73. Stevens, ed., *Mary Taylor*, p. 52.

74. Ainslee T. Embree, 'Boughton, Sir Charles William Rouse- [...] (1747–1821)', *ODNB* (2008).

75. 'A Shropshire Pig', MERL acc. no. 64/100; Museum of English Rural Life, University of Reading.

76. Bedfordshire Archives: OR2298-5b, Theresa Rouse-Boughton to Sir William Edward Rouse-Boughton, 13 June 1853.

77. Quoted in Ronald G. Engle and Daniel J. Watermeier, 'Phelps and His German Critics', *Educational Theatre Journal*, 24:3 (1972), p. 243.

78. *Provinciale Noordbrabantsche en 's Hertogenbossche courant*, 21 July 1877 (my translation). Also *Algemeen Handelsblad*, 19 August 1880.

79. J.P. Wearing, 'Phelps, Samuel (1804–1878)', *ODNB* (2015).

80. *Kentish Gazette*, 23 March 1813, p. 3.

81. *Public Ledger & Daily Advertiser*, 12 September 1814, p. 2. Robert M. Phelps as auctioneer: *Royal Cornwall Gazette*, 24 December 1814, p. 1.

82. W. May Phelps and John Forbes-Robertson, *The Life and Life-Work of Samuel Phelps* (London: Sampson Low, Marston, Searle, & Rivington, 1886), p. 1.

83. Richard Foulkes, 'Macready, William Charles (1793–1873)', *ODNB* (2008).

84. Phelps and Forbes-Robertson, *Life-Work of Samuel Phelps*, pp. 32–3.

85. *Western Times*, 15 March 1828, p. 4; *Globe*, 15 August 1837, p. 1.

86. Phelps and Forbes-Robertson, *Life-Work of Samuel Phelps*, p. 34.

87. John Coleman, assisted by Edward Coleman, *Memoirs of Samuel Phelps* (London: Remington & Co Publishers, 1886), pp. 30–1.

88. Queen Victoria's Journals: 19 November 1847, 6 February 1852, 19 January 1858.

89. Phelps and Forbes-Robertson, *Life-Work of Samuel Phelps*, pp. 56–7; review in *The Times*, 25 October 1842, p. 4. The Senior Curator of Paintings in the Royal Collection, Vanessa Remington, told me that she had not come across a reference to this work. 'There is no watercolour or portrait miniature of Phelps by Ross, or indeed by any other artist, in the Royal Collection at present.' Email 1 August 2019.

90. ACAD: Robert Phelps. Phelps's father is given there erroneously as Robert Millar, which is a corruption of his middle name.

91. 'Institution Supérieure: Chateau de Koekelberg', *Provinciale Noordbrabantsche en 's Hertogenbossche courant*, 21 July 1877: '(20 minutes de distance de Bruxelles) [...] Le Château de Koekelberg est un des points de vue les plus ravissants des environs de Bruxelles'; see also *Algemeen Handelsblad*, 19 August 1880: 'Institut Supérieur, pour un nombre limité de Demoiselles, fondée en 1815, dirigée par Mde. M. Bonnange [...] successeur de Mde. Vve Goussaert, née Phelps [...] situé au milieu d'un immense jardin, sur le point culminant du plateau de Koekelberg'.

92. Belgian Archives: Gegevens van de akte nr. 17, civil marriage certificate.

93. Apparently there are over forty copies of the equestrian statue of San Martín worldwide; the original was erected in Buenos Aires in 1862.

94. I largely follow John Lynch, *San Martín: Argentine Soldier, American Hero* (New Haven and London: Yale University Press, 2009).

95. Lynch, *San Martín*, p. 180.

96. Francisco de Goya, *The 3rd of May 1808 in Madrid* (1814), at Museo Nacional del Prado, Madrid.

97. Lynch, *San Martín*, p. 23.

98. Brontë, *Shirley*, p. 481.

99. John Miller, *Memoirs of General Miller, in the Service of the Republic of Peru*, 2nd edn, 2 vols (London: Printed for Longman, Rees, Orme, Brown, and Green, 1829), vol. I, p. 426. This is partly quoted, without a source, in Lynch, *San Martín*, p. 209.

100. Lynch, *San Martín*, p. 220.

101. Lynch, *San Martín*, pp. 206, 174.

102. Lynch, *San Martín*, p. 180.

103. Captain Basil Hall in June 1821, quoted in Lynch, *San Martín*, p. 151.

104. François-Joseph Navez, *José de San Martín*, 1828, Museo Histórico Nacional, Buenos Aires: Plate 3 in Lynch, *San Martín*.

105. Lynch, *San Martín*, p. 158.

106. Harman, *Charlotte Brontë*, pp. 144–5, source on p. 389.

107. Quoted in Eric Ruijssenaars, *The Pensionnat Revisited: More Light Shed on the Brussels of the Brontës* (printed by NUANCE Zaandam, privately published, 2003), pp. 46–7. I have not found this review in the *Bradford Observer* of 1914 since the newspaper changed its name in 1901 (see BNA); but there are several reviews in other newspapers. I have corrected the punctuation of the letter to follow that in the published book of letters.

108. Barker, *The Brontës*, p. 493 for quote about Heger from Westwood's letter; note 26 on p. 1068.

109. [Thomas Westwood]; Preface by Florence, Lady Alwyne Compton, *A Literary Friendship: Letters to Lady Alwyne Compton 1869–1881 from Thomas Westwood* (London: John Murray, 1914).

110. Kate Flint, 'Soulsby, Lucy Helen Muriel (1856–1927)', *ODNB* (2004). Kate Flint doesn't mention Soulsby's connection with the Thomas Westwood letters, which Soulsby helped prepare for publication, but the link between the headmistress and Lady Alwyne Compton can be found in Lady Layard's Journal (she was the wife and cousin of the archaeologist Sir Austen Henry Layard) in the BL, online thanks to Baylor University, Texas at www.browningguide.org/lady-layards-journal. E.g. Miss Soulsby as head of the High School at Oxford (journal entry written in Lady Layard's Venetian palazzo on 4 September 1896)

and Miss Soulsby as a friend of Bishop and Lady Alwyne Compton (28 August 1904).

111. See Thomas Seccombe, rev. J.-M. Alter, 'Westwood, Thomas (1814–1888)', *ODNB* (2008) for his poetry and bibliographies of angling and anecdotes about Charles Lamb.

112. [Westwood], *Literary Friendship*: letter dated 21 November 1869 is on pp. 1–3; letter dated 21 February 1870 is on pp. 9–16.

113. John Hay Library, Brown University Library: Ms.52.298, T. Westwood, 'Letter, 1869, November 21, Brussels, Belgium'.

114. Email from Tim Engels, Senior Library Specialist, Special Collections – Manuscripts, Brown University Library, 20 October 2017.

115. Eric Ruijssenaars, 'The True Cause of Death of Martha Taylor', *Brussels Brontë Blog* (18 May 2016).

116. 'bright, dancing, laughing Martha': Gaskell, *Life*, p. 175.

117. Gaskell, *Life*, p. 178; CB to Ellen Nussey, 10 November [1842], *Letters* I, p. 302. Mary Taylor's two letters to Mrs Gaskell of 1856 and 1857 seem not to have survived. Stevens has pieced together what Mrs Gaskell used from the letters in her editions of the *Life*: Stevens, ed., *Mary Taylor*, pp. 157–67, but Mrs Gaskell probably used other, shorter extracts without mentioning 'Mary' as the source.

118. Mary Taylor to Ellen Nussey, 30 October and 1 November 1842, *Letters* I, pp. 296–7. Unfortunately Smith was fooled by Gérin and refers the reader to the latter's largely made-up account of Martha Taylor's illness and funeral.

119. CB to Ellen Nussey, 10 November [1842], *Letters* I, p. 302.

120. Gérin, *Charlotte Brontë*, p. 212.

121. Gaskell, *Life*, p. 115.

122. For their father Joshua Taylor as a New Connexion Methodist, see Juliet Barker, 'Taylor, Mary (1817–1893)', *ODNB* (2004); for their mother Anne as a Calvinistic chapel-goer, see Janet Horowitz Murray, 'Introduction' to Mary Taylor, *Miss Miles* (Oxford: Oxford University Press, 1990), p. viii; for their eldest brother Joshua, whom Mary never mentions, marrying in the Moravian church at Gomersal in 1838, see Stevens, ed., *Mary Taylor*, pp. 5, 139 n. 8.

123. Brontë, *Shirley*, p. 436; see also p. 305.

124. e.g. Mary and Ellen Taylor to CB, Wellington, 13 August 1850, *Letters* II, pp. 438–9.

125. 'Would you like to be cracking your head with French & german?' Martha Taylor

in the 'newspaper' letter to Ellen Nussey, March–April 1842, *Letters* I, p. 280.

126. Baptisms solemnized in the Parish of Birstall in the County of York, 1819.

127. Knight, *Nineteenth-Century Church*, p. 25.

128. CB to Margaret Wooler, 28 August 1848, *Letters* II, p. 107.

129. Stevens, ed., *Mary Taylor*, p. 67.

130. Tom Dixon to Mary Dixon, 1842, quoted in Stevens, ed., *Mary Taylor*, p. 32; for Tom see also p. 27.

131. CB to Ellen Nussey, [14 July 1840], *Letters* I, p. 223.

132. Letter 3 in Stevens, ed., *Mary Taylor*, pp. 32–3.

133. Kadoc: BE/942855/2062/144.

134. Mary Taylor to Ellen Nussey, 25 June 1843, in Stevens, ed., *Mary Taylor*, p. 46.

135. CB to Ellen Nussey, 10 November [1842], *Letters* I, p. 302: 'We sailed from Antwerp on Sunday [6 November] – we travelled day & night and got home on Tuesday morning.' They presumably went on the steam packet the *Wilberforce*, which arrived early Monday morning at Blackwall 'after a splendid run of only eighteen hours', *Sheffield and Rotherham Independent*, 12 November 1842, p. 5; see also *Hull Advertiser and Exchange Gazette*, 4 November 1842, p. 4.

136. Brontë, *Shirley*, p. 305.

Chapter 14: Charlotte Returns to Brussels, 1843: A Faithless-looking Youth, a Welsh Pony and Possible Forgery

1. Wyndham: Alward Wyndham to Margaret Wyndham, 31 May [1853].

2. Gaskell, *Life*, p. 162.

3. Patrick Brontë to Mrs J.C. Franks, 6 July 1835, *Letters* I, p. 141.

4. CB to Ellen Nussey, 30 January [1843], *Letters* I, p. 309.

5. Bristed, *Five Years in an English University*, pp. 275, 280.

6. Emails from Mike Morrogh, History Department, Shrewsbury School, 10 April 2014.

7. George William Fisher, *Annals of Shrewsbury School*, rev. J. Spencer Hill (London: Methuen, 1899), pp. 332, 334, 348, 366.

8. *Bell's Life in London and Sporting Chronicle*, 9 June 1861, p. 10.

9. Bracken, 'Football and the Brussels Brontë Story'. Bracken also mentions the Brussels Cricket Club.

10. See Wikipedia: 'Cambridge Rules'.

11. Smith, ed., *Letters* III, p. 78 n. 1.

12. CB to George Smith, 3 November 1852, *Letters* III, p. 77.

13. Brontë, *Villette*, p. 16.

14. Brontë, *Villette*, p. 372.

15. Whitehaven: Eliza Jenkins to Frances Curwen, May 1846.

16. CB to W.S. Williams, 22 February 1850, and CB to Ellen Nussey, [?11 March 1850], *Letters* II, pp. 350, 353.

17. See especially Smith, ed., *Letters* I, 'The History of the Letters', pp. 33–63.

18. Gaskell, *Life*, p. 162.

19. Mary Taylor to Ellen Nussey, 30 October and 1 November 1842, *Letters* I, pp. 296–7.

20. Gaskell, *Life*, p. 176.

21. Brontë, *Professor*, p. 176.

22. Brontë, *Professor*, p. 179.

23. Brontë, *Professor*, pp. 188–9.

24. CB to Ellen Nussey, 13 October [1843], *Letters* I, p. 334.

25. Green, 'The Brontë–Wheelwright Friendship': the link to this useful article was helpfully put on the Brussels Brontë Group website by Eric Ruijssenaars and Brian Bracken: 'Brontë Brussels Past Historians: Joseph Joshua Green' (2015). The bankruptcy is noted in numerous newspapers, e.g. *Morning Post*, 2 January 1843.

26. In the 1841 Census Dr Thomas Wheelwright put his profession as 'surgeon'. The family were then living in South Place, Finsbury, a short walk from the later Liverpool Street Station.

27. Quoted in Green, 'The Brontë–Wheelwright Friendship', p. 118.

28. Caroline Zilboorg, 'Shorter, Clement King (1857–1926)', *ODNB* (2004).

29. National Portrait Gallery, *Clement King Shorter* ('Men of the Day. No. 607') by Sir Leslie Ward, chromolithograph, published in *Vanity Fair*, 20 December 1894. NPG D44730.

30. Smith, ed., *Letters* I, p. 52. See pp. 52–63, especially, for Shorter's involvement.

31. Clement K. Shorter, *Charlotte Brontë and Her Circle*, 2nd edn (London: Hodder and Stoughton, 1896), pp. 25–6.

32. Smith, ed., *Letters* I, p. 58.

33. Trollope, *Belgium since the Revolution*, p. 72.

34. Shorter, *Charlotte Brontë and her Circle*, p. 111.

35. Sue Lonoff, 'The Brussels Experience', in *Brontës in Context*, ed. Marianne Thormählen (Cambridge: Cambridge University Press, 2012), p. 108.

36. Biber, ed., *English Church*, 2nd edn, p. 46; Trollope, *Belgium since the Revolution*, p. 72; Gérin, *Charlotte Brontë*, p. 217.

37. Kadoc: BE/942855/2062/146 2: Burials. This is William Drury's burials register from May 1829 until his death in 1878, which contains Julia Wheelwright's funeral (No. 143). He last signs himself as 'Minister of St George's Church Brussels' on 25 March 1839. For the next burial, on 27 May 1840, he signs himself as 'Officiating Minister'. He is in a different building, shared with Belgian Protestants.

38. Gérin, *Charlotte Brontë*, p. 217 n. 1; *Journal de Bruxelles*, 21 November 1842, p. 4 (above a list of train times); Eric Ruijssenaars, 'The Death of Julia Wheelwright', *Brussels Brontë Blog* (May 2018).

39. CB to Ellen Nussey, 13 October [1843], *Letters* I, p. 334.

40. V.E. Chancellor, 'Dixon, George (1820–1898)', *ODNB* (2013).

41. *Leeds Mercury*, 26 March 1842, p. 8.

42. *British Advertiser*, 22 January 1840.

43. Haworth BPM: Dixon Papers 13, Abraham Dixon to Mary Dixon, 24 July 1843.

44. R.B. Prosser, rev. R.C. Cox, 'Kyan, John Howard (1774–1850)', *ODNB* (2006).

45. Chancellor, 'Dixon', *ODNB*.

46. Haworth BPM: Dixon Papers 14, Abraham Dixon to Mary Dixon, 31 May and 3 June 1842.

47. Batley register has Joseph Walker Jenkins officiating on 22 August and then on 7 September 1842.

48. Haworth BPM: Dixon Papers 13, Abraham Dixon to Mary Dixon, 24 July 1843.

49. Emily Brontë, *Wuthering Heights* (London: Penguin Books, 2003), pp. 131, 134.

50. Margaret Lane, 'Introduction' to Elizabeth Gaskell, *Cousin Phillis* (London: Dent, 1970), p. ix. The seducer Mr Bellingham also has brain fever, in North Wales, in *Ruth*.

51. Brontë, *Professor*, pp. 120–1.

52. CB to Ellen Nussey, 6 August 1843, *Letters* I, p. 327.

53. Smith, ed., *Letters* I, p. 328 n. 5.

54. Chadwick, *Footsteps*, p. 224.

55. The parish register of baptisms in Pudsey has Joseph's baptism on 11 December 1816, and his birth (handwritten in the margin) on 31 October. His ordination as priest in 1842: see Crockford's Clerical Directory.

56. There would have been 'retired' Anglican clergymen in Brussels whom Evan could call on to do the service to enable him to have a break.

57. *Almanach royal* 1845. Joseph was chaplain at Spa 1844–8. He married Margaret Eggleston in Yorkshire a month after his return to England, in May 1848.

58. Biber, ed., *English Church*, pp. 49–50.

59. Thackeray, *Pendennis*, p. 729.

60. W.M. Thackeray to Mrs Carmichael-Smyth, 10 August 1843, in *Letters and Private Papers*, vol. II, p. 116.

61. CB to W.S. Williams, 11 December 1847, *Letters* I, p. 571.

62. See Smith, ed., *Letters* I, p. 582 n. 2, for Charlotte's dedication to Thackeray.

63. Quoted in Ray, *Thackeray: Uses*, p. 11.

64. CB to Emily J. Brontë, [1 October 1843], *Letters* I, p. 331.

65. Queen Victoria's Journals: 18 September 1843.

66. Anthony Trollope, *Barchester Towers* (Oxford: Oxford University Press, 2014), p. 10.

67. Quoted in Gordon N. Ray, *Thackeray: The Age of Wisdom (1847–1863)* (London: Oxford University Press, 1958), p. 36.

68. Ray, *Thackeray: Age*, p. 36; Thackeray, *Pendennis*, p. 1018, note to p. 107.

69. *Messager de Gand*, 13 September 1843, p. 4.

70. *Morning Post*, 19 September 1843, p. 3.

71. *The Times*, 19 September 1843, p. 4.

72. Queen Victoria's Journals: 17 September 1843.

73. *Morning Post*, 23 September 1843, p. 2.

74. Thomas Love Peacock, *Nightmare Abbey* and *Crotchet Castle* (Harmondsworth: Penguin Books, 1969), p. 202.

75. *Cambridge Chronicle and Journal*, 24 September 1842, p. 4; ACAD: John Jessopp, St John's College, Cambridge, BA 1837, in Ostend 1840–4; *Illustrated London News*, 14 August 1858, p. 13.

76. Elizabeth Gaskell, 'My Lady Ludlow', in *The Cranford Chronicles* (London: Vintage Books, 2007), p. 293.

77. Queen Victoria's Journals: 7 March, 21 May 1858, 23 November 1880.

78. Queen Victoria's Journals: 11 June 1873, 17 September 1879, 15 March 1873.

79. Trollope, *Autobiography*, p. 158.

80. Smith, ed., *Letters* I, pp. 92–3, 312 n. 3.

81. Brontë, *Professor*, p. 108.

82. CB to Branwell Brontë, 1 May 1843, *Letters* I, p. 317.

83. CB to Ellen Nussey, [?late June 1843], *Letters* I, p. 325.

84. CB to Emily J. Brontë, 2 September 1843, *Letters* I, p. 329.

85. CB to Ellen Nussey, 13 October [1843], *Letters* I, p. 334.

86. Thomas Westwood to Lady Alwyne Compton, 21 February 1870, in [Westwood], *Literary Friendship*, p. 15.

87. CB to Emily J. Brontë, 19 December 1843, *Letters* I, p. 339.

88. Smith, ed., *Letters* I, p. 339 n. 2.

89. Haworth BPM: Dixon Papers 11, Abraham Dixon to Mary Dixon, 30 December 1843.

90. E.g. Gérin, *Charlotte Brontë*, p. 255; Harman, *Charlotte Brontë*, p. 181.

91. Fraser, *Charlotte Brontë*, p. 201.

92. Eric Ruijssenaars, 'Je me vengerai, or Did Charlotte Really Say that to Madame Heger?', *Brussels Brontë Blog* (29 March 2007).

93. Phyllis Bentley, 'The Hegers: A Brontë Luncheon in Brussels for Dr. Phyllis Bentley', *Brontë Society Transactions*, 12:1 (1951).

94. Smith, ed., *Letters* I, p. 340 n. 1.

95. *L'Indépendance Belge*, 28 December 1843, p. 4; *Le Messager de Gand*, 4 January 1844, p. 4.

96. Emily J. Brontë, Diary Paper [31] July 1845, *Letters* I, p. 408.

97. *Le Messager de Gand*, 30 December 1843, p. 4: 'Mardi 2 janv. 10 du soir'; and *Hull Packet*, 5 January 1844, p. 2: 'Leaving Ostend for London, every Tuesday and Friday Evenings'. See also *British Advertiser*, 22 January 1840, p. 1: 'The General Steam Navigation Company's Packet *Earl of Liverpool*' will 'return from Ostend every Tuesday night [...] The departure from, and arrivals at Ostend, are so arranged as to avoid the expense and inconvenience of embarking or landing in boats.'

98. CB to Emily J. Brontë, 19 December 1843, *Letters* I, p. 339.

99. *Journal de Bruxelles*, 1 January 1844, p. 4.

100. Dalrymple, *Brussels Guide*, p. 6.

101. CB to Ellen Nussey, 10 November [1842], *Letters* I, p. 302.

102. Gérin, *Charlotte Brontë*, p. 255.

103. Haworth BPM: Sotheby, Wilkinson & Hodge, Wellington Street, Strand, *Catalogue of Valuable Illuminated & Other Manuscripts: Autograph Letters, Oriental Drawings and Printed Books* [13–15 December], 1916: Third Day, p. 90.

104. E.g. 'Sale of Bronte Relics and Books', *The Times*, 27 July 1907, p. 7.

105. CB to George Smith, 6 December 1852, *Letters* III, p. 88; also Gaskell, *Life*, p. 395. Charlotte is commenting on whether Lucy Snowe and Graham Bretton's relationship in *Villette* should have blossomed into romance. I apply her words to the whole of this sorry fabrication of how Charlotte left Brussels for the last time.

106. CB to Ellen Nussey, 23 January 1844, *Letters* I, pp. 341, 342 n. 6; Gaskell, *Life*, p. 198. Smith notes that an empty envelope at the Brontë Parsonage Museum is inscribed by Charlotte: 'Diploma given to me by Monsieur Heger Dec 29–1843'. The day placed *after* the month seems to be Charlotte's normal style, and is not consistent with the possible fabrication in the book of poems.

Chapter 15: 'Why should we weep or mourn': Schoolboys and Death

1. Whitehaven: all the letters are in DCU/3.
2. Anon., 'Curwen, John Christian (1756–1828)', *ODNB* (2007).
3. Holmes, *Darker Reflections*, p. 160.
4. Gill, *Wordsworth*, p. 420.
5. Kadoc: BE/942855/2062/146 1.
6. *Who Was Who*: Rev. Edward Hasell Curwen (1847–1929): 'Education Brussels (Jenkins)'; 'Wigton Literary and Scientific Society: Interesting Lecture by Canon Curwen', *Wigton Advertiser*, 15 November 1913, p. 4. Oddly, in the article, Canon Curwen says that he attended a 'military school', also, he remembered how he used to punch an African prince there (he uses a word other than 'African'). See also *L'Indépendance Belge*, 25 June 1850, p. 2 about the African boys in Edward's school and my chapter 16.
7. ACAD: Leonard Becher Morse.
8. Will of Leonard Becher Morse, 1827. Charlotte Brown is the executrix and is identified as a spinster. His legitimate daughter had received money in his father's will and was living with her diplomat husband in Buenos Aires at the time of her father's death in Brussels. Possibly Leonard and Charlotte weren't married for reasons of class.
9. Early 1800s: After she has fled Edward Rochester, St John Eyre Rivers gives Jane, then eighteen, a 'new publication' – Scott's *Marmion* – published in 1808 (Brontë, *Jane Eyre*, p. 396). But see Q.D. Leavis's note in *Jane Eyre* (pp. 487–9) on the confusion about dates, but that it suggests 'the timeless quality of the myth and day-dream [...] we are reading a fairy-tale' (p. 489).
10. Thackeray, *Book of Snobs*, p. 12. Thackeray himself fell prey to the delight of knowing 'Duchesses and Marchionesses', which Charlotte recognized early on: 'he is half their slave'; CB to Amelia Taylor, née Ringrose, 7 June 1851, *Letters* II, p. 633.
11. Wyndham: Eliza Jenkins to Janet Jay, 3 August [1855].
12. Shropshire Archives: 807/568, M. Bright to Augusta Bright, 24 February c.1846.
13. Dalrymple, *Brussels Guide*, pp. 85–6.
14. Dalrymple, *Brussels Guide*, p. 8.
15. Whitehaven: DCU/3/31.
16. Kate Summerscale, *Mrs Robinson's Disgrace: The Private Diary of a Victorian Lady*, paperback edn (London: Bloomsbury Publishing, 2013), p. 253 n. 96, and pp. 95–7 for her account of the letter and the supposed aftermath. Mary Moorman, *William*

Wordsworth: A Biography: The Later Years: 1805–1850 (Oxford: Clarendon Press, 1965), pp. 597–8 n. 3. Moorman (1905–94) was the daughter of the historian G.M. Trevelyan: 'Obituary' by Jonathan Wordsworth, *The Independent*, 1 February 1994 (online).

17. Katie Waldegrave, *The Poets' Daughters: Dora Wordsworth and Sara Coleridge* (London: Windmill Books, 2014), pp. 311–12.

18. Wordsworth Trust: WLL/Wordsworth, Dora/2/17 – Dora Quillinan to Mary Wordsworth, 1 October 1845.

19. Isabella's date of birth is not certain, but in the 1841 census she is thirty.

20. CB to Ellen Nussey, [?20 October 1854], *Letters* III, p. 295. Thankfully Ellen didn't burn the letter. Charlotte then requiring Ellen to write a note to Arthur promising to destroy Charlotte's letters is frankly appalling: see CB to Ellen Nussey, 31 October 1854 and Ellen to A.B. Nicholls, [November 1854], *Letters* III, pp. 296–7.

21. Wordsworth Trust: WLL/Wordsworth, Dora/2/6: Dora and Edward Quillinan to Mary Wordsworth, 27 May 1845.

22. John Worthen, *The Life of William Wordsworth: A Critical Biography* (Chichester: Wiley Blackwell, 2014), p. 446 n. 12.

23. Gill, *Wordsworth*, p. 610 n. 134.

24. Whitehaven: DCU/3/31: Henry Curwen to Edward S. Curwen, 30 to 31 January 1846. I have expanded contractions.

25. The registration of death for Isabella Wordsworth in Italy does not contain the cause of death: I thank Giordano Turchi, Funzionario archivista, Archivio di Stato di Firenze; email 8 October 2019.

26. I am grateful to Poppy Garrett, Assistant Curator, and Jeff Cowton, Curator, of the Wordsworth Trust for sending me a legible copy of Wordsworth's will (the copy I obtained directly from the National Archives is excruciatingly hard to read).

27. *Carlisle Patriot*, 10 January 1857, p. 8.

28. Whitehaven: DCU 3/27: Eliza Jenkins to Frances Curwen, 30 July 1844 and 28 July [1845].

29. Wyndham: Janet Jay to Margaret Wyndham, 25 November 1845.

30. Shropshire Archives: Mary Bright to Augusta Bright, Brussels, 24 February [?1846].

31. *La Belgique Judiciaire*, 10–14 August 1845, column 1212 (my translation).

32. Brontë, *Villette*, p. 197.

33. *London Evening Standard*, 2 April 1846, p. 4.

34. *Leeds Intelligencer*, 22 April 1837, p. 7. See CB's comments on the newspapers that the family read in 1829: Gaskell, *Life*, p. 67, which included the *Leeds Intelligencer*.

'a most excellent Tory newspaper', and the *Leeds Mercury*.

35.   Barker, *The Brontës*, p. 308.

36.   See Matthew Cragoe, 'The Great Reform Act and the Modernization of British Politics: The Impact of Conservative Associations, 1835–1841', *Journal of British Studies*, 47:3 (2008), pp. 581–603.

37.   *Leeds Intelligencer*, 22 April 1837, p. 7.

38.   See also Thomas Love Peacock, *The Misfortunes of Elphin* [1829] (Felinfach: Llanerch Publishers, 1991), pp. 51–2, who comments that 'Some of the Welsh historians are of opinion that [the Christian faith] was first preached by some of the apostles [...] the evidence [is] inconclusive with respect to St. Paul'; he also mentions the 'archbishopric of Caer Lleon, which was, during many centuries, the primacy of Britain' (p. 51). There is no trace of Peacock's usual satire here.

39.   *Leeds Times*, 29 April 1837, pp. 6, 3.

40.   *Leeds Times*, 4 February 1837, p. 5; see also Strong, *Story of Pudsey Church*, p. 21.

41.   *Leeds Mercury*, 20 May 1837, p. 7.

42.   *Bradford Observer*, 27 June 1844, p. 6.

43.   *Y Gwladgarwr* ['The Patriot'], April 1841, p. 123.

44.   *Glamorgan Monmouth and Brecon Gazette and Merthyr Guardian*, 3 April 1841, p. 3.

45.   *Manchester Courier and Lancashire General Advertiser*, 22 April 1846, p. 6.

46.   The number of the house in the Chaussée d'Ixelles had changed because of street renumbering: see Bracken, 'The Jenkinses' House in Ixelles'.

47.   The 1840 *Almanach* lists Simon Salter (rather charmingly) as 'agent de l'united kingdom liffe asse company'; he lived at 56 rue de la Pépinière, near the Porte de Namur. In the 1854 *Almanach*, William Jackson may be listed as 'épic., vins. Chaussée d'Ixelles, 97'. The Jenkinses must have shopped there often for groceries and wine, including the numerous bottles that young Henry Curwen consumed!

48.   e.g. *Indépendance Belge*, 8 October 1849, p. 1: 'Le révérend M. Jenkins, pasteur adjoint du Roi et ministre de l'église anglicane à Bruxelles, est mort ces jours derniers à Ixelles.'

49.   *Elgin Courier*, 13 July 1849, p. 4; newspaper cutting in great-aunt's album with handwritten date 1886, which states that Evan Jenkins had officiated, while his son John officiated at the funeral of 'Miss Cotton', the niece who looked after the museum on the battlefield after her uncle's death.

50.   *Indépendance Belge*, 1 October 1849, p. 1.

51.   *Gentleman's Magazine*, ser. 2 vol. 32, October 1849, p. 436.

52.   Anna [Maria] Calhoun Clemson to John C. Calhoun, Brussels, 12 August 1849,

in Clyde N. Wilson and Shirley Bright Cook (eds), *The Papers of John C. Calhoun*, XXVII, *1849–1850* ([Columbia]: University of South Carolina Press, 2003), p. 23; Thomas G. Clemson to John C. Calhoun, Brussels, 1 August 1849, p. 4; same to same, Brussels, 24 September 1849, p. 64.

53. Lambeth: FP Blomfield 48, fol. 365, Bishop to Eliza Jenkins, Fulham, 26 September 1849.

54. Kadoc: BE/942855/2062/146 2: Burials.

55. Kadoc: BE/942855/2062/146 1: Baptisms, e.g. for John Card Jenkins (junior) on 25 July 1874.

56. *Bury and Norwich Post*, 30 January 1850, p. 4; 26 November 1851, p. 3; *Newcastle Journal*, 23 March 1850, p. 8. Edward Jenkins's Fellowship was awarded on 28 May 1850: email from Catherine Sutherland, Deputy Librarian, Pepys Library & Special Collections, Magdalene College, Cambridge, 2 November 2015.

57. Lambeth: FP Blomfield 48, fol. 364, Bishop to Rev. Maxwell J. Blacker, Fulham, 25 September 1849.

58. Trollope, *Barchester Towers*, pp. 259–60. See also Collins, *Jane Austen and the Clergy*, p. 22, where she comments on *Persuasion* (1817) and the 'tendency [of curates] to be on the look-out for sick and elderly parsons'.

59. Lambeth: FP Blomfield 59, fol. 385, Bishop to Charles Ellis, 6th Baron Howard de Walden, Minister at Brussels, ?28 September 1849. Blacker's appointment in December 1849: *Almanachs royaux* for 1850–2; but *Almanachs* for 1855–6 have instead 29 October 1849. Perhaps he started in October for a trial period and was then confirmed in the post.

60. John Julian, *A Dictionary of Hymnology* (London: John Murray, 1907), p. 1553; *Crockford's Clerical Directory*, 1865.

61. Blacker and Emily Daveney: *Morning Post*, 11 July 1850, p. 8; Rev. Hill and Ellen Daveney: *Royal Cornwall Gazette*, 13 February 1846, p. 3; John Steele of Antwerp to Emma Daveney: *Norfolk Chronicle*, 13 September 1845, p. 2.

Chapter 16: 'between Life & death'

1. 'Annonces. Vente Publique pour cause de décès, d'un beau mobilier', *Journal de la Belgique*, 9 November 1849, p. 4.

2. *Report of Her Majesty's Commissioners Appointed to Inquire into the Revenues and Management of Certain Colleges and Schools* (London: George Edward Eyre and William Spottiswoode, 1864), vol. I, p. 313.

3. Emails from Catherine Sutherland, Deputy Librarian, Pepys Library & Special Collections, Magdalene College, Cambridge, 2 November 2015 to 18 February 2016.

4. *Cambridge Chronicle and Journal*, 22 November 1851, p. 6.

5. Cambridge University Library: Ely, List of Candidates, 17 November 1851.

6. *L'Indépendance Belge*, 25 June 1852, p. 2. See my chapter 15, n. 6.

7. Wyndham: Eliza Jenkins to Margaret Wyndham, 22 February 1853; Charlotte Starky to Margaret Wyndham, undated [?13 October 1851].

8. Kadoc: BE/942855/2062/144.

9. Email from Lesley Park, Searchroom Assistant, Record Office, Whitehaven, 10 November 2015.

10. See Michael Freeman, *A Winter Sanatorium: Ventnor as a Health Resort in the Victorian Era* (Ventnor: Ventnor & District Local History Society, 2009).

11. Michael Freeman, email, 20 August 2015; and e.g. *Oxford Chronicle and Reading Gazette*, 6 November 1852, p. 6.

12. Freeman, *Winter Sanatorium*, pp. 4–5.

13. Wyndham: Jane Bowden Baker [née Livingston] to Margaret Wyndham, Bourn, Burrington, Bristol, 15 August 1861.

14. MacCarthy, *Byron*, p. 183.

15. Bristed, *Five Years in an English University*, pp. 163–4.

16. Wyndham: Charlotte Starky to Margaret Wyndham, undated [?13 October 1851].

17. *Cheltenham Looker-On*, 13 September 1851, p. 13.

18. *Cheltenham Looker-On*, 4 October 1851, p. 10.

19. Brontë, *Villette*, pp. 213, 214.

20. Wyndham: Janet Jay to Margaret Wyndham, 19 August 1856.

21. Wyndham: Eliza Jenkins to Margaret Wyndham, Brussels, 19 January 1852. I have been trying to find her 'Beggar Woman' for years (that is definitely the spelling). It could be from a poem known to her and her sister.

22. Wyndham: Laetitia Wyndham to George Wyndham, 27 June 1833.

23. Elizabeth Gaskell, *Cranford* (Oxford: Oxford University Press, 2011), p. 19.

24. Wyndham: Eliza Jenkins to Margaret Wyndham, [June] 1853 and 30 March 1854.

25. Wyndham: Eliza Jenkins to Margaret Wyndham, Brussels, 30 March 1854.

26. Stapylton, *Eton School Lists, from 1791 to 1850*, p. xii.

27. *Bucks Herald*, 8 August 1840, p. 2.

28. Wyndham: Ella Wyndham to George Wyndham, [15 January 1852].

29. Wyndham: Alward Wyndham to Margaret Wyndham, Dinton, 2 July 1852.

30. *Almanach* 1854: Noms: 'Blackaert Prêtre anglais'. Blacker is not listed under

'Institutions', as the Jenkins pensionnat is.

31. Wyndham: Eliza Jenkins to Margaret Wyndham, Brussels, 22 February 1853.

32. Wyndham: Charlotte Starky to Margaret Wyndham, Yarlington Lodge, August 1855; Charlotte Starky to George Wyndham, Spye Park, 3 October 1855.

33. Wyndham: William Wyndham (V) to George Wyndham, Dinton, 14 November 1858.

34. Wyndham: William Wyndham (VI) to George Wyndham, Dinton, 10 March 1864; bankrupt: John Wyndham to Edward Sandford Wyndham, [December 1867].

35. See Dalwood Restoration Association Newsletters at https://dalwood.org.au/newsletters.html; www.dalwood.org.au/; and Wikipedia, 'Dalwood House', though note that Margaret Wyndham née Jay could hardly be called 'of French extraction', despite the Huguenot ancestors.

36. Wyndham: Eliza Jenkins to Margaret Wyndham, Brussels, 19 January 1852.

37. Wyndham: Janet Jay to Margaret Wyndham, 7 July 1852.

38. Wyndham: Eliza Jenkins to Margaret Wyndham, Brussels, 22 February 1853.

39. Wyndham: Eliza Jenkins to Margaret Wyndham, [June] 1853.

40. Wyndham: Eliza Jenkins to Margaret Wyndham, 30 March 1854.

41. Wyndham: Janet Jay to Margaret Wyndham, 19 August 1856.

42. Wyndham: Eliza Jenkins to Margaret Wyndham, Brussels, 30 August 1856.

43. Wyndham: Jane Bowden Baker to Margaret Wyndham, Bourn, Burrington, Bristol, 15 October 1856.

44. Will of Margaret Bowden, 20 November 1857.

45. Wyndham: Eliza Jenkins to Margaret Wyndham, [June] 1853.

46. CB to George Smith, 18 September 1850, *Letters* II, p. 470.

47. Leaflets from the Church of Christ the King, Gordon Square, London. For Alward Wyndham's involvement: Wyndham: e.g. Charlotte Starky to George and Margaret Wyndham, Spye Park, 25 February and March 1854, where Charlotte Starky calls it a 'strange delusion'.

48. *Bradford Observer*, 24 August 1854, p. 5.

49. Strong, *Story of Pudsey Church*, p. 24.

50. George John Tuck, *Newton Church and John Powell* (1911), online at www.ewyaslacy.org.uk: Newton Church.

51. Probate: Administrations, 1870: The Reverend Joseph Walker Jenkins, effects under £100, late of Newton in the County of Hereford, 'who died 30 September 1860 at Pentwyn Cottage Bacton': Letters of Administration of the Personal estate and effects were granted to Sarah Jane Clara Wilhelmina Jenkins of 116 rue Sans-

Souci Brussels, as they were left unadministered by his widow Margaret. In the 1870 *Almanach* C.E. Jenkins 'pasteur angl.' was at 114 rue Sans-Souci. It's a narrow road near Chaussée d'Ixelles. Mina died in Leicester in March 1926.

52. Elizabeth Gaskell to Fanny Holland, Burrow Hall, Kir[k]by Lonsdale, Thursday [?13 March 1856], in J.A.V. Chapple, 'Two Unpublished Gaskell Letters from Burrow Hall, Lancashire', *The Gaskell Society Journal*, 6 (1992), pp. 68–9.

53. Mrs Gaskell to Lady Kay-Shuttleworth, 7 April [1853], *Letters* III, p. 150.

54. Elizabeth Gaskell to Marianne Gaskell, Victoria Hotel, Euston Square, [?6 May 1856], in *The Letters of Mrs Gaskell*, ed. J.A.V. Chapple and Arthur Pollard (Manchester: Mandolin, 1997), p. 880.

55. Elizabeth Gaskell to Laetitia Wheelwright, 17 Cumberland Terrace, ?13 June 1856, in *Letters*, ed. Chapple and Pollard, p. 391.

56. *Morning Chronicle*, 26 April 1856, p. 6.

57. *Dublin Evening Packet and Correspondent*, 24 April 1856, p. 3.

58. Wyndham: Jane Bowden Baker to Margaret Wyndham, 15 October 1856.

59. *Norfolk Chronicle*, 3 July 1858, p. 5.

60. Wyndham: Charlotte Starky to George Wyndham, Spye Park, 2 August 1856.

61. Wyndham: Janet Jay to Margaret Wyndham, 19 August 1856.

62. Wyndham: Eliza Jenkins to Margaret Wyndham, Brussels, 30 August [1856].

63. Wyndham: Eliza Jenkins to Margaret Wyndham, Brussels, 30 August [1856].

64. Wyndham: Jane Bowden Baker to Margaret Wyndham, Bourn, Burrington, Bristol, 15 August 1861.

65. Wyndham: Jane Bowden Baker to Margaret Wyndham, 15 May 1862.

66. 'History of the Building of the Church of the Resurrection in Brussels' [n.d. c.1876], sent to me by Roger Cox November 2013, in Kadoc: BE/942855/2062/147.

67. 'Church of the Resurrection (Anglican), Brussels', *The Civil Engineer and Architect's Journal*, 28 (July 1865), p. 196.

68. 'Church of the Resurrection (Anglican), Brussels'.

69. Wyndham: Helen Jenkins to Janet Jay, Brussels, Easter Monday [28 March 1864]. The other four letters can be dated 1, 3, 5 and 7 April.

70. H.M. Stephens, rev. H.C.G. Matthew, 'Ellis, Charles Augustus, sixth Baron Howard de Walden and second Baron Seaford (1799–1868)', *ODNB* (2011).

71. Whitehaven: DCU 3/27/2, Eliza Jenkins to Frances Curwen, Brussels, 21 April [1847].

72. ACAD. See also Roger Cox, *Anglicans in Brussels*, rev. edn (Brussels: Holy Trinity, Rue Capitaine Crespel, 2004), for Rowton, though the booklet unfortunately has many errors.

73. Trollope, *The Warden*, p. 63.
74. Arthur Burns, 'Wilberforce, Samuel (1805–1873)', *ODNB* (2009).
75. *Illustrated London News*, 23 April 1864, p. 384. Louis Ghémar and his half-brother had a renowned photo-studio in Brussels c.1859–94 and took many photographs of Belgian and English royalty. I presume Helen refers to Louis Ghémar. Perhaps photos of the stone-laying ceremony will turn up one day.
76. See also 'Etat Civil d'Ixelles. Du 5 au 12 mai' 'Décès' 'E. Jay, directrice d'institution, 66 ans, veuve du révérend Evan Jenkins, rue des Champs Elysées, 14'.

Chapter 17: Coda

1. *Echo du Parlement*, 14 September 1869, p. 2 (my translation).
2. 'History of the Building of the Church of the Resurrection in Brussels', sent to me by Roger Cox, in Kadoc: BE/942855/2062/147. Details in the following paragraph also from here.
3. Thomas Westwood to Lady Alwyne Compton, 7 March 1879, in [Westwood], *Literary Friendship*, pp. 182–4.
4. Newspaper cuttings in the albums of John's daughters, in my possession, as is the 1885 bound book ('address') presented to John. One newspaper cutting adds that the book is signed by 'about 500 persons, including the Bishop of London and Bishop Titcombe, [and] is really a work of art, reflecting the greatest credit upon Mr. Lory-Delaet who engrossed and illuminated it, and upon M. Schavye by whom it was bound'.
5. CB to W.S. Williams, 14 August 1848, *Letters* II, p. 98.

Select Bibliography

Archives

Archives de Bruxelles

Almanacs: https://archives.bruxelles.be/almanachs:
Almanachs; *Almanachs de poche*; *Almanachs royaux*

Balliol College Archives, University of Oxford

Morier Family Papers, Class C, Box 1, 1788–92

Bedfordshire Archives

OR2298-5b: Theresa Rouse-Boughton to Sir William Edward Rouse-Boughton, 13 June 1853

Borthwick Institute for Archives, University of York, York Diocesan Archive

Ord.D.1810, Ord.P.1811: Ordination papers of David Jenkins

British Library, London

Add. MS 61805: Stonestreet journal

Brontë Parsonage Museum, Haworth

Dixon Papers 11, 13, 14

Sotheby, Wilkinson & Hodge, Wellington Street, Strand, *Catalogue of Valuable Illuminated & Other Manuscripts: Autograph Letters, Oriental Drawings and Printed Books* [13–15 December], 1916

Brown University Library, John Hay Library

Ms.52.298: T. Westwood, 'Letter, 1869, November 21, Brussels, Belgium'

Cumbria Archive and Local Studies Centre, Kendal

MS WDS/38/3: Clergy Daughters' School, Admissions Register, 1824–39

Cumbria Archive and Local Studies Centre, Whitehaven

Curwen Family of Workington Hall, 1358–1929: DCU/3

Hampshire Record Office

Malmesbury papers: 9M73/G410, Andrew Dalziel [Dalzel in DNB] (1746–1806), Greek professor at University of Edinburgh, 27 June 1777

Kadoc – Documentatie- en Onderzoekscentrum voor Religie, Cultuur en Samenleving, Leuven, Belgium

United Anglican Church:

BE/942855/2062/143 (Register of Baptisms, Marriages and Burials – Reverends Willoughby and Prince, 1817–22)

BE/942855/2062/144 (Register of Marriages, Baptisms and Burials – Rev. Evan Jenkins et al., 1818–49; including loose pages, 1850s, Reverends Blacker and C.E. Jenkins)

BE/942855/2062/145 (Scrapbook with drafts? of marriages, burials and baptisms, Rev. Evan Jenkins, 1825–49, with index, compiled shortly after his death?)

BE/942855/2062/146 1 (Register of Baptisms, Rev. William Drury, 1828–78)

BE/942855/2062/146 2 (Register of Burials, Rev. William Drury, 1829–78)

BE/942855/2062/147 (Register of Baptisms and Burials, Rev. C.E. Jenkins et al., 1856–1923), also containing an article, 'History of the Building of the Church of the Resurrection in Brussels'.

Kensington and Chelsea Archives, London

F.P. Thompson's map of 1836

'Population Book of St Luke's Parish Chelsea, Middlesex' (1801)

Lambeth Palace Library, London

FP Blomfield 48, 59, 65

FP Howley 4, 5, 7, 24

Lincolnshire Archives

3-SIB/1/18: Letter from Richard Waldo Sibthorp, Brussels, to his sister Mrs Hawkins, Berkeley House, Little Hampton, Arundel, Sussex

London Metropolitan Archives, City of London

Bishop's Act Book, 1809–28: DL/A/A/020/MS09532A/002 and 1828–42: DL/A/A/020/MS09532A/003

Church of the Resurrection, Brussels, Belgium (1874–1914): Papers relating to the consecration of the church [...] an 'Almanack of the Church of the Resurrection' (1914) [...]: DL/E/D/010/MS19230/016

Ordination bundles, Evan Jenkins: DL/A/B/002/MS 10326 (May and December 1825)

Transcripts of baptisms and burials 1818, 1821 and 1825–6 and marriages 1818, 1821 and 1826 at the British Embassy and Chapel Royal, Brussels: DL/E/E/037/MS11199

National Library of Wales/Llyfrgell Genedlaethol Cymru, Aberystwyth

Cardiganshire wills, 1805–1847: 39–52

Jenkin, Evan, yeoman, Llanbadarn Odwyn, Cardiganshire to Davies, Elisabeth, sp., Tregaron, Cardiganshire: marriage bond, 1785, Nov. 18: St. Davids B 18/182

Letters, 1823–1873: 12-21: 'Letters mainly from John Pugh, Llan-gors vicarage, co. Brecon, to his uncle Evan Richards of Nanthenfoel, and one, 1823, from E. Jenkins, Brussels, to David Richards of Glanywern, Lampeter'

Peny Castell in the parish of Llanbadarn Odwyn [cartographic material]: Nanteos 208 132/1/49

Roberts & Evans (solicitors), folders R&E 9/1, 9/3: Peter Felix files

Norfolk Record Office

BUL 1/15/1-54 561 x 9: copy letter to Rev. E. Jenkins 1836 from Sir George Hamilton Seymour GCG His Britannic Majesty's Envoy Extraordinary and Minister Plenipotentiary in Belgium

Northamptonshire Archives Service

C(A) Box 15/95: Papers of the Cartwright family of Aynho, letter from Bishop Howley to Rev. Holworthy, 24 April 1826

Shropshire Archives

807/568: M. Bright to Augusta Bright, 24 February c.1846

State Library of New South Wales, Sydney, Australia

Mitchell Library: Papers of the Clarke and Mann families, 1797–1954, MLMSS 139, volume 5

Trinity College Library, University of Cambridge

Admissions Book for 1817/18

Admission slips for 1817/18

Head Lecturer's Book for 1818–22

University of New England (UNE), NSW, Australia

Regional Collection: Dinton–Dalwood Letters 1827–88, acc. no. A109. [Abbreviated in the notes as 'Wyndham']

Wordsworth Trust

WLL/Wordsworth, Dora/2/17: Dora Quillinan to Mary Wordsworth, 1 October 1845

WLL/Wordsworth, Dora/2/6: Dora and Edward Quillinan to Mary Wordsworth, 27 May 1845

Websites

ACAD: A Cambridge Alumni Database (*Alumni Cantabrigienses*): http://venn.lib.cam.
  ac.uk/Documents/acad/2018/search-2018.html
CCEd: Clergy of the Church of England Database, 1540–1835: https://theclergydatabase.
  org.uk
Dalwood Restoration Association Newsletters: https://dalwood.org.au/newsletters.html
  'Legacies of British Slave-ownership': www.ucl.ac.uk/lbs
Queen Victoria's Journals: www.queenvictoriasjournals.org

Literature

Austen, Jane, *Emma* [1816], ed. Mary Lascelles (London: Dent, 1964).
Austen, Jane, *Mansfield Park* [1814], ed. Kathryn Sutherland (London: Penguin Books, 2014).
Austen, Jane, *Pride and Prejudice* [1813], ed. James Kinsley (Oxford: Oxford University Press, 2008).
Barbauld, Anna Laetitia, *Collected Works*, vol. I: *The Poems, Revised*, ed. William McCarthy (Oxford: Oxford University Press, 2019).
Barnes, Julian, *Flaubert's Parrot* (London: Vintage Books, 2009).
Brontë, Charlotte, *Jane Eyre* [1847], ed. Q.D. Leavis (London: Penguin, 1985).
Brontë, Charlotte, *The Professor* [1856] (Ware: Wordsworth Editions, 2010).
Brontë, Charlotte, *Shirley* [1849] (Ware: Wordsworth Classics, 2009).
Brontë, Charlotte, *Villette* [1853] (Oxford: Oxford University Press, 2000).
Brontë, Emily, *Wuthering Heights* [1847] (London: Penguin Books, 2003).
De Quincey, Thomas, *Confessions of an English Opium-Eater* [1821, 1856], ed. David Ellis (Ware: Wordsworth, 2009).
Dumas, Alexandre, *The Three Musketeers* [1844] [no translator credited] (London: Francis Aldor, n.d.).
Eliot, George, *The Mill on the Floss* [1860] (Oxford: Oxford University Press, 2015).
Gaskell, Elizabeth, *Cousin Phillis* [1864], Introduction by Margaret Lane (London: Dent, 1970).
Gaskell, Elizabeth, *Cranford* [1853] (Oxford: Oxford University Press, 2011).
Gaskell, Elizabeth, *Half a Life Time Ago* [1855] (London: Dent, 1970).
Gaskell, Elizabeth, 'My Lady Ludlow' [1858–9], in *The Cranford Chronicles* (London: Vintage Books, 2007).
James, Henry, *The Aspern Papers and Other Tales*, ed. Michael Gorra (London: Penguin Books, 2014).
Larkin, Philip, 'High Windows', in *The Complete Poems*, ed. Archie Burnett (New York:

Farrar, Straus and Giroux, 2012).

Lever, Charles, *Harry Lorrequer* [1839] (London: Chapman and Hall, 1857).

Scott, Walter, *The Betrothed* [1825] (Edinburgh: Adam and Charles Black, 1886).

Thackeray, W.M., *The Adventures of Philip* [1861–2] [and] *A Shabby Genteel Story* [1840] (London: Smith, Elder, & Co., 1900).

Thackeray, W.M., *The Book of Snobs: Sketches of Life and Character etc. etc.* [1848], in *The Works of William Makepeace Thackeray*, vol. IX (London: Smith, Elder & Co., 1894).

Thackeray, W.M., *The History of Henry Esmond* [1852], Introduction by John Sutherland (London: Penguin, 1985).

Thackeray, W.M., *Lovel the Widower, Etc.*; [*Notes of a Journey from Cornhill to Grand Cairo*] (London: Collins, [1912]).

Thackeray, W.M., *Pendennis* [1848–50], ed. John Sutherland (Oxford: Oxford University Press, 1994).

Thackeray, W.M., *A Shabby Genteel Story and Other Writings* (London: J.M. Dent, 1993).

Thackeray, W.M., *Vanity Fair* [1847–8], Introduction and Notes by Carole Jones and Owen Knowle (Ware: Wordsworth, 2001).

Thomas, Dylan, 'Fern Hill', in *The Loud Hill of Wales: Poetry of Place*, selected by Walford Davies (London: J.M. Dent, 1991).

Trollope, Anthony, *Barchester Towers* [1857] (Oxford: Oxford University Press, 2014).

Trollope, Anthony, *Doctor Thorne* [1858] (Oxford: Oxford University Press, 2014).

Trollope, Anthony, *Framley Parsonage* [1861] (Oxford: Oxford University Press, 2014).

Trollope, Anthony, *The Warden* [1855] (Oxford: Oxford University Press, 2014).

Trollope, Frances, *The Vicar of Wrexhill*, 3 vols (London: Richard Bentley, 1837).

Woolf, Virginia, *The Waves* (Harmondsworth: Penguin Books, 1964).

Wordsworth, William, *Selected Poems*, ed. Stephen Gill (London: Penguin Books, 2004).

Wordsworth, William, 'Simon Lee, the Old Huntsman', in William Wordsworth and Samuel Taylor Coleridge, *Lyrical Ballads* [1798] (London: Penguin Books, 2006).

Primary

Airy, Sir George Biddell, *Autobiography*, ed. Wilfrid Airy (Cambridge: at the University Press, 1896).

Anon., *Memoir of the Rev. John Buckworth, M.A., Late Vicar of Dewsbury, Yorkshire* (London: Messrs. Hatchard [etc.], 1836).

[Atkinson, Solomon], 'Struggles of a Poor Student through Cambridge by a Senior Wrangler', *London Magazine and Review* (1 April 1825), pp. 491–51.

Austen, Jane, *Jane Austen's Letters*, ed. Deirdre Le Faye, 3rd edn (Oxford: Oxford University Press, 1997).

[Beaumont, Augustus Hardin], *Adventures of Two Americans in the Siege of Brussels, September, 1830*, by one of them (London: Edmund H. Beaumont, Printer, St. Michael's Alley, Cornhill, [?1831]).

Biber, Rev. G.E., ed., *The English Church on the Continent: or, an Account of the Foreign Settlements of the English Church* (London: Francis & John Rivington, 1845); 2nd edn in 1846.

Borrow, George, *Wild Wales: The People, Language and Scenery* [1862] (London: Century, 1984).

Bristed, Charles Astor, *Five Years in an English University*, 2nd edn (New York: G.P. Putnam & Co, 1852).

Brontë, Charlotte, *The Letters of Charlotte Brontë*, Volume One: *1829–1847*, ed. Margaret Smith (Oxford: Clarendon Press, 1995).

Brontë, Charlotte, *The Letters of Charlotte Brontë*, Volume Two: *1848–1851*, ed. Margaret Smith (Oxford: Clarendon Press, 2000).

Brontë, Charlotte, *The Letters of Charlotte Brontë*, Volume Three: *1852–1855*, ed. Margaret Smith (Oxford: Clarendon Press, 2004).

Cooper, T. Sidney, RA, *My Life* (London: Richard Bentley and Son, 1891).

Dalrymple, Mrs Wemyss, *The Economist's New Brussels Guide* (Brussels, 1839).

Downey, Edmund, *Charles Lever: His Life in His Letters*, 2 vols (Edinburgh and London: William Blackwood and Sons, 1906).

Faulkner, Thomas, *An Historical and Topographical Description of Chelsea and its Environs* (London: Printed by J. Tilling, Chelsea, 1810); 2nd edn 1829.

Fontaine, Jaques, *Memoirs of the Reverend Jaques Fontaine (1658–1728)*, ed. Dianne W. Ressinger, Huguenot Society n.s. no. 2 (London: The Huguenot Society of Great Britain and Ireland, 1992).

Gaskell, Elizabeth, *The Letters of Mrs Gaskell*, ed. J.A.V. Chapple and Arthur Pollard (Manchester: Mandolin, 1997).

Gaskell, Elizabeth, *The Life of Charlotte Brontë*, ed. Elisabeth Jay (London: Penguin Books, 1997).

Grattan, Thomas Colley, *Beaten Paths; and those who trod them*, 2 vols (London: Chapman and Hall, 1862).

Hall, N. John, *Salmagundi: Byron, Allegra and the Trollope Family* (Pittsburgh: Beta Phi Mu, 1975).

The Harrow School Register, 1800–1911, 3rd edn (London: Longmans, Green, and Co., 1911).

Hucks, J., *A Pedestrian Tour through North Wales, in a Series of Letters* [1795], ed. Alun R. Jones and William Tydeman (Cardiff: University of Wales Press, 1979).

Juste, Théodore, *Memoirs of Leopold I King of the Belgians*, trans. Robert Black, 2 vols (London, 1868).

'Lady, A', *Anecdotes, personal traits, and characteristic sketches of Victoria the first, brought down to the period of her majesty's marriage with his royal highness Prince Albert of Saxe-Gotha* (London: William Bennett etc., 1840).

Mackay, Charles, *Forty Years' Recollections of Life, Literature, and Public Affairs from 1830 to 1870*, 2 vols (London: Chapman & Hall, 1877).

Mackay, Charles, *Through the Long Day, or, Memorials of a Literary Life during Half a Century*, 2 vols (London: W.H. Allen & Co., 1887).

[Marryat, Frederick], 'Diary on the Continent', in *Olla Podrida*, 3 vols (London: Longman, Orme, Brown, Green, & Longmans, 1840).

[Mauvy, A.X.], *The Stranger's Guide through Brussels and its Environs* (Brussels: Ad. Wahlen, Printer to the Court, 1834).

Old Resident, An, *A Week in Brussels: The Stranger's Guide to the Capital of Belgium*, 3rd edn (London: Edwards and Hughes, 1846).

Phelps, W. May, and John Forbes-Robertson, *The Life and Life-Work of Samuel Phelps* (London: Sampson Low, Marston, Searle, & Rivington, 1886).

Romberg, J.B., *Brussels and its Environs* (Brussels: Printed for B. Le Francq, 1824).

Stapylton, H.E.C., *The Eton School Lists, from 1791 to 1850*, 2nd edn (London: E.P. Williams, 1864).

Steven, Revd. William, *The History of the Scottish Church, Rotterdam* (Edinburgh: Waugh & Innes, 1832).

Stonestreet, George Griffin, *Recollections of the Scenes of which I was Witness in the Low Countries and France in the Campaigns of 1814 and 1815 and the Subsequent Occupation of French Flanders: The Journal and Letters of the Reverend George Griffin Stonestreet 1814–16*, ed. Gareth Glover (Godmanchester: Ken Trotman Publishing, 2009).

Taylor, Lieut.-Gen. Sir Herbert, *The Taylor Papers: Being a Record of Certain Reminiscences, Letters, and Journals*, arranged by Ernest Taylor (London: Longmans, Green, and Co., 1913).

Thackeray, William Makepeace, *The Letters and Private Papers*, ed. Gordon N. Ray, 4 vols (Cambridge, MA: Harvard University Press, 1946).

Trollope, Anthony, *An Autobiography and Other Writings*, ed. Nicholas Shrimpton (Oxford: Oxford University Press, 2016).

Trollope, Mrs [Frances], *Belgium and Western Germany in 1833* (Paris: Baudry's European Library, 1834).

Trollope, Frances Milton, *Domestic Manners of the Americans* (London: Whittaker, Treacher, & Co., 1832).

Trollope, Rev. W., *Belgium since the Revolution of 1830: Comprising a Topographical and Antiquarian Description of the Country, and a Review of its Political, Commercial, Literary, Religious, and Social Relations, as Affecting its Present Condition and Future Prospects* (London: How and Parsons, 1842).

Victoria, Queen, *The Letters of Queen Victoria*, ed. A.C. Benson and Lord Esher, 3 vols (London: John Murray, 1908), vol. I: *1837–1843*. Project Gutenberg Ebook, updated 2009.

[Westwood, Thomas]; Preface by Florence, Lady Alwyne Compton, *A Literary Friendship: Letters to Lady Alwyne Compton 1869–1881 from Thomas Westwood* (London: John Murray, 1914).

White, Charles, *The Belgic Revolution of 1830*, 2 vols (London: Whittaker and Co., 1835).

Wordsworth, Dorothy, *Journal of a Tour on the Continent*, in Dorothy Wordsworth, *The Continental Journals*, Intro. by Helen Boden (Bristol: Thoemmes Press, 1995).

Wright, Charlotte May, *Memories of Far Off Days: The Memoirs of Charlotte May Wright 1855–1929*, ed. Peter A. Wright, 2nd edn (privately published, 1988).

[Wright, John Martin F.] A Trinity-Man, *Alma Mater; or, Seven Years at the University of Cambridge*, 2 vols (London: Black, Young & Young, 1827).

Secondary

Altick, Richard, *The Art of Literary Research* [1963], 3rd edn (New York: W.W. Norton, 1981).

Altick, Richard D., *Lives and Letters: A History of Literary Biography in England and America* [1965] (Westport, CT: Greenwood Press, 1979).

Altick, Richard, *The Scholar Adventurers* [1950] (Columbus: Ohio State University Press, 1987).

Barker, Juliet, *The Brontës* [1994] (London: Abacus, 2010).

Benbough-Jackson, Mike, *Cardiganshire and the Cardi, c.1760–c.2000: Locating a Place and its People* (Cardiff: University of Wales Press, 2011).

Bew, John, *Castlereagh: The Biography of a Statesman* (London: Quercus, 2014).

Bracken, Brian, 'Football and the Brussels Brontë Story', *The Brussels Brontë Group: Research* (9 June 2014), online.

Bracken, Brian, 'The Jenkinses' House in Ixelles', *The Brussels Brontë Group: Research* (18 November 2010), online.

Braekman, E.M., *Le protestantisme à Bruxelles: Des origines à la mort de Léopold I* (Brussels: Bibliothèque Royale Albert I, 1980).

Chadwick, Mrs. Ellis H., *In the Footsteps of the Brontës* (London: Sir Isaac Pitman & Sons, 1914).

Collins, Irene, *Jane Austen and the Clergy* (London: The Hambledon Press, 1993).

Colyer, Richard J., *The Teifi: Scenery and Antiquities of a Welsh River* (Llandysul: Gomer Press, 1987).

Davies, John, *A History of Wales*, rev. edn (London: Penguin Books, 2007).

Dixon, Peter, *Canning: Politician and Statesman* (London: Weidenfeld and Nicolson, 1976).

Downey, Edmund, *Charles Lever: His Life in His Letters*, 2 vols (Edinburgh and London: William Blackwood and Sons, 1906).

Edel, Leon, *Writing Lives: Principia Biographica* [1959] (New York and London: W.W. Norton & Company, 1984).

Evans, George Eyre, *Cardiganshire: A Personal Survey of Some of its Antiquities, Chapels, Churches, Fonts, Plate, and Registers* (Aberystwyth: Printed at the 'Welsh Gazette' Offices, 1903).

Fraser, Rebecca, *Charlotte Brontë* (London: Methuen–Mandarin, 1989).

Freeman, Michael, *A Winter Sanatorium: Ventnor as a Health Resort in the Victorian Era* (Ventnor: Ventnor & District Local History Society, 2009).

Gérin, Winifred, *Charlotte Brontë: The Evolution of Genius* [1967] (Oxford: Oxford University Press, 1969).

Gill, Stephen, *William Wordsworth: A Life*, 2nd edn (Oxford: Oxford University Press, 2020).

Gillen, Mollie, *The Prince and His Lady: The Love Story of the Duke of Kent and Madame de St Laurent* (London: Sidgwick & Jackson, 1970).

Grainger, Elena, *The Remarkable Reverend Clarke: The Life and Times of the Father of Australian Geology* (Oxford: Oxford University Press, 1982).

Green, Joseph J., 'The Bronte–Wheelwright Friendship', *Friends' Quarterly Examiner* (1916).

Hague, William, *William Pitt the Younger* (London: HarperCollins, 2004).

Hague, William, *William Wilberforce: The Life of the Great Anti-Slave Trade Campaigner* (London HarperCollins, 2007).

Harman, Claire, *Charlotte Brontë: A Life* (UK: Viking, 2015).

Hibbert, Christopher, *George IV: Regent and King 1811–1830* (London: Allen Lane, 1973).

Holme, Thea, *Chelsea* (London: Hamish Hamilton, 1972).

Holmes, Richard, *Coleridge: Darker Reflections* (London: Flamingo, 1999).

Holmes, Richard, *Coleridge: Early Visions* (London: Harper Perennial, 2005).

Holmes, Richard, *Footsteps: Adventures of a Romantic Biographer* (London: HarperPress, 2011).

Holmes, Richard, *Shelley: The Pursuit* (London: Harper Perennial, 2005).

Holmes, Richard, *This Long Pursuit: Reflections of a Romantic Biographer* (London: William Collins, 2016).

Howells, William H., 'The Library of Edward Richard, Ystradmeurig', *Ceredigion: Journal of the Cardiganshire Antiquarian Society*, 9:3 (1982), pp. 227–44.

Jones, Raymond A., *The British Diplomatic Service 1815–1914* (Gerrards Cross: Colin Smythe, 1983).

Kendall, Monica, 'Brussels, Brontë, Jenkins: My Great-great-grandparents Rev. Evan and Eliza Jenkins and the Brontës', *The Brussels Brontë Group: Research* (26 March 2014), online.

Kendall, Monica, ed., *Miss Cavell Was Shot: The Diaries of Amy Hodson, 1914–1920* (Bristol: SilverWood, 2015).

Knight, Frances, *The Nineteenth-Century Church and English Society* (Cambridge: Cambridge University Press, 1998).

Livingston, Edwin Brockholst, *The Livingstons of Callendar and their Principal Cadets: The History of an Old Stirlingshire Family* (Edinburgh: T & A Constable, at the University Press, 1920).

Lynch, John, *San Martín: Argentine Soldier, American Hero* (New Haven and London: Yale University Press, 2009).

MacCarthy, Fiona, *Byron: Life and Legend* (London: John Murray, 2002).

MacEwan, Helen, *Down the Belliard Steps: Discovering the Brontës in Brussels* (Hythe: Brussels Brontës Editions, 2012).

Moore-Colyer, Richard, *Welsh Cattle Drovers: Agriculture and the Welsh Cattle Trade before and during the Nineteenth Century* (Ashbourne: Landmark, 2002).

Morgan, Gerald, ed., *Nanteos: A Welsh House and Its Families* (Llandysul: Gomer Press, 2001).

Osborne-Jones, D.G., *Edward Richard of Ystradmeurig with the Story of His School and its Associations under its Successive Masters 1734–1934* (Carmarthen: W. Spurrell & Son, 1934).

Philip, Rosemary, 'Lixmount House and its People', *The Scottish Genealogist*, 64:1 (March 2017), pp. 17–29.

Ray, Gordon N., *Thackeray: The Age of Wisdom (1847–1863)* (London: Oxford University Press, 1958).

Ray, Gordon N., *Thackeray: The Uses of Adversity, 1811–1846* (London: Oxford University Press, 1955).

Rees, Rev. D.C., *Tregaron: Historical and Antiquarian* (Llandysul: J.D. Lewis & Sons, Gomerian Press, 1936).

Richardson, Joanna, *My Dearest Uncle: A Life of Leopold: First King of the Belgians* (London: Jonathan Cape, 1961).

Roe, Nicholas, *John Keats: A New Life* (New Haven and London: Yale University Press, 2013).

Ruijssenaars, Eric, *Charlotte Brontë's Promised Land: The Pensionnat Heger and Other Brontë Places in Brussels* (Haworth: The Brontë Society, 2000).

Ruijssenaars, Eric, 'Mapping the Brussels of the Brontës: The Cultural Places', *Brussels Brontë Blog* (28 April 2018).

Russell, John, *The Story of Leith* (London: T. Nelson and Sons [1922]).

Russett, Alan, and Tom Pocock, *A History of Chelsea Old Church: The Church that Refused to Die* (London: Chelsea Old Church, 2004).

Schama, Simon, *Patriots and Liberators: Revolution in the Netherlands 1780–1813*, 2nd edn (London: Fontana Press, 1992).

Shorter, Clement K., *Charlotte Brontë and Her Circle*, 2nd edn (London: Hodder and Stoughton, 1896).

State, Paul F., *Historical Dictionary of Brussels* (Lanham, MD: The Scarecrow Press, 2004).

Stevens, Joan, ed., *Mary Taylor: Friend of Charlotte Brontë: Letters from New Zealand and Elsewhere* (Auckland and Oxford: Auckland University Press, Oxford University Press, 1972).

Stevenson, Lionel, *Dr. Quicksilver: The Life of Charles Lever* (London: Chapman & Hall, 1939).

Strachey, Lytton, *Eminent Victorians* [1918] (Oxford: Oxford University Press, 2003).

Strong, Ruth, *The Story of Pudsey Church* (Pudsey St Lawrence and St Paul Parochial Church Council, 1988).

Sutherland, John, *The Life of Walter Scott* (Oxford: Blackwell, 1995).

Tuffs, J. Elsden, *The Story of Wanstead and Woodford: From Roman Times to the Present* (Published by the Author, 1962).

Tyerman, Christopher, *A History of Harrow School 1324–1991* (Oxford: Oxford University Press, 2000).

Uglow, Jenny, *Elizabeth Gaskell: A Habit of Stories* (London: Faber & Faber, 1993).

Uglow, Jenny, *In These Times: Living in Britain Through Napoleon's Wars, 1793–1815* (London: Faber & Faber, 2015).

Warwick, Andrew, 'The Analytical Revolution from Below: Private Teaching and Mathematical Reform in Georgian Cambridge', in Jonathan Smith and Christopher Stray, eds, *Teaching and Learning in Nineteenth-Century Cambridge* (Woodbridge: The Boydell Press, 2001).

Watson, Marcia, 'In Search of Margaret's Family: Grandmother Elizabeth Hardie', *Dalwood House Newsletter*, no. 102 (September 2018), pp. 2–8.

Watson, Marcia, 'In Search of Margaret's Family: Helen Jay née Livingston', *Dalwood House Newsletter*, no. 107 (December 2019), pp. 15–17.

Watson, Marcia, 'In Search of Margaret's Family: John Jay's School for Boys', *Dalwood House Newsletter*, no. 99 (December 2017), pp. 9–14.

Watson, Marcia, 'To Be or Not to Be', in *A New Tapestry: Huguenot Families in Australia*, ed. Robert Nash (Newtown: NSW Huguenot Society of Australia, 2015), pp. 166–76.

Watson, Marcia, 'What Happened to John Jay's School?', *Dalwood House Newsletter*, no. 100 (March 2018), pp. 5–7.

Weinreb, Ben, and Christopher Hibbert, eds, *The London Encyclopaedia*, rev. edn (London: Macmillan, 1995).

Index

NOTE: Plate numbers appear after page numbers, e.g., Leith, Scotland: St Ninian's Church 133, plate 11. Abbreviations: CB = Charlotte Brontë; EB = Emily Brontë; PB = Patrick Brontë.

Aberdeen, George Hamilton Gordon, 4th Earl of 258, 263–4, 268

Aberdeen, Scotland 96, 97–8

Aberystwyth, Cardiganshire
    challenges of travelling to 21
    coach journey to London via Kington 21, 68–9
    mansions and estates of 42–4
    tourism in Napoleonic era 23
    see also Nanteos estate; National Library of Wales

Adair, Sir Robert 308, 319–20, 321–2, 323, 336, 337, 338

Addison, Joseph 198

Airy, Sir George Biddell 165, 180–2, 186, 190, 194

Airy, Wilfrid 180, 181

Albert, Prince Consort 238, 354, 355, 370, 379, 470
    in Brussels as youth 205, 338–9, 352–3
    royal visit to Belgium 410–14
    travel by train 358

Alexander I, Tsar of Russia 203

Allen, Rev. Joseph (later Bishop of Bristol then Ely) 168–70, 178, 184

Almanack of the Church of the Resurrection 201, 217, 467, plate 24

Althorp, John Charles Spencer, Viscount 169

Altick, Richard 13, 140, 356–7, 362

Andover, Hampshire: Dr and Mrs Jay's school 113, 115, 116–23, 124–5

Andrew, George (of Lixmount House) 134, 135

Anglicanism
    Catholic resistance to Anglican clergy in Brussels 436
    church building programme in early 1800s 225–6
    pull towards Catholicism and Oxford Movement 249–50, 470
    and Taylor family 388–92
    in Wales 31, 32–3, 54, 439, 483*n*.45
        itinerant schools and religious education 58
        landed gentry and church estates 42
        pluralism and economic drivers 60, 73
        poverty and poor education of Welsh clergy 59–60
        teaching as stop-gap for clergy awaiting ordination 53, 61
    see also Brussels: Protestant churches;

curateships; Evangelicalism; Protestantism
Antwerp 447
  and travel to England 393, 418, 421–2
Arbroath, Scotland 128, 131
Arthur, King: and tunic-stealing 20
Atkinson, Solomon 160, 176–8, 198
  admission to Cambridge as sizar 177–8, 180
  on college tutors 184–5
  on degrading duties of Cambridge sizars 182
  dismissive of lecturers and professors 95
  on ease of falling into debt 189
  tutoring job to pay for lodgings 186
  Wright on unimaginative character of 185
Auber, Daniel: *Muette de Portici* (*Masaniello*)
  277–8, 317–18, 320, 321
Austen, Rev. Henry 74
Austen, Jane 115, 251, 252
  Emma 120, 298, 333–4
  Mansfield Park 61–2, 74, 149, 208, 370
  Pride and Prejudice 74–5, 97, 208, 312
Australia
  Dalwood House 6
  Eliza and Evan Jenkins's son in 455, 457–62, 466
  Rev. William Branwhite Clarke in 312–13, 369
  see also Wyndham, George; Wyndham, Margaret
Austrian Netherlands 203
Ayers, Charlotte (née Morse) 424–6, 427, 429, 443, 448
Ayers, William 421, 424, 427, 429, 443, 448

Back, Rev. E. 210
Bagnano, Libry (Libri) 272, 278
Bagot, Sir Charles 236–7, 239, 244, 246, 247–8, 266
Bagot, Lady Mary Charlotte Anne (née Wellesley-Pole) 246, 247
Bagot, Richard, Bishop of Oxford 250
Baker, Rev. Henry Defoe 216, plate 24
Baker, Rev. Samuel Ogilvy 96

Barbauld, Anna Laetitia: *Eighteen Hundred and Eleven* 139
Barker, John 308, 309–10
Barker, Juliet
  The Brontës 222
  on Buckworth as vicar of Dewsbury 83
  on David Jenkins and PB in Yorkshire 75, 76, 79, 81–2, 87
  on 'Diligence' and Brontës' arrival in Brussels 357–8, 359
  on Rev. Jenkins and Brontë family in Brussels 361
  and Westwood's letters as confusing source 384–5, 386
Barker, Sophia 294, 295–9, 302–6, 308–12, 313
Barker, Thomas 296
Barnes, Julian: *Flaubert's Parrot* 2, 334
Barnes, Mr (Cambridge tutor) 178
Bassompierre, Mademoiselle de 10–11
Batley, Yorkshire: Joseph Walker Jenkins as curate at 365, 374, 405, 407, 408
Bauer, Caroline (Karoline) 292
Beaumont, Arthur 282, 283, 284, 524n.46
Beaumont, Augustus Hardin 282–3, 284
Beaumont, Edmund H. 282–4, 524n.46
Belgium xviii
  amalgamation with the Netherlands 199–200, 272
  Belgian Revolution (1830) 270, 272–89
    American radicals as volunteers 282–4
    opera performance as catalyst 277–9
    Prince Frederick and unsuccessful Dutch responses 280–2, 283–4, 284–5, 287
    provisional government and choice of Leopold as king 288–9, 293–4, 299–300, 301–2
  cholera epidemic (1848–9) 443–4
  Dutch invasion and subsequent truce 306–8
  equitable financial control in Belgian marriages 460
  introduction and building of railways in 334–5, 437

visit of Victoria and Albert and press 410–14
  see also Antwerp; Bruges; Brussels; Ostend;
    Spa
Bentley, Dr Phyllis 417–18
Bess of Hardwick (Elizabeth Cavendish) 72
Bevan, Madam Bridget 58
Biber, Rev. G.E. 364, 367, 368–9, 403, 409
Bifrons, Kent 251, 252
Bingley, Rev. William 505*n*.49
biographers and craft
  aptitude for history 7
  consideration of context and people 13
  craving for inclusion 1–2, 304
  repetition of unconfirmed 'facts' 2, 13,
    356–62, 387
  revenge by proxy 2
  value of letters to 125
Birstall, Yorkshire: St Peter's Church and Taylor
  family 388, 390, 391
Blacker, Rev. Maxwell Julius 392, 446–7, 449,
  451, 455–7, plate 24
Blake, Joseph (lodging house proprietor in
  Ventnor) 450
Blomfield, Charles James, Bishop of London
  boyhood and background 261–2
  and controversy over Bishop Luscombe
    261, 262, 263, 265, 266, 268, 269
  letter to Jenkins family on death of Rev. Evan
    Jenkins 444–5
  letter to Rev. Blacker re post of chaplain in
    Brussels 446–7
  mass confirmations in Brussels and Evan as
    tour guide 269, 336
  Trollope's characterization in *The Warden*
    261, 470
Bolívar, Símon 381–2
Bolton, Rev. William Watson 259–60
Borough, Sir Richard 206, 211, 212
Borrow, George: *Wild Wales* 36–7, 55, 486*n*.31
Borthwick Institute for Archives, York 34
Boudin, Dr Hugh 348
Bowden, Albinia Jackson *see* Chave, Albinia Jackson
Bowden, Alfred 143, 144

Bowden, Clara (née Wylde) 341, 349
Bowden, James (d. 1821) 96, 140–1, 143, 144,
  146, 341, 349
Bowden, Margaret (née Livingston) (1779–1811)
  96, 140–1, 143, 248
  deaths of children 143–4
Bowden, Margaret (1806–65): will 144, 461
Bracken, Brian 7
Bradford Observer 440–1
Branwell, Elizabeth
  CB's appeal for support for educational trip
    to Brussels 3, 363, 364, 396, 476
  illness and death and CB and EB's return
    from Brussels 388, 393, 418
Branwell, Maria *see* Brontë, Maria (née Branwell)
Bright, Louisa 374, 416, 417
Bright, Mary (Mrs) 416, 417, 427–8, 436, 449,
  450, 452
Bright family in Brussels 374, 416, 417, 427–8
Bristed, Charles Astor 159, 179–80, 182, 189,
  192, 396–7, 451
Brontë, Anne 3, 357
Brontë, Branwell 33, 393, 437
Brontë, Charlotte 245, 325, 455, plate 20
  admirer of Byron 351
  Angrian stories and mocking of Methodism
    33
  appeal to aunt Branwell to go to Brussels 3,
    363, 364, 396, 476
  ardour fired by Mary Taylor's letters 2–3,
    363–4, 366
  on author's allegiance to truth 476
  in Brussels for first stay and acquaintance
    with Jenkins family 2, 96, 205, 246, 351,
    355, 356–93, 475
    arrival and biographers on transport
      to Brussels 357–60
    assistance from Mrs Jenkins in finding
      school 3, 365–6
    and death of Martha Taylor 387, 388,
      392, 393
    enrolment at pensionnat Heger 3–4,
      5–6, 10–11, 366

first morning and story about Mr and
Mrs Jenkins 8, 360–2, 366, 384
improvement in dress sense 299
on Joseph Walker Jenkins 224
story of shyness in social situations 4,
8–9, 383, 384, 396, 399–400
sudden return on death of aunt 388,
392, 418
in Brussels for second stay as teacher with
Hegers 393, 396–420
friendship with Wheelwright family
400, 401, 402, 403
presentation of diploma from Heger
on departure 420
relations with Hegers and decision to
leave 414–15, 416
and social visits with Jenkins family
396, 399–400, 403, 476
story of gift of poetry book from M.
Heger and inscriptions 418, 419–20
transport, timings and manner of final
departure 417–20, 429–30
career as governess
education at Cowan Bridge school for
230
stifling nature of job 3
on Edinburgh 135
on Irvingites 462
letter to EB on seeing Queen Victoria in
Brussels 410
letters to Constantin Heger 420, 435–6
letters to Ellen Nussey 362, 399, 402, 404,
432
on conveying letter to Martha Taylor
391
on desire to travel and desire to learn
2–3, 363–4, 365
on hearing Rev. Joseph Walker Jenkins's
voice in Brussels 407–8
on Heger's presentation of diploma on
parting 420
on Mrs Jenkins's help with search for
school 365–6

joint letter with Taylor sisters 373–4
on journey from Leeds to Brussels 358
letters to and from Mary Taylor
and description of Rev. Jenkins as
consul 363–4
as inspiration for desire to visit
Continent 2–3, 363
Mary's destruction of CB's letters 362,
399
mistranscription and error about
weather 357
and search for suitable school in
Brussels 363–4, 365, 366
literature on
repetition of unconfirmed facts
357–62, 383–7
Westwood's published letters 383–7
see also Gaskell, Mrs; Gérin, Winifred
marriage to Arthur Nicholls
honeymoon in Snowdonia 171–2
supervision of wife's letters 432
plan to set up school with sisters 3, 363
as pupil at Cowan Bridge school 222, 230
as pupil at Roe Head school 396
royal admirer in Queen Victoria 414
Jane Eyre 104, 425
Cowan Bridge school as Lowood 89,
222, 229
dedication to Thackeray 409–10
Queen Victoria's enjoyment of 414
The Professor 199, 215, 217, 357, 368, 369, 400
on congregation departing Chapel
Royal 406–7
Heger in character of William 415
parallels with Jenkinses' home school
in Brussels 401
on travelling by diligence 359, 360
Shirley 381, 414
charitable fund 535*n*.51
on effects of war and politics in West
Yorkshire woollen towns 80, 138–9
Rev. Roberson as inspiration for Rev.
Helstone 226

satirical view of Methodism 33
scorn for 'gentleman' status of Peter
      Malone 39–40
Taylor family as characters in 3, 362–3,
      389, 393
Villette 6, 100, 104, 205, 220, 357, 359, 371,
      380, 414
   echoes of Rev. Evan Jenkins in 348, 436
   on Louise-Marie, queen of the Belgians
      452
   melancholy portrayal of King Leopold
      290–1
   Mrs Gaskell's research 464
   possible portrait of Edward Jenkins in
      398–9
   on turbulent recent past in Brussels
      285–6
   and Wheelwright family 402
Brontë, Elizabeth 229, 230
Brontë, Emily 3, 234, 419
   biographies and literature on 140
   in Brussels and acquaintance with Jenkins
      family 2, 205, 355, 359, 361, 373–4,
      387, 475
      enrolment at pensionnat Heger and
         stay in Brussels 3–4, 5–6, 10–11, 366
      improvement in dress sense 299
      as piano player and teacher 371, 402
      story of shyness in social situations 4,
         8–9, 383, 396, 400
      sudden return on death of aunt 388,
         392, 418
   at Cowan Bridge school 230
   decision not to return to Brussels 393
   letter from CB on seeing Queen Victoria in
      Brussels 410
   on timing of CB's final return from Brussels
      418
   Wuthering Heights 406
Brontë, Maria (daughter) 89, 223, 229, 230
Brontë, Maria (mother, née Branwell) 3, 89, 223,
   227
Brontë, Patrick
   biography of 7
   clerical career and friendship with Rev.
      David Jenkins in Yorkshire 2, 7–8, 24,
         33–4, 441
      Cambridge education confers
         respectability 40
      curacies in Essex and Shropshire 75
      curacy in Dewsbury and hope of
         Hartshead living 75–6
      and David Jenkins's appointment as
         curate at Dewsbury and Hartshead
         63, 74, 76–9
      duties shared with David Jenkins at
         Dewsbury and Hartshead 78–9,
         81–2, 87–8, 89
      eldest daughters at Cowan Bridge
         with Harriet Jenkins 89, 229–31
      as minister at Hartshead 87, 88, 89,
         222, 223, 226
      as minister at Thornton 222, 223
      move to Haworth and ministry at 89,
         227, 388, 405
      possibly visited by Evan Jenkins 405
   correspondence with M. Heger 371
   escorts CB and EB to Brussels and stays
      with Jenkinses 3–4, 355, 359, 360, 361,
         366, 396
   marriage and children 89, 223, 227, 230–1
   and Methodism 33
Brontë Society 79, 81
Brontë Society Transactions 10
Brown, Mr (Cambridge tutor) 163, 165, 188, 189
Brown, Charlotte (partner of Leonard Becher
   Morse) 425
Bruges 175
   Trollope family in 325, 326, 335
Brussels xix–xxi
   British Ambassadors *see* Adair; Bagot;
      Howard; Seymour
   Chaussée d'Ixelles and Jenkinses' home 7,
      8, 20, 257–8, 351
   cholera epidemic (1848–9) 443–4
   Connie Jenkins's memories of 5–6

Cricket Club and Edward and John Jenkins 397, 456

English charitable fund 367–8

Hôtel d'Angleterre 219, 220

Isabelle Quarter xxi, 7, plate 19

   see also Pensionnat Heger

literary descriptions in early 1800s 214–15

marriages between English nationals in 368–9

museum and contents 428–9

Place Royale 205, 249, plate 18

Protestant cemetery 215–16, 445

   CB's description in *The Professor* 215

   Jay family burials 215–16

   relocation to Evere and removal of bodies 1, 11–13, 216, 462, plate 1

Protestant churches 344

   Catholic resistance to Anglican rites in hospital 436

   and controversy over Bishop Luscombe 258–68, 269

   project to build Church of the Resurrection 11, 201, 467–8, 470–1, 473–4, plate 25

   Senate's refusal of grant for English churches 333, 334

   see also Chapel Royal; Church of the Augustines (King's Church); Church of the Resurrection; St George's Chapel

research visits by Mrs Gaskell 93, 402, 464

revolution

   Jenkinses' experiences in city 271–2, 279–80

   siege of city 282, 283–5, 286–7

   unrest against Orangists and Leopold's attempts to bring calm 320–4

schools *see* Château de Koekelberg; Institut Britannique; Pensionnat Heger; St Bernard's School, Brussels *and also under* Drury, William *and* Jenkins, Evan

visit by Queen Victoria and Prince Albert 410

Brussels Brontë Group 7, 11, 12, 13, 19

Buckworth, Rev. John (d. 1835) 74, 75, 76, 77–8, 82–6, 88, 89

   posthumous *Memoir* on 78, 82–3, 84

Bulwer, Sir Henry Lytton 337, 338, 339

Bunhill Fields, East London 104

Bunyan, John 104

Burge, Rev. Richard 79, 82, 86, 90

Burgess, Thomas, Bishop of St David's (later Bishop of Salisbury) 50, 53, 59, 60–1, 438–9, 441

Burney, Fanny 125

Bury Hall, nr Edmonton, Middlesex 141, 142

Butler, Rev. Dr George: headmaster of Harrow School 66, 255, 256

Butler, Rev. Weeden (1742–1823) 66, 67

Butler, Weeden (1772–1831) 66, 67

Byron, Allegra 327–32

Byron, George Gordon, Lord 98, 195, 236, 263, 286, 339, 343

   as boy at Harrow School 66, 246, 254, 255, 338, 476

   in Brussels 214, 325

   at Cambridge with bear 185–6

   Childe Harold's Pilgrimage 159, 214, 286, 476

   daughter Allegra and burial in Harrow 327–33

Byron, Lady 252

Cadogan, Earl 65

Calverley parish, West Yorkshire 89, 223, 228–9

Calvert, Thomas Jackson (professor at Cambridge) 19, 191

Calvinism

   Calvinistic Methodism in Wales 31, 33, 40, 52, 54

   Huguenots and Revocation of Edict of Nantes 99–100

Cambrian, The (newspaper) 55–6, 60

Cambridge University 15, 158–68, 176–98

   class and ranks of students 188

   and examination requirements for

degrees 160, 168
and lure of drink and debt 189–90
pensioners 150, 163, 167–8, 179, 186–7
sizars 179–82, 185–6, 191, 195
and evolution of football rules 398
examinations and attitudes towards 197–8
extra-curricular lectures 193–4, 195
Master of Arts degree criteria 159–60, 168
mathematics as core subject 159, 162, 165, 166, 178, 188, 189, 197
Norrisian lectures and ordination 19, 191–2, 232
opium use 178
reputation of Shrewsbury students at 396–7
Shrewsbury scholarship for Edward Jenkins 436, 448–9
Wordsworth at 158–9, 180, 187, 189
see also Trinity College, Cambridge
Canning, George 236–7, 246, 248, 260–1, 264, 319
Canvey Island, Essex: Dutch community in 1600s 104–5
Cardiganshire (now Ceredigion) 14
Coleridge and walking tour 27–8
customary pregnancy on marriage 176
Jenkins family land ownership 39–41
landowners and estates 42–4, 49, 58
vagaries of roads 20–1
women in Welsh dress 36
see also Aberystwyth; Llanbadarn Odyn (Odwyn)
Carey, George: *A Complete System of Theoretical and Mercantile Arithmetic* 147–9, 151
Carlyle, Thomas: noise in Chelsea 72
Caron *see* Tregaron (Caron), Cardiganshire
Cartwright, Thomas (Brussels Chargé d'Affaires) 258, 261, 263, 264–5
Castlereagh, Amelia ('Emily') Stewart, Viscountess 252
Castlereagh, Robert Stewart, Viscount 203, 207, 235, 236, 252, 255, 337
Catherine the Great, Empress of Russia 58
Catholic Apostolic Church 462

Ceredigion *see* Cardiganshire (now Ceredigion)
Ceredigion Museum, Aberystwyth 20–1
Chadwick, Mrs Ellis H. (née Esther Alice Miller)
impossibility of meeting Eliza Jenkins 8, 9, 10, 383
In the Footsteps of the Brontës 8–9, 13, 361, 388
copying from Mrs Gaskell's biography 8–9
misconstrual of CB's description of Joseph Walker Jenkins 408
Mlle Bassompierre as source 10–11
story of Brontës' arrival in Brussels 357, 359, 360, 383, 384
story of Edward and John Jenkins escorting Brontë sisters 8, 9, 10
as possible buyer of Emily's accounts notebooks 419
Chadwick, Ellis Henry 9
Chapel Royal, rue du Musée, Brussels 204–13, 216–17, plates 14, 15
committee and contested appointment of Anglican chaplain (1817–18) 201, 204, 206–13
Evan Jenkins as chaplain at 250–1, 257, 277, 351, 352, 367
controversy over authority of Bishop Luscombe and licences 264–8
King Leopold's attendance 205, 303–4, 318, 320, 352–3
misattribution of CB's recognition of voice from home 407–8
missing record of Martha Taylor's funeral 391–2
ordination and testimonials 16, 17–18, 237–8
Prince Albert's attendance 353
registration of death 17, 19–20
subscriptions for new organ 184
successor on death 444–5, 446–7, 449, 465
Evan's son Rev. (Charles) Edward as chaplain 392, 463, 465, 470
list of chaplains plate 24

registers and records
    and funeral of Martha Taylor 388, 389
    Jay family deaths and burials 215
    lack of records on English Anglicans
      at 205–6
    Rev. Evan Jenkins's incomplete set of
      registers 391–2
    Rev. Prince and abduction of register
      206, 211–12, 212–13
Charade, Jacqueline 205
charity schools and education in Wales 57, 58
Charlotte (Augusta), Princess 206, 207, 213, 273
    courtship and marriage to Prince Leopold
      289–90
    death in childbirth 290
Château de Koekelberg (Mme Goussaert's
    school), nr Brussels 244–5, 363, 371–6, 380,
    382
    and death of Martha Taylor at 387–8, 392–3
    wrongly described as finishing school 373,
      375
Chave, Albinia Jackson (née Bowden): 'friend of
    Thackeray' 349–51
Chave, Rev. William 349–51
Chelsea, London 65–8, 69–72, plate 7
    Cheyne House Academy 64–6, 73, 164
    David Jenkins's journey to and arrival in
      68–72
    Felix school 170, 171, 172
    Mrs Gaskell's family in 173–5
    Old Church 70–1, 73, 78, 175, plate 6
    other schools in 66
    St Luke's Church 65, 70
Chelsea Physic Garden 65–6
Cheltenham, Gloucestershire 450–4
    spa cures 451
Chevallier, Rev. Temple 197
Cheyne House Academy, Chelsea, London 64–6,
    72, 73, 164
    see also Felix school
cholera epidemic in Belgium 443–4
Christian, John (later Curwen) (1756–1828) 422
Church of the Augustines (King's Church),

Brussels 203–4, 213, 233–4, 259, 264, 277,
    plate 13
    Evan Jenkins's ordination and curacy at
      237–8, 248
    list of chaplains plate 24
    Revolution and subsequent closure 314, 315
Church Building Act (Million Act) (1818) 225
Church of England *see* Anglicanism
Church Missionary Society 194, 196
Church of the Resurrection, Brussels
    Edward Jenkins's unbuilt church 11, 201,
      467–8, 470–2, 473, 474, plate 25
    list of chaplains plate 24
    new site and church and John Card Jenkins's
      ministry 473–5
'circulating schools' in Wales 58
Clairmont, Claire 328–9, 332, 343
Clancarty, Richard Le Poer Trench, 2nd Earl of
    207, 233, 235, 236
Clare, Suffolk 106–7
Claremont House, nr Esher, Surrey 290, 291, 292
Clarendon, Earl of 465
Clark, Sir James (physician) 449
Clarke, Miss (sister to Rev. Clarke) 299, 300, 304,
    527*n*.131
Clarke, Edward Daniel (lecturer at Cambridge)
    295
Clarke, Maria Moreton (née Stather) 298, 312, 313
Clarke, Rev. William Branwhite 184, 192, 194
    courtship of Sophia Barker and love triangle
      294–9, 300, 302–6, 308–12, 313
    Eliza and Evan Jenkins's letters to 109, 294,
      295, 298, 300–2, 303–4, 304–6, 310–12,
      313, 327, 367
      on aftermath of Belgian Revolution
        288, 299–300
    friendship and stays with Jenkins family in
      Brussels 295, 296, 302–6
    move to Australia and geology studies 193,
      312–13, 369
Clarkson, Catherine (friend of Dorothy
    Wordsworth) 180
Clarkson, John (governor of Sierra Leone) 506*n*.63

Clarkson, Thomas (slavery abolitionist) 180–1
Clarkson, William (of Pudsey) 440
Clemson, Anna Maria Calhoun and Thomas
   (US diplomat in Brussels) 444
Clergy Daughters' School, Cowan Bridge 89,
   222, 227, 229–31
Cobbett, William 112
Cock, Charles (teacher at Drury's school) 339–41
Cockerill, William 257, 275–6, 280, 285
Coleman, John 378–9
Colenutt, Henry and family (of Ventnor) 450
Coleridge, Hartley 152–3, 166, 422
Coleridge, Samuel Taylor 186, 422
   in Brussels with Wordsworth 247
   debt and dissipation at Cambridge 190
   'Frost at Midnight' and despair over son
      152–3
   walking in Wales with Hucks 27–8, 60
commercial education and John Jay's school
   127–8, 144, 145, 146–9, 151, 155–6
Compton, Lady Alwyne 383, 384, 385, 386
Conservatism *see* Tories
Conservative associations in Yorkshire 437–8
Constable, John 295
Conyngham, Elizabeth, Marchioness 252
Conyngham, Henry, 1st Marquess 252
Cooper, Charlotte (née Pearson) 277, 279, 287
Cooper, Thomas Sidney 275–7, 279, 281, 286–7
Cotton, Sergeant-Major Edward 444
Countesswells estate, Scotland 96, 97
Cowan Bridge school, Lancashire 89, 222, 227,
   229–31
Cribs, Mr and Mrs (Jenkinses' gardener and wife
   in Brussels) 424, 425
Cross Keys pub, Chelsea 71–2
Cunningham, Rev. Joseph William 330, 331–2
Cunynghame, Sir David 416–17
curateships
   exploitation of curates in England 234
   in literature 74–5
   poor pay and conditions in Wales 59–60
   teaching posts while awaiting ordination
      53, 61

Curwen, Alfred 400–1, 421–5, 427–30, 435
Curwen, Rev. Edward Hasell 423, 449
Curwen, Edward Stanley 422–3
   as brother-in-law to Rev. John Wordsworth
      430–1, 432–3, 434
   visits to sons in Brussels weather permitting
      430
Curwen, Frances (Fanny) 399, 432, 433
   correspondence with Eliza Jenkins 469
   on sons' progress at school in Brussels
      421–2, 423–30, 434–5
Curwen, Henry (grandfather): letter to son about
   Rev. John Wordsworth 430–1, 432–3, 434, 435
Curwen, Henry (grandson) 400–1, 421–5,
   427–30, 435
Curwen, Isabella Christian *see* Wordsworth,
   Isabella
Curwen, John Christian 422

Dalrymple, Mrs Wemyss: *Brussels Guide* 358,
   360, 428–9
Dalwood House, Hunter Valley, Australia 6,
   243, 341
Dalwood House Newsletter 6
Dalziel, Andrew (professor at Edinburgh) 124,
   125, 174
Darwin, Charles 195, 313
Daveney family in Belgium 446–7
David, Jacques-Louis 5, 6
Davies, Elizabeth *see* Jenkins, Elizabeth (née
   Davies)
Davies, Grace: witness of farmer Evan Jenkins's
   will 26
Davies, John (historian) 33, 38, 39, 58
Davies, Rees (uncle of Evan and David Jenkins)
   38–9
de la Fontaine *see* Fontaine
De Quincey, Thomas 48, 178
   escape to Wales 37–8
Delacroix, Charles 130
des Réaux, Arnold (merchant in South Holland)
   104, 106

des Réaux, Bénigne (née Fontaine) (1665?–1740) 105, 106

des Réaux, Elisabeth *see* Jay, Elisabeth

des Réaux, Ester (1609–83) 101

des Réaux, Jean (1607–61) 101

des Réaux, Rev. Peter (Pierre) (1663–1736) 104–5, 106

des Réaux, Pierre ('le beau') (1636–1702) 102, 104

Devil's Bridge, Cardiganshire 27

Dewsbury

    All Saints Church (now Dewsbury Minster) 79–82

        appointment of David Jenkins as curate at Dewsbury and Hartshead 63, 74, 76–9, 86–8

        Buckworth as Evangelical vicar of 82–6

        PB's curacy assisted by David Jenkins 81–2, 87, 88, 89

        see also Buckworth, Rev. John

    and CB's view of depressed mill towns 80

Dickens, Charles 105, 345, 406

'Diligence' coach in Belgium 357–8, 359–60, 361, 417, 418

Dissenters *see* Nonconformists (Dissenters)

Dixon, Abraham 390, 392, 403–6, 408, 415, 416–17, 418

Dixon, George 404

Dixon, Laetitia 404

Dixon, Mary 390–1, 396, 404–5, 416

Dixon, Tom 390–1, 392, 405

Dixon family in Brussels

    friendship with Jenkins family 390, 396, 403, 416–17

    friendship with Taylor family in Yorkshire and Brussels 363, 374, 388, 392, 400, 404

Dordrecht, Netherlands 109–11

Drury, Arthur 330

Drury, Charles 255

Drury, Rev. Henry 254, 330

Drury, Rev. Dr Joseph 253, 254–6

Drury, Rev. Mark 253–6, 330, 331

Drury, Rev. William James Joseph

    and burial of Byron's daughter at Harrow 330–1, 333

    as Embassy chaplain in Brussels 319, 338, 355, 368

    and Harrow School 253–4, 255, 260, 330, 331, 338, 339, 476

    as minister of St George's Chapel in Brussels 258–60, 264–5, 266–7, 268, 333, 351, 352, 355

        Gladstone attends 314, 315

        and licence from Luscombe 262, 267

        termination of lease and move to Leopold Quarter 367, 403

    officiates at funeral of Rev. Jenkins and note in register 445

    presence at foundation stone ceremony for Church of the Resurrection 471, plate 25

    presence at mass confirmation by Bishop of Oxford 470

    presence at railroad opening celebrations 437

    services in new church in Brussels and CB's attendance 403

    takeover as head of John Jay's school in Brussels 256–7, 258, 325, 327, 333, 423

        Anthony Trollope as teaching assistant 325, 326, 327

        Charles Cock as infamous master 339–41

        Prince Albert and literature lectures 338

        problems and sale of school and house 339, 340, 341

    teaching private pupils in Brussels 341, 351

Dumas, Alexandre: *The Three Musketeers* 98

Duncan, Mr (Glasgow merchant) 138, 157

Dunlop, Alexander (professor at Glasgow) 107

Edel, Leon 7

Edgcumbe, George (at the Brussels Embassy) 239

Edict of Nantes: revocation and Huguenot flight from France 99–100, 102–3, 104

Edinburgh, Scotland

Eliza and Jay family in
  house in New Town 131–2
  Lixmount House nr Leith 132–40,
    157, 174, plate 26
  possible acquaintance with Walter
    Scott 131–2, 140, 174
  possible acquaintance with Stevenson
    family 174–5
  St Ninian's in Leith 133, plate 11
Edmonton, Middlesex: Eliza and Jay family in
  140–4
Edward, Duke of Kent and Strathearn 204,
  207–8, 209, 210, 212, 213, 316
  marriage to Victoria Mary Louisa 291
Edwards, Thomas (Chelsea schoolmaster) 34, 64,
  65, 66–7, 78
Edwards, Thomas (lawyer son) 64–5, 69, 71, 78
Eggleston, Margaret *see* Jenkins, Margaret (née
  Eggleston)
elementary education provision in Wales 57–8
Elen, St 20
Eliot, George: *The Mill on the Floss* 56, 57
Ellis, Charles Augustus *see* Howard, Lord
Elsworth manor, Cambridgeshire 232
Enslie, James (merchant in Rotterdam) 126, 154
Enslie, Jane (née Tod) 109
Enslie, Janet (d. 1820) 122–3, 134, 146, 153–4,
  156
Enslie, Johanna *see* Jay, Johanna
Enslie, Rev. John (Joannes) (1685?–1766) 107–9
Enslie, John (d. 1798) 126, 128, 131
Enslie, Mary *see* Jay, Mary
Enslie, William (merchant in Smyrna, d. 1794)
  113, 114, 116
Ernst II, Duke of Saxe-Coburg and Gotha 205,
  338–9, 345, 352
Eton School 261–2, 455, 456
Evangelicalism 54, 84–6, 249
Evans, Miss (English teacher in Belgium) 373
Evans, Mrs Estyn (of Belfast) 24
Evans, George Eyre 23, 45
Evans, Rev. John (London lecturer) 72–3
Evere, Brussels: cemetery and Protestant graves 1,

11–13, 216, 462, plate 1
Eyton, Rev. John 75

Faber, Rev. Thomas 90
Farrar, John (of Pudsey) 440
Faulkner, Thomas: *An Historical and Topographical
  Description of Chelsea and its Environs* 67–8, 69,
  70, 71, 73, 172
Felix, Rev. David 164, 170, 172, 262
Felix, Rev. Peter 65, 164, 170, 172, 173, 219, 238,
  262
Felix school in Chelsea 170, 171, 172
Flaubert, Gustave 2, 334, 359
Fontaine, Bénigne *see* des Réaux, Bénigne
Fontaine, Rev. Jaques (1603–66) 103
Fontaine, Rev. Jaques (1658–1728, memoirist)
  99, 100–3
  on flight from France 102–3
  on half-brother Pierre 103–4
  on nephew Peter des Réaux 105
  published *Memoirs* 99, 100–1, 102–3, 105
Fontaine, Jaques de la (1547?–1633, of La
  Rochelle) 101
Fontaine, Jean de la (1500?–63, martyr) 100
Fontaine, Rev. Pierre (1634?–1715, of the Pest
  House) 99, 100, 103–4, 105
Fox, Charles James 63, 319
France
  Huguenots and flight from 98, 99–101,
    102–3, 104
  Trois Glorieuses (July revolution, 1830) 273,
    280
François I, king of France 100
Franks, Mrs J.C. (née Elizabeth Firth, friend of
  the Brontës) 396
Fraser, Rebecca 417
Frederick, Prince, of the Netherlands 280, 281–2,
  283–4, 284–5, 287
Freemasons in Belgium 348

Galt, John: *Life of Byron* 338
Gaskell, Elizabeth (Mrs) (née Stevenson) 399,
   plate 21
   birth and family life in Chelsea 173–5
   correspondence with Mary Taylor 359,
   388–9
   'Cousin Phillis' and brain fever storyline 406
   Cranford 454
   'Half a Life Time Ago' (short story) 41
   The Life of Charlotte Brontë 7, 8–9, 357, 359,
   362, 420
      on death of Martha Taylor 387
      Heger reads his letters from CB to 415
      Queen Victoria as reader 414
      research visits to Brussels and Jenkins
      family 93, 402, 464
      on Rev. and Mrs Jenkins in Brussels
      3–4, 361, 363, 365, 366
      on search for suitable school in Brussels
      365, 366
   'My Lady Ludlow' (short story) 413
gentry and estates in Wales 42–4, 49
   as English-speakers 58
   gentlemen farmers 39–40
   poverty of clergy 60
George III, king of Great Britain 34, 63, 73, 319
George IV, king of Great Britain 214, 237, 252,
   292, 293, 319
Gérin, Eugène 7
Gérin, Winifred (née Bourne)
   biographies and plays about Brontë family 7
   Charlotte Brontë: The Evolution of Genius
   7–8, 9–10, 13, 222
      on 'Diligence' and Brontës' arrival in
      Brussels 357, 359
      on Drury and Julia Wheelwright's
      funeral 403
      fabricated account of arrival in Brussels
      357, 359, 383, 384
      on first morning in Brussels and Mr
      and Mrs Jenkins 8, 360–1
      on Martha Taylor's death and burial
      388–9, 392

   repetition of misinformation from
   earlier biographies 8–9, 357
   and school in Brussels 372
   as source for misinformation in other
   biographies 10, 361, 387
   as source for supposed meeting
   between Mrs Chadwick and Mrs
   Jenkins 8, 9, 10, 383
   story of Edward and John Jenkins
   escorting Brontë sisters 8, 9, 10
   story of gift of book to CB from M.
   Heger 418, 419, 420
Ghémar, Louis 471
Gill, Frances (formerly Barker) 296, 297, 303
Gill, Francis Turner 296, 305
Gill, James 296, 297, 302, 303, 305, 308
Gill, James Sebastian 296, 300, 305
Gill, Stephen: *William Wordsworth: A Life* 55,
   433, 434
Gladstone, John 133
Gladstone, William Ewart 250
   in Brussels 314–15
Gladstone family in Leith 133
Gladstones, Thomas 133, 137
Glan y Gors (Glangors) farm, Cardiganshire 39,
   40, 41, 57, 483n.50
Godwin, Mary *see* Shelley, Mary
Goldney, Rev. John Kellow 354
Goldsmid, Abraham 139
Gomersal, Joseph 442
Gomersal, Mary Ann *see* Jenkins, Mary Ann
Goode, Rev. William 17
Gordon, George Hamilton, 4th Earl of Aberdeen
   258, 263–4, 268
Gordon, Pryse Lockhart 247
Goussaert, Catherine (née Phelps) 416
   background and family 376–80
   school nr Brussels 244–5, 363, 371–6, 380,
   382
      and death of Martha Taylor 387–8,
      392–3
Goussaert, Norbert 372, 380, 389
Goya, Francisco de: *The 3rd of May 1808 in*

Madrid 381
Granville, Lord 236, 237
Grattan, Thomas Colley 246–7, 319–20
Green, Joseph J. 401–2
Greenwich, London: Jay family in 354, 369, 406,
      408
Guiccioli, Contessa Teresa 329

Habsburgs and Low Countries 199, 200
Hague, William 130, 159, 160, 165
Hall, Rev. John 88
Hallam, Arthur Henry 187
Hammond, Dr John 142
Hammond, Dr Thomas 140, 141–3, 144
Harcourt, Edward Venables-Vernon *see* Venables-
      Vernon, Edward
Hardenbroek, Baron 289
Hardie, Elizabeth *see* Livingston, Elizabeth
Hardiviller, Charles-Achille d' 140
Harris, James (1709–80) 124, 125
Harris, James (later 1st Earl of Malmesbury)
      (1746–1820) 125, 127
Harrow-on-the-Hill: St Mary's church and
      Byron's daughter 327–8, 329–31
Harrow School
      Byron at 66, 246, 254, 255, 338, 476
      and Drury family 253–6, 260, 330, 331,
            338, 339
Hartshead, Yorkshire
      St Peter's Church 63, 75–7
            appointment of David Jenkins and
                  time as curate 77–9, 86–8, 89
            PB as minister with living at 87, 88, 89,
                  222, 223, 226
Hawkshead grammar school, Cumbria 55
Haworth, Yorkshire 7, 9, 357, 420
      Parsonage Museum 226, 419–20
      PB's living at 89, 227, 388, 405
      Top Withens 29
Hazlitt, William 236
Heald, Rev. William Margetson and family 388,
      390, 391

Hefford, John (teacher at John Jay's school) 147
Heger, Constantin 7, 234, 371, 393
      CB's feelings for 414–15
      Gérin's play 7
      letters from CB 435–6
            later publication 420
            reads letters to Mrs Gaskell 415
      presents CB with diploma on departure 420
      story of gift of poetry book to CB and
            inscriptions 418, 419–20
      in Westwood's letters 384, 385–6
Heger, Madame (Zoë Claire, née Parent)
      and story of CB's departure from school 414,
            415, 417–18
      see also Pensionnat Heger, Brussels
Henderson, Robert (death in Ventnor) 450
Heneage, George Fieschi 166–7
Henri IV, king of France 101
Henslow, John Stevens (botany professor at
      Cambridge) 195
Hill, Rev. Pascoe Grenfell 447
Hodson, Ernest Rust 12, 476
Holland *see* Netherlands
Holloway, Thomas (engraver) 155
Holmes, Richard (biographer) 1–2, 27, 152, 153,
      190, 203, 235, 295, 304, 328
Holmes, Richard (military historian) 200
Holworthy, Rev. William Henry 232–3, 235,
      247, 264
      concern over authority of Bishop Luscombe
            261, 262, 265–6, 268
      as Embassy chaplain 277, 315, 319, plate 24
      Evan Jenkins as curate for 231, 232, 233,
            237, 238, 248, 250
            succeeds as chaplain 240–1
      testimonial for Evan Jenkins's ordination
            18, 217
Holworthy family 232–3
Hook, Rev. Walter Farquhar 260, 262
Hornby, Rev. George 206, 209–10, 211, 212,
      213, 216, plate 24
Howard, Lord (Charles Augustus Ellis, 6th
      Baron Howard de Walden) 469–70, 471

Howard, Lucy, Lady (Lady Lucy Cavendish-
Scott-Bentinck) 469–70, 471, 472
Howley, William, Bishop of London (later
Archbishop of Canterbury) 202
and contested appointment of Anglican
chaplain to Chapel Royal in Brussels
204, 207, 208, 210, 212
and controversy over Luscombe as bishop
in Europe 258, 260–1, 263, 266–7, 266–8
and ordination of Evan Jenkins 16, 17, 232,
238
Howorth, Rev. William (at Pudsey) 89–90, 224
Hucks, Joseph: in Wales with Coleridge 27–8,
59–60
Hughes, Hugh (insane agent) 43
Hughes, Rev. John (pupil at Ystrad Meurig)
53–4, 60
Hugo, Victor 214
Huguenots
flight from France 98, 99–101, 102–3
as refugees in London 100, 103, 104
Hunt, Leigh 235
Hurd, Douglas 254–5
Hustler, James Devereux (tutor at Cambridge)
163, 167, 168, 181, 184
Hustler, William (tutor at Cambridge) 184, 295
Hutchinson, Mary *see* Wordsworth, Mary
Hutchinson, Sara 150
Hutton, Catherine 20–1, 23, 36
Hutton, William 23
Huxley, Thomas 470

Institut Britannique, Brussels 155–6, 213, 215,
218, 242
Rev. Evan Jenkins as head of classics 231,
237, 238, 239, 257–8
William Drury at 256–7, 258, 327
Irving, Rev. Edward 462
Isle of Wight 449–50
itinerant schools in Wales 58

Jackson, William (Brussels shopkeeper) 443
James, Henry 333
'The Aspern Papers' 25, 332
Jay, Elisabeth (née des Réaux) (1704–65) 105,
106, 109, 110–11
Jay, Eliza *see* Jenkins, Eliza
Jay, Helen (née Livingston) (1777–1821) 95, 96,
97, 154
death and burial in Brussels 215, 216, 466
marriage to John Jay in Rotterdam 128–9
move to Edinburgh and Lixmount House
131, 132, 174
move to Edmonton and stay with sister's
family 140–1, 143
Jay, Isabella (née Layel) 129, 136, 154
Jay, Janet (Jenny/Jen) (1810–81) 92, 141, 143,
154, 244
friendship with Sophia Barker 296, 297, 298
letters from niece Helen 468–9, 469–70,
470–2
letters to sister Margaret in Australia
369–70, 371, 435–6, 452–3, 458, 460
on death of niece Mina 465–6
and death of sister Eliza 468–9
life in Greenwich with brother John 347,
353, 467
visits to Greenwich from Eliza and Evan
Jenkins 354, 369, 406, 408
Jay, Johanna (née Enslie) 126, 216, 238, 346–7
Jay, John (1770–1838) 6, 19, 92, 98, 111, 112,
115, 244, 296
career in family mercantile business in
Rotterdam 126–31
death 347
marriage to Helen and children 128–9, 130,
131, 133
move to Scotland and family business John
Jay & Co. 131–40, 174
bankruptcy and misfortune ends
business 137–40, 145, 157, 347
return from Rotterdam on mother's death
122–3, 127
school for commercial education in Essex

127–8, 144–9, 231, 347–8
  masters and subjects 147–9, 151
  relocation of school to Brussels 148–9, 155–7
  sale of Prospect House and contents 153–5, 156–7
  second marriage to Johanna Enslie 126, 216, 238
  starts and runs Institut Britannique in Brussels 155–6, 213, 215, 218, 231, 238, 239, 242
    parting of ways with Evan Jenkins 257–8
    sale of school to William Drury 256–7, 258, 327
  Utrecht school for young ladies 346–7
Jay, John Livingston (1802–81) 92, 132, 135, 141, 148, 199, 213, 243
  admission to Cambridge and non-appearance 239, 242
  as clerk at Royal Hospital, Greenwich 91, 242
  and Eliza's son Evan and repayment of debt 458, 459
  on lack of social advantage of Eliza's life in Brussels 91, 353, 370
  life in Greenwich with sister Janet 91, 353–4
  unsuccessful courtship of Sophia Barker 294–5, 309–10, 312
  visits to Greenwich from Eliza and Evan Jenkins 354, 369, 406, 408
Jay, Lucy-Hermione 238
Jay, Margaret *see* Wyndham, Margaret
Jay, Maria (née Spicer) 369
Jay, Mary (née Enslie) (1741–90) 107, 109, 112, 114, 126
  death 122, 123
  school in Andover 113, 115, 116–22
Jay, Mary (1799–1812) 131, 141, 143, 144
Jay, Rev. Samuel (1694?–1751) 106–7, 109, 110
Jay, Dr Samuel (1737–93) 107, 109, 111–25, 126
  death 123
  school in Andover 113, 115–23, 124–5
Jay, Samuel (Sam) (1767–96) 114, 116–17, 118,

122, 126, 129
Jay, Samuel (1800–81) 92, 131, 141, 148, 215, 353, 458
  marriage to Maria Spicer 369
  Oxford education and career as barrister 150–2, 153, 198, 213, 244
Jay, William (1771–1844) 126, 129, 131, 133, 136, 145, 146, 154
Jay, William (1805–22) 141, 146, 213, 215, 216, 466
Jenkins, Alexander Livingston (1829–51) 96, 279, 396, 436, 443, 459
  illness and cures in Isle of Wight and Cheltenham 449–54
    death and burial in Cheltenham 450–4
Jenkins, Constance ('Connie', née Hodson) (1881–1963) 5–6, 234
Jenkins, David (d. 1791) 26, 39, 40
Jenkins, David (d. 1842, last of Jenkins male line in Wales) 40
Jenkins, Rev. David (1787–1854) 31, 63–90, 176
  affidavits from mother on birth date 35, 37, 38, 78, 88
  appearance 90, plate 8
  classical education at Ystrad Meurig school 34, 38, 52–3, 54, 57, 58
  death and will 442, 462–3
  early career as schoolmaster in Chelsea 34, 53, 57, 61, 63, 64–5, 67–8, 73, 164
    coach journey and arrival in Chelsea 68–72
    possible acquaintance with Stevensons 173, 175
  and Evan's certificate of baptism 18, 232, 241
  family wills and lack of legacy 25, 38–9
  friendship with PB and curacies in Yorkshire 2, 7–8, 24, 33–4, 61, 441
    begins ordination process 69, 72–3, 74
    ordination as deacon 76–7, 88
    ordination as priest 88
    ordination records and testimonials 33–5, 64, 67, 72–3, 77–8, 88
    PB and appointment to curacies at

Dewsbury and Hartshead 63, 74, 76–9
as PB's co-curate in Dewsbury and Hartshead 34, 78–9, 81–2, 86–9
as perpetual curate in Pudsey 89–90, 222–3
request from PB to help find school in Brussels 365
see also Pudsey ministry *below*
marriage to Harriet and children 89, 223, 224, 226
Pudsey ministry 89–90, 218, 222–3, 364
building programme and new Gothic church 81, 90, 224, 225–9, 463
last years and legacy 462–3
petition to House of Commons re St David's College 441–2
political partisanship and defence of church rates 437–41
and Smiting and Brawling Case 440
visits from brother Evan and family 238, 405, 435–6, 437
second marriage to Rebecca 22, 442
Jenkins, David (1818–47, 'woolsorter') 225, 442
Jenkins, Dorice Margaret *see* Kendall, Dorice Margaret
Jenkins, Rev. (Charles) Edward (Ned) (1826–73) 6, 93, 279, 304, 395, 466
appearance 398–9, plates 22, 23, 24
choice of name by Eliza and Evan 247, 251, 300
clerical career
assists at Chapel Royal 449
father's death and future plans 445
ordination and testimonials 449
post as chaplain at Chapel Royal in Brussels 392, 463, 465, 470
project to build Church of the Resurrection 11, 201, 467–8, 470–2, 473, 474, plate 25
and Cricket Club in Brussels 397, 456
death and grave in Brussels 11, 12, 473, plate 1

as escort to Mrs Gaskell on research visit 402
family acquaintance with Brontë sisters in Brussels 222, 386, 400, 417, 476
story of escorting CB and EB in Brussels 8, 9–10, 13, 383, 384, 387
family concerns over brother Evan in Australia 458–9, 460, 461
friendship towards Bayntun Starky 456, 457
marriage to Lora 467
possible portrait as young John Graham Bretton in CB's *Villette* 398–9
as pupil at Shrewsbury School 396–8, 435
scholarship to Cambridge 436, 448–9
as student at Magdalene College, Cambridge 435, 436, 443, 448–9
teaching posts in Brussels 423, 448
at pensionnat in rue des Champs Elysées with mother 455–6, 457
Jenkins, Rev. (Charles) Edward (1873–1931) 11, 41–2
Jenkins, Eliza (née Jay, 'Mrs Jenkins') (1797–1864) 5, 19, 91–157
background and ancestors 91–125
family accounts of character 91, 92
French Huguenot ancestors xxiii, 98–106
Scottish ancestors xxiv, 91–8
staunch Protestant pedigree 105–6, 109
childhood and early life 126–57
birth in Rotterdam 130–1
father's business and home nr Leith 131–40
father's school in Woodford, Essex 141, 144–57
move to Brussels and Institut Britannique 155–6, 213, 215, 216, 242
death
and final illness 468–9, 472, 473
grave in Brussels 11, 12
on equality in Belgian marital finances 460
facts and fiction of Brontës in Brussels 3–4, 12, 96, 363

Brontës' first morning and story about
Mr and Mrs Jenkins 8, 360–1, 362,
366, 384
impossible meeting between Eliza and
Mrs Chadwick 8, 9, 10, 383
recommendation as respectable
personage 3, 364
and search for suitable school for CB
and EB 3, 365–6
and shyness of CB and EB in social
situations 4, 8–9, 13, 383, 384, 396,
399–400
visits by CB during second stay in
Brussels 396, 399–400, 403, 415,
417, 476
letters to Rev. William B. Clarke 109, 288,
294, 295, 298, 299–300, 303–4, 334
letters to and from Frances Curwen 421–2,
423–30, 434–5, 469
concern with social status 425–7
letters to sister Margaret Wyndham 338,
453–4, 455, 458, 459–61, 466
marriage to Evan in Brussels 140, 199, 238,
242
Embassy wedding 239–40
registration document 19, 20
married life and family in Brussels 264,
317–18, 334
choice of children's names 35, 42, 96,
247–8
concerns over son Alexander 436
death of Mary Jane Wilhelmina in
Ostend 348–9
experience of rioting and Belgian
Revolution 271–2, 279–80,
299–300
family holidays in Belgium 175, 263,
406, 416, 435, 457
financial concerns 435, 436
friendship with Dixon family 390, 396,
403, 416
home in Chaussée d'Ixelles 7, 20, 93,
257–8, 351

involvement with Rev. Clarke's love
triangle 296–306
on Mina as bridesmaid 399
see also facts and fiction of Brontës in
Brussels *above and* school in home
in Brussels; widowhood in
Brussels *below*
return visits to England
nurses son Alexander in Cheltenham
451–4
visits Jay relatives in Greenwich 354,
406
school in home in Brussels 93, 271, 279,
296, 300–1, 400–1, 421–47
correspondence with Frances Curwen
and sons as pupils 421–2, 423–30,
434–5
fluctuations in numbers and success
427–8
sale of school on husband's death 448
staff 424–7
techniques for evading customs 429–30
travel arrangements for Curwen boys
421–2, 429
widowhood and new school on rue
des Champs Elysées 92–3, 455–7
widowhood in Brussels
appearance and 'shrivelled' description
92, 93–5, 395, plate 10
death of husband Evan 443–5, 447, 448
financial concerns and repayment of
son Evan's debt 459–60
hospitality to Bayntun Starky 455–7
letter from Bishop Blomfield on
chaplain's position 444–5
and move to rue des Champs Elysées
92–3, 95, 448, 455
nephew Alward Wyndham's account
of visit 395–6
opens pensionnat with son Edward as
teacher 455–7
sadness on death of daughter Mina
465–6

slowing down in middle age 467

son Alexander's ill-health and death
451–4

son Evan's tribulations in Australia
458–62, 466

visit from Mrs Gaskell 93, 464

Jenkins, Elizabeth (née Davies) (1760–1822) 25,
36, 56, 58, 68, 226

affidavits on birth date of son David 35, 37,
38, 78, 88

death 219, 220–1

marriage bond 35

Jenkins, Elizabeth (b. 1821) *see* Lloyd, Elizabeth

Jenkins, Evan (d. 1806?) 30–1, 38–9, 56, 57, 58

legacies from parents 40–1

marriage bond 26, 35

as tenant farmer at Penycastell 26–7, 41,
43, 176

unknown grave 15, 32

will 14–15, 25–7, 30

Jenkins, Rev. Evan (1794–1849) 4–5, 6, 7–8,
14–44

amiable character 333

birth and background in Cardiganshire
14–15, 18, 19, 68, 96

early home at Penycastell 20, 22, 24

education at Ystrad Meurig school 38,
52–3, 54–5, 56, 57, 59–61, 62, 164

father's will 25

as Cambridge student at Trinity College 4,
17, 18, 54, 163–8, 194, 197, 216, 244, 339

admission and confusion over age
15–16, 19, 45, 159, 163, 168, 178

possibility of teaching post before
Cambridge 170, 172–3

possibility of tutoring alongside studies
187, 190–1

return for Commencement and
collection of MA 262–3

status as sizar student 179–80, 182,
187, 191

teaching in Brussels after graduation
198, 217–19, 231

clerical career in Brussels

baptism certificate and brother David's
mission 18–19, 232, 241

CB's visits to Chapel Royal 407–8

confusing records and frustrating
research 15–19

initial teaching posts and Institut
Britannique 217–19, 231, 237, 238,
242, 257–8

licence in Brussels (1835) 16, 19, 266,
269, 336

marries Catherine Phelps and Norbert
Goussaert 380

ordination as deacon and post as
curate in Brussels 16, 17, 18–19,
231–3, 234–5, 237–8

ordination as priest in London 16, 17,
18, 240–2

ordination records and testimonials
16–19, 216–17, 231–2, 237–8

post as chaplain of Chapel Royal in
Brussels 250–1, 257, 264–8, 277,
320, 333, 351, 352, 353, 367,
391–2

post as Embassy chaplain in Brussels
336–7, 338, 352, 355, 367, 368

post as honorary chaplain to Leopold I
4, 16, 108, 269, 336–8, 352, 355,
367, plate 24

presence at railroad opening
celebrations 437

prospect of cathedral stall in England
370–1

questioning of Bishop Luscombe's
authority to issue licences in
Brussels 265–6

questioning of Bishop Luscombe's
consecration of St George's Chapel
264–5, 266–7, 268

resistance to Bishop Luscombe's
authority in Brussels 262, 264–9

sickbed duties and deposition on
treatment of Protestants in

Catholic hospitals 436, 444
social duties and lovesick parishioner
416–17
and Victoria and Albert in Ostend
410, 411–14
death in Brussels 443–5, 452
funeral and note in Drury's register 445
grave in Protestant cemetery 11, 12,
445, plate 1
registration record 17, 19–20
as director of English charitable fund in
Brussels 367–8
facts and fiction of Brontës in Brussels 3–4,
7, 12, 13, 96
CB's description of Evan as consul not
clergyman 363–4
CB's intention to inquire after schools
364–5
CB's visits to home 396, 415, 417, 476
first morning and story about Mr and
Mrs Jenkins 8, 360–1, 362, 366,
384
misattribution of familiar voice heard
by CB in Chapel Royal 407–8
illness in 1843 406, 408
joins Freemasons in Brussels 348
letters to Rev. William B. Clarke 294, 295,
300–2, 304–6, 310–12, 313, 327, 334,
367
marriage in Brussels 140, 239–40, 242
registration document 19, 20
married life in Brussels 334, 348–9
choice of children's names 35, 42, 96,
247–8
concerns over son Alexander 436
death of Mary Jane Wilhelmina in
Ostend 348–9
experience of rioting and Belgian
Revolution 271–2, 279–80
home in Chaussée d'Ixelles 7, 20,
257–8, 351
and love triangle and Rev. Clarke
296–306

marriage registration 19–20
see also facts and fiction of Brontës in
Brussels *above and* school in home
in Brussels *below*
return from Brussels on mother's death
220–1
school in home in Brussels 93, 257–8, 271,
279, 296, 300–1, 305, 400–1
escorts pupils to and from England
299, 300, 369, 370, 406, 421
reputation of school and Evan as
teacher 333, 351, 369
sale on death 448
staff 424–7
visit to Eliza's family in London and letters
for Victoria and Albert 369–70
visits to Pudsey to see brother David 238,
405, 437
Jenkins, Evan (1832–68) 96, 318, 395, 443, 453
excluded from Margaret Bowden's will 461
move to Australia and dissolute life 455,
457–62, 466
return and death and burial in Brussels 462
Jenkins, Harriet (née Walker) (1788?–1824) 89,
223, 224, 227, 374
Jenkins, Harriet (1814–34) 176, 222, 223
at Cowan Bridge school 89, 227, 229–31
Jenkins, Helen Eliza (1827–1911) 35, 93, 279,
403, 405, 435–6, plates 10, 25
at Château de Koekelberg school 374–5,
376, 387
and death of mother 468–9, 472
and death of sister Mina 465, 466
delicate constitution 452–3
guest of Starky family at Spye Park 457
as headmistress of a school 94, 95
letter to Bishop Blomfield on death of
father 444–5
letters to aunt Janet in Greenwich 469–70
on building of new church 468, 470–2
on death of mother 468–9
piano lessons and playing 371, 395–6, 476
and project to build Church of the

Resurrection 468, 470–2, plate 25
to England in later years 10, 476
Jenkins, John (d. 1765) 39, 40
Jenkins, John (d. 1822) 221
Jenkins, John (d. 1832) 39, 40, 41, 57, 482*n*.26, 483*n*.50
Jenkins, Rev. John Card ('Co'/'Coco') (1834–94) 93, 349, 387, 395, 424, 443, 457, 458, 461, plates 24, 25
　choice of name by Eliza and Evan 247–8
　and Cricket Club in Brussels with brother Edward 397
　death and registration in Brussels 41–2, 402, 476
　and family Bible 4–5
　grave in Brussels and relocation of family graves 11, 12, 462, 466
　at Magdalene College, Cambridge 466–7
　marriage and children 197, 459
　ordination and clerical posts 467
　photography hobby 94
　post as assistant chaplain to brother at Chapel Royal 467, 470, 471, 475
　relocated Church of the Resurrection and ministry 473–5
　school in rue St-Bernard, Brussels 6, 12, 462, 476
　story of escorting CB and EB in Brussels 8, 9–10, 13, 383, 384
Jenkins, John Card ('Jack') (1874–1958) 5, 41–2, 190, 476
Jenkins, Rev. Joseph Walker (1816–60) 176, 224–5
　CB's recognition of voice in Brussels 407–8
　as curate in Batley 365, 374, 405, 407, 408
　as English chaplain at Spa 408–9, 442
　marriage to Mary 442
　as minister in Newton, Herefordshire 463
Jenkins, Magdalen (d. 1823) 221
Jenkins, Magdalen (d. 1825) 221
Jenkins, Margaret (d. 1805) 39, 40–1
Jenkins, Margaret (née Eggleston) 442, 463
Jenkins, Margaret Wilhelmina (1877–98) 226

Jenkins, Mary (1789?–1860) *see* Roderick, Mary
Jenkins, Mary (née Tompson, wife of John Card Jenkins) (1843–1907) 4, 197
Jenkins, Mary Ann (née Gomersal) 442
Jenkins, Mary Jane Wilhelmina (1830–8) 12, 35, 279, 297, 348–9, 463
Jenkins, Meliora Georgina ('Lora', née Tinling) 10, 467, 471, 473, 476
Jenkins, Mina (Sarah Jane Clara, daughter of Joseph Walker Jenkins) (d. 1926) 225, 463
Jenkins, Mina Janet ('Jeannette') (1839–56) 35, 349, 354, 395, 399, 457, 463
　illness and death 452, 461, 462, 464, 465–6
Jenkins, Susannah (b. 1823) 227
Jenkins, Thomas (b. 1819) 226
Jenkins family xxii
　Bible and family records 4–5
　family albums and scrapbooks 5, 12, 93
　friendship with Dixon family in Brussels 390, 396, 403, 416–17
　graves at Llanbadarn Odwyn 39
　graves in Brussels and relocation to cemetery at Evere 1, 11, 12, 216, 462, plate 1
　land ownership in Wales 39–41
　wills in National Library of Wales 24–6, 38–9
Jennings, Alice (Keats's grandmother) 142
Jessopp, Rev. John 410, 411, 412–13, 414
John Jay & Co. import and export business 131, 132, 136, 137–40, 157
Johnes, Thomas, of Hafod 26, 483*n*.50
Johnson, Samuel: *Lives of the Poets* 356–7
Johnston, Dr (minister of St Ninian's, Leith) 133–4
Johnston, Henry McKenzie: *Ottoman and Persian Odysseys* 112, 113, 115
Jones, Rev. Griffith ('Llanddowror') 58
Jones, Rev. Lewis (pupil at Ystrad Meurig) 171
Jowett, Dr Joseph 75
Juste, Théodore 293, 321

Kaye, Bishop John (professor at Cambridge) 193–4

Kean, Edmund 246, 276

Keats, Frances 142

Keats, John 140, 141–2, 143, 144

Keble, John 153

Kelting, Captain Frederick Andreas 138, 140, 157

Kendall, Dorice Margaret (née Jenkins) 4, 5, 247

Kennedy, Ann *see* Livingston, Ann

Kennedy, Benjamin Hall (headmaster of Shrewsbury School) 397

Kennedy, William (professor at Aberdeen) 494–5*n*.45

Kent, Duke of *see* Edward, Duke of Kent and Strathearn

Kilvington, Rev. Edward 88

King's Church *see* Church of the Augustines, Brussels

Kington, Herefordshire: coaching stop 68–9

Knight, Frances 225, 234

Knox, Mary *see* Taylor, Mary (née Knox)

Koekelberg school *see* Château de Koekelberg school

Kyan, John Howard 404

La Fontaine *see* Fontaine

La Rochelle and siege (1627–8) 98, 101

Lane, Rev. Charlton 216, plate 24

Lane, Emma 271–2

Lauderdale, James Maitland, 8th Earl of *see* Maitland

Lawrence, Sir Thomas: portrait of Lord Aberdeen 263

Lawrence, T.E.: *Revolt in the Desert* 22

Lax, William (professor at Cambridge) 194

Layel, Rev. Alexander 129

Layel, Elizabeth *see* Livingston, Elizabeth

Layel, Isabella *see* Jay, Isabella

Lebeau, Dr (Eliza's doctor in Brussels) 468

Lee, Samuel (professor at Cambridge) 194

Leeds Intelligencer 438

Leeds Mercury 440

Leeds Times 439

Leichhardt, Ludwig (explorer, disappeared 1848) 95, 341

Leiden, Netherlands 111–12

Leith, Scotland
  Jay family at Lixmount House 133–40, 157, 174, plate 26
  St Ninian's Church 133, plate 11

Leland, John 46

Lennox, Charles *see* Richmond, Charles Lennox, 4th Duke of

Leonardo da Vinci 100

Leopold I, King of the Belgians 383, plate 17
  background and life as prince 289–93
  Belgian revolution (1830) and installation as king 273, 288–9, 293–4, 299–300, 301–2, 303
    valiant defence of Dutch invasion 307–8
    violence towards Orangists and Leopold's attempts to bring calm 320–4
  and building of railways and travel by train 334, 358
  and Rev. Evan and Eliza Jenkins 311, 427
    attendance at Evan's services at Chapel Royal 205, 303–4, 318, 320, 352–3
    Evan as courier for royal missives 299, 370
    Evan as honorary chaplain to 4, 16, 108, 269, 336–8, 352, 355, 367
  and Lever's medical career 344, 345
  marriage to Princess Charlotte and tragedy 207, 213, 289–91
  and Prince Albert 4, 370
    Brussels stay with uncle as youth 205, 338–9
    Leopold's plans for marriage to Victoria 339
    pre-wedding visit to Brussels 352–3
    and royal visit to Belgium 411, 412
  and Queen Victoria 370
    fondness of niece for uncle 291, 339

Leopold's description of new wife as
homily 315–16
Leopold's marriage plans for niece 293,
339
and royal visit to Belgium 411, 412
refusal of throne of Greece 292–3
second marriage to Louise-Marie d'Orléans
315–18, 366
death of first child as infant 324–5
Leopold, Prince (later Leopold II of Belgium) 337
Lethbridge, Sir John 328
Lever, Charles 257, 312, 341–6, 355, 423
Harry Lorrequer 341–3
letters on social life in Brussels 343–5
Lewis, Rev. Dan. 176
Lisburne, Earl of 42, 483*n*.50
literacy skills in rural Wales 37, 38
elementary education provision 57–8
Liverpool, Lord 70, 203, 237
Liversedge, Yorkshire: Gothic church 226
Livingston, Alexander (bap. 1716–83) 95–8
portrait of 94–5, plate 9
Livingston, Alexander (1781–1856) 92, 96, 97,
141, 150
Livingston, Ann (née Kennedy) 95, 98
Livingston, Elizabeth (née Hardie, later Layel)
(1744–1824) 95–6
Livingston, Helen *see* Jay, Helen
Livingston, Jane Benger (née Ogilvy, 'Aunt Jane')
(1774?–1855) 91, 92, 96, 97, 150
Livingston, Margaret *see* Bowden, Margaret
*The Livingstons of Callendar and their Principal
Cadets* 96
Lixmount Cottage, nr Leith 136, 137
Lixmount House, nr Leith: Jay family home
133–40, 157, 174, plate 26
Llanbadarn Fawr, nr Aberystwyth: St Padarn's
Church 20
Llanbadarn Odyn (Odwyn), Cardiganshire
Evan Jenkins's birth at Penycastell 18, 19, 20
St Padarn church 20, 31–2, 35, 38, plate 2
Jenkins family graves 39, 176, 221
Llangeitho, Cardiganshire 31, 32–3, 52, 176

Lloyd, Elizabeth (née Jenkins) 226, 442
Lloyd, Erasmus 226, 442
Llwynpiod Methodist chapel 31, 40, 58, 176
Lockhart, John Gibson 53
London *see* Chelsea, London; Greenwich, London
London Evening Standard 437
Lorrington, Meribah (headmistress in Chelsea) 66
Louis-Philippe I, Duc d'Orléans, king of the
French 273, 289, 316
Louise-Marie d'Orléans, queen of the Belgians
315–18, 324–5, 337, 366, 412, 427
death from tuberculosis 452
Lovelace, Ada, Countess of 252
Lovell, John 145
Low Countries *see* Belgium; Netherlands
Lucas, Rev. William Hanwell 76, 87
Luscombe, Matthew Henry Thornhill, Bishop
258, 259, 343
questionable powers as bishop in Europe
260–1, 262–9
Lynch, John: *San Martín* 382

Mabinogion, The 20
Macaulay, Thomas Babington 166, 186, 190,
196, 197–8
MacCarthy, Fiona 185–6, 255
McCarthy, William 139
MacEwan, Helen 7, 11–12, 19
Mackay, Charles 256–7, 276, 278, 280, 285, 341
Macready, William Charles 378
Maitland, James, Viscount (later 8th Earl of
Lauderdale) 124, 174
Malcolm, Janet 125
Malthus, Robert 260
A Man for All Seasons (film) 71
Marlow, Michael (President of St John's College,
Oxford) 207, 212
Marryat, Captain (Frederick) 334–5, 423
Marsh, Herbert (professor at Cambridge) 195
Marx, Karl 6
Master, Elizabeth (née Mosley) 217
Master, Rev. Streynsham 18, 216–17, 237, 238,

248, plate 24

Melbourne, Lord 437, 439

Mellish, William 154–5, 156

merchants *see* commercial education

Mérimée, Prosper 99, 102

Methodism in Wales 31, 32–3, 38, 52, 176
  Calvinistic Methodism 31, 33, 40, 52
  Sunday schools and literacy 58

Meyrick, Sir Samuel Rush (antiquarian) 480*n*.7

Miller, General William 382

Million Act (Church Building Act) (1818) 225

Milner, Dr Isaac 177–9, 180, 182, 194

Milner, Joseph 178, 180

Milnes, Richard Monckton 144

Milton, Ann (nurse in Cheltenham) 452

Monboddo, James Burnett, Lord 124, 125

Monk, James Henry (Cambridge professor) 163,
  168, 188, 192

Monmouth House, Chelsea 71

Moorman, Mary 430

More, Sir Thomas 70–1

Morgan, Rev. William 441

Morier, Clara (née Van Lennep) 112, 113, 115–16,
  116–17, 120–1

Morier, Isaac 112, 113, 115–16, 118, 119, 120,
  121–2, 127

Morier, Jack (John Philip) 113, 115, 116–17, 118,
  119, 120, 121, 122, 123, 127

Morier, James 11, 112–13, 115, 116–17, 118, 119,
  120

Morning Post and Queen Victoria in Belgium
  410–14

Morrogh, Mike 397

Morse, Charlotte *see* Ayers, Charlotte

Morse, Leonard Becher 425

Mosley, Sir Oswald 217

La Muette de Portici (*Masaniello*) (opera) 277–8,
  317–18, 320, 321

Murray, John 329, 331

Murray-Prior, Thomas (pupil of William Drury)
  341

Nanteos estate, Cardiganshire 30, 42–4, 49
  Powells as trustees at Ystrad Meurig school
    49, 52
  records and Penycastell 26, 41, 43

Nanteos Mansion, Aberystwyth 42–3, 43–4

Napoleon I and Napoleonic Wars 23, 27, 34, 64,
  80, 138–9
  Peninsular War 73, 92, 97, 381
  and redistribution of Low Countries 200
  Waterloo (1815) 203–4, 214, 249, 400

National Library of Wales, Aberystwyth 22–3,
  23–7

Netherlands xviii, 199–200
  Eliza Jenkins's Huguenot ancestors 104–5,
    106, 107–12
  Jay family in 126–31
  'Patriot Revolt' (1781–7) 126–7
  and Revolutionary France 130–1
  unrest and Belgian Revolution (1830) 270,
    272–89, 320–4

New York: St Bernard's School 5, 476

Newell, Rev. R.H.: *Letters on the Scenery of Wales*
  (1821) 28

Newman, John Henry (later Cardinal) 54, 153,
  248, 250, 316

Newton, Herefordshire: St John's Church 463

Nicholls, Arthur 402
  honeymoon in Snowdonia 171–2
  supervising CB's letters to friends 432
  widow's sale of Brontë memorabilia 419–20

Nonconformists (Dissenters)
  burials in Bunhill Fields in London 104
  limits on university education 107
  Rev. David Jenkins and defence of church
    rates 439, 440

North, Rev. Brownlow, Bishop of Winchester 67

Nussey, Ellen 355, 387
  assistance with address of Rev. Jenkins in
    Brussels for CB 365
  CB's letters to 362
    on conveying letter to Martha Taylor 391
    crossing out of names in CB's letters
      404

on desire to travel and desire to learn
2–3, 363–4, 365
on hearing Rev. Joseph Walker
Jenkins's voice in Brussels 407–8
on Heger's presentation of diploma on
parting 420
on husband vetting letters 432
on Mrs Jenkins's help with search for
school 3, 365–6
joint letter with Taylor sisters 373–4
on journey from Leeds to Brussels 358
as resource for Brontë industry 362,
399, 402
on spineless ?George Dixon 404
on improved dress sense of CB and EB
post-Brussels 299
Martha Taylor's letter on meeting up in
Yorkshire 391
Mary Taylor's letter on death of her sister
Martha 387–8, 392–3
as pupil at Roe Head school 362

Ogden, Rev. Joseph (officiating minister at
Hartshead) 87
Ogilvy, Jane Benger *see* Livingston, Jane Benger
'Old Church' *see* Chelsea, London: Old Church
Operative Conservative Society in Yorkshire
437–8
Oriel College, Oxford University 150–1, 166
Hartley Coleridge at 152–3
Osborne-Jones, D.G. 49, 52, 54
Ostend
burial of Mary Jane Wilhelmina Jenkins
at 348–9
Eliza Jenkins and family holidays in 406,
416, 457
story of CB's departure from Belgium
417–20
transport options to and from Brussels
357–60, 417, 418
Victoria and Albert's visit and minister on
duty 410–14

Owen, Rev. John, Chaplain General 202
Oxford Movement 250, 470
Oxford University
as respite from mathematics at Cambridge
165
and Ystrad Meurig school 48, 54
see also Oriel College, Oxford University

Padarn, St 20
Paganini, Niccolò 324
Paley, William 192, 193, 195
Palin, Will 354
Palmerston, Lord 319, 323–4
Pantbeudy ('Pantyboidy') Hall, Cardiganshire
220–1
Parker, Hon. Colonel Thomas 206, 207, 208,
209–10, 211–12
Parsonage Museum, Haworth, Yorkshire 226,
419–20
'Patriot Revolt' (1781–7) in Dutch Republic
126–7
Peacock, Thomas Love: *Crotchet Castle* 413
Pearse, Brice (army clothier and slave owner) 149
Pearse, Charlotte (née Raikes) 149
Peel, Sir Robert 253–4, 254–5, 439
Peninsular War 73, 92, 97, 381
Pensionnat Heger, Rue d'Isabelle, Brussels 375
CB and EB study at 3–4, 8, 10–11, 360,
361, 366, 393
CB's return as teacher 393
Mme Heger and story of CB's departure
from school 414, 415, 417–18
Wheelwright children at 401, 402
Pentre Padarn (Pentre-Padarn) farm,
Cardiganshire 39
Penycastell (Peny Castell), Llanbadarn Odyn
(Odwyn), Cardiganshire 18, 19, 21–2
baptism of David Jenkins at 35
on death registration of John Card Jenkins
senior 42
Evan Jenkins senior leases farm from
Nanteos estate 26–7, 41, 43

map in Nanteos estate records 26, 39, 41, 43
Rodericks continue farming tradition 176
search for remains of farm 29–31
Pest House, London and Huguenot refugees
100, 103, 104
'Peterloo' Massacre (1819) 235
Peters, Charles Henry (teacher at John Jay's
school) 147
Phelps, Catherine *see* Goussaert, Catherine
Phelps family 376–80
Phelps, Peter Turner 378
Phelps, Rev. Robert 376, 377, 379
Phelps, Samuel 376, 377–9
Philip, Rosemary 134–5, 139–40
Pierce, Rev. William Matthews and family 239,
240
Pitt, William, the Younger 63, 130, 159, 319
Ponsonby, Lord John 293
Porteus, Thomas (secretary to Archbishop of
York) 63, 76
Pott, Joseph Holden, Archdeacon of London 202
Powell, Avarina 42, 43
Powell, Eleanor 43
Powell, George (1842–82) 42
Powell, John 463
Powell, Thomas, MP (d. 1752) 43
Powell, Thomas (d. 1797) 43
Powell, William 42, 43
Powell, Rev. Dr William (d. 1780) 43, 49
Powell, William Edward (d. 1854) 30, 43
Powell family and Nanteos estate 41, 42–4, 49
press: Queen Victoria and Prince Albert in
Belgium 410–14
Priestley, Joseph 23, 178
Prince, Rev. Dr Thomas 206, 207, 209–13, 233,
248, plate 24
Proctor, Jonas (of Pudsey) 440
Prospect House, Woodford, Essex 144–6, 153–6
Protestantism
Evan Jenkins's deposition on treatment of
Protestants in Catholic hospitals 436, 444
see also Anglicanism; Brussels: Protestant
cemetery; Brussels: Protestant churches;

Calvinism; Nonconformists
(Dissenters); Puritanism
Pudsey, Yorkshire 171
David Jenkins as minister 88–90, 218,
222–3, 364
building programme and new Gothic
St Lawrence's Church 81, 90, 224,
225–9, 463
last years and death 462–3
political involvement and defence of
church rates 437–41
visits from brother Evan and family
238, 405, 435–6, 437
Puritan preaching of Elkanah Wales 223–4
reform and political allegiances 437–8, 439
Smiting and Brawling Case 440
Pugh, Rev. John 48
Puritanism
in East Anglia 107
Elkanah Wales in Pudsey 223–4

Quillinan, Dora *see* Wordsworth, Dorothy (Dora)
Quillinan, Edward 431–2

railways in Belgium 334–5, 437
and Brontës' arrival in Brussels 357–8,
359–60, 361
Réaux *see* des Réaux
Rees, Rev. D.C. 55, 480–1*n*.13
Reform Act (1832) and political unrest 437–8
religion
Evangelicalism as movement 84–6
Roman Catholicism and High Anglicanism
249–50
in Wales 31–2, 32–3, 439
see also Methodism in Wales
see also Anglicanism; Protestantism
Reyroux, Rev. Frederick 82
Richard, Abraham 48
Richard, Edward 47–50, 50–1, 52, 54, 59, 60,
plate 4

Richard, Thomas and Gwenllian 48, 49

Richards, David 25, 26, 172–3, 218–19

Richards, Evan 24, 25

Richards, John (aspiring schoolteacher in London) 218–19

Richards, Rev. Thomas (pupil at Ystrad Meurig) 54

Richardson, Joanna 292

Richmond, Charles Lennox, 4th Duke of 206, 207, 213

Richmond, Charlotte, Duchess of 5, 203

Ricks, Christopher 186–7

Ridge, William (banker) 401–2

Ritchie, John and family (Thackeray's relations) 350

Roberson, Rev. Hammond 226

Robinson, David 46

Robinson, Mary 'Perdita' 66

Roderick, Evan 176

Roderick, Mary (née Jenkins) (1789?–1860) 24, 25, 30–1, 40, 57, 68
  grave at Llanbadarn Odwyn 31, 32
  inheritance of feather bed from uncle 38
  inheritance of Penycastell lease 41
  literacy 57
  marriage to Moses 176

Roderick, Moses (1790?–1851) 24, 40, 57, 176, 220
  grave and son's grave at Llanbadarn Odwyn 31, 32

Roe Head school, nr Mirfield, Yorkshire 362, 396

Rogerson, Joseph (Yorkshire textile entrepreneur) 224

Roman Catholicism and High Anglicanism 249–50, 470

Romberg, J.B.: *Brussels and its Environs* (1824) 203–4

Rose, Rev. Joseph Patten (London lecturer) 72–3

Rothman, Richard ('Ricardus') Wellesley (Cambridge student) 167–8

Rotterdam, Netherlands 111
  Rev. John Enslie in 107–9, 114
  John Jay in family business in 126–31

Rouse-Boughton, Theresa (pupil at Château de Koekelberg) 375–6

Rowland, Rev. Daniel 32, 33, 52, 58

Rowton, Rev. Rupert 470, 471

Ruijssenaars, Eric 7, 383–4, 385, 387, 388, 403, 417–18

Rush, Rev. John 67, 72, 73, 87, 172

Russell, Lord William 308, 527*n*.127

Russell, Rev. Whitworth 216, plate 24

St Bernard's School, Brussels 6, 12, 462, 476

St Bernard's School, New York 5, 476

St David's College, Lampeter 60–1, 441–2

St George's Chapel, Brussels 351, 352
  consecration by Bishop Luscombe 258–60, 264–5, 266–7, 268
  Gladstone attends 314, 315
  termination of lease and Drury's departure 367, 403

St John's College, Cambridge 158, 160, 180, 187

Saint-Laurent, Madame de 206, 213

Salter, Simon (banker in Brussels) 443, 547*n*.47

San Martín, General José de 380–3

San Martín, Mercedes de 382, 383

Sarn Helen (Roman road in Wales) 20, 29, 39, 40

Sarnele land belonging to Jenkins family 40–1, 57

Schama, Simon 127, 130

schools: charitable provision in Wales 57–8

Scott, Charlotte (née Charpentier) 131–2

Scott, Sir Walter 52, 99, 134, 140, 413, 480*n*.7
  in Brussels 214
  John Williams and Welsh setting for *The Betrothed* 53, 485*n*.26
  possible acquaintance with Jay family in Edinburgh 131–2, 174

Sedgwick, Adam (professor at Cambridge) 181, 193, 194–5, 295

Seymour, Sir George Hamilton 322, 337–8, 340, 343, 368, 370

Shawe, Isabella *see* Thackeray, Isabella

Shelley, Harriet (née Westbrook) 61, 62, 328

Shelley, Mary (née Wollstonecraft Godwin) 61, 328–9

Shelley, Percy Bysshe 61, 62, 235, 328–9

Shorter, Clement King: *Charlotte Brontë and her Circle* 402–3

Shrewsbury School, Shropshire 396–7, 398, 448–9

Shrewsbury House, Chelsea 72

Sibthorp, Rev. Richard Waldo 248–50

Simeon, Rev. Charles 195–6, 230

Sinden, Donald 376

sizar students at Cambridge 179–82, 185–6, 191, 195

Skene, Dr David (at Marischal College, Aberdeen) 112, 123, 494–5*n*.45

Sloane, Sir Hans 66, 71

Smith, George (publisher) 398

Smith, Margaret 15, 363, 374, 398, 402, 407, 419

Smiting and Brawling Case in Pudsey 440

Smollett, Tobias 71

Smyrna (now Izmir), Anatolia and Jay family 113, 114, 115–16

Snowdonia 171–2

Society for Promoting Christian Knowledge (SPCK) 57, 58, 60

Sotheby's: auction of Brontë memorabilia (1916) 419–20

Soulsby, Lucy (headmistress in Oxford) 385

Southey, Robert 214

Spa 408–9, 435

Spanish Netherlands 199–200

'Spencer, Mr' (buyer of Brontë memorabilia) 419–20

Spencer, John Charles *see* Althorp

Spicer, Maria *see* Jay, Maria

Starky, Rev. Andrew 457, 465

Starky, (John) Bayntun 451, 455–6, 457

Starky, Charlotte (née Wyndham) 451, 455, 456, 457, 465

Stather, Maria Moreton (later Clarke) 298, 312, 313

Stephenson, George 334, 335

Stephenson, Robert 334

Steven, Rev. William: *The History of the Scottish*

Church, Rotterdam (1832) 107, 108–9, 114, 128, 129, 130

Stevens, Joan 371–3, 374, 375

Stevenson, Elizabeth Cleghorn *see* Gaskell, Elizabeth

Stevenson, Robert Louis: *Kidnapped* 137

Stevenson, William and family 173, 174–5

Still, Eliza 243, 245

Still, Rev. John (father) 243

Still, Rev. John (son) 243, 244

Still, Mary *see* Taylor, Mary (née Still)

Stockmar, Christian Friedrich, Baron 290, 292, 311

Stonestreet, Rev. George Griffin 206

    as Chaplain to the Forces in Brussels 201–3, 206–7, 233

        ministry to Anglican community and Chapel Royal 202, 203, 204, plate 24

    school in Brussels 203

Stopford, Hon. Henry Scott (student at Cambridge) 168

Strachey, Lytton 248, 250, 362

Strata Florida abbey, Cardiganshire 46

Strong, Ruth 463

Stuart, Sir Charles 202, 233, 236, 237, 260

Summerscale, Julia 430–1

Sunday schools and literacy 58

Sussex, Augustus Frederick, Duke of 163

Sutherland, John 131–2

Swift, Jonathan 66

Swinburne, Algernon 42

Sydonie (at Jenkins home) 468, 471

Symons, Rev. J. (in Boulogne) 262, 268

Tait, Archibald, Bishop of London, later Archbishop of Canterbury 53

Taylor, Sir Brook 252

Taylor, Rev. Edward, of Bifrons, Kent (1734–98) 251–2

Taylor, Edward (1774–1843) 250–2, 300, 308, 319, 321–4, 337

Taylor, Hannah (in Rome) 243

Taylor, Lieutenant-General Sir Herbert (1775–1839) 251–2, 303, 321, 323

Taylor, Joe (CB's 'Martin Yorke') 3, 374

Taylor, John (of Yorkshire, then New Zealand) 390

Taylor, Joshua (CB's 'Mr Yorke') 362–3, 389

Taylor, Martha (CB's 'Jessy Yorke')
  birth and baptism record 390
  and Dixon relatives in Brussels 363, 364, 390, 391, 392
  family as characters in CB's *Shirley* 3, 362–3
  as model for 'Jessy' 363, 389, 393
  letter to Ellen Nussey on meeting up in Yorkshire 391
  as pupil at Mme Goussaert's school 245, 391
    information relayed to CB on schools 363–4, 365, 477*n*.7
    joint letter to Ellen Nussey with Mary and CB 373, 374
    sudden death at school 387–8, 392–3
    unreliable accounts of death and burial 387, 388–9, 392
  as pupil at Roe Head school 362

Taylor, Mary (daughter of Hannah Taylor) 243

Taylor, Mary (née Knox) 390

Taylor, Mary (née Still) 243, 245

Taylor, Mary (sister of Martha, CB's 'Rose Yorke')
  and arrival of Brontës in Brussels 359, 361
  birth and baptism record 390
  burial at Birstall churchyard 390
  and Dixon relatives in Brussels 368, 388, 390, 391, 396, 400
  family as characters in CB's *Shirley* 3, 362–3, 389, 393
    as model for Rose Yorke 363
  in Germany 415, 416
  letters to and from CB
    and description of Rev. Jenkins as consul 363–4
    inspires CB to visit Continent 2–3, 363
    later destruction of CB's letters 362, 399
    mistranscription and mistake about

    weather 357
  and role in CB's departure from Heger household 415
  and search for suitable school in Brussels 363–4, 365, 366
  letters to Mrs Gaskell 359
    on contrasting religions of CB and Taylor family 388–9
  letters to Ellen Nussey
    on death of sister Martha 387–8, 392–3
    joint letter from Brussels school with Martha and CB 373, 374
    on quiet evening with CB and EB after visit to Martha's grave 400
  in New Zealand 372, 390
  as pupil at Mme Goussaert's school 3, 245, 371–6, 391
  as pupil at Roe Head school 362

Taylor, Samuel (husband of Mary Still) 243, 244

Taylor, Thomas (architect) 225–6

Taylor, William Waring (of Yorkshire, then New Zealand) 390

Teifi, river 46

Tennyson, Alfred, Lord
  at Cambridge 160, 166, 186–7
  'Timbuctoo' prize poem 262

Tennyson, Charles 186

Tennyson, Frederick 186

Thackeray, Isabella (née Shawe) 268, 349–50, 409

Thackeray, William Makepeace 257, 349–50
  The Adventures of Philip 359
  Barry Lyndon 409
  Book of Snobs 160, 426–7
  on Brussels 214
  crossing paths with CB 409–10
  The History of Henry Esmond 187, 198
  and Lever 343
  on lure of debt at Cambridge 189
  Luscombe officiates at wedding in Paris 268, 269
  on Macaulay 166

and newspaper gossip columns 410
Pendennis 112–13, 214, 409
A Shabby Genteel Story 246, 268–9
on Smyrna 114
Vanity Fair 113, 146, 203, 373
Thelwall, John Hampden (student at Cambridge)
167
Thomas, Aeronwy 32
Thomas, Caitlin 32
Thomas, Dylan 32, 58, 72, 477*n*.1, 514*n*.82
Thompson, Miss (first wife of Rev. Jaques
Fontaine) 103
Thornhill, Yorkshire 89
Thornton, Yorkshire: PB as minister 89, 223
Tierney, George (at the Brussels Embassy) 239,
246
Times, The: Queen Victoria in Belgium 410, 412,
414
Tinling, Meliora Georgina *see* Jenkins, Meliora
Georgina
Tod, Jane *see* Enslie, Jane
Top Withens, nr Haworth, Yorkshire 29
Tories: reform and political uncertainty 437–8,
439
Tourettes, Alexandre Ferrier de 358
trains *see* railways in Belgium
Tregaron (Caron), Cardiganshire 22, 55
accounts of primitive nature 27, 28
droving town 28–9
fireplace in church 55
records for Elizabeth Jenkins's family (Davies)
38–9
Trench, Richard Le Poer *see* Clancarty
Trinity College, Cambridge 75, 159–68, 176–98
admission procedure and registration
162–3, 167–8, 178
Airy as sizar student 181–2, 186
chapel 182–3, 183–4
Rev. Evan Jenkins at 4, 17, 18, 54, 163–8,
194, 197, 198, 216, 244, 339
admission and confusion over age
15–16, 19, 45, 159, 163, 168, 178
possibility of tutoring alongside
studies 187, 190–1
return for Commencement and MA
262–3
status as sizar 179–80, 182, 187, 191
testimonials for curateship in Brussels
231–2
examinations and attitudes towards 197–8
geology and Sedgwick as professor 193,
194–5
lodgings for sizar students 185–6
pensioners at 182, 186–7
ten-year-men 170–1
Wright as sizar student 185–6
Trollope, Anthony 75, 156, 254, 325, 341
Autobiography
on being a sizar at Cambridge 179
on CB's true passion in *Villette* 414
and floggings at Harrow 66
Barchester Towers 410, 446
in Brussels as assistant at Drury's school
325, 326, 327, 333
and Byron's daughter's burial and Fanny
Trollope's poem 327–8, 329–32, 333
on charms of his friend Charles Lever 345–6
Doctor Thorne 40, 303
Framley Parsonage 306, 370–1
The Warden 261, 470
Trollope, Frances (Fanny) 156, 254, 325–6, 335
Domestic Manners of the Americans 326
poem on burial of Byron's daughter 327–8,
329–31
The Vicar of Wrexhill 84–6, 331
Trollope, Sarah (née Clarke) 308, 369
Trollope, Thomas Adolphus 268–9
Trollope, Rev. William 192, 272, 308–10
Belgium since the Revolution of 1830 367–8,
369, 403
Tunney, Rev. R.W. plate 24
Turner, J.M.W. 71–2
Tyerman, Christopher 255–6, 259, 260
Tyrwhitt, Rev. Thomas: death from cholera 444
Tyson, Ann and Hugh: and William
Wordsworth 55

Uglow, Jenny
  Elizabeth Gaskell 174
  In These Times 139

Valpy, Abraham John 341, 349–50
Valpy, Harriet (née Wylde) 341, 349–50
Van Lennep, Clara *see* Morier, Clara
Van Lennep, Coco 121–2
Van Lennep, Cornelia Jacoba *see* Waldegrave, Cornelia Jacoba
Van Lennep, David 112, 113, 116
Van Lennep, George 121
Van Lennep, Peter 113, 115, 116, 120, 121, 122, 127
Van Snick, François 294, 301
Vaughan family in Cardiganshire 42, 49, 58
Venables-Vernon, Edward, (later Harcourt) Archbishop of York 225, 227–8
Venn, John, the younger 15
Vent, Rev. Chrétien-Henri (in Brussels) 388
Ventnor, Isle of Wight 449–50
Verböckhoven, Eugène Joseph 277
Verdi, Giuseppe: *Don Carlos* 200
Victoria, queen of United Kingdom and Ireland 238, 354, 355, 470
  correspondence with Leopold I
    Evan Jenkins as courier 299, 370
    fondness for uncle 291, 339
    Leopold's description of new wife as homily 315–16
    Leopold's marriage plans for 293, 339
  enjoyment of *Jane Eyre* and interest in CB 414
  on Rev. Robert and Samuel Phelps 379
  royal visit to Belgium and press coverage 410–14
Victoria & Albert Museum, London: costume collection 93–4
Victoria County History 66, 145
Victoria Mary Louisa, Duchess of Kent 291

Wainewright, Rev. Latham 191
Waldegrave, Cornelia Jacoba (née Van Lennep) 118, 121
Waldegrave, Katie 431, 432
Waldegrave, Captain William (later 1st Baron Radstock) 118, 121
Wales, Rev. Elkanah (in Pudsey) 223–4
Wales
  charity schools and elementary education provision 57–8
  gentlemen farmers 39–40
  landed gentry and estates 42, 49, 58
  St David's College, Lampeter and petition to award degrees 441–2
  small size of Welsh according to Borrow 55
  travellers and historical accounts 20–1, 23, 27–8, 36–8, 59–60
  Welsh dress for women 36
  see also Cardiganshire (now Ceredigion); Welsh language
Walker, Harriet *see* Jenkins, Harriet (née Walker)
Walraven, Arnout: similar name to CB's Madame Walravens 104
Waterloo, Battle of (1815) 203–4, 400
  site as tourist attraction 214, 249, 328
Watson, Marcia 6, 19–20, 24, 105–6, 135, 220, 231
Weightman, Rev. William (Haworth curate) 388
Wellesley, Rev. Gerald Valerian 67, 69–70, 73
Wellington, Arthur Wellesley, 1st Duke of 69, 70, 246
  Peninsular War 73, 97
    Battle of Salamanca 381
  response on hearing of Napoleon's defeat 200
  return of Napoleon and Battle of Waterloo 203, 400
    as George IV's battlefield guide 512*n*.54
  and revolution in Belgium 270, 280
  see also Napoleon I and Napoleonic Wars
Welsh language
  literacy skills in rural Wales 37, 38, 58

and teaching at Ystrad Meurig 49
Welsh Methodism *see* Methodism in Wales
Wesleyan Methodism 33
Westbrook, Harriet *see* Shelley, Harriet
Westney, Dr Paul 50, 51, 54
Westwood, Rosa 385
Westwood, Thomas 383, 384–7, 399, 415, 474–5
Wethersfield, Essex: PB as curate 75
Weyhill Fair, Hampshire 119
Whately, Richard, Archbishop of Dublin 351–2
Wheelwright, Frances 10
Wheelwright, Julia 402, 403
Wheelwright, Laetitia 401, 402, 403
Wheelwright, Dr Thomas 401–2
Wheelwright family in Brussels 10, 401–3
Whigs: reform and political uncertainty 437–8,
    439
White, (Captain) Charles 326
    background and family 271
    first-hand account in *The Belgic Revolution*
        270–5, 288
        on adverse publicity of theft of
            Princess of Orange's jewels 274–5
        on anti-Dutch August riots (1830)
            and flawed response 277, 278–9,
            280, 281–2, 284–5
        assistance in negotiations for Leopold
            as king 293–4
        on inauguration of Leopold as king
            (July 1831) 302
        on invasion by Dutch troops (August
            1831) 306–8
        on Van Snick's courage 294, 301
White, Patrick: *Voss* 95
Whitecombe, Captain (of steam packet *Soho*) 421
Whiteley, Doug 226–7
Whitmore, William (godfather to John Jay's last
    son) 146
Wilberforce, Samuel, Bishop of Oxford ('Soapy
    Sam') 166, 467, 468, 469, 470–2, plate 25
Wilberforce, William (1759–1833) 63, 97, 165,
    166, 178, 180, 230
Wilberforce, William (son) 165–6

William IV, king of Great Britain (the 'sailor
    king') 291, 293, 311–12, 321–2, 339, 438
William I, king of the Netherlands 108, 130, 249
    church attendance in Brussels 233, 258, 259
    exhibition of national industry 275–6
    unrest and Belgian Revolution (1830) 272,
        273, 280
        and renewed hostilities 320, 323
William II, Prince of Orange, later king of the
    Netherlands ('Slender Billy') 202, 277, plate 16
    adverse publicity from theft of wife's jewels
        273–5
    and Belgian Revolution (1830) 273, 280
William IV, Prince of Orange, Stadtholder 108
William V, Prince of Orange, Stadtholder
    126–7, 130
Williams, Dr Daniel (Welsh Presbyterian) 107
Williams, David (1785?–1823) 52
Williams, Evan (publisher) 51–2
Williams, Rev. John (1745–1818) 45, 49, 50,
    51–2, 54–5, 59, plates 3, 4
Williams, Rev. John (1792–1858) 52–3, 54, 55, 61
Williamson, Charles (d. 1820) 171
Williamson, Thomas (1756–1838) 139, 157, 347
Williamson Ramsay, 'Lieutenant' George ('of
    Lixmount') 139–40
Willoughby, Rev. E.C. 206, 208, 209–10,
    211–12, 213, plate 24
Wilson, Romer 140
Winchester House, Chelsea 72
Withers, Robert Jewell (architect) 467–8, 471
Wood, Charles, 1st Viscount Halifax 151
Woodford, Essex: Jay family at 141, 144–57, 347
Woodford Historical Society 145, 154
Wooler, Margaret 362, 388, 390
Woolf, Virginia: *The Waves* 2
'woolsorter's disease' (anthrax) 442
Wordsworth, Charles 259, 260, 262
Wordsworth, Christopher 159
Wordsworth, Dorothy (1771–1855) 180
    on Brussels 214–15
Wordsworth, Dorothy (Dora) (1804–47) 150,
    247, 431–2

Wordsworth, Isabella (née Curwen, d. 1848) 422, 430, 431–5

Wordsworth, Rev. John 165, 194, 422
   misconduct and Henry Curwen's letter 430–5

Wordsworth, Mary (née Hutchinson) 214, 431, 434

Wordsworth, William (1770–1850) 60, 150, 165, 422
   at Cambridge 158–9, 180, 187, 189
   in Brussels 214–15, 247
   'Composed Upon Westminster Bridge' 64
   lodgings at Hawkshead grammar school 55
   The Prelude 158–9, 187, 189
   son's conduct and change to will 431, 432–3, 434

Wordsworth, William 'Willy' (1810–83) 434

Worthen, John 432–3

Wren Library, Trinity College, Cambridge 160–1, 162–3, 165

Wright, Charlotte May: *Memories of Far Off Days* 106, 243

Wright, John Martin Frederick
   guide to Trinity College, Cambridge in *Alma Mater* 161–3, 182–4, 190
      on admission process and Wren Library 162–3
      on Atkinson's lack of imagination 185
      on chapel 182–3, 183–4
      on dining experience in hall 183
      on fear of final examinations 197
      hesitant definition of 'ten-year-men' 171
      on King's Gate and Great Court 182
      on lectures and exams in mathematics and classics 188–9, 197
      on lectures and exams on New Testament in Greek 192
      lodgings in turret room 185–6, 187
      on Norrisian lectures and failure to complete 191
      on Rev. Simeon 196
      on sympathetic examination in

      mathematics 197
      on temptations and 'gay-men' 189, 191

Wylde, Clara *see* Bowden, Clara

Wyndham, Alward 92, 456, 458, 462
   letters to parents and Jenkins family in Brussels 394–6

Wyndham, George 92, 338, 456, 457
   background and family in Wiltshire 6, 19, 97, 167, 239
   home and vineyard in Australia 6
   letters from sister Charlotte Starky 465
   letters from son Alward 394
   meeting with Margaret Jay and marriage 97, 242–4
   and nephew Evan in Australia 458, 459

Wyndham, Margaret (Meg, née Jay) (1803–70) 19, 106
   appearance 95, plate 12
   childhood and youth 141, 150, 154, 213, 242–3, 244–5
   letters from Alward (son) 394–6
   letters from Eliza Jenkins (sister) 92, 338, 455
      concerns for son Evan in Australia 458, 459–61, 466
      on death of her daughter Mina 466
      on death of her son Alexander 453–4
   letters from Janet Jay (sister) 369–70, 371, 435–6, 452–3, 458, 460
      on death of niece Mina 465–6
      and death of sister Eliza 468–9
   letters from John Livingston Jay (brother) 353–4
   letters from Livingston family 450
   letters from Samuel Jay (brother) 151, 152, 353
   letters from Wyndham family 455–6
   marriage and children 97, 242–4, 454
   move and life in Australia 6, 271–2, 459
   and nephew Evan in Australia 457–8, 459–61, 466

Yates, Richard Vaughan: 'A tour in Wales'
   (1805) 28
York: Borthwick Institute for Archives 34
Ystrad Meurig (Ystradmeiric) school,
   Cardiganshire 22, 45–62
      church building as original school 45–6,
         50–1, 55
      classical subjects and scholarly teaching
         47–8, 49, 54, 60, plate 5
      for education of clergymen 48, 52, 54, 59,
         60–1
      endowment as grammar school 49
      fees in 1820s 56
      founding by Edward Richard 47–50
      illustrious careers of alumni 54
      library and range of books 49, 50
      new school building (1812) 50–1, 54–5,
         plate 4
      numbers of pupils and size of school 54–5
      pupils boarding nearby 55–6
      pupils progressing to Oxford and
         Cambridge 45, 54, 164, 171, 173
      teaching in Welsh language 49